Latin American
Government and
Politics

THE DORSEY SERIES IN POLITICAL SCIENCE

EDITOR   NORTON E. LONG   *Brandeis University*

BROWN & WAHLKE (eds.) *The American Political System: Notes and Readings*

DRAGNICH *Major European Governments* rev. ed.

EDELMANN *Latin American Government and Politics: The Dynamics of a Revolutionary Society* rev. ed.

GRIPP *Patterns of Soviet Politics* rev. ed.

FROHOCK *The Nature of Political Inquiry*

JACOB & ATHERTON *The Dynamics of International Organization: The Making of World Order*

JACOBINI *International Law: A Text* rev. ed.

LUTTBEG (ed.) *Public Opinion and Public Policy: Models of Political Linkage*

MACRIDIS & BROWN *The De Gaulle Republic*

MACRIDIS & BROWN (eds.) *Comparative Politics: Notes and Readings* 3d ed.

MANGONE *The Elements of International Law* rev. ed.

MEEHAN *Contemporary Political Thought: A Critical Study*

MEEHAN *Explanation in Social Science: A System Paradigm*

MEEHAN *The Theory and Method of Political Analysis*

MINAR *Ideas and Politics: The American Experience*

MURPHY *Political Theory: A Conceptual Analysis*

NAGEL *The Legal Process from a Behavioral Perspective*

ROBINSON *Congress and Foreign Policy-Making: A Study in Legislative Influence and Initiative* rev. ed.

ROELOFS *The Language of Modern Politics: An Introduction to the Study of Government*

SIGLER *An Introduction to the Legal System*

SPIRO *World Politics: The Global System*

POLITICAL
MAP
of
LATIN
AMERICA

Latin American Government and Politics The Dynamics of a Revolutionary Society

ALEXANDER T. EDELMANN

Professor of Political Science
University of Nebraska

1969 · Revised Edition

THE
DORSEY
PRESS   Homewood, Illinois
Irwin-Dorsey Limited, Georgetown, Ontario

Revised Edition

First Printing, June, 1969

Library of Congress Catalog Card No. 70–78393

Printed in the United States of America

To Dot—*Mi Esposa, Querida, y Colaboradora*

PREFACE

In this revised edition the overall, institutional approach is followed as before. Several basic changes have been made, however, to afford a more balanced treatment and to introduce significant new developments. To avoid some duplication, the part of Chapter 3 dealing with social classes in the colonial era has been integrated into Chapter 2, "People"; and Chapter 4, much condensed, has been combined with Chapter 3. New developments in the economic realm are treated in a new chapter entitled "Foreign Aid, Economic Planning, and Economic Integration."

In bringing the text up to date, I have tried to take advantage of the many scholarly contributions of the past four years. More than a third of the authors cited did not appear in the first edition.

In conclusion I wish to thank Professor Erwin W. Bard of Brooklyn College and Professor Roger Anderson of Bowling Green State University for their helpful criticisms and suggestions for the revised edition.

Lincoln, Nebraska   ALEXANDER T. EDELMANN
May, 1969

PREFACE TO FIRST EDITION

Anyone who has the temerity to write a basic text about Latin American Government and Politics is immediately confronted with a dilemma. Should he adopt the plan of treating each country individually, or should he deal with the region as a whole? The first approach has some obvious advantages. A picture of each country can be drawn clearly and distinctly, and the pitfalls of questionable generalization avoided. On the other hand, the overall approach has its advantages too. The nations in many respects have common cultural backgrounds, values, and social institutions, including a similarity in the organization and operation of government. As a result, the overall approach obviates a duplication of treatment, and enables a good view of the forest as a whole without the necessity of climbing every tree.

While either one of the two approaches is quite valid for studying the government and politics of the region, I have chosen to follow the second, in the belief that the overall, institutional approach affords a broad, interdisciplinary understanding of the subject.

In presenting this text, I am deeply indebted to a host of scholars—political scientists, historians, sociologists, economists, anthropologists, and others for their labors and dedicated scholarship, whether boldly treating the institutions and problems of the entire region, a whole state, or a minuscule but significant community high in the Andes or deep in Brazil's imposing vastness. I have generously availed myself of their works, as is shown by the many quotations, citations, and suggested readings. I am also grateful to friends in Latin America who have made our trips there so delightful, and whose assistance has been as fervent as their *abrazos*.

I want to express my gratitude too to the Research Council of the University of Nebraska which has awarded me grants for travel, research assistants, and a leave of absence during the academic year 1964–1965 to continue my research on land reform, a project which has broadened my perspective and served generally to enrich this textbook.

Lincoln, Nebraska　　　　　　　　　ALEXANDER T. EDELMANN
June, 1965

x

TABLE OF CONTENTS

Exercising Presidential Control. Presidential Responsibility. Exposure to the Public—a Risk of the Game. Succession to the Presidential Office When Vacant. Ex-Presidents.

Legislative–Executive Relations. Legislative Experimentation. Selection of Members: *Qualifications. Apportionment. Method of Election.* Organization of the Legislature. The Legislative Process. Sessions. Powers and Functions: *Legislative. Constitutive. Electoral. Judicial.* Legislative Privileges and Immunities.

Peculiar Attributes of Latin American Law: *A Blend of Legal Systems. Extensive Borrowings. Embodiment of the Law in Codes.* Organization and Operation of the Courts: *The Supreme Court. The Lower Courts. Special Courts.* Independence of the Judiciary. Civil and Criminal Procedure. Judicial Review. Criticisms of the Courts.

INDEXES

LIST OF TABLES AND FIGURES

TABLES

FIGURES

PART I

Bases of National Power
and Development

1

THE LAND AND RESOURCES:
Challenges to Ingenuity

In addition to Canada, our Anglo-Saxon neighbor to the north, the United States has other neighbors that share with it the land and destiny of the western hemisphere. The 20 countries that will be studied in this textbook lie to the south and southeast of the United States. They are: Mexico; the 6 nations of Central America—Guatemala, El Salvador, Honduras, Nicaragua, Costa Rica, and Panama; the 3 insular Caribbean countries—Cuba, Haiti, and Dominican Republic; and the 10 nations of South America—Argentina, Bolivia, Brazil, Chile, Colombia, Ecuador, Paraguay, Peru, Uruguay, and Venezuela.

This vast area, extending from Mexico's northern boundary, the Rio Grande, all the way to Cape Horn on the southern tip of Argentina, has long been called Latin America. But, like many other things about the region, its very name is controversial. The name came into vogue during the 19th century, after the young nations had won their independence, and it reflected their admiration for the French (Latin) political idealism and culture—values that still appeal to many intellectuals. To them, the name is quite appropriate. As F. García Calderón, one of the region's distinguished writers, expresses it, the Latin Americans ". . . belong to the great Latin family; they are the children of Spain, Portugal, and Italy by blood and by deep-rooted tradition, and by their general ideas, they are the children of France."[1]

However, "Latin America," although generally used, is resented by many who regard it as inaccurate and inappropriate. Among these is Luis

---

[1] F. García Calderón, *Latin America: Its Rise and Progress,* trans. Bernard Miall (London: T. Fisher Unwin, 1913), p. 288.

Alberto Sánchez, a Peruvian writer. In his book *¿Existe América Latina?*, Sánchez concluded that Latin America in reality does not exist. Its culture, he reasoned, is by no means entirely Latin but is a blend with the Indian.[2]

Obviously, the name Latin America does not adequately designate the region, but neither do the other commonly used synonyms, Hispanic America and Ibero-America, which also fail to recognize the Indian and his contributions to the area's culture. Yet, the term Indo-America, advocated by some, is equally inadequate because it ignores the Spanish and Portuguese altogether. To compound the confusion, all of them are inaccurate because they completely neglect one of the main racial and cultural ingredients—the African.

Yet, just as most Southerners (especially those who have held onto their Confederate currency) continue to refer to everything north of the Mason and Dixon line as The North, so do most of us in the United States regard the before-mentioned nations south of the border as Latin America. In the absence of agreement among our neighbors, that is the name we shall use.

GEOGRAPHICAL ASPECTS

The area of Latin America is approximately 8 million square miles, which amounts to about 10 percent of the world's inhabited continental territory. South America proper is the fourth largest continent—a fairly respectable showing as continents go. The individual countries vary considerably in size. Brazil, with more than 3¼ million square miles, is the giant. Containing almost half the total area of South America, it is larger than the continental United States. At the other extreme is El Salvador, the midget, with only 7,700 square miles, approximately the size of New Jersey. Figure 1–1, which superimposes the area of Central America on that of Texas, and the areas of other nations on that of the United States, shows the comparative sizes of the countries.

The relative location of Latin America has greatly affected its development and relations with other nations. From the beginning, its southerly latitude played a large part in determining that it would be Spanish and Portuguese instead of, perhaps, English. The region is much closer to Spain and Portugal, located in the extreme southwestern part of Europe, than to the British Isles, which are far to the north. Columbus, venturing forth from Spain in his quest to reach the Orient, was somewhat south of his westward course when he landed in the Bahamas, triumphantly planted the Spanish flag, and claimed the territory for Spain, all the while assuming it was India. In somewhat similar fashion, the English explorers

---

[2] Luis Alberto Sánchez, *¿Existe América Latina?* (Mexico City: Fondo de Cultura Económica, 1945).

FIGURE 1-1

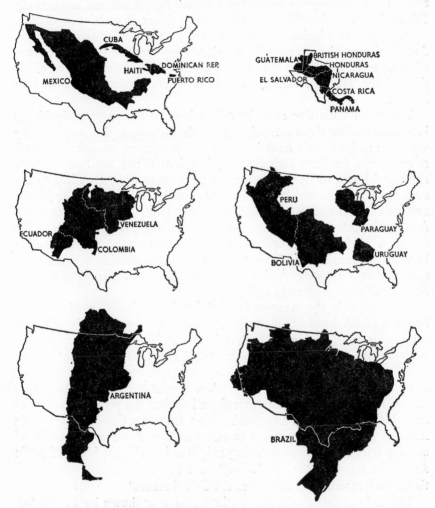

SOURCE: *Center of Intercultural Formation* (CIF), *Study No. 1. Socio-Economic Data—Latin America in Maps, Charts, and Tables* (compiled by Yvan Labelle and Adriana Estrada) (Cuernavaca, Mexico, 1963), p. 30. Reproduced by permission.

sailed westward too, landed in upper North America, and proudly claimed that territory for England.

The location of Latin America was also influential in aiding these colonies to break away from the mother country. Far from the Old World, which for decades was convulsed in the Napoleonic struggle, they were able to declare and successfully assert their independence. The support of the swashbuckling young United States, embodied in the Monroe Doctrine, was a verbal deterrent against the Old World's henceforth attempting to colonize the New or to extend its political system there. The more tangible support of seasoned British tars and battle-ready British ships was the effective 19th century threat of massive retaliation.

From the standpoint of international trade, the location of Latin America is not advantageous. The region is remote from the main centers of commercial activity of the modern world, which are situated on either side of the North Atlantic, in eastern North America and western Europe.

The region's location opposite Africa has also been a very significant influence. During three centuries of the slave trade, Africa involuntarily supplied much of Latin America's population, coloring its culture as well as its people. Itself an underdeveloped region, Africa has been of little commercial help to Latin America. In fact, because it grows largely the same tropical crops and has similar raw materials it is in many respects a competitor—and one to be seriously reckoned with. Realizing this, Latin America is understandably concerned about the growing strength of the Common Market in Europe and the close commercial ties developing between its members and their former African colonies—a relationship that threatens to give Africa a strong advantage and deprive Latin America of some of its main markets.

Its location in the western hemisphere, in proximity to the United States, has also been of momentous consequence to Latin America. In some ways, this location has been quite beneficial, providing markets for its products and supplying foreign capital needed for its development. Yet, the propinquity to a far stronger, muscle-flexing neighbor has often resulted in domination and exploitation. It was the United States that unilaterally promulgated, interpreted, and applied the protective Monroe Doctrine—in a spirit of big brotherliness that sometimes forgets Latin America too has grown up. The resentment resulting from continued overexposure to an overshadowing neighbor is a tie that binds all Latin Americans together. "Poor Mexico," goes a familiar lament often heard there, "so far from God, so close to the United States."

The main surface features in Latin America, as shown by Figure 1–2, are the Andes Mountains; the plateaus of Brazil, Mexico, the Guianas and the Andean uplands of Bolivia and Peru; the tropical jungles or rain forests; and the broad fertile plains or pampas. The Andes and the jungles are as fiercely individualistic and assertive as their Spanish and Portuguese conquerors, and as uncooperative as the Indians. The mountains, with their many defiant peaks, and the jungles, with their overwhelming growth, are antisocial, flaunting their contempt for man. They may appear on the map as belonging to Brazil or Ecuador, but they have never been really conquered. Indeed, a large part of the territory still remains outside the effective control of the states that claim it.

Unlike the mountains and jungle, the pampas and plains are sociable

FIGURE 1–2.   RELIEF MAP: NORTH AND SOUTH AMERICA

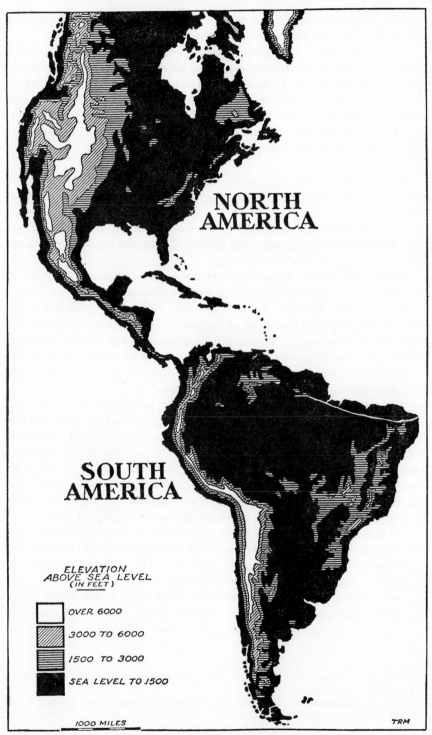

NORTH
AMERICA

SOUTH
AMERICA

ELEVATION
ABOVE SEA LEVEL
(IN FEET)

OVER 6000

3000 TO 6000

1500 TO 3000

SEA LEVEL TO 1500

1000 MILES

TRM

SOURCE: Hubert Herring, *A History of Latin America from the Beginnings to the Present* (2d ed. rev.; New York: Alfred A. Knopf, Inc., 1961), p. 9. Reproduced by permission.

and responsive to man's overtures. The fertile, grass-covered expanses meet him with open arms and make him feel welcome.

The Andes have the distinction of being the longest continuous mountain chain in the world, extending all the way from the northern part of Colombia and Venezuela to Tierra del Fuego on the extreme southern tip of the continent, a distance of more than 4,000 miles. The Andes are much narrower and much higher than the Rocky Mountains in the United States. Throughout most of their length they are approximately 200 miles wide, except in Bolivia where they bulge out to about 400 miles.

They are among the highest mountains in the world. At least 14 of the peaks are more than 21,000 feet high, and Mount Aconcagua, which boasts an elevation of 22,835 feet, is the highest peak in the western hemisphere. Most of the passes across the mountains are above 10,000 feet, making crossings much more difficult than in the Rockies, where the passes are only 6,000 to 7,000 feet high.

With their heights capped by glaciers and ice sheets, the Andes in some places are split by raging river torrents into several separate ranges, making passage through them even more difficult. "Colombia is an obstinately perpendicular kind of country," says Kathleen Romoli, describing its topography. "Crossing it from west to east has all the dizzy variety of a roller coaster of the Gods. Sea level to 8,000 feet, down to 3,000, up to 10,000 or so, down to 800, up a mile and three quarters, down to 1,000—the whole in a little over 200 air miles."[3]

Tall and gangly, the Andes as well as the mountains of Mexico and Central America are geologically young, undisciplined by time and the elements. And with all the impetuosity and unpredictability of youth, the obstreperous upstarts occasionally go on a tear, pitching an earthquake, a volcanic eruption, or an avalanche. The narrowness and great height of the young mountains account for potential subterranean stresses and strains that make disasters of nature an ever-present menace in the whole region of the Cordillera from northern Mexico to southern Chile.

Of these cataclysmic scourges, earthquakes have been by far the most devastating in their effects, both material and psychological. It is difficult to imagine how awful they can be. "The face of the country was entirely changed," said W. B. Stevenson, describing a very severe quake, ". . . mountains rose where cultivated valleys had existed, the rivers disappeared or changed their courses. The face of the country was so completely altered that no one knew the site of the largest farm in the province."[4]

---

[3] Kathleen Romoli, *Colombia: Gateway to South America* (Garden City, N.Y.: Doubleday, Doran Co., 1941), pp. 6-7.
[4] W. B. Stevenson, *A Historical and Descriptive Narrative of Twenty Years' Residence in South America* (London, 1825), Vol. II, p. 267.

Smitten by nature, many cities have been destroyed or heavily damaged by earthquakes, including Lima, Caracas, Santiago, Arica, Cuzco, Concepción, and Mendoza. Some have been destroyed a number of times: Concepción, in 1570, 1730, 1751, and 1835; and the capital of Guatemala in 1541, 1773, and 1917.

In recent years, Chile has suffered two destructive earthquakes that caused great damage and loss of life. In 1939, Chillán was reduced to a pile of rubble and 30,000 of its residents killed. In 1960, the nation was struck by a series of earthquakes, tidal waves, and volcanic eruptions that killed almost 10,000 people. The 1960 disasters that struck Chile show the full magnitude and extent of seismic destruction. In all, 2 million people—more than a fourth of the population—were left homeless, and half of the nation's farmland was damaged. The total loss was estimated at $500 million—more than the annual national budget.[5] If comparable damage were suffered by the United States, it would be more than $100 billion—the amount of our nondefense expenditures.

The material losses, however large, can be estimated and statistically shown; yet nothing can measure the tragic psychological effects these calamities have on the people. "Mass hysteria and paroxysms of terror," says William Lytle Schurz, "are often followed by a state of fatalism and resignation. The hypertension of panic may result in outbursts of fanatical religious fervor or end in downright madness as the mind breaks from the memory of horrors and the suspense of waiting for the repetition of disaster."[6]

Another important surface feature is the plateau: extensive ones are those in Mexico and Brazil, and the vast altiplano in Peru and Bolivia; smaller ones are those in the southern parts of Venezuela and Argentina.

The Mexican plateau covers most of the country. The northern part, lightly populated and containing much of the nation's mineral resources, is desert and semidesert with a very low or seasonal rainfall. The central part of the plateau is far more important; although it contains only about one seventh of the area of the nation, this includes half of its arable land. And crowded into a series of intermont basins, at elevations of 5,000 to 8,000 feet, are half of the nation's population and most of its industry.

The Brazilian plateau, located in the southeastern part of the country, is one of the major upland masses in the world. Four times the size of Texas, it has an average elevation of 2,500 feet. The highest part, the Great Escarpment, extends along the coast for about a thousand miles, rising to a height of 10,000 feet back of Rio de Janeiro. So steep is the escarpment here that a train crossing it can make the ascent only by the aid of cables.

---

[5] *New York Times,* "Hemisphere Economic Review," January 11, 1961, p. 49, col. 1.
[6] William Lytle Schurz, *This New World: The Civilization of Latin America* (New York: E. P. Dutton & Co., Inc., 1954), p. 30.

In the highlands, or along the coastal area just over the Great Escarpment, live most of Brazil's population; the region contains all the large cities, with the exception of Rio de Janeiro on the southeastern coast, and Belem at the mouth of the Amazon. Much of the area is rolling grassland or brushland, except in the southern part where there are large stretches of fine forests.

With three fourths of its area lying in the equatorial belt, Latin America's many rain forests extend from southern Mexico, through the coastal plains of Central America and the Choco country of Colombia, into the very heart of the continent. By far the largest such forest—in fact, the largest tropical jungle in the world—is the huge Amazon basin.

All the rain forests follow a similar pattern of tall, thick, tree growth, dense tangled foliage, incessant rain, and debilitating heat. These vast and seemingly endless jungles are like Doctor Jekyll and Mr. Hyde, showing one face to the naturalist but quite a different one to the settler.

To the naturalist, they are fascinating and challenging—a tropical paradise.[7] Among the many distinguished naturalists interested in the area was Henry Bates, who spent 11 years there, studying and collecting specimens. During this time, he collected the enormous total of almost 15,000 species, including 52 mammals, 350 birds, 140 reptiles, 120 fishes, 35 mollusks, and 14,000 insects. Approximately 8,000 of these, according to Bates, were species new to science.[8]

However, the settler bent on carving out his own small private domain and developing it by courage and *cruzeiros* has found the jungle to be Mr. Hyde at his worst. Ready and anxious to combat man, his crops, and his domestic animals is a heavy mass of verdure. Stimulated by heat and moisture, the trees and vines rudely trample and elbow one another in a frantic effort to reach the sun, shutting out all sunlight on the vastness below. The settler's hope of substituting crops for creepers and reaping the benefits of a copious fertility always seemed a good idea, but the jungle usually won out, closing in again and asserting itself once more.

The profuse vegetation is only one of the many enemies of man in the jungle. Snakes are ready to challenge him on every hand, from the large boa constrictors, reaching 30 feet in length (adversaries to be respected,

---

[7] Another paradise for the naturalist is the Galapagos Islands, located about 600 miles west of Ecuador and belonging to that nation. They were described by Charles Darwin as "the living laboratory of evolution." Most of the species are endemic, unique to the archipelago; of the 89 species and subspecies of birds that live in the islands, 77 exist nowhere else. Animals that belong to the Antarctic live side by side with those that belong to the tropical zones; fur seals and penguins are neighbors with tropical marine iguanas. See Irenaus Eibl-Eibesfeldt, *Galapagos: The Noah's Ark of the Pacific*, trans. Alan Houghton Brodrick (Garden City, N.Y.: Doubleday & Co., Inc., 1961); and Roger Tory Peterson, "The Galapagos: Eerie Cradle of New Species," *National Geographic*, Vol. 131 No. 4 (April, 1967), pp. 540–85.

[8] Paul Russell Cutright, *The Great Naturalists Explore South America* (New York: Macmillan Co., 1940), p. 5.

although they do not usually attack man), to the rattlesnakes, the most poisonous and the boldest of all, who never retreat from humans but daringly crawl toward them and strike with little or no warning.

In the jungle waters, where man bathes and sometimes has to work, the stinging ray attacks him with its poison and the electric eel with its power charge. Also infesting the waters is the piranha, the most ferocious fish in the world, whose sharklike teeth, sharp as a buzz saw, can tear a man to shreds within minutes.

Also ready to pester and torment him are the 14,000 species of insects, including mosquitoes, chigoes, and red ants. Besides causing discomfort, the mosquitoes are carriers of chills and fevers. Although Bates identified many varieties of the insect, according to one traveler in the jungle there are just two kinds—the day shift and the night shift.

About the most dreaded insects of all are the tambochas. When the natives sense their approach, they flee in terror and submerge themselves in the nearest stream. Like Sherman's Army on its march to the sea, the tambochas devastate the land, devouring everything in their path, including people, animals, plants, and trees. Before them, even the earth trembles, say some who lived through their awesome destruction.[9]

Latin America has two extensive plains, the llanos and the pampas. The llanos in Venezuela is a vast, almost featureless plain approximately 600 miles long and 200 miles wide, consisting of a mixture of savannah and scrub woodland. Although used primarily for grazing, it is not good pastureland because of the extremes of rainy and dry seasons.

The pampa, located in northeastern Argentina, Uruguay, and parts of Paraguay and southern Brazil, contains about 250,000 square miles. Comprising some of the most fertile land in the world, its soil would do as fertilizer for the poorer land of less favored nations.

Until the middle of the 19th century, this large plain, lying mostly in Argentina and sometimes called the Sea of Grass, was inhabited mainly by Indians, outlaws, range cattle, and gauchos. Everything there was wild and tough: the wiry prairie grass, the hardy far-ranging cattle, and the husky lawless gauchos who were so ". . . rowdy that the drinking houses where they caroused had iron grills to protect the bar man from their patrons."[10]

This primitive and undeveloped world of the gaucho was completely transformed by the immigrants who came into the area during the 1870s. They were searching, not for El Dorado, but for good land to farm. For the first time, fences were put up, utilizing barbed wire that

---

[9] For a graphic account of their onslaught, see José Eustacio Rivera, "The Vortex," *The Green Continent: a Comprehensive View of Latin America by Its Leading Writers*, ed., Germán Arciniegas (New York: Alfred A. Knopf, Inc., 1944), pp. 39–40.

[10] Lewis Hanke, *South America* (Princeton, N.J.: D. Van Nostrand Co., Inc., 1959), p. 64.

had been invented only shortly before, and pastures were planted in alfalfa. Purebred English longhorn cattle with as proud a pedigree as any member of the peerage were brought over from England; their offspring returned later as choice steaks and roasts on the recently invented refrigerated ships. Supplying English and other European markets, Argentina soon became the world's leading exporter of meat.[11] By 1900, however, wheat and other grains were more important to the nation's economy than were meat and other animal products.

Argentina, which in Spanish means "land of silver," was named in the expectation that the precious metal would be found there. When none was found, however, Argentina was pitied for its lack of resources and long regarded by its neighbors as a poor relative. But its pampa, although tapped belatedly, has proved to be an asset far more valuable than any mineral resource of the New World.

CLIMATE

One of the many misconceptions North Americans often have concerns the climate of Latin America. Since most of the region lies within the equatorial zone, they jump to the conclusion that it must be stiflingly hot and humid. This is not the case at all (see Figure 1–3). On the contrary, most of the area has a wide range of climates, especially in the Andes. While there are many local variations, depending on exposure to sunlight and rain-bearing winds, there are general altitude zones where the temperature decreases as the elevation increases. In fact, in the Andes climate is primarily a matter of altitude and varies as the elevation increases or decreases.

The differences in climate are so distinct at the different elevations that Latin Americans living in the Andes and toward the equator describe their climate in terms of vertical zones. The lowest zone, *tierra caliente* or hot country, extends from sea level to about 3,000 feet. Here, the average annual temperature is usually between 75 and 85 degrees, with a difference of only 3 or 4 degrees between the averages of the warmest and coldest months.

Above the hot country, the next zone, *tierra templada* or temperate country, extends from approximately 3,000 to 6,000 feet. At this elevation, the average annual temperature is between 65 and 75 degrees, but the difference between the coldest and warmest months is even less than in *tierra caliente*.

Still higher, a third zone, *tierra fría* or cold country, extends from approximately 6,000 to 10,000 feet. Here, the average annual temperature

---

[11] The development of the cattle industry in Argentina is treated by Morton D. Winsberg, *Modern Cattle Breeds in Argentina: Origins, Diffusion and Change* (Manhattan: University of Kansas, 1968).

FIGURE 1–3. TEMPERATURE AND RAINFALL

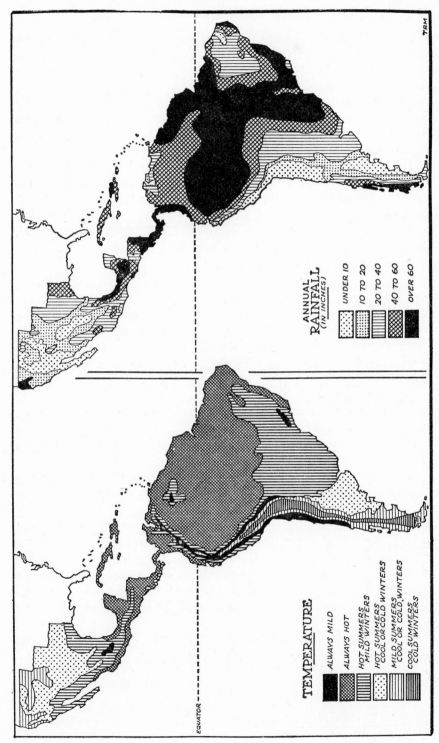

SOURCE: Hubert Herring, *A History of Latin America from the Beginnings to the Present* (2d ed. rev.; New York: Alfred A. Knopf, Inc., 1961), p. 11. Reproduced by permission.

is between 55 and 65 degrees, with practically no difference in temperature from one month to another.[12] Perhaps the extreme of high altitude monotony exists in Quito, located above 9,000 feet. Here, the average annual temperature is an invigorating 54.6 degrees, and the average temperatures of the coldest and warmest months vary by only 0.3 of a degree. Above the cold country, extending from approximately 10,000 feet to the snow line at about 15,000, lies the zone of the Alpine Meadows, or treeless *páramos*.

The vertical zones that exist throughout the long stretch of the Andean chain are especially noticeable in Colombia, located on the equator with mountain peaks reaching up to the snow line. The result? At sea level it is gaspingly hot; yet, at Medellín, 5,000 feet up, there is a pleasant 70 degree year-round temperature. Still higher up, at Bogotá, located above 9,000 feet, it is refreshingly brisk topcoat weather.

Wrote Vernon L. Fluharty:

Bogotanos occasionally take a day off to go down to "hot country" to drive the chill from their bones, and residents of *tierra caliente* who swelter in a perpetual Turkish-bath climate on the coastal littorals, go up to "temperate country" or "cold country" for a spell to activate sluggish livers and regain their vigor in the bracing air of the *altiplano*.[13]

The other mountain areas and upland plateaus benefit by the same moderating influence that high elevation has on temperature in the tropics. The elevation of Mexico City and the rest of the plateau is responsible for the region's pleasant, bracing climate. Similarly, the elevation of Brazil's extensive highland assures a temperate climate for a large part of the country which would otherwise be as tropical as its latitude implies.

Nowhere in the equatorial regions are there such extremes of hot weather as one finds during a summer heat wave in the North American corn belt, where it is sometimes more than 110 degrees. At the equator, temperatures rise into the 80's, occasionally the 90's during the day, and at night fall into the 70's or 60's. Yet, according to climatic records for the Amazon region, a temperature of 100 degrees has never been recorded there. Moreover, nowhere in Latin America does the temperature go above 110 degrees, except in several areas in Mexico, mainly in the northeast, and in northern Argentina—areas a considerable distance from the equator.

In the southern part of South America, the prevailing moderate seasonal climate is roughly comparable to that of similar latitudes in the

---

[12] For these zones, see Preston E. James, *Latin America* (3d ed.; New York: The Odyssey Press, Inc., 1959), pp. 79–80.

[13] Vernon L. Fluharty, *Dance of the Millions: Military Rule and the Social Revolution in Colombia, 1930–1956* (Pittsburgh, Pa.: University of Pittsburgh Press, 1957), pp. 11–12.

northern hemisphere, yet is neither so cold in winter nor so hot in summer. For example, average temperature of Buenos Aires in January, a summer month there, is 73.6 degrees—about the same as that of New York City in July. But in July, Buenos Aires' cold season, the average temperature is 48.9 degrees—about the same as that of Charleston, South Carolina, in January.

Latin America's moderate, pleasant climate in the higher altitudes located near or even on the equator, with year-round temperatures that vary but little, is very provocative to the social scientist. While he regards temperatures of around 60 to 70 degrees as ideal for energetic, healthful living, he contends that considerable seasonal variations are necessary too. But could the delightful year-round climate of Medellín be improved by the sleet and slush of Boston? A citizen of Medellín would doubtless laugh at the very idea. And most Americans who long to live in Florida or California would probably feel the same way.

Despite the moderate climate in large areas, the climate elsewhere has sometimes been a cause of concern. In the opinion of some scholars, the South American continent by virtue of its size and climate should be able to support many different species of large animals. Instead, it has

. . . a prodigality of inferior life, aggressive and useless. . . . Still incipient studies lead to the conclusion that the higher animals degenerate in South American regions, sometimes because of the altitude, as in Bolivia and Peru, sometimes because of the grave disease prevalent in the torrid lowlands of the rest of the country. . . .[14]

Evidence does exist that living in the high Andes was quite difficult for the early conquering whites. Most of them suffered from the bitter cold; some were bothered with acute nervous tensions; and others were stricken by *soroche* (mountain sickness), becoming so nauseated that they staggered or even threw down their arms.

Another disconcerting problem was male sterility; it was a long time before any Spanish babies were conceived and born in Potosí, high up in the Bolivian Andes.[15] Speaking of Cerro de Pasco, located in the Peruvian Andes at an elevation of almost 15,000 feet, Lieutenants Herndon and Gibbon observed: "The temperature is so rigorous here that the hens do not hatch nor the llamas procreate; and women at the period of their confinement are obliged to seek a more congenial climate or their offspring will not live."[16]

Leaving the subject of temperature, we find that the rainfall of the region varies considerably over its large territory with its wide range of latitude and elevation. The Atacama Desert on the west coast is one of the

---

[14] In Romoli, *op. cit.*, pp. 8–9.
[15] Schurz, *op. cit.*, p. 9.
[16] Quoted, *ibid.*, p. 34.

driest places on earth. During a 20-year period, Iquique in northern Chile had a total of only 1.1 inches of rain, and in some regions of the Atacama no rainfall has ever been recorded.[17] In these very lightly populated areas, the lack of rain has occasioned little hardship. But in heavily populated northeastern Brazil, where most of the inhabitants depend on farming for at least a bare sustenance, the long periods of severe drought have caused thousands to perish from sheer starvation and thirst. The result has been mass migration from this region of abject poverty and fierce struggle for existence. This part of Brazil is understandably one of the most fertile breeding places for communism in all Latin America.

Some areas instead of suffering from lack of rain go to the other extreme. In an average year, the Caribbean side of Nicaragua has a rainfall of more than 250 inches, or almost 21 feet. But over the main agricultural region, the broad and fertile pampa of South America, fortunately no such extremes exist. There, the rainfall is apt to be 30 to 40 inches a year, enough to ensure the region's being one of the great granaries of the world.

NATURAL RESOURCES

Minerals and other natural resources have played an important and often exciting role in Latin America. With their venturesome spirit, the conquerors of the new world were impelled by Gold, God, and Gusto. Gold unquestionably had top billing. The lure of enormous riches, sometimes realized but usually illusory, emboldened men to trudge across blazing deserts, plod through savage jungles, and tackle perilous mountain heights. "Spanish America was born in a gold rush . . ." says Hubert Herring. "Hunger for precious metal was the propulsive force which cleared the way for the Spanish American empire."[18]

After appropriating by sword and fire the gold treasures of the Indians, the newcomers began an intensive exploitation of the many valuable mineral resources of the region. They discovered, however, that all that glitters is not gold; sometimes it is silver. The rich find at Potosí, Bolivia, in 1545 has been called "the most fabulous pile of silver ever uncovered by man. A 2,000 foot hill of silver." The treasure was so vast that the expression, *vale un Potosí* ("worth a Potosí"), came to mean "indescribably wealthy."[19]

More than four centuries later, Latin America is still a colossal storehouse of basic minerals. Chile has the only sizable deposits of natural nitrates known to exist; it is also the world's second largest producer of

---

[17] James, *op. cit.*, p. 256.

[18] Hubert Herring, *A History of Latin America from the Beginnings to the Present* (2d ed. rev.; New York: Alfred A. Knopf, Inc., 1961), p. 198.

[19] *Ibid.*, p. 109.

copper. Mexico is the world's largest producer of silver, and Bolivia's tin deposits are among the largest in the world. Venezuela is now the world's third major producer of petroleum, the new black gold which is found in most of the countries and which provides greater wealth than the early seekers of gold ever dreamed of.

Equally as impressive are the rich deposits of iron ore found in many of the countries. Brazil's Itabira deposit is estimated to contain more than a billion tons of ore, and Venezuela has several whole mountains of iron, the largest of which contains an estimated 2 to 2½ billion tons, with an iron content of more than 50 percent. Indeed, it is believed to be the richest iron deposit in the world. These recently discovered ores are now pouring into the United States to make up for the dwindling output of the formerly highly productive Mesabi Range. The production of industrial metals—zinc, mercury, graphite, antimony, arsenic, cadmium, cobalt, vanadium, and bismuth, as well as industrial diamonds—is becoming of increasing importance in many of the countries.

These numerous and extensive resources have been of inestimable value in the development of the countries. As exports, they have provided much or most of the foreign exchange needed to pay for imports. Copper represents more than half of Chile's total exports; tin constitutes three fourths of Bolivia's; and petroleum accounts for 95 percent of Venezuela's.

On the domestic front, the production of minerals stimulates internal development and provides jobs for many people. Moreover, as the mining communities grow into towns and cities, they become important markets for local products. Agriculture benefits as farms and ranches spring up around the mining communities to supply their food. Roads and railroads have to be built to transport the minerals to a port of embarkation, and hauling provides a large part of the freight of the railroads and other carriers.

Moreover, taxes paid on mining enterprises are an important source of government income, sometimes the major source. In Chile, nitrates were a bonanza to the government; during the four decades following the 1880's, they provided most of the national revenue, sometimes as much as 68 percent of the total.

Today, foreigners own the greater part of the mineral resources in Latin America. Much foreign capital has entered the region to speed up and extend exploitation, particularly in the latter half of the 19th century. Foreign money was needed because of the relatively little domestic capital accumulated in the countries, and also because of the traditional preference of local investors for putting their money in land and commercial enterprises rather than in mines.

The resulting foreign ownership has caused widespread and bitter resentment that increases as the Latin Americans become more nationalistic. The tirades against foreign exploiters are sometimes vehement. You have gotten wealthy . . . built up your own high standard of living at our expense, many Latin Americans charge. You take our invaluable, irreplaceable natural resources . . . pay us little for them—just about whatever you wish . . . and reduce us to economic colonialism. You meddle in our politics too . . . try to tell us what kind of government we should have . . . even the policies we should follow. While these charges are sometimes exaggerated, a student of United States history is apt to conclude that there is considerable justification for the resentment.[20]

Yet, however justified this attitude may be, the intense nationalism that today tends increasingly to shut out foreign investments in Latin American mining has some risky implications. Unable herself to supply the capital needed for development, Latin America may tarry too long—miss taking advantage of the brisk world demand for her resources until some new technological advance comes along that makes them obsolete and unneeded.

Chile knows from sad experience the awful impact that a new and radical technological change can have on a national economy. For decades, the nation had enjoyed a world monopoly of the production of natural nitrates, an industry that was the backbone of its economy and responsible for its boomtime prosperity. However, the bubble suddenly burst in the 1920's, when a process for making synthetic nitrogen from the air was discovered, causing the large demand for natural nitrates—their high price, too—to plummet. New techniques could similarly affect other mineral resources if they are not utilized while the brisk demand for them exists.

In many ways, their valuable mineral resources are not fulfilling the expectations of the Latin Americans. Instead of being processed and used by manufacturers at home, their ores are usually shipped to the United States or some other foreign country to be processed and utilized. The prices paid for them, determined in the highly competitive world market, are sometimes disappointingly low and often fluctuate widely—conditions that both hurt and infuriate the Latin Americans. The drop of just one cent per pound in the price of copper on the world market costs Chile a much-needed $6 million a year in its foreign exchange; a drop of a few cents may completely unbalance its national budget and seriously dislocate its economy.

Nevertheless, mineral resources have generally benefited the nations possessing them. In Mexico, says Frank Tannenbaum, ". . . the mines—

---

20 A main area of conflict today is foreign (which means mainly American) exploitation and marketing of petroleum. For the main issues involved and national policies of the several producing states, see Peter R. Odell, "Oil and State in Latin America," *International Affairs*, Vol. 40, No. 4 (October, 1964), pp. 659–73.

chiefly silver—paid for most of Mexico's imports for nearly four centuries, made possible the development of Mexico into a modern nation, justified the building of most of the railroads, and gave Mexico its distinctive place in the outside world."[21]

But some nations have not been so fortunate as Mexico—Bolivia, for example. Neither its fabulous deposits of silver at Potosí, exhausted and drained off to Spain before the end of the colonial period, nor its valuable, more recently exploited tin mines have contributed much to the nation's development. In fact, some contend that these misused mineral assets are primarily responsible for its serious economic problems. The legacy of Potosí, they believe, is "responsible for fastening upon Bolivia a pernicious economic-social system which exalted quick profits from the mines and left agriculture so little regarded that its growth was dangerously neglected and a feudal-type society prolonged for centuries."[22]

Bolivia's wealth in tin has served the nation little, if any, better than did its treasure of silver. The tin mines were controlled by Patiño, Hochschild, and Aramayo, a powerful, ruthless alliance popularly known as the *rosco* (a yoke around the neck of oxen). The tycoons dominated the nation's government and economy, dictating to presidents and cabinets alike. Members of the clique and a few others made immense fortunes; Patiño, who owned the biggest share of the tin produced, was reputedly one of the richest men in the world. But, their sole motive was profit. They paid paltry wages to their underfed, overworked miners, who lived short, wretched lives.

Since Latin America does have many important natural resources, it might understandably be concluded that it will some day be one of the highly industrialized areas of the world, comparable to the eastern United States or to western Europe. Much as Latin Americans would welcome this, prospects for its happening are not good at present. Because of the lateness of industrialization or other factors, the nations have been slow in utilizing their deposits of coal and in assessing their reserves. Argentina, which had long been dependent on Great Britain for coal, was faced with such a serious crisis during World War II, when its fuel supply was cut off, that its railroads were forced to use wood as fuel and sometimes even maize and other grains soaked in linseed oil. The most important deposit of Argentine coal is that of the Rio Turbio, located about 1,800 miles from Buenos Aires. The reserve has been estimated at more than 400 million tons, and the exploitation of the deposit is in the hands of the state.[23]

---

[21] Frank Tannenbaum, *Mexico: The Struggle for Peace and Bread* (New York: Alfred A. Knopf, Inc., 1954), p. 201.

[22] Hanke, *op. cit.*, p. 31.

[23] For Argentina's problem with coal, see Marcelo Isacovich, *"Carbón," Argentina Económica y Social* (Buenos Aires: Editorial Quipo, 1961), pp. 103–5.

While the total amount of coal available in Latin America cannot be considered small, coal which can be directly converted into coke is scarce. Most of the coal produced is of low quality, having a high ash content and containing sulphur. The iron and steel plants at Volta Redonda in Brazil and Huachipato in Chile manage to operate by mixing, in the ratio of 80 to 20, the low quality coal produced locally with high quality coal imported from the United States. Moreover, to compound the problem, the coal that exists in the region is usually located far from the iron ore where it is needed.[24]

Due to the lack of coal, special attention has been paid to the development of hydroelectric power. Thanks to the towering Andes along the west coast and the high escarpment along the east coast, the area has a very large power potential, estimated at approximately 120 million kilowatts.

Of the countries of Latin America, Brazil has the best prospects for extensive development of water power. The engineering feat of redirecting the Tieté River to flow eastward and plunge 2,000 feet down the Serra do Mar mountain was one reason why São Paulo has become the industrial center of the nation. The large hydroelectric plant located at the Paulo Alfonso Falls on the São Francisco River is designed to aid in the economic development of the northeastern section, which has suffered so greatly from periodic droughts. Among the spectacular falls available for the generation of hydroelectric power are the Guaira Falls of the Paraná and the Iguaçu Falls on the Río Iguaçu. The nation's hydropotential, one of the largest in the world, is estimated to be more than 60 million kilowatts. In 1964, it produced a total of 29 million kilowatts, of which 22 million was hydroelectric power.[25]

Still another of Latin America's important resources is its farmland. In the absence of extensive land-use studies and soil surveys, it is not definitely known just how much of the land is cultivable. Irrespective of surveys and statistics, the definition of cultivability is itself a pertinent consideration. How do you define "arable land"? Should it include such arid areas as northern Mexico, where although the rainfall is too little for crops the land supports drought-resistant grasses that provide limited grazing for cattle? Should it include large areas that might be cultivated if cleared or irrigated, although at considerable expense?

However arability is defined, it is obvious that large areas in Latin America cannot be so classified. The terrain consists largely of mountains and hills, jungles and deserts, leaving relatively little land with the

---

[24] For the problem of coal in Latin America's industrial development, see Bruno Leuschner, "Technological Research in Latin America," *Economic Bulletin for Latin America*, UNESCO, Vol. 8, No. 1 (March, 1963), pp. 68–69.

[25] *Documents on Brazil: Survey of the Brazilian Economy, 1965* (Washington, D.C.: Brazilian Embassy, 1966), pp. 134 and 142.

combination of topography, soil, and climate necessary for agriculture. In fact, this area is estimated to be only 5 percent of the total, or about 1½ acres per person. This figure is small compared with that of western Europe or the United States; it is large, however, compared with that of Asia, whose cultivable area amounts to less than one-half acre per person.[26]

The 1½ acres per person for Latin America is, of course, only a statistical average. Uruguay, blessed with fertile, level land and a favorable climate, can use 86 percent of its land for farming—a whopping 15.1 acres per capita. At the other extreme is Bolivia, saddled with a mountainous terrain and a cold climate; as a result, only 0.3 percent of its land area is presently used for farming—a mere 0.2 of an acre per person. Thus, Uruguay has about 75 times the amount of arable land per capita as Bolivia, whose situation will improve in time as its fertile Oriente is developed.

South America is sometimes called the Vanishing Continent, and for good reason. Little attention has been given to conservation of the soil since the days of the Incas. As a result of heavy, relentless rains beating down on unterraced cultivated slopes, the topsoil of large areas has been swept down the slopes and into rushing rivers to be deposited far out in the Atlantic—a most difficult region to farm! Completely ruined by erosion or by leaching, as in the Paraná and Amazon River basins, many areas formerly used for agriculture have had to be abandoned entirely.

In striking contrast to such wastage, both Mexico and Paraguay in the last two decades have shown what can be accomplished by good land-use practices. By means of irrigation and better methods of farming, they have expanded their harvested area by almost 50 percent.

The amount of land suitable for agriculture is always important, affecting as it does a region's standard of living and its prospects for economic development generally. Of even greater significance at the moment than the amount of arable land in Latin America are such pressing problems as the need for wider distribution of land ownership and the better use of cultivable areas that already exist. These problems will be dealt with at length in Chapter 7, Agriculture and Land Reform.

TRANSPORTATION AND COMMUNICATION

The high mountains, impenetrable jungles, and desert wastes that cover most of the area of Latin America have been great obstacles to transportation, making the building of railroads a very difficult and expensive undertaking. Sometimes, the most complicated engineering

---

[26] F. Benham and H. A. Holley, *A Short Introduction to the Economy of Latin America* (Royal Institute of International Affairs) (New York: Oxford University Press, 1960), p. 20.

problems are involved, as in the case of the Peruvian Central Railroad. At a distance of only 106 miles from the sea, its trains laboriously reach an elevation of 15,680 feet, the highest rail line in the world, by the use of 65 tunnels, 67 bridges, and a series of 16 switchbacks over which the trains move alternately forward and backward. The rail line—a product of Henry Meiggs, world-renowned builder of railroads—runs to Cerro de Pasco, the famous old silver mine in Peru. Struggling to reach the heights, the little cars cling for dear life to the sides of almost vertical cliffs, teeter around kinky curves, grope their way in dark tunnels through high mountain peaks, gingerly cross bridges above bottomless chasms. In one place, they do a dervish dance and spiral upward in a tunnel inside a mountain in order to reach the top.

Although railroads are the main mode of inland transportation—with a total of 84,444 miles of track, according to the most recent data available[27]—in many respects they are inadequate for the needs of the region. Less than one fifth of the territory is within 20 miles of a railroad, and many of the older towns that sprang up at road junctions or river crossings are not served by a railroad at all. Moreover, the rail lines which have been constructed tend to be very concentrated within the small populous areas. In Brazil, nine tenths of the nation's mileage is in a narrow coastal belt 300 miles long, serving the region from Santos and São Paulo to Rio, and leaving an area half the size of the United States with only 35 miles of railway.

Another serious shortcoming of the railroads is their haphazard planning and construction. Built decades ago by foreign interests to connect a mine or plantation with a port, they were not designed to develop a region as a whole or to promote intercourse between regions. Consequently, there were few, if any, connections between different railroads. In Argentina, all lines converged on Buenos Aires, often necessitating a long and circuitous journey to cover a short distance as the crow flies. To remedy this, in recent years connecting lines have been constructed between major interior points. In August, 1961, Colombia celebrated one of its proudest achievements—the completion of its first through rail line of 418 miles, which connected the seven existing railroads, the major cities, and the Pacific and Caribbean ports.

An even more serious problem is the use of different gauges, necessitating expensive and time-consuming transfers. In many of the countries there are three gauges: the narrow, of 1 meter; the standard, 4 feet 8½ inches; and the broad, 5 feet 3 inches. Brazil even has five gauges. "Caramba!" one may exclaim. "What a way to run a railroad!" Realizing the importance of railroads to industrial development, Mexico between 1945 and 1950 spent a tremendous sum to modernize the railroads and institute a uniform standard gauge.

---

[27] Vision, *latin america '68: The Annual Review of Latin American Business and Development* (New York: Vision, Inc., 1968), pp. 98–101.

High freight rates are still another problem of the rail lines. Necessitated by the heavy cost of construction and maintenance and the prevalent pattern of one-way payloads and return deadheading, the rates are so high that some commodities cannot stand the cost. To ship an article from Buenos Aires to Asunción, about 1,000 miles, costs as much as it would to send it all the way to Yokohama, halfway around the world.

Besides modernizing and expanding the railroads, since World War II, the governments have been progressively taking them over from private ownership. In Argentina and Uruguay, the railroads have been nationalized; in Brazil, Chile, Mexico, and many other countries, the government lines dominate the railroad systems.

Generally speaking, Latin America is not very well endowed with usable rivers. Those of Mexico, Central America, and the west coast of South America are studded with rapids and falls in their abrupt descent from the mountains. Although possibly useful for irrigation and power, none of them is truly navigable.

The best known of the rivers, the Amazon, dwarfs all other rivers of the world. Fed by countless thousands of small streams that collect water from snow melting high in the Andes and from the torrential rains constantly drenching the huge basin, it drains an area of more than 2.7 million square miles—about 40 percent of all Latin America. The volume of muddy water that pours into the Atlantic—five times that of the Mississippi—is so huge that it turns the salt water fresh for 200 miles from shore. The Amazon is navigable by ocean vessels all the way to Iquitos in eastern Peru, 2,000 miles from its mouth—the longest navigable distance of any river of the world.

Yet, for all its mighty volume of water and long navigable distance, the Amazon is of comparatively little value to Brazil or the other countries as a water highway for trade and economic development. For Amazonia is so lightly populated and undeveloped that its output of goods provides only a very small volume of freight to be transported on this remarkable waterway.

Second in size among the river systems of Latin America is the Paraná-Paraguay, which drains an area of about 1.5 million square miles of northern Argentina, Paraguay, southern Brazil, and Uruguay. Despite many problems of navigation similar to those on the Amazon, oceangoing vessels use the river as far inland as Santa Fe—about 300 miles—and slightly smaller vessels can make it up to Asunción, about 700 miles farther upstream. Although the Paraná-Paraguay is not as large or as long as the Amazon, it is easily the most important river in South America, serving a population of more than 20 million and carrying much of northern Argentina's grain and meat and Paraguay's lumber and *quebracho.*

There are other important rivers, too, including the Magdalena and the Orinoco, but like the Amazon they are of limited value as highways of travel and commerce. Often, they are in the wrong place or perhaps flow in the wrong direction. The São Francisco, for example, rises in south-eastern Brazil only a short distance from the coast; because of the 10,000 foot escarpment along the coast, it flows northward and away from the populous developed areas of São Paulo and Rio de Janeiro that could well use a navigable river and a supporting inland territory.

For the past two decades, rivers have played a decreasingly important role in transportation as expanded highway, rail, and airway systems carry much of the traffic formerly handled by ships.

The long coastline of Latin America and the concentration of most of its population near the ocean have made coastwise shipping very impor-tant to the region. Much of the trade between the countries is carried by ocean vessels, and some of the nations have sizable merchant marines. Argentina's state-owned fleet, totaling about 1 million tons, visits most of the other Latin American ports, as well as those of many other nations.

As in the case of usable rivers, Latin America has also been noticeably shortchanged in the possession of good natural harbors. At most of the ports on the west coast, ships are forced to anchor in the open ocean a mile or more offshore and load or unload their cargoes by means of lighters—a slow, expensive, and sometimes risky undertaking. In striking contrast is the magnificent harbor of Rio de Janeiro, considered one of the finest in the world. Its value as a harbor is greatly diminished by the high mountains that literally rise out of the ocean to hem in the city and make access to the interior both difficult and costly.

Unlike Rio, Buenos Aires does not have a good natural harbor. In order for oceangoing vessels to be able to reach its artificial harbor, dredges must work constantly to maintain a channel across the shallow mudbank of the Plata. Despite this disadvantage, however, Buenos Aires has become the leading port in Latin America. It was established on a strategic site that could benefit from the large inland area served by the Paraná-Paraguay River, which virtually assured its becoming one of the important ports of the world.

Roads are another main means of transportation. When the early conquerors reached the Andes, they found that the Incas, like the Romans, had magnificent roads to all parts of their far-flung empire. Easy, rapid communication was an important technique of political control; and a swift courier service, maintained by relays of runners, interlaced the country to carry reports and orders. Gaping gorges and raging rapids were easily crossed by bridges built of wood or bamboo suspended from dizzy heights by liana vines. Not appreciating the value of the Inca roads, the conquerors let them deteriorate into complete ruin; travel in the area was not as safe or as fast again until the advent of the airplane.

The construction of highways in modern times has been handicapped by the same geographic obstacles that made railroad building so difficult and expensive; consequently, the area is deficient in good roads. According to the most recent data available, the region (excluding Cuba) has a total of approximately 697,200 miles of roads, of which 67,600 are paved; 105,100, gravel, stone, or stabilized earth; 382,400, dry season; and 142,100, unimproved.[28]

Large areas in the region have no roads at all, and in many instances the roads duplicate and compete with existing rail lines instead of taking care of areas not served by trains. In the past two decades, great strides have been made in the building of new roads, which today has a high priority on the region's program of economic development. Since such programs are very expensive, the countries are able to undertake them only with the assistance of large loans obtained from international and foreign agencies.

The new roads are proving most beneficial. Those constructed across the Andes into eastern Bolivia, Colombia, and Peru have opened up large virgin tracts whose fertile soil attracts the landless peons spilling over from the high, crowded valleys, and whose rich resources greatly increase the national wealth, promising a better life for all. As the roads reach out into new areas, they also stimulate industry by expanding the national market, and they aid in national unification by facilitating intercourse between formerly isolated regions.

An exciting new road, stretches of which have already been completed, is the Marginal Highway of the Jungle. Located on the eastern slope of the Andes, the highway will extend from Venezuela southward through Colombia, Ecuador, Peru, and Bolivia; it will not have to scale the mountains but will run at elevations of between 1,200 and 4,500 feet along the escarpments and through the valleys that cut the mountain ranges. The road will be a tremendous boon to colonization and development of the nations' vast but hardly tapped eastern resources.[29]

Another road of especial interest is the Pan American Highway, which extends from Laredo, Texas, in the north to Puerto Montt, Chile, in the south and to Buenos Aires, Montevideo, and Rio de Janeiro in the east, connecting all the capitals of continental Latin America.[30] When completed, this highway is expected to enable tourists to travel freely between the countries, thus providing a powerful stimulus to mutual understanding and hemispheric solidarity.

---

[28] Vision, *latin america '67, op. cit.*, p. 148. This source also gives the breakdown by countries.

[29] *Ibid.*, pp. 67–73; and Earl Parker Hanson, "New Conquistadors in the Amazon Jungle," *Americas*, Vol. 17, No. 9 (September, 1965), pp. 1–8.

[30] For information about the total length of the highway, including alternate routes, as well as the mileage paved, all weather, dry weather, or impassable, see *The Pan American Highway System* (Washington, D.C.: Pan American Union, 1963), p. 86.

One of the first successful airlines in the world was established in Colombia in 1920 by an Austro-German group. Since then, airlines, whose main routes and distances are shown in Figure 1–4, have been the fastest growing form of transportation in Latin America. "The great distances," said Simon G. Hanson, "meager development of surface transportation, physical barriers to construction of surface facilities, high

FIGURE 1–4

MAIN AIRWAY SYSTEMS AND COMPARATIVE DISTANCES

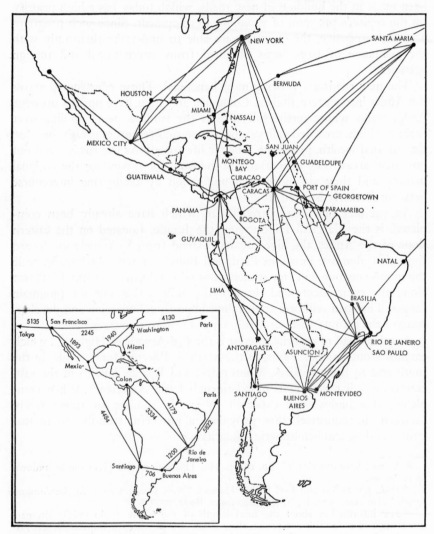

SOURCE: *Center of Intercultural Formation* (CIF) *Study No. 1*, pp. 32, 105. Reproduced by permission.

cost and poor service of existing transportation forms . . . all helped to promote air-mindedness."[31]

The advent of the plane was revolutionary in Latin America as elsewhere, only more so. A small, level clearing sufficed for takeoffs and landings, without the laborious, backbreaking, or dangerous toil needed to hang a puny railroad line foot by foot onto an Andean precipice—or hewing, clawing, or fighting through a tropical jungle, either. With their three-dimensional simplicity of operation, airplanes take up the challenge of topographical obstacles, shrink distances, and whittle down barriers to man-sized proportions, opening up completely new horizons and bringing all Latin America much closer together. Until the coming of the plane, if one wanted to travel in Peru from Lima to Iquitos he had to endure a two months' sea voyage around Cape Horn or through the Panama Canal, and then a long river trip of 2,000 miles up the Amazon. Today, one can board a plane in Lima and step off in Iquitos just two hours later.

Planes carry most of the passenger traffic, and a large part of the freight, too. Air freight in South America represents a much greater percentage of the total scheduled air traffic than that for the world as a whole; in 1963, for the world as a whole this figure was 19 percent. All South American countries except Argentina and Uruguay exceeded this percentage. In Venezuela, air freight represented 45 percent of total scheduled air traffic in 1963.[32]

Planes have proved themselves best as carriers, serving areas that are inaccessible by conventional means of transportation. For these areas, airplanes seem the perfect answer. Casting their punctual shadows on jade forests or opal heights that have never known the feet of men, they vie with the condors for use of the rarefied air space, swooping down and landing atop a mountain crag where a village perches with its head in the clouds. There is no road of any kind to the village. The Indian living there would be shocked at the sight of an automobile, for he has never seen one. However, the sight of a plane is commonplace to him. He may hop one every morning to get to his work on a neighboring height a few minutes away, a trip that by foot or muleback would take days—perhaps weeks.

In these lofty regions of the Andes, many villages and towns have come into existence as a result of the airplane and can endure only with its help. They depend on it for practically everything, even their sustenance. In addition to the passengers, the planes are apt to carry a motley

[31] Simon G. Hanson, *Economic Development in Latin America* (Washington, D.C.: Inter-American Affairs Press, 1951), p. 334.

The role aviation has played in the development of Latin America is briefly discussed in Pan American Union, *Air Transport in Latin America* (Washington, D.C.: Organization of American States, 1961), pp. 11–14.

[32] Robert T. Brown, *Transport and the Economic Integration of South America* (Washington, D.C.: Brookings Institution, 1966), p. 207.

cargo, including ducks and chickens, sheep and goats, llamas and burros.

Years ago, pilots in Brazil drew the line at carrying certain things on their planes. Sometimes a native would carry onto a plane a baby boa constrictor 10 feet or so long to sell to a buyer for a zoo. "The pilots got to the point where they flatly refused to carry them unless they were boxed. They didn't like the idea of a boa constrictor chasing around loose in their planes."[33]

GEOPOLITICS OF INDIVIDUAL NATIONS AND THE REGION

The various aspects of geography have had a great impact on the political development and policies of individual nations and the region as a whole.

While sheer size is only one of the indexes of national power, it is a very important one. Brazil with its area of 3,286,470 square miles, which makes it the fifth largest nation in the world, has an excellent chance because of this and its other assets to become in time one of the great powers of the world, with a strong voice in international decisions. In fact, the United States strongly urged that the nation be accepted as one of the permanent members of the United Nations Security Council—a proposal vetoed by the Russians. Conversely, El Salvador with its tiny area of 7,700 square miles can hardly expect to ever play more than the role of a small nation in a world of sovereign states and power politics.

The shape of a state also has important political implications. Compactness is ordinarily an advantage for many reasons—efficient national administration, social and cultural mobility, and defense against aggression by other states. Evaluated by these criteria, the configuration of Chile is plumb cockeyed; a shoestring of land 110 miles wide and 2,600 miles long is hardly the ideal shape for a state. But, paradoxically, Chile's unique shape turned out to be far more an asset than a liability.

For bordering the narrow strip of land throughout its length is an excellent line of communication—the Pacific Ocean—that enabled the government to maintain easy contact with the outlying provinces. Consequently, if a provincial *caudillo* or officer in charge of a garrison began an insurrection, the ocean waterway enabled the government to rapidly dispatch to the scene a naval task force with troops, and put down the revolt before it became a serious threat to the government. The ocean bordering on the west and almost impassable mountains on the east were deterrents to insurrection for another reason: when the leader of a rebellion was defeated, he had no remote, inaccessible region he could flee to, regroup his forces, and strike again. The only victorious insurrection was that of 1891, when the insurgents had naval superiority because part of

---

[33] Kathleen McLaughlin, *New Life in Old Lands* (New York: Dodd, Mead & Co., 1954), pp. 132–33.

the fleet defected.[34] "No other Nineteenth-Century Latin American country," says Ernst Halperin, "afforded geographical conditions so favorable to the maintenance of a strong centralized system of government."[35]

With regard to boundaries, the vague haphazard delineation after independence was of little concern to the new nations. Most of the population clustered in towns or cities close to the coast; the hinterland was practically deserted. Burdened with their many problems, the governments were little concerned about what the boundaries really were. But boundaries became a matter of vital national interest when important natural resources were discovered in the vicinity of vague boundary lines. The rich deposits of nitrates sparked the War of the Pacific;[36] the rumored deposits of oil in the Chaco sparked the war between Bolivia and Paraguay.[37]

Disputes about boundaries and riparian rights are seldom definitively and finally settled; most of them smolder and periodically flare up to disturb the peace and possibly provoke open conflict. Indeed, the highly charged disputes that statesmen play down and politicians play up are a barometer of nationalism and social unrest. The territorial disputes today include the following areas: the wilds of Laguna del Desierto and other parts of the ill-defined frontier between Argentina and Chile; a three-mile strip which includes the isolated Guaira Falls, important because of its vast hydroelectric potential and claimed by both Brazil and Paraguay; the large Amazon region which Ecuador finally conceded to Peru by treaty signed in 1942—a treaty it later vehemently denounced; and remnants of Britain's empire in Latin America, especially British Honduras claimed by Guatemala, the Falkland Islands claimed by Argentina, and a large part of British Guiana claimed by Venezuela.[38] Argentina and Chile, two of the 12 signatories of the Antarctic Treaty of 1959, both claim large parts of the Antarctic region.[39]

Other disputes have arisen over rivers flowing between or through two

[34] Ernst Halperin, *Nationalism and Communism in Chile* (Cambridge: The Massachusetts Institute of Technology Press, 1965), p. 28.

[35] *Ibid.*

[36] The effects of the war on each of the three combatants is summarized by Herring, *op. cit.*, pp. 542–43, 555, and 585–86.

[37] The claims of each nation to the Chaco, as well as the conduct of the war, are given by Harris Gaylord Warren, *Paraguay: An Informal History* (Norman: University of Oklahoma Press, 1949), chaps. xvii–xviii. A recent account of the war from the Bolivian point of view is Roberto Querejazu Calvo, *Masamaclay: Historia Política Diplomática y Militar de la Guerra del Chaco* (La Paz, 1965).

[38] The disputes are summarized in Harry Robinson, *Latin America: A Geographical Survey* (New York: Frederick A. Praeger, Inc., 1967), pp. 211–16; and *Vision Letter* (February 16, 1966).

[39] For the terms and significance of the Treaty, see Manuel Amaro, "Symbol of Good Will: The Antarctic Treaty," *Américas*, Vol. 19, No. 2 (February, 1967), pp. 1–9.

or more of the nations. Bolivia is trying to win from Chile control of the headwaters of the Lauca River and use of its waters. Paraguay has long attempted to win from Argentina recognition of her right of free, unrestricted navigation of the Paraná River, its vital link to the sea. On January 19, 1966, Argentina and Uruguay amicably resolved the issues, often bitter since 1830, arising from their common but imprecisely defined boundary, the Uruguay River. Besides establishing the exact boundary between the two nations, the treaty provides for complete freedom of navigation, even for warships.[40]

Of all the nations involved in territorial disputes, probably the one most disturbed by its claims is Bolivia. Landlocked since Chile took its coastline after winning the War of the Pacific in 1883, Bolivia bears its historic cross with increasing national resentment.[41] A coastline for sovereign access to the outside world is claimed to be absolutely essential to national development; moreover, "it rightfully belongs to Bolivia" rings the popular theme, as enunciated by Alipio Valencia Vega.[42] If Bolivia had the military might to achieve victory, she would fight if necessary to regain her lost coastline.

Just as boundary disputes can embitter relations between nations, the satisfactory settlement of a dispute can do much to promote cordial interstate relations. The 1964 settlement of the century-long dispute over the Chamizal "removed a major emotional irritant from United States–Mexican relations."[43]

The location of a nation has also had an important effect on its public policy, especially its relations with other states. Panama's location, together with other geographical aspects, made the nation the logical site for the transisthmian canal and served to bring it under the tutelage of the United States.[44]

The nations located in or bordering on the Caribbean, America's Mare Nostrum, repeatedly suffered from American intervention and economic exploitation. The Good Neighbor policy portended the end of intervention; but the cold war and possibilities of communist regimes in the area were a renewed justification for intervention.[45] Of course, the nation

---

[40] The novel provisions relating to the river boundary are given by Homero Martínez Montero, in "Of Law and the River," *Américas*, Vol. 18, No. 2 (February, 1966), pp. 1–4.

[41] Abdon S. Saavedra asserts Bolivia is "a nation crucified . . . a nation in mourning." *Reivindicación Marítima* (La Paz, 1966), pp. 161–64.

[42] Alipio Valencia Vega, *Geopolítica en Bolivia* (La Paz, 1965), pp. 341–43.

[43] Sheldon B. Liss, *A Century of Disagreement: The Chamizal Conflict, 1864–1964* (Washington, D.C.: The University Press, 1965), p. 102. For the terms of the settlement, see pp. 90–98.

[44] For a brief account of United States–Panamanian Relations prior to 1946, and a detailed treatment of relations since the beginning of the cold war, see Sheldon B. Liss, *The Canal: Aspects of United States–Panamanian Relations* (Notre Dame, Ind.: Notre Dame University Press, 1967).

[45] For the successful interventions in Guatemala and the Dominican Republic, see, respectively, Ronald M. Schneider, *Communism in Guatemala, 1944–1954* (New

that has suffered most from proximity to the United States is Mexico; it lost about half of its total territory as a result of its defeat in 1848 and the harsh terms of the Treaty of Guadalupe Hidalgo.[46]

Location at a considerable distance from the United States has been one of the factors responsible for Argentina's independent, often anti-United States policies.[47] On several occasions, the United States did intervene in Argentine affairs, as in the Falkland Islands case and the Paraguayan War; but the interventions were mild compared with most others the United States has been guilty of.[48] Chile's distant location also served to make the nation relatively immune to intervention by the United States; the main instances of intervention, as during the War of the Pacific and the Civil War of 1891, were flagrant and deeply resented by the nation.[49]

The location of Paraguay and Uruguay as buffer states between powerful neighbors has directly affected their public policies, which have sometimes had to be modified so as not to antagonize these neighbors. However, Uruguay has also benefited by its buffer status. With its independence virtually guaranteed by the mutual rivalry of Argentina and Brazil, the nation has not had to expend a large part of its resources on defense. The weakness of the army is both a reflection of and a cause of the truly democratic government Uruguayans are so proud of.

Still another aspect of geography, topography, has had important effects on policy. The many topographical barriers are largely responsible for both regionalism and nationalism as well as *caudillismo* and insurrectionary guerrilla uprisings.

Regionalism has sometimes been so intense as even to pose the threat of civil war and the breakup of a nation. In Brazil, when it appeared that João Goulart might not be allowed to succeed to the presidency after Jânio Quadros' resignation, the state of Rio Grande do Sul prepared to

---

York: Frederick A. Praeger, Inc., 1958); and Dan Kurzman, *Santo Domingo: Revolt of the Damned* (New York: G. P. Putnam's Sons, 1965).

For the unsuccessful intervention in Cuba, see Haynes Johnson, *et al.*, *The Bay of Pigs* (New York: Dell Co., Inc., 1964).

The interventions and economic exploitation during the first two decades of the century are treated by Dana G. Munro, *Intervention and Dollar Diplomacy in the Caribbean, 1900–1921* (Princeton, N.J.: Princeton University Press, 1964).

[46] Increasingly popular demands in the United States for annexing the whole nation subsided when the Mexican Government acceded to the suggested American terms, which were made public. Henry Bamford Parkes, *A History of Mexico* (3d ed. rev.; Boston: Houghton Mifflin Co., 1960), p. 221.

[47] For a graphic portrayal of many displays of this, see Samuel Guy Inman, *Inter-American Conferences 1826–1954: History and Problems* (Washington, D.C.: The University Press of Washington and the Community College Press, 1965), chaps. 3–19.

[48] For these interventions, see Harold F. Peterson, *Argentina and the United States 1810–1960* (New York: State University of New York, 1964), chaps. viii and xii.

[49] For these instances of intervention, see Fredrick B. Pike, *Chile and the United States, 1880–1962* (Notre Dame, Ind.: Notre Dame University Press, 1963), chap. 3.

secede from the nation, and probably would have if an acceptable compromise had not been reached.[50]

Topographical barriers between nations have also had the effect of
stimulating nationalism and making cooperation with neighbors more
difficult. Isolation from one another and absorption with national interests
after independence shattered the dreams of the liberators for a strong,
unified Latin America patterned after the successful United States, which
had won its independence only several decades before.[51] Nationalism was
also one of the main causes of the failure of the Central American Federation, comprising the five Central American Republics, 1824–1838, as well
as of the many attempts made since then to form a new federation.[52] The
Central American Common Market, a going regional enterprise,[53] has
been jeopardized by the threats of Honduras and Nicaragua, emphasizing
national interests, to secede from the market unless given preferential
treatment.[54]

Topography has also been one of the influences favorable for the rise
and rule of *caudillos.* Capitalizing on rugged topography to the utmost
enabled José Antonio Páez to become one of the renowned *caudillos* of
Venezuela—a leader in the Wars for Independence, and dictator-president from 1830 to 1846 and 1861 to 1863.[55]

Terrain that is mountainous and has poor communications has been
regarded in recent years as ideal for a base for guerrilla warfare aimed at
overthrowing the government.[56] But principles governing terrain favor-

---

[50] Thomas E. Skidmore, *Politics in Brazil 1930–1964: An Experiment in Democ-
racy* (New York: Oxford University Press, 1967), pp. 209–10; and Jordan M. Young,
The Brazilian Revolution of 1930 and the Aftermath (New Brunswick, N.J.: Rutgers
University Press, 1967), pp. 109–10.

[51] At the four Latin-American conferences held in 1826, 1847, 1856, and 1864 on
problems of common interest, attendance was so poor as to preclude any semblance
of a common front. For these conferences, see Inman, *op. cit.,* pp. 1–31.

[52] For the history of the Federation and the many attempts at union since 1838,
see Thomas L. Karnes, *The Failure of Union: Central America 1824–1960* (Chapel
Hill: University of North Carolina Press, 1961).

[53] This is discussed in Chap. 9 of this book.

[54] Joseph S. Nye, Jr., "Central American Regional Integration," *International
Conciliation,* No. 562 (March, 1967), p. 48.

[55] For a colorful account of Páez' background and shrewd tactics, see Raymond
E. Crist, "Geography and Caudillismo: A Case Study," *Dictatorship in Spanish
America,* ed. Hugh M. Hamill, Jr. (New York: Alfred A. Knopf, 1965).
   Thoroughly familiar with the territory, Páez won one battle by waiting until he
was upwind from the Royalists, then having his men set fire to the dry grass; the
flames with a terrific roar completely routed the enemy. On another occasion, Páez
used another unique tactic that was successful. He had his men lasso four wild horses,
tie their tails together, take them close to the sleeping enemy, and release them with a
few shots fired into the air. The confusion among the terrified enemy, Páez asserts,
was as great as that caused by the 2,000 bulls that Hannibal released against the
Romans. *Ibid.,* pp. 81–82.

[56] *Che Guevara on Guerrilla Warfare,* intro. by Major Harries-Clichy Peterson
(New York: Frederick A. Praeger, Inc., 1962), pp. 20–27; and Régis Debray, *Revolution in the Revolution?* (New York: Grove Press, Inc.), pp. 59–65.

able for such operations are easier to formulate them to apply; the Sierra Maestra Mountains of Cuba proved to be a wise selection for Castro's eventually successful guerrilla campaign; but the mountainous province of Santa Cruz in Bolivia was a poor choice for Che Guevara's guerrilla dream of overturning the governments of South America from the heartland.[57]

Adverse geographical features have also been severe obstacles to national development and regional cooperation. Many more roads, such as the Atlantic Highway in Guatemala, the Cochabamba-Santa Cruz Highway in Bolivia, and the Literol Highway in El Salvador, will have to be built to afford the ease of communication and transportation so urgently needed within nations.[58] And "regular, frequent, and economical transport" between nations is absolutely necessary if the dream of the Latin America Free Trading Area is to be realized.[59]

SUGGESTED READINGS

Arciniegas, Germán (ed.). *The Green Continent: A Comprehensive View of Latin America by Its Leading Writers,* Part I. Trans. Harriet de Onís and others. New York: Alfred A. Knopf, Inc., 1944.

Bates, Marston. *Where Winter Never Comes: A Study of Man and Nature in the Tropics,* chaps. vi–xiv. New York: Charles Scribner's Sons, 1952.

Benham, F., and Holley, H. A. *A Short Introduction to the Economy of Latin America,* chaps. iv–vi. Royal Institute of International Affairs. New York: Oxford University Press, 1960.

Brown, Robert T. *Transport and Economic Integration of South America.* Washington, D.C.: Brookings Institution, 1966.

Butland, Gilbert J. *Latin America: A Regional Geography.* New York: John Wiley & Sons, Inc., 1960.

Cline, Howard F. *Mexico: Revolution to Evolution: 1940–1960,* chaps. iv–vi and xxix. Royal Institute of International Affairs. New York: Oxford University Press, 1962.

Cole, John P. *Latin America: An Economic and Social Geography.* Washington, D.C.: Butterworths, 1965.

Cutright, Paul Russell. *The Great Naturalists Explore South America.* New York: Macmillan Co., 1940.

Eibl-Eibesfeldt, Irenaus. *Galapagos: The Noah's Ark of the Pacific.* New York: Doubleday & Co., Inc., 1961.

---

[57] For the guerrilla operations in Cuba and Bolivia, see Chap. 11 of this book.

[58] Case studies of the impact of these highways on development in the three nations are given in George Wilson, Barbara R. Bergmann, Leon V. Hirsch, and Martin S. Klein, *The Impact of Highway Investment on Development* (Washington, D.C.: Brookings Institution, 1966).

[59] Robert T. Brown, *Transport and the Economic Integration of South America* (Washington, D.C.: Brookings Institution, 1966).

Furtado, Celso. *The Economic Growth of Brazil: A Survey from Colonial to Modern Times*, Part III. Trans. Ricardo W. de Aguiar and Eric Charles Drysdale. Berkeley: University of California Press, 1963.

International Bank for Reconstruction and Development. *The Economic Development of Venezuela*, chaps. 1, 8, 11–13. Baltimore: Johns Hopkins Press, 1961.

James, Preston E. *Latin America*. 3d ed. New York: The Odyssey Press, Inc., 1959.

Kalijarvi, Thorsten V. *Central America: Land of Lords and Lizards*, chap. 2. Princeton, N.J.: D. Van Nostrand Co., Inc., 1962.

Leonard, Olen E. *Bolivia: Land, People and Institutions*, chap. i. Washington, D.C.: The Scarecrow Press, Inc., 1952.

May, Stacy (dir.), *et al. Costa Rica: A Study in Economic Development*, chaps. 5 and 7. New York: Twentieth Century Fund, 1952.

Monge, Carlos. *Acclimatization in the Andes*. Trans. Donald F. Brown. Baltimore: Johns Hopkins Press, 1948.

Odell, Peter R. "Oil and State in Latin America," *International Affairs*, Vol. 40, No. 4 (October, 1964), pp. 659–73.

Osborne, Harold. *Bolivia: A Land Divided*, pp. 1–43; 71–82. Royal Institute of International Affairs. New York: Oxford University Press, 1954.

Owens, R. J. *Peru*, pp. 1–6; 114–32. Royal Institute of International Affairs. New York: Oxford University Press, 1963.

Pan American Union. *Air Transport in Latin America*. Washington, D.C.: Organization of American States, 1961.

———. *Pan American Highway System*. Washington, D.C., 1963.

Peterson, Roger Tory. "The Galapagos: Eerie Cradle of New Species," *National Geographic*, Vol. 131, No. 4 (April, 1967), pp. 540–85.

Pohl, Irmgard; Zepp, Josef; and Webb, Kempton E. (eds.). *Latin America: A Geographical Commentary*. London: John Murray, Ltd., 1966.

Robinson, Harry. *Latin America: A Geographical Survey*. New York: Frederick A. Praeger, Inc., 1967.

Schurz, William Lytle. *Brazil: The Infinite Country*, chaps. 1 and 2. New York: E. P. Dutton & Co., Inc., 1961.

———. *This New World: The Civilization of Latin America*, chap. i. New York: E. P. Dutton & Co., Inc., 1954.

Stark, Harry. *Social and Economic Frontiers in Latin America*, chaps. 17, 19, and 20. 2d ed. Dubuque, Ia.: W. C. Brown Co., 1963.

Wagley, Charles. *An Introduction to Brazil*, chaps. 1 and 2. New York: Columbia University Press, 1963.

Whetten, Nathan L. *Guatemala: The Land and the People*, chap. 1. Caribbean Series, 4. New Haven, Conn.: Yale University Press, 1961.

Wilgus, A. Curtis (ed.). *The Caribbean: Venezuelan Development; A Case History*, Part I. The Caribbean Conference Series, 1, Vol. XIII. Gainesville: University of Florida Press, 1963.

Wilson, George W.; Bergmann, Barbara R.; Hirsch, Leon V.; and Klein, Martin S. *The Impact of Highway Investment on Development.* Washington, D.C.: Brookings Institution, 1966.

Winsberg, Morton D. *Modern Cattle Breeds in Argentina: Origins, Diffusion and Change.* Manhattan: University of Kansas, 1968.

Wolf, Eric R. *Sons of the Shaking Earth,* chap. i. Chicago: University of Chicago Press, 1959.

2

THE PEOPLE:
Demographic Potpourri of
a Society in Transition

The region's towering peaks, overwhelming jungles, and spacious plains provide a vivid setting for the drama that is Latin America. Equally interesting and picturesque are the people who live in the 20 republics, numbering about 240 million, or 9 percent of the total population of the world. Brazil has by far the largest number, 81 million; Mexico is next with 41 million; and Panama is the smallest with only about 1 million.

Considering the large size of the region, its population is relatively small. In fact, it has the lowest density of any major region except Africa and Australia. The density is estimated to be 30 persons per square mile, compared with 45 for the world as a whole, 59 for the United States, and 196 for Europe exclusive of Russia. In Latin America, the density varies considerably among the 20 nations; Bolivia with only 8 persons per square mile has plenty of elbow room, but El Salvador with 315 persons per square mile represents one of the most densely populated areas in the world. Figure 2–1 gives the density and spatial distribution of population.

Representing three of the races of mankind—Caucasian, Indian, and Negro—the people of Latin America range in color from alabaster white to bronze red to jet black, with every conceivable variation in between. Figure 2–2, which gives the ethnic composition of each country, shows that in some nations the population is homogeneous: Haiti is approximately 90 percent Negro, and most of the rest of the population Negroid; Guatemala is 50 percent Indian and 30 percent mestizo; and Argentina is approximately 90 percent white—"the only white country south of Canada," Argentines sometimes like to boast. In striking contrast to these nations is Brazil, whose population is one of the most heterogeneous of all.

FIGURE 2–1

DENSITY AND SPATIAL DISTRIBUTION OF POPULATION

SOURCE: *Center of Intercultural Formation* (CIF) *Study No. 1*, pp. 57, 59. Reproduced by permission.

It is 12 percent Negro, 20 percent mulatto, 8 percent mixed (including Indians, Orientals, and many others), and 60 percent white—a veritable demographic potpourri.

FIGURE 2–2

Ethnic Composition of Each Country

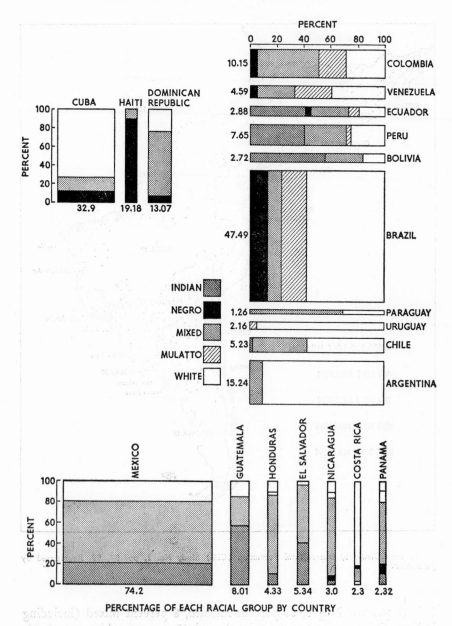

Source: *Center of Intercultural Formation* (CIF) *Study No. 1*, p. 76. Reproduced by permission.

THE WHITES

In colonial Hispanic America, the society, consisting of various races and nationalities, was highly stratified. The *peninsulares* (men of the peninsula, or Spaniards born in Spain), were the bulwark of Spanish rule in the New World; they were entrusted by the crown and the papacy with the highest offices in the government, the army, and the Church. Consequently, they became the viceroys, captains-general, governors, intendants, judges, generals, archbishops, and bishops.[1]

Besides monopolizing the higher offices, they were granted many *fueros* or special privileges, including exemption from taxes, despite their enormous wealth, and immunity from imprisonment for debt, however it had been contracted.

The privileges and preferences bestowed on the *peninsulares* were bitterly resented by the *criollos*, the whites born in the New World, who were excluded from most of the responsible and prestigious offices. Although they were children or descendants of Spanish parents, the unfortunate accident of being born on the wrong side of the tracks—in this case ocean—they felt unfairly denied them their birthright, no matter how proud their lineage. In Mexico, they derisively referred to *peninsulares* as the *gachupines* (the men with spurs) and in South America as the *chapetones* (the tenderfeet).[2] But this derision was little balm to their pride, often insulted without limit.

The *criollos*, denied an important role in political administration, became the dominating influence in the *cabildos*, the municipal councils in the colonies. Although seats were largely honorific, being sold to the highest bidder, the *cabildos* turned out to be very significant in the wars for independence, since they functioned as legislative bodies in many of the colonies during the protracted struggle. The *criollos*, rebuffed in their frequent demands for self-government, cast in their lot for independence and provided the leadership for achieving it.[3]

Long before the break with Spain, the *criollos*, excluded from most positions of leadership and prestige, entered the professions in increasing numbers, becoming the doctors, lawyers, and traders of colonial society. Many became quite wealthy from their ownership of productive plantations, profitable mines, and lucrative businesses.

Despite the political differences between *criollos* and *peninsulares*, all members of the upper class had one thing in common—their affluence.

[1] J. Fred Rippy, *Historical Evolution of Hispanic America* (3d ed.; New York: Appleton-Century-Crofts, Inc., 1945), p. 107.

[2] Hubert Herring, *A History of Latin America from the Beginnings to the Present* (2d ed., rev.; New York: Alfred A. Knopf, Inc., 1961), p. 187.

[3] Donald E. Worcester and Wendell G. Schaeffer, *The Growth and Culture of Latin America* (New York: Oxford University Press, 1956), pp. 536–37.

They very much enjoyed conspicuous consumption, setting the tone for future Latin American society. Indeed, descriptions of their efforts to outdo one another in showy displays whet the imagination. Baptism offered just such an occasion. "The traditions relate how it was a customary thing," said Riva Palacio, "for the rich to lay down a path of silver bars from their houses to the nearby parish church or at least from the vestibule to the alcove, for those who carried the capitalist's baby for baptism."[4]

Today, the whites inhabit Costa Rica and the southern temperate region of South America, consisting of Argentina, Uruguay, southern Brazil, and Chile. In these areas, the climate, crops, and social patterns were not suitable for importing and using large numbers of Negro slaves, as in eastern Brazil and the Caribbean nations.

The scattered Indian groups in these countries disappeared long ago. In Uruguay, they were assimilated into the predominantly white population. In Costa Rica, they succumbed to disease, and the Spanish settlers, instead of importing Negro slaves for the large estates, evolved into a community of mainly small farmers.

In Argentina, after a long series of Indian depredations and killings, the Red Men were exterminated by a military campaign that began in 1879. Its slogan, according to its leader, General Julio A. Roca was, "For the Argentine Republic there is no frontier in the West and the South than the peaks of the Andes and the Ocean." The mere 2,000 Indians that survived the fierce war of extermination were captured, shipped to Buenos Aires, and imprisoned or indentured as domestic servants.

In Chile, the whites encountered the roughest going in all Latin America. The Araucanian Indian defiantly risked extermination to avoid the shame and ignominy of being conquered.

His spirit was indomitable. Said an Araucanian prisoner to the Spaniards:

I am your captive, . . . [but] the Araucanian is never subdued. He is born free. You may put chains on his body, but you cannot put chains on his spirit. You may kill our warriors and make our country a desert; but you will marry our women, and your children will have the strong blood of the Araucanian. . . . The Araucanian has always triumphed, and he will still triumph. . . . You may tear us in pieces with your horses; you may burn us with hot irons; you may pull out our tongues by the roots; but the Araucanian will not be conquered.[5]

Fighting with savage ferocity and a contempt for death, the Araucanians made the Spaniards pay dearly for their victories. According to

---

[4] Vicente Riva Palacio (ed.), *México a través de los siglos* (5 vols.; Barcelona: 1888–89), Vol. II, pp. 724–25, in Bailey W. Diffie, *Latin American Civilization: Colonial Period* (Harrisburg, Pa: Stackpole Sons, 1947), pp. 482–83.

[5] In Bernard Moses, *The Spanish Dependencies in South America* (2 vols.; New York: Harper & Bros., 1914), Vol. I, pp. 358–59.

General Indalicio Tellez, the campaign against them cost Spain the lives of more than 42,000 soldiers up until the 17th century alone. This was a heavier loss of life than Spain suffered in the discovery and conquest of all the rest of Latin America. The Araucanians continued to inhabit the southern half of the country until 1883, when they were assigned certain lands in perpetuity, similar to the reservations of the United States.

With the Indians largely or completely exterminated and with only a few Negroes imported, the population of these five countries is predominantly white because of intensive emigration from Europe. From southern Europe came some 5 million Italians, about 4 million Spaniards, and a little more than 2 million Portuguese. Of the northern European nations, Germany supplied the largest number, which accounts today for the predominantly German populations in southern Brazil and in parts of southern Chile.

These and other groups of hopeful immigrants packed the steerage of passenger boats or worked their way over on freighters to pioneer a new world frontier—South America. Ships from the west brought Chinese and Japanese to settle in Peru and other nations on the Pacific coast, and also in Brazil. Ships from the east brought a large variety of nationals that included English, Scotch, Irish, Poles, Ukranians, Yugoslavs, French, Swiss, Dutch, Syrians, Lebanese, and others.

Up to World War II, more than 12 million immigrants entered the area. At least half of them, between 6 and 7 million in all, settled in Argentina, and most of the rest settled in southern Brazil and Uruguay.

Bringing with them their skills, their strong arms, and their eagerness to work, the newcomers contributed much to the prosperity and development of their adopted nations. The Italians for the most part soon became assimilated, transferring their allegiance and loyalty to their new-found home. Most of the other nationalities in time became assimilated too. But there are notable exceptions. The Japanese in Brazil remain separate and organized; and the German colony south of Valdivia, Chile, numbering some 30,000 to 40,000 persons, remains an isolated economic and cultural group, retaining its German language and customs.

THE INDIANS

The Indians were the largest group in colonial society. Although free men, at least in theory, they were subjected in reality to a prolonged slavery dating from the first days of the conquest. When the conquistadors landed, triumphantly claiming the territory for Spain, "they fell first on their knees and then on the Indians."

Almost from the very first, the crown was confronted with a puzzling problem. Its empire in the New World depended on the labor of the Indians; but, they would not work unless they were forced to, fleeing to the mountains or forests if necessary to escape their taskmasters. As a result, throughout the colonial period the crown was continually attempting to find a satisfactory policy that would permit the use but not the abuse of the Indians.

In the colonies, several institutional arrangements developed for utilizing this unwilling working force.[6] Under the *repartimiento,* natives could be temporarily allotted to an individual for the purpose of performing some work in the public interest, a purpose interpreted liberally enough to include work on private plantations, mines, or factories. In effect, the *repartimiento* was little more than legalized slavery; the authorities would even aid in rounding up the number of Indians the colonists needed and in compelling them to work.

Another arrangement devised in the colonies was the *encomienda,* a grant of authority to collect tribute from and use the personal services of the Indians;[7] the grant, made to the Spanish colonists, in time resulted in their expropriation of the Indians' land.

Still another device designed to provide labor for the colonists was the *mita,* a sort of corvée. Under this, the Indian communities were required to supply a certain number of workers for a specified task, such as tilling the fields, digging in the mines, or weaving in the textile plants.

Rapidly reduced to servitude, the Indians were the victims of widespread cruelty and mistreatment. In an effort to protect them, the crown passed many laws and regulations; they were legally regarded as minors, were not subject to military service or the Inquisition, and were exempt from paying taxes except for a small annual personal tax. If they got into trouble, they were entitled to lawyers to defend them free of charge.[8]

Besides being accorded a special status, the Indian was the beneficiary, nominally at least, of many laws specifically relating to his employment, including minimum wages, maximum hours, and provision for adequate food and shelter, as well as an education and religious instruction. Repeatedly declared to be a free man, he was to be given humane treatment and not to be used as a beast of burden without his consent, except possibly in emergencies. Although in some measure effective, the many laws to protect the Indians were essentially just so much verbiage, violated with impunity by greedy, rapacious colonists, overseers, and colonial administrators.

As a result, the enslavement suffered by the Indian was far worse than that of the Negro.[9] Purchased at a high price, the African represented a

---

[6] For these arrangements, see Herring, *op. cit.,* pp. 190–92; and William Lytle Schurz, *This New World: The Civilization of Latin America* (New York: E. P. Dutton & Co., Inc., 1954), pp. 58–60.

[7] The history of the *encomienda* is given by Lesley Byrd Simpson, *The Encomienda in New Spain* (Berkeley: University of California Press, 1950).

[8] Lucas Alamán, *Disertaciones sobre la história de la república Mexicana desde la epoca de la conquista, México, 1844–49* (3 vols.), Vol. I, pp. 22–25.

[9] For the many brutalities inflicted on the Indian, see Diffie, *op. cit.,* pp. 200–203, 462–64, and 467–69.

big investment that a slaveowner or overseer, however cruel, would not willfully destroy. But not so the Indian; he was expendable. When he died in the factory, still holding the weaving in his hands, or collapsed in the mine from overwork or hunger, he was hauled out like cattle and left exposed to the elements.

With the cruel and inhuman treatment often inflicted on them, millions of Indians died from starvation, overwork, and punishment. In fact, the race was exterminated in large areas.

Those fortunate enough to escape such a fate, possibly legal slavery too, usually found themselves entrapped in the most insidious form of servitude of all—debt slavery.[10] It was so easy to become enmeshed in it. The landlord who kept the books knew how to figure—and how to outfigure too. He could charge his workers for expenses they did not incur, force them to buy such useless things as silk hose or Parisian hats, maybe advance them money for *chicha* or a *fiesta*. Easy to get into, debt slavery was most difficult to escape from. For it was, in effect, a legalized form of servitude. The law upheld the right of creditors to obtain payment for such debts, which usually lasted for the full lifetime of the worker and could even be passed on to his children, putting them too into legal servitude.

The mistreatment of the Indian is the most unsavory chapter of the colonial era, and its aftermath persists even today in the Indian Problem that is such a burden to much of Latin America. Today, their number is a matter of conjecture, depending primarily on how one defines Indian. If the definition is based on physical characteristics only, as color of the skin, texture of the hair, or shape of the head, the figure arrived at will be relatively high, close to 30 million. If, however, one classifies as a mestizo every Indian who has picked up a few words of Spanish, wears sandals, and has adopted some of the customs of the whites, one will get a much smaller figure, closer to 14 million.

Two of the recent censuses of Mexico show how widely the figures may vary within a nation, depending on the criteria used. In 1921, when Indian-ness was based on physical characteristics alone, more than 4 million persons, approximately 24 percent of the population, were classified as Indians. In 1940, however, when Indian-ness was defined in terms of social characteristics, the number dropped drastically to less than a million and a half, approximately 7½ percent of the population. In the determination of the number of Indians in the Latin American nations today, the cultural yardstick is the one usually used.

Most of the Indians live in Mexico, Guatemala, Honduras and El

---

[10] See Diffie, *op. cit.*, pp. 471–72; and Frank Tannenbaum, "Toward an Appreciation of Latin America," *The United States and Latin America*, ed. Herbert L. Matthews (American Assembly) (2d ed.; New York: Columbia University, 1963), pp. 34–35.

Salvador, Bolivia, Peru, Ecuador, and Paraguay. Almost no Indians, on the other hand, are found in the insular republics of Cuba, Haiti, and the Dominican Republic or in the predominantly white areas of South America. A few of them are found in the remaining countries.

The reaction of the Indians to the Spaniard's culture and domination is one of the most significant influences in Latin America today. In a few areas, they are still wholly beyond the reach of white culture and rule. Such a group is the Camayuras of Brazil, who live near the geographical center of South America in the midst of the dense jungle of the Mato Grosso (thick forest). Most of this country is so wild it is still uncharted and unexplored. Secluded in their isolated refuge, the Camayuras maintain a way of life as primitive as that of the Stone Age. Indeed, neighboring tribes are so hostile to white men that they have been known to shoot arrows at low-flying planes.[11]

Some of the other Indians, as the Otavalos who live on the lower slopes of Mount Imbabura in Ecuador, have gradually adopted many of the ways of the white society but without discarding the values of their ancient culture. The Otavalos fare well from their thriving small farms and a prosperous textile industry carried on in their homes. They are also learning Spanish and seeking an education when schools are available. The achievements of these self-reliant citizens are lyrically described in *The Awakening Valley*, whose authors believe that the success of the Otavalos "could be shared throughout the Andes, for their vitality is born of universal energies."[12]

Most of the Indians, however, react quite differently. Except for those who have moved to urban areas, they shun any association with whites and steadfastly resist their influence.

It is difficult to blame them. Over the centuries of Spanish rule, they have been brutally and heartlessly exploited. Because of this, and because of neglect by the rest of society, the Indian adamantly refuses to be Europeanized. Determined to remain an Indian in his culture and way of life, he clams up in his shell—his native community in the sierra. When necessary to escape the influence of the advancing intruder, he "has climbed to altitudes so high and terrains so barren that white exploiters have found it unprofitable to follow."[13]

As a result of his self-chosen isolation, the Indian in reality is not a citizen or member of the national society. He is not the least interested in politics; in fact, he feels an intense dislike for government. To him, government is simply the tax collector who chisels in on his meager

---

[11] "Stone Age Brazilians," *Life*, Vol. 25 (September 20, 1948), pp. 88–91.

[12] John Collier, Jr., and Aníbal Buitrón, *The Awakening Valley* (Chicago: University of Chicago Press, 1949), p. 2.

[13] W. Stanley Rycroft (ed.), *Indians of the High Andes* (New York: Committee on Cooperation with Latin America, 1946), p. 81.

living, or the law who slaps him in the calaboose when he gets too much *chicha* under his belt. But even if the Indians desired to participate in the political life of the nation, they would often be prevented by law from doing so. Thus, they are barred from voting by literacy qualifications in many of the constitutions. Ecuador's Constitution contains such a qualification, and since an estimated 95 percent of the nation's Indians are illiterate, they are legally excluded from the suffrage.[14]

In only two countries of Latin America, Mexico and Bolivia, has the Indian really come into his own. Since Mexico's 1917 revolution, he has had a recognized, influential, even honored role in society. He is "a symbol of oppression, and the redemption of the Indian has been a major theme of the Mexican revolution. In sentiment most Mexicans identify their nation with the Indian rather than the Spanish heritage."[15] And since Bolivia's 1952 revolution that completely swept aside the old order, the Indian there too for the first time stands erect and holds up his head in human dignity, a respected member of society who owns land and participates in the government of his country.

THE NEGROES

Most of the Negroes were slaves during the colonial era; Negro slavery in the New World followed close on the heels of the conquistadors. In 1502, Nicolás de Ovando, commissioned governor of Hispaniola, was authorized by the Spanish crown to take to the New World a few Christian Negroes born in the Iberian peninsula. The number of blacks was destined to increase greatly as the slave trade expanded.

The Indians on whom the colonists depended for labor on plantations proved unable to stand the hot sun; as a result, many died from heatstroke and exhaustion. The Negroes, on the other hand, were inured in their native Africa to working long hours under the tropical sun, growing crops in an agrarian society. In the New World, large numbers were needed on plantations for growing sugarcane and for operating the many sugar mills, each of which required from 50 to 100 hands.

With so much labor needed, the slave trade increased in volume like the fierce tropical hurricanes that spawn in the Caribbean.[16] For the next three centuries, the tropical winds when calm were to slowly waft many slavers' ships, burdened with their suffering human cargo, to their des-

---

[14] George I. Blanksten, *Ecuador: Constitutions and Caudillos* (Berkeley: University of California Press, 1951), p. 19.

[15] Oscar Lewis, "Mexico Since Cárdenas," *Social Change in Latin America Today* (Council on Foreign Relations) (New York: Harper & Bros., 1960), p. 290.

[16] For graphic accounts of the slave trade, see Basil Davidson, *Black Mother: The Years of the African Slave Trade* (Boston: Atlantic–Little, Brown & Co., 1961); and Daniel P. Mannix in collaboration with Malcolm Cowley, *Black Cargoes: A History of the Atlantic Slave Trade, 1518–1865* (New York: The Viking Press, 1962).

tination in the New World. Large fortunes were to be made not only in sugar but also in the slave trade itself. Hardy adventurers, risk capital too, enthusiastically engaged in it; slaves were sold in the New World for as much as 30 times what they cost in Africa![17]

Originating in economic necessity, the slave trade in its early years was sanctioned by the Church. The importation and use of Negro slaves were designed to protect the Indians, a purpose regarded as wholly compatible with Christian ethics.[18] In later years, however, the Church condemned the slave trade and prohibited Catholics from engaging in it, but did not interfere with slavery itself where domestic law permitted it. In fact, the Jesuits themselves owned a considerable number of slaves; these comprised much of their property when they were expelled from America in 1767.

While there were undoubtedly many instances of cruelty and brutality to slaves in Latin America, laws did exist to protect them and give them certain rights. For slavery had been recognized for centuries by both Spain and Portugal, and such codes as *Las Siete Partidas,* adopted about 1265, recognized the slave as a human being whose moral status was equal to that of his master; his spirituality might be even greater. When the Negro was transplanted to the New World, he automatically became the beneficiary of this ancient legal heritage.[19]

This heritage and its protection were invaluable to the slave, as Frank Tannenbaum concludes.

He was no stranger to the law. His obligation and freedom within the code were both known. In fact, the element of human personality was not lost in the transition to slavery from Africa to the Spanish or Portuguese dominions. He remained a person even while he was a slave. He lost his freedom, but he retained his right to become free again, and, with that privilege, the essential elements in moral worth that make freedom a possibility. He was never considered a mere chattel, never defined as unanimated property, and never under the law treated as such. His master never enjoyed the powers of life and death over his body, even though abuses existed and cruelties were performed. Even justice proved to be blind, and blindness was not incurable. The Negro slave under this system had both a juridical and moral personality, even while he was in bondage.[20]

The number of Negroes today is variously estimated at between 25 and 30 million—figures that are at best only approximations, for one encounters many difficulties in trying accurately to ascertain the number.

---

[17] For a vivid account of the slave trade, with its incredible profits and horrible brutalities, see Herring, *op. cit.,* pp. 100–109; and Frank Tannenbaum, *Slave and Citizen: The Negro in the Americas* (New York: Alfred A. Knopf, Inc., 1947), p. 33.

[18] Diffie, *op. cit.,* pp. 192–93 and 473.

[19] Tannenbaum, *Slave and Citizen: The Negro in the Americas, op. cit.,* pp. 48–52.

[20] *Ibid.,* pp. 97–98.

Census records are notoriously unreliable, often incomplete or not up-to-date. Sometimes the census questionnaire is purposely designed to keep from showing the nation's racial composition. Since 1890, the year after the Negro slaves in Brazil were given their freedom, the censuses there have contained no questions whatever relating to racial background. Still another difficulty is the lack of a uniformly accepted definition as to who is a Negro or mulatto; as with the Indian, this depends mainly on the criterion followed, whether physiological or cultural.

Whatever their number, Negroes constitute a large and important part of the population in many of the nations. Brought over from Africa in one of the greatest forced migrations in history, their habitat in the New World is usually the warm tropical areas similar to their native land. Brazil has the largest number, probably 10 million or so, or about an eighth of the population. Haiti, with a population of more than 3 million, has the largest percentage of Negroes, being almost entirely Negroid. Large numbers are also found in Cuba, the Dominican Republic, Colombia, Venezuela, Mexico, and Panama.

The Negro in Latin America has been assimilated to a remarkable degree, especially in Brazil. Among the several factors that have greatly aided assimilation in Brazil are the many opportunities for obtaining freedom; the extensive miscegenation that has taken place; the temperament, physical courage, and ability of the Negroes; and the liberal definition of white as applied to race.

Regarding opportunities for freedom, manumission existed from the earliest days, and accounted for the large number of freedmen of color. According to some estimates, there were actually more Negro freedmen than slaves, thanks to the many ways by which freedom could be attained. The slave had two days a week to work for himself, and could accumulate property as well as buy his liberty by paying the original purchase price. Sometimes, liberty was a gift bestowed by the owner either during his lifetime or on his death. Often, the fathers of illegitimate offspring freed their children at the baptismal ceremony, or the owners of female slaves "freed the womb" of servitude, assuring freedom to their offspring.

Manumission was sometimes granted as a reward for faithful service; from 1864 to 1870, many of the male slaves in Brazil were granted their freedom for serving in the prolonged bloody war against Paraguay. But the Negro women had to earn their freedom the hard way. Under the law, they were automatically free after rearing 10 children;[21] the lucky 10th child was their passport to freedom.

Assimilation by the process of gradualism was furthered primarily by

[21] For the many ways a slave could obtain his freedom, see Donald Pierson, *Negroes in Brazil: A Study of Race Contact at Bahia* (Chicago: University of Chicago Press, 1942), pp. 51–52.

miscegenation, the great social equalizer. The Portuguese pioneer who sought his fortune in the new world usually came without his wife and was apt to pick his Negro slaves, particularly the females, on criteria quite different from those followed by the English colonist in North America. The Englishman, who brought along his wife to be his companion, selected his slaves to work in the field; they had to have plenty of physical strength and stamina, and be cheap.[22]

But the Portuguese colonist had other things in mind. Besides needing all kinds of skilled workers and specialists for his society, including ironworkers, mining technicians, cattle raisers, schoolmasters, and priests, he also needed attractive females; one might end up as the mistress of his house. In his ads for Negroes he wished to buy, he was unabashedly explicit in his preference for physical attractiveness. He wanted females who were tall, well-built, "comely of face and body," and "with all the teeth in front."[23]

In meeting these exacting requirements, it was no accident that the Portuguese colonists "skimmed off the topsoil of the African people."

The temperament and personality of the Negro were also favorable to his assimilation into society. Unlike the Indian, characteristically an introvert with a tendency to withdraw from contact with the European, the Negro was basically an extrovert, sociable, expansive, and easygoing. Also unlike the Indian, he was adaptable, interested in learning the language of his masters, adopting their customs and habits, and in general identifying himself with them.

His physical courage and military prowess won him great respect. Henrique Días, one of Brazil's two national heroes, had immortalized himself by the valor he displayed in the early colonial wars against the Dutch. Later, in the wars of independence other Negroes valiantly aided the cause of freedom by fighting in the ranks of the armies. Still later, in the War of the Triple Alliance they loyally volunteered in large numbers to aid Brazil in crushing Paraguay.

The Negro has also proved to be an industrious and useful member of society. In Brazil many of them were artisans and skilled workers; some became quite wealthy, owning businesses, mines, or other valuable property. Occasionally, they themselves owned slaves and even invested their savings in the slave trade, sending money, tradable goods, and arms to a designated individual in Africa to "get up raids in their old homes or amongst neighboring tribes."[24]

In the realm of the arts, too, the Negroes and their mulatto offspring

---

[22] Gilberto Freyre, *The Masters and the Slaves: a Study in the Development of Brazilian Civilization*, trans. Samuel Putnam (2d Eng. ed. rev.; New York: Alfred A. Knopf, Inc., 1956), p. 308.

[23] *Ibid.*, pp. 320–21.

[24] Pierson, *op. cit.*, p. 68.

often distinguished themselves, contributing many of the leading musicians, artists, and sculptors. The sculpture of Aleijadinho in the churches of Minas Geraes is world renowned for its unique artistry. Aleijadinho, which means "little cripple," was the nickname given to Antônio Francisco Lisboa, a poor crippled mulatto. Having no hands, he had to tie the hammer and chisel to his wrists with ribbons to carve painfully and laboriously the stone shapes of angels and saints whose faces bore the mark of his suffering soul. A whole school of art developed around Aleijadinho, a tribute to his rare ability in designing churches and sculpturing.[25]

The Negro's—especially the mulatto's—rise and acceptance in Brazilian society has also been facilitated by the definition of race. The Brazilian definition of white is almost as broad as the definition of Negro in the United States, where one drop of Negro blood, if it is known, makes a man a Negro. In Brazil, one may have decidedly Negroid features and still be accepted as white. *"Ele tem dedo na cozinha"* ("He has a finger in the kitchen"), the Brazilians may say facetiously about one suspected of having Negro blood. But even if it is known that he has a close Negro ancestor, this is not likely to affect his social standing. In his tactful, "so what?" manner, the Brazilian may simply answer, "We never go very far into a person's past . . . that would be impolite."[26]

Although the Negro in Brazil is often handicapped by low income, illiteracy, and a low standard of living, which consign him to the lower class, he nevertheless has the opportunity to compete in the whole community despite his color.

Racial prejudice is common in Latin America; it exists to some degree in Brazil, too. But the many contributions of the versatile Negro, brought over as a humble slave, are recognized as largely responsible for the progressive new society that Brazilians are so proud of—a society that gratefully recognizes him as "the white man's greatest and most plastic collaborator in the task of agrarian colonization." The whole society, too, feels a close affinity with him. "Every Brazilian, even the light-skinned fair-haired one," says Gilberto Freyre, "carries about with him on his soul, when not on soul and body alike . . . the shadow, or at least the birthmark, of the aborigine or the Negro."[27]

THE MESTIZOS, MULATTOS, AND ZAMBOS

Following the arrival of the conquistadors and colonists in Latin America and the introduction of Negro slaves, miscegenation became so common and widespread as to radically change the character of the

---

[25] Freyre, *op. cit.*, p. 295.
[26] Pierson, *op. cit.*, pp. 128 and 139.
[27] Freyre, *op. cit.*, p. 278.

component groups. The indiscriminate sexual activity of Spaniards and Portuguese with Indians and Negroes produced so many varieties of racial mixtures as to defy complete classification. The offspring of the unions were of three general castes: the mestizo, a cross between a white and an Indian; the mulatto, between a white and a Negro; and the zambo, between an Indian and a Negro.

There were several reasons for this widespread miscegenation. For one thing, white women were very scarce. Since the conquistadors were engaged in a military mission of exploring and conquering a vast, hitherto unknown region, they did not take their wives and families with them in the first stages of the conquest. To alleviate the shortage of women, the government sent some from the mother country, mainly prostitutes and girls from orphanages.

Miscegenation was also facilitated by the fact that Moors had ruled the Iberian peninsula for centuries, tending to remove any racial prejudice on the part of both the Spanish and Portuguese. Indeed, even members of the royal family regarded it as an honor to mate with the dark-skinned Moors, who not only exercised political control but also possessed a superior culture.

Also contributing to miscegenation were the easy standards of sexual relations characteristic of many of the Indian tribes. "The milieu in which Brazilian life began," wrote Gilberto Freyre, "was one of sexual intoxication." He quotes Father Anchieta: "The women go naked and are unable to say no to anyone but they themselves provoke and importune the men . . . for they hold it to be an honor to sleep with the Christians."[28]

Fraternization between the races was so unrestrained that the mestizos increased much more rapidly proportionately than either the whites or the Indians. These *naturales* did not have the status of either the Spaniards or natives. And when unacknowledged by their fathers—often unknown in the many casual unions—or ignored by their mothers, they were so many pack rats who had to fend for themselves at the expense of society. "Lost and vagrant people," for they had no roots and could not find jobs, they tried to escape from a society which mercilessly repressed them; at times they staged violent rebellions against society.[29]

Lastly, the importation of Negro slaves inevitably resulted in sexual depravity, a concomitant of slavery wherever it exists. The woman slave, subject to the commands or desires of young sons of the family, usually initiated them precociously into physical love. The owner, too, used them to satisfy his sexual desires, and encouraged dissoluteness in order to increase the number of his *crias* (young slaves). "The most productive

---

[28] *Ibid.*, pp. 85–86.
[29] Magnus Mörner, *Race Mixture in the History of Latin America* (Boston: Little, Brown & Co., 1967), pp. 75–78.

feature of slave property," said Joaquim Nabuco, "is the generative belly."[30]

POPULATION TRENDS

In Latin America, the population is distributed most unevenly; some areas have far too few people, others have far too many. The huge Amazon basin, almost two thirds the size of the United States, has a population less than the Dominican Republic—too few people to develop the area economically. Haiti, on the other hand, has so many crowded together that they cannot support themselves adequately by the agricultural economy they must depend on for a livelihood. In the region as a whole, the population tends to be heavily concentrated in certain areas. Most of the inhabitants live in communities located near the coast, easily accessible from the sea, or in the highlands that afford a moderate climate.

Although Latin America is commonly regarded as a region whose population is predominantly rural, the picture is changing rapidly. As Figure 2–3 shows, 8 of the nations (including the most populous) have about 50 percent or more of their population in urban areas. In Venezuela, Chile, Uruguay, and Argentina, the percentages, respectively, are: 67.4, 68.7, 72.5, and 74.1.

While all urban areas have grown in size, the larger cities have grown much more rapidly. Today, at least 71 cities have populations between 100,000 and 1 million—43 in South America and 38 in Middle America. The number of such cities almost doubled between 1948 and 1958.[31]

In some instances, the growth has been spectacular. Mexico City shot up from about 1.4 million inhabitants in 1940 to an estimated 5 million in 1963, and is now vying with Buenos Aires for the distinction of being the largest city in Latin America. There are several other large cities: Rio de Janeiro and São Paulo each boast of about 4 million; Santiago and Havana approximately 2 million; and Bogotá, Caracas, Lima, and Montevideo over 1 million.

Such statistics, impressive though they are, tell us nothing of the human drama behind them. The phenomenal growth of the cities—some of the most beautiful in the world—is a source of much pride to Latin Americans. But this growth is also the cause of many serious social problems resulting from the vast internal migration to the cities from rural areas that are burdened with poverty, illiteracy, and lack of opportunity.[32]

---

[30] Freyre, *op. cit.*, p. 324.

[31] Preston James, *Latin America* (3d ed.; New York: The Odyssey Press, Inc., 1959), p. 9.

[32] Two undesirable by-products of urbanization in Latin America are (1) the transfer of unemployment, underemployment, and low-productivity employment

FIGURE 2-3

PERCENTAGES OF URBAN POPULATION, 1965

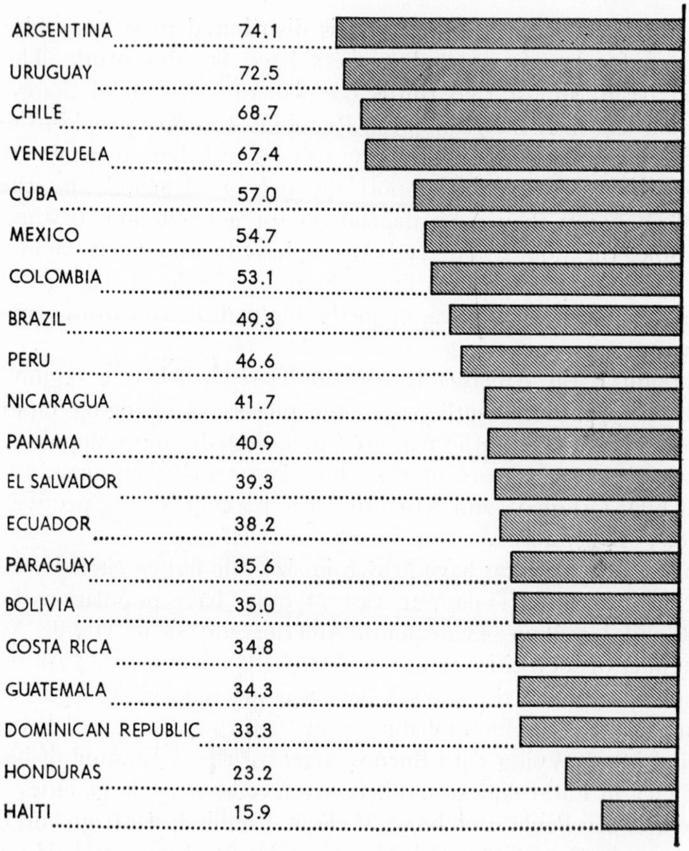

Country	Percentage
ARGENTINA	74.1
URUGUAY	72.5
CHILE	68.7
VENEZUELA	67.4
CUBA	57.0
MEXICO	54.7
COLOMBIA	53.1
BRAZIL	49.3
PERU	46.6
NICARAGUA	41.7
PANAMA	40.9
EL SALVADOR	39.3
ECUADOR	38.2
PARAGUAY	35.6
BOLIVIA	35.0
COSTA RICA	34.8
GUATEMALA	34.3
DOMINICAN REPUBLIC	33.3
HONDURAS	23.2
HAITI	15.9

SOURCE: Inter-American Development Bank, *Social Progress Trust Fund* (Fifth Annual Report) (Washington, D.C., 1965).

The trek to the city is often the gamble of a lifetime. Speaking of Peru, J. Halcro Ferguson says:

Entire Indian villages, impelled by the poverty of their highland holdings, pack up and take train or truck, or even walk, to Lima, to them the capital

from farm to city, and (2) the frustration of a main purpose of moving to the city—to be near a variety of activities—because of the difficulty of transportation and the necessity of living far from the center of the city.

Benjamin Higgins, "The City and Economic Development," *The Urban Explosion in Latin America,* ed. Glenn H. Beyer (Ithaca: Cornell University Press, 1967), p. 142.

of the world, where they have heard that it is possible to live like human beings. Usually they arrive with little or no money, and knowing nobody except some *compadre* (a word denoting some friendly person from outside) of whose very address they have probably only the haziest notion.[33]

They soon found out, however, that the city is far from the land of their dreams. Everything there is in short supply. There are not enough houses, not enough jobs, not enough schools. There is not enough food, not enough transportation—in fact, not enough of anything! Worst of all, the newcomers feel friendless, lonely, and bewildered in a busy, impersonal society too preoccupied with its own interests to know or care about their problems.

"Where do these people go?" asked an editorial in *La Prensa*, one of Lima's daily newspapers. "To fill the crime pages of the daily Press? To . . . live in the primitive and promiscuous condition of animals? . . . To crowd the tubercular wards of the hospitals? To form new gangs of juvenile delinquents? . . . To increase the population of the prisons?"[34]

Flooding the cities and seething with discontent, the newcomers are social dynamite of megaton proportions.

The population explosion, a worldwide demographic phenomenon of our age, has greater significance for Latin America than for any other region. Its population is increasing at the prodigious rate of 2.8 percent or more a year, the highest in the world. "If our last two censuses are accurate," exclaimed one official in the Dominican Republic, "the period of gestation here is three months!"[35]

As Table 2–1 shows, the countries that are chiefly contributing to the great increase are those of Central America and tropical South America. In 12 of the 13 countries of these 2 regions, which contain 72 percent of Latin America's population, the increase between 1960 and 1965 was more than 15 percent, or an average annual increase of between 2.9 and 3.9 percent.

The significance of Latin America's high rate of increase is seen by comparing its predicted growth with that of the United States. In 1969, Latin America has approximately 240 million people, about equal to the population of the United States and Canada combined. By the year 2000, however, according to a United Nations estimate, it will probably have 600 million, almost double that estimated for the United States and Canada.

This explosive growth in Latin America is primarily the result of a

---

[33] J. Halcro Ferguson, *Latin America: the Balance of Race Redressed* (Institute of Race Relations) (New York: Oxford University Press, 1961), p. 63.

[34] *Ibid.*, p. 64.

[35] "How Many Babies Is Too Many?" *Newsweek*, July 23, 1962, p. 32.

TABLE 2-1

POPULATION INCREASES, 1960-65

	Average Annual Increase 1960-65	Total Increase 1960-65	Total Population 1965	Percent of Total Latin America
Argentina ⎫ Puerto Rico ⎬ Uruguay ⎭	1.7%	8.5%	28,100,000	11.8%
Bolivia ⎫ Cuba ⎬ Haiti ⎭	2.2%	10.1%	16,300,000	6.8%
Chile ⎫ Paraguay ⎬ Peru ⎭	2.5%	12.5%	22,200,000	9.3%
Brazil ⎫ Columbia ⎪ Ecuador ⎪ El Salvador ⎬ Guatemala ⎪ Panama ⎭	2.9%	14.5%	112,700,000	47.3%
Dominican Republic ⎫ Honduras ⎪ Mexico ⎬ Nicaragua ⎪ Venezuela ⎭	3.4%	17.0%	57,600,000	24.2%
Costa Rica	3.9%	19.5%	1,400,000	.6%
Latin America as a whole	2.8%	14.0%	238,300,000	100.0%

SOURCE: J. Mayone Stycos and Jorge Arias (eds.), *Population Dilemma in Latin America* (Washington, D.C.: Potomac Books, Inc., 1966), p. 17.

drastic fall in the death rate without a corresponding decline in the high birthrate. For centuries, both the birth and the death rates were high. "Women gave birth to children with a frequency close to that possible in the human organism." Indeed, during the last century, the birthrate was probably as high as 40 to 50 per 1,000, and the mortality rate was almost as high; up to half of all the babies died before reaching the first birthday.[36]

The present decline in the death rate is attributable to a large number of modern advances, including better medical facilities and care, public health campaigns stressing the importance of sanitation, more adequate diets, a higher level of living for the masses, and, most important of all, better care and feeding of infants.

[36] T. Lynn Smith, "Current Population Trends in Latin America," *American Journal of Sociology*, Vol. LXII (January, 1957), p. 401.

One of the main reasons for the region's high birthrate has been the attitude of the Roman Catholic Church toward the use of contraceptives and effective family planning. The Church favors family planning, provided that the methods used are natural and that the aim is regulation of the size of the family consistent with responsible parenthood.[37]

The traditional opposition of the Catholic Church to birth control by artificial means, and even to dissemination of information regarding sex, makes birth control by natural means completely unrealistic in view of the prevailing ignorance about sex on the part of most of the populace. According to a study made in Costa Rica, one of the several most literate nations in Latin America, 71 percent of a national sample thought that a man's fertility varies with the weather, and 77 percent that a woman's fertile period occurs just before and after menstruation.[38]

But despite the doctrines and precepts of the Catholic Church, the women of Latin America have clearly indicated their preference for having smaller families. Studies made in 8 cities by the United Nations Latin American Demographic Center in collaboration with Cornell University show their preference ranges from an average of 2.4 children in Rio de Janeiro to 4.1 in Mexico City.[39] Moreover, a large majority of the Catholic women not only favor birth control by artificial means but also use contraceptives of some kind.[40] One widely prevalent form of birth control is quite dangerous—abortion. According to a study made in Chile, almost one out of every four women had had at least one induced abortion; of the total number aborting, a fourth had already had three or more abortions.[41]

Family planning in the region is slowly getting under way. Active organizations that give limited services regarding contraception, mostly in the urban communities, are functioning in a dozen or so of the nations. However, only in Chile and Colombia are these organizations well coordinated and attempting to cover the entire country. Honduras is in the process of setting up such a comprehensive program.[42]

The attitude of the Roman Catholic Church toward birth control and

---

[37] A detailed and objective presentation of the attitude of the Catholic Church is given by Father Gustavo Pérez Ramírez, "The Catholic Church and Family Planning—Current Perspectives," *Population Dilemma in Latin America*, eds. J. Mayone Stycos and Jorge Arias (Washington, D.C.: Potomac Books, Inc., 1966), chap. 8.

[38] J. Mayone Stycos, "Birth Control," *Integration of Man and Society in Latin America*, ed. Samuel Shapiro (Notre Dame, Ind.: Notre Dame University Press, 1967), p. 14.

[39] *Ibid.*, p. 17.

[40] A summary of the findings made by the cooperative study are given by Ramiro Delgado García, "Prospectives of Family Planning Programs in Latin America," *Population Dilemma in Latin America, op. cit.*, chap. 9.

[41] J. Mayone Stycos, "Demography and the Study of Population Problems," *Population Dilemma in Latin America, op. cit.*, p. 238.

[42] The Chilean and Colombian programs are given in *ibid.*, pp. 222–26.

IRRESISTIBLE FORCE, IMMOVABLE OBJECT

SOURCE: Herblock, *The Lincoln Star,* July 31, 1968.

the limitation of population seemed to have been changing in recent years. At the third session of the Vatican Council in 1964, the problem of population and use of contraceptives was fervently debated.[43] But expectations that the Vatican would reverse its unrealistic, medieval stand on birth control—a stand that bordered on hypocrisy because the Church even bitterly opposed the dissemination of information that might possibly make the rhythm plan work—were shattered on July 29, 1968, with the Papacy's unequivocal condemnation of birth control by other than natural means, whatever that is. The ruling precipitated another crisis within the Church even greater than that of the ban against the marriage of priests.[44]

While the Catholic Church has undoubtedly been an influence affecting the increase in population, especially by inhibiting public consideration

[43] Stycos, "Birth Control," *op. cit.,* p. 13; and Pérez Ramíres, *op. cit.,* pp. 205–6.

[44] For a critical analysis of the stand of the Roman Catholic Church on birth control, see Father James Kavanaugh, *A Modern Priest Looks at His Outdated Church* (New York: Trident Press, 1967), pp. 135–45.

of the problem, Latin American intellectuals, too, have had considerable influence on public policies regarding population growth. The intellectuals generally, following a Marxist line that postulates that an excess population is impossible in an efficient socialist state, regard the peopling of Latin America's large open spaces as a kind of manifest destiny which will bring power and recognition to the relatively weak nations of the region. The editor of El Salvador's newspaper *El Diario de Hoy*, N. Viera Altamirano, maintains that Latin America needs 2 billion more inhabitants to reach an optimum level.[45]

The individuals most interested in birth control and in restricting the growth of the population, insists Luis Alberto Sánchez, are the large landowners and the backward capitalists; although a larger number of consumers would constitute a larger market, the landowners and capitalists are afraid that a mass demand for distribution of economic and social benefits would be a threat to their profits.[46]

In time, increasing urbanization and industrialization will likely lead to lower birthrates—a trend that usually accompanies the change from an agricultural to an industrial economy. For the foreseeable future, however, no reduction in the high birthrate or in the high annual population increase is anticipated.[47] If anything, this increase will probably go even higher as the death rate continues to decline further with improved sanitation, better medicine, and healthier diets.

Meanwhile, the population explosion, whatever its local or general effects and whatever problems it may cause, is like an atomic detonation: once the atom is unleashed, only time can tell the full effects of the fallout.

Besides being much larger, the population of Latin America in the future will probably be quite different racially from its composition today. According to Table 2–2, the proportion of Indians is decreasing, of Negroes is about the same, and of whites (or those regarded by the society as whites) is increasing. This ethnic change is attributable to several causes. The upper classes have families as large as the other classes,

---

[45] Stycos, "Demography and the Study of Population Problems," *op. cit.*, p. 229.
For attitudes of other intellectuals opposed to birth control, see J. Mayone Stycos, *Human Fertility in Latin America: Sociological Perspectives* (Ithaca, N.Y.: Cornell University Press, 1968), pp. 43–48.

[46] Luis Alberto Sánchez, "Urban Growth and the Latin American Herritage," *The Urban Explosion in Latin America, op. cit.,* p. 2.

[47] "A spontaneous decline in the birthrate cannot take place in a country where the majority of the population is plunged in such misery that they have neither the incentive nor the material possibilities of practicing birth control, and are too superstitious and improvident to care. Another important fact is that sexual intercourse is the only pleasure which the very poor can afford." Stanislav Andreski, *Parasitism and Subversion: the Case of Latin America* (New York: Pantheon Books, Inc., 1967), p. 17.

TABLE 2-2

EVOLUTION OF THE ETHNIC COMPOSITION OF THE POPULATION BETWEEN
1650 AND 1950

(population figures in millions) *

| | 1650 | | 1825 | | 1950 | |
Groups	Population	%	Population	%	Population	%
Indians	9.13	80.4	8.2	35.6	14.3	8.8
Negroes	0.83	7.3	4.07	17.8	13.7	8.0
Whites	0.72	6.4	4.3	18.8	72.0	44.5
Mestizos	0.67	5.9	6.2	27.1	61.6	38.1

* W. S. and E. S. Woytinsky, *World Population and Production: Trends and Outlook* (New York: Twentieth Century Fund, 1953).

and what is particularly significant, with their higher standard of living and better medical care, manage to save a far greater proportion of their children. Also, the mores of Latin America that sanction extramarital relations of the male are responsible for the upper class whites' siring many of the children born to lower class women of color. "The net result of all this is that the population of Latin America is 'bleaching' rapidly. . . ."[48]

Yet in spite of all this bleaching, the whites may still fail to assimilate the Indians, who have managed over the centuries to maintain their own race and way of life. Like the captured Araucanian warrior, they may refuse to capitulate.

Frank Tannenbaum says:

. . . the Indian is in all probability increasing more rapidly than the urbanized population. . . . That the Latin will ultimately absorb the American has been taken for granted from the beginning which is more than four centuries ago. And so it may prove in the end, but the end is a long way off and history has shown itself capable of many an unexpected turn.[49]

Perhaps it is too early to tell yet whether the Indians and Negroes will be bleached or whether the whites will be colored. But from many indications, the race emerging in Latin America today will probably be a new breed, different from any of its ancestors. It will likely be part white, part red, and with at least a little "finger in the kitchen."

IMPLICATIONS FOR PUBLIC POLICY

The complexion and size of the population in the nations of Latin America have many important bearings on public policy. The presence of

[48] Smith, *op. cit.*, p. 406.
[49] Tannenbaum, "Toward an Appreciation of Latin America," *op. cit.*, pp. 20–21.

millions of Indians, mainly in the highland regions from Mexico south-ward, has been a great obstacle to national unity. When living in their isolated *communidades*, whether from the neglect of society or self-imposed isolation, the Indians speaking only in Indian dialect, illiterate, knowing little about the outside world, and caring even less—wanting only to be left alone—contribute little or nothing to the society.[50] This large segment of the population must be brought into the national life and aspirations.

The several races with their different cultures, mores, and interests have often felt a strong animosity toward one another. The tensions resulting from racial differences and interests have often been tempting targets for demagogues who rise to power by capitalizing on such differences.

The national complexion of large immigrant sectors of the population have sometimes had a strong influence on foreign policy. In Argentina, it was debatable what effect the large, rich, and influential German community had on the nation's policy of neutrality in World War I—a policy widely regarded as pro-German and anti-American.[51] In World War II, however, the government was obviously pro-Nazi, pursuing a policy of aiding Germany, as later shown by documentary evidence in the German archives.[52]

The rapid urbanization and growth of a few large cities, especially the capitals, poses a basic question: What policy should the government adopt toward such growth? In Chile, the government has tried to hold back the growth of Santiago by not establishing any important industries there and by locating them in cities far removed from the capital. In Mexico, on the other hand, the government has encouraged the growth of Mexico City by subsidizing food, fuel oil, and electricity and natural gas to hold down the cost of living with a view of attracting industry.[53]

A possible counteractant to the unwieldy growth of a few large cities is a policy of regional development and regional distribution of cities. This reorientation, if possible, would have many advantages but would encounter much opposition, including a commitment of the central government to provide urban services and the embellishments of metro-politan living, as well as the large costs that would have to be borne by a planned program of dispersing the cities and having them contribute to

---

50 *Ibid.*, pp. 14–15 and 17.

51 Harold F. Peterson, *Argentina and the United States, 1810–1960* (New York: State University, 1964), p. 309.

52 J. Lloyd Mecham, *A Survey of United States–Latin American Relations* (Boston: Houghton Mifflin Co., 1965), p. 146; and J. Lloyd Mecham, *United States and Inter-American Security, 1889–1960* (Austin: University of Texas Press, 1961), pp. 194 and 215.

53 Glenn H. Beyer (ed.), *The Urban Explosion in Latin America: A Continent in the Process of Modernization, op. cit.*, pp. 165–66.

regional development.[54] A dispersion of cities throughout the nation might in time even modify the unitary, centralized form of government that prevails over most of the region. Populous distant provinces or states might well demand a large measure of autonomy, leading to the adoption of a federal system of government.

The cities are to a large extent parasitic, and live on the countryside without contributing much to its welfare. This is particularly true of the national capitals, "with their absentee landowners, generals, politicians, clergymen, officials, troops, lawyers, students, and the enormous numbers of servants attending to the needs of all these categories."[55] To distribute national benefits more equitably, and to encourage agricultural production and assure that farm products are paid what they are really worth, the governments might well institute some sort of parity, maybe even price supports and acreage controls when feasible.

The population explosion in most of Latin America is not a stimulating but a retarding influence, absorbing the results of increased production and limiting the growth in per capita income. But ". . . it is doubtful whether an increase in population can shock an economy into growth unless it is already well advanced, or there is a shortage of labor in proportion to land and capital."[56]

In confronting the population explosion while at the same time trying to promote economic development, Chile has decided to curb its rate of growth, relatively low by Latin American standards, in order to assure the economic growth of the nation and thereby provide its people with a better standard of living.[57] Mexico, on the other hand, has followed a very different policy; there has been no effort to raise Mexican per capita income by reducing the rate of population growth, among the highest in the world. With this rate of growth, in another 20 years Mexico will outstrip France, Italy, and the United Kingdom and become one of the 10 most populous nations in the world. "From the Mexican viewpoint, the population explosion is a benign event that may well lead to larger domestic markets and a larger role in world affairs."[58]

Whether Latin America should try to curb its high rate of population growth or should even encourage it, with the expectation of receiving certain benefits, is no longer just a social or economic issue but a political

---

[54] *Ibid.*, pp. 157–63.

[55] Andreski, *op. cit.*, p. 8.

[56] William Withers, *The Economic Crisis in Latin America* (New York: Free Press of Glencoe, 1964), p. 70.

[57] The nation's extensive program of family planning is given by Thomas G. Sanders, "Family Planning in Chile: Part I, The Public Program; Part II, The Catholic Position," *American Universities Field Staff*, Vol. XIV, Nos. 4 and 5 (West Coast South American Series, December, 1967).

[58] Robert J. Shafer, *Mexico: Mutual Adjustment Planning* (Syracuse, N.Y.: Syracuse University Press, 1966), p. xiii.

one as well. The Christian Democratic parties, on the ascendancy throughout most of Latin America, are in most nations unequivocally opposed to birth control. Their rationale is not that of traditional theology but that Latin America is underpopulated and needs a larger population in order to fully exploit the region's resources.[59]

SUGGESTED READINGS

Adams, Richard N. *A Community in the Andes: Problems and Progress in Muquiyauto.* Seattle: University of Washington Press, 1959.

Arciniegas, Germán. *The Green Continent: A Comprehensive View of Latin America by Its Leading Writers,* Part V. Trans. Harriet de Onís and others. New York: Alfred A. Knopf, Inc., 1959.

Beyer, Glenn H. (ed.). *The Urban Explosion in Latin America.* Ithaca, N.Y.: Cornell University Press, 1967.

Collier, John. *The Indians of the Americas,* Part Two. New York: W. W. Norton & Co., Inc., 1947.

———, and Aníbal Buitrón. *The Awakening Valley.* Chicago: University of Chicago Press, 1949.

Davidson, Basil. *Black Mother: The Years of the African Slave Trade.* Boston: Atlantic–Little, Brown & Co., 1961.

Fals-Borda, Orlando. *Peasant Society in the Colombian Andes; A Sociological Study of Saucío,* chaps. 4 and 9. Gainesville: University of Florida Press, 1957.

Ferguson, J. Halcro. *Latin America: The Balance of Race Redressed.* Institute of Race Relations. New York: Oxford University Press, 1961.

Fitzgibbon, Russell H. *Uruguay: Portrait of a Democracy,* chap. v. New Brunswick, N.J.: Rutgers University Press, 1954.

Freyre, Gilberto. *The Masters and the Slaves: A Study in the Development of Brazilian Civilization,* pp. 3–80 and 185–277. Trans. Samuel Putnam. 2d ed. rev. New York: Alfred A. Knopf, Inc., 1956.

Gruening, Ernest. *Mexico and Its Heritage,* pp. 69–90. New York: D. Appleton-Century Co., Inc., 1934.

International Labour Office. *Indigenous Peoples: Living and Working Conditions in Independent Countries,* Parts I and II. Studies and Reports, New Series, No. 35. Geneva, Switzerland, 1953.

Leonard, Olen E. *Bolivia: Land, People and Institutions,* chaps. ii–iv. Washington, D.C.: The Scarecrow Press, Inc., 1952.

Mannix, Daniel P. in collaboration with Malcolm Cowley. *Black Cargoes: A History of the Atlantic Slave Trade; 1518–1865.* New York: The Viking Press, 1962.

Mörner, Magnus. *Race Mixture in the History of Latin America.* Boston: Little, Brown & Co., Inc., 1967.

---

[59] Edward J. Williams, *Latin American Christian Democratic Parties* (Knoxville: University of Tennessee Press, 1967), pp. 95–96.

Nelson, Lowry. *Rural Cuba,* chaps. ii and iv. Minneapolis: University of Minnesota Press, 1950.

Osborne, Harold. *Indians of the Andes: Aymaras and Quechuas.* Cambridge, Mass.: Harvard University Press, 1952.

Pierson, Donald. *Negroes in Brazil: A Study of Race Contact at Bahia,* chaps. ii–v and ix–xi. Chicago: University of Chicago Press, 1942.

Rycroft, W. Stanley (ed.). *Indians of the High Andes.* New York: Committee on Cooperation with Latin America, 1946.

Sanders, Thomas G., "Family Planning in Chile: Part I, The Public Program; Part II, The Catholic Position," *American Universities Field Staff,* West Coast South American Series. Vol. XIV, Nos. 4 and 5 (December, 1967).

Schurz, William Lytle. *Brazil: The Infinite Country,* chaps. 3 and 7. New York: E. P. Dutton & Co., Inc., 1961.

———. *This New World: The Civilization of Latin America,* chaps. ii–vi. New York: E. P. Dutton & Co., Inc., 1954.

Smith, T. Lynn. *Brazil: People and Institutions,* Part II. Rev. ed. Baton Rouge: Louisiana State University Press, 1963.

Steward, Julian H., and Farón, Louis C. *Native Peoples of South America.* New York: McGraw-Hill Book Co., Inc., 1959.

Stycos, J. Mayone. *Human Fertility in Latin America: Sociological Perspectives.* Ithaca, N.Y.: Cornell University Press, 1968.

———. "Birth Control," *Integration of Man and Society in Latin America* (ed. Samuel Shapiro). Notre Dame, Ind.: Notre Dame University Press, 1967.

Stycos, J. Mayone and Arias, Jorge (eds.). *Population Dilemma in Latin America.* Washington, D.C.: Potomac Books, Inc., 1966.

Tannenbaum, Frank. *Slave and Citizen: The Negro in the Americas.* New York: Alfred A. Knopf, Inc., 1947.

Taylor, Carl C. *Rural Life in Argentina,* chaps. iii–vii. Baton Rouge: Louisiana State University Press, 1948.

Wagley, Charles. *An Introduction to Brazil,* chap. 7. New York: Columbia University Press, 1963.

Whetten, Nathan L. *Guatemala: The Land and the People,* chaps. 2 and 3. Caribbean Series, 4. New Haven, Conn.: Yale University Press, 1961.

———. *Rural Mexico,* chaps. ii and iii. Chicago: University of Chicago Press, 1948.

PART II

Social Fountainheads
of Political Action

3

THE SOCIAL CLASSES AND THE FAMILY:
Fermentation in the Structure

THE SOCIAL CLASSES

In most of Latin America, the rigid class structure of the colonial era was very slow to change. The boldly proclaimed declarations of independence and idealistically inspired professions of equality and rights seemed to scarcely make a dent in the hard-shell social structure. But the class structure has been undergoing considerable change, especially in the last several decades. This is mainly true in those nations where industrialization and urbanization are advancing at a fast pace. In Brazil's changing society, while the old pattern persists, it no longer prevails; the new one, however, although becoming stronger, is not yet dominant in the society.[1] Even in the nations industrializing relatively slowly, as Colombia, the composition and attitudes of the social groups are noticeably changing.[2]

Determinants of Social Status

Among the several determinants of one's social status in Latin America today, education and culture are easily the most important. In fact, they are the open sesame to achievement and prestige. Illiteracy and little or no

---

[1] Irving Louis Horowitz, *Revolution in Brazil: Politics and Society in a Developing Nation* (New York: E. P. Dutton & Co., Inc., 1964), p. 225.

The changing social structure of Brazil under the impact of industrialization and urbanization is given in chap. viii.

[2] Robert H. Dix, *Colombia: The Political Dimensions of Change* (New Haven, Conn.: Yale University Press, 1967), pp. 72–73.

schooling, on the other hand, are characteristic of the large lower class and virtually destine its members to poverty, meniality, and servility.

Language is one of the most important cultural criteria of status. Throughout Hispanic America, Spanish is the accepted language of polite society; in Brazil, it is Portuguese; in Haiti, it is French. The millions of Indians who speak nothing but one of the hundreds of Indian languages or dialects are, in effect, social outcasts beyond the pale of polite society.

Of all these Indian languages, only Guaraní spoken in Paraguay is sanctioned by polite usage. It is one of the principal Indian contributions to Paraguayan culture, and it gives the nation the distinction of being the only truly bilingual country in Latin America. While Spanish is the official language of the country and is used on more formal occasions, even the best families speak Guaraní at home. "The Paraguayans love, hate, and fight in Guaraní. In this tongue they shout on the football field and whisper their declarations of love in the dark corners of the patios of their old colonial houses."[3] When debate becomes heated in Parliament, the members may suddenly lapse into their ancestral tongue.

Another cultural requirement for social status is that one belong to the Roman Catholic Church. Although it has lost much of its earlier influence and has been the target of widespread anticlericalism, Catholicism is nevertheless regarded as the religion of higher status.

As in other societies, the Latin American's dress, home, and manners are also important in determining the class he belongs to. To achieve a higher status, he must wear the conventional attire of the West and live in one of the better neighborhoods in a substantial home or at least in a dwelling of permanent construction with floors made of something better than packed earth. He must also use polite language, as well as have good manners and social *savoir faire*.

As in other socially conscious societies, occupation is another important determinant of social status. The ideal is not to have any occupation at all. For work is regarded as simply a means to an end—a sort of necessary evil to obtain a livelihood. There is nothing noble or dignifying about it. Rather, as the Latin Americans view it, "Idleness is the mother of a delightful life," and, "Work is sacred, don't touch it."

But if one has to work for a living, he should select something dignified, possibly enter one of the professions, as law, medicine, teaching, writing, artistic achievement, military service, or the priesthood. Only as a last resort would he choose manual labor; it would immediately stamp him as belonging to the lower class.

"Money talks" it is often said. In Latin America, it shouts in a stentorian voice. Money alone does not assure a high social status, but if one has even a modicum of culture and social graces he will find that having plenty of money will get him nowhere socially but to the top.

---

[3] George Pendle, *Paraguay: A Riverside Nation* (The Royal Institute of International Affairs) (London: Oxford University Press, 1954), p. 93.

Money can even change one's color, too. In Brazil with its large Negro and Negroid population, it changes black to white and white to black. *"Negro rico é branco, e branco pobre é negro"* ("A rich Negro is a white man, and a poor white man is a Negro").[4]

In Colombia, lack of money can change white to red. "The term 'Indian' designates a social status, and not an ethnically identifiable biology," asserts Gerardo Reichel. "An individual with predominantly Caucasian physical characteristics [still] is designated as an 'Indian' if he lives on an aboriginal cultural level, or if he *occupies a low rung on the social scale.*"[5]

Race also has an important bearing on a person's social position. While there is no race problem in the same sense that it exists in many other nations, in every country of Latin America the ruling classes are whiter than the lower classes; and usually the whiter the individual is, the higher his status is in the social hierarchy.

White blood is highly prized by the ruling classes, who sometimes boast of *pureza de sangre* (purity of blood). Vernon Fluharty wrote:

The concupiscent conquistadors and their descendants took the native and slave women to their beds, but scarcely ever to their bosoms; they used them, but did not marry them. Rather, they made of "whiteness" a yardstick by which all social, economic, and political preference was measured. Children of cross-matings had better social chances than did the aborigine; and further "whitening" might bring them even closer to the select circle. Still, from the beginning down to the present in Colombia, the circle has been select.[6]

White blood is also prized by the dark-skinned persons in the lower classes. In Brazil, for example, a Negroid woman who bears a whiter child considers herself fortunate; her status and her child's are improved. "I don't want to go back to Africa," she may say to express her preference for lighter offspring. And as a sort of justification for her action, if any were needed, she is apt to add, *"Estou limpando a minha raça"* ("I am cleansing [i.e., whitening] my race"), or *"Melhorando a raça"* ("improving the breed").[7]

In most of the Latin American countries, being either Indian or Negro is a distinct handicap because these racial groups have been relegated to the lower classes through the denial of social and economic opportunity. As a result, their very physical characteristics continue to be symbols of low social rank, of descent from slaves or peons.

Yet, in the highly stratified society, class lines are actually greater

---

[4] Donald Pierson, *Negroes in Brazil: A Study of Race Contact at Bahia* (Chicago: University of Chicago Press, 1942), p. 152.

[5] In Vernon L. Fluharty, *Dance of the Millions: Military Rule and the Social Revolution in Colombia, 1930–1956* (Pittsburgh, Pa.: University of Pittsburgh Press, 1957), p. 179.

[6] *Ibid.,* p. 175.

[7] Pierson, *op. cit.,* pp. 120–22.

barriers than racial differences. Since Latin America defines race in terms of cultural traits rather than physical differences, and since culture is such an influential factor in determining social status, neither Negro nor Indian blood has been an insuperable bar to acceptance in high social circles. Individual competence is more important than social background in the determination of one's status. According to Donald Pierson,

Color is undoubtedly a handicap. But it always tends to be discounted if the individual in question possesses other characteristics of upper-class identity, such as professional competence, intellectual ability, educational achievement, wealth, an "engaging" manner, personal "charm," poise, "breeding," and, especially with the females, beauty.[8]

Even in the sensitive area of marriage, class is a more important consideration than race. Where there is opposition to marrying a black, it is based on class rather than on racial grounds concludes Donald Pierson, speaking of the Negroes in Brazil. Indeed, when the color black does not ". . . identify an individual as a member of the lower class, opposition to him tends to disappear. Virtually no opposition attaches to the marriage of light mixed-bloods into even the upper class, especially if they do not show in their features or color too obvious evidence of Negro origin."[9]

Indeed, the Moreno is regarded in Bahía as the ideal type of feminine beauty. With her dark-brown eyes, dark wavy hair, and *café com leite* (coffee with milk) complexion, she is the toast of poets and songwriters and the overwhelming preference in marriage over mulatto or even white girls.

Upper Class

The upper class consists of two groups—the old landed aristocracy and the new moneyed elite. Most members of the old group, who own the *haciendas* and plantations, enjoy their status by virtue of birth—*el privilegio de la cuna* (the privilege of the cradle).[10] Some, however, have entered the group by virtue of a fortunate marriage. But since its members have strongly tended to intermarry, it has been virtually a closed circle, almost as select as that of the earlier Inca whose status was so exalted that only his full sister was qualified to be his wife.

Belonging to this closed circle, however achieved, has been all-important. Its members have had a monopoly of the political power, wealth, education and culture, prestige and influence in the countries. Capable, cultured, and cosmopolitan, the landed aristocrats are versatile individ-

---

8 *Ibid.*, pp. 204–5.
9 *Ibid.*, p. 151.
10 Ironically, among the poorer classes where infant mortality is very high, *cuna*, cradle, means "coffin."

uals.[11] Besides managing their haciendas, supervised in their absence by overseers, they sometimes become interested in urban economic opportunities—no ordinary jobs, of course, but something befitting their status, such as president of a bank or director of a railroad. Sometimes they enter politics, and play a prominent role in the national congress or perhaps in the president's cabinet. Sometimes they prefer to dabble in a profession, delving deeper into law, philosophy, or some other love of their student days. But whatever they do, it is with the love of a dilettante who does not have to depend on it for a living.

The lords and masters of all they surveyed (most of the farmland in Latin America and practically all of the good land), the *hacendados* have been a powerful force in the painful evolution of Latin America.

A few of them, able to see beyond their own immediate interests, have been idealistic champions of reform. Galo Plaza, a wealthy liberal landowner and president of Ecuador from 1948 to 1952, was a model president, promoting democracy, prosperity, and progress. And Pedro Aguirre Cerda, a wealthy intellectual radical and president of Chile from 1938 to 1941, promoted an extensive program of social legislation that made his nation one of the model welfare states of the world.

But most of the *hacendados* have opposed social reforms because they cost a lot of money—money for schools, hospitals, medical clinics, housing, and social security, as well as for higher wages that would enable the peons to live like human beings. The cost would inevitably have to be borne mainly by the aristocrats, since they possess most of the wealth.

Determined to safeguard their privileges, they have used every weapon in their aristocratic arsenal. They have organized powerful pressure groups, such as the Sociedad Nacional de Agricultura, to elect members to the national congress and to fight any proposed legislation considered inimical to their interests. They have also cultivated the armed forces, winning their support by granting them privileges and large budgets. And whenever it served their interests, which was often, they have openly or tacitly supported dictators who could be counted on to preserve the status quo and, although repressive in their rule, to stave off the hideous specter of change.

In some countries, the aristocracy has had notable reverses: in Paraguay, it never recovered from the body blows inflicted by Francia; in Venezuela, it was reduced to virtual impotence by the long, ruthless dictatorship of Gómez; in Brazil, its economic base was obliterated by the abolition of slavery. There, the Big House, for all its pomp and planning for posterity, is an empty, decaying reminder of a slave society that, like our own, has "gone with the wind."

The whirlwinds of social change have had their effects, too. The social

---

[11] For a sympathetic, yet penetrating, critical evaluation of the privileged upper class, see Fluharty, *op. cit.*, pp. 183–87.

revolutions in Mexico, Bolivia, and, most recently, Cuba, have apparently jolted the complacency of the oligarchs, creating some misgivings about their traditional opposition to social reform. In Peru, the oligarchy played an important role in ending the military dictatorship of General Manuel Odría in 1956, possibly fearing that change is inevitable and that it had better come gradually through the democratic process rather than by violent revolution as in neighboring Bolivia.

In most of the countries, however, the oligarchy remains an adamant, usually decisive force in determining national policies and objectives. Even when it is unable to muster large blocks of votes and loses direct control of government, it usually manages, with its great economic power, influence, and prestige to exercise an effective veto over any measures it opposes. Its intransigent attitude toward social reform, especially land and tax reform, threatens to defeat the ambitious objectives of the Alliance for Progress.

The entrenched oligarchs are veritable roadblocks to progress. In fact, after long service in the region a seasoned diplomat concluded: "They are willing to tie down the safety valve and to wait for the boiler to burst."[12]

In addition to the aristocratic landed elite, many of the countries have a new upper class that consists of industrialists, entrepreneurs, business-men, and bankers who have risen to prominence in the more industrially developed nations. Often from humble backgrounds, they are self-made men who had no family name or prestige to rely on, only their ability, vision, and driving ambition for success and recognition. Many of them are *arrivistas*, or recent arrivals—European immigrants who despaired of their opportunities in the old world and were attracted to Latin America by the chance to begin a new life, setting up their own small businesses, becoming financially independent, possibly even amassing a fortune.

With seemingly unlimited resources ready to be exploited and with insatiable wants for new products and services, Latin America offered boundless opportunity—the proverbial "tide in the affairs of men"—for those astute and daring enough to grasp it. Staking their all on hard work, ingenuity, and unscrupulous methods if necessary, they sometimes suc-ceeded beyond a young hopeful's wildest dreams. The sagas of their rise from rags to riches are Horatio Alger exploits in a Latin American setting.

Among those particularly favored by fortune's wide smile was Fran-cisco Matarazzo, an energetic, imaginative emigrant from Italy. On his trip over in 1881, he lost his initial capital, the merchandise he was bringing with him. Undaunted by this setback, after settling down in

---

12 John M. Cabot, "Social Evolution in Latin America—the Necessity for Mutual Understanding," *Toward Our Common American Destiny* (Fletcher School of Law and Diplomacy, 1954), p. 21.

Sorocaba, Brazil, he began to experiment with new methods for processing and putting up foods. As each new venture succeeded, he branched out into others. During World War I, already one of the nation's leading industrialists, he plunged headlong into many new enterprises, reaping such great profits that he was accused by his countrymen of desiring to aid both sides so as to prolong the conflict and pyramid his profits.[13] Before his death in 1937, Matarazzo was reputedly the wealthiest man in Latin America, heading the world's largest personally managed industrial empire.[14]

Other enterprising individuals were eminently successful too, and soon came to constitute a new upper class, a respected and envied plutocracy. With the prestige of his wealth and influence, the new industrialist sometimes marries a member of the landed aristocracy. With his grandiose plans, he is giving a momentum to economic development that augurs well for the future of the countries. All segments benefit from his goals. In order to develop a larger internal consumer market that will buy his products and augment the profits of his enterprise, he is interested in increasing the purchasing power of the mass, developing new wants of many kinds, and promoting a higher standard of living for all.

And just as he has taken over some of the prestige formerly monopolized by the old landed elite, he has also made inroads on its political power and influence. In Brazil, he is the dominant figure in society. To further his objectives, he usually allies himself with the liberal parties that champion social reform. He has often supported the Partido Social Progressista led by Adhemar de Barros, and the Partido Trabalhista Brasileiro founded by Getulio Vargas, both of which are strongly supported by the urban lower class. It is, observes Charles Wagley,

an unusual political alliance, an alliance . . . between the wealthiest segment of the population, the new business and industrial groups, and the urban lower class who often live in outright misery. For different reasons, both seem to be united against what they consider the special privileges of the old oligarchy."[15]

Middle Class

The rise and growth of the middle class in Latin America have been very uneven among the 20 countries. In five of them—Argentina, Brazil, Chile, Uruguay, and Mexico—the class is growing rapidly, as shown by

[13] Richard M. Morse, *From Community to Metropolis: A Biography of São Paulo, Brazil* (Gainesville: University of Florida Press, 1958), pp. 176 and 228–29.

[14] *Ibid.*, p. 229.

[15] Charles Wagley, "The Brazilian Revolution: Social Changes Since 1930," *Social Change in Latin America Today* (Council on Foreign Relations) (New York: Harper & Bros., 1960), pp. 226–27.

the great increase in the demand for consumer goods and services, and is playing an important role in the progress of these nations. In Argentina, Chile, and Uruguay, the class is estimated to be 50 percent or more of the population; in Mexico and Brazil, about 30 percent.[16] These countries are the most progressive in the region, and also the most important in terms of population, area, wealth, and international prestige.

Studying the middle class in other countries, one is tempted to ask: "*¿Existe la clase de media?*" One scholar, after spending a year observing and investigating in Cuba, was not sure that it did. "One has the general feeling," said Lowry Nelson, "that Cuban society has not 'set' or 'jelled.' "[17]

Another scholar was apparently even more frustrated. "The most difficult task in studying the Colombian middle class," wrote Vernon Fluharty, "is to find it."[18]

In those countries—the less advanced ones burdened by illiteracy, poverty, and dictatorship, as well as the more progressive ones that have large Indian populations—the embryonic middle class has had difficulty pecking its way through the hard shell of social stratification. Between the extremes of wealth and culture, there is no sizable middle group that even resembles a class.

Even in the five countries where the middle class constitutes a sizable part of the population, it is not a middle class in the sense that it is usually regarded in the more advanced nations—the group politically dominant, economically powerful, numerically large, and the group to which most members of society belong emotionally as well as economically. Since the middle group in Latin America differs so markedly from this, even in those countries where it is most powerful, some writers prefer to use other terms to describe it, such as middle sectors, middle groups, middle segments, middle components, middle elements, and the like.

In several respects the middle class does not have the usual characteristics of a social class, and it lacks a class consciousness that results from a common background and similar interests. This is partly the result of the great difference in the income and standard of living among members of the class. In Mexico, some earn 50,000 pesos a year or more, enabling them to live opulently in the finest mansions in the city; most of them,

---

[16] The Brazilian social pyramid, according to L. C. Bresser Pereira, is as follows: upper class, 1 percent; upper-middle, 2 percent; middle, 6; lower-middle, 18; and lower, 70 (leaving 3 percent undistributed). See L. C. Bresser Pereira, "The Rise of Middle Class and Middle Management in Brazil," *Journal of Inter-American Studies,* Vol. IV, No. 3 (July, 1962), p. 320.

[17] Lowry Nelson, *Rural Cuba* (Minneapolis: University of Minnesota Press, 1950), p. 139.

[18] Fluharty, *op. cit.,* p. 187.

In the opinion of Robert H. Dix, Colombia does have a small but increasing middle class—15 percent of the populace, according to the Lebret Report of 1958, and a higher percent according to some other studies. Dix, *op. cit.,* p. 56.

however, have very modest incomes, as little as 5,000 pesos or less, forcing them to live in undesirable sections.[19] It is also partly the result of the very heterogeneous composition of the group: those rising from the lower class; members of the old aristocracy whose families have lost their landed fortunes; and the spillover from the aristocracy whose wealth, however great, was limited in the number it could support in elite fashion.[20]

Several factors are responsible for the rise of the middle class; probably the most important is industrialization. The industrial revolution was slow to get to Latin America, but when it did, technology and machines went far toward recreating society and its values. In the new industries that were established, a wide range of new positions was provided—clerical, supervisory, statistical, analytical, research, and many others. The white collar, the trademark of the middle class, was as symbolic of the new order as was the machine.

The great expansion of government resulting from its assumption of many new activities was also a powerful stimulus to the rise of the new class; as in the case of industry, it created many new white-collar positions. The spread of public education also served to promote the new class. By obtaining a high school, technical school, or perhaps university education, large numbers could prepare for the professions or the many desirable new jobs in industry and government. Too, teaching became one of the most important professions that furnished employment for many.[21]

Many occupational opportunities are open to members of the class. Professional men and intellectuals play a prominent role as doctors, lawyers, professors and school teachers, writers and journalists, painters, scientists, actors, and radio and television performers. Others in the class are associated with industry and trade, and include small industrialists, businessmen, salesmen, engineers, and technicians. The more influential

---

[19] Oscar Lewis, "Mexico since Cárdenas," *Social Change in Latin America Today, op. cit.*, p. 336.

[20] The swarm of minor officials who occupy posts in the national, state, and local governments, and the host of lawyers who constitute the overwhelming majority of professional men, are the sons, grandsons, and great-grandsons of persons who formerly occupied positions at the apex of the social pyramid in Colombia. T. Lynn Smith, *Colombia: Social Structure and the Process of Development* (Gainesville: University of Florida Press, 1967), pp. 339–40.

In Brazil, a government position at any level confers prestige far out of proportion to its modest stipend; any employee usually holds two or more positions to earn an adequate income. Rollie E. Poppino, *Brazil: The Land and People* (New York: Oxford University Press, 1968), pp. 304–5.

[21] According to a study made in the state of Rio de Janeiro, Brazil, the upper and upper-middle class contributed 26 percent of the primary teachers and 40 percent of the secondary; the lower-middle, 53 percent of the primary and 56 percent of the secondary; and the lower class, 20 percent of the primary and 3 percent of the secondary. Robert J. Havighurst y colaboradores, *La sociedad y la educación en América latina* (Buenos Aires, 1962), p. 328.

labor leaders, although beginning as proletarians, move up into the class by acquiring skills and symbols mandatory for the national influence they need.

Still other members are engaged in politics or are employed by the large governmental bureaucracy as administrators, supervisors, clerks, and a wide range of specialists, including farm extension workers, labor advisers, nurses, and hygienists and social workers. Many other occupational groups, such as army officers and clergymen, belong to the class.

There are no set criteria to determine precisely who will be in the middle class. In most countries, however, it does not include persons engaged in any kind of manual labor. But this is not true in Mexico. Due to the country's industrial expansion and constant upgrading of labor, the Mexican blue-collar worker performing skilled labor is considered middle class. Similarly, although in most countries the farmer of a few acres is relegated to the rural lower class, in Mexico the small landowners and *ejidatarios* are regarded by some as belonging to the middle class. In the areas of Colombia where family-size farms constitute the nucleus of the prevailing rural social system and where social stratification is slight, the farm owners enjoy a middle class status. With the egalitarian personal relations and the great incentive to work and save, manual labor on the farm is considered dignifying.[22]

Most members of the middle class, regardless of their backgrounds, aspire to the old aristocratic values of the landed gentry. For the great majority, this beer income but champagne appetite is the cause of much frustration. They regard telephones, electric stoves, refrigerators, and washing machines as not merely conveniences but necessities; but the cost of these products is extremely high when compared with their incomes. A small electric refrigerator, for example, may cost the equivalent of five or six months' salary; the prices of other conveniences are likewise very high.[23]

As in the United States, better housing is an important status symbol, but it is often impossible for a family to obtain a home befitting its status. Building or buying one is very difficult. A prospective builder or buyer can get a loan for only 40 to 60 percent of the value, must pay 20 percent interest a year, and must repay the entire mortgage within 5 or 6 years. As a result of inadequate long-term financing, most of the urban property in many cities is rental, and many middle class families must live cramped in one- or two-room apartments. In the fast-growing cities, building has

---

22 Smith, *op. cit.*, p. 11.

23 Wagley, *op. cit.*, p. 219.

Moreover, to aggravate the financial difficulties of the middle class, its savings, if any have possibly been accumulated, are often wiped out by inflation. Sometimes, too, its jobs, which are the basis of any real security, are jeopardized by political instability. Charles Wagley, "The Dilemma of the Latin American Middle Classes," *Proceedings of the Academy of Political Science* (Economic and Political Trends in Latin America), Vol. XXVII, No. 4 (May, 1964), pp. 2–10.

not been able to keep up with population growth, and millions of new dwellings are urgently needed. Families that could afford better places are often forced to live in undesirable quarters because nothing else is available.[24]

The disdain of Latin Americans for manual labor makes it even more difficult for them to live within their incomes. Regardless of the tight squeeze on its budget, the family must have at least one domestic servant, preferably several, since they are visible proof to the world that it has arrived. To be able to afford them and keep up appearances, the husband may have to work long hours, possibly moonlight too, with at least one other job in addition to his regular one.

Caught between the squeeze of extravagant wants and limited financial means, the middle class is being forced to modify some of its traditional values and to discard some of its long-standing prejudices. The woman's place is in the home, they have long believed; but in order to afford a higher standard of living, wives and daughters in increasing numbers have had to go to work to supplement the family income.

Owing its very existence to change and progress, the middle class professedly supports a broad program of social change.[25]

1. It supports public education, exerting strong pressure for the allocation of more resources to it, and influences the content of education not only directly through its demands but also indirectly through the predominance of its members among teachers, administrators, and planners.

2. It accepts the need for industrialization as a self-evident truth, the one accomplishment most likely to solve all national problems and ensure economic progress. This will also give the class a deciding voice in national affairs.

3. Intensely patriotic, it stresses national goals and interests, and embraces nationalism as a major ideology in its efforts to assert national sovereignty and dignity. Pursuing these ends, it is often antiforeign and particularly anti-American.

4. Rejecting the laissez-faire philosophy, it accepts the concept of the welfare state and advocates a strong, active role for government in the attainment of social goals. Government should plan for the public welfare, and where necessary, should provide the machinery and investment for establishing any enterprise the nation needs. Also, where necessary for the public interest, government should nationalize basic industry, mining, or public services.

5. Aiming to help all the broad segments of society, it supports

---

[24] "Needed: Millions of Houses," *Américas*, Vol. 13, No. 7 (July, 1961), pp. 19–23.

[25] See especially John J. Johnson, *Political Change in Latin America: The Emergence of the Middle Sectors* (Stanford, Calif.: Stanford University Press, 1958), pp. 5–11; and Victor Alba, "The Latin American Style and the New Social Forces," *Latin American Issues: Essays and Comments,* ed. Albert G. Hirschman (New York: Twentieth Century Fund, 1961), pp. 50–51.

agrarian reform and improvement of the lot of the rural masses, collective bargaining and other rights for labor, and a comprehensive program of social security to aid the aged, unemployed, sick, and disabled.

For decades past, the middle class has been regarded as a truly progressive, democratizing force in society, which spurred the nations to the realization of their political, economic, and social goals. But from recent evaluations of the role of the middle class, it is hardly living up to earlier expectations.

In Argentina, Juan Perón largely ignored the middle class and appealed directly to the *descamisados*, "the shirtless ones," for support. In Brazil, Getulio Vargas, too, during both his 15-year tenure as benevolent dictator and later term as constitutional president neglected the class, looking to the mass for support.[26] Whether its interests were threatened by presidential favoritism or by the widening popular suffrage, the middle class has increasingly tended to be less and less a progressive force and more concerned with maintaining the status quo in order to safeguard its hard-won gains. In Victor Alba's opinion, the class as presently constituted lacks the economic means to support its desire for progress.[27] Whatever the reason for its changed attitude, the class is so concerned with preserving its status and gains that it will call on the military—itself mainly middle class—to intervene when these are seriously threatened.[28]

Lower Class

The lower class, popularly referred to as the masses, has been intensively studied by reformers and graphically portrayed by writers. It is definitely the class to be from, not in. Usually illiterate, its members are ordinarily unskilled and can perform only some sort of manual labor, which automatically consigns them to the class. They are the most poorly paid in society, earning so little and often paid in scrip good only at plantation store that they are not an effective part of the consumer economy. Unlike members of the middle class who ambitiously strive

---

26 The resulting dilemma of the middle class in Brazil is given by Thomas E. Skidmore, *Politics in Brazil, 1930–1964: An Experiment in Democracy* (New York: Oxford University Press, 1967), pp. 118–20; and Hélio Jaguaribe, "The Dynamics of Brazilian Nationalism," *Obstacles to Change in Latin America*, ed. Claudio Veliz (New York: Oxford University Press, 1965), pp. 168–72.

27 Victor Alba, *Alliance Without Allies: The Mythology of Progress in Latin America* (New York: Frederick A. Praeger, Inc., 1965), p. 81.

28 José Nun, "The Middle-Class Military Coup," *Obstacles to Change in Latin America, op. cit.,* p. 103; and Irving Louis Horowitz, "The Military Elites," *Elites in Latin America,* eds. Seymour Martin Lipset and Aldo Solari (New York: Oxford University Press, 1967), p. 152.

The evolution of the middle class and its increasing reliance on the military are given in more detail on pp. 340–41 of this book.

For the role the middle class played in the politicization of the military in Argentina and Chile, see Liisa North, *Civil-Military Relations in Argentina, Chile, and Peru* (Berkeley: University of California Press, 1966), chaps. 5–7.

to get an education and maintain a minimum standard of decency, they are too busy scratching for a living to have time or thought for the niceties and amenities of life.

Since most of the countries of Latin America are predominantly rural, and since a few wealthy persons own most of the land, the largest group in the whole population is the landless peons and others who work on the haciendas and plantations. The peon is a stable, permanent worker. Usually in debt to the *hacendado* who keeps the books, he stays put like his forefathers who have lived on the same hacienda for generations. Obedient and uncomplaining, he is the work horse of the hacienda, laboring from can till can't. He patiently performs all his tasks by hand, just as his ancestors have done for centuries before him, eking out a meager existence for himself and his family.

He nevertheless enjoys a warm personal relationship with the *hacendado* who is his *patrón* (*patrão* in Brazil) and who shows a paternalistic regard for his problems and welfare. This relationship affords a sense of security to him; he knows that in time of extreme need or trouble he and members of his family will receive the help they ask for.

Another segment of the rural class consists of laborers who are employed on the large, corporate, highly mechanized farms, sometimes called factories in the field. There, the worker, enjoying stable employment, punches a time clock, works regular hours, and is paid fairly and honestly in coin of the realm that is good anywhere he may choose to spend it.[29]

Often, he is there only for a harvest season or so and then moves on, usually in the hope of somehow bettering himself. During his stay, his relations with management are businesslike and impersonal, with no tinge whatever of paternalism. Lacking an understanding *patrón* to turn to in time of trouble, he feels unsure and insecure, rootless and alone. As a result, he is apt to respond readily to the labor leader or political radical who promises to befriend him. He also tends to look increasingly to government as a new *patrón* who will take care of his problems.

Since early colonial days, there has also been an urban lower class; a mudsill society always needs plenty of hewers of wood and many drawers of water. The urban group, although not presently as large as the rural in most of the nations, is increasing much faster than the total population, whether from natural increase or from migration.

Although never seeming to have enough jobs, the city does offer a wide variety of work for persons in the lower class. The construction going on everywhere on public buildings, factories, and homes provides many jobs for skilled and unskilled laborers. The increasing number of factories also provide many such jobs. And there are various other

---

[29] The new pattern of work on a large corporate farm is described by Harry W. Hutchinson in *Village and Plantation Life in Northeastern Brazil* (Seattle: University of Washington Press, 1957), p. 107.

employment opportunities for manual laborers, as stevedores and truck drivers, domestics and laundresses, candy peddlers, newsboys, and shoe shiners.

While their jobs pay three or four times as much as those in the rural areas, the cost of living is much higher and housing is a critical problem, especially for the new arrivals. As a result, they usually end up as squatters in one of the many *favelas* mushrooming like cancerous growths on the periphery of the cities. These slums cling to the hillsides in Caracas, Rio de Janeiro, and São Paulo, rest on the mud flats in Recife. As rude shelter for protection against the elements and for providing a semblance of family living, *favelados* throw up a one-room shack of whatever material is available: scraps of lumber, found or stolen; flattened gasoline cans; poles, thatch, and mud. Crates, drums, and boxes usually serve as furniture. Maybe there is one old iron bed on which six sleep, three at the head and three at the foot. Others sleep in hammocks hung over the bed or on mats strewn about the earthen floor. "There they endure their afflictions, pains, and personal dramas in silence . . . the sadness etched on every face."[30]

Yet, whatever the privation and discomfort, migrants from the country, having once tasted city life, seldom go back to the farm.

In most of the countries, the large lower class has very little political power or influence. Most of the members are illiterate, a handicap that precludes an effective awareness of the ramifications of economic and political problems. And since in many countries literacy is a requisite for voting, they are prevented from participating in politics. But even when given the suffrage and possibly encouraged to exercise it, they often show very little interest. Their struggle for sheer existence leaves little time or concern for the privileges and duties of an articulate, politically conscious citizen.

The peons on the haciendas and plantations are the ones who have the least political power and influence. In most countries where the big landowners still determine public policy or, at least, effectively veto reforms, the rural workers have been prevented by law from organizing and presenting a united front. Thus disorganized and weak, they are easily controlled, even used to promote the interests of the *hacendados*. In fact, the strong conservative parties in Brazil, Chile, Colombia, Ecuador, Nicaragua, and Uruguay, representing the interests of the big landowners, ". . . get their electoral strength mainly from the ability of landowners to march their peons to the polls to vote as their masters instruct them."[31]

---

[30] Walmyr Maranhão, "Recife Carnival," *Américas*, Vol. 12, No. 3 (March, 1960), p. 17.

[31] Charles O. Porter and Robert J. Alexander, *The Struggle for Democracy in Latin America* (New York: Macmillan Co., 1961), p. 27.

The workers in the cities are more independent and better able to promote their interests. Under their right to organize, guaranteed in most of the countries, large segments of labor have formed cohesive, powerful units that exercise considerable influence on public policy. In several countries, governments that depended on the support of labor have come into power, including the governments of Jacobo Arbenz Guzmán of Guatemala, Lázaro Cárdenas of Mexico, and Juan Perón of Argentina.

THE FAMILY

The family is easily one of the most important institutions in Latin America. As the primary group in society, it exerts a greater influence on the individual than does any other group. It determines what class he will belong to, what rank he will have within his class, and what cultural background he will be exposed to during the most formative years of his life. The family is of interest to us not only as a key social unit but also as one of the major influences shaping the nations' political and economic development.

Types of Marital Unions

In Latin America, there are three usual types of marital unions: civil marriages, church marriages, and consensual or free unions. The three, very different in their contraction and sanction, reflect in many ways the social and economic chasm between the haves and the have-nots, the somebodies and the nobodies. They also reflect the long struggle of the state to circumscribe the powers of the Church and to put the family under its control and protection.

The civil marriage is performed in accordance with the laws of the state and by a government official, usually a justice of the peace, in a ceremony that is simple, brief, and inexpensive. If he and his clerk, however, have to go out to a village to perform the ceremony, their traveling expenses together with the fee, cost of papers, and stamps may amount to more than a small farmer or sharecropper earns in a month.[32]

The civil marriage is popular with many in the rising middle class and is almost invariably the one that members of the lower class have, if they have any formal ceremony at all.

Since their attainment of independence, the republics have strongly promoted civil marriage. It is the only form recognized by Mexico since the 1910 revolution, which drastically limited the influence and activities

---

[32] Marvin Harris, *Town and Country in Brazil* (New York: Columbia University Press, 1956), p. 161.

of the Roman Catholic Church. According to the constitution of 1917, "Marriage is a civil contract. This and other acts of a civil nature concerning persons are within the exclusive competence of the civil officials and authorities."[33] In other Latin American nations, the church ceremony must be supplemented by a civil ceremony, which usually must be held first, and in still others the religious service alone is sufficient when it is properly registered with the authorities. In Guatemala, under a law of June 2, 1959, priests and ministers may obtain authorization to perform marriages that are legally recognized by the government.[34]

If most Latin Americans about to be married had a choice, they would probably choose a church wedding. This is the only marriage that has the blessing and sanction of the Catholic Church. According to Catholic doctrine, the family has a divine and natural origin, which gives the Church alone the authority to perform marriages. The state, it contends, has no right to require only a civil ceremony.[35] But despite the Church's emphasis on religious marriage, the number of persons united in wedlock by the priest is but a very small minority of the total population. Apparently, most of those who might be expected because of their social and religious background to prefer a religious ceremony are deterred from it largely by one thing—the cost.

Much as the state stresses civil marriage and much as the Church stresses religious marriage, both types are limited mainly to the upper and middle classes of society. In the lower class, which is by far the largest in most countries, the great majority of persons live in what is known as the consensual or free union. In effect, it is a common-law marriage where the man and woman live together as husband and wife, exhibiting toward each other and also toward the community the responsibility that a legal marital relationship imposes. Neither sanctioned by the state nor blessed by the Church, this do-it-yourself union is sometimes known as "living in friendship."

Sometimes, the friendship is quite stable, and the couple live together as blissfully and loyally as though they had been married by the justice of the peace, the priest, or perhaps both. Sometimes, in fact, after having lived together many years, they finally get married. This may be the consequence of some good fortune, as getting a better paying job, persuasion on the part of their grown children who regard marriage as important, or possibly refusal of the priest to give extreme unction unless they are married. Other free unions may last for years and then for some reason or another break up. Still others are so short term as to be mere

---

[33] Mexican Constitution of 1917, Article 130.

[34] Nathan L. Whetten, *Guatemala: The Land and the People* (New Haven, Conn.: Yale University Press, 1961), p. 244.

[35] John J. Kennedy, *Catholicism, Nationalism, and Democracy in Argentina* (Notre Dame, Ind.: University of Notre Dame Press, 1958), p. 202.

passing fancies and, whether by design or by accident, are little more than shacking up.[36]

But a more important consideration than the cost of a wedding is the sanction given the free union by public opinion. Within the community, whether rural or urban, the relationship is accepted with little or no disapproval by the rest of society. No social stigma results from living *amancebados* (in concubinage) or *apalabrados* (promised). In fact, in many areas either relationship is considered to be almost as respectable as a legal union itself. And still another important consideration is that divorce is forbidden in most countries, except on very narrow grounds; marriage is generally regarded as indissoluble.

Although consensual unions are formed outside the purview of the law, it is forced to take cognizance of the common-law relationship that has been freely assumed by such a large part of the populace in every country. Once the relationship is legally recognized, its status under law is definite and enjoys most of the advantages of a legal marriage. The difficulty, however, has been to decide when and under what conditions such a union becomes a legally recognized relationship.[37]

The constitutions and laws of the different nations have established various criteria for determining this. A provision in the Panamanian constitution of 1946 specifies: "A union in fact between persons legally capacitated to contract matrimony, maintained during ten consecutive years in conditions of singularity and stability, will have all the effects of civil matrimony."[38] Other countries have similar laws that differ mainly in the duration required of the union. Guatemala, for example, specifies three years[39] and Bolivia only two.[40]

Upper and Middle Class Family

In the upper and middle classes, the family is strongly authoritarian and patriarchal. The father is the unquestioned head of his brood; his word is law with his wife, his children, his relatives that live with them, and of course with his servants. Virtually on his own he makes the important decisions for the group or any one of its members.

The highly authoritarian control he exercises is the result of several historic influences. On the Iberian peninsula, the father was a little dictator within the family circle—a tradition the colonists brought over to

---

[36] For a good account of the several types of marital unions, see Elman R. and Helen S. Service, *Tobatí: Paraguayan Town* (Chicago: University of Chicago Press, 1954), pp. 142–44 and 158–61.

[37] Melvin M. Tumin, *Social Class and Social Change in Puerto Rico* (Princeton, N.J.: Princeton University Press, 1961), p. 249.

[38] Constitution of 1946, Article 56.

[39] Whetten, *op. cit.*, p. 240.

[40] Constitution of 1961, Article 131.

the New World. Here, the father on occasion even exercised the momentous power of life and death, and there are cases where he actually had his own son put to death. "It was that God's will might be done that I had my son killed," wrote patriarch Pedro Vieira, who ordered an older son to slay his younger brother. "God's will" with Vieira was his jealous discovery that one of his sons was having relations with his favorite slave girl.[41] Catholicism has also contributed to the strong role of the father, stressing as it does the necessity of obedience and submission on the part of other members of the family.

The father maintains his position and asserts his authority within the family in several ways. One, he would not deign to perform any of the household chores. As the undisputed master of his household, he vaunts his authority and independence in yet another way—the many extramarital affairs he engages in. Convinced that he is more virile than men of other races, he worships at the shrine of *machismo* (masculinity) and takes great pride in his feminine conquests. Whether he is the driver of a bus or president of a bank, he is apt to show his sexual prowess not only by occasional forays of seduction but also by supporting a *querida* (mistress) or a *casa chica* (little house). John and Mavis Biesanz conclude:

> The *querida* is a prestige item, like a Cadillac. Men flaunt their mistresses, take other men to call on them, provide them with luxuries usually far more expensive than those they give their wives. Panamanians boast, "We do not hide our mistresses like the Costa Ricans." *Queridas* are the subject of gossip at the market and in the park; everyone seems to know all about such relationships and to tolerate them. It is generally agreed that a man has a right to as many mistresses as he can afford."[42]

As the position of women continues to improve in Latin America, however, *machismo*, *queridas*, and *casas chicas* are expected to be less and less prevalent until they cease to be institutions that are characteristic of the society. In fact, changes are already in evidence, as in Panama where women enjoy a relatively independent role, thanks largely to the foreign influences the society has been exposed to. From the observation of John and Mavis Biesanz,

> More and more in Panama . . . young men are coming to believe that wife and sweetheart can be one and the same, for they have increasing freedom of choice in marriage and less likelihood of social ostracism and disinheritance if they marry a pretty lower-class sweetheart. Also, with increasing education and freedom of action, women are better companions to their husbands; since they practice birth control they are less tied down. They are also less resigned to male infidelity.[43]

---

[41] Gilberto Freyre, *The Masters and the Slaves* (2d Eng. ed. rev.; New York: Alfred A. Knopf, Inc., 1956), p. xxxix.

[42] John and Mavis Biesanz, *The People of Panama* (New York: Columbia University Press, 1955), p. 300.

[43] *Ibid.*, p. 299.

In decided contrast to the husband, the wife leads a relatively circum-scribed life. Her place is in the home; her principal duties are to adore and obey her husband, to bear and raise his children, and to supervise the domestic operation of the household. With her responsibilities at home, she does not share in the freedom of Hispanic-American individualism so enjoyed by her husband. Put on a pedestal by him, she is always expected to be a model of virtue and feminine behavior. In this exalted status, she is under constant social pressure to avoid doing anything, however slight, that might make her honor subject to the least suspicion.

Although they lead circumscribed lives, wives have appeared to be contented with their lot and to accept gracefully their confining, double-standard existence. They value the love and devotion of their children—the passionate affection of their philandering husbands, too—and do not appear to attach much importance to fidelity on the part of their hus-bands. Indeed, according to some opinions, "Women expect their hus-bands to have *queridas* just as they expect their children to have measles."[44]

A poll conducted in Costa Rica to ascertain feminine attitudes on the subject of traits desired in a husband, showed that married women rated fidelity 14th! In their scale of feminine values, the most important quality was believed to be culture, defined as "manners, courtesy, some degree of formal education."[45]

Such attitudes result from centuries of conditioning by the home, the Church, and society generally. From early girlhood, females are imbued with the conception of a double standard of marital fidelity and with the expectation of philandering by the mate. The Catholic Church, too, is partly responsible for the situation; although it condemns infidelity, it has done little to enforce this condemnation. Indeed, by counseling patience, submission, and resignation on the part of the wife, and by denying her right to a divorce, the Church, in effect, buttresses the husband's liber-tinism.

But while society is quite willing to overlook male infidelity, unfaith-fulness on the part of the wife is abhorred as a cardinal sin. In fact, the husband considers it such an unforgivable insult to his masculine dignity that he feels compelled to divorce an unfaithful wife to preserve his good name before society.[46] Nevertheless, some retaliate against their unfaith-ful husbands with extramarital ventures of their own.

Some countries have attempted to provide legal equality of the sexes. In Cuba, according to the 1940 constitution, there is an "absolute equality

---

[44] *Ibid.*, p. 300.

[45] John and Mavis Biesanz, *Costa Rican Life* (New York: Columbia University Press, 1944), p. 62.

In Cuba today, wives resent the extramarital affairs of husbands, but are resigned to this behavior. José Yglesias, *In the Fist of the Revolution: Life in a Cuban Country Town* (New York: Random House, 1968), p. 256.

[46] Biesanz, *The People of Panama, op. cit.*, p. 301.

of rights of both husband and wife. . . . The married woman enjoys the full advantages of equal civil capacity, with no necessity for marital permission or authorization in order to manage property, freely to engage in trade, to enter industry or a profession, to practice an art, to hold office, and to dispose of the product of her work."[47]

With the many social changes sweeping over Latin America today, the status and role of women are inevitably changing too. In decided contrast to earlier times, many women have shaken off the confines of the home and have taken jobs of one sort or another. In Panama, approximately a third of them work—about the same percentage as in the United States. Women seek employment for several reasons: sometimes, they are forced to provide the entire livelihood for the family; sometimes, they supplement the family income so they can have things they could not otherwise afford; often, they go to work simply because they are bored and desire challenging interests to be found outside the home.

In their newly found freedom, they are following a wide variety of occupations. Many are white-collar workers employed as secretaries or clerks in government offices, businesses, or industries. Others have invaded the professions and are making contributions to their society as teachers and journalists, doctors and lawyers.

In the realm of politics, too, they are becoming increasingly active. Some have been elected mayors—as in San Juan, Puerto Rico, and Santiago, Chile—or elected members of the national congress. Others have held some of the highest appointive positions in their countries, including membership in the cabinet, judgeships, or diplomatic assignments.

In at least one country, the new role and influence of women in politics has been the cause of publicly expressed concern. In an attempt to stem the obvious tide of feminine influence, the Panamanian constitution of 1946 expressly forbids the formation of any political party established solely on the basis of sex, race, or religion.[48] This constitutional restriction was regarded by some feminist leaders as a masculine trick to prevent them from forming a militant reform party that might put an end to governmental corruption and inefficiency.[49]

In the more urbanized and industrialized nations, women have achieved a relatively high degree of freedom, have many interests outside the home, and are well on their way toward a position of equality in the society, as a visitor in Mexico City, Rio de Janeiro, Montevideo, Buenos Aires, or Santiago can observe for himself. However, in the less urbanized and less industrialized nations, such as Peru, the large majority of women

---

[47] Constitution of 1940, Article 43.
[48] Constitution of 1946, Article 103.
[49] Biesanz, *The People of Panama, op. cit.,* p. 164.

still regard their place as in the home and do not contribute much to public life.[50]

Cuba's egalitarian society undoubtedly represents the greatest effort to give women full equality. The government has championed the rights of women, has encouraged them to take jobs, establishing centers to take care of their children while they are at work, and has taken many of them into the militia.[51]

Lower Class Family

In the lower class conventional family, as in the middle and upper class family, the husband is the undisputed head. He makes all the important decisions for the group, and enforces obedience on the part of his wife and children. The wife does the cooking, the washing, the cleaning, as well as helping with the garden. In some rural areas, she is not expected to work in the field, but in others she helps her husband with the planting and harvesting.

A large percentage of the households are matrifocal or matrilineal families headed by women. In some communities, women head almost half the total number of households.[52] In such cases, the mother earns the living, usually working in some menial capacity as a cook, maid, washerwoman, or the like. And on her meager income she must support her children—sometimes a houseful of them—possibly one or both of her parents, and maybe even some of her other relatives.

There are several causes for the widespread existence of the matrifocal family. Foremost among these is the popularity of the free union, a large majority of which are quite unstable. The husband lives with the wife only long enough to have a child or two, often as a freeloader, then heads for some greener pasture, leaving her with the offspring. Sometimes, he may not only live with his common-law wife, known as a *conviviente*, but may also even have another woman or two with whom he maintains a similar relationship and who also bears him children.[53]

Another cause of the matrifocal family is the decided imbalance between the number of men and women in some areas. Paraguay has long been regarded as a land of women because of a very real shortage of men at different times. The tragic War of the Triple Alliance, 1865–70, consumed most of the manpower of Paraguay, leaving many women but

50 Nelly Festini, "Women in Public Life in Peru," *Annals of the American Academy of Political and Social Science*, Vol. 375 (January, 1968), pp. 58–60.

51 Maurice Zeitlin, *Revolutionary Politics and the Cuban Working Class* (Princeton, N.J.: Princeton University Press, 1967), p. 126.

52 Service, *op. cit.*, p. 45.

53 Richard W. Patch, "The Role of a Coastal Hacienda in the Hispanization of Andean Indians," *American Universities Field Staff*, March 15, 1959, pp. 8–9.

few males except very young boys and doddering old men. The more recent bloody war over the Chaco, 1928–35, again cost Paraguay many thousands of casualties. And still more recently, the cruel tenacious dictatorships and economic stagnation have driven many thousands of young men to Argentina, Uruguay, or Brazil in search of political exile or economic opportunity, again resulting in a noticeable imbalance of the sexes and a predominance of women in Paraguayan town life.[54]

Another cause of the matrifocal family generally is that the women tend to live longer than the men, especially among the lower classes. There, the males often burn themselves out in early middle age by grueling manual labor. As a result, a large number of widows automatically become the heads of their households.[55]

Extended Family and Compadre Relationship

When the Latin American speaks of his family, he is referring to a large group, a sort of clan that scholars term the "extended family." This consists not only of the immediate family—the parents, the children, and possibly one or several grandparents living with them—but also of a host of other relatives. So great is the Latin American's interest in his family that it is not unusual for him to keep up closely with 100 or more relatives. According to a survey made in São Paulo, he might even be able to identify as many as 500![56]

In addition to its large size, the traditional family is also noted for its cohesiveness and closeness. This is shown by the frequent marriages that take place between members of the group. In Brazil, consanguineous marriages have been common since the first century of colonization. Often, a man married a niece or a cousin, usually for the purpose of preventing the dispersal of the family property or to preserve the purity of the family bloodstream of noble or illustrious origin.[57] Marriage between first cousins still occurs occasionally, more frequently in the upper class than in the lower, sometimes to keep estates from being dispersed and sometimes because mates of equal social position are just not available.[58]

As large and closely knit as it is, the extended family is socially self-sufficient and does not have to look outside for its social interests or gratifications. In fact, most of the social activities of its members are

54 *Ibid.*, pp. 44–45.

55 Raymond T. Smith, "The Family in the Caribbean," *Caribbean Studies: A Symposium*, ed. Vera Rubin (Seattle: University of Washington Press, 1960), p. 70.

56 Morse, *op. cit.*, p. 216.

57 Freyre, *op. cit.*, p. 356.

58 Harris, *op. cit.*, p. 103; and Service, *op. cit.*, p. 165.

carried on strictly within the family circle and between its many members.

With their many close ties, the members of a family have a strong sense of responsibility for one another. Standing together one for all and all for one, they help to bear each other's burdens and also share in each other's successes. If a member of the family is stricken with a serious illness or loses his job, all the other members will pitch in and render aid in every possible way. If a member of the family is fortunate enough to acquire wealth or high position, he is expected to share the benefits of his good fortunate with all his relatives. If he becomes a government official, for example, he is expected to use his influence and whatever authority he may have to get them appointed to good positions in the government service.[59]

Another distinctive characteristic of the family in Latin America is *compadrazgo*, the relationship of coparenthood, and *padrinazgo* or godparenthood. Godparents are known as *padrinos* (masculine) and *madrinas* (feminine) by their godchildren, and as *compadres* (masculine) and *comadres* (feminine) by the parents.

These coparents, honored by being invited into the close family circle, are carefully selected by the parents for certain important ceremonial occasions within the family, especially baptism, confirmation, and marriage.[60] The godparents assume a weighty responsibility for the concern and welfare of their godchild. If death or other serious misfortune to the parents should leave the child sorely in need of help, the godparents would step in as auxiliary or substitute parents, willing, ready, and able to assume the responsibility of parenthood. In appreciation of this broad commitment on his behalf, the godchild is expected to show respect, affection, and devotion toward his *padrino* and *madrina*.

The significance of the godparenthood relationship depends largely on the relative social status of the *compadres*, and whether they live in the country or in the city. Among persons of the middle and upper classes, the parents usually select another member of the family or possibly a close friend to act as the godparent of their child. The only considera-

---

[59] Nelson, *op. cit.*, p. 184.

[60] Others, special occasions long revered and scrupulously observed by the indigenous population, include occasions such as the first cutting of hair, the opening of ear lobes, and the first cutting of fingernails. Orlando Fals-Borda, *Peasant Society in the Colombian Andes* (Gainesville: University of Florida Press, 1957), p. 199.

For a vivid description of the *quitanaqui*, celebrated at the first haircutting of a child, see Patch, *op. cit.*, p. 6.

These ceremonies have long been of great significance to primitive and superstitious peoples of the world; how to dispose of the shorn hair or cut nails was a problem as critical to them as how to dispose of the dangerous waste resulting from the production of fissionable materials is for us today. For the great significance of these ceremonies, see Sir James George Frazer, *The Golden Bough: A Study in Magic and Religion* (1 vol. abridged ed.) (New York: Macmillan Co., 1951), pp. 272–76.

tions in the selection are affection, congeniality, and trust; and ordinarily the responsibility that the godparent assumes is fairly light and nominal. In the lower class, the parents usually select as godparents some wealthy or influential persons who are in a position to help their children, and themselves, too, if help is needed. In rural areas, the owner of the hacienda or *tienda* (store) or the cacique (local political boss) is very often invited to assume this responsibility.

BEARINGS ON PUBLIC POLICY

With the widespread social unrest prevalent in most of Latin America today—whether due to the determination of upper and middle classes to maintain their positions now threatened by the popular class or to the military to safeguard their privileged status—[61] the governments, both civilian and military, are sorely pressed to maintain order and a semblance of political stability. The masses in the more dynamic nations show an increasing determination to share in the benefits of the society; no government, civilian or military, can deny them these benefits very long. Fidel Castro, the idol of much of the populace, has proved that basic social changes can be made—quite rapidly, too.

Governments can take many steps to improve the lot of the mass of citizens. A more effective tax system that calls on the wealthy—now very lightly taxed in most nations—to assume a larger burden and particularly to invest their profits at home instead of abroad would be a great stimulus to industrialization and such critically needed social services as an adequate number of schools at all levels.

A severe pruning of the top-heavy government bureaucracies—largely parasitic and contributing little to society—and an allocation of funds saved to economically productive enterprises needed by the society and subsidized or run by government would provide productive jobs for the excess bureaucrats, as well as for many who are either unemployed or underemployed.

The exclusiveness of the upper class family has had notably adverse effects on the society. Besides tending to perpetuate the heavy concentration of ownership of land, it has also tended to concentrate control of industrial enterprises, even to the extent of hindering the formation of capital that is necessary in an industrializing society. Most enterprises are so largely family owned that there is little incentive to place stock in them on the market, except for a proportion sufficiently small to ensure that the family's control is not affected. Thus, in Lima, Caracas, Bogotá, Santiago, and other capitals, the stock markets do not really represent an incentive for the mobilization of savings; a large majority of the stocks traded are in the few enterprises not controlled by a family.[62]

---

[61] These are discussed on pp. 340–41 of this book.

[62] Economic Commission for Latin America, *The Process of Industrial Development in Latin America* (New York: United Nations, 1966), pp. 211–12.

The preference for governmental positions given when possible by members of the family to one another and to close friends is undisguised nepotism, favoritism, and paternalism, all of which thwart the development of an effective civil service and an efficient public administration.

Many measures can be taken to benefit and help strengthen the family. An office for keeping an accurate legal record of births, marriages, deaths, and other vital statistics is very much needed.[63]

The government can encourage legal marriage by such means as giving preference to married couples in public housing—already done in several nations—and by nationwide campaigns, as Castro conducted in Cuba.

The enactment of stronger laws with adequate sanctions could establish a father's responsibility toward his offspring, and ensure that he discharges this responsibility adequately.[64]

The recognition of equal rights for women would serve many useful purposes: remedy an obvious social injustice, enable women to make a greater contribution to the society, and establish the family on a firmer basis.

Elimination of the two- or three-hour midday siesta and establishment of an eight-hour or so workday, with definite hours for husbands to report to work and definite hours when they could be expected home, would go far toward eliminating the opportunity for visiting *queridas*—might in time even revolutionize the Latin American family. President Eduardo Frei's government took the bold step of abolishing the long siesta—a measure widely applauded by Chilean wives—but male pressure was so great that the order later had to be rescinded.

A Ministry of Family Affairs, of which there are 11 in Europe and 1 in Canada, would help bolster the family.[65] Surely, the family deserves as much consideration as public transportation, urban housing, and the other new areas that are receiving governmental attention and assistance.

SUGGESTED READINGS

Adams, Richard N. *et al. Social Change in Latin America Today.* Council on Foreign Relations. New York: Harper & Bros., 1960.

Azevedo, Thales de. *Social Change in Brazil,* chaps. i and ii. Latin American Monograph Series, No. 22. Gainesville: University of Florida Press, 1963.

Biesanz, John, and Biesanz, Mavis. *The People of Panama,* pp. 202–323. New York: Columbia University Press, 1955.

---

63 J. Mayone Stycos, "Demography and the Study of Population Problems," *Population Dilemma in Latin America,* eds. J. Mayone Stycos and Jorge Arias (Washington, D.C.: Potomac Books, Inc., 1966), p. 231.

64 UNICEF, *Children and Youth in National Development in Latin America* (Santiago, Chile: United Nations Children's Fund, 1965), p. 81.

65 Pedro Richards, "Latin America's Christian Family Movement," *Social Revolution in the New Latin America,* ed. John J. Considine (Notre Dame, Ind.: Fides Publishers, Inc., 1965), p. 208.

Cline, Howard F. *Mexico: Revolution to Evolution: 1940–1960*, chap. xi. Royal Institute of International Affairs. New York: Oxford University Press, 1962.

Dix, Robert H. *Colombia: The Political Dimensions of Change*, pp. 42–73. New Haven, Conn.: Yale University Press, 1967.

Fals-Borda, Orlando. *Peasant Society in the Colombian Andes: A Sociological Study of Saucío*, chap. 13. Gainesville: University of Florida Press, 1957.

Fluharty, Vernon L. *Dance of the Millions; Military Rule and Social Revolution in Colombia: 1930–1956*, pp. 174–201. Pittsburgh, Pa.: University of Pittsburgh Press, 1957.

Freyre, Gilberto. *The Masters and the Slaves: A Study in the Development of Brazilian Civilization*, pp. 81–184 and 278–467. Trans. Samuel Putnam. 2d Eng. ed. rev.; New York: Alfred A. Knopf, Inc., 1956.

――――. *New World in the Tropics: The Culture of Modern Brazil*, chap. iv. New York: Alfred A. Knopf, Inc., 1959.

Harris, Marvin. *Town and Country in Brazil*, pp. 96–178. New York: Columbia University Press, 1956.

Hutchinson, Harry W. *Village and Plantation Life in Northeastern Brazil*. Seattle: University of Washington Press, 1957.

Leonard, Olen E. *Bolivia: Land, People and Institutions*, chap. ix. Washington, D.C.: The Scarecrow Press, Inc., 1952.

Lewis, Oscar. *The Children of Sánchez: Autobiography of a Mexican Family*. New York: Random House, Inc., 1963.

――――. *Five Families: Mexican Case Studies in the Culture of Poverty*. New York: Basic Books, Inc., 1959.

McBride, George McCutchen. *Chile: Land and Society*, chap. i. American Geographical Society Research Series, No. 19. New York, 1936.

Nelson, Lowry. *Rural Cuba*, chaps. vii, ix and x. Minneapolis: University of Minnesota Press, 1950.

Pierson, Donald. *Negroes in Brazil: A Study of Race Contact at Bahia*, chaps. vi–viii. Chicago: University of Chicago Press, 1942.

Poppino, Rollie E. *Brazil: The Land and People*, chap. 8. New York: Oxford University Press, 1968.

Schurz, William Lytle. *This New World: The Civilization of Latin America*, chap. viii. New York: E. P. Dutton & Co., Inc., 1954.

Service, Elman R., and Service, Helen S. *Tobatí: Paraguayan Town*, chaps. ix–xii. Chicago: University of Chicago Press, 1954.

Smith, T. Lynn. *Brazil: People and Institutions*, chap. xviii. Rev. ed. Baton Rouge: Louisiana State University Press, 1963.

――――. *Colombia: Social Structure and the Process of Development*, chap. 9. Gainesville: University of Florida Press, 1967.

Taylor, Carl C. *Rural Life in Argentina*, chap. xiii. Baton Rouge: Louisiana State University Press, 1948.

Wagley, Charles. *Amazon Town: A Study of Man in the Tropics*, chaps. iv and v. New York: Macmillan Co., 1953.

———. *An Introduction to Brazil,* chap. 3 and pp. 184–203. New York: Columbia University Press, 1963.

Whetten, Nathan L. *Guatemala: The Land and the People,* chaps. 4 and 12. Caribbean Series, 4. New Haven, Conn.: Yale University Press, 1961.

———. *Rural Mexico,* chaps. 4 and 16. Chicago: University of Chicago Press, 1948.

4

EDUCATION:
The Open Sesame
to Individual Advancement

ELEMENTARY, SECONDARY, AND ADULT EDUCATION

Elementary and Secondary

Latin America's achievement of political independence was regarded at the time as the dawn of a new democratic society in which education would have a most important role. "Public instruction is the primary need of all pupils," declared San Martín in a decree of February 23, 1822. "Any government that does not promote it is guilty of a crime which later generations, however long after, have the right to avenge while cursing its memory."

In keeping with San Martín's ideal, the constitutions of Latin America boldly and unequivocally proclaimed that providing an education is one of the main responsibilities of government. "It is a fundamental duty of the state," says Panama's constitution of 1946, "to subserve national education in all its aspects—intellectual, moral, civic, and physical." In conformance to the constitutions, many laws have been enacted to provide an education for young citizens, and to make it obligatory for them to take advantage of the opportunity afforded.[1]

In March, 1961, considerable impetus was given to planning educational programs by the important Conference on Education and Economic and Social Development in Latin America held in Santiago, Chile, and

---

[1] Ecuador's efforts are given in Emilio Uzcátagui, *Compulsory Education in Ecuador* (UNESCO: Studies on Compulsory Education Series, VII) (Paris, 1951), pp. 13–16 and 23–26.

attended by 15 ministers of education. Considering economic possibilities and educational needs, the conference established several objectives that have helped the countries of the region to draw up their own plans and programs. The educational targets embodied in the national plans cover the entire field of education—primary, secondary, university, teacher and technical training, and literacy in general.[2]

With the high rate of growth in most nations of the region, the percentage of the population that is age 15 or under is quite high, too. As Table 4–1 shows, in 17 of the 19 countries for which information is

TABLE 4-1

EDUCATIONAL DATA*

	Children under 15 (% of Total Pop.)	Literate (% of Total Pop.)	Education Expenditures (% of National Budget)
Argentina	30	92	12.8
Bolivia	42	33	25.2
Brazil	43	61	17.0
Chile	40	84	14.4
Colombia	57	62	16.1
Costa Rica	48	84	28.7
Dominican R.	47	64	14.9
Ecuador	45	68	14.5
El Salvador	53	48	22.1
Guatemala	45	30	14.0
Haiti	46	20	10.8
Honduras	48	50	21.2
Mexico	45	71	24.3
Nicaragua	48	50	15.6
Panama	43	79	22.4
Paraguay	42	68	16.3
Peru	45	61	17.5
Uruguay	37	91	16.4
Venezuela	45	80	12.3

* Most recent data available, 1960–65.

SOURCES: ECLA; Social Progress Trust Fund, given in *latin america '67: The Annual Review of Latin American Business and Development* (New York: Vision, Inc., n.d.), p. 132.

available this percentage is 40 or more. In two of the nations, El Salvador and Colombia, the percentages are 53 and 57, respectively. This high percentage of the total population that either is of school age or soon will be has presented a tremendous challenge to the governments to cope with rapidly increasing enrollments, to provide the teachers, schools, instructional materials, and many other necessities, and to provide, of course, the huge sums of money required to finance the educational systems.

[2] A summary of the targets in the national plans is given in Economic Commission for Latin America, *Economic Bulletin for Latin America*, Vol. XI, No. 2 (October, 1966), p. 10.

TABLE 4-2

PRIMARY EDUCATION

(total enrollment as a percentage of age group 7-12 and private enrollment)

	1957		1960		1962		Enrollment as Percentage of Age Group 7-12‖			Private Enrollment§ as Percentage of Total	
	Thousands§ Enrolled	Index‖	Thousands§ Enrolled	Index‖ (1957=100)	Thousands§ Enrolled	Index‖ (1957=100)	1957	1960	1962	1957	1962
Argentina	2,783	100	2,948	106	3,056	110	113	113	114	10	12
Bolivia	317*	100	424	134	511*	161	60	76	87	15*	30*
Brazil	6,466	100	7,529	116	7,846	121	68	74	72	10*	11*
Chile	997	100	1,108	111	1,274	128	94	98	107	33	30
Colombia	1,381	100	1,674*	121	1,904	138	62	68	73	15	15
Costa Rica	168	100	198	118	222*	132	108	110	113	5	5*
Cuba	756	100	1,368	181	1,177†	156	83	141	116	16*	—
Dominican Repub.	462	100	499	108	487	105	108	105	96	4	5
Ecuador	502	100	595*	119	642*	128	80	86	87	20	19
El Salvador	237	100	290	122	354	149	71	80	89	8	4
Guatemala	250	100	297	119	335	134	45	46	47	19	19*
Haiti	200	100	238	119	260*	130	37	41	43	23	31*
Honduras	147	100	205	139	238	162	56	73	80	10	7
Mexico	3,826	100	4,807	126	5,620	147	74	84	92	9	8
Nicaragua	132	100	168	127	194*	147	65	75	78	9*	15*
Panama	143	100	162	113	180*	126	97	101	104	7	5*
Paraguay	287	100	305	106	323	113	117	117	120	7	8
Peru	1,202	100	1,433	119	1,562	130	78	86	88	9	15
Uruguay	302	100	322	107	343	114	104	107	112	18	21
Venezuela	694	100	1,095	158	1,277	184	71	101	109	19	12
Total	21,249	100	25,664	121	27,804	131	75	84	86	12	—‡

* Estimate.
† Public schools only.
‡ Not available.
§ Data kindly provided by Sebastián Ferrer Martin, Expert in Educational Statistics, Latin American Institute for Economic and Social Planning. Based on answers to questionnaires submitted in connection with the Report of the Intergovernmental Consultative Committee for the UNESCO Major Project.
‖ Indexes and percentages calculated by the IIEP secretariat on the basis of data provided by Sebastián Ferrer Martin.

SOURCE: In UNESCO, Problems and Strategies of Educational Planning: Lessons from Latin America, ed. Raymond L. Lyons (United Nations, 1965), p. 36.

As Table 4–2 shows, the increase in enrollment at the primary level between 1957 and 1962 is indeed impressive in most countries, especially Bolivia, Honduras, and Venezuela. In Bolivia, whose average annual population increase during 1960–65 was 2.2 percent, the increase occurred mainly because a larger percentage of the school age population attended school. In Honduras and Venezuela, both with average annual population increases during 1960–65 of 3.4 percent (and approximately the same rate earlier), the increase occurred because a larger percentage of the school age population attended school and because the birthrate was higher. In these nations, and all the others, too, the construction of many new schools in communities that formerly had none has served to swell the enrollment.

Enrollment in the secondary schools has grown faster than in the primary schools. In 1955, there were 2,270,000 secondary students; in 1960, 3,960,000; and in 1962, 4,787,000. During the period 1960–62 alone, enrollment as a percentage of the age group 13–19 increased from 15 to 17 percent.[3]

The high rate of dropout continues to be a problem, almost as much as in years past. In Colombia, where in 1950 an analysis was made of the cohort of all children enrolled in the first grade, it was found that for every 100 children who started in the first grade only 59 entered the second grade the next year. The percentage that continued in school declined in each succeeding year, to 25 in the third grade, 18 in the fourth, and 11 in the fifth. These figures, incidentally, included pupils in both urban and rural areas. In rural areas, the dropout rate was especially high; there, the percentages left in succeeding grades after the first were: 50 in the second, 6 in the third, 1.2 in the fourth, and 0.2 in the fifth.[4]

In recent years, there has been a slight decrease in the percentage of dropouts. In 1965, an estimated 2 million pupils completed their primary educations; this was an increase of 3 percent after discounting the increase in enrollment.[5]

If recent figures are reliable, absenteeism is not nearly as high as it was a decade or more ago. Then, absenteeism in the primary grades as shown by the records of reporting nations usually varied between 40 and 60 percent.[6] According to recent statistics, it has dropped to a low of about 10 percent in some nations and to a high of 40 percent in others.[7]

---

[3] UNESCO, *Problems and Strategies of Educational Planning: Lessons from Latin America* (United Nations: International Institute for Educational Planning, 1965), p. 37.

[4] UNESCO, *World Survey of Education, II: Primary Education* (Paris, 1958), p. 265.

[5] Economic Commission for Latin America, *op. cit.*, p. 28.

[6] UNESCO, *La Situación Educativa en América Latina*, pp. 211 and 225.

[7] Jorge V. Arévalo, "Population Growth and Education," *Population Dilemma in Latin America*, J. Mayone Stycos and Jorge Arias, eds. (Washington, D.C.: Potomac Books Inc., 1966), p. 131.

The burgeoning enrollments have taxed the educational system to provide enough teachers. As recently as 1960, it was estimated that in Latin America as a whole at least 400,000 additional qualified teachers were critically needed. A large percentage of those who were teaching were not well prepared; approximately one third of them did not have professional teaching certificates. Indeed, lay or provisional teachers were so common that often there was not a single teacher in a school qualified by recognized standards to hold a teaching position. Many of them had finished only primary school.

The shortage of teachers, especially acute in the rural areas, was attributable to many causes, especially: low salaries, as low as $60 a month in 4 countries and $18 a month in Haiti;[8] an uncomfortable, dull existence in the hinterlands, with no inside plumbing, no outside interests; a host of responsibilities—in Brazil, at least 29 positive requirements;[9] and the need to learn an Indian dialect if assigned to one of the native communities.[10]

In recent years, much progress has been made toward providing an adequate number of well-trained teachers for the schools. The 10-year program launched by UNESCO in 1957 for the improvement of primary education in Latin America was largely responsible for the increased number of teachers; from 1957 to 1965, teacher training schools nearly doubled their enrollments.[11] In many countries, priority in the field of higher education has been given to the establishment of normal schools for the training of teachers. As Table 4–3 shows, in some of the countries the number of students enrolled in the normal schools is larger than the number attending the universities. This is true of Brazil, Colombia, Cuba, and especially El Salvador and Nicaragua.

In seeking to make teaching a more attractive profession, the governments have appealed to a sense of idealism and loyalty. Salary increases, as 33 percent in Ecuador in 1960 and the same in Peru in 1965, have helped to get the message across.

The tremendous number of new schools needed has posed a problem, too. Until rather recently, public education was not taken seriously enough to justify the building of schools as such; and most classes were held in old private houses, in buildings constructed for offices, or in any other space that the government might acquire by leasing or renting. With such makeshift arrangements, the accommodations provided for the schools were often rundown and ill-kept, since neither the state nor the private owner felt responsible for making repairs. Even Chile did not

---

[8] M. B. Lourenço Filho, *et al., The Training of Rural School Teachers* (Paris: UNESCO, 1953), p. 12.

[9] T. Lynn Smith, *Brazil: People and Institutions* (rev. ed.; Baton Rouge: Louisiana State University Press, 1963), pp. 497–99.

[10] For an interesting account of the many languages, see Clarence W. Hall, "Two Thousand Tongues To Go," *Reader's Digest*, August, 1958, pp. 195–215.

[11] UNESCO, *Problems and Strategies of Educational Planning, op. cit.*, pp. 9 and 38.

TABLE 4–3

Higher Education: 1964–66

Country	Colleges and Universities			Teacher Training, Normal Schools		
	Number of Institutions	Number of Teachers	Number of Students	Number of Institutions	Number of Teachers	Number of Students
Argentina	363	14,301	225,653	690	20,239	172,632
Bolivia	7	—	11,090	20	454	6,109
Brazil	1,257	30,872	142,386	1,656	20,782	175,384
Chile	—	11,005	36,503	18	505	6,225
Colombia	261	6,049	37,462	348	4,303	52,319
Costa Rica	1	—	5,133	1	26	2,332
Cuba	3	2,520	23,284	15	1,262	26,977
Dominican Republic	1	204	5,322	5	43	346
Ecuador	15	1,611	12,486	34	715	11,918
El Salvador	—	—	3,624	—	—	7,571
Guatemala	1	608	7,014	99	1,075	5,873
Haiti	—	—	1,705	4	46	192
Honduras	6	—	2,239	—	—	2,966
Mexico	283	17,170	133,406	212	6,808	63,561
Nicaragua	6	397	2,770	27	355	4,756
Panama	3	321	6,306	1	56	1,351
Paraguay	1	553	3,759	38	909	8,131
Peru	—	—	46,334	—	—	—
Uruguay	24	—	14,947	24	—	3,884
Venezuela	10	4,723	58,954	117	1,750	17,336

Source: *Statistical Yearbook, 1966* (United Nations, 1967).

recognize until 1937 the need of modern, utilitarian buildings designed for the particular needs of students, with sufficient light and ventilation, adequate space for teaching and recreational activities, and easy egress in case of fire, earthquake, or other emergency.

In recent years, many large modern schools have been built in the cities and towns, and modest ones in the rural areas. In 1965, Chile constructed 5,712 classrooms, the equivalent of 1,461 state schools—in effect, an increase of 33 percent in a single year.[12] Mexico, to take care of the many thousands of isolated, scattered Indian communities with only several hundred inhabitants, has built many new one-teacher schools. Sometimes, transportation and breakfast are provided for the pupils.[13]

The shortage of schools and teachers is complicated by the prevailing mores, requiring that boys and girls be separated in their instruction—a practice rigidly followed in private schools and in most public schools as

[12] UNICEF, *Children and Youth in National Development in Latin America* (Santiago, Chile: United Nations Children's Fund, 1965), p. 89.

[13] *Ibid.*, p. 19.

well. Separation of the sexes is deeply ingrained in the educational tradition of Latin America. "The ideal of education," said a member of the Secretariat of Public Education in Mexico, "is to make woman more feminine and man more masculine; in other words: education should enable the boy and the girl to emphasize the characteristics proper to their sex instead of blunting, nullifying, or substituting them."[14]

Separation of the sexes is not much of a problem in the cities, where large enrollments and many schools can fairly easily be divided between members of both sexes. But in rural areas, fortunate to have even one school, separation of the sexes often works a real hardship; as a result, many of these schools teach boys and girls together.

For one reason or another, coeducation has gotten a firm toehold and threatens to make further inroads on the traditional pattern of separation of the sexes. Some Latin Americans have even given coeducation enthusiastic approval. "The boys and girls of our school go to class, study and play together, as well as participate in an active social program," said Galo Plaza, referring to the American School in Quito, an Ecuadorian institution, 80 percent of whole student body is Ecuadorian. "Coeducation has made possible a wholesome, normal, and happy relationship between girls and boys that was not thought possible before."[15]

The Roman Catholic Church, however, is strongly opposed to coeducational schools. A decree issued by the Sacred Congregation of the Religious in 1958 forbids "any member of a religious order from becoming head of an elementary or secondary coeducational school except in case of dire necessity." And where coeducation is unavoidable, "there should be scrupulous separation of the sexes for lessons on the Sixth Commandment which forbids sins of the flesh and on biological and psychological subjects." Boys and girls should never participate together in gymnastics, sports, or games; moreover, they should be seated separately in class and have separate doors and gateways for entering and leaving school.[16]

To meet the needs of students in agrarian but rapidly industrializing societies, the curriculum has undergone considerable change. Traditionally designed to serve a small elite and give them a cultural background befitting their status, the curriculum in both the elementary and secondary schools has been broadened to include subjects that are utilitarian. However, secondary school students continue to follow the traditional pattern of an academic education, leading to one of the professions rather than the many specialized and technical forms of training the region

---

[14] In William S. Stokes, *Latin American Politics* (New York: Thomas Y. Crowell Co., 1959), p. 54.

[15] Galo Plaza, "Two Experiments in Education for Democracy," *Responsible Freedom in the Americas,* ed. Angel del Rio (Garden City, N.Y.: Doubleday & Co., Inc., 1955), p. 76.

[16] *New York Times,* March 11, 1958, p. 7, col. 6.

sorely needs. The enrollment by type of study is: academic, 58 percent; commercial, 21; teacher training, 12; technical-industrial, 5; and miscellaneous, 4.[17]

In the elementary schools of rural areas, as Bolivia and Ecuador, the emphasis is strongly and unabashedly on practicality.[18] Galo Plaza, commenting on Ecuador's problems, said:

If the Indian is to become a free human being, a full citizen of his country, and if his country is to become a true democracy by incorporating him into political and civic activities a large sector of its population, the only effective course of action is to give the Indian an education along practical and sensible lines.[19]

In addition to practicality, other measures have been taken to strengthen the educational program. Chile has extended its elementary program to eight years, and Uruguay has added three years to its secondary cycle. In Guatemala, when surveys conducted by the Rockefeller Foundation and Michigan State University showed that students graduating from the secondary schools and entering the University of San Carlos were poorly prepared in languages, history, science, and mathematics, a two-year program of basic studies was set up for high school graduates as a prerequisite to taking courses in these fields at the university.[20]

Like curriculum, teaching methods are changing, too. The newer methods are being promoted at teacher training schools, are incorporated in the educational plans of each nation, and are spelled out in detail in voluminous curriculum guides issued by the ministries of education. Some teachers use the new methods of encouraging discussion and pupil participation. However, many teachers ignore the guides and methods prescribed by the government and teach from their own copybooks that have been handed down from one teacher to another, often friends and relatives, and contain an outline of the subject matter arranged in questions and answers. Using the copybook, the teacher requires the pupils to

---

[17] UNESCO, *Problems and Strategies of Educational Planning, op. cit.,* p. 38.

[18] In Bolivia's rural schools, the guidebook for rural teachers contains the following subjects: Our Cleanliness; How We Protect Ourselves from Disease; Cultivation of the Potato, Maize, Rice, the Banana, and Sugar Cane; Manures and Fertilizers; The Care of the Rabbit, the Ewe, the Cow, and the Bee; also, How We Improve Our Home. *Guía Didactica de Educación Rural No. 2* (Preparada por la Dirección General de Educación Rural en Cooperación con el SCIDE, Ministerio de Asuntos Campesinos) (La Paz, Bolivia: Alianza Para El Progreso, 1963), p. 233.

[19] Galo Plaza, "Two Experiments in Education for Democracy," *Responsible Freedom in the Americas, op. cit.,* p. 69.

[20] *New York Times,* October 23, 1965, p. 10, col. 4. The program had to be discarded in August, 1968 because of the vehement opposition of students, some attacking it as an effort of the CIA to make them nonpolitical, others charging that it caused a delay in starting professional courses.

copy, in the course of the year, all the questions and answers and to memorize them carefully.[21]

The whole elementary and secondary system is under highly centralized control. The national government dominates all phases of education. Ordinarily, it makes all decisions of any importance: the school buildings to be constructed, the curriculum to be taught, the text books to be used, the teachers to be employed, the teaching guides to be used, the timetable of instruction to be followed, and even the tests or examinations to be given. So extensive is the national control exercised from the top that teachers are usually expressly forbidden to omit any part of the instructional program, alter the order of recitations, or even change the distribution of time among the various subjects.[22]

The tight control from the top precludes the development of much local concern with the activity and welfare of the local school. There is no locally elected school board whose public discussions and decisions tend to whip up interest on the part of the community. There is seldom a parent-teacher association to give the school strong grass roots support.

Moreover, centralized control has many directly harmful effects on the educational system. The minister of education is usually a political appointee, with no training or experience in education. Consequently, the entire system is vulnerable to political influence, as is shown by the disproportionate amount of funds allocated to administration as compared with teaching. The minister and his staff change with each new administration, which because of the region's political instability means frequently. So the planning and execution of a program hardly get under way before a new minister takes office, scraps the old plan, and institutes one of his own, which is also likely to be short-lived.

The conference at Santiago, Chile in 1961 recommended that national expenditures for education be considerably increased—a recommendation that according to available statistics has been followed in all the countries, with the possible exception of Brazil. Ecuador's rate of increase of public expenditure on education for the period 1961–65 was 20 percent; Peru's was 20.5 percent. The rate of increase for other nations, with the exception of Brazil, was from 7 to 12 percent. Even before the increase in accordance with the recommendations of 1961, the total public expenditure on education in all the nations in 1960 was $1.32 billion—a tremendous increase over earlier years.[23] The percentage of the national budget

---

[21] UNESCO, *Problems and Strategies of Educational Planning, op. cit.,* p. 25. "As these notebooks have been copied and recopied for years and years, many errors have slipped into the transcription, and the children are taught many quite meaningless or contradictory statements." *Ibid.*

[22] For a chart showing Chile's highly centralized organization of education, which other national systems resemble, see UNESCO, *World Survey of Education, 1958 op. cit.,* p. 233.

[23] The figures of the annual rate of increase for the several countries are given in *World Year Book of Education 1967: Educational Planning* (New York: Harcourt, Brace & World, Inc., 1967), p. 373.

devoted to education in the several countries in recent years is given in Table 4–1.

Of the total public expenditure for education, about half goes to primary education. In terms of cost per pupil, it is low. In reality, it is high because only a small fraction of those initially enrolled complete the full cycle of "compulsory" education.[24]

A large part of the money spent for education is dissipated by the top-heavy bureaucracy that administers the program. In its department of education, a nation may have more administrators and inspectors than teachers on the payroll. In one country with 1,448 full-time secondary teachers, there were 3,250 administrative officials for the program—two for each teacher—and 1,797 auxiliary service employees—one for each teacher. Salaries—mainly for bureaucratic officials—consume most of the budget expenditures, leaving very little for books and necessary equipment, thus reducing the effectiveness of those who teach.[25]

Adult Education and Literacy Campaigns

The high rate of illiteracy that prevails over most of Latin America (as shown by Table 4–1 and Figure 4–1, which give the newspaper circulation) has been the cause of much concern, as evidenced by the many national campaigns that have been launched to teach adults to read and write.[26]

Sometimes, a nationwide campaign designed to reduce illiteracy turns out to be merely *projectismo*. In 1945, Ecuador enacted a sweeping literacy law under which all illiterate Ecuadorians between the ages of 16 and 50 were required to learn to read and write and to understand the elements of arithmetic within five years. All persons who had illiterates in their employ were to send their names to the appropriate authorities and to assist in their attending classes. But the great mass of illiterates were not noticeably affected by the law. Unable to read even the simplest government posters or pronouncements, they never knew anything about it! And many of those who could read did not bother to tell them about it![27]

Mexico's continuing literacy campaign launched in 1944 has been very successful. It has reduced illiteracy from 53 percent of the population age 6 years and over in 1944 to 36 percent in 1960 and 28 percent in 1964.

---

[24] UNESCO, *Problems and Strategies of Educational Planning, op. cit.*, p. 89.

The rate of retention at the primary school level has varied in recent years from a low of 7 percent in the Dominican Republic to a high of 48 percent in Panama. These and retention rates for the other nations are given in UNICEF, *op. cit.*, p.130.

[25] UNESCO, *Problems and Strategies of Educational Planning, op. cit.*, pp. 102–3.

[26] The targets of these campaigns, also of the elementary schools, secondary schools, and universities, are given in Economic Commission for Latin America, *op. cit.*, pp. 10–17.

[27] Uzcátegui, *op. cit.*, pp. 34–35.

FIGURE 4-1

NEWSPAPER CIRCULATION IN 1965

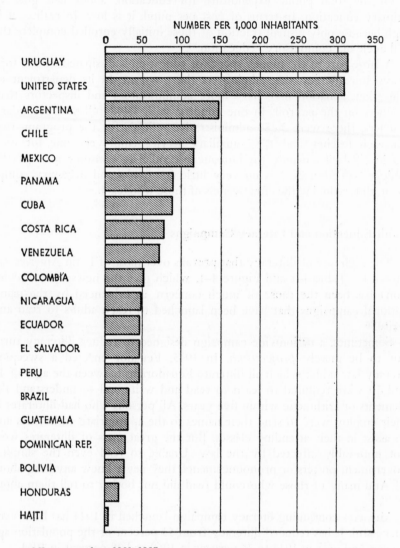

NUMBER PER 1,000 INHABITANTS

° Years range from 1961–1965.
SOURCE: *United Nations, Statistical Yearbook, 1966* (1967).

Easily the most intensive literacy campaign undertaken to date is that
of Cuba. Having proclaimed 1961 as The Year of Education, Castro
launched a massive drive intended to wipe out illiteracy in the nation and
to provide technical training. For those between 12 and 18 years of age,

formal classes were abandoned for the year as 271,000 school children, teachers, and volunteer workers went out to teach, often into remote areas of Oriente, under the slogan, "If You Know, Teach; If You Don't Know, Learn."[28]

In the tremendous effort, most army barracks were turned into schools, and large school towns were built; one near the Sierra Maestra was supposed to take care of 20,000 pupils, although it never reached this number.[29] Massive public support was given to the drive by television, radio, and the press, which daily kept education in the public eye. Civic groups and committees whipped up interest by supporting the effort.[30]

By the end of the year, 707,000 adults had been taught to read and write, "alphabetized" to the level of the first grade. In December, the government proudly proclaimed that Cuba was the first Latin American country practically without illiterates. According to government statistics, the number of illiterates had been reduced from 14 to 3.9 percent of the total population, with only 271,000 adults remaining illiterate.[31]

Assessments of the goals and accomplishments of the drive differ widely among scholars. In the judgment of Edward Boorstein, they constituted an epic campaign to bring literacy and opportunity to even the most isolated, forsaken regions, such as the Ciénaga Swamp and the mountains of Oriente.[32] Boris Goldenberg, however, assesses the whole effort quite differently.

Looked at critically, this campaign must be described as a typical "fidelista" enterprise, designed to fill the masses with enthusiasm, to indoctrinate them with the communist ideas which filled the official textbooks, and to make propaganda for the Revolution abroad, rather than to perform the essential, urgent tasks with a maximum of rationality, taking into account the real priorities of economic and social reconstruction.[33]

---

[28] Richard Jolly, "Education," *Cuba: The Economic and Social Revolution,* ed. Dudley Seers (Chapel Hill: University of North Carolina Press, 1964), pp. 181 and 189.

[29] Boris Goldenberg, *The Cuban Revolution and Latin America* (New York: Frederick A. Praeger, Inc., 1965), p. 215.

[30] Jolly, *op. cit.,* pp. 187–89.

[31] Goldenberg, *op. cit.,* p. 217.

[32] Edward Boorstein, *The Economic Transformation of Cuba* (New York: Monthly Review Press, 1968), pp. 40–41.

[33] Goldenberg, *op. cit.,* p. 217. Political indoctrination schools were particularly important for the formation of cadres in the state farms, the trade unions, and teacher organizations; among their functions was dissemination of the principles of Marxism-Leninism. *Ibid.,* p. 216.

As Dudley Seers concludes, "the intention to use the Cuban educational system for political and social purposes has been openly declared." The summary outline of the social studies program for grade 4 to 6 bears out Seer's observation. The broad topics to be included cover: The Revolution in Power; The Democratic, Anti-imperialist Revolution and The National Liberation; and World Projection of Our Socialist Revolution. Dudley Seers (ed.) *Cuba: The Economic and Social Revolution, op. cit.,* pp. 346–58.

However widely assessments may vary, the literacy campaign apparently did accomplish much. Besides winning worldwide sympathy, the drive served not only to teach illiterates how to read and write but also to further pursue an education. In 1962, the number of pupils in the primary schools greatly increased with the government's program of trying to get every child of primary school age to enroll. The number in secondary schools also greatly increased, and many attended special schools or took special courses for the training of managers, technicians, and semiskilled or skilled labor.[34]

HIGHER EDUCATION

General Characteristics

There are approximately 2,500 institutions of higher education in Latin America; of these, 1,257 are located in Brazil, 363 in Argentina, and 283 in Mexico. Of the total number of institutions, about 125 are of university rank. In 10 of the nations, there is only 1 university; in Brazil, Colombia, and Mexico, however, there are 15 or more. The total number of colleges and universities has increased tremendously during the last several decades. In Brazil, for example, it was not until 1920 that the first university was created, but by 1965 there were 30 in the nation.

Likewise, the number of students in colleges and universities has greatly increased in recent decades. In Brazil, which well reflects the general trend, the number increased from about 26,000 in 1935 to about 75,000 in 1955, and 115,000 in 1962. In all the Latin American nations, approximately 750,000 students are enrolled in institutions of higher learning. Although the number of students in higher education increased approximately 50 percent during the decade, 1955–64, the number as a percentage of the age group 20–24 has remained constant—about 3 percent.

Among the significant recent developments in Latin America's higher education is the University of Chile's program of decentralization, which established seven regional university centers located throughout the country. The total enrollment of the university from 1961 to 1966 increased by 83 percent. The spectacular annual increase of 17.2 percent was due in large measure to the establishment of the regional branches, which enabled ambitious students in the provinces to obtain an education—a privilege enjoyed before only by those who could afford to go to Santiago.[35]

The curriculum in Latin America has undergone considerable change.

---

[34] Jolly, *op. cit.*, pp. 177, 181, and 247, and Goldenberg, *op. cit.*, p. 266.

[35] Kent A. Herath, "Chile's Regional Universities," *Américas*, Vol. 19, No. 11 (November, 1967), pp. 18–20.

In colonial days, the universities were primarily schools of theology that trained priests, and the main fields of study were theology, law, and medicine. Sometimes, other courses were given, such as astronomy, botany, chemistry, and mineralogy. In recent years, as man's scientific and general cultural horizons have expanded, the curriculum has been broadened to include many new fields of study, such as electrical, mechanical, aviational, and petroleum engineering, geology, public administration, business administration, oceanography, and nuclear physics.

As a result of the broadened curriculum, students in Latin America today have many challenging fields to choose from in preparing for their future careers. However, they are not choosing the fields that will contribute most to the region's development. For example, since agriculture is the mainstay of most of the countries, and since poor farming practices are largely responsible for low productivity, abuse of the soil, and calamitous effects from drought, the nations need a large number of agricultural experts, such as agronomists, soil specialists, and conservationists. Yet, despite this great need only 2 percent of the students are specializing in agriculture; it is not regarded as having high status, being too closely associated with manual labor and dirty hands. Not even all this 2 percent would be studying agriculture were it not for the more dignified title of "agricultural engineer" that graduates of colleges of agriculture now receive.

The unwillingness of students to enter fields in which they are critically needed is the cause of much concern. The Task Force Report of the OAS Special Commission for the Programming and Development of Education, Science, and Culture in Latin America concluded:

Latin America has a fertile University tradition. Since colonial days, the universities have molded the leading social sectors and have played an important part in political life. At present, however, it may be said that the university has failed to keep pace with the social and economic evolution of the Latin American countries, and has made little effort to promote the "new" professions needed for accelerating development. Although there is a critical shortage of trained, high-level manpower, Latin American universities continue to emphasize the traditional professions, many of which are neutral towards development and have failed to train enough persons capable of leadership or to contribute to the mobility of societies. . . .[36]

The method of instruction is mainly by lecture. This method is followed even in such courses as engineering and medicine, which are taught primarily from a theoretical point of view, with little or no opportunity of practical application. As a result, most medical doctors get their degrees without ever having actually performed, assisted in, or even seen

---

[36] Betancur-Mejía, *op. cit.*, p. 4. The report and recommendations of the OAS Special Committee are embodied in *Latin American Higher Education and Inter-American Cooperation* (Washington, D.C.: Pan American Union, June, 1961).

an operation. The theoretical tenor of instruction is adequate for the purposes of most med students, who obtain an M.D. degree only because of the prestige that it confers without any intention of ever practicing medicine.

One of the big problems of higher learning in Latin America is lack of adequate financial support. Many of the institutions, publicly supported, are resigned to an economically precarious existence, since the government has limited funds available for higher education. Sometimes a university lives a hand-to-mouth existence, facing the prospect of having to dismiss classes and close its doors any day because the governmental appropriation it depends on has not been received. The University of San Carlos, Guatemala's only institution of higher learning, was confronted with just such a prospect in 1960, when government payments for its support were three months overdue.[37]

Some of the newer universities have spacious campuses and modern, utilitarian buildings. Among these are universities in Mexico, Brazil, Panama, Colombia, and Venezuela. The older institutions, however, are located in business districts, noisy and crowded parts of the cities. Indeed, the typical college or university, with its classrooms, administrative offices, and few cubbyholes for professors, is housed in a single building in the downtown area.

Organizationally, the Latin American university is a mere federation of independent faculties, an artificial, formal amalgam of preexistent schools, each with its own traditions, prerogatives, and fields of learning. As a result, the several colleges often provide instruction in the same subjects, with a consequent duplication of teaching staff and research facilities. Thus fragmented, any subject requires a large number of professors, scattered throughout the different faculties, who are not consolidated to form complete, cooperative teams.[38]

In most of the Latin American colleges and universities, only a small part of the teaching staff are full-time professors who have no other outside jobs and can devote to the institutions their full time and energy. At the Greater University of San Simón, in Cochabamba, Bolivia, for example, there are only 4 full-time professors and 164 who teach part time. The part-time staff members are often called "taxi" professors because they rush to the classroom for an hour or so, read a prepared lecture, then rush away to another job they depend on for a livelihood to make up for the meager salary they are paid for teaching.[39]

---

[37] *New York Times,* January 18, 1960, p. 12, col. 8.

[38] Darcy Ribeiro, "Universities and Social Development," *Elites in Latin America,* eds. Seymour Martin Lipset and Aldo Solari (New York: Oxford University Press, 1967), pp. 358–59 and 361.

[39] As shown by Table 4–3, the widespread use of part-time professors results in a disproportionately large number of professors for the number of students enrolled. In colleges and universities in Chile, for example, the professor–student ratio is just over 3 to 1; in Brazil, 4.6 to 1; and in Mexico, 7.7 to 1. (*Footnote continued on page 107.*)

The full-time professors, rare in most Latin American nations, have often brought disrepute on the profession. "Proprietors of a chair," as they are commonly dubbed, they seldom go to class. Darcy Ribeiro says:

> The occupant of a Brazilian University Chair is a feudal overlord with absolute powers in university life, whose security from dismissal and right to life occupancy of his post are guaranteed by the Constitution itself. He obtains his *latifundia* in the learned world through a public competitive examination which represents a "bloodless tournament" in which no scholar would deliberately choose to take part.[40]

In reality, the vast majority of professors never take the examinations, but win a teaching position by taking advantage of many legal stratagems. One commonly used is to be virtually selected by the reigning professor, who has great discretion in selecting or promoting his subordinates, a practice that practically nullifies the system of selection by competitive examination.[41]

The rigid organization of the university into independent, competing faculties has many adverse effects on students. Before matriculating, they must choose their course of study once and for all, often with no objective information about the professional scope and opportunities of their choice. Since each faculty is allowed to decide the number of students it will take, and selection is on the basis of competitive examinations, competition for admission to many of the colleges is indeed fierce. To improve his chances for acceptance, a would-be matriculant often takes special preparatory courses. Because they are usually private and expensive, they are, in effect, social barriers to obtaining a higher education. Aware of the problems that confront entering students, some universities have established a system of vocational guidance as well as centralized services for the selection of students to be admitted.[42]

Several nations are trying hard to make teaching a full-time profession. Venezuela is outstanding in this respect; it has one of the highest percentages of full-time faculty members. But even there, absenteeism of professors has become such a problem that regulations put into effect specify that any professor who is absent for more than 25 percent of the time is subject to dismissal.[43]

For the salaries that professors receive in the several nations, see Harold R. W. Benjamin, *Higher Education in the American Republics* (New York: McGraw-Hill Book Co., Inc., 1965), pp. 63–66, 94, 120–21, and 145–48.

[40] Ribeiro, *op. cit.*, p. 363.

[41] *Ibid.*, pp. 363–64.

[42] *Ibid.*, pp. 366–67.

In Brazil, it is nearly impossible for students who attend only public schools to enter the universities. Rollie E. Poppino, *Brazil: The Land and People* (New York: Oxford University Press, 1968), p. 310.

[43] George I. Sánchez, *The Development of Education in Venezuela* (U.S. Department of Health, Education, and Welfare) (Washington, D.C.: U.S. Government Printing Office, 1963), pp. 107–8.

Student Reform Movement

One of the most significant developments in the history of Latin American education is the University Reform Movement, born at the university at Córdoba, Argentina, in June, 1918. Picking up momentum as its objectives were publicized, it spread in time to Lima, to Santiago, and eventually to all the centers of higher learning in Latin America. In essence, the movement was the outgrowth of the region's antiquated system of higher education and the determination of students to force basic, much-needed measures of reform.

The University Reform Movement as espoused by the students was a very ambitious program. Its main objectives were: (1) to make the university democratic and open to all students, regardless of class, race, or family; (2) to enable the students to participate in the government of the university in order to end the monopoly over professorships which the upper class had long enjoyed; (3) to limit a professor's term of appointment to from 5 to 10 years in order to afford a periodic review of his competence, and to "break down the impermeability of a dogmatic faculty that failed to reflect changes in its respective disciplines"; (4) to encourage seminars, round tables, and group discussions to stimulate thought among students and professors alike; and (5) to involve the university more closely with the actual problems in each country and locality.[44]

Thanks to the Reform Movement, many much-needed changes have been made in the universities of Latin America. No longer the private preserve of the elite, their doors are now open to students from the middle and lower classes. Students are represented on the ruling council of the university, along with the rector, deans, and representatives of the faculty and alumni; thus they have a voice in all decisions made on university policy and operations.

However, the Student Reform Movement has been responsible for many questionable practices, even grave abuses. Largely because of student pressure, standards of admission were lowered, with no attempt to weed out students who were not of university caliber. Also, examinations were either abolished or watered down so as to be of little value in measuring accomplishment. Indeed, if a student failed to pass an examination, he was authorized to take it again in a few months; and if he failed then, he could continue to take it until he finally passed it or lost interest and left the university. Moreover, many courses that would strengthen the university curriculum have failed to be adopted or have been discarded because of student opposition.

---

[44] Luis Alberto Sánchez, "The University in Latin America: Part III: The University Reform Movement," *Américas,* Vol. 14, No. 1 (January, 1962), pp. 13–14.

To force acceptance of their point of view, students often resort to crude, rough tactics, ranging from badgering and hectoring to demonstrating, striking, and burning in effigy.[45] Student obstreperousness often had unfortunate consequences. In Brazil, a visiting American professor of geology at the University of Recife incurred the wrath of students in his class in economic geology when he gave some of them low grades. The students retaliated by striking, hoisting banners that read "Down with the Dishonest Professor," refusing to go on a field trip, and, finally, issuing an ultimatum to the university rector, demanding that the grades be raised. Student pressure became so great that in February, 1960, the United States finally had to withdraw all three American professors engaged in a technical assistance program of great importance to Brazil. Striving to develop her subsoil resources, the nation needs trained geologists, of which there are only about 100 in the country. Yet, this program had to be abandoned because of student opposition.[46]

Such actions by students have often been deplored in both Latin America and the United States. William Benton concludes:

> . . . one of the greatest needs of Latin America is the establishment—and strengthening—of private universities which can set standards. Most Latin American universities are national universities, financed by their governments. The problems of improving their standards are often exacerbated by the powerful role of the students in their management. Characteristically, student representatives sit on their ruling councils, often in such numbers as to make effective faculty control of curricula and discipline exceedingly difficult if not impossible. A proposal that I believe has great merit calls for an attempt to help a single privately run Latin American university, free of political or student control, reach such a peak of distinction that it will serve as an example for others. This was the theory on which Johns Hopkins was founded and on which John D. Rockefeller later founded the University of Chicago. Such a private university in Latin America could quickly exercise a powerful influence over the course of higher education.[47]

Student Activism and University Autonomy

In Latin America, university students are one of the most politically conscious and politically active groups in society. This had been the case ever since the wars for independence, which began in the early part of the 19th century. In the struggles to throw off the yoke of Spanish rule,

[45] According to Focion Febres Cordero, the enemies of the reform which have largely thwarted its fulfillment are: university factions; timid, unsuitable professors interested only in the prestige of their position; "academic feudalism"; and abuses on the part of the students. Focion Febres Cordero, *Reforma Universitaria* (Caracas: Universidad Central de Venezuela, 1959), pp. 73–79.

[46] *New York Times,* February 15, 1960, p. 6, col. 3.

[47] Committee for Economic Development, *Cooperation for Progress in Latin America* (New York: April, 1961), p. 24.

the university was the "cradle of republican thought." In fact, students and professors alike were among the principal promoters of independence for Latin America.[48] Since independence, the university has continued to live up to its tradition of liberal, freewheeling thought and action. It is the spawning place of political philosophies. Thus, it was at the venerable University of San Marcos in Lima that Aprismo was conceived by Victor Haya de la Torre.

But students and professors do more than philosophize; they often aid or maybe foment revolutions. Sometimes they are the sole intransigent force in the nation that dares to oppose a dictator—an opposition that is apt to mean imprisonment, torture, or liquidation. Even when such sacrifices are not immediately successful, they leave their mark. For even the worst dictators have learned to respect and fear students, and because of their efforts, a later revolution often succeeds. Perón in Argentina and Jiménez in Venezuela were both overthrown largely as a result of the determined opposition of the students.

Just as the university is the cradle of political philosophies, so is campus politics the cradle of national politics. Richard Patch concludes:

Politics is not a game in the university, it is a completely serious business for students and professors alike. Student politicians are playing for larger stakes than campus offices. They are beginning careers which may take them to power or exile within a few years. Most student politics is directed to national goals and the students expect to become national figures.[49]

Those most active in campus politics and elections are the "professional students" who may operate on campus for a decade or more. Usually on the payroll of a political party, they have little or no interest in academic life; their jobs as political activists are to recruit members to the party, manage student elections, and act as liaison between the university party and the national party.

A student election is therefore regarded as a serious test of strength between rival political parties and candidates. And in the absence of local elections that would reflect grass roots sentiments, an election at the university is regarded as a political weather vane, a sort of Latin American New Hampshire primary. Interest is heightened by the realization that student parties, in effect, are national parties; they are generously aided financially by the national party organizations, which may even specify the strategy and tactics to be followed. The student election thus becomes a matter of national interest and is followed closely by the

---

[48] Luis Alberto Sánchez, "The University in Latin America: Part II: Cradle of Republican Thought," *Américas*, Vol. 13, No. 12 (December, 1961), pp. 20–23.

[49] Richard W. Patch, "Fidelismo in Peruvian Universities: Part I: A New Platform for Old Causes," *American Universities Field Staff Reports Service*, Vol. VIII, No. 2 (West Coast South American Series, Peru) (New York: AUFS, Inc., January, 1961), pp. 2–3.

public via all the nation's media of mass communication, including radio and television stations, newspapers, and magazines.[50]

The student's absorbing interest in politics and his pronounced revolutionary spirit can be attributed to several factors. Luis Alberto Sánchez, Rector of San Marcos University in Lima, concludes:

. . . a Latin American student . . . is, above and beyond everything, a young person who is dissatisfied with the society in which he lives, . . . with the means available to him for achieving his objectives. . . . he will be dominated by the feeling of protest against the injustice that he feels binds him, and he will be carried away by the impulse to rebel against the powers that block the way to what he thinks are his ultimate goals.[51]

Whatever the reason for the student's antagonistic attitude, "student violence in politics has a romantic appeal in Latin America," says William S. Stokes. "In practice, the idea of direct action means the use of pistols, rifles, bombs, machine guns, even light artillery. It means that students have to become arsonists, murderers, and assassins in order to achieve their political ideals."[52]

The willingness of students to resort to violence has made them vulnerable to criticism, even by those who agree with their objectives. As another scholar, George I. Sánchez, concludes:

. . . students are led into riots hither and yon; some are employed to manufacture Molotov cocktails and to engage in terrorism and guerrilla activities. Strikes are called; marches are organized—these often being expressions of sympathy for the little understood issues being argued. Irresponsible and unbridled, the political action of some groups of students in Venezuela are making a mockery of university autonomy and educational discipline.[53]

---

[50] For an interpretative account, see *ibid.*, and Richard W. Patch, "Fidelismo in Peruvian Universities: Part II: "The Fidelistas Take Power," *op. cit.*, No. 3 (February, 1961).

[51] Luis Alberto Sánchez, "The University in Latin America: Part IV: As It Looks Today," *Américas*, Vol. 14, No. 2 (February, 1962), p. 16.

Three conditions incline Latin American students to political activity, according to S. Walter Washington: Latin Americans have respect for the educated; many students, coming from the poorer classes, are impatient for social reform; the population is young—more than 70 percent of the Venezuelans, for example, are under 30 years of age. S. Walter Washington, "Student Politics in Latin America: The Venezuelan Example," *Foreign Affairs*, Vol. VII, No. 3 (April, 1959), p. 463.

[52] William S. Stokes, *Latin American Politics* (New York: Thomas Y. Crowell Co., 1959), p. 82.

For many acts of violence by and against university students in Cuba, see William S. Stokes, "National and Local Violence in Cuban Politics," *Southwestern Social Science Quarterly*, Vol. 34, No. 2 (September, 1953), pp. 59–60.

[53] George I. Sánchez, *op. cit.*, pp. 108–9.

Chilean students, on the other hand, have been a beneficial influence. "Students have been a force for progress within the university," concludes Frank Bonilla; "their dedication to democratic ideals, their readiness to protest injustice, and their resistance to political repression have helped keep Chile politically moderate." Frank Bonilla, "The Student Federation of Chile: 50 years of Political Action," *Journal of Inter-American Studies*, Vol. 11, No.. 3 (July, 1960), p. 315.

Student activists are bafflingly ambivalent in their interests and goals. They profess to demand a reform of their frequently archaic universities, yet they vehemently resist attempts made to change the system, and are mainly responsible for the practices and structure that exist today. They profess to want a more stimulating and meaningful education, but they go on strike when a university administration takes any step to improve the quality of education. In April, 1966, the National University of Mexico attempted to raise academic standards. After a prolonged strike, the students forced the resignations of Rector Ignacio Chavez, also of the newly appointed Director of the College of Law, Ignacio Medina Lima, whom they had pelted with tomatoes.[54] They profess a demand for an overhaul of the universities' disjointed structure but any changes proposed, especially if based on a United States' model, are regarded as unwarrantable interference.[55] Even when the university attempts to focus on academic pursuits, as by excluding professional political agitators from campus—"students" who often hang around campus for a decade or more—the students are adamantly opposed.

Students supposedly champion the rights of the masses, yet those from the upper and middle classes and those who aspire to this status almost from the moment of receiving their degrees take their places in the stratified society, enjoying their status and helping to preserve the status quo, even if it means allying themselves with the military to protect their interests when threatened by proletarian demands.

The students idolize Castro with his sense of purpose and total commitment for remaking society. Yet with the high value they place on status and their disdain of anything resembling or related to manual labor, if a Castroite regime rose to power, establishing an egalitarian society and demanding that all citizens roll up their sleeves and go to work, maybe in the sugarcane fields, the Latin American students would probably be among the first to book passage on an international airline, seeking refuge in another Latin American nation, or perhaps the United States they so much criticize.

Student activism is for the most part a negative activity, giving vent to students' frustrations and expressing what they are against, not what they are for. It is an opposition movement that has to oppose in order to justify its very existence. When the Christian Democratic Party in Chile won in the 1964 presidential election—the only clear case in which a national election has echoed a student election—the Christian Democratic students were in a unique position: they were the only student group in control to

---

[54] *New York Times,* April 28, 1966, p. 11, col. 1; June 2, 1966, p. 44, col. 1; July 24, 1966, p. 22, col. 1; and August 19, 1966, p. 2, col. 4.

[55] Alistair Hennessy, "University Students in National Politics," *The Politics of Conformity in Latin America,* ed. Claudio Veliz (New York: Oxford University Press, 1967), pp. 122–24, 125, 132, and 139.

be affiliated with a party in power. But since student parties have little viability and dynamism unless they are an opposition party, the Christian Democratic students are wary of supporting their own administration.[56]

In Latin America, the public university prides itself on having a unique status known as "autonomy." Under this status, the university, although supported by public funds, traditionally claims the right to be completely independent in its operation and control, immune from any interference by the government, even by law enforcement authorities. Autonomy, a major aspiration and achievement of the Student Reform Movement, "was designed to free the administration and students from government control and to make of the university an island or a fortress within society where none of the other general agents of order had a right to meddle."[57] Students in Latin America have been renowned as valiant fighters against dictatorship and oppression. The grant of autonomy was public acknowledgment of its great contribution to the cause of freedom.

Autonomy is largely responsible for the intense political activity of students and their freedom to criticize or oppose the government; they are sometimes the only group that has this privilege. Of the many student activists operating under the protective umbrella of autonomy, some have in later years become dynamic, democratic heads of their nations—notably, Rómulo Betancourt and Raúl Leoni of Venezuela and Eduardo Frei of Chile.

From the standpoint of promoting healthy political ferment, autonomy has for the most part served a very useful purpose. But in recent years, many are convinced that this privileged, extraterritorial status of the university has become more a liability than an asset to society. Instead of becoming a renovating force in society, the university has alienated much of its popular support and has found that as an autonomous institution it has no way to affect society.[58]

Autonomy has become the most sensitive and crucial issue between the universities and the state. Students, with their volatile, activist enthusiasm, may challenge almost any decision made, whether at the national, state, or local level, by the university administration, a private enterprise such as the bus company, or the national or local government. The resulting student strikes or riots, which frequently paralyze important activities, pose a grave problem to government concerned with how to contain them without making martyrs of the student agitators, a martyrdom which feeds on itself and generates a more violent response. But however great the damage caused by student riots, the governments have usually re-

---

[56] *Ibid.*, pp. 134–39.

[57] Ricardo Arias Calderon, "The Universities," *Integration of Man and Society in Latin America*, ed. Samuel Shapiro (Notre Dame, Ind.: University of Notre Dame Press, 1967), p. 69.

[58] *Ibid.*, p. 70.

spected the inviolability of the campus as a safe refuge for rioting students and sometimes for common criminals, too.

In recent years, a bitter and divisive gap has opened between many governments and the autonomous state universities. The governments resent the hostile and often irresponsible criticism and action from the academic sanctuaries, also the inability of universities to provide the technical experts required for development programs.[59]

The governments, frustrated in their attempts to make changes in universities that are jealous of their autonomous prerogatives, tend to avoid a direct confrontation by by-passing the universities. They either establish institutes under their close control to produce the technicians needed, or they encourage establishment of private universities where autonomy is no problem. Ten years ago, there were only about 13 Roman Catholic universities in Latin America; now, there are 31—10 of them in Brazil, compared with only 4 a decade or so ago.[60]

In several countries, the governments have dared to challenge the hitherto sacrosanct status of autonomy, either ending it or severely circumscribing it. In Argentina, the military government of Lieutenant General Juan Carlos Ongania in 1966 intervened in the federal universities, and assumed direct responsibility not only for law and order but also for academic decisions.

More significant is the action several democratic regimes have taken to curb autonomy. In Colombia, when student activists threw stones and bottles at President Carlos Lleras Restrepo and his guest, John D. Rockefeller, III—the School of Veterinary Medicine was established with assistance from the Rockefeller Foundation—daring them to come onto campus, President Lleras responded decisively. He ordered police to enter the campus, where they arrested the ring leaders who had fled there for sanctuary. President Lleras Restrepo later announced that the inviolability of the National University and other public universities was ended. Police would have the same authority on the campuses as anywhere else in the nation.[61]

In Venezuela, too, the government acted decisively to limit the autonomy of the Central University in Caracas. It had been obvious for some time that the university was the privileged staging area for the many terrorist acts of subversion and sabotage calculated to discredit and, if possible, to topple the democratic government. Pro-Castroite rebels who wrecked their vengeance on the government by blowing up supermarkets, refineries, and oil pipelines, or by robbing banks or assassinating government officials usually fled to the university, where they found sanctuary.

---

[59] Hennessy, *op. cit.*, p. 126.
[60] *Ibid.*, pp. 126–27.
[61] *New York Times*, October 25, 1966, p. 2, col. 4.

Determined to end the terrorism, President Raúl Leoni, himself an activist in his student days, ordered troops to take over the campus and thoroughly check it as a base for sabotage. Caches of arms were found in several of the university buildings—caches that included pistols and revolvers, rifles and machine guns, grenades, electronic detonators, and explosives for making bombs.

President Leoni's sending troops onto the campus, a drastic reversal of policy, apparently won popular acceptance both in the nation and on campus. Professors of the College of Medicine were so frequently beaten up at night when leaving the university that they stayed in the hospital instead of going home. "Something had to be done; it was impossible for professors to teach and it was impossible for students to learn."

In a nationwide television and radio address to the nation, President Leoni laid down the new line: "I do not accept the thesis that pretends to make the University a State within a State. The University will remain autonomous only as far as teaching and administration are concerned."[62]

Responsible for many excesses, autonomy has apparently outlived its usefulness. In any event, it is unquestionably on the defensive and may be on the way out.

Relevance to Public Policy

The allocation in recent years of an increasing proportion of the public revenues to education serves a very important social goal. But this emphasis, some believe, is at the expense of other social needs that are also very important.[63]

The governments provide free public education at the primary level, where 87 percent of the pupils take advantage of it, and at the university level, where 90 percent of the students enroll in public universities; but they leave secondary education mainly to private schools supported by tuition and catering to the more affluent. Such neglect largely vitiates the primary and university systems.

The limited financial means of students who are working their way through school often forces them to major in such fields as economics and law—both with so many graduates that they cannot utilize their training—rather than in medicine, engineering, and other fields whose graduates are sorely needed in the nations. Some form of financial aid to students might well correct the imbalance.[64]

---

[62] For details of the government's action against the Central University, see *New York Times*, December 17, 1966, p. 3, col. 3; December 19, 1966, p. 3, col. 5; and December 23, 1966, p. 12, col. 5.

The Mexican government, usually meticulous in respecting autonomy despite frequent provocation, in October, 1966, sent troops into the University of Morelia.

[63] *World Book of Education, 1967, op. cit.,* p. 372.

[64] *Economic Commission for Latin America, op. cit.,* p. 9.

The failure of the universities to recognize the importance of training in public administration is largely responsible for the inefficient administration in most of the nations. Even when a university tries to initiate such programs, as did San Andrés University in Bolivia, student opposition may be so strong as to compel the university to discontinue the program. The students in Bolivia and elsewhere are not interested in efficient public administration; they want and expect jobs in the already swollen government bureaucracy.

The universities' failure to recognize the importance of demography in teaching and research has played an important part in the rapid population increase. Due to the peculiar development of the social sciences in the universities, where sociology has followed nonempirical, humanistic, and literary lines, the governments have not had comprehensive scientific data on which to base a rational policy.[65]

The provincial universities in the several nations, though useful in decentralizing higher education, could become so closely identified with regional interests as to be involved in a political struggle of the region against the central government. When many of their students are drawn from an awakened peasantry, the provincial universities may well become the powerhouses of rural revolution.[66]

With the failure of the universities to produce the number of technicians needed by the industrializing nations, the younger officers in the technical branches of the armed forces have helped to fill in the gap. Their campaigns of Civic Action, though useful to the nation, could eventually establish the armed forces as the levers of a technocratic revolution.[67]

The governments' encouragement of private universities, most of which are ecclesiastical but receive public funds, may result in strong competition for available government support and the uneconomic dispersion of money devoted to education, and may considerably change the content of education.[68]

SUGGESTED READINGS

Adams, Richard N., and Cumberland, Charles C. *United States University Cooperation in Latin America.* Institute of Research on Overseas Programs. East Lansing: Michigan State University, 1960.

Benjamin, Harold R. W. *Higher Education in the American Republics.* New York: McGraw-Hill Book Co., Inc., 1965.

[65] J. Mayone Stycos, "Demography and the Study of Population Problems in Latin America," *Population Dilemma in Latin America,* eds. J. Mayone Stycos and Jorge Arias (Washington, D.C.: Potomac Books, Inc., 1966), pp. 233–34.

[66] Hennessy, *op. cit.,* pp. 123 and 125.

[67] *Ibid.,* p. 128.

[68] Ribeiro, *op. cit.,* pp. 372–73.

Biesanz, John, and Biesanz, Mavis. *The People of Panama,* pp. 157–61, 324–51. New York: Columbia University Press, 1955.

Bonilla, Frank. "The Student Federation of Chile: 50 Years of Political Action," *Journal of Inter-American Studies,* Vol. 11, No. 3 (July, 1960), pp. 311–34.

Bunkley, Allison Williams. *The Life of Sarmiento.* Princeton, N.J.: Princeton University Press, 1952.

Cline, Howard F. *Mexico: Revolution to Evolution: 1940–1960,* chaps. xx and xxi. Royal Institute of International Affairs. New York: Oxford University Press, 1962.

Economic Commission for Latin America. *Economic Bulletin for Latin America* Vol. XI, No. 2 (October, 1966).

Fitzgibbon, Russell H. *Uruguay: Portrait of a Democracy,* chap. xiv. New Brunswick, N.J.: Rutgers University Press, 1954.

Holmberg, Allan R. "Changing Attitudes and Values in Peru: A Case Study in Guided Change," *Social Change in Latin America Today,* chap. 2. Council on Foreign Relations. New York: Harper & Bros., 1960.

Jolly, Richard. "Education," *Cuba: The Economic and Social Revolution* (ed. Dudley Seers), Part II, pp. 161–280. Chapel Hill: University of North Carolina Press, 1964.

Lipset, Seymour Martin and Solari, Aldo (eds.). *Elites in Latin America,* chaps. 10–13. New York: Oxford University Press, 1967.

MacGaffey, Wyatt, and Barnett, Clifford R. *Cuba: Survey of World Cultures,* chap. 8. New Haven, Conn.: American University, HRAF Press, 1962.

Organization of American States. *Latin American Higher Education and Inter-American Cooperation.* Washington, D.C.: Pan American Union, June, 1961.

Patch, Richard W. "Fidelismo in Peruvian Universities," *American Universities Field Staff Reports Service.* West Coast South American Series, Part I: "A New Platform for Old Causes," Vol. VIII, No. 2 (Peru); January, 1961. Part II: "The Fidelistas Take Power," Vol. VIII, No. 3 (Peru), February, 1961.

Pierson, William W., and Gil, Federico G. "Education," *Governments of Latin America,* chap. 16. New York: McGraw-Hill Book Co., Inc., 1957.

Rio, Angel del (ed.). *Responsible Freedom in the Americas,* "Part One: Elementary, Primary, and Secondary Education"; "Part Two: University Education"; "Part Five: The Government in Education." Garden City, N.Y.: Doubleday & Co., Inc., 1955.

Sánchez, George I. *The Development of Education in Venezuela.* United States Department of Health, Education, and Welfare. Washington, D.C.: U.S. Government Printing Office, 1963.

Sánchez, Luis Alberto. "The University in Latin America," *Américas:* "Part I: The Colonial Period," November, 1961; "Part II: Cradle of Republican Thought," December, 1961; "Part III: The University Reform Movement,"

January, 1962; "Part IV: The University As It Looks Today," February, 1962.

Schurz, William Lytle. *Brazil: The Infinite Country*, chap. 10. New York: E. P. Dutton & Co., Inc., 1961.

Shapiro, Samuel (ed.) *Integration of Man and Society in Latin America*, pp. 61–73. Notre Dame, Ind.: University of Notre Dame Press, 1967.

Smith, T. Lynn. *Brazil: People and Institutions*, Part 5, chap. xix. Rev. ed. Baton Rouge: Louisiana State University Press, 1963.

Stokes, William S. *Latin American Politics*, chaps. 5 and 6. New York: Thomas Y. Crowell Co., 1959.

Tannenbaum, Frank. *Mexico: The Struggle for Peace and Bread*, chap. 10. New York: Alfred A. Knopf, Inc., 1954.

———. *Peace by Revolution: An Interpretation of Mexico*, chaps. 24–26. New York: Columbia University Press, 1933.

———. *Ten Keys to Latin America*, chap. 6. New York: Alfred A. Knopf, Inc., 1962.

UNESCO. *Problems and Strategies of Educational Planning: Lessons from Latin America.* United Nations, 1965.

UNICEF. *Children and Youth in National Development in Latin America.* Santiago, Chile: United Nations Children's Fund, 1965.

Uzcátegui, Emilio. *Compulsory Education in Ecuador.* UNESCO: Studies on Compulsory Education Series, VII. Paris, 1951.

Veliz, Claudio (ed.). *The Politics of Conformity in Latin America*, pp. 119–57. New York: Oxford University Press, 1967.

Wagley, Charles. *An Introduction to Brazil*, pp. 204–31. New York: Columbia University Press, 1963.

Whetten, Nathan L. *Guatemala: The Land and the People*, chap. 13. Caribbean Series, 4. New Haven, Conn.: Yale University Press, 1961.

Wilgus, A. Curtis (ed.). *The Caribbean: Venezuelan Development, A Case History*, Part II. Gainesville: University of Florida Press, 1963.

5

THE CHURCH:
An Influence for Standpatism or Progress

The Church in Latin America, meaning until recent decades the Roman Catholic Church, has been one of the strongest influences on the development of each nation and the lives of its citizens. This influence began in the very first days of conquest and colonization and has continued until today. In fact, the questions of just what authority the Church should enjoy in the society and what functions it should exercise have been very controversial issues ever since independence, and have not been completely settled to date.

THE CHURCH IN COLONIAL SOCIETY

At the time America was discovered, the Roman Catholic Church enjoyed a position of great power and prestige in both Spain and Portugal. The successful campaigns that had been waged to oust the Moors and crush Mohammedanism had long been a holy crusade, greatly aided by members of the clergy. Exhorting their parishioners to fight as a Christian duty and threatening punishment to those who shirked, members of the clergy could justifiably claim much of the credit for victory. As a reward for their invaluable assistance, they were given a large part of the land that was reconquered. Consequently, the Church became exceedingly wealthy, with a prestige and influence commensurate with its great wealth.

After Columbus accidentally bumped into America in his quest for the East Indies, the Spanish and Portuguese crowns lost no time in laying claim to this new, large, hitherto undiscovered part of the world. In

119

conquering its vast domain and exploiting its rich resources, even more valuable than those of the East Indies, the monarchy and the papacy worked hand in hand as a close partnership; the crown furnished the manpower and material necessary for conquering the region, while the Church assumed the responsibility of Christianizing and educating the "heathen" natives.

While the partnership between the monarchy and the Church was very close, the monarchy was unquestionably the senior partner, determined to enjoy the temporal power Spain as a new nation-state could exercise independently of the papacy. In effect, the king was the secular head of the Church, with control over most of its activities in the new world. This control was recognized in three papal documents issued soon after the discovery of America. A bull of Alexander VI issued in 1493 divided the New World between Spain and Portugal, granting to them the exclusive privilege of Christianizing and civilizing the natives. Another bull of Alexander VI in 1501 granted to the Spanish monarch the right to ecclesiastical tithes in all his New World dominions on condition that he be responsible for establishing and maintaining the Church. Still another bull, issued by Julius II in 1508, conferred on the king the right of universal patronage over the Church in the New World.

These three papal documents constituted a firm basis upon which the Spanish crown was able to maintain its control over the Church. The first bull gave papal confirmation of the crown's territorial claims, making a contest with Portugal less likely; the second vested in the crown the all-important power of the purse; and the third, probably the most significant of all, in effect gave the crown the power to select all the clergy in America—the archbishops, bishops, and abbots, as well as lower members of the clergy.

Known as the *Patronato Real,* or royal patronage of the Church, the king had the authority to nominate a cleric for any vacant benefice. If an archbishop, bishop, canon, or other high officer was to be selected, the king's nomination was made to the pope. However, if an individual was to be selected for one of the lower benefices, the royal nomination was made to the archbishop or bishop of the diocese that contained the vacancy. Until 1574, the king himself made all nominations for vacant clerical offices. But as the administration of the colonies became more complex, the crown delegated to the viceroys, presidents, governors, and captains-general the authority to make nominations for the lesser benefices.

The crown's control over the patronage was one of its most highly prized powers. As "the richest stone, the most precious pearl in the royal diadem," it was a prerogative that was zealously guarded, and any threatened infringement was sure to evoke vigorous royal action.[1]

---

[1] For the significance and exercise of the patronage, see J. Lloyd Mecham, *Church and State in Latin America* (rev. ed.; Chapel Hill: University of North Carolina Press,

In the joint exploitation of Latin America, the king was determined to sit in the driver's seat, holding the reins tightly to control the temporal and ecclesiastical team in the new domain. Referring to the crown's control over the Church, J. Lloyd Mecham concludes, ". . . it is difficult to conceive of a more absolute jurisdiction than that which the kings of Spain exercised over the ecclesiastical affairs of the Indies. . . . Never before or since did a sovereign with the consent of a pope so completely control the Catholic Church within his dominions."[2]

During the colonial period, the crown had the deciding voice in practically all the Church's many activities. Not a single church or monastery or hospital could be built by the Church unless the crown approved it; no priest could come to the New World unless licensed by the government and directed where to serve; no church councils could be held or papal bulls issued applying to the new world unless the monarch first gave his stamp of approval.

But while the state in its impersonal way governed the people, the Church by its close personal touch with them actually ruled them, catering to their everyday needs from the cradle to the grave. Frank Tannenbaum writes:

The Church was everywhere and with every individual all his life. The day began with early morning mass and ended with Ave Maria. . . . The Church was . . . the school, the university, the hospital, the home for the aged, the sick, and the abandoned. It served the individual and the community in many ways. In the absence of newspapers, libraries, museums, and theaters, the religious ritual of the churches . . . gave the individual a place in an enchanted and meaningful world.[3]

In addition, the Church was a strong influence in trying to protect the helpless Indian against the predatory conquistador. Las Casas, the bishop of Guatemala, made more than a dozen trips across the Atlantic to plead with the king for justice to the Indians, asserting that the conquistador was not different or better by nature than the Indian, and that "all men are men and nothing more."

The Indian, thanks to the Church's interest in Christianizing him and interceding for him against the conquistador, certainly enjoyed a much more humane treatment than he would have otherwise received. Consequently, many Indians flocked to the priests, quite willing to be converted in return for protection they sorely needed. When the spirit was willing, conversion was a relatively easy process, often accomplished en masse.

1966), pp. 3–23; also Carlos E. Castaneda, *Church and Society: Catholic Social and Political Thought and Movements,* ed. Joseph N. Moody (New York: Arts, Inc., 1953), pp. 735–52.

[2] Mecham, *op. cit.,* pp. 12 and 36.

[3] Frank Tannenbaum, *Ten Keys to Latin America* (New York: Alfred A. Knopf, Inc., 1962), p. 57.

But when the spirit was not receptive, conversion was often an ordeal for both the priests and members of their refractory flock. Sometimes the Indians had to spend five to seven years in a mission before they were ready for baptism. It was difficult for the priests to hold them that long, as they were not accustomed to such a sedentary life. As a result, they often tried to escape. Occasionally, the entire mission population of Indians quietly decamped, heading back for the forests and hills. The missionaries would go after them in hot pursuit with one or two soldiers and perhaps a few trusties. Sometimes it was a long chase before the fugitives were caught and persuaded or forced to return.[4]

In addition to aiding the Indians (sometimes rather against their will), the Church did much to ease the lot of the Negro slaves. In the early days of the conquest, the Church advocated the importation of slaves from Africa, intending thereby to protect the Indians from exploitation at the hands of colonists. But as the slave trade became more inhumane and barbaric, the Church forbade any of the faithful to engage in it. Regarding slavery itself, opinion within the Church was sharply divided as to whether it was justifiable or should be abolished.[5] Some of the religious orders themselves owned slaves, who were invariably treated most kindly.

In its overall policy regarding slavery, the Church was one of the most influential forces in ameliorating its effects and standing up for the human dignity and rights of the slave. It emphasized the moral equality of all persons, including the slave, and stressed the obligation of protecting his rights, even that of manumission itself.[6]

Thus, the Church played a leading role during the long colonial period, performing many functions which the society very much needed, and enjoying great influence and prestige. Its influential, privileged position was to bring it into bitter conflict with the new states after they had won independence from Spain.

THE CHURCH DURING THE WARS OF INDEPENDENCE

The outbreak of the revolutions against Spain found the clergy bitterly divided in their sympathies and support. Most of the hierarchy were unswerving in their loyalty to the crown, loyalty that is quite understandable. For although exercising a strong degree of control, the

---

4 Clarence H. Haring, *The Spanish Empire in America* (New York: Oxford University Press, 1947), p. 197.

5 For the difference of opinion in Brazil, see Donald Pierson, *Negroes in Brazil: A Study of Race Contact at Bahia* (Chicago: University of Chicago Press, 1942), pp. 54–57.

6 Frank Tannenbaum, *Slave and Citizen: The Negro in the Americas* (New York: Alfred A. Knopf, Inc., 1947), pp. 62–64, 92, and 98–99.

king had nevertheless been a faithful friend and ally, furnishing protection to the Church and granting it many valuable privileges for which it was very grateful. Moreover, its prestige and privileged position were assured under the dominion of the crown. But how well would they fare under a new revolutionary regime bent on change?

As a longtime copartner in the whole colonial undertaking, the hierarchy threw its great influence and power solidly behind the royal cause, determined to make it a battle to the death if necessary to win. By impassioned exhortations or fearful threats, the members of the higher clergy strove to prevent defections from allegiance to the crown. Their financial contribution to the cause was considerable too.

A very large part of the lower clergy, however, ardently espoused the aspirations of the revolutionists, giving them invaluable encouragement and assistance, and often capable leadership. Most members of the lower clergy were Creoles who greatly resented the favoritism shown by the crown to the *gachupines,* or clergy born in Spain and sent over to monopolize the higher church offices. Also, the great majority of the Creole clergy were very poor, with incomes of only a hundred or so pesos a year—pathetic when compared with the very large incomes, often in the hundreds of thousands of pesos, of the higher clergy, whose affluence enabled them to live like princes. Another tie that bound many of the Creole clergy to the revolutionaries was that they had risen from the humblest ranks of society and were bitter about the many discriminations and exploitations inherent in the colonial system.

Dedicated to the ideals of the revolution, many of the lower clergy aided it in various ways. After celebrating Mass, they explained the principles and ideals of the struggle and exhorted the faithful to give it their full support. Besides supporting the fight verbally, they greatly aided it materially, donating personally a large part of the funds needed to sustain the armies in the field. Some of the priests went even further. Forsaking their parishes and congregations, they took up arms to join the armies on the firing line or possibly to lead them.

In Mexico alone, besides the revered national heroes, Father Hidalgo and Father Morelos, more than 100 parish priests and some 50 members of the religious brotherhoods left the pulpit or cloister and took to the field. Many of these, including Hidalgo and Morelos, were to lose their lives in battle or before a firing squad. Indeed, so active were the clergy of Mexico in fighting for independence that Lucas Alamán, the distinguished Mexican scholar, credits them with sustaining the revolution almost alone.[7]

---

[7] For the role of the clergy as portrayed here, see Mecham, *op. cit.,* pp. 50–55; and Ernest Gruening, *Mexico and Its Heritage* (New York: D. Appleton-Century Co., Inc., 1934), pp. 184–89.

ANTICLERICALISM

When independence was finally won after years of bitter, bloody fighting, it was almost inevitable that the newly independent states and the Church would clash headlong on many crucial issues. For one thing, the Church as an institution was on the losing side, which hardly helped its position in the new states. More importantly, its privileged position, affluence, and influence were matters of serious concern to many leaders of the new states. Anticlericals, as they are commonly referred to, were opposed to the influence of the Church in political and social affairs, and advocated complete separation of religious authority from civil government, with the ultimate goal of subordinating the Church to the control of the state.

The anticlerical liberals were by no means anti-Catholic or antireligious. In fact, they usually regarded themselves as devout members of the faith, with a mission of reforming the Church and adapting it to contemporary society. Bernardo O'Higgins, Chile's national hero, was just such a Catholic from his point of view. So also were many other national leaders, such as Benito Juárez of Mexico and José Batlle y Ordóñez of Uruguay.

While some of the anticlericals were undoubtedly mere opportunists, seeking to benefit themselves at the expense of the Church, others were very sincerely concerned about the status and role of the Church, as well as its many activities. They deplored the Church's extensive ownership of land that could never be privately owned or developed, as well as its operation of many commercial enterprises. This control of so much of the national wealth, all exempt from taxation, would in the opinion of the anticlericals make it difficult, if not impossible, for the state to have a sufficiently large economic base to maintain its very existence.

Also, the anticlericals were convinced that the Church should devote itself solely to spiritual matters, and that many of its activities, especially those of education, welfare, and control over the family, should be taken over by the state. Furthermore, they were determined that religious authority should be separated completely from that of the civil government, that the Church should be subordinated to state control, and that the Church as an organization should stop interfering in politics. J. Fred Rippy succinctly summarizes the issues.

The conflict involved both ideals and interest. In part it was a struggle for revenues, power, property, and prestige and for the creation of conditions that would attract immigrants accustomed to religious toleration; in part it was a struggle for greater intellectual freedom, the curtailment of special privileges, and the creation of wider opportunities for at least some of the people. In the end, the functions, privileges, and wealth of the Church were reduced in the interest of the State, and in the interest of those it governed. . . .[8]

Since independence, the concern and activities of the anticlericals have been directed mainly toward the following: reform of the priesthood, expropriation of the Church's great wealth, assumption by the state of the Church's many secular activities, separation of church and state, and preclusion of the Church from participating in politics.

REFORM OF THE PRIESTHOOD

One of the oft-stated objectives of the anticlericals was to reform the priesthood. Many of the clergy and members of the religious orders— probably a very large majority of them—were persons of excellent character, wedded to the Church and consecrated to a life of celibacy. But many of the priests and members of the religious orders were opportunists of low morals who regarded their vow of chastity very lightly. The resulting licentiousness among the clergy may have been aggravated by the primitive conditions of the frontier and the many native women of a submissive people who could easily be had.

However, the moral laxity of many of the clergy did not originate in the New World. In Spain, Queen Isabella herself attempted to cleanse the monasteries, convents, and secular clergy of violations of the rule of celibacy. For there had grown up in Spain, in spite of all the laws against it, a system of clerical "marriage," simply concubinage, known as *barragania*. The practice was so common and strongly embedded, however, that it was impossible to eradicate.[9]

In Argentina, soon after independence, Bernardino Rivadavia instituted a Civil Constitution of the Clergy patterned after the French prototype and intended to remedy the degraded condition of the clergy. When Rosas became dictatorial head of the nation in 1829, he acted summarily to end licentiousness in the lower clergy. Instituting a thorough housecleaning, he issued numerous decrees that suspended, removed, and even jailed priests for immoral conduct.[10]

In Brazil, the ancient question of sacerdotal celibacy was widely debated during the time of the Empire. A large part of the Brazilian clergy

---

[8] J. Fred Rippy, *Latin America: A Modern History* (Ann Arbor: University of Michigan Press, 1958), p. 185.

[9] Bailey W. Diffie, *Latin American Civilization* (Harrisburg, Pa.: Stackpole Sons, 1945), p. 266.

[10] Mecham, *op. cit.*, pp. 226–28.

Though posing as a champion of the Catholic faith, Rosas ruled the Church with an iron hand, appointing all the members of the Argentine Church from the highest to the lowest, and forcing them to serve his regime of absolutism. For a detailed account of his relations with the Church, see A. Curtis Wilgus (ed.), *South American Dictators During the First Century of Independence* (Washington, D.C.: George Washington University Press, 1937), pp. 473–88.

had never made the least pretense of observing the rule of clerical chastity; in fact, they had lived quite openly with their wives or concubines. Accustomed to such clerical hypocrisy, the general public was prone to accept such arrangements as being in accord with human nature, the climate, and long-established custom. Indeed, many persons, both lay and clerical, openly declared themselves in favor of legitimizing the practice, even if it meant setting up a separate Brazilian church divorced from the authority of the Vatican.[11]

Another condition among the clergy which the anticlericals aimed to correct was their widely known venality. Many of the clergy had apparently entered the priesthood in the New World solely because of the opportunity it offered for making an easy living. Indeed, if a priest could wangle a concession from the crown to build a church or monastery, obtain a grant of land to go with it, and then gather a group of Indians whose labor he could exploit without charge, his comfort was assured.

Posing as the protector of the Indians, he was often in reality a burdensome oppressor, collecting stiff fees from them for each and every clerical service he performed, especially the high fee for High Mass on the saints' days, with an equal amount collected for the sermon.

To this is to be added the customary offering which the overseers are compelled to make to the curate on every saint's festival, which consists of two or three dozen hens, as many chickens, guinea-pigs, eggs, sheep, and a hog if they happen to have any; so that when the saint's day arrives, the curate sweeps off all that the Indian has been able to collect in money during the whole year, and also all the fowls and animals which his wife and children have reared in their huts, so that his family are left almost destitute of food, and are reduced to wild herbs and to the grains which they cultivate in their small gardens.[12]

The venality of many of the priests was recognized by the more conscientious ones as imposing an extreme hardship on the natives. The Augustinian friar, Júarez de Escobar, advised Philip II that the clergy should not charge for the sacraments because, "besides smacking of simony, it works great injury to the Indians, since, if two *reales* is charged and the native has not that to give, he must remain without the sacrament; or requiring a *tostón* for marrying, the natives remain unmarried for lack of money; and the children die without baptism simply because the parents have not the four or five *tomines* which is charged for the rite."[13]

---

[11] William Lytle Schurz, *Brazil: The Infinite Country* (New York: E. P. Dutton & Co., Inc., 1961), p. 192.

[12] In Bernard Moses, *South America on the Eve of Emancipation* (New York: G. P. Putnam's Sons, 1908), 186–87.

[13] "Colección de Documentos Inéditos Relativos al Decubrimiento Conquista y Colonización de las Posesiones Españoles . . . ," Sacadas en su Mayor Parte del Real Archivo de Indias. 1 Series, 42 vols., Madrid, 1864–84, in Charles S. Braden, *Religious Aspects of the Conquest of Mexico* (Durham, N.C.: Duke University Press, 1930), p. 218.

Still another condition that has sometimes aroused resentment against the Catholic Church is the foreign character of the priesthood. During colonial days, most members of the clergy were foreigners; the king preferred to nominate persons from Spain whose loyalty and dependability could be counted on for carrying out the crown's policies. However, the appointment of Spaniards for the more responsible positions meant that the Creoles were eligible only for the lower church offices, while the mestizos and Indians were excluded altogether.

Since independence, the Church has continued the practice of appointing foreigners as members of the hierarchy, as well as of the lower clergy. Such appointments have been necessary, the Church has explained, because of the high level of illiteracy in most of the Latin American nations, which has seriously hampered efforts to establish seminaries in the region for the training of native-born priests. However much justified, the foreign character of many of the clergy has greatly impaired their effectiveness, since Latin Americans tend to regard their presence as a hangover of colonial days and a reminder of colonialism they would like to forget.

In recent years, the papacy has frankly recognized that the sending of priests from Spain, Italy, the United States, or elsewhere to the Latin American nations, very nationalistic and sensitive about their sovereignty, is a practice to be discontinued at the earliest possible moment. In his fourth encyclical letter, Pope John XXIII expressed confidence in the native clergy at a time when "the aspirations of the peoples to self-rule and independence is becoming general." The missionary bishops and priests sent to the underdeveloped areas, asserted His Holiness, must educate the native clergies so that they can "take the government of the new churches in their own hands as soon as possible."[14]

The earlier shortcomings of the priesthood have been recognized and corrected by the papacy. But their existence at an earlier date is a fact of life which the Catholic Church must reckon with in its relations with the region's 400 million inhabitants, most of whom are at least nominal Catholics.

EXPROPRIATION OF THE CHURCH'S GREAT WEALTH

The tremendous wealth of the Church was another problem that worried many of the new leaders. When the colonial period ended and the young nations achieved independence, the Church was a fabulously wealthy institution. In Mexico, it owned at least half of the total real estate of the entire nation, and held mortgages on much of the remaining property. Its financial interests were quite varied, and consisted of all kinds of commercial enterprises, including cattle ranches, corn and wheat farms, sugar and flour mills, and even factories and silver mines.

---

[14] *New York Times,* November 29, 1959, p. 1, col. 5.

This great wealth came from a number of sources. In addition to large gifts of land or money made by the crown or affluent philanthropists, the Church benefited greatly by bequests. In fact, most of the extensive domain possessed by the monasteries had been willed to them, for as the Chilean Barros Arana remarked, "a will which did not include some legacy in favor of the monastery passed for an act against religion."

In an effort to prevent members of the religious orders from unduly influencing their parishioners or charges, the crown in 1774 expressly forbade ecclesiastics from interfering in the drawing up of wills, and in 1775 forbade confessors or their converts to be heirs or legatees. The decrees were not enforced, however, and the Church continued to amass a fortune in real estate and other valuables.

This great wealth of the Church posed serious problems for the development of the new nations. Ownership of such a large part of the land aggravated the effects of the economically unsound *latifundios* or large estates by further reducing the amount of land available for small independent farmers. This discouraged the best use of the land and also the immigration the region greatly needed. The legal principle of mortmain further aggravated the scarcity of land available for small owners. Under the principle of mortmain (dead hand, in French), once property was acquired by the Church it could never be alienated or distributed to other owners. Moreover, since all the Church's properties, including its commercial enterprises, were exempt from taxation, the government did not have a sufficiently large economic base from which to obtain the taxes it needed.

As a result of these problems, in nation after nation the extensive properties of the Church were in time expropriated by the government, which sometimes took over even the churches and other buildings used solely for religious purposes. These buildings were used for a variety of purposes. In Guatemala, many of them became public schools or military academies. Others became mental asylums, reformatories, or prisons. Still others were used for government offices or barracks for the army.[15]

While the society as a whole derived some benefit from the properties taken over, this benefit was apparently small compared with the heavy loss the Church suffered. In Guatemala, the Church was so financially despoiled that it has not even been able to keep its buildings in good repair or to restore them completely after severe earthquake damage. The gain that accrued to society as a whole was far from proportionate to the Church's loss. If the properties expropriated had been administered in such a way as to avoid the temptations of public and political greed, concluded Manuel Montufar y Coronado, they would have served to

---

[15] Mary P. Holleran, *Church and State in Guatemala* (New York: Columbia University Press, 1949), pp. 59–60.

"repair the losses of the state, substituting in place of the convents . . . loans for the development of agriculture, commerce and highways; but the disorders of the first days and the confusion of the first measures taken impaired everything, and finally only a small number of individuals profited by it."[16]

In brief, it was much easier for the anticlericals to tear down the Church's financial empire than to conserve its valuable assets for the benefit of the nation. For as might have been suspected, some of the anticlericals were merely selfish opportunists, interested only in feathering their own nests.

STATE ASSUMPTION OF THE CHURCH'S SECULAR ACTIVITIES

Another goal of the anticlericals was to divest the Church of what are commonly regarded in democratic countries today as secular functions and activities, transferring them to the jurisdiction of the state. The main ones they strove to have secularized were the following: the family, particularly its establishment by marriage and its dissolution by divorce; education at all levels; welfare programs for the less fortunate; cemeteries available to all; banking and credit; and civil registry of wills, deeds, and contracts.

In most of the nations today, a couple that marries must have a civil ceremony, performed by a justice of the peace or some other official of the government in a simple, inexpensive ceremony. This civil ceremony, performed under the auspices of the government, constitutes a legal marriage entitled to the full protection and support of law. The couple may desire to have a religious wedding performed by a priest in the Church, but this can take place only after the civil ceremony and is in no wise a substitute for it. Indeed, a priest joining a couple in wedlock before they have already been married in a civil ceremony is in most countries subject to fine or other punishment by the state.

An exception to the requirement of a civil ceremony is sometimes made for Indians. In Bolivia, a law passed in 1920 allows them to be married by a religious ceremony alone, without the necessity of a civil marriage. This exception was made because of "the fanatical attachment of the ignorant Indians to the priests, and their inability to regard anything other than the religious ceremony as being binding."[17]

The Indians in Guatemala are so suspicious of government officials that they avoid having any dealings with them whenever possible, even for a civil wedding to legitimize their union in the eyes of the law. But because of the relatively heavy expenses of the religious ceremony, they are

---

[16] In *ibid.*, p. 58.
[17] Mecham, *op. cit.*, pp. 186–87.

unable to afford being married by the Church. As a result, very few of them are married in the eyes of the state or the Church.[18]

Another form of union that most states recognize as legal marriage under certain conditions is the consensual or common-law marriage, discussed in Chapter 3. This recognition was dictated by the very large percentage of couples in most of the countries who live together without the blessing of either a civil or a religious ceremony. In order for these common-law unions to be regarded as legal, the couple must have lived together as man and wife for a specified minimum number of years.

The state has further exercised its control over the family by providing for its dissolution under certain conditions. Divorce is now permitted in many of the nations; sometimes, as under the Cuban constitution of 1940, the wife has about the same grounds for divorce as does the husband.[19]

Another function of the Church which the state usually decided to take over is that of providing an education for students at all levels, with religious instruction being forbidden in the public schools. This policy has invariably provoked bitter controversy, for the Church and its partisans were loath to surrender this important function. In states where the Church enjoyed a privileged status, it was sometimes given control of the educational system. In Colombia, the constitution of 1886 empowered the Church to exercise such control, which it did until 1936 when the Liberals succeeded in revising the constitution.

Argentina has traditionally followed quite a different course from Colombia. After a prolonged and bitter church-state controversy, it was finally decided in 1884—or so the nation thought—that the public schools were to be completely secular, with the Church exercising no control over them. No religious instruction could be given in public schools during the regular school day but could be given at the end of the day to children who voluntarily chose to remain at school to receive it. The sensitive issue of compulsory religious instruction in the public schools was revived in 1943 when the military junta, after taking over the government, reversed the congressional act of 1884 which provided for religious neutrality in the public schools and instituted compulsory instruction in the Catholic religion for all primary and secondary schools. Only those pupils would be exempted whose parents professed other

---

[18] In some parts of Guatemala, only an estimated 2 percent of the Indians are formally married, according to Mary P. Holleran. The complication of having to use *ladino* agents for making all arrangements, also being very discourteously treated by them, discourages Indians from desiring to have a formal marriage, civil or religious. (Holleran, *op. cit.*, p. 245.)

[19] For a survey of divorce in the several republics, see Gordon Ireland and Jesús Galíndez Suárez, *Divorce in the Americas* (Buffalo, N.Y.: Dennis and Co., Inc., 1947).

religions and asked that their children be excused. Those exempted would receive moral instruction.[20]

In addition to the family and the school, another area to which the government often extended its authority was the welfare program for helping the less fortunate members of society—the orphanages, hospitals, and other agencies of mercy. Argentina was one of the first nations to take over these eleemosynary institutions from the Church. Bernardino Rivadavia, one of the ablest leaders in the early days of the republic and president from 1826–27, confiscated the properties of several religious orders engaged in welfare activities of one sort or another; in his opinion, their zeal for discharging these functions was flagging. Rivadavia, a humanitarian, established *La Sociedad de Beneficencia* (Society of Charity) to have jurisdiction over orphanages, hospitals, and other welfare agencies, entrusting its direction to prosperous, socially conscious matrons of Buenos Aires society, who did an excellent job in discharging their responsibility.[21]

Flexing the muscles of their sovereignty, the states also took over other important functions which had previously been performed by the Church. Banking was one of these. Recognizing that credit was the economic lifeblood of society, governments established public banks that would operate directly under their control or authorized private ones that would function under their close supervision. No longer were loans to be a monopoly of the Church, granted under its own terms and conditions— lenient and considerate, it should be noted—but would be provided by agencies which the state either controlled or regulated.

Another church activity the state decided to take over was control of the cemeteries. At first glance, the government's action may appear to be picayune and its interest in cemeteries provocative and contentious. Far from it; the Church's ownership and operation of cemeteries had long been one of its most effective controls over society. Burial of a loved one in consecrated ground is essential to a family's peace of mind; according to popular belief in Latin America, unless the dead are buried in such ground, they cannot go to heaven. Thus, denying the deceased the privilege of being buried there was tantamount to consigning his soul to hell. But interring him in the cemetery involved a continuing expense that bore heavily on the poor.

To eliminate possible abuses, the governments have provided for the establishment, under municipal supervision, of public cemeteries open to all without restrictions and providing a respectable resting place at very modest cost.

---

[20] For a discussion of the justification and impact of this law, see George I. Blanksten, *Perón's Argentina* (Chicago: University of Chicago Press, 1953), pp. 188–90.

[21] Hubert Herring, *A History of Latin America from the Beginnings to the Present* (2d ed. rev.; New York: Alfred A. Knopf, Inc., 1961), p. 623.

Whatever activity the government sought to take over, whether control of education or of cemeteries, it was sure to provoke a vehement no-holds-barred struggle. The Church, regarding each new design of the government as a further encroachment on its hallowed prerogatives, fought back with every weapon at its disposal. Thus, when the Congress of Chile in 1875 abolished the Church courts and gave the civil courts jurisdiction over priests, the Church excommunicated every congressman who voted for the measure; and when civil marriage was legalized in 1883, the Church excommunicated the president, members of his cabinet, and all congressmen who supported it.[22]

In earlier times, excommunication or even the threat of it was such a potent weapon that it could make a powerful monarch crawl on his knees to the papacy seeking pardon. But the formerly potent weapon apparently has had little effect on the undisciplined, ultraindividualistic society of Latin America. Moreover, in the strong secular social current, time and tide were on the side of the state.

SEPARATION OF CHURCH AND STATE

Another measure ardently advocated by anticlericals was separation of church and state, which has been accomplished in a number of the countries. Colombia in 1853 was the first to proclaim separation, a radical step proposed by President José Hilario López and approved by his liberal adherents in the Congress; but this action was reversed in 1887 when the Conservatives managed to regain control of the government. Mexico was the first nation to disestablish permanently the Church, and its lead was followed by several of the Central American republics. In reality, however, the Church was usually not actually separated from the state and allowed to operate independently; rather, it was kept under the thumb of the state and often subjected to very oppressive controls.

Brazil in its Federal Republican Constitution promulgated in February, 1891, proved that disestablishment could be accomplished peaceably and amicably. In accordance with the constitution, church and state are completely separated. The government relinquished its control over the national patronage and has no voice whatever in the selection of the Church's personnel. The Church has title to its properties, and all buildings used exclusively for religious purposes are exempt from taxation, although other realty owned by the Church is not. Religious instruction may be given in the public schools after school hours to any children who want it, but the government does not pay the teachers for this service.[23]

The solution of the knotty, complex problem of the relationship

[22] *Ibid.*, p. 583.
[23] Mecham, *op. cit.*, pp. 275–77.

between church and state by amicable separation of the two was typically Brazilian. As one student of colonial art remarked: "In Brazil, even Christ hangs comfortably on the cross." In keeping with the general absence of violence and extremes of passion in Brazilian history and with the generally mild and non-political role the Church has played in society, the pattern of violent clericalism and anti-clericalism found elsewhere in Latin America simply does not exist in Brazil.[24]

Friendly separation of church and state has taken place in other nations too: in Cuba in 1902; Panama, 1904; Uruguay, 1919; and Chile, 1925.

Contrasting with the peaceable disestablishment of the Church in the above states is the long-drawn-out, bitterly fought battle over separation in Mexico, which began in 1855 and still has not been settled. The Reform Movement led by Benito Juárez, a full-blooded Zapotec Indian and the nation's venerated national hero, aimed to establish a secular state with democratic, constitutional government. A number of far-reaching reforms were adopted, including: expropriation of the Church's immense holdings, dissolution of the religious communities, public control of education and cemeteries, civil marriage, civil registry of births and deaths, and restrictions on political activities of the clergy.

These reforms were adopted over the most vehement ecclesiastical opposition, which culminated in open revolt against the government. According to J. Lloyd Mecham:

The War of the Reform was essentially a religious conflict, and for that reason, perhaps, it was characterized by excessive plunder, rapine, brutal reprisals, and a general spirit of extermination. Prisoners were slaughtered in cold blood, doctors and nurses were killed, and churches were sacked. The clergy made it a holy war.[25]

During the long dictatorship of Porfirio Díaz, which lasted from 1876 to 1910, the transfer of many of the Church's functions to the government and the imposition of various restrictions on the Church were not enforced; as a result, the Church regained most of its former power and influence. It owned property; operated schools, convents, and monasteries; and in general ignored the laws of the Reform with the tacit acquiescence of Díaz.

But the revolution of 1910, the first social revolution to occur in Latin America, once again tested relations between church and state. The constitution of 1917, like its predecessor of 1873, contained many provisions designed to increase the power of the state at the expense of the Church; but until 1926 these provisions were practically ignored.

---

[24] In Lewis Hanke, *South America* (Princeton, N.J.: D. Van Nostrand Co., Inc., 1959), p. 89.

[25] Mecham, *op. cit.*, p. 366.

When the archbishops and bishops of Mexico, in a joint statement issued in January, 1926, criticized the articles in the constitution relating to religion, President Calles acted swiftly and decisively. The government promptly nationalized all property the Church held, closed all church schools, required all private schools to register with a stern prohibition against religious instruction, and deported the foreign-born clergy.

Many of the laws passed by the state governments were minutely restrictive, as those which set such low limits on the number of priests to be allowed so as to make impossible the performance of their clerical duties. The state of Tabasco even went so far as to require that all priests must marry. "It was merely an effort to legitimize the existing children," Governor Tomás Garrido alleged.

Once again, Mexico became an open battlefield between the intransigent forces of those who championed the cause of the state or of the Church. A nationwide economic boycott instituted by the Catholic League for the Protection of Religious Liberty was a peaceful movement that petered out. But the *cristero* revolt that broke out cost many lives and required more than a year to subdue.

After 1930, relations between the Church and the state began to improve under an unwritten gentlemen's agreement, whereby it was understood that each would try to avoid as far as possible provoking any open conflict with the other. This arrangement has apparently proved satisfactory to most Mexicans. While the constitution contains many restrictive provisions against Catholicism or any other religion, its provisions are not rigidly enforced. Consequently, church schools and seminaries have quietly been allowed to reopen throughout the country,[26] and church buildings and other properties have been quietly returned. In fact, there has been such an increased attendance at Mass as to burden the priests limited in number by law.

From surface indications, relations between the Church and the Mexican state have improved; but it is an uneasy truce at best, which can be upset by any one of many highly inflammatory issues. Just such an issue was the government's establishment in 1959 of a free textbook commission, designed to improve instruction in the schools by providing textbooks at government expense, since three fourths of the pupils cannot afford to buy them. However, the program of providing uniform free textbooks aroused vehement opposition on the part of the Church and many Catholic organizations, which claimed that the program of one text is totalitarian and dangerous, is Marxist-oriented, attempts to separate the child from the family, and indoctrinates the students with the supremacy of the state.

---

[26] In 1962, some 30,000 church schools flourished as private institutions, according to the Copley News Service. (*Hispanic American Reports*, Vol. XVI, No. 4 [July, 1963), p. 431.)

The Church expressed its opposition in mass demonstrations; 150,000 participated in the one at Monterrey in February, 1962. The government met this opposition head-on by organizing counterdemonstrations in support of its program. President López Mateos himself departed from his usually mild, conciliatory attitude toward the Church by castigating its efforts to thwart his program, terming the Church and its related Catholic organizations "the forces of darkness."[27]

Although the 20 Latin American republics are all predominantly Catholic, there are great differences in their relationships with the Church. On the basis of these relationships, the states may be classified into three general groups.

1. States which have expressly or implicitly retained Catholicism as the established privileged religion in the society. There are seven states in this group: Argentina, Colombia, Costa Rica, Ecuador, Paraguay, Peru, and Venezuela. In these states, the constitutions may require that the president and other officials be Roman Catholics, a requirement that is broadly interpreted and is apparently satisfied by their having been baptized in the Church. Moreover, the Church is the recognized protector of the family; consequently, in accordance with Catholic doctrine, divorce is either difficult or impossible to obtain. The Church may also administer the national program of education or give religious instruction in Catholicism that is compulsory for all students, sometimes with specified exceptions. The government usually has certain peculiar functions, such as nominating members of the clergy, levying and collecting tithes, and using tax money for the support of the Church.

2. States that have dissolved their former union or close association with the Church, which is recognized as nominally independent or actually so—a free church in a free state, as we have in the United States. Comprising this group are the following 12 nations: Bolivia, Brazil, Chile, Cuba, the Dominican Republic, El Salvador, Guatemala, Haiti, Honduras, Nicaragua, Panama, and Uruguay.

3. One state, Mexico, where the Church has been separated from the state but kept under its close control. In addition to the restrictions already mentioned, members of the clergy in Mexico may not wear clerical garb in public, engage in politics, hold office, or even vote.

PARTICIPATION BY THE CHURCH IN POLITICS

The Catholic Church in Latin America has since early colonial days been accustomed to taking an active role in the government and politics of the region. Often the archbishops and bishops were assigned govern-

---

[27] For these details regarding the uniform free textbook controversy, see *ibid.,* April, 1962, p. 112; October, 1962, p. 962; March, 1963, p. 19; and July, 1963, p. 413.

Summaries of the bitter conflict between Church and state in Mexico are given by Mecham, *op. cit.,* chaps. xv and xvi; and more briefly by Charles C. Cumberland, *Mexico: The Struggle for Modernity* (New York: Oxford University Press, 1968), pp. 276–86.

mental responsibilities by the crown, and their discharge of these duties greatly contributed to the effective administration of the colonies. After independence, members of the clergy continued to play a prominent role in government. Among the best-educated and most qualified members of society, they participated in the constituent assemblies which formulated the constitutions of the new nations. Besides playing this important role, they took an active part in both local and national government. Sometimes in the selection of members of congress, it was simply a question of whether to send educated members of the clergy or settle on rural clodhoppers.

In Oaxaca, Mexico, a citizen contemplating the election for members of Congress moaned:

In my Department you have . . . three kinds of men: first, the rich, usually ignorant . . . and egotistical; second, persons more or less well-known, who are the only ones suitable to discharge public duties, and who for this reason are almost all employed in public office; and third, those absolutely without property, who, destitute of all knowledge, are useless for public affairs. Except, then, the second class and Oaxaca will have to send to the general Congress a representation of asses, or else ten good clergymen to make up a delegation.[28]

As the Church's temporal activities have been increasingly circumscribed by the state, ministering to the spiritual needs of the faithful has taken up a larger share of the clergy's time, and there is less opportunity for them to be personally involved in dispensing personal ideas and expressing personal convictions on nonspiritual issues. Consequently, clergymen are usually not as politically influential in most of the nations today as earlier, except as they reflect the policies of the hierarchy, which may or may not conform to the thinking of the politically dominant segments of the society.[29]

But although the Church's spiritual role is unquestionably its main concern today, the Church sometimes still finds it difficult to give up its earlier political role. In the Cuban Revolution beginning in January, 1959, the Church in Cuba wittingly or unwittingly assumed an active, antigovernment role. Indeed, according to Leslie Dewart, it was one of the parties responsible for pushing Cuba toward communism; in fact, it was perhaps more responsible than any other single one.[30]

---

[28] Fran co Bas [?] met to Valentín Gómez Farías, August 16, 1846, Farías Papers. In Wilfred Hardy Callcott, *Church and State in Mexico: 1822–1857* (Durham, N.C.: Duke University Press, 1926), p. 180.

[29] John J. Johnson, *Political Change in Latin America: The Emergence of the Middle Sectors* (Stanford, Calif.: Stanford University Press, 1958), pp. 12–13. His observations regarding Argentina, Brazil, Chile, Uruguay, and Mexico are applicable to the other nations of Latin America.

[30] The following comments on the relation of the Roman Catholic Church to the Cuban Revolution are from Leslie Dewart, *Christianity and Revolution: The Lesson of Cuba* (New York: Herder and Herder, 1963), especially pp. 91, 122, 140, 142, 164–66, and 174–75.

In the early stages of the revolution, the Church, apparently emboldened by its help, demanded that instruction in Catholicism be given in the public schools—a demand unprecedented in the history of the nation. But in deference to the hierarchy, the government agreed to it.

With this important concession made to it, the Church before long began to evidence deep concern over the emergence of the Communist Party which Castro legalized. Soon the Church was captivated by the conviction that its only duty toward the revolution was to oppose communism. And although many Catholics and Catholic lay organizations voiced support of land reform—the heart of the new revolutionary movement—in time a majority of them took a vigorous stand in opposition to it.

In April, 1961, relations between the Church and Castro were severely strained. Catholic cooperation with the CIA in the Bay of Pigs fiasco was all too evident: the shoulder patches on the uniforms of the invaders, in the shape of a shield with a Latin Cross in the center; three captured Catholic priests whose duty was to minister to the religious needs of the invaders; and a document taken from the head chaplain and apparently intended to be a proclamation to be broadcast to the Cuban people, stating, "The liberating forces have landed on the beaches of Cuba. We come in the name of God, Justice, and Democracy to restore the rights that have been subjugated and slandered."

The antagonism between the Church and Castro came to a boil on September 10, 1961, when several thousand Catholics turned a religious procession into a vociferous, anti-communist demonstration which soon became a riot. The entire sequence of events was apparently planned in the church of Monsignor Boza, one of the leading prelates. Castro retaliated swiftly and vehemently against the Church. He had the monsignor arrested on September 12, held incommunicado, and on September 17 put bodily aboard the Spanish liner Covadonga bound for Spain, and along with him 135 priests.

Thus, according to Dewart, the Catholic Church by its intransigent opposition to the revolution and its insistence on strong ties with the United States rather than with Russia, was largely responsible for Cuba's becoming a communist nation allied with the East, and also for the Church's being thrown out of Cuba.

In regard to its policy of interfering in politics in Latin America, the Catholic Church might do well to ponder the conclusion of a prominent scholar.

Perhaps it is too much to expect, but it would seem that after all that time, cognizance would be taken of the lessons that history teaches. One of the greatest of these lessons is that when the Church acts like a political party, it will be treated like one. When churchmen become politicians, they will be regarded as politicians.[31]

---

[31] Holleran, *op. cit.*, p. 243.

Besides participating in politics generally, the Catholic Church has also on occasion supported dictators. This support in no sense represented a preference for dictators as such. Rather, the interests of the Church were often best served by a strong ruler who maintained the status quo and respected vested interests or who gave the Church favored treatment.

A classic example of such support was the Church's policy toward the regime of Juan Perón. There is no valid evidence to show that the Church did anything to help establish the dictatorial regime which governed Argentina's destiny from 1943 to 1955. But the decision of the military junta in late 1943 to make the teaching of Catholicism compulsory in all public schools was enough to win the sympathy and support of the Catholic Church. To show its appreciation, it gratefully thanked the government for the largess it had received. However, the government, which soon meant Colonel Juan Perón, needed more than thanks; it critically needed help in the presidential election scheduled for February 7, 1946.

Whether or not the Church intended to do so, it virtually decided the outcome of the election. Throwing its influential weight solidly behind Perón, the Argentine Episcopate addressed a pastoral letter to all the clergy and faithful, forbidding them to vote for any parties or candidates that advocated measures contrary to the interests of the Church. This letter was the kiss of death to the moderate, anti-Perón Democratic Union, generally conceded to be the only party that had a chance of defeating Perón. In appreciation for this support, Perón's government later gave the Church many unusual privileges, such as staging religious parades in Buenos Aires during religious week and unrestrictedly using loudspeakers to cover neighborhoods with hymns, slogans, and sermons—activities that until then had been strictly forbidden.

Whatever the *quid pro quo*, if any, the Church displayed an obvious bias thereafter in its attitude toward Argentine politics. It saw nothing wrong with permitting Father Virgilio Filippo to campaign actively for Perón in 1946. This ecclesiastical firebrand's fervent and fanatical support was recognized in 1948 when he was elected a Peronista member of the Chamber of Deputies from Buenos Aires. But while condoning, if not sanctioning or even promoting, this sort of pro-Perón activity, it was at the same time throttling any ecclesiastically expressed opposition to the regime.

When in September, 1948, Perón threatened to hang the enemies who opposed his proposals for constitutional reform, Father José María Dunphy had the courage to chide the dictator-president from his pulpit and in his letters to the Catholic newspaper *El Pueblo*. "It is not Christian for those in high places to foment or incite to civil war," he said. "Nor is it Christian to elevate hatred to the extreme of wanting to annihilate those who hold differing opinions."

For his bold stand, which ran counter to Church policy, Father Dunphy was summarily removed from his parish; Cardinal Copello even refused to put in writing the reasons for his dismissal. An appeal for an ecclesiastical trial in accordance with canon law was not answered, nor was an appeal made directly to the Vatican.[32]

But when, toward the end of his administration, Perón committed such blasphemies as legalizing divorce and even prostitution, the Church reappraised its position. It excommunicated Perón, adding its weight to help topple a regime that was already beginning to fall.[33]

If the policy of supporting Perón and other dictators was a short-sighted one, we must remember that the Catholic Church was not alone in pursuing this policy. Until 1961, the government of the United States often followed the same course. President Franklin Roosevelt, apologetic for his support of Trujillo, the long-time dictatorial boss of the Dominican Republic, is said to have remarked: "I know he is an S.O.B., but at least he is *our* S.O.B."

Since 1955, the Catholic Church in Latin America, reversing its course, has opposed dictators and time after time has helped to overthrow them. In Colombia, in 1957, it was in the forefront of the fight against Rojas Pinilla. During High Mass on a fateful Sunday morning, Father Severo Velásquez delivered a fiery denunciation of the repressive regime. Before a packed congregation, with many standing in the doorways, he proclaimed: "It is the duty of all Catholics, with the pastors at their heads, to fight against criminals, and not only those from below, but also, and principally, those from above." After the service, with Father Velásquez leading them, the congregation poured out of the edifice chanting "Cristo, si! Rojas, no!" to face a barrage of tear gas from the police and sprays of red dye from tank trucks standing nearby.[34]

In other nations, too, the Catholic Church has had a principal role in helping to topple such dictators as Pérez Jiménez of Venezuela in early 1958 and Fulgencio Batista of Cuba not long afterward. Moreover, it has not hesitated to express its strong disapproval of other dictatorial regimes, such as those of Fidel Castro in Cuba and François Duvalier of Haiti, where members of the clergy who boldly spoke out against the government at great personal risk to themselves were expelled from the country.

The Catholic Church's new look at dictators extended even to Paraguay, whose government for many years has been so dictatorial that an estimated one third of the total national population lives abroad as exiles in a "continual state of tourism." In Asunción, a young priest, Father

---

[32] *New York Times,* September 27, 1948, p. 13, col. 4; and *Time,* January 17, 1949, p. 28.

[33] For a detailed account of the relationship between the Church and the Perón government, see Blanksten, *op. cit.,* pp. 229–37.

[34] John D. Martz, *Colombia: A Contemporary Political Survey* (Chapel Hill: University of North Carolina Press, 1962), pp. 238–39.

Ramón Talavera, at great danger to himself defied the government by making a public appeal from a loudspeaker-equipped truck before a large crowd in front of the National Pantheon of Heroes, pleading for the restoration of freedom. Citing the many evils in the country that needed to be corrected, the priest urged "active resistance against acts of tyranny."[35]

The Catholic Church has often been criticized for its earlier support of dictators. But after its change of policy in the mid-1950's, while the government of the United States continued for several years longer to support dictators, the question was sometimes facetiously asked with as much truth as humor: "Why can't the State Department be as democratic as the Vatican?"

RELIGIOUS ELITES[36]

The religious elites, as Ivan Vallier conceives them in the Roman Catholic Church, are not necessarily those who have top positions in the religious system—cardinals, bishops, and others—but rather those who have the capacity "to exert a decisive influence on the development of the Catholic system or the wider social order, whether this influence is resistive, innovative, or neutralizing." According to Vallier, there are four identifiable types of elites within the Catholic Church: the traditional elites termed the "politicians," and three new types—the "papists," the "pastors," and the "pluralists."

The politicians represent the traditional Catholic structure and values. Concerned principally with maintaining the prestige of the Church and their own positions as influential members of the hierarchy, they ally themselves with the vested interests of the social power structure. The laity are ignored. Social problems are too, for they can be circumvented by manipulating public opinion, the politicians reason.

The papists, one of the three new elites, also embrace the hierarchical organization of the Church, but for a reason quite different from that of the politicians. Working as a team, the hierarchy, the clergy, and the laity constitute a missionary elite for promoting Catholicism. The papists frown on the Church's traditional involvement in politics, and even forbid activities in direct support of a political party. Hoping to chart a new course, they concentrate on building a Church that can rely on its own authority and its own resources to achieve its religious goals.

The pastors, unlike the other two elites, prefer a cooperative rather

---

[35] *New York Times*, March 3, 1958, p. 10, col. 3.

[36] The information in this section is from Ivan Vallier, "Religious Elites: Differentiations and Developments in Roman Catholicism," *Elites in Latin America*, eds. Seymour Martin Lipset and Aldo Solari (New York: Oxford University Press, 1967), pp. 190–91 and 203–6.

than a hierarchical form of organization. Seeking to develop a strong, worship-centered congregation, they encourage laymen to take active roles in the liturgy, and attempt to integrate priests, parishioners, and the sacraments into a spiritual body. Solidarity within the congregation is a major objective.

The fourth elite group, the pluralists, are not primarily concerned with the Church's traditional authority and political ties, with hierarchy and clericalisms, or even with worship and the sacraments. Rather, the pluralists frankly admit that Catholicism in Latin America is really a minority faith—one religion among many others. Accordingly, they stress the critical importance of Catholics' joining with other like-minded groups to cope with the many pressing social problems of the region.

THE ROMAN CATHOLIC CHURCH TODAY

Any attempt to accurately evaluate the strength of the Roman Catholic Church in Latin America as a whole or in any specific nation is at best an estimate. One fact is obvious: its strength varies considerably among the 20 republics, being notably strong in some and weak in others. Colombia has staunchly remained one of the strongest bastions of the Church. Its loyalty might be deflected during liberal regimes, but over most of its national history the nation has been a dedicated supporter of Catholicism. Many of the other nations too, especially Peru and Paraguay, have given the Church strong support.

But in some of the other nations, the Catholic Church is undeniably quite weak. In Bolivia, it has had such slight prestige that it has never been persecuted. In Brazil, it was completely overshadowed by the Big House, an expression of enormous feudal might with an "arrogant solidity of form and material." Yet, it must be noted that the pomp of the Big House has turned to dust, gone with the wind, while the Church has survived and is continuing with its work.[37]

In Cuba, the Church, threatened as it was by secularism, freemasonry, Protestantism, and indifference, was poor and impotent. A rural priest would have starved if he had had to depend on his parishioners for support. It was the fashion to make fun of the Church and the clergy, even ridicule them; organized religion was generally regarded as a matter for women and children. Any male who regarded himself as *macho* did not want to be seen speaking civilly to a priest or entering a church on Sunday. For if he violated the *macho* code, he might be charged with effeminacy and lack of virility. Aware of the national mores, a Cuban

---

[37] Gilberto Freyre, *The Masters and the Slaves: A Study in the Development of Brazilian Civilization,* trans. Samuel Putnam (2d Eng. ed. rev.; New York: Alfred A. Knopf, Inc., 1956), xxxv, and p. 192.

priest realized that one of the few ways he could hope to earn a modicum of respect from other Cuban men was to maintain a *querida*.[38]

In Panama, too, religion has not been a very influential factor in national life. The clergy does not play an important role, nor do religious issues often disturb the populace. Most Panamanians tend to keep church and state strictly separated in their thinking.[39]

Uruguay is another nation where Catholicism is weak. In large measure, this situation reflects "the lengthened shadow of a man," writes Russell Fitzgibbon, "that of José Batlle y Ordóñez—which helps account for how Uruguay worships, or fails to worship, today. Batlle early developed a skeptical and questioning attitude toward the Catholic Church."[40] Through the medium of his newspaper, *El Dia*, Batlle took advantage of his opportunity to minimize the influence of the Church. As a result of his persuasiveness, a divorce law was passed in 1907, the teaching of religion in public schools was prohibited in 1909, and finally, in 1917, church and state were completely separated. "His measures against it [the Church] set a pattern of anticlericalism that has persisted to the present day and has left the Catholic establishment in Uruguay in as debilitated a position as it is anywhere in Latin America."[41]

In Latin America as a whole, the population is sometimes referred to as being 90 percent or so Catholic—a Catholic stronghold, in fact, where approximately one third of the total Catholic population of the world resides. But according to other estimates, probably no more than 10 to 20 percent of the population are actually practicing Catholics who understand the teachings of the Church and apply them in their daily lives.

Only a very small percentage of the nominal parishioners attend a weekly mass. In the rural areas of Peru and Venezuela, it is only about 3 to 5 percent of the total population. In the cities, it is somewhat better; in Buenos Aires, between 7 and 10 percent; and in Rio de Janeiro, about 10 percent.[42]

Poor attendance at mass, for whatever reason, is one evidence of nominal Catholicism. Another is the widespread practice of "folk Catholicism." Handed down from generation to generation with only a minimal influence of the priests, it bears little resemblance to official Church doctrine. It does not stress man's sinfulness, the necessity of salvation from hell, or the ethics of everyday life. Rather, its aim is to establish control over nature, especially adversities that man cannot cope with in a human manner. Concerned only with the satisfaction of natural daily

[38] Dewart, *op. cit.*, pp. 94, 95, and 99.

[39] John and Mavis Biesanz, *The People of Panama* (New York: Columbia University Press, 1955), pp. 161–62.

[40] Russell H. Fitzgibbon, *Uruguay: Portrait of a Democracy* (New Brunswick, N.J.: Rutgers University Press, 1954), p. 231.

[41] Johnson, *op. cit.*, p. 51.

[42] François Houtart and Emile Pin, *The Church and the Latin American Revolution*, trans. Gilbert Barth (New York: Sheed and Ward, Inc., 1965), p. 152.

needs, folk Catholicism endows the virgin and the saints with characteristics very similar to those of Indian spirits or ancestral African gods.[43]

Still another evidence of nominal Catholicism is the baffling resurgence
in some of the nations of the African pagan fetishistic cults. These pagan
cults and rites, which are hundreds, perhaps even thousands of years old,
have long been practiced by many members of the poor, illiterate lower
class. But in recent years, spiritism and cultism have spread to embrace
many in the middle class and even the very top of society. President François Duvalier of Haiti, even after expelling the Catholic clergy and being
excommunicated by the Church, still regards himself as a faithful Catholic. But he makes no bones about also practicing voodoo.[44]

Approximately 30 percent of the entire population of Brazil is in one
way or another affiliated with spiritism. According to a study made in the
favellas of Rio de Janeiro, although 80 percent declare themselves to be
Catholics, 67.3 percent occasionally take part in Umbanda sessions.[45]

Several factors account for the fact that the great mass of the population is only nominally Catholic. The region has long suffered from a
severe shortage of priests; it has only about 37,000 of them, and according
to officials of the Church, from 4 to 5 times that many are urgently
needed. In North America, there is 1 priest for approximately 700 Catholics, but in Latin America there is only 1 priest for 5,000 of the faithful.
In some areas there, a priest may have as many as 30,000 or more people
in his nominal flock, and thousands of villages and towns have no church
or resident priest. The average geographical area of a parish is about 400
square miles; the rural parish, usually far larger than its urban counterpart, may be 700 or more square miles.

As Table 5–1 shows, the shortage of priests has eased somewhat during
the past two decades; the total number of priests, diocesan and religious,
increased from 24,381 in 1945 to 37,636 in 1960. The remarkable increase
was due largely to the heavy influx of priests from other countries—
namely, Spain, 7,352; Germany, 1,480; the Netherlands, 1,208; United
States, 1,106; France, 583; Italy, 470; Canada, 312; Belgium, 268; Switzerland, 102; and Austria, 82.[46]

---

[43] Emanuel de Kadt, "Religion, the Church, and Social Change in Brazil," *The
Politics of Conformity in Latin America*, ed. Claudio Veliz (New York: Oxford
University Press, 1967), pp. 193–97.

[44] For an extensive account of the nature and impact of such pagan cults in Brazil,
see T. Lynn Smith, *Brazil: People and Institutions* (rev. ed.: Baton Rouge: Louisiana
State University Press, 1963), pp. 531–49. For their practice in Cuba, see Wyatt
MacGaffey and Clifford R. Barnett, *Cuba* (New Haven, Conn.: HRAF Press, 1962),
pp. 205–10.

[45] Boaventura Kloppenburg, "The Prevalence of Spiritism in Brazil," *The Religious Dimension in the New Latin America*, ed. John J. Considine (Notre Dame,
Ind.: Fides, Inc., 1966), pp. 77 and 81.

For the many reasons why Spiritism appeals to so many people, see *ibid.*, pp.
85–87.

[46] Houtart, *op. cit.*, pp. 156–57.

TABLE 5-1

NUMBER OF PRIESTS IN LATIN AMERICA BETWEEN 1912 AND 1960

Year	Diocesan Priests	Religious Priests	Total
1912	11,776	4,578	16,354
1945	12,992	11,389	24,381
1950	14,270	13,282	27,552
1955	16,145	16,010	32,155
1960	18,451	19,185	37,636

SOURCE: François Houtart and Emile Pin, *The Church and the Latin American Revolution*, trans. Gilbert Barth (New York: Sheed and Ward, Inc., 1965), p. 146.

The fact that more than half of the imported priests came from reactionary fascist Spain had a decided impact on at least one of the recipient nations. In Cuba, any hope the Catholic Church might have had for training a native clergy did not materialize. In fact, there were four or five Spanish clergymen for every native priest. Many of these Spaniards nurtured an admiration for reactionary, staunchly Catholic Franco—even hoped to bring Cuba back into the Spanish fold, Leslie Dewart is convinced. Indeed, they were largely responsible for the Catholic Church's early and unjustifiably intransigent opposition to Castro—an opposition that helped to push him into the communist camp.[47]

Besides suffering from a shortage of priests, the Catholic Church has also been greatly hampered by the lack of funds needed to carry on its work—a condition resulting mainly from the expropriation of its properties and the prevailing poverty of many areas. In Venezuela, the plight of the Church was so serious that President Gómez restored some of its former properties to improve its financial condition. In Guatemala, to help relieve its financial distress President Ydígoras in July, 1959, decreed that the Church could own property designed exclusively for religious, social welfare, or educational purposes—the first time since 1879 that the Church has been allowed to own property.

The needs of the Church in Latin America have worried not only the Vatican but also the faithful in many countries. The situation has been soberly surveyed by a number of conferences held in Rome, the United States, Latin America, and elsewhere to consider measures urgently needed for strengthening the Catholic Church in Latin America. The call to action was sounded by Pope John XXIII in his fourth encyclical letter, when he urged all Catholic missions throughout the world to increase their missionary efforts. In response, the Church has planned and is executing a worldwide program calculated to give the spiritual, educa-

---

[47] Dewart, *op. cit.*, pp. 95 and 98.

tional, and material assistance so greatly needed in Latin America. Under the program of Papal Volunteers for Latin America, many members of the faithful have been encouraged to go to the region to aid the lay organizations there.[48] Moreover, the Grail, an international group of laywomen, has been training young women for the lay apostolic in the region.

THE PROTESTANT CHURCHES—TRADITIONAL AND PENTECOSTAL

For centuries, Catholicism was the only faith recognized in Latin America. Even when freedom of conscience was recognized, as in Argentina's first constitution, in effect it meant freedom only from a Catholic conscience and point of view. One of Perón's greatest insults to the Church, ranking with legalized divorce and prostitution, was authorizing the Seventh-Day Adventists to come in and compete with the Catholic Church.

Emphasizing the social gospel, the Protestant missions and missionaries in Latin America are carrying it to the neglected lower classes and to the rural areas which priests with their large parishes have found it difficult to take care of. In proselytizing, they have catered to the physical and intellectual needs of the people. To this end, they have built many hospitals, as in Quito, among the most modern in Latin America, whose facilities are available to even the humblest peon who does not have a peso in his pocket but who needs treatment. They have also established a large number of schools and colleges; some of the institutions of higher learning, as the Presbyterian MacKenzie College in São Paulo, have made outstanding contributions.

For many years after their missions were first established, the Protestant churches in Latin America experienced a very slow growth. In Brazil, after 18 years of missionary work the Baptists at the turn of the century had only 734 members; the Presbyterians, despite 43 years of intense proselytism, had only 14,000.[49] Beginning in 1938, when the

---

[48] The Latin American Catechetical Institute established in 1961 as a unit in the College of Sacred Theology of the Pontifical Catholic University of Santiago, Chile, and a second Latin American Catechetical Institute established in 1966 at Manizales, Colombia, train laymen from the southern and northern countries, respectively. For the selection of candidates, the training they receive as seminarians, and their later important role as village laymen, see Thomas W. Verhoeven, "New Army of Catechists in the Andes," *The Religious Dimension in the New Latin America, op. cit.*, chap. 10.

For the continental training course for catechetical leaders, see Onesimo O'Gorman, "Continental Program for Religious Education," *ibid.*, chap. 15.

[49] Emilio Willems, "Protestantism and Culture Change in Brazil and Chile," *Religion, Revolution, and Reform: New Forces for Change in Latin America*, eds. William V. D'Antonio and Fredrick B. Pike (New York: Frederick A. Praeger, Inc., 1964), p. 94.

FIGURE 5-1

GROWTH OF PROTESTANT CHURCHES IN BRAZIL
(total communicant figures to 1964)

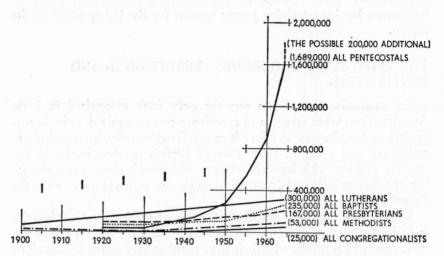

SOURCE: William R. Read, *New Patterns of Church Growth in Brazil* (Grand Rapids, Mich.: William B. Eerdmans Co., 1965), p. 18.

missionary field in Asia was closed by developmnts on the international scene, the Protestant churches turned to Latin America as a favorable area to concentrate on. As a result, they enjoyed much faster growth.

Since the socioeconomic changes affecting Latin American society have brought few if any benefits to the lower classes, it is understandable that they are in a state of latent or overt rebellion against the status quo. The Catholic Church, often regarded as a symbol of the traditional order because of its close ties with the landed aristocracy, has become the target of much hostility on the part of the masses. One of the ways by which they express their hostility is conversion to Protestantism, especially to its sectarian varieties. Since Pentecostalism is better equipped to channel and symbolically express mass rebellion, from its inception it has been very popular with the lower classes, especially in Brazil and Chile.[50]

As Figure 5–1 shows, missions of the traditional Protestant churches in Brazil experienced a fairly steady but slow growth—this despite the efforts of hundreds of missionaries and the expenditure of many millions of dollars. By 1964 there were approximately 300,000 Lutherans, 235,000 Baptists, 167,000 Presbyterians, 53,000 Methodists, 25,000 Congregationalists, and 13,000 Episcopalians (not shown on the figure). But while these

[50] *Ibid.*, pp. 103 and 106; and Emilio Willems, *Followers of the Faith: Culture Change and the Rise of Protestantism in Brazil and Chile* (Nashville, Tenn.: Vanderbilt University Press, 1967), pp. 122–31 and 144–53.

denominational groups enjoyed relatively modest gains, despite the out-pouring of missionary effort and money, the Pentecostal churches, which started from scratch about 1920 and grew rather slowly until about 1940, have since then experienced a phenomenal growth. By 1964 they had approximately 1,689,000 communicants—double the membership of all other Protestant churches combined. The main Pentecostal churches are: The Assemblies of God, with 950,000 communicants; Congregacão Cristã no Brasil, with 300,000; and Independent Pentecostals, of which the main one is Brasil para Cristo, all with 389,000. Besides being the largest Pentecostal church, The Assemblies of God are growing at a fantastic rate—about 25 percent a year.[51]

Aiming their message only to the lower classes, the Pentecostal churches frown on any kind of learning beyond mere literacy and are notably suspicious of intellectual interests. In fact, any learning except knowledge of the Bible is suspect as dangerous to the true faith. Conse-quently, very few of the pastors have attended a seminary and been exposed to its teachings. In one of the main Pentecostal churches, the Christian Congregation of Brazil, there is no clergy; all church positions, including the ministry, are open to all members without regard to educa-tional background, occupation, or economic achievement.[52]

To qualify for an office in the congregation, one must have experi-enced *tomada de Espirito,* or seizure by the Spirit. Having "received the Holy Spirit"—by a direct line, of course—one can then be elected or appointed to any office by the congregation, or possibly begin a profes-sional career within the organizational framework of the sect.

Also basic in Pentecostalism are the powers of the Spirit, which are not the privilege of a few, but rather a Divine gift democratically bestowed on all Pentecostals. There are a half dozen or so main powers of the Spirit—powers that dramatically energize an otherwise powerless indi-vidual or group. These are: the *tomada,* thaumaturgy, *discernimiento,* *persuasión,* speaking in tongues, and prophetizing.

The *tomada,* or seizure by the Spirit, affords one "visions of celestial beauty"; he may also hear "heavenly music" and even be privileged to have God and the angels speak to him. With thaumaturgy, or the power to heal, one seized by the Spirit may find himself cured of an "incurable" ailment, or, if he has previously received the Spirit, may be able to perform the miracle of healing another.

Discernimiento is a power that enables an individual, inspired by the Spirit, to recognize and understand the Truth. *Persuasión,* another power bestowed by the Spirit, transforms the recipient into such a convincing

---

[51] William R. Read, *New Patterns of Church Growth in Brazil* (Grand Rapids, Mich.: William B. Eerdmans Co., 1964), pp. 11–12, 18, 142, 175, 177, and 217.

[52] This information, also the following powers of the Spirit, is from Willems, in D'Antonio and Pike, *op. cit.,* pp. 106–7.

evangelist that he finds himself under an almost irresistible compulsion to spread the Gospel.

Speaking in tongues and prophetizing are the most respected and coveted powers conferred by the Holy Spirit. The tongues are unknown languages through which the Spirit sends messages to the congregation or certain of its members. When the speaker of tongues transmits his message, he is in a trancelike state and usually not aware of what he is saying. In this case, a prophet who may also have heard the message translates it to the other members. The prophet may also use tongues to communicate his inspirations, which are believed to come directly from God. Indeed, the voice of the prophet or of one speaking in tongues *is* the voice of God.

There are many indications that Protestantism has become an indigenous faith in Latin America. In fact, the Pentecostal churches are completely autonomous and govern themselves. If they have relationships with other churches, they are of a fraternal nature and not of dependence or subordination. They do not depend at all on aid from abroad. The churches are self-supporting, and expand spontaneously with their own resources, personnel, and funds. Culturally, their expressions of Christian faith and congregational life are not foreign but close to the ways of the people. Their songs, musical instruments, and rituals have a kinship with their folkways. In short, the Pentecostal movement is self-governing, self-supporting, and self-propagating.[53]

Many criticisms have been leveled at The Assemblies of God. Among these are: they proselyte and grow at the expense of other evangelical churches by sheep-stealing; they "have a big back door," and many who join later leave; some of them have loose morals, resulting in public scandals that divide churches; they have too much emotion, shown in loud preaching, singing, and praying; they aim to reach only the lower classes; they interpret the Bible literally, and therefore their theology is wrong; and they lack a ministry that is trained in the tenets of Protestantism.[54]

As Table 5–2 shows, Protestantism's main strength lies in Brazil, Chile, and Mexico. More significant than statistics on church membership are those relating to the clergy. As Table 5–2 shows, 13,526 of the clergy are natives—84 percent of the total number.

Now that Protestantism has been embraced by three or four generations in the region, it is acquiring a maturity and status. Young members of the faith have a feeling of belonging to the culture and life of their native land. Their religious faith has given them greater self-assurance,

---

[53] Key Yuasa, "Indigenous Expressions of Protestantism," *Integration of Man and Society in Latin America,* ed. Samuel Shapiro (Notre Dame, Ind.: University of Notre Dame Press, 1967), p. 202.

[54] Read, *op. cit.,* pp. 139–42.

TABLE 5-2

PROTESTANTISM IN LATIN AMERICA (1961)*

Country	Churches	Membership	Clergy Foreign	Native
Argentina	2,067	414,323	245	732
Bolivia	544	46,663	200	253
Brazil	20,990	4,071,643	687	8,403
Colombia	1,618	92,728	96	236
Costa Rica	290	22,902	51	109
Cuba	1,416	264,927	112	527
Chile	2,490	834,839	119	277
Dominican Republic	611	19,289	95	116
Ecuador	186	11,499	77	34
El Salvador	1,144	57,691	14	197
Guatemala	1,553	149,081	44	265
Haiti	2,418	327,140	75	78
Honduras	438	34,488	39	117
Mexico	3,515	897,227	77	789
Nicaragua	297	37,666	20	28
Panama	358	41,778	58	219
Paraguay	270	36,560	99	258
Peru	1,178	94,053	168	258
Puerto Rico	934	174,707	29	203
Uruguay	243	42,594	38	93
Venezuela	60	26,042	133	82
Total	42,420	7,710,412	2,556	13,526

* Prudencio Damboriena, S.J., *El Protestantismo en América Latina* (Fribourg: FERES, 1963) Vol. 2, p. 18 (reprinted from Kenneth Grubb, H. W. Coxill, World Dominion Press, London), in François Houtart and Emile Pin, *The Church and the Latin American Revolution*, trans. Gilbert Barth (New York: Sheed and Ward, Inc., 1965), p. 264.

destroyed some of their prejudices, and stimulated them to worthy goals.[55]

The future of Protestantism in Latin America? It is bright, in the opinion of John MacKay, a distinguished Presbyterian missionary who went to Lima in 1916 with his bride and spent most of his life spreading the faith there. But it must give unswerving allegiance to certain imperatives. Among these, evangelism must be given priority status. Also, Protestants in Latin America must respect a theological education so that students in seminary and Bible schools acquire an intelligent understanding of the Christian faith. Too, concern for social justice must be the responsibility of all Protestants of whatever denomination.[56]

[55] José Miguez-Bonino, "Main Currents of Protestantism," *Integration of Man and Society in Latin America, op. cit.*, p. 199.
[56] John MacKay, "Historical Perspectives of Protestantism," *Integration of Man and Society in Latin America, op. cit.*, pp. 184–90.

THE CHALLENGE OF SOCIAL REFORM

Besides Protestantism, another great challenge that the Roman Catholic Church faces in Latin America is the critical need for social reform, which is largely responsible for the widespread unrest and instability throughout the region. In the past, the Church has been a staunch supporter of the status quo, frequently aligning its great power and prestige with the economic strength of the *hacendados* and the weapons of the military to prevent any radical change in the existing order. In its role as spiritual mother to the large underprivileged mass, it was the most influential of the three. By stressing the rewards to be obtained in the hereafter rather than in the present life, it used its great spiritual influence to get the mass to accept its lot in society as its Christian duty.

If the Church's interests were threatened, priests or members of the hierarchy might resort to drastic measures. When Mexico was struggling to introduce land reform in the La Laguna region, priests in the area carried on an intensive campaign of propaganda against it. A peasant union (*Sindicato de Campesinos de Durango*) complained in 1922 to the archbishop of the state because of the biased political activities of the priests. "Fr. Reyes of Gómez Palcio is so violently anti-agrarian that he refused to administer the last rites to Eulalio Martínez merely because in life he had been an agrarian," charged one complaint. "Fr. Santiago Zamora of Mapimí sustains on every occasion that taking possession of idle land is theft, and that the government which authorizes it as well as the *campesinos* and their families who benefit by it, are bandits," alleged another complaint.[57]

The seemingly inflexible attitude of the Church toward social change was, in the opinion of many, a serious portent for the future of democracy and of the Church as well. "Since Hispanic Catholicism doesn't seem to be able to make the continent suitable for normal human life," concluded Roger E. Vekemans, "and since, despite the papal encyclicals, the social situation in Latin America is one of the worst in the world, it is obvious that the people of Latin America look for other solutions."[58]

But whatever policy the Church has followed in the past, others are convinced that Catholicism will successfully meet the challenge of the pressing need for reform in Latin America. "Even though the Church stresses the eternal and the intemporal," said Jorge Mañach, professor of philosophy at the University of Havana, "and keeps its doctrine aloof from historic relativity, in practice it has always shown itself much more flexible than its own theories imply. Just because it feels that its vocation

---

[57] Clarence Senior, *Land Reform and Democracy* (Gainesville: University of Florida Press, 1958), p. 60.

[58] *Ave Maria*, in *Time*, January 18, 1960, p. 58.

is that of eternity, it will take care to adjust itself to the will of the world, to the inescapable design of history."[59]

During the past decade, Roman Catholicism in Latin America has been busy "adjusting itself to the will of the world." By precept and by practice, it is using its great influence in the region to promote social reform. In the several Rural Life Conferences held in Latin America, the Church, with the aid of Protestant and Catholic experts, has studied the problems of the area at the grass roots to attempt to build a solid basis for future policy and activities.

Mobilizing its resources throughout the region, the Catholic Church is giving its strong support to a wide range of social reforms. In Ecuador, the clergy in a pastoral letter dealing with agrarian reform advocated the immediate elimination of both *latifundios* and *minifundios*. Emboldened by Pope John XXIII's papal encyclicals, "Mater et Magistra" and "Pacem in Terris," they reaffirmed man's rights to private property, but firmly asserted that the state could rightfully expropriate any land if the action was necessary for the common good, since human dignity had precedence over the right of private property. Going even further, they advocated a progressive income tax and stressed the social obligations of businessmen and property owners toward labor.[60]

In Colombia, the Church placed itself squarely behind land reform; representatives of the Church participated in the formulation of Law 135 of 1961, embodying the nation's program of agrarian reform.[61] In Chile, the Catholic Church strongly supported President Frei's program of land reform adopted in July, 1967—a program that promises to be one of the most effective in all Latin America.[62]

In northeastern Brazil, so plagued by drought and poverty that the Peasant Leagues were tempted to embrace Castroism, Maoism, or other radical solutions, the archbishop in 1961 appointed four priests to organize Catholic *sindicatos* in the rural areas. Within several years, the movement was so successful that the Federation of Christian Unions had a membership of 200,000 and afforded its members various benefits, including legal services.[63] Father Melo, one of the priests active in the movement and renowned for his interest in agrarian reform, faced the issue of reform quite realistically. "The agrarian revolution has to be carried out neither peacefully, as the Capitalists say, nor violently, as the Communists say. Historical circumstance itself will prescribe the form of the revolu-

---

[59] Jorge Mañach, "Religion and Freedom in Latin America," *Responsible Freedom in the Americas*, ed. Angel del Rio (Columbia University Bicentennial Conference Series) (Garden City, N.Y.: Doubleday & Co., Inc., 1955), pp. 359–60.

[60] Hispanic American Report, Vol. XVI, No. 4 (July, 1963), p. 482.

[61] Robert H. Dix, *Colombia: The Political Dimensions of Change* (New Haven, Conn.: Yale University Press, 1967), p. 316.

[62] *New York Times*, July 17, 1967, p. 14, col. 3.

[63] De Kadt, *op. cit.*, p. 214.

tion. If results cannot be gained peaceably, then we shall have to face up to the reality of outright struggle."[64]

In confronting the pressing issues of social reform in Latin America, the Catholic Church has not been able to take a united stand, Fredrick B. Pike observes. For as the Church attempts to become a force for change, in many of the countries its leaders—whether bishops, priests, or laymen —are often bitterly divided with regard to changes that should be made. Many churchmen, preferring to retain a nondemocratic, hierarchical structure, are appalled at the idea of social mobility and class competition. With more effective measures of charity and paternalism, they reason, the underprivileged mass can be made to be content to remain always a lower class. But other Catholic leaders are convinced that political democracy accompanied by genuine social pluralism is the only solution. Social pluralism for them connotes a system in which all social classes and functional interest groups can freely, equally, and democratically compete with one another in attempting to gain their goals.[65]

In striking contrast to such sharp, often bitter divisiveness within the Catholic Church on issues of social reform, the Protestant Churches are united in favor of fundamental, far-reaching changes throughout the society. Decades ago, the Protestant Churches in Mexico endorsed the principles of the social revolution which the nation was struggling to achieve; as a result, their properties were usually respected, and many of the Protestants became educational leaders or held positions of prominence.[66]

Today in Latin America, the Protestant Churches are doing more than bringing the social gospel to the region. Aiming their message at the underprivileged masses, they are according them full recognition as members of the society, worthy of sharing in its responsibilities and benefits.

The dramatic growth of Protestantism in recent years has been about as neglected by scholars as has been another very significant development—the dramatic rise of the Christian Democratic Parties.[67] Protestantism, like Christian Democracy, is on the move. Its revolutionary message and tactics may well turn out to be one of the basic forces that will transform Latin American society.

---

[64] In Josué de Castro, *Death in the Northeast* (New York: Random House, Inc., 1966), p. 181.

On the issue of land reform, the progressive wing of the Catholic Church has rejected extremists' views, whether of the right or the left. Thomas E. Skidmore, *Politics in Brazil, 1930–1964: An Experiment in Democracy* (New York: Oxford University Press, 1967), pp. 232 and 247.

[65] Fredrick B. Pike, "Introduction," *Religion, Revolution, and Reform: New Forces for Change in Latin America, op. cit.,* p. 7.

[66] Wilfred Hardy Callcott, *Liberalism in Mexico, 1857–1929* (Stanford, Calif.: Stanford University Press, 1931), pp. 251–52.

[67] These parties are discussed in Chapter 12.

SUGGESTED READINGS

Azevedo, Thales de. *Social Change in Brazil,* chap. iii. Inter-American Studies, Monograph Series No. 22. Gainesville: University of Florida Press, 1963.

Blanksten, George I. *Perón's Argentina,* pp. 65–66; 188–90; 229–37. Chicago: University of Chicago Press, 1953.

Castaneda, Carlos E. "Social Developments and Movements in Latin America," *Church and Society: Catholic Social and Political Thought and Movements* (ed. Joseph N. Moody). New York: Arts, Inc., 1953.

Considine, John J. (ed.). *The Religious Dimensions in the New Latin America.* Notre Dame, Ind.: Fides, Inc., 1966.

———— (ed.). *Social Revolution in the New Latin America: A Catholic Appraisal,* chaps. 11–13, 16, and 18. Notre Dame, Ind.: Fides, Inc., 1965.

D'Antonio, William V., and Pike, Fredrick B. (eds.). *Religion, Revolution, and Reform: New Forces for Change in Latin America,* pp. 1–128. New York: Frederick A. Praeger, Inc., 1964.

Dewart, Leslie. *Christianity and Revolution: The Lesson of Cuba.* New York: Herder and Herder, 1962.

Houtart, François, and Pin, Emile. *The Church and the Latin American Revolution.* Trans. Gilbert Barth. New York: Sheed and Ward, Inc., 1965.

Kadt, Emanuel de. "Religion, the Church, and Social Change in Brazil," *The Politics of Conformity in Latin America* (ed. Claudio Veliz), pp. 192–220. New York: Oxford University Press, 1967.

Kavanaugh, Father James. *A Modern Priest Looks at His Outdated Church.* New York: Trident Press, 1967.

Mañach, Jorge. "Religion and Freedom in Latin America," *Responsible Freedom in the Americas* (ed. Angel del Rio), pp. 349–60. Garden City, N.Y.: Doubleday & Co., Inc., 1955.

Martz, John D. *Colombia: a Contemporary Political Survey,* pp. 24–27; 214–17; 219–21; 238–40; 317–19. Chapel Hill: University of North Carolina Press, 1962.

Mecham, J. Lloyd. *Church and State in Latin America: A History of Politico-Ecclesiastical Relations.* Rev. ed. Chapel Hill: University of North Carolina Press, 1966.

Pike, Fredrick B. (ed.). *The Conflict between Church and State in Latin America.* New York: Alfred A. Knopf, 1964.

Read, William R. *New Patterns of Church Growth in Brazil.* Grand Rapids, Mich.: William B. Eerdmans Co., 1965.

Rice, Sister M. Elizabeth. *The Diplomatic Relations Between the United States and Mexico, as Affected by the Struggle for Religious Liberty in Mexico, 1925–1929.* Washington, D.C.: Catholic University of America Press, 1959.

Rycroft, W. Stanley. *Religion and Faith in Latin America.* Philadelphia: The Westminster Press, 1958.

Sejourne, Laurette. *Burning Water: Thought and Religion in Ancient Mexico.* Trans. Irene Nicholson. New York: Vanguard Press, 1956.

Shapiro, Samuel (ed.). *Integration of Man and Society in Latin America,* pp. 149–223. Notre Dame, Ind.: University of Notre Dame Press, 1967.

Smith, T. Lynn. *Brazil: People and Institutions,* chap. xx. Rev. ed. Baton Rouge: Louisiana State University Press, 1963.

Stokes, William S. "Catholicism and Democracy in Latin America," *Responsible Freedom in the Americas* (ed. Angel del Rio), pp. 361–80. Garden City, N.Y.: Doubleday & Co., Inc., 1955.

Tucker, William P. *The Mexican Government Today,* chap. 3. Minneapolis: University of Minnesota Press, 1957.

Vallier, Ivan. "Religious Elites: Differentiations and Developments in Roman Catholicism," *Elites in Latin America* (eds. Seymour Martin Lipset and Aldo Solari), chap. 6. New York: Oxford University Press, 1967.

Whetten, Nathan L. *Rural Mexico,* chap. xix. Chicago: University of Chicago Press, 1948.

Willems, Emilio. *Followers of the New Faith: Cultural Change and the Rise of Protestantism in Brazil and Chile.* Nashville, Tenn.: Vanderbilt University Press, 1967.

6

THE ARMED FORCES:
Big Brother in Action

In an international order where each nation may have to rely ultimately on its own resources for survival, the armed forces perform very useful functions. They serve as a bulwark against aggression by other nations and also as a backstop for the police in maintaining internal order. In Latin America, they also discharge other responsibilities such as assisting with the periodic censuses, presiding over elections, and engaging in a wide variety of public works.

INTERFERENCE IN POLITICS

Despite the many useful services they perform, the armed forces—traditionally, the army—have been one of the greatest impediments in the laborious, century and a half struggle of the region to attain democracy. Unlike the armies of other democratic nations, the military establishments in most of Latin America have a record of frequent interference in politics.

This interference is evidenced in a number of ways: the military's active, often decisive, role in the selection of the president; its strong voice in the determination of national policy; its recognized right to decide virtually all matters that pertain to itself, a right that, in effect, amounts to self-regulation; and its large proportion of the national budget.

Accustomed as a rule to exerting its influence, the military nowhere enjoys this more than in the selection of the nation's executive. Does the military boss want the presidency for himself? If so, he has not only the inside track but also the only sure one to the presidential palace. The recent histories of several of the republics show this quite well.

Venezuela has a most unenviable record of being governed by ambitious generals who aspired to crown their military careers by occupying the presidential office. When the civilian statesman Rómulo Betancourt was elected president in December, 1958, for a 5-year term and succeeded by Raúl Leoni, elected in December, 1963, it was a welcome phenomenon; in the preceding 50 years the nation had been governed by military men for all but 3 years—the short period 1945–48.

Paraguay, Nicaragua, and the Dominican Republic are other nations in which the military have been able to virtually corner the presidential office. In Paraguay, military dictators have been presidents or have controlled civilians who were presidents since the end of the Chaco War with Bolivia in 1936. General Alfredo Stroessner who led a successful army coup in 1954 was elected President later the same year, and re-elected by an overwhelming majority in 1958, 1963, and 1968. He is only 55 years of age, and is apparently in good health.

In Nicaragua, the military has exercised unquestioned control ever since the withdrawal of the United States Marines in the early 1930's. General Anastasio Somoza, head of the armed forces, either governed as president or exercised a controlling voice until his assassination in 1956. Since his death, the Somoza family continues to maintain its tight grip on the country. Luis, a civilian, filled the office of president for the six-year term May, 1957–May, 1963, and was succeeded by René Schick Gutiérrez, who was careful to respect the interests of the Somoza family before his demise by a heart attack in August, 1966, when Vice President Lorenzo Guerrero became president. All the while, the real power rested with Luis' brother, Colonel Anastasio Somoza, Jr., who was commander in chief of the national guard. In the February, 1967, election, Anastasio left the army barracks to serve a six-year stint in the presidential palace.

Instead of assuming the presidency himself, the military leader who has the office within his grasp may prefer to call the tune from behind the scenes and exercise control through a civilian who is president in name only, a mere puppet who moves precisely as the military puppeteer manipulates the strings. Sometimes the military leader who remains in the background may exercise control over the government through the office of the secretary of war. This is a very powerful post, which is usually filled by a general who can speak authoritatively for the military. Ensconced in his cabinet office, strategic vantage ground, he is a sort of fifth column within the civilian stronghold, in a position to keep the closest tab on the president.

Sometimes the control exercised by the military takes the form of a veto to prevent someone distasteful to them from attaining the presidential office, even though he has been elected to it or is constitutionally entitled to it by virtue of being the nation's vice president. When Jânio

Quadros unexpectedly resigned as president of Brazil in May, 1961, military leaders took steps to prevent João Goulart, the vice president, from assuming the presidential responsibilities because of his alleged leftist tendencies. They finally allowed him to take office only to avert the serious threat of imminent civil war, after requiring the establishment of a parliamentary government where most of the executive power was exercised by a prime minister responsible to congress instead of by the president.

While control of the presidency is undoubtedly the *pièce de résistance* in Latin America, the military bosses are sometimes content to dine on lesser fare—the less spectacular but equally meaty formulation of national policy. In democratic nations, this is a responsibility of the legislative branch of the government, which has been popularly elected and represents the opinions and desires of the majority of the citizens.

In most of the Latin American nations, however, public policy is formulated quite differently. While there are other politically strong pressure groups, such as political parties and organized labor, ordinarily the decisive voice is that of the armed forces.

The issues that confront the country may be of the greatest importance. Should foreign companies be allowed to develop the nation's petroleum resources, so critically needed, or should development be postponed until and if domestic capital is able to do it? Should the nation maintain economic and diplomatic ties with the United States and other Western countries only, or should it have relations with the Communist nations as well, deriving the benefits that might come from dealing with both groups? Although these are critical questions that tax the wisdom of the most dedicated Latin American statesmen, for them to make a decision without first consulting the military is like playing Russian roulette with their careers at stake—possibly their lives, too.

Perhaps no Latin American statesman in recent times has so stood up to the fierce pressures of the military as did Arturo Frondizi, president of Argentina from 1958 until his overthrow by the military in March, 1962. After withstanding onslaught after onslaught on his presidential prerogatives, and after making one concession after another, he finally took his stand, a brave and bold one: while he welcomed the military's suggestions regarding national problems as a contribution to the government's policies and course of action, he did not intend to give up his prerogative of "directing policies in the economic and social area, in the national affairs, and in those matters that are properly in the President's domain."[1]

Frondizi's bold stand against the military, even though he was eventually forced out, is in striking contrast to the subservient attitude of presidents in some of the countries, who dare not make any decision of importance without first consulting the military powers that be.

---

[1] *New York Times,* October 16, 1960, p. 36, col. 1.

In one area of public policy in particular, the military exercise virtually complete and unchallenged control. This is the important area of matters that relate solely or primarily to the armed forces themselves. In such questions as rank, salary, promotion, and retirement benefits, the desires of the military leaders are determining and final.

Whatever the armed forces may be lacking, it certainly is not high rank. Military back scratching assures that there will be suitable top brass positions for all the deserving. In this respect, Paraguay easily takes the lead. Although its navy consists of only three small river gunboats, there are seven admirals to assume responsibility for them. Like the lord of the admiralty in *H.M.S. Pinafore*, apparently four of the admirals stick close to their desks and never go to sea.

The armed forces, besides deciding matters that relate only to their internal organization and functioning, also preempt for themselves such critical decisions as how large the several branches should be and what weapons and equipment they should have—basic questions of defense policy that are decided by civilian authorities in democratic nations.

In Latin America, however, any interference by civilian officials in the broad area of military interests is regarded as a presumptuous invasion of the military's prerogatives. Several presidents, including Bustamente of Peru and Gallegos of Venezuela, have been summarily thrown out of office for presuming to make decisions relating to the military establishment. As a consequence, however strongly reform regimes may feel about the need for change in this area, they are obliged to confine their reform activities to nonmilitary matters.

The military show their interference in politics in still another way—by the large amount of their annual appropriations, a disproportionately large share of the national revenue. Operating on the premise that to the victor belongs the spoils, they in effect cut the budget pie, or at least one large slice for themselves.

As a result, the armed forces in most of the nations receive the largest share of the budgetary take, a share that averages as much as 10–20 percent annually. Sometimes it is considerably larger. As poor as Paraguay is, virtually bankrupt and dependent on the largesse of international financial institutions to keep her afloat, the nation under its military dictatorship has spent more than half its total revenue on the armed forces. Even these reported expenditures in Paraguay and elsewhere, large as they are, do not reveal the full picture. For much of the appropriations designated for public works, interior, and communications actually goes to support the military establishment and its activities.

The extravagant financial demands of the military, a sort of fiscal hijacking, have had a very harmful effect on the social and economic progress of the nations. Although many of the nations have a high rate of illiteracy, they spend about as much or more for the armed forces as for public education, as Figure 6–1 shows. Forced to divert much of their

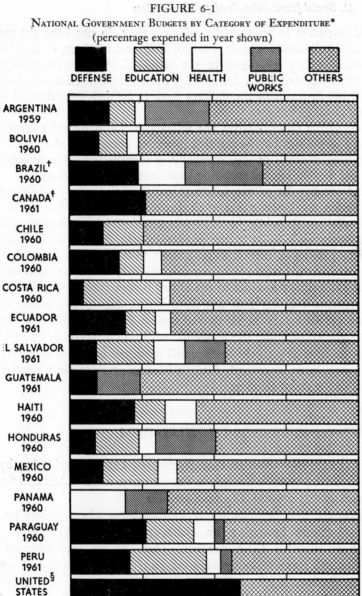

FIGURE 6-1
NATIONAL GOVERNMENT BUDGETS BY CATEGORY OF EXPENDITURE*
(percentage expended in year shown)

DEFENSE   EDUCATION   HEALTH   PUBLIC WORKS   OTHERS

ARGENTINA 1959
BOLIVIA 1960
BRAZIL† 1960
CANADA† 1961
CHILE 1960
COLOMBIA 1960
COSTA RICA 1960
ECUADOR 1961
:L SALVADOR 1961
GUATEMALA 1961
HAITI 1960
HONDURAS 1960
MEXICO 1960
PANAMA 1960
PARAGUAY 1960
PERU 1961
UNITED§ STATES 1961
VENEZUELA 1961

0   25   50   75   100
PERCENT

* Data not available for Dominican Republic, Nicaragua, and Uruguay.

† Education and health included in one category.

‡ Percentages for specified categories, in addition to defense, are: debt interest, 13.0; subsidies, 2.1; social security, 11.4; veterans' benefits, 5.1; and transfers to provincial governments, 9.4.

§ Percentages for specified categories, in addition to defense, are: debt interest, 11.2; agricultural subsidies, 4.6; veterans' benefits, 6.6; health, education, welfare, social security, labor, 5.6; foreign aid, 2.2.

SOURCE: *Américas*, July, 1963, pp. 42, 43. Reproduced by permission.

limited resources to appease the military, they do not have the money needed to build more schools, provide additional teachers, or build roads that are necessary for pupils to get to school. As a result, millions of children throughout Latin America are denied the benefit of an education because the demands of the military have to be met, regardless of other pressing needs of society.

Thus, as the record shows, the military in Latin America frequently interfere in politics by the positive means of controlling the presidency, determining national policy, especially as regards the military establishment, and demanding and receiving huge annual appropriations.

Paradoxically, the military's interference in politics may take the form of no action whatever—a sort of sit-down strike. Just such a situation in the Dominican Republic in 1930 was responsible for initially putting Rafael Leonidas Trujillo in the presidency—the first act in the nation's drama of prolonged dictatorship. Thanks to his military ingenuity and driving ambition, Trujillo had been able to rise through the ranks until he became commander in chief of the armed forces, transformed by United States Marine training into a well-equipped, highly disciplined army. When a revolutionary horde moved against President Horacio Vásquez in 1930, the army under the leadership of Trujillo stayed in its barracks, refusing to give help to the beleaguered president who was consequently overthrown. Soon afterward, Trujillo became president in a thoroughly rigged "democratic" election.

ALTERNATING TRENDS OF MILITARISM

The intense militarism so characteristic of Latin America has by no means followed an even course; on the contrary, it has ebbed and flowed like the tides that rise and fall on the seashore.

During the first half-century of independence, characterized by disorder sometimes bordering on chaos, militarism was at flood tide throughout most of Latin America. Then, as the prevalent political instability and turmoil slowly subsided, an ebb tide set in and militarism began to decline. A substantial evidence of this was the long period of international peace which began during the second half-century after independence. Although five major wars were fought in South America during the tumultuous period from 1825 to 1883, none occurred after 1883 until the Chaco War began in 1932.

The decline of militarism, so welcome to the region and lasting until the beginning of the Great Depression, is attributable to many causes.

Perhaps as Herbert Spencer and some others believed, the transition from a military to an industrial period was natural and inevitable. In Latin America, wrote F. García Calderón,

. . . invariably we find the sequence of the two periods, one military and one industrial or civil. The independence realized, the rule of militarism sets in throughout the republics. After a period of uncertain duration the military caste is hurled from power, or abdicates without violence, and economic interests become supreme. Politics are then ruled by "civilism."[2]

While evolution was doubtlessly a factor in the decline of militarism, other causes were at work too.

Militarism partly consumed itself through its own outrageous excesses, partly it was mitigated by rising new civilian forces. Much of Latin America began to enter a new epoch. The chaotic aftereffects of the long wars for independence began to subside. Political experience was accumulated, culture diffused, illiteracy reduced. Immigrants began to come in. A heavy influx of foreign capital financed construction of telegraph lines and railroads. And along with people, capital, and technology came modern European ideas.[3]

Still other causes contributed to the decline. The unification of the armed forces into truly national bodies tended to lessen the strength of regional military factions. Also, the acquisition by the armed forces of new weapons, including artillery and planes, tended to give them a preponderance of strength over most would-be insurrectionary groups. The beginning of professionalism in the armed forces was an important influence too. Members of the officer corps now began to concentrate on their military functions rather than on political interests, and to regard themselves and their troops as the servants rather than the masters of the state.[4]

Professionalism developed much later in some countries than in others. In Venezuela as late as the 1850's, many military chiefs were self-commissioned leaders of personal armies or prominent civilians awarded a military title in recognition of their faithful support. It was not until 1895 that the Artillery School was founded, laying the groundwork for a trained, permanent army, and not until 1910 that the Military Academy was established to provide a corps of professional officers for a modern army.[5] But whether early or late in developing professionalism, the nations were quite convinced of its value. In 1864 Brazil had a large, professional, well-trained officer corps, while Paraguay had no such reservoir of professional, trained officers; this proved to be one of the decisive factors in the outcome of the bitter, hard-fought Paraguayan War.[6]

---

[2] F. García Calderón, *Latin America: Its Rise and Progress,* trans. Bernard Miall (London: T. Fisher Unwin, 1913), pp. 86–87.

[3] Edwin Lieuwen, *Arms and Politics in Latin America* (Council on Foreign Relations) (rev. ed.; New York: Frederick A. Praeger, Inc., 1961), pp. 28–29.

[4] *Ibid.,* pp. 30–31.

[5] Robert L. Gilmore, *Caudillism and Militarism in Venezuela, 1810–1910* (Athens: Ohio University Press, 1964), p. 78.

[6] Charles J. Kolinski, *Independence or Death! The Story of the Paraguayan War* (Gainesville: University of Florida Press, 1965), chap. iv.

Militarism continued to decline until the end of the 1920's, when it reached neap tide. At that time military regimes exercised control in only six of the countries, and these represented only about 15 percent of the total population.

Then, following the onset of the depression of 1929, there abruptly began a striking relapse into militarism. This relapse, which saw new military regimes instituted in many formerly democratic countries, was due to several conditions. The devastating effects of the depression, acutely felt in the form of economic stagnation, unemployment, and even hunger, resulted in widespread demands for social reform. While some army officers, particularly the junior ones, sided with the advocates of reform, the conservative ranking officers not only backed the oligarchs and other entrenched interests but sometimes even moved into the presidency to assure continuance of the status quo.[7]

As a result of the bitter schism within the society, militarism was once again in the saddle.

The advent of World War II served to further aggravate the region's unfortunate relapse into militarism.

The net effect of the War upon Latin American politics was to freeze traditionalist regimes in power as long as the security of the hemisphere was threatened. The wartime emergency provided dictatorial regimes with justification for outlawing social experimentation and major social or economic reform for the duration. Also, the United States, whose overriding consideration was strategic, did its best to maintain stability in Latin America, sought the cooperation of incumbent regimes which were willing to help the war effort, and provided them with military and economic aid.[8]

Although World War II served to strengthen the control of the military, it paradoxically resulted in a new cycle of revolt against the old vested interests. In some cases the revolt was led by a civilian leader, such as Rómulo Betancourt of Venezuela; in other cases it was led by a reformist military officer, such as Juan Perón in Argentina. Then, as the strokes of the pendulum became shorter, the few years of revolt and reform were hurriedly followed by a period of counterrevolution and opposition to social change. This counterrevolution, lasting from approximately 1947 to 1957, reached a crest in 1954, when 12 of the 20 republics were ruled by military presidents.[9]

But in the next several years, militarism receded at a rapid rate as one military regime after another was toppled. In six of the nations, colonels or generals were ousted from office by revolution: Juan Perón in Argentina in 1955, Paul Magloire in Haiti in 1956, Rojas Pinilla in Colombia in 1957, Pérez Jiménez in Venezuela in 1958, Fulgencio Batista in Cuba in

---

[7] Lieuwen, *op. cit.*, p. 59.
[8] *Ibid.*, pp. 62–63.
[9] *Ibid.*, pp. 59–60 and 122.

1959, and María Lemus in El Salvador in 1960. In four of the nations, military heads of state were eliminated by assassination: Antonio Remón of Panama in 1955, Anastasio Somoza in Nicaragua in 1956, Castillo Armas in Guatemala in 1957, and Rafael Trujillo of the Dominican Republic in 1961. In one nation, Peru, General Manuel Odría left office peacefully after a civilian opposition candidate was elected in 1956.

By mid-1961, only one of the 12 military heads of state was still in office—General Alfredo Stroessner of Paraguay. The prospect seemed indeed bright for civilian constitutional government in the region. This welcome prospect was one of the main reasons for optimism favoring a democratic social revolution, which the Alliance for Progress attempted to initiate at Punta del Este, Uruguay, on August 17, 1961.

However, beginning the next year the pendulum once again swung strongly toward intervention by the military. From 1962 to 1969, 11 regimes that held office constitutionally were overthrown by the intervention of the military: in 1962, Arturo Frondizi of Argentina and Manuel Prado of Peru; in 1963, Ydígoras Fuentes of Guatemala, Carlos Julio Arosemena of Ecuador, Juan Bosch of the Dominican Republic, and Ramón Villeda Morales of Honduras; in 1964, João Goulart of Brazil and Paz Estenssoro of Bolivia; in 1966, Arturo Illia of Argentina; and in 1968, Arnulfo Arías of Panama and Fernando Belaunde Terry of Peru. The relapse into escalated intervention by the military is a bad omen for the future of constitutional government.[10]

In the first seven interventions referred to above, the professed purpose of each was to protect the nation against presidents sympathetic to communism. The real reason, however, was institutional self-interest, Edwin Lieuwen is convinced. "The military acted primarily to prevent the coming to power of civilian political groups they considered inimical to the interests of the armed forces."[11]

In several of the nations, the military's fear of greater influence or power of the masses is basically a fear of what the military might expect if certain strongly antimilitaristic parties managed to win control of the government—as the Peronistas in Argentina and the Apristas in Peru. For these parties would probably obliterate the existing military as completely as Castro did Batista's hated army. The military have another reason for fear of the masses. The officers enjoy a high status in the region's strati-

---

[10] For the successful military coups, 1920–1966, by country and date, see Claudio Veliz (ed.), *The Politics of Conformity in Latin America* (New York: Oxford University Press, 1967), p. 278.

For the illegal and unscheduled changes of heads of state, 1930–1965, giving country, head removed, date, and type of action, see Willard F. Barber and C. Neale Ronning, *Internal Security and Military Power* (Columbus: Ohio State University Press, 1966), Appendix.

[11] Edwin Lieuwen, *Generals Vs. Presidents: Neomilitarism in Latin America* (New York: Frederick A. Praeger, Inc., 1964), p. 107.

fied society, but if the distinction between class and mass broke down because of industrial development, urbanization, and the opportunity for an education for all, the military elite would be hurt more than any other group in society. Truly, their very survival might depend on their ability to ride the crest of social and economic development, somehow preserving their traditional advantages during the transition.[12]

ACCEPTED CAUSES OF MILITARISM AND MILITARY INTERVENTION IN POLITICS

Militarism and the interference of the military in politics have been persistent and tenacious characteristics of the Latin American society. In only a few of the nations is democratic government so firmly established that the civilian authorities can govern with assurance that the military are their loyal, obedient servants. Since Latin America was one of the first large areas in the world to embrace democratic government, how can we account for this continued prevalence of militarism, which is the very antithesis of true democracy?

According to many scholars of the past, among the many causes of militarism and the active role of the military in politics the most important have been: (1) the effects of the wars of independence; (2) the lack of a tradition of separation of civil and military power; (3) the social environment, including especially poverty, illiteracy, and localism; (4) the better social status that could be gained by military service; (5) the economic perquisites available to the military; (6) the influence of German, Italian, and certain other military missions; (7) the few wars in Latin America, with politics as a needed outlet for activity; (8) the tradition of the military's serving as guardians of the nation's honor; (9) the social and economic crises that invite military intervention; and (10) the established role of the military as arbiters in national life.

1. In the long struggle for independence, dynamic military leaders of the revolutionary armies rose to the forefront in the rough and tumble of combat. Renowned in their regions, or perhaps in the entire nation, for their prowess and heroic exploits, they were the recognized leaders in the young republics. For the *peninsulares*, who represented Spanish authority, had already fled or been liquidated, leaving a power vacuum that the victorious leaders of the revolution would naturally be the ones to fill. The draughts of victory and power were heady wine for leaders and soldiers alike. "The Generals could not be reconciled to the obscurity of private life under civilian rule," says J. Fred Rippy, "and the common soldiers, accustomed to the adventure, the plunder, and the excitement of

---

[12] Irving Louis Horowitz, "The Military Elites," *Elites in Latin America*, eds. Seymour Martin and Aldo Solari (New York: Oxford University Press, Inc., 1967), pp. 166–67.

military combat, were loath to exchange the camp for the field and the shop."[13]

2. Unfortunately for the newly established republics, there was no deeply rooted tradition that the civil and military power should be separate and distinct entities, with the military subordinate to the civil. Bifurcation of the two authorities and the assured supremacy of civil power were part of the American colonies' treasured political heritage from England. Lacking such a tradition, however, the liberators of Latin America were seldom willing to follow the example of George Washington in the United States, and they did not hesitate to seize control of the nation when they had the military force to do so.

3. The social environment, especially poverty, illiteracy, and localism have also taken their toll. In their battle with poverty, the masses were forced to spend most of their time grubbing for the bare essentials of existence. Unable to read, they knew little if anything about the civil rights established in the new constitutions and had not the least conception of civic responsibilities, so essential if democratic government is to be effectual.

4. One's social status could be immeasurably improved by service in the army. Authoritarian and hierarchical though it was, the army was paradoxically one of the region's most democratizing influences. In all the countries, military service was one of the main avenues to a higher social position in the society. Civilians were taught to look up to members of the military, who were among the respected Somebodies in society. "In Francia's time," says C. D. Mansfield, "everybody was forced to take off their hats to every soldier, and the country boys, who wear no clothes at all, were obliged to wear hats for the purpose of saluting them."[14] Even the most ignorant recruit whose Indian race and culture had always been a millstone around his neck would emerge from his military service magically transformed into a cultural mestizo.

An especially prized privilege of the military is the *fuero militar,* which, in effect, gives them a status above the law. The *fuero,* which exempts them from the jurisdiction of the civil courts, tends to create a privileged caste that is exempt from public liability and from civil responsibility. In Mexico, says Henry Bamford Parkes, the officers "resplendent in blue and white uniforms, enjoying, like the clergy, the *fuero* of being tried only in their own military courts . . . soon began to think of themselves as an independent and privileged caste."[15]

---

[13] J. Fred Rippy, "Dictatorships in Spanish America," *Dictatorship in the Modern World,* ed. Guy Stanton Ford (Minneapolis: University of Minnesota Press, 1935), pp. 54–55.

[14] In George Pendle, *Paraguay: A Riverside Nation* (Royal Institute of International Affairs) (London: Oxford University Press, 1954), p. 20.

[15] Henry Bamford Parkes, *A History of Mexico* (3d ed.; Boston: Houghton Mifflin Co., 1960), p. 117.

5. Important as were the social opportunities open to members of the military, the economic perquisites weighed more heavily. Oftentimes a peon got his first suit of clothing, his first pair of shoes, when he joined the army. For the poor and humble, the army was by far the safest and most lucrative career. And what made it particularly appealing, no special training was needed to enter it.

While the enlisted man had "never had it so good," the officers were naturally the ones favored with "the gravy." Besides receiving high salaries, they were given such valuable additional benefits as housing, medical care, recreational facilities, and commissary privileges which enabled them to buy many items not generally on the market at a relatively low cost. They also enjoyed membership in a luxurious officers' club, and had many opportunities for travel to the United States, Europe, or elsewhere. Early retirement was encouraged to provide opportunities for younger officers, and sometimes the retirement pay was actually larger than the regular salary.

6. The German, Italian, and certain other military missions have also had considerable influence on the development of militarism in Latin America. Not only did they increase the efficiency and fighting ability of the Latin American armies, but they also noticeably affected the thinking of the officer corps. Thanks to their influence, officers often felt even greater contempt for democratic government than before and were convinced that they had an extramilitary responsibility and destiny to fulfill.

7. The Russian grand duke who said that he hated war "because it spoils armies,"[16] hardly expresses the sentiments of the Latin American military. They fairly spoil for a fight. Wars have occurred so rarely in Latin America that the life of the officer has tended to become, oh, so humdrum! Peaceful settlement of boundary disputes may be good for the statesmen and the nation as a whole, but they tend to put the armed forces out of business. Barrack fatigue, the officers find, is more damaging to morale than battle fatigue. As a result, a little war now and then is relished by the military men. It gives them an opportunity to show their daring, their skill with strategy, their mastery of military tactics.

Consigned to barracks boredom, the officers crave a means of self-expression, a feeling quite akin to the creative urge of the artist. The outlet that most of them seize on is plotting a little revolution or drawing up demands to be made upon the president.

8. The military also take pride in their tradition of being guardians of the nation's honor. Feeling their deep responsibility for defending its territorial integrity and sovereignty, they are particularly conscious of the nation as an ideal and as a concept of value. Consequently, they feel very strongly about its sacred honor, and are convinced that they are

---

[16] Alfred Vagts, *A History of Militarism* (New York: W. W. Norton & Co., Inc., 1937), p. 13.

responsible for preserving it. If the politicians use power in any way that detracts from the dignity of the nation, the military feel they must intervene and set things right.

9. The fundamental social and economic changes occurring in Latin America during the past several decades, resulting in strong tensions and deep bitterness, have also invited military intervention. The surge of industrialization, the revolution of rising expectations, and the cry for land have created pressing problems and social crises that the governments have been unable to cope with. Often in the class struggle between the upper class attempting to maintain the status quo and labor and other new social forces attempting to alter it, the armed forces have been called on to intervene by one group or the other.

10. Finally, in some countries, such as Brazil, the military have established for themselves a recognized role and peculiar responsibility as arbiters in the nation's affairs. "The position of the Brazilian armed forces is in many ways unique," says Edwin Lieuwen. "Politically, they are above partisan politics. As supreme guarantors of constitutional processes, they sit in judgment over presidents, judges, legislators, and all nonuniformed mortals. When it becomes necessary to correct a political situation which they regard as illegal or unconstitutional, they do not descend to the street level, operating with brute force. Rather they quietly issue a dignified ultimatum, from which there is no appeal, and which astute politicians have learned to respect. In other words, a president's policies, especially if they involve significant innovations, are, in practice, subject to veto by the military."[17]

THEORIES ADVANCED IN RECENT YEARS TO EXPLAIN INTERVENTION BY THE MILITARY

In recent years many theories have been advanced to attempt to explain why the military intervene in politics. According to S. E. Finer, the military is motivated mainly by its concern for: the national interest, a regional interest, a class interest, the self-interest of the military as an entity, and the self-interest of individual officers.[18]

The application of Finer's motives to the *golpe* staged in Ecuador, July, 1963, showed that individual self-interest may have played a role, and the national interest apparently did. The corporate self-interest was obviously a significant factor: the military, strongly anti-communist, feared that in the event of a communist take-over the army would be

---

[17] Lieuwen, *Arms and Politics in Latin America, op. cit.*, pp. 166–67.

For a brief treatment of these several causes of intervention, see Claudio Véliz, *Latin America and the Caribbean: A Handbook* (New York: Frederick A. Praeger, 1968), pp. 365–69.

[18] S. E. Finer, *The Man on Horseback: The Role of the Military in Politics* (New York: Frederick A. Praeger, 1962), chap. 4.

disbanded and replaced by a militia, as happened in Cuba when Fidel Castro came to power.[19]

The application of Finer's motives to the *golpe* in Bolivia, November, 1964, showed that while all of the motives apparently operated to some extent, no one of them was dominant. Even the military's perception of its corporate self-interest was "less of a factor than might have been expected," and obviously less than in the 1963 coup in Ecuador.[20]

More recently, Robert D. Putnam has sought to explain military intervention in politics by examining four categories of factors that appear to be causes of or conditions for intervention or abstention. These categories are: aspects of socioeconomic development, aspects of political development, characteristics of the military establishment itself, and foreign influences. Social development as measured by literacy and urbanization was found to inhibit intervention, but economic development as measured by the GNP and employment of labor appeared to encourage it. Most aspects of political development, including constitutional and legal restrictions to prevent the military from engaging in political activity and the percentage of the qualified electorate that votes, apparently have little effect. In the military establishment itself, there is a strong positive relationship between military spending and military intervention, but a negative relationship between the size of the armed forces and intervention. Finally, foreign military missions appear to have little if any influence on intervention.[21]

INFLUENCES TENDING TO LESSEN THE POWER OF THE MILITARY

While many influences in the region have unfortunately tended to stimulate militarism, other influences have served to contain, lessen, or even eliminate it. These counteracting influences are: the constitutional and legal restrictions imposed on members of the military regarding political activity, the increasingly strong democratic civilian groups, and rivalries between the several branches of the armed services.

The constitutions of the various countries contain many provisions explicitly designed to restrain the military. One can almost visualize the idealistic constitution makers as they rack their brains, hoping somehow to be able to assure civilian control.

In Colombia, the armed forces are specifically declared to be "obedient" and "not deliberative." They are not to assemble except by order of

---

[19] Martin C. Needler, *Anatomy of a Coup d'Etat: Ecuador 1963* (Washington, D.C.: Institute for the Comparative Study of Political Systems, 1964), pp. 40–41.

[20] William H. Brill, *Military Intervention in Bolivia: The Overthrow of Paz Estenssoro and the MNR* (Washington, D.C.: Institute for the Comparative Study of Political Systems, 1967), pp. 59–64.

[21] Robert D. Putnam, "Toward Explaining Military Intervention in Latin American Politics," *World Politics*, Vol. XX, No. 1 (October, 1967), pp. 83–110.

legitimate authority, nor are they to address any petition to the government except on matters related to their efficiency and morale.[22]

In Chile, the constitution attempts to protect the president, the congress, and the judiciary from any direct coercion by the military.

Every decision that the President of the Republic, the Chamber of Deputies, the Senate, or the tribunals of justice may agree to in the presence or on demand of an army, an officer at the head of an armed force, or of any assembly of people, with or without arms, and in disobedience of the authorities, is null in law and cannot produce any effect.[23]

Many other constitutional restrictions commonly adopted are also designed to limit political activities of members of the armed forces. They are not allowed to run for public office, to be active in a political campaign, or to exercise their franchise while on active duty. They may be restricted from even taking part in political discussions. In Nicaragua, so restricted is a member of the armed forces that he may not "collectively or individually express an opinion on matters relating to the service or which in any way attacks or criticizes the laws of the Republic."[24]

Although the constitutional restrictions have usually been just so much verbiage, they nevertheless do serve a useful purpose. Written not only on paper but also in the aspirations of liberty-loving citizens, they serve notice on the military of what their fellow countrymen expect—and for what they will try to exact punishment if the military violate their trust.

Important as these constitutional principles are in attempting to hold the military to account, more tangible restrictions are represented by civilian groups that are opposed to participation by the military in politics.

Political parties, with their democratic programs and leadership, usually have interests that are quite antithetical to those of the military. They advocate many basic reforms in society—reforms to be achieved by evolution if possible but by revolution if no other course is open. Their main tenet is constitutional, democratic government, a *sine qua non* of their very existence. They also support free elections, freedom of speech, the press, and assembly, and universal suffrage. In short, free political parties advocate that civilians control the government and decide public policy—objectives that toll the knell of arbitrary, irresponsible military rule.

The rising middle class is another large group regarded in the past as opposed to the military's taking an active part in politics. This class, mainly responsible for the growth of industrialism and economic development generally, depends on sound economic policies for its prosperity and well-being. Some of its most influential members, the industrialists and businessmen, also need governmental stability as a political

---

[22] Constitution of 1886, Article 168.
[23] Constitution of 1925, Article 23.
[24] Constitution of 1950, Article 317.

climate favorable to their enterprises. But serious questions have been raised as to whether the middle class, instead of opposing intervention by the military, as supposed, has not actually promoted it in recent years to protect their interests threatened by the masses that are demanding more of the society.[25]

The most serious threat of all to the power of the military is that posed by the labor unions, highly organized and often led by fiery leaders capable of inciting mass action and commanding the intense loyalty of great blocs of the underprivileged. While others speak feelingly of liberalism and profess its idealistic tenets, the workers are the one group in society willing to fight, bleed, and die for their liberal principles if necessary. They have a potent weapon too, the general strike, which can paralyze the economic life of the nation and bring its multifarious activities to a standstill. It is a weapon that cannot be countered by the heaviest tanks, the deadliest bazookas, or even bombs dropped by flashing jet planes. It is a weapon as potent as Gandhi's renowned passive resistance in India which brought the mighty British Empire to terms. The military are well aware of the potency of the general strike; it has often triggered the overthrow of an established military regime.

Interservice rivalries have also aided in curbing militarism. When the armed forces are united, they are practically irresistible. But they are sometimes as much concerned with cutting each other's throats as with coping with a common enemy. Division within the camp has often proved to be the Achilles' heel of the military. In Brazil, when the military chiefs of staff in 1961 attempted to prevent Vice President João Goulart from becoming president after the resignation of Jânio Quadros, a division within the armed forces almost provoked civil war. The Third Military District, which comprised the state of Rio Grande do Sul, refused to obey orders of the minister of war; and armored divisions from the Second Military District were ordered against the rebellious state. A last-ditch compromise was worked out by the military to avert open conflict. Under the compromise, Goulart would be permitted to become president, but a prime minister operating under a parliamentary system would actually exercise the executive power.[26]

THE MILITARY AS SOCIAL REFORMERS

During the past several decades, many members of the military, especially the younger officers, have sided with the new rising groups struggling to change the status quo and initiate programs of reform. This new

[25] See pp. 340–41 of this book.
[26] Jordan M. Young, *The Brazilian Revolution of 1930 and the Aftermath* (New Brunswick, N.J.: Rutgers University Press, 1967), pp. 109–10; and Thomas E. Skidmore, *Politics in Brazil: 1930–1964: An Experiment in Democracy* (New York: Oxford University Press, 1967), pp. 209–10.

social alignment is quite different from the army's leanings during the 19th century and the first quarter of the 20th. Its sympathies then were unmistakably with the oligarchy, whose power and interests it could invariably be counted on to support and protect.

This earlier military support of the propertied elite came about quite naturally. Only members of the Creole aristocracy could become officers. With their aristocratic background, they naturally sided with the class they came from. Moreover, the officers, especially the higher ones, often used their positions to amass fortunes. Becoming wealthy from perhaps controlling a state monopoly or acquiring a large landed estate, it was easy for them to become staunch supporters of the prevailing social and economic order in their society.

After World War I, however, many of the officers, especially the younger ones, now gave their loyalty and support to the new groups rising in society and struggling for recognition and power. Various factors account for this changing social attitude. Many of the young officers were now coming from a middle class that included industrialists and managers, bureaucrats and professional men, technicians, proprietors, and others. Representing these new urban elements, the young officers had no ties with the landed oligarchy and no interest in perpetuating the traditional social order. Rather, they identified themselves with the middle class and accepted its social values.

They also approved of the economic policies of their class—policies that emphasized industrialization as the key to national development. John J. Johnson says:

Under the widening impact of nationalism, both the civilian and military elements have tended increasingly to equate industrial growth with national progress. Officers, thanks to their training in organization, have found employment as directors of state-controlled economic enterprises, and the armed forces look forward to domestic production of war matériel. Thus, despite differences in their approach to politics, the military and the civilian components of the middle sectors tend to agree on their broad social and economic objectives.[27]

The tie between the young officers and the urban middle class they came from was probably the main cause of the junior officer uprisings in the second quarter of the 20th century. "In general," concludes Edwin Lieuwen, "the ideological conflict was between the old and the new generation, between the generals, on the one hand, and the majors, captains, and lieutenants on the other, with the colonels often pulled in both directions. Such cleavages were nothing new in Latin America; what was new was their origin in social conflict."[28]

---

[27] John J. Johnson, *Political Change in Latin America: The Emergence of the Middle Sectors* (Stanford, Calif.: Stanford University Press, 1958), p. 14.

[28] Lieuwen, *Arms and Politics in Latin America, op. cit.,* p. 126.

In the social conflict of the past several decades, the popular revolutions of Latin America have usually been led by the young officers who sponsored public welfare measures and basic social reforms. It was they who precipitated the break that occurred in Brazil between the old landed aristocracy and the army. In the early 1920's, the *Tenentes* (lieutenants) began to advocate changing the status quo in the nation. Although unsuccessful in two revolutionary attempts, they later succeeded in a third, the revolution of 1930, which brought Getulio Vargas to power.[29]

Vargas was the outspoken champion for the large mass of underprivileged Brazilians. During his 15-year dictatorial rule, he recognized the plight of the masses; by edict or by arm-twisting members of congress, he bestowed many rights and benefits on the popular class. After he was overthrown by the military in October, 1945, he staged a comeback; held office as duly elected president from 1951 until, still championing the cause of the masses and about to be overthrown by the military, he chose to commit suicide.[30] In his approximately 20 years in office, Vargas succeeded in incorporating the working class into the meaningful national society, accomplishing what the heads of state in Argentina were either unable or unprepared to do—make possible, without violence, the transition of the working class to participation in the political activities of the country.[31]

In Argentina, too, it was the younger officers led by Colonel Juan Perón who instituted the sweeping movement for social and economic development in the nation. Belonging to the middle class himself, Perón was quite contemptuous of the landed aristocracy. Consequently, his program was largely aimed at undermining their vested power and benefiting the urban masses of Argentina.

Perón's program in behalf of the workingman had a powerful appeal.

It was not surprising that by October 1945 the majority of workers considered Colonel Perón to be a more important man than their traditional leaders. And, no matter how demagogic his methods, he had accomplished more for them in two years than the Socialist Party had achieved in decades of patient and constantly obstructed legislative effort. . . . "Social justice" was certainly a worthy ideal; and under Perón—especially in the first phase of his rule—not only did the workers appreciate that the state was mindful of their needs, but

[29] For the development and program of the *Tenentes* movement, see Robert J. Alexander, "Brazilian Tenentismo," *Hispanic American Historical Review*, Vol. XXXVI, No. 2 (May, 1956), pp. 229–42.

[30] For a perceptive appraisal of Vargas' accomplishments and tactics, see John W. F. Dulles, *Vargas of Brazil: A Political Biography* (Austin: University of Texas Press, 1967), pp. 341–48.

The shift of emphasis from cultural and political nationalism to economic nationalism during the Vargas era is given in E. Bradford Burns, *Nationalism in Brazil: A Historical Survey* (New York: Frederick A. Praeger, Inc., 1968), chap. 5.

[31] Young, *op. cit.*, p. 96.

they also felt that they themselves were at last being allowed to share in the responsibilities of Government.[32]

In Colombia, another military reformer, General Rojas Pinilla, took over the presidential power in June, 1953, with general popular approval. Rojas was the able and respected head of the nation's armed services. His country had been ravaged for five long years by internecine civil war, and he appeared to be the only one who could end the fratricidal strife and bring order out of chaos.

The program of reform he initiated was popular with the mass of citizens. Under it, the workers were to accept discipline, and the struggle between the classes was to cease. Labor unions were to devote their efforts to protecting the workers' rights rather than to supporting any political party. Small businesses were to be encouraged and aided to survive amid the flourishing monopolies. Land was to be provided for the landless farmers, who would be trained in modern farming methods. In short, the goal of Rojas' program was social justice that would benefit all classes of society. "The ideal is not that there be fewer rich men," said Rojas, "but rather, fewer poor people."[33]

But however sincere the officers might be in their espousal of reform, they faced almost insuperable odds in attaining their objectives. In Colombia, the reforms Rojas proposed to correct basic weaknesses in the nation would perforce be very costly. To pay for these extensive social benefits for the underprivileged, he proposed that the tax structure be reformed to impose most of the costs of his program on the wealthy, who were best able to bear them. But the oligarchs bitterly resented being called upon to shoulder this burden and fought Rojas with every weapon at their command.[34]

Yet, their opposition was by no means solely responsible for the failure of Rojas' program and his removal from office by the military in 1957. Like many another reform-minded general, especially Juan Perón, he had but little competence in the realm of economics. Consequently, his ambitious programs of social security, public works, and economic develop-

---

[32] George Pendle, *Argentina* (Royal Institute of International Affairs) (3d ed.; London: Oxford University Press, 1963), pp. 99 and 177.

"For the first time in Argentine history," says John J. Kennedy, "the factory hand, the bus driver, and the packing-house worker could feel that he was participating in public affairs and that his participation was not only accepted, but eagerly solicited." John J. Kennedy, "Accountable Government in Argentina," *Foreign Affairs*, Vol. VII, No. 3 (April, 1959), pp. 455–56.

A good summary of Perón's and Evita's many reforms in favor of the masses is given by Samuel L. Baily, *Labor, Nationalism, and Politics in Argentina* (New Brunswick, N.J.: Rutgers University Press, 1967), pp. 96–105.

[33] Vernon L. Fluharty, *Dance of the Millions: Military Rule and the Social Revolution in Colombia, 1930–1956* (Pittsburgh, Pa.: University of Pittsburgh Press, 1957), pp. 265–66.

[34] For the opposition of the oligarchy to Rojas' program, see *ibid.*, pp. 237–45.

ment, laudable though they were, threatened to plunge the country into bankruptcy.[35]

In recent years the military in only two of the nations have played a conspicuous role in furthering social reform. In Venezuela, the civilian regimes of Rómulo Betancourt, 1959–64, and Raúl Leoni, 1964–69, have been able to win the support of the military for the nation's extensive program of reform.[36] In El Salvador the military regime headed by Colonel Julio Rivera, 1962–67, and his military successor, Colonel Fidel Sánchez Hernandez, 1967–date, is promoting a broad program of economic development, social change, and democratic freedom.[37]

In fact, a study of military interventions during the three decades, 1935–64, shows there has been a significant decline in the number aimed at reforming the society. During the decade 1935–44, 8 of the 16 successful insurrections, or 50 percent, were reformists. In the decade 1945–54, 5 of the 22 successful coups, or only 23 percent, were reformists. And in the decade 1955–64, only 3 of the 18 successful interventions, or 17 percent, were reformists.[38]

Even though military reformers and their programs were generally popular in their nations, they nevertheless had one weakness that invalidated all their good intentions. They were very contemptuous of democracy—"decadent democracy," as they often referred to it. Scorning the ability of the people to govern, they established authoritarian governments that became increasingly oppressive when they encountered difficulties or suffered reverses. An outstanding example of this is the regime of Rojas Pinilla, which began as a blessing to Colombia but ended as a curse.

Among other social reform-minded military presidents who eventually became very unpopular and lost their following because of their authoritarian methods were: Carlos Ibáñez, Chile, 1924–32; Rafael Franco, Paraguay, 1936–37; Germán Busch, Bolivia, 1937–39; Gualberto Villarroel, Bolivia, 1943–46; Juan Perón, Argentina, 1945–55; and Jacobo Arbenz Guzmán, Guatemala, 1950–54.

Many so-called reformers among the military were not genuinely interested in promoting reform and did not conscientiously concern themselves with the social and economic betterment of their people. In many instances, they were mainly interested in bolstering vested interests or perhaps feathering their own nests.

---

[35] Lieuwen, *Arms and Politics in Latin America, op. cit.,* pp. 146–47.

[36] For the techniques used, see Lieuwen, *Generals Vs. Presidents, op. cit.,* pp. 86–91; and John Martz, *Acción Democratica: Evolution of a Modern Political Party in Venezuela* (Princeton, N.J.: Princeton University Press, 1966), pp. 310–14.

[37] Lieuwen, *Generals Vs. Presidents, op. cit.,* pp. 91–94.

[38] Martin Needler, "Political Development and Military Intervention in Latin America," *American Political Science Review,* Vol. LX, No. 3 (September, 1966), pp. 616–26.

But even when their motives were of the best, military reformers almost invariably turned out to be poor presidents. Eduardo Santos, distinguished statesman and former president of Colombia, eloquently explains the reasons for their notorious incompetence in governing. "The military profession," he says, "is not exactly the best school in which to learn the difficult art of government. If governing were merely commanding, as the military believe, the role they assume would be justified. But to govern means to interpret, to reconcile, to respect the rights of all, to give freedom of expression to every opinion, to abide by the laws and never subordinate them to personal caprice. To govern—to govern well—often means to have the courage to rectify a mistake; to ask for and listen to advice; to have patience; and to realize that one owes one's power to the will of the people and exercise it for the period they have determined and within the limitations they have established. All of this is difficult for the military to understand and accept, accustomed as they are to the blind obedience of their inferiors, the dry voices of command, and the narrow horizon of their profession, which rarely encompasses the element of humanism."[39]

Does the incompetence of the military in governing mean, then, that military reformers have failed completely? Far from it. Although their programs are usually swept away by the counterrevolutions that oust them from office, they nevertheless often leave behind them enduring monuments in the minds and hearts of their underprivileged fellow countrymen—a faint ray of hope of better days to come . . . a glimmer of faith in the eventual triumph of justice . . . a glimpse of the freedom that ignites human aspiration. Vernon L. Fluharty wrote:

Rojas has turned the clock forward on social achievement for the masses. He has given them status, and a sense of their importance, if only because his government has emphasized their welfare. That lesson they will never forget, and nothing less will be acceptable from other governments to come. No regime in Colombia's future will be able to ignore successfully the needs of the "95 percent."[40]

---

[39] Eduardo Santos, "Latin American Realities," *Foreign Affairs*, Vol. 34, No. 2 (January, 1956), p. 256.

Since World War II, direct intervention by the military has tended to take the form of government by juntas, representing all branches of the armed forces. The juntas have been just as inept in governing as has the single traditional military dictator—perhaps even more so. They have been notoriously incompetent as administrators intrusted with public responsibility, have stifled public debate and thwarted a democratic solution of problems they inherited from democratic leaders, and have flubbed at promoting industrial development. Johnson, *The Military and Society in Latin America, op. cit.*, pp. 252-53.

[40] Fluharty, *op. cit.*, pp. 316-17.

THE THINKING OF THE MILITARY ON MAJOR NATIONAL ISSUES[41]

Since the armed forces in most of the nations have much influence on public policy, often shaping it, their thinking on major national issues is indeed important. Major areas of policy that have felt the impact of their thinking are education, industrialization, state intervention, nationalism, communism and *fidelismo*, and agrarian reform.

Since representative democracy is not a primary objective of the military, they have not really promoted education for the masses. In fact, no military government in Latin America has made an outstanding record in the field of education, and illiteracy is highest in those nations traditionally dominated by the military. Because students are likely to be leaders of the civilian opposition, military governments are apt to deal harshly with higher education. However, they have probably been more favorable to Catholic schools than have been the civilian regimes.

The attitude of the military toward industrialization apparently depends on the degree of industrialization in the nation. In the more developed states, they favor industrialization; in those less developed, however, they are so little concerned with industrial development that they prefer to have their uniforms made abroad instead of by a local industry. In states where they are actively promoting industrialization, they tend to be divided on the issue of the extent to which foreign capital should be permitted to participate.[42]

In the matter of intervention by the state in economic development, the military believe that the state has responsibility for the development of certain basic sectors, such as transportation and power, which have been neglected by domestic and foreign private capital and which are vital to national defense. The military also favor state control of natural resources, and endorse state intervention in general because governmental enterprises provide many desirable high administrative positions officers like to fill.

The more institutionalized and professionalized the military are, the more likely they are to be strongly nationalistic, as in the case of the Argentine armed forces. However, where the military do not have such an institutional and professional status, they have few nationalistic tendencies, as is shown by Honduras.

---

[41] Most of the information in this section is from John J. Johnson, *The Military and Society in Latin America, op. cit.*, chap. v.

[42] Sometimes the military, although in favor of industrialization, are divided on how economic development should take place. In Brazil, the liberal officers fervently support state-run enterprises in the basic sectors; the conservative officers are sympathetic to the agrarian-mercantile interests; and the others, sympathetic to the need for a national effort, take a middle position. Thomas E. Skidmore, *op. cit.*, p. 121.

Concerning communism and *fidelismo*, the military are usually on record as being very anti-communist. In fact, with the exception of Cuba, Costa Rica, and Uruguay, every Latin American republic would be politically more to the left were it not for the strong stand taken by the military. But their opposition is often more noise than substance, more emotion than intelligence, and not very effective. Sometimes instead of opposing communism, the military find it expedient to have the communists as allies, as was true of Pérez Jiménez of Venezuela and Fulgencio Batista of Cuba, who sought thereby to obtain the support of labor, and the military junta of Peru, which preferred to accept the communists rather than the apristas, their bitter foes.

Lastly, the military have hardly been sold on the necessity or even the desirability of agrarian reform. The very professionalism of officers makes them gradualists, afraid of disorder, social ferment, and revolutionary change. Moreover, officers believe that they have nothing to gain by rapid change but would have to bear part of the financial burden which reform would entail. Even the yearning of officers to acquire and retire to a landed estate of their own has predisposed them to private ownership represented by the status quo.

THE MILITARY ELITE

As in the case of some other significant subjects, very little attention has been paid to the matter of military elites in Latin America. But a study made by José Luis de Imaz on the officer corps of the Argentine armed forces affords interesting, though limited, insights into the subject.[43] The corps has tended to become urbanized along with the rest of the population: for example, the percentage of generals coming from the urban areas as compared with the rural has noticeably increased over the past three decades. Regarding social background, the overwhelming majority of the higher officers come from the middle or upper classes; in fact, only 2 percent of them came from the lower class. The educational orientation of higher officers is noticeably changing, too. During the 1930's and 1940's, almost all the generals received their higher education at the Military War College. However, during the 1950's, a large percentage received their education at the Military Technical College; by 1961, almost half of them attended the Technical College or other technical schools.

In Latin America as a whole, the several branches of the armed forces have their own degree of prestige. In most of the nations, the army has traditionally been the main or only military power; this is why in referring to the armed forces many speak of them as "the military." In those

---

[43] Imaz's conclusions are summarized by Irving Louis Horowitz, "The Military Elites," *op. cit.*, pp. 160–64.

nations where the army is dominant, it, of course, enjoys the highest prestige. But in those nations, such as Argentina and Chile, that have built up strong navies for national defense, naval service on a tidy ship is prestigious compared with army duty on wearisome and dangerous terrain. Thus, in Argentina, Edwin Lieuwen observes,

While the army officers have been petty-bourgeois in class origin, the navy officers have come from the upper-middle class, a class traditionally opposed to any socio-political advance of the labor-left, which Perón supported. As a result, it took Perón nearly a year to find a high ranking officer willing to head the Navy Ministry. The navy, besides participating in the plots of 1944 and 1945 to oust Perón, refused his gestures of cooperation, and continued to work for his downfall.[44]

In the jet and space age of 1969, the elite branch of service is the air force. René Barrientos, the talented and ambitious Bolivian air force general who engineered the overthrow of Paz Estenssoro in November, 1964, and later took over the destiny of the nation, is a prototype that the nations will probably see more often in the future.[45]

THE POLITICIZATION OF THE ARMED FORCES IN CUBA[46]

In a communist nation, it is not enough for most of the cadres of the armed forces to be party members. It is also necessary to establish a party organization paralleling that of the military in order to enable the leadership to indoctrinate and impose its will from top to bottom. Prior to 1964, Castro had many times considered the advisability of organizing the United Party of the Socialist Revolution (known as PURS) within the framework of the Revolutionary Armed Forces. However, the decision to do so was not made until after his second visit to Moscow in January, 1964, indicating that the decision was a result of his trip.

The organization and methods used in politicization of the armed forces are similar to those used in Russia, with the modifications needed in Cuba. There is a political department in each of the three army corps, each department is headed by a chief, and the three chiefs are subordinate to a single overall chief.

Within a department, the principle of a single chain of command is observed, just as in the armed forces. A political directive or interpretation given by any superior is binding all down the line and must be

---

[44] Lieuwen, *Generals Vs. Presidents, op. cit.,* p. 15.

[45] A highly complimentary biography, which calls Barrientos "the courageous knight," is that of José Antonio Llosa, *René Barrientos Ortuño: Paladín de la Bolivianidad* (La Paz, 1966).

[46] The information in this section is from Andrés Suárez, *Cuba: Castroism and Communism, 1959–1966,* trans. Joel Carmichael and Ernst Halperin (Cambridge: Massachusetts Institute of Technology Press, 1967), pp. 196–97 and 227–29.

followed. If members of the cells, established at different levels comparable to the military echelons, have any criticisms to make, they must do so in writing and only to the secretary of the cell. They are forbidden to raise such questions at the meetings. Party cells are supposedly formed after the soldiers of every unit have held meetings to select "model fighters," and indulge in self-criticism and self-analysis.

While the political departments have important responsibilities of indoctrination and control, they are nevertheless subordinate to the Military Department of the National Directorate of PURS. And when the safety of the nation is threatened by either internal or external elements, the armed forces assume complete authority. All the party organs from top to bottom cease to function, and the military chain of command takes over.

The politicization of the armed forces was intensified in 1965 when the Communist Party replaced PURS as the only political party in the nation, structured conformably to the model of a governing communist political organization. Members of the armed forces were appointed to each of the Soviet-type political organs that were established—the Central Committee, the Politburo, and the Secretariat—and constituted a majority of the membership of each body.[47] The new Soviet political structure with the military participating is apparently another measure designed to strengthen Castro's control over the nation.

THE MILITARY IN THE SEVERAL NATIONS TODAY[48]

The degree of political control exercised by the military varies widely among the 20 republics. Between Paraguay, which maintains the most obvious military dictatorship in Latin America, and Costa Rica, which is so nonmilitaristic that it does not even have an army, there are 18 gradations representing the other nations in the region. However, they may all be classified into three main groups—dominated by the military, transitional, and apolitical—approximately equal in number but varying considerably in importance.[49]

The nations in which the military dominate politics are Dominican

---

[47] This political affiliation is treated in greater detail in Chapter 12.

[48] For extensive discussions of this subject see Lieuwen, *Arms and Politics in Latin America, op. cit.,* pp. 154–72; and Theodore Wyckoff, "The Role of the Military in Latin American Politics," *Western Political Quarterly,* Vol. XIII, No. 3 (September, 1960), pp. 745–63.

[49] Martin Needler basically follows this classification, grouping the states according to minimal involvement in politics, intermittent military intervention, and continuing military rule. Martin C. Needler, *Latin American Politics In Perspective* (rev. ed.; Princeton, N.J.: D. Van Nostrand Co., Inc., 1967), pp. 64–70.

Robert D. Putnam establishes four categories: states essentially apolitical or, at the other extreme, ruled directly by the military; and two levels of intervention between these extremes. Robert D. Putnam, *op. cit.,* pp. 89–90.

"He sure looks lifelike doesn't he?"

Republic,[50] El Salvador, Haiti, Honduras, Nicaragua, and Paraguay. These nations, which constitute only about 8 percent of the region's population and 4 percent of its area, are the least influential in Latin America. They all have generally similar social and economic characteristics, including a high rate of illiteracy, low per capita income, primitive agricultural economy, great concentration of wealth, very little industry, little or no middle class, and a weak labor movement.

In the realm of government, these nations are frequently threatened with dictatorial rule by the military, accompanied by the suspension of private rights, the suppression of civilian political activity, and the elimination of the opposition by incarceration, assassination, or exile.

Sometimes the military do not even bother to disguise their naked dictatorial intent. In Honduras, although accepting a civilian president, they clearly showed their determination to maintain a stranglehold on the nation. In the proclamation they issued on the eve of the 1957 election, they bluntly stated that they would "assume the irrevocable functions of

---

[50] Although Joaquín Balaguer, a civilian, was elected president in 1966, and the municipal elections of 1968 showed support for his administration, the Dominican Republic is hardly yet qualified to deserve classification other than domination by the military.

permanent guarantors and zealous keepers of the integrity of the country's institutions."

The nations in which the military are in a state of transition from political to nonpolitical bodies are Argentina, Bolivia, Brazil, Cuba, Ecuador, Guatemala, Panama, Peru, and Venezuela. This group is especially important because it contains several of the largest nations in Latin America, as well as more than 60 percent of the region's population, 70 percent of its area, and the greater part of its natural resources. They have certain characteristics in common, including: a social structure that is more complex; wider variety of crops, occupations, and industry; economic power that is more widely diffused; stronger political parties; and personal freedoms that are usually respected.

In these states, the armed forces themselves are apt to be torn by disunity regarding the role they should take in resolving social crises. One group of officers, usually the senior, conservative ones, prefers to maintain the status quo. To this end, these officers prefer to have a dominant role in politics in order to thwart social change if possible, or at least to tone it down. A second group of officers would completely remove the

Courtesy of Mirochi and The Wall Street Journal

"O.K. Raise your hand if you haven't been president yet."

Courtesy of Berry and The N.E.A.

"Remember, I'm running this show."

Courtesy of Aldor and El Tiempo,
Bogotá

The Peruvian junta: "Why don't they
realize that we follow in the steps of
democracy?"

military from politics. Some of these are dedicated professionals who feel
that the armed forces should eschew politics; others, remembering the
failure of military presidents to resolve economic and social crises, are
convinced that government and politics should be left to civilians. Still a

third group consists of young officers imbued with strong social con-
sciences and sympathy for the masses. They believe the military should
take up the cause of social revolution and actively intervene to better the
condition of the underprivileged.[51]

Nations in which the military are nonpolitical are Chile, Colombia,
Costa Rica, Mexico, and Uruguay. These five nations are quite important
too, containing approximately one third the population and one fourth
the area of the region, as well as many of its important natural resources.
They have a number of features in common, including political and economic stability; a fair degree of social mobility; a high degree of literacy
and culture; effective constitutional government; a meaningful political
opposition; and freedom of speech, religion, and the press, as well as many
other personal rights.

In these countries the military have a politically neutral, professional
status that removes them from a decisive role in politics.

In Chile and Colombia, the armed forces have a unique status. They
have long been aloof from politics—in Chile, except for the brief period
1924–32, and in Colombia, for the period 1948–58[52]—and are, in effect,
autonomous bodies, not really under the direct control of the civilian
governments. Rather, under a sort of gentlemen's agreement that exists in
both countries, they are allowed to operate without interference and to
make their own military decisions, in return for which they strictly mind
their own business and remain aloof from political activity.

Easily one of the most nonmilitaristic states of Latin America is
Uruguay. "The ministry of national defense," says Russell Fitzgibbon,
"does not call the tunes in Uruguay, as is unhappily often the case in
other Latin American countries."[53] Its demilitarization is primarily the
result of two influences. The nation is a buffer between two giants and
has always been able to depend on their mutual animosities to guarantee
its existence and borders. More specifically, its abolition of militarism was
primarily the work of its great national patriot and statesman, José Batlle,
who established the framework of most of its contemporary political
institutions.

Another country that has been very successful in throttling militarism
and firmly establishing the control of civilian authorities is Costa Rica. In

---

[51] Lieuwen, *Arms and Politics in Latin America, op. cit.,* pp. 163–64.

[52] The Leticia controversy between Colombia and Peru during 1932–33 resulted in
the beefing up of the nation's weak army; and preparedness during World War II as
an ally of the United States served to further strengthen it. During the tragic civil
war that raged from 1948 to 1958, "the army became the rock upon which the state
clung for survival." J. León Helguera, "The Changing Role of the Military in
Colombia," *Journal of Inter-American Studies,* Vol. III, No. 3 (July, 1961), pp. 353
and 355.

[53] Russell H. Fitzgibbon, *Uruguay: Portrait of a Democracy* (New Brunswick,
N.J.: Rutgers University Press, 1954), p. 158.

fact, the nation does not even have an army. It was abolished shortly after the 1948 revolution was suppressed, and in its place was substituted a small National Police Force equipped only with side arms. Purposely lightly armed, its functions are only to provide ordinary police protection for the inhabitants, and to furnish a corps of officers for the civilian militia charged with defending the nation in case of invasion.

Relieved of the heavy expense of maintaining an army, Costa Rica is using its resources for peaceful development. Less than one eighth of the national budget is spent on the National Police Force—very low for Latin America. Quite symbolically, the former Bella Vista Barracks have been turned into a museum of fine arts, and the nation in 1959 initiated a program to trade its surplus arms to a United States company in return for farm tractors—a modern version, Costa Rican style, of converting swords into plowshares.

Perhaps the best expression of the nation's attainment of true constitutional government is the power of the president over the police force. In exercising his authority, the president does not mince words or pull punches. In November, 1960, President Echandi, sure of his constitutional prerogatives, did not hesitate to order the arrest of the police force's commanding officer, Colonel Fernandez, on disciplinary charges.

Among the larger nations of Latin America, Mexico is the only one that has managed to throw off the shackles of militarism. Its achievement, historic in the annals of Latin America, affords a provocative case study of militarism.

HOW MEXICO SUCCEEDED IN CURBING MILITARISM[54]

Subjecting the military to civilian control is one of the most dramatic achievements of Mexico's sweeping social revolution that began in 1910. If any nation in Latin America is qualified to write authoritatively on How to Succeed in Curbing Militarism, it is Mexico. In a region where most of the countries are still plagued with the vicious affliction, this success story should be a best a seller—required reading too!

Mexico has probably suffered more from the ravages of rampant militarism than any other country in Latin America. Flourishing lustily there, the weed seed of militarism early extended its tenacious taproot of military control deep down into the political and economic subsoil of the nation. The results were as harmful as noxious weeds in a field of sweet clover.

Responsible democratic government, an ideal embodied in the first constitution, was almost completely stifled after independence because the military refused to demobilize. Instead, the leaders and their ragged

---

[54] For a comprehensive treatment of this subject, see Lieuwen, *op. cit.*, pp. 101–21; and Virginia Prewett, "The Mexican Army," *Foreign Affairs*, April, 1941, pp. 608–20.

armies now fought each other for the prized privilege of controlling the government. As a result, every established government soon found itself confronting military rebellions on every side, instigated by generals who were greedy for power, prestige, and property. During the first century of independence, the nation was plagued with more than 1,000 armed uprisings, many of which were successful. The result was political and economic chaos.

The new head of the nation hardly had an opportunity to unpack in the presidential palace and get acquainted with the problems of government before he was thrown out by a revolution, just as he had seized power only a short while before. The turnover in heads of state was fantastic. According to William Robert Shepherd, during Mexico's first 55 years of independence it was governed by at least 74 different executives! These included two emperors, some 36 presidents, 9 provisional presidents, 10 dictators, 12 regents, and 5 supreme counselors.[55]

The continued rivalry of military chieftains who sought to control the government did far more than prevent any possible political stability; it jeopardized the very survival of the nation.

With every *jefe político*, commander, general, governor, cacique, or other military leader seeking to establish control over his locality, to make and enforce its laws, and to levy and collect its taxes, the country was in danger of imminent dismemberment. For years at a time, large regions controlled by local leaders were completely independent of the federal government. In fact, since the whole country was threatened with dismemberment, it is nothing less than miraculous that Texas was the only region that permanently separated itself from the rest of the country.[56]

Besides causing political chaos, the numerous military uprisings kept the nation in a state of continual bankruptcy. An established government was forced to spend most of its revenues in quelling uprisings against it. In addition, vast sums were lavished on its own troops in the hope, often futile, of holding their loyalty. So extreme were the demands of the military that during Mexico's first quarter century of independence the military budget was greater than the total government revenue in two out of every three years. In fact, in the 23 years from 1823 to 1846 the total income of the nation was $291,236,796; during this time the army was allocated $326,506,715.[57]

The greed of the military leaders seemed insatiable.

All wanted to be cavalry colonels, or at least infantry colonels. All wanted to be heads of military expeditions against real or imaginary bandit groups, against

---

[55] William Robert Shepherd, *The Hispanic Nations of the New World* (New Haven, Conn.: Yale University Press, 1919), p. 123.

[56] Frank Tannenbaum, *Peace by Revolution: An Interpretation of Mexico* (New York: Columbia University Press, 1933), pp. 82, 85, 89–90.

[57] *Ibid.*, p. 85.

peaceful or savage Indians, with unlimited expense accounts. All wanted to have the income from ports or fiscal offices, all wanted gold, either private or public, all wanted concessions, *haciendas,* houses, titles, to establish gambling houses, all wanted their exemptions to cover past, present and future crimes. All wanted everything and the president, instead of being the leader of a government and governor of an army, became the servant and slave of an army of an unstable group of bandits.[58]

Often forced to spend the amount of its annual collected revenue, it is no wonder that Mexico never once achieved a balanced budget until 1894. According to Francisco Bulnes, there was a revolution whenever the deficit exceeded 25 percent.[59] Yet, however extravagant the demands of the military were, and however disastrous their effects on the public treasury, they were always satisfied, even by resorting to forced borrowing if necessary. Although the nation was sadly in need of roads and railroads, schools and hospitals, public utilities and industries, it was bludgeoned into dissipating its limited resources on the profligate military.

Despite the huge public outlays for the nation's armed might, its military effectiveness was a farce. The army was ludicrously top-heavy in brass. According to one description of it, "For every two men that carried a gun, there were two commanders that ordered them about, one official who commanded the commanders, one musician who played the tune, and one retired officer who criticized the operations and collected his gratuity."[60]

Despite the great expenditures on the military, the rank and file of the army were a miserable rabble. Ragged, barefooted, little disciplined, and poorly armed, they were so scantily paid—only three or four pesos a month—that they were often forced to scrounge around and live off the country. The generals, given a daily allowance for troops' rations, often pocketed most of it. Indeed, the general who commanded an army of several thousand engaged in suppressing a Maya rebellion managed within three years to accumulate a private fortune of 10 million pesos at the expense of his men, who were reduced to filth and semistarvation.[61]

Few of the soldiers had voluntarily entered the military service; none of them had received a courteous, ceremonial notification from their local draft board beginning, "Greetings." Rather, the ranks were filled with a motley assortment of agitators and beggars, bandits and criminals, adventurers and vagabonds, many of whom had been thrown into the army by local political bosses as a convenient way of getting rid of them.

In the decades preceding the 1910 revolution, the president, General Porfirio Díaz, accomplished the seemingly miraculous by providing the

---

[58] *Ibid.,* pp. 84–85.
[59] Parkes, *op. cit.,* p. 179.
[60] Tannenbaum, *op. cit.,* p. 80.
[61] Hubert Herring, *A History of Latin America from the Beginnings to the Present* (2d ed. rev.; New York: Alfred A. Knopf, Inc., 1961), p. 342.

nation with sorely needed stability. Imposing tyranny and organized violence—"Díaz-potism," many called it—he maintained peace and order in the land by rigidly controlling the army.

But when Díaz was overthrown after the revolution of 1910, the nation reverted to its previous state of chaos. Once again, reminiscent of the first half-century of independence, the government was beset with hundreds of ambitious, self-seeking military leaders who sprang up all over the country. Commanding his own private army, each was an irresponsible autocrat in his own state or region. Entirely independent of the central authority, each exercised complete control over the lives, property, and destinies of those who lived within his authority; in brief, he was the law and government.[62]

Controlling the noxious weed of militarism was in many respects the most difficult part of the revolution, and credit for the achievement belongs to four of the nation's outstanding leaders—presidents Obregón, Calles, and Cárdenas, and General Joaquín Amaro, the able and zealous Indian general of the revolution who was as ardently pro-professional as he was antimilitaristic.

Álvaro Obregón, president from 1920–24, was a civilian—a self-made, well-to-do farmer who had risen to heroic stature in the revolution. Popular with the army and the masses alike, he capitalized on his popularity and personal prestige in his measures designed to curb the rampant militarism. A shrewd politician as well, he knew when it was advisable to give. When his minister of war, General Francisco Serrano, lost 80,000 pesos in one sitting at the gambling table, Obregón magnanimously authorized the treasury to pay the debt.

But if he diplomatically knew when to bend, he just as astutely knew when and how to apply needed pressure.

As an apparently magnanimous gesture, he had all the revolutionary generals put on the government payroll and incorporated into the national army. This was a shrewd act, for it put under governmental authority the hundreds of irascible generals who had mushroomed during the many years of civil war and internal strife. In deciding who was entitled to what, President Obregón was too smart to quibble about details, holding that "if a man calls himself a general, he must be one."[63]

Meanwhile, professionalism was being astutely promoted among the lower officers of the army. The old Colegio Militar at Chapultepec was reopened for new officers, who could take a three-year specialized course to prepare them for the infantry, cavalry, or artillery. Also, many of the promising young officers were sent abroad, particularly to Spain or France, Germany or the United States, to study military science and tactics. Another significant sign of demilitarization was Obregón's reduc-

---

[62] Frank Tannenbaum, *Mexico: The Struggle for Peace and Bread* (New York: Alfred A. Knopf, Inc., 1954), p. 95.
[63] *Ibid.*, p. 63.

ing the size of the army, and also its share of the federal budget, from 142 million pesos in 1921 to 117 million in 1924.[64]

The number of generals was conveniently reduced, too, especially after the unsuccessful uprising of 1923 led by the military. Some of the leaders were exiled, others were simply shot. This unceremonious treatment of the hitherto sacrosanct generals was no graduated deterrent. Rather, it was a form of massive retaliation that magically diminished the enthusiasm of the military for instituting insurrections against the government.

Plutarco Calles, president from 1924 to 1928 and behind-the-scenes ruler until 1934, continued the work of deemphasizing the military that Obregón had so successfully begun. General Joaquín Amaro, a dedicated professional officer, was made secretary of war, "to transform Mexico's semi-feudal Army into a truly national body."

Initially, General Amaro shrewdly avoided a direct challenge to the powerful revolutionary generals whom he aimed eventually to break. Instead, he concentrated mainly on winning over the other military elements in the army. More of the younger officers were sent abroad for training, and on their return to Mexico were used to build up an efficient staff. In addition to advanced training, emphasis was placed on loyalty to the military profession and to the nation. For President Calles was convinced that loyalty and national pride were the ultimate cures for the country's persistent militarism.[65]

In addition to bettering the training and career opportunities of the younger officers, President Calles and his able secretary of war were very concerned about the men in the ranks. To win them over, President Calles saw that they were given better uniforms, better food and barracks, as well as better equipment.

With the morale of the rank and file thus greatly improved and the younger officers favorably disposed, President Calles and General Amaro were now ready to tackle the old revolutionary generals. Accordingly, they deliberately launched the policy of shifting military commands—a radical change that was shrewdly calculated to provoke the generals. It had long been customary for a general to regard his troops as his very own—in effect, belonging to him. He had recruited, trained, and equipped them; they were as much a part of his military prerogatives as were his title, decorations, and emoluments—so much so that he always expected to move only with his own troops. In fact, it was unthinkable that he be transferred to command a strange new outfit that owed him no personal loyalty whatever.[66]

---

[64] Lieuwen, *Arms and Politics in Latin America, op. cit.,* p. 110.
[65] *Ibid.,* pp. 110–11.
[66] Tannenbaum, *Mexico: The Struggle for Peace and Bread, op. cit.,* p. 91.

The administration's intentionally provocative move encountered vehement resistance, just as Calles and Amaro had expected. But they were fully prepared for it. Assured of the loyalty of the younger officers and of the men in the ranks, they effectively crushed the two uprisings that occurred—the first in 1927, the second in 1929—and dismissed the errant generals. This time, the civilian leaders were so sure of themselves that they did not bother to shoot the military insurrectionists.

With militarism reeling from these body blows, General Lázaro Cárdenas, president from 1934 to 1940, succeeded in delivering still other telling punches. Realizing that the remaining revolutionary generals had become large landowners and big businessmen who would naturally oppose his radically new land and labor reforms, President Cárdenas determined to build up other forces that could counteract and defeat any pressure these generals might exert. Confident that the landless peons were sold on his land reform program and that he could count on their loyalty, Cárdenas equipped them with weapons and organized them into powerful army reserves. In like fashion, he organized into an independent labor militia the mass of workers who benefited from his regime's social reforms.[67]

Still other measures were taken to establish the army as a professional, nonpolitical career. Beginning in 1936, competitive examinations were required for the promotion of all officers, and the following year it became unlawful for them to have a civilian occupation. This emphasis on professionalism was accompanied by rigid restrictions on the political activities of all military personnel. They were prohibited from participating in public political activities of any kind, whether meetings, discussions, or public expressions of their opinion. Moreover, the officers were specifically forbidden to exercise any political influence whatever over their subordinates.[68]

In addition to arming the agrarian and labor groups, promoting professionalism, and forbidding political activity, President Cárdenas gave another mighty punch to militarism by his reorganization of the Revolutionary Party in December, 1937. The new federated party, as reorganized, was composed of four equal groups: labor, peasant, popular, and military. Under this new arrangement, the army could always be outvoted and its political strength could be nullified by pitting the other three forces against it. When President Cárdenas was soundly criticized by some for allegedly bringing the army into politics, his retort was shrewdly to the point: "We did not put the army in politics," he said, "it was already there. In fact, it had been dominating the situation, and we did well to reduce its influence to one vote out of four."[69]

---

[67] Lieuwen, *Arms and Politics in Latin America, op. cit.*, p. 113.
[68] *Ibid.*, p. 118.
[69] *Ibid.*, p. 114.

In 1940, after less than three years of existence, the military sector was dissolved. This did not mean that the army was completely divorced from politics but that henceforth its influence, still strong though less obvious, would be exerted through the popular sector of the party.[70]

Curbing the nation's erstwhile unrestrained militarism has proved to be one of the most beneficial reforms accomplished by the Mexican social revolution. No longer are the military a serious drag on the economy, consuming a disproportionate share of the national budget, as is unfortunately the case in most of the other Latin American countries. The size of the army—about 50,000 men—has been purposefully kept small in comparison to the size of the rest of the population. And it is allocated only about 9 percent of the national budget in 1967—one of the smallest proportions in all Latin America. Precious national revenues, seemingly always too meager for the nation's burgeoning needs, can now be beneficially used for building roads or hospitals, financing schools or literacy campaigns, rather than squandered on a bloated, parasitic, unneeded military machine.

No longer does the military interfere in politics, either overturning or threatening to overturn the government at will. Instead, civilian officials, now firmly in control, run the government and decide national policy without interference from the armed forces, which may be freely overridden, even on strictly military issues.[71]

Although the political power of the army has been effectively curbed, its efficiency and effectiveness have been greatly increased. Its organization, discipline, and training, all patterned after the armed forces of the United States, have been greatly strengthened, and its leadership now consists of a well-trained, highly professional corps of capable, loyal officers.

Instead of impeding national progress as earlier, the armed forces are now engaged in many constructive activities, including a widespread public works program. They build schools and hospitals, conduct reforestation and irrigation programs, and help with maintenance of the nation's road system. All in all, their changed role has been largely responsible for the great progress that Mexico is very proud of.

"For the past generation," says Edwin Lieuwen, "the entire nation, including the armed forces, has been reaping the rewards of this basic political reform and will almost certainly continue to do so. . . . In dealing with militarism, Mexico has set an example which other Latin American nations might be well advised to follow."[72]

---

[70] Robert E. Scott, *Mexican Government in Transition* (rev. ed., Urbana: University of Illinois Press, 1964), pp. 133–34; and William P. Tucker, *The Mexican Government Today* (Minneapolis: University of Minnesota Press, 1957), pp. 43 and 193.

[71] Lieuwen, *Arms and Politics in Latin America, op. cit.,* p. 119.

[72] *Ibid.,* p. 121.

To which conclusion the many friends of Latin America concur in a fervent Amen.

SUGGESTED READINGS

Alexander, Robert J. *The Bolivian National Revolution,* chap. 8. New Brunswick, N.J.: Rutgers University Press, 1958.

———. "The Army in Politics," *Government and Politics in Latin America* (ed. Harold Eugene Davis), chap. 6. New York: Ronald Press Co., 1958.

———. "Brazilian Tenentismo," *Hispanic American Historical Review,* Vol. XXXVI, No. 2 (May, 1956), pp. 229–42.

Arciniegas, Germán. *The State of Latin America,* chap. xvii. Trans. Harriet de Onís. New York: Alfred A. Knopf, Inc., 1952.

Barager, Joseph R. (ed.). *Why Perón Came to Power.* New York: Alfred A. Knopf, Inc., 1968.

Brill, William H. *Military Intervention in Bolivia: The Overthrow of Paz Estenssoro and the MNR.* Washington, D.C.: Institute for the Comparative Study of Political Systems, 1967.

Dulles, John W. F. *Vargas of Brazil: A Political Biography.* Austin: University of Texas Press, 1967.

Gruening, Ernest. *Mexico and Its Heritage,* pp. 280–331. New York: D. Appleton-Century Co., Inc., 1934.

Horowitz, Irving Louis. "The Military Elites," *Elites in Latin America* (eds. Seymour Martin Lipset and Aldo Solari), chap. 5, New York: Oxford University Press, Inc., 1967.

Johnson, John J. The *Military and Society in Latin America.* Stanford, Calif.: Stanford University Press, 1964.

——— (ed.). *The Role of the Military in Underdeveloped Countries.* Princeton, N.J.: Princeton University Press, 1962. Chaps. on the Latin American military by Victor Alba, Edwin Lieuwen, and John J. Johnson.

Kolinski, Charles J. *Independence or Death! The Story of the Paraguayan War,* chap. iv. Gainesville: University of Florida Press, 1965.

Lieuwen, Edwin. *Generals Vs. Presidents: Neomilitarism in Latin America.* New York: Frederick A. Praeger, Inc., 1964.

———. *Arms and Politics in Latin America.* Rev. ed. Council on Foreign Relations. New York: Frederick A. Praeger, Inc., 1961.

———. "The Changing Role of the Military in Latin America,' *Journal of Inter-American Studies,* Vol. III, No. 4 (October, 1961), pp. 559–69.

McAlister, L. N. "Civil-Military Relations in Latin America," *Journal of Inter-American Studies,* Vol. III, No. 3 (July, 1961), pp. 341–50.

———. "Changing Concepts of the Role of the Military in Latin America," *Annals of the American Academy of Political and Social Sciences,* Vol. 360 (July, 1965), pp. 85–98.

Needler, Martin C. *Anatomy of A Coup d'Etat: Ecuador 1963*. Washington, D.C.: Institute for the Comparative Study of Political Systems, 1964.

———. *Latin American Politics in Perspective*, pp. 64–88. Rev. ed. Princeton, N.J.: D. Van Nostrand Co., Inc., 1967.

———. "Political Development and Military Intervention in Latin America," *American Political Science Review*, Vol. LX, No. 3 (September, 1966), pp. 616–26.

North, Liisa. *Civil–Military Relations in Argentina, Chile, and Peru*. Berkeley: Institute of International Studies, University of California, 1966.

Potash, Robert A. "The Changing Role of the Military in Argentina," *Journal of Inter-American Studies*, Vol. III, No. 4 (October, 1961), pp. 571–78.

Prewett, Virginia. "The Mexican Army," *Foreign Affairs*, April, 1941, pp. 608–20.

Putnam, Robert D. "Toward Explaining Military Intervention in Latin American Politics," *World Politics*, Vol. XX, No. 1 (October, 1967), pp. 83–110.

Santos, Eduardo. "Latin American Realities," *Foreign Affairs*, Vol. 34, No. 2 (January, 1956), pp. 244–56.

Skidmore, Thomas E. *Politics in Brazil, 1930–1964: An Experiment in Democracy*. New York: Oxford University Press, 1967.

Stokes, William S. *Latin American Politics*, chap. 7. New York: Thomas Y. Crowell Co., 1959.

Veliz, Claudio. *Latin America and the Caribbean: A Handbook*, pp. 265–78. New York: Frederick A. Praeger, Inc., 1968.

Wyckoff, Theodore. "The Role of the Military in Latin American Politics," *Western Political Quarterly*, Vol. XIII, No. 3 (September, 1960), pp. 745–63.

Young, Jordan M. *The Brazilian Revolution of 1930 and the Aftermath*. New Brunswick, N.J.: Rutgers University Press, 1967.

PART III

Promotion of the General Welfare: by Evolution or Revolution

AGRICULTURE
AND LAND REFORM:
The Cry for Land and Its Portent

Agriculture is very important in every nation. In the United States, the farmers like to regard it as the backbone of the economy. In the 20 Latin American republics, agriculture is of special significance to the society. It serves primarily, of course, to feed the region's rapidly increasing population, which is leading the field in the worldwide population explosion. Moreover, it provides a livelihood for a large majority of the people; 60 percent or more are engaged in farming for a living,[1] as shown by country in Figure 7-1. And, as in other underdeveloped nations, it provides most of the capital which the countries must rely on for industrialization. Furthermore, the sale of agricultural products abroad enables the nations to buy the consumer goods they do not produce themselves, and the machines and tools they must have in order to industrialize.

CONCENTRATION OF OWNERSHIP OF LAND

One of the most distinctive features of agriculture in Latin America is the highly concentrated ownership of land. In fact, a handful of *hacendados,* or large landowners, has controlled a large proportion of the farmland in most of the nations.

The hacienda, known in Argentina as the estancia and in Brazil as the fazenda, was the prevailing pattern of land ownership in most of Latin America until World War I, and in many of the countries it continues

---

[1] In the United States today, despite its unmanageable agricultural surpluses only about 12 percent of the population farms for a living.

FIGURE 7–1

PERCENTAGE OF POPULACE ENGAGED IN AGRICULTURE

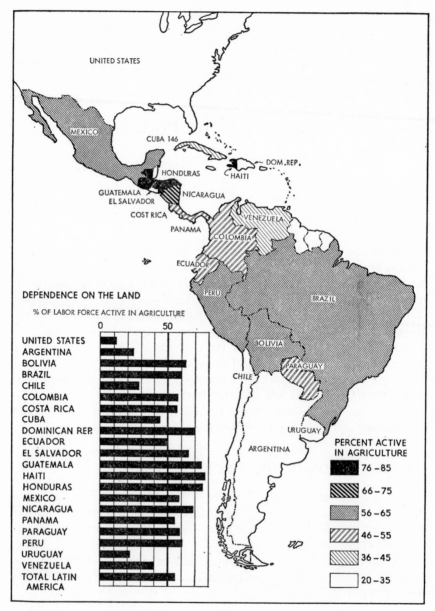

Source: *Center of Intercultural Formation* (CIF) *Study No. 1,* p. 125. Reproduced by permission.

today with hardly diminished vigor. According to a United Nations estimate in 1951, only 1.5 percent of the total number of farm properties, averaging more than 15,000 acres each, contained 50 percent of the total agricultural land in the whole region. In Chile, one of the many nations where the *latifundios* still flourish, 1 percent of the landowners control 43 percent of the total farmland. In Bolivia, according to the 1950 census taken just 2 years before the revolution, 4.5 percent of the population owned 70 percent of the total farm acreage. One *hacendado* reportedly owned 16.3 million acres of land; a second, 3.4 million acres; and a third, 2.2 million. In Ecuador and Peru, other Andean nations with relatively little developed tillable land, the situation was about the same. Some estimates, however, as Table 7-1 indicates, suggest an even higher degree of concentration.

Ownership is very concentrated in Argentina, where some 500 or so owners possess 18 percent of the total national farmland. The stranglehold that the small number of *hacendados* exercise over the whole agricultural economy has often been severely criticized. One of its most

TABLE 7-1

Minifundios and Latifundios

Country (In Order of Total Area of Farmland)	Year of Census	Percentage of Total Number of Farms		Percentage of Total Area of Farmland	
		Less than 5 Hectares (12.36 Acres)	More than 2,500 Hectares (6,177.6 Acres)	Less than 5 Hectares (12.36 Acres)	More than 2,500 Hectares (6,177.6 Acres)
Brazil	1960	34.0*	—	1.0*	—
Argentina	1960	15.7	2.6	0.1	59.8
Mexico	1950	72.6	1.3*	0.9	77.0*
Bolivia	1950	59.3	3.8	0.2	81.8
Colombia	1960	62.5	0.1	4.5	20.2
Chile†	1955	36.9	1.1*	0.3	63.7*
Peru	1961	82.9	0.1	5.2	64.5
Uruguay†	1961	14.7	1.4	0.2	33.4
Cuba	1952	13.9	—	—	—
Ecuador	1954	73.1	0.1	7.2	25.9
Guatemala	1950	81.0*	0.1	11.0*	27.5
Honduras	1952	57.0	0.0	8.1	13.2
Nicaragua‡	1952	26.0	0.1*	1.5	20.0*
Dominican Republic	1960	86.3	0.0	—	—
Costa Rica‡	1955	36.0*	0.1	2.0*	21.0
El Salvador	1961	85.1	0.0	15.0	7.2
Panama†	1950	52.0	0.1*	8.3	10.0

— Data not available. 0.0 represents magnitude less than half of the unit employed.
° Estimate.
† Excludes farms of less than 1 hectare.
‡ Excludes farms of less than 0.7 hectare.
Source: *Américas*, November, 1964, p. 47. Reproduced by permission.

trenchant critics was Juan Perón. Quite contemptuous of the landed oligarchy, he did not hesitate to castigate it. An attempt had been made, he contended, to mislead the public into believing that the oligarchy, an unruly bunch of demagogues, were the "ruling class in the country, its elite, and as such was made up of wise, rich, and good people. We must observe that 'the wise are seldom rich, and the rich seldom good.' Nor must we forget that neither the wise nor the good found a place among Argentine politicians."[2] But not even Perón, with his strong dictatorial rule of 10 years and his many restrictive measures applying to agriculture, was able to dislodge the landed oligarchy from their long entrenched position of power.

Concentration of ownership has been especially pronounced in Mexico where, prior to the 1910 revolution, just 1 percent of the population owned 97 percent of the land. Even since the revolution, one of whose major aims was to break up the large landed estates and give land to the landless, a small handful of owners still hold a large proportion of the farmlands. Although the agrarian laws of the nation limit owners to 100 hectares of irrigated land and 200 of nonirrigated land, the agricultural census of 1940 showed that properties of 1,000 hectares or over, constituting only 0.3 percent of the total number of holdings, comprised 61.9 percent of the whole farmland of the nation. Of these large farms, 301 each had an acreage of more than 40,000 hectares.[3]

Despite the widespread concern about the problem frequently expressed in Latin America, ownership of land continues to be highly concentrated in many of the nations. In 1969, of Colombia's approximately 1.2 million farms, 40 percent are *minifundios* of 5 acres or less. On the other hand, some of them are vast holdings; the 15 largest range from 250,000 acres to almost 2 million. About half of the land in these vast tracts is not cultivated at all simply because the owners lack the needed capital.[4]

What is perhaps more disconcerting, the high degree of concentration of ownership is actually increasing instead of decreasing in several of the most important nations, squeezing out many of the small farmers. This is true of Argentina,[5] and also of Brazil despite the intent of its inheritance laws to disperse ownership.[6]

---

2 *Perón Expounds His Doctrine*, trans. Argentine Association of English Culture (Buenos Aires, 1948), p. 49.

3 For statistics on the number and size of *latifundios* and *minifundios* in most of the countries, see Joâo Gonçalves de Souza, "Land for the Farmer: Problems of Agrarian Reform in Latin America," *Américas*, Vol. 12, No. 8 (August, 1960), p. 14.

4 The need for land reform in Colombia is discussed by T. Lynn Smith, *Colombia: Social Structure and the Process of Development* (Gainesville: University of Florida Press, 1967), pp. 242–49.

5 Felix J. Weil, *Argentine Riddle* (Latin American Economic Institute) (New York: John Day Co., 1944), pp. 93–94.

6 Josué de Castro, *Death in the Northeast* (New York: Random House, Inc., 1966), p. 154.

TYPES OF LARGE-SCALE AGRICULTURAL ENTERPRISES

Corporate Mechanized Farms

There are two main types of large-scale agricultural enterprises in Latin America. One consists of the relatively new, large mechanized plantations often referred to as "factories in the field." Usually foreign owned and foreign managed, they are models of intensive, scientific farming requiring a high degree of managerial and technical skill. Representing a large investment, these efficiency-expert farms use modern methods and machinery, thereby achieving a high level of production.

Relations between management and labor are on a strictly business basis. On arriving at work, the laborer punches an impersonal time clock instead of deferentially saying, "Buenos días, patrón," and a scrupulously accurate record of his labor is kept by a timekeeper. The corporation usually provides houses for the workers, as well as a school, chapel or church, soccer field, clinic for medical assistance, and a system for supplying water and electricity. Many of the workers, migrants from backwoods rural areas, have grown up under the paternalistic *patrón* system, and have difficulty in adjusting to this revolutionary, impersonal economic enterprise.

Haciendas

The old traditional hacienda as it has long existed in Latin America is the very antithesis of this efficient, productive, and impersonal agricultural enterprise. In most cases, the hacienda has been inherited for generations, and has long been accustomed to a slow, poky, easygoing way of life. It is never worried about making a return on an investment, since little or no capital has ever been put into it. Its main objective has always been to be as economically self-sufficient as possible, producing on the place everything that is needed there.

The hacienda does not have to worry about labor problems, either. The hands were born on the estate; their ancestors have lived there for generations, sometimes by choice but often because they owe their souls to the plantation store. And quite unlike the businesslike "factory in the field," the hacienda is the essence of paternalism. The *hacendado* is no impersonal labor boss. Rather, he is the *patrón* of all the families who live on his place; he gives them help when they need it, chastizes them when he thinks they deserve it, and in general directs their work and life. He is also the godfather to many of the children born on the place.

In Brazil, the fazenda was the result of an ultragenerous policy of the Portuguese monarch in making grants of land in the New World. After Portugal's title to the region of what is now Brazil was recognized, the monarch granted all the land from the coast to the line of demarcation to 12 noblemen; but these king-sized grants accomplished very little in the way of encouraging immigration to the area or increasing the revenue the monarch hoped to receive from the overseas empire. Accordingly, the king later modified the original agreement by designating a viceroy to head the government of Brazil and providing that land would be available to all Portuguese who applied for it, with generous limits to the grants.

As a result of this policy, the fazendas of Brazil tower in size above the other large acreages in Latin America. One *fazendeiro*, or large land-owner, possessed an agrarian domain larger than the whole area of the mother country, Portugal. Another huge estate was that owned by the Costa Ferreiras in the vast Amazon region; it was bigger than England, Scotland, and Ireland combined.[7]

Large grants of land were likewise made in Spain's colonial empire, accounting for haciendas that have existed for centuries in most of the nations. But Argentina's problem of *latifundios* today is of relatively recent origin, and is the result of a very shortsighted governmental policy. *Latifundismo* made a strong beachhead there soon after independence when the government made large grants of land to individuals and companies in order to add to its short-term income, settle the interior of the country, and push forward the frontier against the Indians. These large acreages were granted at very nominal prices, and sometimes without any charge whatever.

Indeed, the 1826 Act of the Argentine Congress was one of the biggest giveaways in all the history of Latin America. According to the law, public lands could be distributed without being put up for sale, with no restriction at all as to the amount of land any individual could obtain. As a result of this myopic policy, many speculators were able to grab huge acreages, with no thought of farming or developing them, but solely for holding them for a profit or the personal prestige of the owner. The nation's precious resource of fertile land was further dissipated by Rosas, who either gave away large acreages of frontier land or sold them for a ridiculously low price to be paid in installments and without interest. Other large tracts were given to military veterans who had participated in the war of extinction against the Indians. Thanks to these reckless grants, many an Argentine became a multimillionaire by taking advantage of shortsighted governmental policies, hogging a large part of the nation's agricultural wealth without any work or investment whatever on his part.

Argentina's policy regarding grants of public land was very different from that of the United States. Here, the policy was to promote an agrarian

---

[7] Gilberto Freyre, *The Masters and The Slaves: A Study in the Development of Brazilian Civilization*, trans. Samuel Putnam (2d Eng. ed. rev.; New York: Alfred A. Knopf, Inc., 1956), p. *liv*.

community of small- and medium-size farmers who owned and worked their properties. The Homestead Act of 1862, enacted to reward veterans who fought in the Union Army, was a milestone in American history, since free land had long been the ardent goal of many citizens. But the act was not designed to benefit speculators who had no intention of farming. Each veteran was eligible to receive only up to a quarter section, 160 acres, about enough for a family-sized farm; and he did not receive full title to it until he had lived on it for five years and had made certain specified improvements.

In Mexico, the large landed estates began and have continued in quite a different fashion. As in most of the other Hispanic colonies, large grants of land were made by the crown. Many such grants were made to the Church, which by this and other means in time became by far the largest landowner in Mexico, controlling in some areas an estimated 80 percent of the land. After independence had been won, many of the secular *latifundistas* took advantage of laws or decrees requiring the Church to sell its vast holdings; they often bought valuable properties for a pittance. If they had been divided into small tracts, those properties might well have started the nation on the road to becoming a stable society of small- and medium-size farmers.

Equally as significant were the predatory tactics the *latifundistas* used against the native Indian communities. Before independence, the Indians were able to look either to the crown or to the Church for protection of the meager ancestral lands they had somehow managed to preserve. After independence, however, the Indians were without the protection either of the clergy or of the government. In fact, under the guise of liberalism and individual initiative the *latifundistas* further expanded their holdings by getting possession, by one means or another, of most of the remaining farmland and woodland which had been recognized for centuries as the propertied heritage of the Indian communities.

In expanding their holdings at the expense of the helpless Indians, they had no scruples against using the most ruthless and savage tactics, when necessary for gaining their ends. Ernest Gruening writes:

Government and *hacendados* were one. Obstreperous villagers were sentenced to the army by the local judge or *jefe político*, and sent to remote regions as soldier-convicts. Often they never saw their families again. In Hidalgo, when the spokesmen for a pueblo became threatening, they were seized by order of the governing and landowning Cravioto dynasty, and buried to their necks in the center of the *ejido* they were trying to save. Then the *Rurales* [mounted police] galloped over them.[8]

---

[8] Ernest Gruening, *Mexico and Its Heritage* (New York: D. Appleton-Century Co., Inc., 1934), p. 129.

For the "Rape of the Pueblos," as Eyler N. Simpson terms it, see his *The Ejido: Mexico's Way Out* (Chapel Hill: University of North Carolina Press, 1937), pp. 29–33.

The *hacendados* and their families, the privileged, aristocratic elite of the society, enjoyed a life of luxury and leisure. Lords over all they surveyed, they enjoyed the prestige and fruits of their landed empires. Henry Bamford Parkes writes:

> Outside the cities, the valleys of central and southern Mexico were dotted with enormous white houses where creole *hacendados* lived in lonely grandeur, owners of estates which might cover hundreds of square miles of mountain and forest and in which grazed herds of oxen which were sometimes numbered by tens of thousands. They spent their days on horseback, hunting and shooting, or supervising the peons who worked in the wheatfields or the sugar plantations; and any traveler who broke in upon their solitude was greeted with a Castilian courtesy and entertained with a bullfight, a picnic with music in the fields, or an exhibition of the skill of the *vaqueros* in throwing their master's cattle."[9]

Separated by many miles of territory from adjoining haciendas, with only rarely used paths connecting them, each hacienda is an isolated, self-sufficient social unit. All of those who live on the place, both the many peons and the residents of the Big House, have to depend on one another for entertainment and pleasure. Sunday is always a big day, when the peons, dressed in their Sunday best, attend services at the chapel located near the Big House. A christening or wedding or saint's day of the owner or another member of his family is celebrated as a festive holiday that is long remembered. On these occasions, everyone on the place turns out to enjoy the carefree festivities, including dancing to a hot beat and drinking all he can handle—often more.

Such occasions are the highlights the peon likes to remember. But his everyday life is quite different from this; it is a monotonous, humdrum existence of sweat and toil from early sunup to late sundown. He and his family live in a rude hut or shack that usually has only one room, sometimes two, with only the simplest of furnishings: a crude table and several crudely made chairs, a box or trunk for clothing, a chest of drawers, and an iron bedstead or two.

In return for cultivating a small plot of his own and possibly pasturing an animal or two, the peon obligates himself to farm a certain number of hectares, raising such crops as the landlord specifies and on terms mutually agreed on. These agreements vary widely in their terms, as there are many different kinds of land tenure in the whole region.[10] Under the

---

[9] Henry Bamford Parkes, *A History of Mexico* (3d ed. rev.: Boston: Houghton Mifflin Co., 1960), p. 117.

For colorful accounts of visits to haciendas, see George McCutchen McBride, *Chile: Land and Society* (American Geographical Society Research Series No. 19) (New York, 1936), pp. 3–8 and 47–54.

[10] For a summary of the various forms of land tenure in the several nations, see International Labour Office, *The Landless Farmer in Latin America* (Geneva, Switz., 1957), chaps. i–iv.

For the forms of tenure in Peru, see Thomas R. Ford, *Man and Land in Peru* (Gainesville: University of Florida Press, 1955), chap. 4.

more customary form of agreement, the landowner provides the land, seed, tools, and maybe work animals; in return, the peon raises the crop, which is divided between the landlord and himself on a previously agreed on basis. Usually, the peon as well as members of his family agree to give a certain number of days of free labor every year, performing such chores as mending fences, rounding up and checking cattle, digging wells, or possibly working in the Big House.

The hacienda and the landed aristocracy it supports have had far-reaching effects on the society. For the most part, the hacienda has been a tremendous obstacle to the economic development of the nations. Because of its agricultural practices, land that is the main natural resource of the region is only partially utilized. Despite the abundance of farm manpower and the need of the region for agricultural products, most of the land is allowed to lie idle. For under the system there is no incentive—or pressure—for putting all the fertile acres to work. Self-sufficient as the hacienda is, and incurring practically no outside expenses in making a crop, whatever the crop brings when sold on the commercial market is clear profit, which the *hacendado* and his family use to enjoy a very affluent standard of living. In planning his farming program, the *hacendado* is concerned only with this, and not with the productivity per acre, per worker, or per man-hour employed. Nor does he have any incentive to invest in modern machinery and tools, or to require the workers to use efficient methods for the various farming operations. As a result, the yield of crops raised is usually extremely low per acre or per worker. The low productivity of the peon compared with that of the worker in other major fields is shown by Figure 7–2.

These poor farming practices are very different from the efficient ones used more than four centuries ago by the Incas. Masters of efficient, productive farming, the Incas used ingenious methods. Every square foot of tillable soil was cultivated, even the steep slopes by means of the construction of masonry terraces, which provided narrow stretches of flat land and kept the soil from eroding. The crops planted there were fertilized by fish and guano, and were irrigated by an elaborate system of aqueducts that tapped mountain streams far above the agricultural lands and carried their cold, nourishing waters to the intensively cultivated terraces—a sort of staircase system of farming.

Besides inefficiency of production and very low yields for the land's potentiality, the hacienda poses another problem because of its concentration on money crops that can be sold on a national or world market. The concentration of effort on such crops has prevented even a semblance of diversified farming. As a result, little or no attempt has been made to raise fruits, vegetables, dairy products, or many other foodstuffs, which are sorely needed to feed the population. Consequently, foodstuffs often must be imported at a heavy cost, although most of the population is engaged in agriculture. Because the hacienda fails to raise the food needed

FIGURE 7–2

Size of Labor Force and Worker Productivity

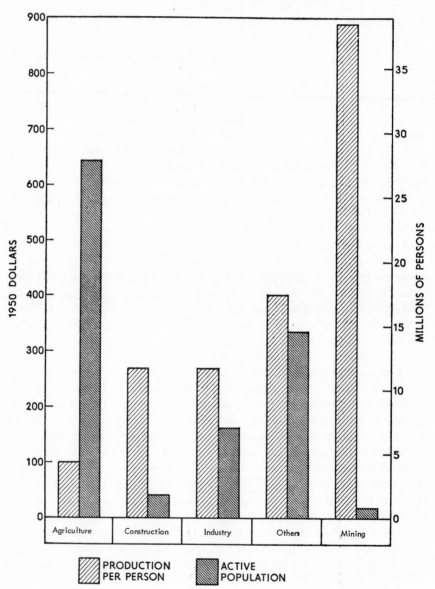

Source: *Center of Intercultural Formation* (CIF) *Study No. 1*, p. 216. Reproduced by permission.

by the populace, it is mainly responsible for the lack of a balanced diet, which plagues most of Latin America and consigns a large part of its populace as expendables to low efficiency, sickness and disease, and an early death.

The hacienda has been a harmful influence on another score. Having helpless and servile labor within its grasp, it has often exploited this labor to the fullest. A low grade of liquor was usually one of the main commodities sold by the store on the hacienda. Sometimes the workers, paid for their labor in wooden or metal tokens good only on the plantation, were required to buy a prescribed minimum amount of the booze, sold at exorbitant prices. Sometimes the workers in the fields were even given a glass of liquor free of charge during their rest period "as a tonic or energizer." The coca drug was also sold at plantation stores; part of the wage often was paid in coca leaves. These leaves have a potent effect on the user, anaesthetizing the gustatory and digestive nerves and spurring him to a level of activity that transcends all normal human bounds of endurance. ". . . coca-chewing workers have been found to exert themselves sometimes as much as twenty hours a day over a period of weeks and even months in a state of serious undernourishment."[11]

Sometimes, the exploitation of labor was more systematic and complete. In Peru, a descriptive Spanish term, *gamonalismo,* was used to connote the exploitation of Indians. According to Moisés Sáenz, *gamonalismo* was a social attitude and mores that supported "the condition of inequality of the Indian with respect to the other social classes of the country . . . it is colonialism and clericalism projected through a century of independent life; it signifies spoliation . . . the connivance of . . . authorities, clergy, and landholders in exploiting the Indians without conscience and without scruple."[12]

In still another respect, the hacienda has greatly retarded the region's economic development. Although it represents a considerable part of the income and wealth of most of the nations, it contributes very little in the form of taxes for the support of local or national government. As is well known, the tax rates on farm properties are extremely low throughout Latin America; and sometimes even the low taxes assessed against the properties are not paid. In Paraguay, 53 percent of the taxes levied on land were delinquent for more than 1 year, 34 percent for more than 6 years, 14 percent for more than 11 years, and 8 percent for more than 21

---

[11] George Soule, David Efron, and Norman T. Ness, *Latin America in the Future World* (National Planning Association) (New York: Farrar & Rinehart, Inc., 1945), p. 27.

For the history of cocaism, its medical and social causes and effects, and legislation on the coca leaf, see *International Labour Office, Indigenous Peoples: Living and Working Conditions of Aboriginal Populations in Independent Countries* (Studies and Reports, New Series, No. 35) (Geneva, Switz., 1953), pp. 153–78.

[12] In Ford, *op. cit.,* p. 111.

years. What is especially significant, delinquency in paying taxes on farmland was much more habitual among the large owners than among the small ones.[13]

Furthermore, the hacienda with its far-flung acres is a problem for the rest of society because of its very size. Some haciendas would be regarded as inordinately large by any criterion; the Terrazas in the state of Chihuahua, Mexico, owned 30 million acres of land—an estate about the size of the whole state of Mississippi. Of course most *hacendados* own nothing like this much property. But as a group, constituting only 1 or 2 or maybe 3 percent or so of the total landowners, they control most of the cultivable land in the nation. Their tight control handed down from generation to generation has made it impossible for a large number of individuals to own moderately small- or medium-sized acreages—a dispersion of ownership that has contributed so importantly to the agricultural economy of many nations.

Indeed, one of the worst effects the *latifundios* have had on the society is the inevitable existence of a great number of *minifundios* or tiny holdings of land. Since a small number of *hacendados* owned most or a disproportionate amount of the land, the relatively small balance had to be shared by a large number of small farmers. The acreage they possess is minute by comparison; it is but a few acres at most and often far less. In fact, some of these "farms" are so minuscule that they are calculated in terms of so many rows in the field, or maybe just so many square feet of space.

The haciendas with their spacious acreages have done more than corner most of the land—they have also gotten by far the best part of it. As one rides through the countryside, pausing now and then to admire the fertile land and lush crops, one soon realizes that the haciendas contain all the rich lands in the valleys, also the acreages on the gentle slopes and low rolling hills, obviously the best land of all. The rest usually comprises the *minifundios* whose owners cling tenaciously to the land. The grade is often so steep that after several seasons of cultivation the topsoil has completely washed away and the owner must seek a tiny patch elsewhere. As one looks at these farms high up on the steep mountainside, one wonders how a farmer manages to keep his footing there while growing his crop or harvesting it. He wonders too; sometimes he has to even hold onto a rope in order to keep his balance!

Also on the debit side of the ledger, the hacienda has served to perpetuate servility on the part of a large majority of the populace. In Bolivia prior to the 1952 social revolution, it was customary and in accordance with the tradition of lordly master and humble servant for the

---

[13] Haskell P. Wald, *Taxation of Agricultural Land in Underdeveloped Economies* (Cambridge, Mass.: Harvard University Press, 1959), p. 53.

Indians on a hacienda to bend their knees and kiss the hands of the *hacendado*.

The hacienda has done more than perpetuate servility. It has continued to maintain a form of debt slavery that violates the letter and spirit of the constitutions of all the republics. Even within recent years, advertisements have appeared in newspapers telling of a hacienda for sale and specifying how many peons "go along with the place."[14]

Yes, the hacienda is vulnerable on many counts. Frank Tannenbaum asserts:

Perhaps most serious of all is that it fostered and maintained a social ideal in which the hacendado was the representative type—ideally a superior being possessed of broad acres and numerous servants, dominant, domineering, patronizing, and paternal, with nothing between himself and the peon on the plantation. All other elements in society . . . were looked upon with disdain as a necessary affliction that had at best to be suffered. . . . The hacienda system was thus a major influence in preventing either the democratic or economic development of Latin America. If Latin America has fallen behind the United States and Western Europe in industrial expansion, politically stable and democratic government and in the growth of an educational system adequate for the present time and present need, much of the fault lies with the hacienda system.[15]

PIECEMEAL ATTEMPTS AT REFORM

Many Latin American countries, realizing the harm done to their society by the haciendas, have enacted into law a number of changes intended by one means or another to correct the situation. Sometimes a frontal attack was made in an effort to correct the obvious abuses that existed. Thus in Peru, the Law of Yanaconaje, passed in 1947, provided for written contracts, freedom of the *yanacona* to sell his crop in whichever market he preferred and to trade wherever he chose, and a prohibition against any form of unpaid labor expected to be rendered on the place. If the provisions of the law had been enforced, they would have gone far toward transforming the hacienda in Peru into a modern progressive economic institution. However, only lip service has been

---

[14] One does not have to go as far away as Latin America to find peonage in recent years. In 1950, the author purchased a plantation in south Georgia, on which he put in a stint of several years of dirt farming. In order to keep some of the tenant families that "went with the place," he had to pay their alleged indebtedness to the seller. When at the end of the first year of farming the tenants not only completely paid up their debts but also had a little money besides, they could hardly believe that for the first time in their lives they were free men—and could really move if they wanted to.

[15] Frank Tannenbaum, "Toward an Appreciation of Latin America," *The United States and Latin America*, ed. Herbert L. Matthews (The American Assembly) (2d ed.; New York: Columbia University Press, 1963), p. 39.

given the law, with the result that the hacienda in Peru continues with its four-centuries-old attitude of business as usual.

Another possible means of accomplishing needed reform is the imposition of an adequate and effective tax on land. Such a tax would have many advantages over other forms of revenue[16] and would serve to promote the efficient use of land. "We feel that the most effective method of achieving maximum utilization of land is a system of taxation which would penalize poor use of good land," concluded the World Bank Mission to Colombia. "The important thing is that these evaluations be made and the rate of progression determined in such a way as to provide an immediate and positive incentive to correct a present misuse of the best lands of Colombia, which constitute much of the largest part of the national patrimony."[17] In Colombia, as in many of the other nations, a substantial tax on the lands of rich absentee landowners who now graze cattle on very fertile farmland or simply hold on to it as profitable investment would force them either to fully utilize their land by planting it in crops or to sell the land to farmers or to the government for distribution to peasants.

Such proposals for the effective taxation of land, both to obtain needed governmental revenue and to promote efficient use of the land, have been made so often that they sound like a record with the needle continuing to grind away in the same groove.[18] For the oligarchy with their great power have always been able somehow to thwart the levy of such a tax.

Still another means of at least partially remedying the great concentration of ownership in a few hands is for the government itself to undertake a program of purchasing farmlands from the *hacendados* and reselling them in small parcels to eager would-be owners. Many such programs have been instituted in Latin America, usually without any opposition from the *hacendados*. In fact, from the outcome of the programs one

---

[16] For these advantages in detail, see Wald, *op. cit.*, pp. 184–85.

Referring to Chile's programs for stimulating subdivision of the land by taxes on farmland, on real income derived from the land, and on inheritance of property, James Becket concludes: "The tax approach sounds better in theory than it works in actuality. The best and simplest measure would be a stiff real-estate tax. This suffers from the same 'political reality' as does the matter of assessments." James Becket, "Land Reform in Chile," *Journal of Inter-American Studies,* Vol. V, No. 2 (April, 1963), pp. 202–3.

[17] International Bank for Reconstruction and Development, *The Basis of a Development Program for Colombia: Report of a Mission* (Washington, D.C., 1950), pp. 384–86.

[18] A conference on fiscal policy, which may be very fruitful, however, was held at Santiago, Chile, in December, 1962, under the auspices of the Joint Tax Program of the Organization of American States, Inter-American Development Bank, and Economic Commission for Latin America. For a summary of the problems of tax reform considered and the conclusions reached, see *Economic Bulletin for Latin America* (UNESCO), Vol. 8, No. 1 (March, 1963), pp. 89–94.

would suspect that they were the very ones who initiated them. For the land was usually sold to the government at exorbitant prices, which were passed on to the unsuspecting dirt farmers who purchased the small parcels. When they were unable to meet the high payments necessitated by speculative, jacked-up prices, they had to give up their properties, along with all improvements which had been made. The improved property reverted back to the *hacendado*, who gained handsomely by both of the transactions.[19]

Still another method of reform intended to improve agriculture and provide more land for the landless is colonization. Every one of the nations has had at least one colonization scheme of some sort. Sometimes the plan provides for bringing in skilled farmers from abroad to increase the nation's agricultural output and to set up model farms with modern methods and machinery to serve as examples for the rest of the farming populace. Thus in Bolivia, a colony of Okinawans established in the fertile Santa Cruz area operates, in effect, model experimental farms that can be of great help to native farmers. Another plan for colonizing a part of the national farmland with farmers brought in from abroad is the arrangement made by Paraguay with the Japan Overseas Immigration Promotion Company. Under this plan, the company has purchased several large acreages of land and has brought in many Japanese families to farm it.

Most of the colonization projects, however, were designed for quite a different purpose—to provide land for small native farmers by opening up new areas of farmland. Although often boldly conceived, these projects have usually failed to provide land for many new farmers or to perceptibly increase the total agricultural output of the nation. As one studies these projects, the reasons for their failure are soon obvious. Sometimes, the projects are merely sops to the vociferous demands of idealistic visionaries. For the most part, however, the projects are simply diversionary tactics promoted by the landed powers that be for taking the heat off the haciendas and appearing to give a sincere solution to the widespread popular demand for land to be distributed among many small farmers. In effect, most colonization projects merely brush off the region-wide problem of the intense yearning for land felt by tens of millions of farm laborers who sweat out their whole lives toiling on the land, all for the benefit of the affluent *hacendado*.

As diversionary tactics, the colonization projects have achieved a calculated measure of success in forestalling basic changes, even when they were complete flops. In their real impact on the great landless society, however, they have usually been a mere spit in the bucket as far as the big problem of equitable land distribution is concerned.

---

[19] Soule *et al., op. cit.*, pp. 78–79.

THE CRY FOR LAND: ITS REVOLUTIONARY SIGNIFICANCE

As a result of the many harmful effects of the haciendas on society and the inflexible determination of their owners to maintain their vested interests at all costs, a revolutionary ferment exists throughout most of Latin America today. This is the cry for land whose ominous rumblings of discontent are jarring many nations and threatening to turn their societies upside down. Heedless of these warnings, however, the vested interests appear determined to maintain their long privileged positions, scarcely deigning to yield an inch. They are convinced that "it cannot happen here."

But it has happened in several of the countries whose masses got tired of paper constitutions and laws, empty promises of politicians, and diversionary tactics designed to mislead them. To date, three of the republics have had to resort to social revolution to achieve their democratic ideals and give all citizens an equal opportunity under the law.

Mexico, Bolivia, and Cuba have undergone the excruciating ordeal of social revolution in order to achieve a more democratic society. In every one of these nations—and in Guatemala as well, where an abortive social revolution did not succeed—land reform was the primary goal. Agricultural specialists in the United States and elsewhere may differ as to the exact meaning of land reform; does it mean simply providing the peasant with land of his own, or does it mean also furnishing him with many auxiliary services, such as agricultural credit, technical advice, marketing facilities, and many other forms of governmental assistance that would greatly help the new landowner? The concept of land reform may be "a semantically intriguing topic" to the agricultural specialist,[20] but to the simple peasant in Latin America, land reform means *just one thing*—a few acres of ground that he can really call his own.

The cry for land and need for agrarian reform were largely responsible for the revolutionary ferment which completely destroyed the existing social order and culminated in the radical agrarian reform programs of Mexico, Bolivia, and Cuba. Speaking of Bolivia's social revolution, which began in 1952, Robert Alexander says: "Agrarian reform is the cornerstone of the National Revolution. Social justice demanded it. Economic development was impossible without it. Advance toward a democratic society was inconceivable until it had been accomplished. Bolivia would not truly be a modern nation until agrarian reform had been achieved."[21]

---

[20] For the different opinions as to what land reform means, see Roland R. Renne, *Land Economics: Principles, Problems, and Policies in Utilizing Land Resources* (rev. ed.; New York: Harper & Bros., 1958), p. 559; and Thomas F. Carroll, "The Land Reform Issue in Latin America," *Latin American Issues: Essays and Comments,* ed. Albert O. Hirschman (New York: Twentieth Century Fund, 1961), p. 162.

[21] Robert L. Alexander, *The Bolivian National Revolution* (New Brunswick, N.J.: Rutgers University Press, 1958), p. 57.

Courtesy of Yardley and The Baltimore Sun

"He's not the biggest threat to this Hemisphere, señor!"

MEXICO'S REVOLUTIONARY PROGRAM OF LAND REFORM

Breaking up the haciendas and distributing their large acreages to many small farmers were two of the major objectives of Mexico's social revolution, which began in 1910. Seeking to advance these basic goals, the Constitution of 1917 established radically new norms and concepts about land. According to Article 27 of the constitution, the ownership of land is vested originally in the nation, which alone has the power to grant titles to private persons, thereby constituting private property. But in constituting this private property, the nation has the right to impose certain limitations on it in the public interest. And to serve this interest, the large landed estates may be divided up to provide small holdings for many landless farmers.

The idea that the title to all land was originally vested in the nation, which could freely exercise its power of expropriation in order to promote the public interest, was a completely new concept of property. In establishing this norm, Mexico was blazing the trail for other social revolutions; its own revolution was already seven years old when the more renowned Russian Revolution began.

In Mexico's pioneering venture, most of its program was without precedent. The "Mexican Revolution had no prophet and no body of positive theory; it was obliged to formulate its own ideology and its own program as it went along, a halting, fumbling, misdirected series of experiments. . . ."[22]

The lands expropriated from the *hacendados* were utilized in a unique fashion. They were not granted to individuals as private property which they could control and dispose of as they saw fit. Rather, the land was distributed by the government to small agrarian communities known as *ejidos*, whose populations might vary from less than 100 inhabitants to several thousand. The land that the *ejido* possesses may be farmed either as a collective enterprise or as small individual plots.

The collective *ejidos*, which constitute only about 5 percent or less of the total number, are located in the cotton land of the La Laguna region, in the rice-growing country of Lombardia and Nueva Italia, and in the henequen plantations on the Yucatán peninsula. The lands given to these collectives are among the most fertile in the entire nation. Most of these lands formerly belonged to the more progressive *hacendados*, who farmed the properties by means of machinery and modern methods, and accounted for much of the commercial production in the nation. In expropriating these properties, the government wisely decided that they should be collectively owned and farmed in order to retain most of the advantages the units had enjoyed by virtue of their large-scale operations.

In these collectives, a careful daily record is kept of the work that each member of the group performs, and he is paid for this at the end of every week in accordance with an established wage scale.[23] This payment is really not a wage or salary but an advance against his total contribution for the year as a member of the cooperative. At the end of the year, when the books are balanced and closed, he may receive another payment as his share of the profits.

The cooperative *ejidos* have certain distinct advantages and disadvantages as compared with the individually owned plots. On the plus side, they use modern farm machinery, which would be uneconomical on small tracts; utilize the skills and aptitudes of the *ejidatarios* as managers, mechanics, bookkeepers, or tractor operators, rewarding each individual

---

[22] Carleton Beals, *Mexican Maze* (Philadelphia: J. P. Lippincott Co., 1931), p. 45.

[23] For an explanation of the working arrangements made in the *ejidos* in the La Laguna region, see Clarence Senior, *Land Reform and Democracy* (Gainesville: University of Florida Press, 1958), pp. 96–98 and 112–16.

according to his contribution; make possible the rotation and specialization of crops; temporarily withhold products from the market when advisable to obtain a better price; establish a uniform quality for their products, thereby obtaining a better price; develop supplementary enterprises, which can provide employment during slack seasons; and provide various types of social services for their members, including social security for widows and disabled members of the group.

The cooperatives have some recognized disadvantages, too; the most important are the lack of adequately trained local leaders, the lack of discipline on the part of members, and the longing on the part of many members for a plot of their own to work as they please.[24]

In contrast to these cooperative one for all and all for one ventures, approximately 95 percent of the *ejidos* provide for parceling of their total allotment into small plots, which the individual farmer or *ejidatario* cultivates and manages pretty much as his own. He does not really own the land but, rather, has a use title to it. Thus, he can will it to an heir, but he cannot sell, lease, rent, mortgage, or alienate the land in any way. About the only way he can lose the title to his land is by not working it for two years.

Each *ejido* is supervised in general by the Ministry of Agriculture, the Agrarian Department, and the National Ejido Bank, and enjoys a large measure of self-government. Its general assembly, which usually meets once a month, comprises all members of the group and is authorized to discuss and decide various matters of interest to them. The day-to-day management of the business of the *ejido* is vested in an executive committee made up of three members and three alternates elected by the assembly for a term of three years. Still another body, the vigilance committee, is charged with the duty of checking on the activities of the executive committee to see that they conform to the regulations of the Agrarian Code and that the decisions of the general assembly are carried out.[25]

A presidential decree of October 6, 1936, established certain procedures and requirements for obtaining land for *ejidos*. In order to obtain a grant of land from the government, at least 20 persons must join together and apply for it. If their application is successful, they receive a grant amounting to approximately 4 hectares, or 10 acres, per person. In order to be eligible to receive land, a peasant must have worked for at least 6

---

[24] Nathan L. Whetten, *Rural Mexico* (Chicago: University of Chicago Press, 1948), pp. 211–14.

For an assessment of how well the collective *ejidos* of La Laguna have accomplished their purposes, see Senior, *op. cit.*, pp. 185–212.

[25] For a detailed discussion of the organization of the *ejido* and the supervision exercised over it, see Whetten, *op. cit.*, pp. 187–200.

months in the region and must live within 7 kilometers (approximately 4⅓ miles) of the property to be expropriated.

The owner of the land to be expropriated was allowed to retain as inalienable private property a minimum of 150 hectares, or approximately 370 acres. Moreover, he had the privilege of deciding exactly which land he chose to retain. As a result of this provision of the law, the land of an *ejido* was the leavings and usually was divided into various scattered tracts.[26]

As regards payment, the law provided that any property expropriated would be paid for at its assessed valuation plus 10 percent, with payment to be made in the form of agrarian bonds. In shrewdly deciding on the assessed valuation of properties as the basis for payment, the government could buy many a hacienda for virtually a song—confiscation, some would regard it.

But a song was all the property was worth, according to the self-declared valuation of *hacendados* who had lived off the fat of the land for generations but had contributed very little to society in the form of taxes. In the case of the *ejidos* of La Laguna, the owners of expropriated lands were paid for improvements to their property, such as wells and warehouses, in 10 annual installments that totaled 10,566,000 pesos ($2,893,-150). But the owners chose not to take agrarian bonds as payment for the land itself, figuring that by accepting such bonds they would compromise their claims against the government.[27]

Payment for expropriated properties on the basis of assessed valuations was rough on the *hacendados*, but it might have been worse. From the viewpoint of many a peasant, the land returned him by the government was simply a matter of restitution, since it had earlier been stolen from him or his ancestors. Indeed, according to one sympathizer, the gentlemanly nature of the revolution was proved by the fact that no compensation was demanded from the *hacendados* for their long use of the land![28]

Progress in accomplishing land reform, as well as the other revolutionary goals the society aspired to achieve, was dearly paid for. The tremendous cost in fratricidal bloodletting and insensate destruction paralyzed the nation for more than a decade. Says James G. Maddox:

It was a hard, and often bloody, struggle all through the twenties and early thirties. Landlords were recalcitrant; the peons and their representatives were often hoodwinked; sometimes the peons were patient, but generally they were adamant that they receive land; laws were not clear, and were constantly being changed; the courts often sided with the landowners almost regardless of how the laws were drafted. The struggle shifted from battlefields to govern-

---

[26] For maps showing how land of some of the *ejidos* is distributed, see Senior, *op. cit.*, p. 92, and Whetten, *op. cit.*, p. 183.

[27] Senior, *op. cit.*, pp. 93–94.

[28] *Ibid.*, p. 25.

ment offices and courtrooms. Two systems of social values were locked in a death struggle.[29]

Faced with an intransigent opposition and forced to battle for any gain made, however slight, the government was able to make only slow and laborious progress in land reform during most of two decades, as Table 7–2 shows.

TABLE 7–2

LAND DISTRIBUTION IN MEXICO: 1916–64

	Number of Hectares* Distributed (Thousands)		Number of Persons Receiving Land (Thousands)	
Period	Total	Average per Year	Total	Average per Year
1916–34	7,800	410	783	41
1935–40	17,900	2,982	815	136
1941–58	17,800	988	800	44
1959–64	16,000	2,666	760	127
Total ...	59,500	1,214	3,158	65

* One hectare = 2.47 acres.

SOURCE: Compiled from James G. Maddox, "Mexican Agrarian Reform," *American Universities Field Staff Reports Service* (July, 1957); Howard F. Cline, *Mexico: Revolution to Evolution: 1940–1960* (Royal Institute of International Affairs) (New York: Oxford University Press, 1962), pp. 213–14; and state of the union messages of the presidents. Used by permission.

Until Lázaro Cárdenas became president in 1934, the program of land redistribution merely limped along, doing well to keep going at all. There were many reasons for this. Without question the main reason was the determination of landowners to fight their cases in court, using the writ of *amparo* and every other legal weapon at their disposal. A large majority of the disputes were actually decided in favor of the *hacendados*. But whether the court's action was favorable or unfavorable, it delayed execution of the law, often for many years.

In 1929, however, the Supreme Court changed its mind about the agrarian disputes. In rapid-fire order, it rendered five decisions that ruled adversely against the *hacendados*, thereby dealing them a severe blow. These five decisions established a precedent in Mexican judicial practice which was as binding on future actions as a decision handed down by the Supreme Court of the United States.[30] In effect, the Mexican Supreme Court established a self-denying principle that cases involving agrarian reform were not to be subject to judicial review but were to be decided

---

[29] James G. Maddox, "Mexican Agrarian Reform," *American Universities Field Staff Reports Service* (July, 1957), p. 22.

[30] Simpson, *op. cit.*, pp. 118–20.

by administrative discretion without right of appeal to the courts, except for issues of evaluation and compensation.

This action by the court, together with President Cárdenas' zeal for stepping up the tempo of land reform, served to greatly increase the number of properties expropriated and distributed in small acreages to the peasants. In fact, during Cárdenas' term of six years more than twice as many hectares of land were distributed to peasants as during the whole preceding 18-year period. After 1940, however, the distribution of land again proceeded at a slow tempo.

Governmental policy was primarily to blame for this, although there were extenuating circumstances. There was hardly enough land to go around. Mexico is one of the most mountainous countries in the world; a large proportion of its area is either too steep to farm or is intensely hot and arid or stifling and humid. Consequently, only about 10 percent of the land is arable, as compared with more than 50 percent in the United States. The tempo of redistribution was again greatly speeded up under the administration of President López Mateos, 1958–64. Most of the land distributed during these years was in new agricultural areas opened up by the government. Many colonization projects have been promoted in these areas.[31]

During the first two decades of the nation's land reform program, it was a highly controversial issue and constantly under fire.[32] Within the past two decades, however, the *ejidos*, the basis of agrarian reform, have become such a revered part of the revolution as to be politically sacrosanct. In 1954, however, a great debate as to their value erupted when Professor Antonio Díaz Soto y Gama declared that the *ejidal* system of land tenure should be scrapped. All *ejidatarios* except the most primitive Indians should be converted to small landowners, with the right to use and dispose of their land individually as they saw fit. The *ejido* was not working well for the whites or mestizos, he charged, and only the isolated, backward Indians who "need state protection against their own irresponsibility" should have to continue under the *ejido* system. Professor Díaz' criticisms of the *ejido* were a bombshell, for he had been very active in promoting land reform from the early days of the revolution, and had even helped design the *ejidal* system under which the lands distributed were held communally instead of individually.

Among those who sided with Professor Díaz was José Vasconcelos,

---

[31] For several promoted in connection with an experimental plan of regional development, see Thomas T. Poleman, *The Papaloapan Project: Agricultural Development in the Mexican Tropics* (Stanford, Calif.: Stanford University Press, 1964), chap. 7.

[32] For the many criticisms made of the laws enacted and procedures followed in carrying out the agrarian reform, also the changes made to meet these criticisms, see Frank Tannenbaum, *The Mexican Agrarian Revolution* (Washington, D.C.: The Brookings Institution, 1930), chap. x.

former minister of education and a renowned philosopher. "The case is as clear as water," he said. "The *ejido* has been effective politically because it organizes farmers behind the government party, but it has been disastrous economically as thousands of *braceros* who left not only their land but their country have shown."[33]

As these and many other critics realized, the *ejidos*—certainly, those farmed in individual plots—can hardly be regarded as a success from a strictly economic point of view. The hundreds of thousands of small land units have contributed practically nothing to the nation's economy; in fact, they have not even grown sufficient food for the *ejidatarios* themselves. Indeed, many of them have turned out to be simply part-time farmers, depending on work off the place for much of their livelihood. Others migrated annually to the United States for seasonal farm work, entering the country legally or sometimes slipping across the river as wetbacks. Many others have moved to the city, giving up their claims to their parcels.

Proponents of the *ejido* have rushed to its defense. Instead of being abolished, they maintain, it should be strengthened and its deficiencies remedied. The poverty of *ejidatarios* and their low productivity, they contend, are no fault of the system of landholding, but are the result of inadequate credit,[34] lack of education, and too small acreages to farm.

It is the fervent conviction of its partisans that the *ejido* has contributed greatly to Mexico's progress. The guaranteed possession of even a modest acreage afforded the humblest peons a measure of independence and security which they had never enjoyed before and could not otherwise be sure of. Moreover, their participation in the discussions and decisions of the *ejidal* assemblies, as well as possibly their service on one of the two main committees, was grass-roots training in responsible citizenship—a far cry from their servile days under the *hacendados*.[35]

Whatever decisions are made regarding the future of the *ejidos*, the government has for the past two decades followed the policy of continuing to distribute land to many landless farmers, but in such a way as to benefit by its past mistakes. As a means of preventing future *minifundios*, the size of grants made by the government has been considerably increased. In December, 1949, the Agrarian Code was amended to establish a minimum size of 25 acres of irrigated land or approximately 50 acres of other land.

---

[33] *New York Times*, March 19, 1954, p. 11, col. 1.

[34] Some of them are able to obtain loans from official banks at interest rates of 6 to 8 percent per annum; some of them obtain credit from private banks, which charge 12 percent. But more than half of them have to depend for credit on private lenders whose rates run from 120 to 240 percent per year. (Senior, *op. cit.*, p. 29.)

[35] For the participation of the *ejidatarios* in the self-government of La Laguna *ejidos*, see *ibid.*, pp. 86–87, 131–32, and 185–87. For an assessment of the Laguna experiment in terms of the goals of democracy, see pp. 185–212.

Besides aiding small farmers, the Mexican government has also been paying particular attention to the individual landowners who constitute the private agricultural sector of the economy. It is this group that produces most of the foodstuffs for market. To assure them of secure ownership of their properties, changes made in the Agrarian Code in 1949 provided that private holdings would be given legal protection by being granted certificates of "inaffectibility," which exempted them from future expropriation. In accordance with this policy, most of the land now being granted to the landless comes from publicly owned lands instead of expropriated haciendas as formerly. In order to obtain the large amount of land needed for distribution, the government has aggressively promoted colonization in new areas of the nation. As of 1958, there were more than 900 such colonies, farming more than 16 million acres of land. In fact, the nation's program of colonization is unquestionably one of the most successful in Latin America.

Furthermore, while the government has apparently been neglecting the *ejidos* as regards credit and other forms of assistance, which certainly would have helped them, it has by no means neglected agriculture generally. Rather, it has been channeling most of its limited resources to aid the large private farms on which the nation so critically depends. These commercial farms have been helped in every way possible: by a greatly expanded governmental program of irrigation, by whatever assistance was needed in obtaining the most modern equipment, adequate fertilizer, and improved varieties of seed. This policy of aiding and encouraging the private sector has paid off well. Between 1945 and 1957, agricultural production more than doubled while the population grew by only 40 percent.[36]

In the opinion of many, Mexico's revolutionary program of land reform is primarily responsible for the striking progress the nation has made. As James G. Maddox well expresses it:

. . . most of the available evidence points toward the conclusion that Mexico has made giant strides in becoming a united nation, in speeding up economic, social and political development, and in raising the levels of living of at least 95 per cent of her people, *precisely because* of her Revolution. Moreover, land reform was the single most important ingredient of the Mexican Revolution, and it is quite probable that its other component parts, such as a national program of public education, the building of a national highway system, the fostering of an organized labor movement, and heavy emphasis on industrializing the country, would not have gone forward with anything like the speed that they have, if there had not been a redistribution of the land.[37]

---

[36] For the nation's noteworthy progress in agriculture, see Oscar Lewis, "Mexico Since Cárdenas," *Social Change in Latin America Today* (Council on Foreign Relations) (New York: Harper & Bros., 1960), pp. 312–19.

[37] Maddox, *op. cit.*, p. 22.

Regarding the nation's social revolution as a whole, opinion is divided as to whether it has gone too far, has not gone far enough, or has accomplished much and should be proud of its achievements.[38] Frank Brandenburg is among those in the last group. The revolution has accomplished a great deal for the nation, he is convinced. Among the many achievements, it has broken the vicious circle of poverty, abolished the monopolistic hold on the economy by the traditional privileged interests, and tied a higher standard of living for the masses with economic development.[39]

BOLIVIA'S REVOLUTIONARY PROGRAM OF LAND REFORM

Bolivia was the second nation in Latin America to tackle the thorny problem of land reform as one of the goals in a sweeping social revolution. The experiment was indeed a "bold one," observed John Lindberg. "Nevertheless . . . it appears to be the least dogmatic and one of the most flexible attempts so far tried in the solution of basic problems of economic growth under modern conditions. It should be carefully watched by all those who are concerned with the development of substandard areas."[40]

The program of land reform adopted by the new revolutionary regime was a relatively moderate one. The MNR, then in the driver's seat as a result of the April, 1952, revolution, could hardly have undertaken any other kind of program. For it was no tightly knit, cohesive party, but rather a loose coalition of groups with the most divergent interests and goals. The left wing of the party advocated an extreme program of agrarian reform; the right wing, on the other hand, opposed any real reform whatever. Caught in the middle were the moderates, led by such middle-of-the-roaders as President Victor Paz Estenssoro and Vice President Hernán Siles. Split wide open on the issue of what kind of land reform to adopt, the new regime stalled for time. Meanwhile, landless peasants around Cochabamba took matters into their own hands, seizing farms by force and keeping the properties, livestock, and equipment as their own. Goaded into immediate action, the president hastily appointed the Agrarian Reform Commission, giving it only 120 days in which to

[38] These different points of view are given in Stanley Ross (ed.), *Is the Mexican Revolution Dead?* (New York: Alfred A. Knopf, Inc., 1966).

[39] Frank Brandenburg, *The Making of Modern Mexico* (Englewood Cliffs, N.J.: Prentice-Hall, Inc., 1964), pp. 7–8, 79, 208–24.

James W. Wilkie's provocative statistical evaluation of the progress made by the Revolution is given in *The Mexican Revolution: Federal Expenditure and Social Change Since 1910* (Berkeley: University of California Press, 1967).

[40] John Lindberg, "Bolivia: Mines Without Industry," *Current History*, Vol. 22 (March, 1952), p. 149.

study the land problem and draft a comprehensive program of reform.[41]

The Agrarian Reform Law, promulgated on August 2, 1953, was a milestone in the nation's history, and determined much of its later policy and action. "Law Number 03464," says Eduardo Palomo, referring to the new agrarian law, ". . . in its magnitude and historic importance can only compare with the Proclamation of Independence in 1825. Actually it represented the liberation of more than 2 million human beings from a state of semi-slavery."[42]

The moderate tone of Bolivia's land reform is also shown by the method used to obtain land from the large landowners for distribution among the landless peons. For obtaining the needed land, the government decided on a policy of expropriation rather than one of confiscation, which the left wing of the party strongly advocated. Any land taken for redistribution would be paid for at its assessed tax valuation by bonds, which would mature in 25 years and bear interest at 2 percent per annum. The bonds would have two kinds of collateral: a mortgage on the land the peasant received, as well as a lien on his cattle, crops, and farming equipment; and the guarantee of the government that the bonds would be honored.

The program of land redistribution was not intended to be a national giveaway. Payment for lands expropriated would not be a burden on the government, but would be borne by those who received the land. This requirement in itself was a radical departure from earlier programs of land reform in Latin America. A peasant who received land expropriated by the government would pay for it over a maximum period of 25 years. He would make his payments semiannually, and if he missed making four payments, his land would automatically revert to the government, which might then grant it to another individual.

The strict requirements for repayment by grantees of land were a matter of serious concern to some who helped formulate the land reform program. In their opinion, 25 years to pay for land was regarded as a very short period, especially in view of the many serious hazards Bolivian farmers face. Indeed, the stringent provisions for repayment could burden the state with unpaid-for lands, thus defeating the very purpose of the program, since the government might have to decree a moratorium

---

[41] For the decree that created the commission, the general plan for its study of agrarian reform, the report to the president, the text of Decree Law 03464 and Decree Law 03471, which created the National Service of Agrarian Reform, see *Revista Juridica* (Organo Oficial de la Facultad de Derecho, Universidad de Cochabamba), Cochabamba, Bolivia (Imprenta Universitaria, 1953), Año XVII, Nos. 63–66.

[42] "Agrarian Reform," by Eduardo Palomo, Associate Director, Servicio Agrícola Interamericano, in collaboration with Eugene C. Reichard and Clifford Belcher (La Paz, Bolivia, January 20, 1961), p. 2.

to relieve farmers in distress, thereby setting a potentially dangerous precedent.[43]

The ensuing inflation that engulfed Bolivia benefited all debtors, who could easily pay off their debts in the highly inflated currency. To compensate for this trend, the government decreed in the early days of the land reform program that former owners would be paid on the basis of five times the assessed valuation of their property. But as inflation skyrocketed, no further efforts were made to equate the value of expropriated properties with that of the *boliviano*.[44]

Still another feature of the nation's agrarian reform which shows its essentially moderate character is the status of farmlands after redistribution. Charting a course different from that of earlier programs of reform, Bolivia distributed land to the peons to be owned as private property, except in the case of communal land that was restored to the Indians under the age-old pattern of common ownership and control.

Said Dr. Ñuflo Chávez, the minister of rural affairs:

Before drawing up this law, we made a careful study with the help of United Nations experts because we wanted to avoid the mistakes made in Mexico and Guatemala. In Mexico, peasants were given the communal use of land, but not the title to it. In Guatemala the government became the landlord. Under our law the peasant becomes the owner, except where groups of Indians preferred communal ownership.[45]

The various safeguards established by the government to protect the rights of landowners and to assure that any expropriation would be made in accordance with law further attest to the moderate nature of the reform program. Any landowner who wanted to contest the expropriation of his property would have four opportunities to do so: to the topographer who made the survey, and thus possibly have the survey invalidated; to the local agrarian board, as to how much of his land, if any, would be expropriated and how it should be divided; to the National Agrarian Council, to review these same issues; and even to the president himself. Most of the landowners whose properties were affected took full advantage of their right to appeal. As a result, many cases lingered on for years until they were finally disposed of—a painful revolutionary concession to legality.

In its day-to-day operations, the agrarian reform program has shown various weaknesses of administration. Intending to remove the program as

[43] Edmundo Flores, "Land Reform in Bolivia," *Land Economics*, Vol. 30, No. 1 (February, 1954), pp. 122–23.

[44] The failure of the government to give fair compensation for lands expropriated adversely affected the land reform program, creating a climate of distrust between owners and *campesinos*. Arturo Urquidi, *El Feudalismo en América y la Reforma Agraria Boliviana* (Cochabamba, Bolivia: Imprenta Universitaria, 1966), p. 240.

[45] In "Bolivia's Revolutionary Regime: Political and Economic Development," *The World Today*, Vol. XI, No. 4 (April, 1955), p. 172.

far as possible from political pressure, the government early established the *Servicio Agrario*, or Land Reform Organization, and put it under competent professional leadership. Eduardo Arce, who was made head of the body, was a qualified technician and not even a member of the MNR. Moreover, his assistant, Edmundo Flores, was a Mexican and a member of the American Technical Aid Mission.

But as was perhaps inevitable in the revolutionary society, political considerations have influenced the administration of the program. The lands of persons who belonged to the MNR or were sympathetic to it were apt to be regarded as inviolate and exempt from the provisions of the expropriation law, however large their estates might be. But the lands of political opponents of the regime were likely to be expropriated.

"The agrarian reform in Bolivia," charged Alberto Ostria Gutierrez, ". . . had as its primary objective the economic ruin of the adversaries of the regime, whatever the size of the property they owned."[46]

Another hindrance to the effective administration of the program was the severe shortage of trained engineers qualified to accurately delineate the boundaries of acreages to be distributed. And equally as serious was the shortage at both the local and appellate levels of judicial personnel qualified to render competent and impartial decisions on intricate points of law.

Furthermore, local officials were apparently not averse to using their privileged position to engage in petty but profitable boondoggling. Alleged Fausto Beltran and José Fernandez:

The rural councils, interpreting the law to suit their whims, brought insecurity and anarchy into the country. Their trips for the verification of hearings were virtually expeditions of pillage. Aside from special "gifts," the members of the council collected many *"viaticos"* [provisions for a journey] from the *campesinos*. As for verification of the data, one can say that it was incomplete, superficial, and partisan. The council gathered the data during a visit of a few hours in the house of the *hacienda*, changed it to suit themselves in their offices, and usually slanted it so that *campesinos* and their leaders would be swayed by it.[47]

But despite the many obstacles agrarian reform has encountered, the program has moved ahead, as shown by Table 7–3.

During the first several years of the program, when progress was made at a snaillike pace, a nationwide organization was being established to administer the program, and engineering surveys were being made to ascertain boundary lines of parcels to be expropriated and allocated. Since 1957, however, the program has really been rolling. In fact, progress since

---

[46] Alberto Ostria Gutierrez, *The Tragedy of Bolivia: A People Crucified* (New York: Devin-Adair Co., 1958), pp. 169–70.

[47] Fausto Beltran and José Fernández, *¿Donde Va La Reforma Agraria Boliviana?* (La Paz, Bolivia: Talleres Graficos Bolivianos, 1960), p. 61.

TABLE 7-3

INCREASING TEMPO OF LAND REFORM IN BOLIVIA

Calendar Year	Number of Properties Expropriated	Number of Titles Granted	Number of Families Benefiting	Number of Hectares Distributed
1953–54	0	0	0	0
1955	32	3,400	2,809	51,811.33
1956	75	4,463	3,863	47,183.65
1957	281	11,400	8,028	276,395.66
1958	216	9,193	5,709	201,997.71
1959	313	18,380	12,097	320,502.13
1960	904	38,897	22,410	852,770.55
1961	1,186	45,511	28,210	1,167,820.78
1962	1,880	50,129	28,843	1,280,714.59
1963	1,185	47,461	40,641	1,363,590.90
1964	626	18,317	11,295	565,442.77
1965	202	15,600	9,652	388,282.93

SOURCE: *RESUMEN GENERAL:* Numero de Títulos Ejecutoriales, Jefes de Familia, Superficies Individuales y Colectivas Entregadas a Campesinos por Años 1953–1965, Servicio Nacional de Reforma Agraria, Departamento de Estadistica, La Paz, 8 de julio de 1966.

1960 has been at such a fast pace that Raul Alfonso García, president of the National Council of Agrarian Reform, confidently predicted on July 11, 1963, that the entire program of land redistribution and validation of titles would be accomplished within another 10 years.[48] As Table 7–3 shows, the number of properties expropriated and hectares distributed has declined since the peak years, 1962 and 1963, with the decrease in the amount of land eligible for expropriation.

Expropriating the properties of the *latifundios,* outlawed under the 1953 Agrarian Reform Law, provided small tracts of land for many new farmers throughout the nation. But the government realized from the beginning of its land reform program that merely breaking up the *latifundios* would fall far short of satisfying the hunger for land felt by the large mass of citizens. Fortunately, the nation's eastern area, the Oriente, is a large virginal, fertile expanse, which eventually, with considerable labor and expense, can be developed into highly productive farmland. This area is large enough to provide sufficient land for all the *campesinos*—in fact, to support a population several times that of Bolivia's today. Colonization of the area by *campesinos* from the crowded altiplano and upland valleys is recognized to be the real solution to the problem of providing land for all who want it.

In Alto Beni and Chaparé, two of the main colonization projects, as well as in the Oriente generally, Bolivia is boldly pioneering in a program

---

[48] Interview with the author in La Paz, July 11, 1963.

of extensive colonization. "Its experiments in colonization are among the most significant in all Latin America and give probably the best promise of a sound, workable solution to basic agricultural problems."[49]

In Alto Beni, the government plans, finances, and supervises the whole project, and maintains considerable control over all phases of its development. It carefully screens and selects the colonist; provides him with 12 hectares of land, one of which is cleared before his arrival and planted in bananas, rice, corn, and yucca; builds for him a home suitable for his temporary needs; provides a small amount of needed credit; and builds at government expense a school and a hospital to provide education and medical services free of charge.

In return for these generous measures of assistance—the colonists must repay practically all, except the cost of the school and hospital—the government not only exercises general supervision over the project but also specifies what crops are to be raised on 10 of the 12 hectares. The crops specified are those that are well adapted to the area, can usually be grown successfully, and are reasonably sure of a market, especially a foreign one.

In striking contrast to Alto Beni, the colonization of Chaparé is an unplanned, uncontrolled, unsubsidized, haphazard type of resettlement—a sort of wildcat operation. In this resettlement program, the colonists have cleared every hectare of their land, built their homes by their own labor, and completely supported themselves while getting a toehold in farming. They have even built their own schools as well as most of the roads. The national government does not have an office or even a representative in the area. Local self-government is exercised through the half-dozen *sindicatos* or locally organized groups of citizens in the area. Each *sindicato*, at a meeting of all the men who belong to the group, elects a council of from six to eight members, as well as a secretary-general who is recognized to be the group leader. In the absence of national governmental authority, the *sindicato* exercises extensive control, allocating to each family who moves to Chaparé, as well as to each person capable of working the land, a plot of 10 hectares of ground. All the national government does is to send out a technician from La Paz later to see that the requirements of two years' residence and clearing at least a third of the land have been complied with; if so, it grants the individual a title to the property.[50]

After the revolution, agricultural production on the *altiplano* and upland valleys declined by 15 percent, but by 1964 it was up to at least the prerevolution level. For the nation as a whole, production in 1964 was

---

[49] Ñuflo Chávez, "Bolivia's Revolutionary Regime . . ." *op. cit.*, p. 182.

[50] These and newer colonization projects in Bolivia are treated by the author in "Colonization in Bolivia: Progress and Prospects," *Inter-American Economic Affairs,* Vol. 20, No. 4 (Spring, 1967), pp. 39–54.

33 percent above that of 1952, thanks to the great expansion of farming in the Oriente. The output has more than kept up with the growth in population, unusual in Latin America. In fact, Bolivia is confronted with the problem of overproduction of certain crops, as sugar and rice.[51]

Just how much Bolivia has really benefited economically from the revolution is still a matter of controversy. In the judgment of Cornelius H. Zondag, the revolution has unquestionably proved that profound social changes can be brought about relatively rapidly, and some of the conditions necessary for self-sustaining economic growth can be achieved when all the components of society are given the opportunity to participate. In brief, the Bolivian Revolution has accomplished this "in a far more efficient manner than the Mexican Revolution, which was followed by a 20–25 year period of instability and disorder."[52]

The future of the revolution was temporarily clouded when President Paz Estenssoro was overthrown by a *golpe* in November, 1964, and the MNR was supplanted by a new coalition party in the election of July, 1966. However, the new party has accepted the goals of the National Revolution, and is continuing its programs. General René Barrientos, while leader of the junta that succeeded Paz, and later as president, has often declared his strong support of the revolution's goals. Speaking to the *campesinos* in the village of Trinidad Pampa in November, 1965, he made his position clear. "We never cast the Bolivian National Revolution aside; we would never change it . . . We made a Revolution within the Revolution . . . accomplished the restoration of the Revolution."[53]

CUBA'S REVOLUTIONARY PROGRAM OF LAND REFORM

Cuba is the third nation in Latin America to institute and apparently accomplish a comprehensive revolutionary program of land reform.[54] Land ownership and agriculture generally in the small island republic were sadly in need of reform. Approximately half of the total cultivable

---

[51] Cornelius H. Zondag, *The Bolivian Economy, 1952–65: The Revolution and Its Aftermath* (New York: Frederick A. Praeger, Inc., 1966), pp. 144–48.

[52] *Ibid.*, pp. 243–47.

[53] René Barrientos, *Discurso pronunciado . . . en la pequeña localidad de Trinidad-Pampa, el dia 20 de Nōviembre 1965* (La Paz: Presidencia de la Republica, 1965), pp. 6–11.

[54] Guatemala also attempted a broad program of land reform in 1952 under President Jacobo Arbenz. Its chief aim was to expropriate lands not actually used for farming and distribute them among many small holders. A principal target of its reform was the United Fruit Company, from which the government expropriated 160,000 hectares of uncultivated land. When President Arbenz and his communist backers were ousted in June, 1954, very largely by American backing, Guatemala's short-lived land reform went down the drain. For an account of this abortive land reform, see Richard N. Adams, "Social Change in Guatemala and U.S. Policy," *Social Change in Latin America Today, op. cit.*, pp. 266–73.

area was owned by sugar plantations, the largest of which belonged to American companies. Atlantica del Golfo and the Riondo group each owned 500,000 acres; the Cuban-American Sugar Company, 330,000 acres; and the United Fruit Company, 266,000 acres. In addition to owning half of the total cultivable area, the sugar plantations rented another 800,000 acres, thereby giving them control over three fourths of the total farmland of the country.

This top-heavy ownership by large corporations and emphasis on the production of a single crop had many adverse effects on the nation.[55] Only about one half of the total farmland was cultivated, even though farm laborers were unemployed for most of the year and subsisted on a very poor diet, mainly beans and other starchy foods, with little meat, fruits, vegetables, and dairy products. Indeed, so little attention was given to the production of adequate foodstuffs that the nation had to import a large part of what it consumed—almost $100 million worth a year.

A sweeping program of land reform was one of the first goals of the new revolutionary regime. As promulgated in May, 1959, the Agrarian Reform Law made radical changes in the ownership and tenure of farmland. According to the provisions of the law, only citizens were permitted to purchase such land, and no foreigners were allowed to inherit it. No cane plantation could be operated by a corporation unless every stockholder was a Cuban citizen, and even then the plantation could not be connected in any way with the sugar refineries.

The law also restricted the amount of land any single individual or corporation could own for general farming. The maximum was 393 hectares, approximately 980 acres. A more generous limit was set for cane and rice plantations, also cattle ranches. If the government approved their operation, these specialized farms would be allowed to have up to 3,333 acres. However, any farm, whatever its size, could be expropriated if cultivated by tenants or squatters. Under this provision, the government could legally take almost any of the farms in the nation, as the many tobacco growers in Pinar del Rio Province soon realized. Their holdings, although small, were the first to be expropriated, since they were cultivated by sharecroppers.

The law also established a certain "vital minimum" of land a farm family should own in order to have a reasonable level of living. This minimum was 67 acres, which was given to a tenant or squatter without cost. The land he received was often part of the very acreage he cultivated for one of the large corporations or absentee landowners.

---

[55] According to Ramiro Guerra y Sánchez, the *latifundium* strangled the independent farmer, "ruining him economically, lowering his standard of living, and making his existence intolerable." *Sugar and Society in the Caribbean: An Economic History of Cuban Agriculture* (New Haven, Conn.: Yale University Press, 1964), p. 93.

Lands distributed under the Agrarian Reform Law could not be sold or mortgaged and could be inherited by only one member of a family. By setting a generous minimum of 67 acres for a farm holding and stipulating that this could not be subdivided among heirs, the government intended to avoid creation of *minifundios*, which in the past have hampered both Mexico and Bolivia in accomplishing their programs of reform.

The first anniversary of the Agrarian Reform Law was celebrated in May, 1960, with much bravado when approximately a thousand landless *campesinos* were granted land by the government. But the promise of land to the landless—plots they could call their own—soon soured. For the government decided that instead of distributing land individually to the *campesinos* it would set up cooperatives and *granjas del pueblo*, state farms. The term "cooperative" was a misnomer; the enterprise was directly operated by the Institute for Agrarian Reform, with no voice being given to the workers who were merely wage hands.[56] The sugar *latifundia* were kept intact, apparently to ensure efficient production. The large cattle farms were kept intact too, for fear that if the cattle were divided up among small farms, the protein-hungry peasants would immediately eat them and deplete the supply.[57]

Beginning in 1961, there was a sharp decline in the production of food, leading to shortages, rationing, inflation, and considerable social unrest. The shortages occurred largely because the many small farmers responsible for most of the production were determined to sell their products on the open market—really the black market—at the highest price they could get instead of turning them over to the government at much lower fixed prices. When the government clamped down on the peasants, seizing their goods and in some cases confiscating their land, they sowed less and grew less.[58] The shortages were also largely due to the inefficiency of the state farms. Most of the managers had only a third to fifth grade education; in time, 80 percent of them had to be removed.[59]

The volume and quality of virtually all products declined severely—corn, sorghum, peanuts, milk, tobacco, and even matches. Since the matches produced in 1963 were as poor as those of Soviet Russia in 1928, the Cubans jokingly boasted that they had achieved as much in 4 years as the Soviets had in 11![60]

---

[56] Edward Boorstein, *The Economic Transformation of Cuba* (New York: Monthly Review Press, 1968), p. 45.

According to Boris Goldenberg, profit sharing and a voice in the operation did exist in some of the cooperatives. *The Cuban Revolution and Latin America* (New York: Frederick A. Praeger, Inc., 1965), pp. 221–24.

[57] Boorstein, *op. cit.*, p. 45.

[58] Theodore Draper, *Castroism: Theory and Practice* (New York: Frederick A. Praeger, Inc., 1965), pp. 135–37.

[59] *Ibid.*, p. 140.

[60] *Ibid.*, p. 164.

By 1962, the state farms embraced most of the nation's socialized agriculture. The Second Agrarian Reform, proclaimed in November, 1963, liquidated the so-called medium farmers who owned more than 165 acres of land. When their properties were incorporated into state farms, the government controlled approximately three fourths of the nation's farmland. Since 1963, the continuing liquidation of independent farmers is advancing toward the goal of complete collectivization of agriculture— an objective that not even Russia has been able to accomplish.[61]

In instituting the program of land reform, Castro made one decision that was almost catastrophic for the nation. To liberate Cuba from dependence on one crop—on the United States, too—he decided to reduce the acreage devoted to sugar cane and produce a diversity of crops needed domestically. Plowing under thousands of acres of cane and diversifying with other crops resulted in a sharp decline in the output of sugar, which earned most of the nation's foreign exchange. Production declined from 6.7 million tons in 1961 to 4.8 million tons in 1962 and only 3.9 million in 1963. The balance of payments soon became Cuba's main economic problem as well as the key to its sugar policy, its agricultural and industrial policy, and its long-run economic policy in general.[62]

After 1963's small sugar crop and its disastrous consequences, Castro completely reversed his policy. The government then decided on a spectacular increase in the output of sugar—10 million tons by 1970. "We have lost our fear of monoculture," explained the Vice Minister of Economy, Albán Lataste, at the end of 1964. "We are now aware that we can overcome monoculture solely by developing that same monoculture further."[63]

THE PROSPECTS FOR LAND REFORM BY PEACEFUL MEANS

To date, only two nations in Latin America have been able to plan and initiate extensive programs of land reform by legal, peaceable methods. Venezuela and Chile are the nations that enjoy this distinction.

The Agrarian Reform Law promulgated by the Venezuelan government in March, 1960, was the result of long and painstaking deliberation. The nonpartisan commission that spent seven months carefully drafting the law was chosen so as to reflect all shades of public opinion. The Archbishop of Caracas was one of the members, and several well-known communists were also members. Dividing itself into four subcommittees, charged with studying the legal, economic, social, and agrotechnical

---

[61] *Ibid.*, p. 169–73.
[62] Boorstein, *op. cit.*, p. 191.
[63] Draper, *op. cit.*, p. 173.

aspects of land reform, the nonpartisan group reflected, so far as could be determined, the thinking of the entire nation. Thus, the extensive program of land reform the commission proposed was approved by the Congress with only a few modifications.[64]

The new law recognizes the concept of the "social function of landed property." Under this concept, all property must be held and used in such a way as to benefit the whole society. If it is not so owned and used, it may be expropriated, but only under such conditions and in accordance with such procedures as are prescribed by law. Only three kinds of land may be expropriated by the government: lands not being cultivated; farms cultivated by renters, sharecroppers, or day laborers; and lands being used to graze livestock, although they are fertile enough to grow crops.

Judged by any criteria, Venezuela's democratically inaugurated land reform is a moderate program. The law does not contain any provisions limiting the size of farms, discriminating against foreign owners, or breaking up the large estates unless they are unproductive. Moreover, no land can be expropriated except in accordance with due process of law, with the courts passing on the legality of the procedure. Also, any lands taken over are paid for in cash up to a value of $30,000; for properties valued above this amount, payment is made partly in cash and the rest in bonds.

What most of all sold the government's program to the large, powerful landowners was the provision that any lands expropriated will be paid for at their current market value. Approximately 2,500 large farms, totaling some 45 million acres, contain more than half of the farmland in the nation. The unique provision of the law enabling these large owners to sell their surplus properties to the government at current market value has made the land reform program quite acceptable to them, and many have availed themselves of the opportunity for selling their excess lands, which the government is buying and distributing to make many new small landholders.

The reform law also established a scale of graduated land taxes, which, in effect, tells landowners, "you must either cultivate your properties intensively and efficiently or sell them to the government."

Venezuela has just cause to be proud of its unique, peacefully instituted program of land reform. The reform law was "made for Venezuela," said Dr. Victor Jimínes Landinez, minister of agriculture. "The agrarian problems of Venezuela should not be guided by norms in other countries. The Law is neither leftist nor rightist—it is simply just. The only limit to property is the limit of social function; nobody will be

---

[64] For a full account of the deliberations of the four subcommittees, see Venezuela, Ministerio de Agricultura y Cria; Comisión de Reforma Agraria, *Reforma agraria*, Vols. I–IV (Caracas, 1959).

permitted to maintain land idle or uncultivated when others need it." The aim of the bill was "to put land in the hands of those who work it."[65]

Adequately financed by revenues from its rich oil properties, Venezuela's ambitious program of land reform was originally calculated to benefit approximately 300,000 rural families within 10 years. Since this figure included practically all the landless families in Venezuela, the government by carrying out its scheduled program of dispersed ownership would be able to provide land to all farmers who wanted it.

During 1960 the government came close to achieving its ambitious goal, as Table 7–4 shows.

TABLE 7-4

DISTRIBUTION OF LAND IN VENEZUELA: 1959–62

Year	Number of Properties Acquired	Number of Families Benefited	Number of Hectares Granted
1959	53	5,874	460,769
1960	308	25,221	748,933
1961	141	11,074	156,089
1962	135	14,603	167,283
Total	637	56,772	1,533,074

SOURCES: *Reforma Agraria y Desarrollo Agropecuario en Venezuela: 1959–63* (Ministerio de Agricultura y Cría) (Caracas, 10 al 14 de junio de 1963), p. 7; and *Instituto Agrario Nacional: Informe Anual, 1962* (Caracas, 1963), p. 3.

In 1961 and 1962, as the above figures show, the government fell considerably short of its planned pace, thanks largely to the violence and subversion that convulsed the nation prior to the December, 1963, election—a calculated Castroite campaign of destruction and terror intended to paralyze the nation and prevent by whatever means necessary the democratic, constitutional transfer of authority from one popularly elected administration to another.[66] But the program has continued to move ahead; by mid-1966, 124,154 families received approximately 2,569,000 hectares of land. John Duncan Powell concludes:

Whether the agrarian revolution accomplished in rural Venezuela will be permanent remains to be seen. And if, under almost ideal historic circumstances,

---

[65] *New York Times*, July 24, 1959, p. 7, col. 1.

[66] For the organization of the nation's National Agrarian Institute, see *El Instituto Agrario Nacional y Su Organización* (Caracas: Febrero, 1962). And for its well-heeled budget and accounting of expenditures, see *Instituto Agrario Nacional: Balance General*, 31 de Diciembre de 1962 (Caracas, 1963).

A good background account of the nation's hangover from dictatorship, the critical need of land reform, and the bold program advocated by Democratic Action is given by Ramón Quijada, *Reforma Agraria en Venezuela* (Caracas: Editorial Arte, Mayo de 1963).

the most noted democratic agrarian reform in Latin America fails in its ultimate purpose of liberating the peasant masses from the tyranny of the land, what hope is there for the peasants in the rest of the hemisphere?[67]

Another comprehensive program of land reform by peaceful means was that initiated in July, 1967, by Chile under the statesmanly perseverance of President Eduardo Frei.[68] In his 1964 campaign for the presidency, Frei stressed that land reform would be one of the main goals of his administration, both to increase agricultural output and to distribute the land more equitably. Unlike the many politicians who have been elected largely on such a promise, Frei meant what he pledged; for almost three years, he doggedly strove to get his program of land reform adopted, bucking powerful and vehement opposition, much of it within his own Christian Democratic Party.

In signing the bill before a jubilant crowd of 12,000, President Frei said: "This reform is made to bring an end to the disequilibrium in the Chilean farmlands, where there has been so much neglect that in some cases it was feudal. There was neglect of the man and also of the land, and because of this, production was below one-half of what it should have been in a number of properties."

Under Chile's program, regarded by many as the most ambitious undertaken to date in Latin America, the Agrarian Reform Corporation is authorized to expropriate farmlands now privately owned; approximately 15 million acres of private land will be taken within 5 years and distributed to landless *campesinos*. Anyone who owns more than one basic unit of land will be subject to expropriation, unless his operation is very productive and he is treating his workers well. The size of the basic unit depends on the productivity of the land; it is 200 acres in the fertile Central Valley of the nation. Land expropriated will be paid for at its present market value, with 10 percent paid down and the balance in 30-year government bonds.

To prevent the usual drop in production after expropriation, the Agrarian Reform Corporation will administer the land for two or three years, while the resident *campesinos* farm it on a collective basis under the guidance of the Reform Corporation's technicians and the former landowner. At the end of the period, the land will be divided among the peasants in approximately equal plots, averaging 25 acres of good farmland.[69]

---

[67] John Duncan Powell, "Agrarian Reform or Agrarian Revolution in Venezuela?" *Reform and Revolution*, ed. Arpad von Lazar and Robert R. Kaufman (Boston: Allyn and Bacon, Inc., 1969), p. 290.

[68] The nation's several earlier experiments with reform projects—communal, individualistic, and mixed—are given in William C. Thiesenhusen, *Chile's Experiments in Agrarian Reform* (Land Economics Monograph) (Madison: University of Wisconsin Press, 1966), chaps. 3–6.

[69] This summary of Chile's program is given in *The New York Times*, July 17, 1967, p. 14, cols. 3–6.

Surveying the whole Latin American situation realistically, just what are the chances of accomplishing much-needed reforms by peaceful methods? Frankly, they are very slim, one studying the problem is forced to conclude.

While Chile and Venezuela deserve much credit for conceiving and instituting comprehensive programs of land reform by peaceful, constitutional means, their reforms can hardly be regarded as pilot programs that will set an example for other Latin American nations, as some tend to regard them.[70] With its fabulously productive oil lands, Venezuela is filthy rich compared with the other nations of Latin America. With that sort of bankroll to rely on, just about any nation, if it chose, could institute a peaceful, acceptable, constitutional program of reform. Moreover, such statesmanly leaders as those in Venezuela and in Chile are rare in Latin America. The widespread regression, beginning in 1961, to conservatively minded military dictators determined to put a brake on social change bodes ill for land reform. Moreover, the hacienda system itself seems impervious to efforts to change it.

Frank Tannenbaum reasons:

The hacienda system has in fact reached an impasse from which it cannot escape. The pressure for economic, political, and social change is building up so rapidly that the system cannot avoid the challenge to its traditional ways, and it cannot meet it. *The hacienda has no built-in device that will allow for reform of the system*, that will enable it to transform itself so as to survive and propitiate the new ways that are undermining a traditional and age-old form of social organization.[71]

Despite the gravity of the situation and the widely recognized need for reform, the *hacendados* have been so inflexible in their thinking and in their unwillingness to concede even an inch that there has been scarcely a semblance of a meeting of minds between them and the landless mass. Today, just as centuries ago, the basic problem still is men without land and land without men.

Instead of facing the problem squarely and attempting to arrive at genuine solutions, the *hacendados* continue to fiddle while peasant resentment burns fiercely. Either unaware of the intensity of this resentment or determined, as we noted earlier, to hold down the safety valve of the boiler and take a chance on its bursting, the big landowners continue to rely on diversionary tactics. While peons cry for land, politicians appoint still more committees "to study the problem" and dangle the bait of tax reform or colonization before the peons as adequate to solve the agrarian ills of the society.

---

[70] In the case of Venezuela with its going program, see Carroll, *op. cit.,* p. 188.

[71] Frank Tannenbaum, "Toward an Appreciation of Latin America," *The United States and Latin America, op. cit.,* p. 40.

In Latin America, as elsewhere, "undoubtedly everyone would be happier," says Clarence Senior, "if land could be distributed on a Sunday afternoon with the ceremonies followed by pretzels and beer, or hot dogs and soda pop, or *tortillas* and *pulque,* or rice cakes and *sake.*"[72] The *hacendados* with their recalcitrant attitude may have some such idealized concept of how land reform may operate. But the numerous members of the poverty-stricken, landless mass have no such illusions. From one end of Latin America to the other, they are showing their determination to take matters into their own hands.

In country after country, masses of peasants led by fiery leaders have moved onto the large estates to take them over for their own use. These tactics have become so prevalent in the whole region that members of the invading horde are popularly known as "parachuters," since they seemingly swarm out of nowhere by the hundreds, sometimes thousands.

Sometimes such a peasant invasion is so serious that the government hastily purchases the property and distributes it among the invaders, hoping thereby to temporarily relieve the explosive situation. Far more often, however, determined to dislodge the would-be landowners, the government uses whatever force is necessary for this purpose, whether heavily armed members of the civilian police or units of the nation's armed forces. The frequent invasions of private property often involve bloodshed and sometimes heavy loss of life. Any one of them could easily trigger another revolutionary program of land reform, even another social revolution—such as the Mexican, Bolivian, or Cuban—which completely remakes the society.

For an increasing number of the desperate landless mass are becoming convinced, as one of Zapata's followers stirringly expressed it, that *it is better to die on your feet than to live on your knees.*

SUGGESTED READINGS

Alexander, Robert J. *The Bolivian National Revolution,* chaps. 4 and 5. New Brunswick, N.J.: Rutgers University Press, 1958.

———. *The Venezuelan Democratic Revolution: A Profile of the Regime of Rómulo Betancourt,* chaps. 12–14. New Brunswick, N.J.: Rutgers University Press, 1964.

Biesanz, John, and Biesanz, Mavis. *The People of Panama,* pp. 119–36. New York: Columbia University Press, 1955.

Carroll, Thomas F. "The Land Reform Issue in Latin America," *Latin American Issues: Essays and Comments* (ed. Albert O. Hirschman), pp. 161–96. New York: Twentieth Century Fund, 1961.

---

[72] Senior, *op. cit.,* p. 6.

Cline, Howard F. *Mexico: Revolution to Evolution: 1940–1960,* chaps. xxii and xxviii. Royal Institute of International Affairs. New York: Oxford University Press, 1962.

Cumberland, Charles C. *The Meaning of the Mexican Revolution.* Boston: D.C. Heath & Co., 1967.

Draper, Theodore. *Castroism: Theory and Practice,* pp. 135–73. New York: Frederick A. Praeger, Inc., 1965.

Edelmann, Alexander T. "Colonization in Bolivia: Progress and Prospects," *Inter-American Economic Affairs,* pp. 39–54. Vol. 20, No. 4 (Spring 1967).

Fals-Borda, Orlando. *Peasant Society in the Colombian Andes: A Sociological Study of Saucío,* pp. 64–82, 114–31, and 172–73. Gainesville: University of Florida Press, 1957.

Ford, Thomas R. *Man and Land in Peru.* Gainesville: University of Florida Press, 1955.

Gruening, Ernest. *Mexico and Its Heritage,* pp. 111–67. New York: D. Appleton-Century Co., Inc., 1934.

Guerra y Sánchez, Ramiro, *Sugar and Society in the Caribbean: An Economic History of Cuban Agriculture.* New Haven, Conn.: Yale University Press, 1964.

Gutierrez, Alberto Ostria. *The Tragedy of Bolivia: A People Crucified,* pp. 158–73. New York: Devin-Adair Co., 1958.

Holly, Marc Aurele. *Agriculture in Haiti,* with Special Reference to Rural Economy and Agricultural Education. New York: Vantage Press, Inc., 1955.

Holmberg, Allan R. "Changing Community Attitudes and Values in Peru: A Case Study in Guided Change," *Social Change in Latin America Today,* pp. 63–105. Council on Foreign Relations. New York: Harper & Bros., 1960.

Horowitz, Irving Louis. *Revolution in Brazil: Politics and Society in a Developing Nation,* chaps. 2 and 3. New York: E. P. Dutton & Co., Inc., 1964.

Lazar, Arpad von, and Kaufman, Robert R. (eds.). *Reform and Revolution: Readings in Latin American Politics,* pp. 267–90. Boston: Allyn and Bacon, Inc., 1969.

Leonard, Olen E. *Bolivia: Land, People and Institutions,* chaps. vii and viii. Washington, D.C.: The Scarecrow Press, Inc., 1951.

Maddox, James G. "Mexican Agrarian Reform," *American Universities Field Staff Reports Service* (July, 1957).

May, Stacy (dir.) *et al. Costa Rica: A Study in Economic Development,* chaps. 3 and 4. New York: Twentieth Century Fund, 1952.

McBride, George McCutchen. *Chile: Land and Society.* American Geographical Society Research Series, No. 19. New York, 1936.

Nelson, Lowry, *Rural Cuba,* chaps. v–vii and xiii. Mineapolis: University of Minnesota Press, 1950.

Parsons, Kenneth H.; Penn, Raymond J.; and Raup, Philip M. (eds.). *Proceedings of the International Conference on Land Tenure and Related*

Problems in World Agriculture, Madison, 1951. Madison: University of Wisconsin Press, 1956.

Patch, Richard W. "Bolivia's Developing Interior," *American Universities Field Staff Reports Service.* West Coast South American Series, Vol. IX, No. 3, Bolivia (March, 1962).

Poleman, Thomas T. *The Papaloapan Project: Agricultural Development in the Mexican Tropics.* Stanford, Calif.: Stanford University Press, 1964.

Ross, Stanley R. (ed.). *Is the Mexican Revolution Dead?* New York: Alfred A. Knopf, Inc., 1966.

Senior, Clarence. *Land Reform and Democracy.* Gainesville: University of Florida Press, 1958.

Simpson, Eyler N. *The Ejido: Mexico's Way Out.* Chapel Hill: University of North Carolina Press, 1937.

Smith, T. Lynn (ed.). *Agrarian Reform in Latin America.* New York: Alfred A. Knopf, Inc., 1965.

———. *Brazil: People and Institutions,* Part IV. Rev. ed. Baton Rouge: Louisiana State University Press, 1963.

———. *Colombia: Social Structure and the Process of Development,* chaps. 2–6. Gainesville: University of Florida Press, 1967.

Stokes, William S. *Latin American Politics,* chap. 9. New York: Thomas Y. Crowell Co., 1959.

Tannenbaum, Frank. *The Mexican Agrarian Revolution.* Washington, D.C.: The Brookings Institution, 1930.

———. *Mexico: The Struggle for Peace and Bread,* chaps. 6 and 9. New York: Alfred A. Knopf, Inc., 1954.

———. *Peace by Revolution: An Interpretation of Mexico,* chap. 14. New York: Columbia University Press, 1933.

Thiesenhusen, William C. *Chile's Experiments in Agrarian Reform.* Land Economics Monograph No. 1. Madison: University of Wisconsin Press, 1966.

Weil, Felix J. *Argentine Riddle,* chap. iii and Appendix A. Latin American Economic Institute. New York: John Day Co., 1944.

Whetten, Nathan L. *Guatemala: The Land and the People,* chaps. 7 and 8. Caribbean Series, 4. New Haven, Conn.: Yale University Press, 1961.

———. *Rural Mexico,* Part II, chaps. iv-xi. Chicago: University of Chicago Press, 1948.

Wilgus, A. Curtis (ed.). *The Caribbean: Venezuelan Development, A Case History,* Part V. Caribbean Conference Series, One, Vol. XIII. Gainesville: University of Florida Press, 1963.

Wolf, Eric R. *Sons of the Shaking Earth,* chap. x. Chicago: University of Chicago Press, 1959.

Young, Maurice de. *Man and Land in the Haitian Economy.* Inter-American Studies, Monograph Series No. 3. Gainesville: University of Florida Press, 1958.

Zondag, Cornelius H. *The Bolivian Economy, 1952–65: The Revolution and Its Aftermath,* chaps. 12, 13. New York: Frederick A. Praeger, Inc., 1966.

8

INDUSTRY:

The Revolution of Rising Expectations

Industrialization and technological progress have been characteristic features of the Western way of life for more than a century and a half. But not all the nations in the region have enjoyed the benefits—or suffered the afflictions—of the Industrial Revolution. Indeed, the revolution was quite late in coming to Latin America. Since its arrival, however, its influence has been momentous; there, as elsewhere, it is reshaping the society and reorienting its values and goals.

THE DRIVE FOR INDUSTRIAL DEVELOPMENT: BACKGROUND AND MOTIVATIONS

It was not until the last quarter of the 19th century that Latin America really felt the impact of the industrial revolution. But as immigrants poured in, together with foreign investors and traders, technological advances and new ways of thinking in manufacturing, transportation, and communications were brought into the region. During this first period of industrialization, many enterprises were established to manufacture or process commodities. There were cotton gins and cottonseed oil mills, flour mills and grain elevators, sugar mills and refineries, canneries for fruits and vegetables, laboratories for producing pharmaceuticals, plants for bottling carbonated soft drinks, and breweries that utilized the potent grain and fruit of the vine. The large hat and shoe factories of São Paulo, Brazil, made it renowned as the Pittsburgh of South America. There were even some small iron foundries and steel fabricating plants.[1]

---

[1] Harry Stark, *Social and Economic Frontiers in Latin America* (2d ed.; Dubuque, Ia.: Wm. C. Brown Co., 1963), p. 250.

Although Latin America was not directly involved in World War I, the war had a decided impact there as on the rest of the international economy. The war and its aftermath disrupted international trade and changed the whole complexion and international investment. As a result of the war, Latin America, which had long been closely tied to Europe by friendly bonds of trade and investment, was pretty much on its own. "In a very real sense Latin America had lost its moorings," concluded Miron Burgin. "It could no longer count upon Europe to maintain intact the order in which Latin America had grown and prospered, and had felt secure. In the aftermath of World War I Latin America was forced to mobilize all its moral and material resources in order to adjust itself to a new, tortuously emerging world environment."[2] The deprivation of needed imports during the four years of conflict and the necessity later of having to adjust to alien patterns of trade were great stimuli to the development of a variety of industries throughout the region.

The depression of the 1930's was another big stimulus to industrialization. As nation after nation in the region felt its blighting effects and futilely tried to cope with it by restricting imports by such devices as quotas, licenses, clearing agreements, and higher tariffs, the international trade that was the economic lifeblood of Latin America shrank to a fraction of its former volume. In some of the nations the drop in exports was of fantastic proportions. From 1929 to 1932, Chile's exports dropped 88 percent; during those years her foreign trade suffered more than that of any other nation in the world. During the same period, Bolivia's exports fell 80 percent; Cuba's, 70 percent; and those of the 20 republics as a whole, 65 percent.[3]

The nations suffered acutely from the inability to export their products and import the goods they needed. Indeed, the depression confirmed and strengthened the conviction of many Latin Americans that their economic salvation lay in self-sufficiency, which could be achieved only by establishment of new industries and diversification of production to take care of the needs of the domestic market. In the United States, too, where the high Smoot-Hawley tariff greatly aggravated and probably prolonged the depression, there were many who advocated a similar course of action.[4]

World War II and the ensuing cold war were other strong incentives to the development of industrialization in the region. During World War II, the manufacturer or would-be manufacturer of any commodity from diapers to doughnuts could operate freely without fear of foreign com-

---

[2] Miron Burgin, "New Fields of Research in Latin American Studies," *Responsible Freedom in the Americas,* ed. Angel del Rio (Garden City, N.Y.: Doubleday & Co., Inc., 1955), p. 189.

[3] Sanford A. Mosk, *Industrial Revolution in Mexico* (Berkeley: University of California Press, 1954), p. 11.

[4] One of these was Charles Beard, whose *Open Door at Home* would make the United States economically self-sufficient and let the rest of the world go by.

petition. For the United States, one of Latin America's main markets and also the source of most of its imports, was now devoting its productive capacity to manufacturing weapons of war and taking care of the needs of its own civilian population. Engaged in a titantic struggle on two fronts, the nation had very little in the way of manufactured goods that could be spared for Latin America. England and the other European nations were in the same boat. Moreover, much of the small part that could be diverted from the war effort to the needs of the region was sunk by Hitler's submarines which prowled the eastern seaboard, sinking merchant ships at will.

In addition to affording the industrialist a heyday for establishing or expanding an enterprise, the war favored him in other ways. Whatever surplus the region produced during and for several years after the conflict and could sell abroad was worth its weight in gold; the high price it brought on the world market afforded a measure of prosperity that some of the nations had never enjoyed before.

World War I, the Depression, and World War II were strong environmental influences prodding the nations to industrialize. The deeply felt aspirations of the population have also been spurs in the same direction. The industrialized nations enjoy a much higher standard of living, Latin Americans were convinced after seeing movies from Hollywood, watching television, or seeing tourists from abroad with their obvious affluence. They, too, would like to enjoy the same advantages. In fact, the revolution of rising expectations is as strongly felt in Latin America as in any other part of the world.

Another strong motivation for industrialization is the determination of the nations to free themselves from economic colonialism. Every one of them has the essential attributes of a colonial economy and is quite dependent upon foreign trade and investment. In most of them, the economy is based largely on the production of one or two staple commodities, such as bananas in Honduras, coffee in Brazil and Colombia, copper and nitrates in Chile, and oil in Venezuela.

Such reliance on one or several commodities, most of which are exported rather than consumed at home, places the nations in a very disadvantageous position. The prices of the commodities fluctuate widely and are often severely depressed by factors in the international market completely beyond the control of the producing states. Russia's dumping of tin on the market in 1958, causing a sharp decline in its price, was a severe blow to Bolivia, whose economy is dependent on foreign exchange derived from the sale of the metal. To compound the Latin American's grievances, the prices he receives for his products may hit rock bottom; yet, the prices he must pay for the machines, tools, and consumer goods he imports remain the same or, if they change, climb higher.

Still another motivation for industrializing is the impact on the region of the population explosion. The population is increasing at an annual rate of 2.8 percent or more. Every year there are millions of new mouths to feed, taxing to the fullest the ability of the agricultural sector to produce the food needed by the proliferating population. Every year millions of new jobs must be created for the region's rapidly increasing number of young men and women, challenging to the fullest the ability of industry and other parts of the society to measure up to their responsibilities.

Still another incentive for industrializing is the intense feeling of nationalism that pervades Latin America. Whether in Argentina or Chile, Panama or Guatemala, there is an increasing sense of pride in the nation and confidence in what it stands for and hopes to achieve. "Made in Germany or Japan" stamped on the bottom of a percolator or rear of a washing machine may indicate high quality as well as where it was produced. However, it suggests to the Latin American his inability to produce this product, and reminds him of his condition of economic colonialism. What warms his heart is to see "Made in Argentina" or whatever his nation is. The growing feeling of national pride has played a part in the establishment of many an industry.

Industrialization is an accepted goal in most of the nations. The new moneyed elite consisting of industrialists, entrepreneurs, businessmen, and bankers, many of whom have made fortunes and are recognized as belonging to the upper class, are staunch supporters who believe that industrialization will advance the nation's interests and their own. Members of the middle class for the most part have the same attitude; the realization of their ambitions for an education and a higher standard of living depend mainly on progressive economic development. Labor leaders and their many union members heartily favor industrialization, realizing how much they gain from each new industry established.

But other groups have been far from enthusiastic about industrialization and its effects on society; in fact, for one reason or another they are covertly or openly opposed to it. The large landowners, primarily interested in a plentiful supply of cheap labor, are wary of industrialization, fearing that it may siphon off their labor and force them to pay higher wages. In Venezuela, landowners complained bitterly about the many effects of the petroleum industry on their labor. One complaint was that instead of paying their farmhands once a month as formerly, they now had to pay them every week, as the oil companies did their labor. Consequently, their hands now went on a binge once a week instead of just once a month as formerly.[5]

The large landowners have another gripe against industrialization. The social infrastructure of an industrial society means more schools, libraries,

---

[5] Rodolfo Luzardo, "Farming and Ranching vs. Petroleum," *Venezuela: Business and Finances* (Englewood Cliffs, N.J.: Prentice-Hall, Inc., 1957), chap. 15.

hospitals, and roads, all of which represent a considerable cost, much of which they would have to bear as wealthy members of society.

While the landed oligarchy usually does not openly oppose industrialization and technological progress, intellectuals do not hesitate to do so. In most underdeveloped nations, these individuals have played a major role in promoting the industrial revolution and in winning popular acceptance for it.[6] But not in Latin America. There, values of Hispanic culture are basically antagonistic to the technology that is the very foundation of industrialization. Indeed, the *pensadores* look down their long Hispanic noses at technology and all the values and activities related to it. They decry the very thought of a technical education, necessary for training the many administrators, engineers, scientists, and specialized experts who are needed in an industrial society. Moreover, they are very critical of mechanization, specialization, and concern with profits, all of which, in their opinion, destroy artistic appreciation and creativity, dehumanize the individual, and make him a money-minded member of a materialistic society.

PROGRESS MADE IN INDUSTRIAL DEVELOPMENT

The economic development of Latin America has been one of the most colorful aspects of its colorful history. In Brazil:

. . . the history of [the] economy is a sensational record with amazing fluctuations. It is a history of the appearance and disappearance of entire industries. Its leitmotif is the perpetual change of the "kings." Sugar, cacao, gold, tobacco, cotton, rubber, coffee—each of these products has its place in the history of the country and was at one time the axis of the national (or state) economy, lending to Brazil a temporary world supremacy.[7]

In measuring economic development in Latin America, as elsewhere, three of the indexes frequently used are the GNP (gross national product) per capita, consumption of electricity per capita, and amount of steel produced.[8] On the basis of these indexes, some of the nations are making good progress but others are not faring so well.

---

[6] John H. Kautsky (ed.), *Political Change in Underdeveloped Countries: Nationalism and Communism* (New York: John Wiley & Sons, Inc., 1962), pp. 24 and 44–49.

[7] J. F. Normano, *Brazil: A Study of Economic Types* (Chapel Hill: University of North Carolina Press, 1935), p. 18. In chap. 2, "The Perpetual Change of Leading Products," the author gives a graphic account of the ups and downs—mostly downs—of the products that have been virtually a history of Brazil.

[8] Other indexes besides these are: number of doctors per 1,000 inhabitants; newspaper circulation, also number of radios, telephones, and vehicles in proportion to population; percent of total population in cities over a certain size; and percent of literacy and ratio of enrollment in primary schools to population of school age. Everett E. Hagen, "A Framework for Analyzing Economic and Political Change," *Development of the Emerging Countries: An Agenda for Research* (Washington, D.C.: Brookings Institution, 1962), p. 5.

In the years following World War II, the prosperity enjoyed by many of the nations was very favorable for economic development. The GNP increased at the rate of about 4.7 percent annually—a rate maintained through the period 1955–59, as Table 8–1 shows. However, during the

TABLE 8–1

PERCENTAGE GROWTH OF POPULATION AND GROSS NATIONAL PRODUCT (1955-64)

| | Population Growth* | | Gross National Product | | | |
| | | | Overall Growth† | | Growth per Capita | |
	1955–59	1960–64	1955–59	1960–64	1955–59	1960–64
Latin America (except Cuba) ..	2.9	2.9	4.7	4.0	1.8	1.1
Uruguay	1.2	1.2	0.3	0.1	—0.9	—1.2
Argentina	1.9	1.8	2.7	1.2	0.8	—0.6
Bolivia	2.2	2.3	—0.2	5.0	—2.4	2.7
Chile	2.4	2.4	3.8	4.0	1.4	1.6
Paraguay	2.5	2.5	2.4	3.6	—0.1	1.1
Peru	2.6	2.7	4.7	6.4	2.1	3.7
Colombia	2.8	2.8	5.3	5.3	2.5	2.5
Panama	2.7	2.8	5.3	5.3	2.5	2.5
Guatemala	2.9	2.9	5.1	5.4	2.2	2.5
Brazil	3.1	3.0	5.8	3.9	2.7	0.8
Ecuador	3.2	3.1	4.5	3.7	1.3	0.5
El Salvador	3.0	3.2	3.0	8.3	0.0	5.1
Mexico	3.3	3.4	6.2	6.2	2.9	2.8
Honduras	3.3	3.5	4.8	4.3	1.5	0.8
Venezuela	3.9	3.5	6.5	5.3	2.5	1.7
Nicaragua	3.5	3.5	1.7	7.3	—1.8	3.8
Costa Rica	4.2	4.0	4.9	3.3	0.8	—0.7

* Based on estimates published by the *Bulletin of Statistics of* CEPAL, Vol. I, No. 1.

† CEPAL, *Economic Study* 1964, Table 1–2.

SOURCE: Octavio Cabello, "Housing, Population Growth, and Economic Development," *Population Dilemma in Latin America*, eds. J. Mayone Stycos and Jorge Arias (Washington, D.C.: Potomac Books, Inc., 1966), p. 107.

following 5 years the annual rate of growth declined to 4 percent. This decline in GNP, together with the high annual rate of population growth, also shown on the table, has resulted in a decline of the GNP per capita from 1.8 percent in 1955–59 to only 1.1 in 1960–64. While several of the nations—especially Mexico,[9] Peru, Nicaragua, and El Salvador—had high

---

[9] For a summary of Mexico's steady, healthy growth, see Gustavo Romero Kolbeck, *Economic Development Issues, Latin America* (Committee for Economic Development, Supplementary Paper No. 21, August, 1967), pp. 173–209: and *Mexico's Recent Economic Growth,* trans. Marjory Urquidi (Essays) (Austin: University of Texas Press, 1967).

The Mexican Revolution has sacrificed agriculture to industry and the countryside to the city, contends Moisés González Navarro. The Mexican Revolution is based on the capitalist pattern except for the *ejido*. *Obstacles to Change in Latin America*, ed. Claudio Veliz (New York: Oxford University Press, 1965), p. 225.

rates of per capita growth, others, including Argentina and Brazil—two of the most important industrial nations of the regions—were either barely keeping up with the increase in population or falling behind.

This disappointing performance in most of the nations has occurred despite the assistance of the Alliance for Progress, whose goal is to help the nations attain a GNP per capita annual increase of 2.5 percent or more. The slowdown in the rate of economic growth in the face of the low standard of living and the high increase in population is the number one problem in Latin America, in the opinion of Dr. Raúl Prebisch, one of its leading economists.[10]

In the production of electrical energy,[11] another index of economic development, the region is rapidly moving ahead. In 1965, it generated more than 94 billion kilowatt hours of electric energy—an increase of 27 percent over that generated in 1962. Experts predict that by 1970 the region will need 200 billion KWTs—more than triple the production of 1959. The necessary expansion would require a gross investment of $13 billion.[12]

The increase in production in recent years is shown by Table 8–2, which gives statistics for representative states.

Some of the nations rely mainly on hydroelectric power; among these are Brazil, Chile, Colombia, and Peru. Others rely mainly or almost entirely on coal or oil; nations in this group include Argentina, Mexico, and Venezuela.

The consumption of electric power per capita is shown in Figure 8–1. Consumption varies from a high of approximately 910 kilowatt hours per capita for Venezuelans to 24 for the Haitians, who wash their clothes by hand and go to bed with the chickens. In addition to hydroelectric power, nuclear reactors may be feasible in large interconnected systems, such as the São Paulo–Rio de Janeiro region in Brazil or the Buenos Aires seaboard area in Argentina. They may also be useful in smaller systems that serve industrial complexes situated in areas devoid of hydroelectric resources and dependent on coal with its high transportation costs, such as in the northern part of Chile.[13]

---

[10] Expressed in an interview in *U.S. News and World Report*, August 14, 1961, p. 62.

[11] For a history of the development of electric power in Latin America by nations, see Lloyd Hughlett (ed.), *Industrialization of Latin America* (New York: McGraw-Hill Book Co., Inc., 1946), pp. 319–45. This work also contains histories of the other important industries in Latin America.

[12] United Nations Economic Commission for Latin America, *Report of the Latin American Electric Power Seminar in Mexico City* (Santiago, Chile, February, 1962), p. 12.

[13] *Report of the Latin American Electric Power Seminar in Mexico City, op. cit.,* p. 112.

FIGURE 8-1

ELECTRIC POWER CONSUMPTION (1960)
(total for public and private generating plants)

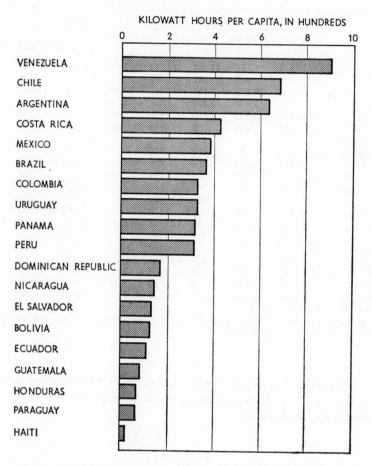

SOURCE: Adapted from *latin america '67: The Annual Review of Latin American Business and Development* (New York: Vision, Inc.), p. 128–31.

TABLE 8–2

ELECTRIC POWER: GENERATING CAPACITY
(millions of kilowatt/hours)

	1962	1963			1964			1965
	Total	Hydro-electric	Thermal	Total	Hydro-electric	Thermal	Total	Total
Argentina	11,873	1,176	11,167	12,343	1,140	12,442	13,582	14,700
Bolivia	496	410	122	532	414	120	534	554
Brazil	27,158	20,278	7,141	27,869	22,097	6,997	29,094	31,600
Chile	5,286	3,404	2,219	5,623	3,724	2,204	5,928	6,250
Colombia	4,247	3,050	1,820	4,870	3,500	2,000	5,500	6,100
Costa Rica ...	492	480	69	549	500	97	597	640
Dominican Republic ...	390	50	410	460	51	529	580	640
Ecuador	451	239	256	495	248	304	552	590
El Salvador ..	302	319	15	334	365	15	380	410
Guatemala ...	324	120	244	364	130	250	380	430
Haiti	100	—	100	100	—	110	110	110
Honduras	108	20	98	118	50	100	150	170
Mexico	12,507	5,803	7,904	13,707	6,866	8,882	15,748	17,400
Nicaragua ...	209	50	196	246	1	269	270	290
Panama	325	20	310	330	27	363	390	390
Paraguay	110	—	125	125	—	129	129	136
Peru	2,900	2,100	1,167	3,267	2,237	1,279	3,516	3,846
Uruguay	1,670	1,102	598	1,700	1,267	457	1,724	1,850
Venezuela	5,900	1,106	5,665	6,771	1,222	6,378	7,600	8,250

SOURCE: *latin america '67: The Annual Review of Latin American Business and Development* (New York: Vision, Inc., n.d.), p. 136.

In the production of steel, still another index of industrial development, the region is forging ahead, as the following statistics of the main producing nations indicate.

TABLE 8–3

PRODUCTION OF CRUDE STEEL, 1966
(thousands of metric tons)

Country	1948	1960	1961	1962	1963	1964	1965
Argentina	483	1,843	1,995	2,396	2,737	2,939	2,896
Brazil	122	277	441	644	913	1,267	1,360
Chile	30	422	363	495	489	544	441
Colombia	157	176	137	194	200	200	204
Mexico	270	1,500	1,725	1,851	1,974	2,280	2,403
Peru	—	60	76	73	72	75	81
Uruguay	—	10	9	9	7	14	13
Venezuela	—	47	75	225	364	441	625

SOURCE: United Nations, *Statistical Yearbook, 1966.*

A plant for producing steel is regarded as the hallmark of an industrialized society.[14] The Chileans take great pride in Compañia de Acero del Pacifico, the steel plant at Huachipato, which began production in 1950, and the Brazilians are equally proud of the Volta Redonda Iron and Steel Plant, which began production in 1946. But the production in these and other more recently built plants has been unable to keep pace with the increasing requirements of the secondary transforming industries engaged in the manufacture of automobiles and trucks, the construction of skyscrapers and bridges, and the shipbuilding programs and modernization of railways.

In 1958 the first semi-integrated steel mills began operation in El Salvador and Panama; since then, the production of steel has had an even higher priority in every one of the more industrialized nations. Mexico, which is second only to Brazil in the output of steel ingots, produced 2,403,000 tons in 1965—an increase of almost 900 percent over its production of 1948.[15]

Industrialization and economic independence are goals that most of the nations of Latin America are striving hard to attain. Their measure of success is reflected by the percentage of the gross national product accounted for by manufacturing compared with that of agriculture, trade, services, and public administration and defense, as given in Table 8–4. The nations with the largest percent of their GNP derived from manufacturing are: Chile 18.6, Colombia 18.9, Uruguay 23.3, Brazil 24.7, Mexico 24.8, and Argentina 35.7.

The high degree of industrialization in some of the nations is well shown by their massive hydroelectric projects, steel mills, aluminum plants, automotive factories, and oil refineries. The nations less industrially advanced mainly have enterprises that process food, make clothing or furniture, or produce other consumer goods for the local market. In Brazil, the concentration of industry and income in São Paulo, with a consequent reduction in industry and income elsewhere, especially in the northeast, has been one of the nation's serious problems.[16]

---

[14] Economists maintain, however, that developing or underdeveloped countries should not try to develop heavy industries, such as integrated steel mills, because these require large capital outlays and a big supply of highly skilled workers. For this viewpoint, see Eugene Staley, *The Future of Underdeveloped Countries* (Council on Foreign Relations) (New York: Harper & Bros., 1961), p. 305; Committee for Economic Development, *Economic Development Abroad and the Role of American Foreign Investment* (A statement by the Research and Policy Committee) (New York: February, 1956), p. 13; and DeVere E. Pentony (ed.), *The Underdeveloped Lands: A Dilemma of the International Economy* (San Francisco: Chandler Publishing Co., 1960), p. 13.

[15] For a brief but graphic account of the Mexican steel industry, see Dennis J. Cipnic, "More Mexican Steel: Monterrey Plan Develops New Process," *Américas*, Vol. 14, No. 10 (October, 1962), pp. 13–16.

[16] Celso Furtado, *The Economic Growth of Brazil: A Survey from Colonial to Modern Times*, trans. Ricardo W. de Aguiar and Eric Charles Drysdale (Berkeley: University of California Press, 1963), pp. 264–66.

TABLE 8-4

ORIGIN OF GROSS NATIONAL PRODUCT
(percentages)

	Agriculture, Fishing, and Forestry	Manufacturing	Mining	Electricity, Gas, and Water	Construction	Transport and Communications	Wholesale and Retail Trade	Banking, Insurance, and Real Estate	Ownership of Dwellings	Government and Defense	Services
Argentina	15.1	35.7	1.7	2.0	4.2	5.6	16.4	2.1	2.0	6.3	8.9
Bolivia	33.6	11.9	13.2	1.0	1.8	9.1	10.4	1.0	3.0	9.3	5.7
Brazil	27.1	24.7	0.5	0.9	1.2	8.4	12.3	3.0	3.9	7.1	10.9
Chile	10.1	18.6	6.3	0.9	3.9	8.5	21.2	3.0	7.7	8.7	11.1
Colombia	31.4	18.9	3.5	1.0	2.9	6.7	15.2	2.6	5.6	5.0	7.2
Costa Rica	29.2	14.4	...	2.9	3.1	4.8	15.3	3.0	5.4	10.0	11.9
Ecuador	35.0	16.6	2.3	1.3	3.5	4.2	12.5	2.8	6.7	6.5	8.6
El Salvador	30.9	17.7	0.8	0.9	2.1	2.9	25.0	2.1	5.0	6.7	5.9
Guatemala	28.5	14.6	0.1	0.9	1.9	5.0	25.0	2.0	8.0	4.6	5.7
Honduras	45.7	13.2	1.3	0.8	3.4	6.0	13.9	1.0	7.0	4.0	3.7
Mexico	17.4	24.8	5.1	1.4	3.8	4.3	25.8	3.0	3.0	2.8	8.6
Nicaragua	36.3	14.0	1.5	1.6	2.7	5.1	20.0	2.2	5.7	5.3	5.6
Panama	20.4	16.5	0.3	1.8	5.4	6.0	14.5	2.7	7.1	2.6	22.7
Paraguay	37.0	17.4	0.2	0.8	2.3	4.3	18.8	2.0	3.5	3.9	9.8
Peru	21.4	19.6	7.6	0.8	4.1	5.4	17.6	3.7	7.4	7.8	4.6
Uruguay	15.3	23.3	0.05	2.1	3.9	8.8	14.6	5.0	6.0	10.2	10.8
Venezuela	7.0	14.1	28.5	2.0	4.6	3.9	14.1	2.0	10.4	2.7	10.7

SOURCES: National; Agency for International Development (AID). In *latin america '67: The Annual Review of Latin American Business and Development* (New York: Vision, Inc., n.d.), p. 134.

TRADITIONAL METHODS FOR PROMOTING INDUSTRY[17]

Mercantilism during colonial days was a far more potent force in the New World possessions of Spain and Portugal than in the British colonies. The crowns of Spain and Portugal were omnipresent, closely supervising the trade of the colonies to make sure that it would accrue to the benefit of the mother country.

Mercantilism has never died in Latin America. To protect their infant home industries and encourage industrialization, the nations have adopted many measures designed to this end, including customs duties, import quotas, exchange controls, licensing, embargoes, loans, subsidies, and tax exemptions.

The protective tariff has been the most widely used method of promoting domestic industries; in fact, the young manufacturing enterprises in Latin America grew up behind the sheltering barriers of high tariff walls. The more industrially advanced nations were the first to adopt a protectionist trade policy—Argentina in 1876, Brazil in 1889, and Chile in 1897. The other nations in time followed a similar policy.

Venezuela's import duties, for example, were originally designed solely to obtain revenue, but were adjusted stiffly upward in order to promote industrialization. From the standpoint of their policy objective, the nation's customs duties and commodities can be classified into three main categories: (1) furniture, apparel, and processed foods, protected by a tariff so high as to make it impossible for foreign imports to compete with them; (2) vegetables, lard, beer, and many other items protected by a tariff of from 50 to 100 percent of the domestic wholesale price, which protected the home industry but did not preclude foreign competition; and (3) capital equipment, tools, and semifabricated products which the nation did not produce, admitted at a low rate.

The survey of Venezuela's tariff policy concludes: "Venezuelan protective policy has in general been successful in creating the basic socioeconomic framework within which domestic manufacture could develop and experience be gained in management and skills."[18]

In Latin America generally, a tariff schedule usually contains four levels of duties: protective duties on agricultural commodities and manufactures produced or suitable for production in the nation concerned; high duties on luxuries; revenue duties on articles that cannot be feasibly produced in the country; and nominal duties on machinery, raw materials, and semimanufactures not produced in the nation concerned.

---

[17] Much of the following information and treatment is from George Wythe, *Industry in Latin America* (2d ed.; New York: Columbia University Press, 1949), pp. 65–76.

[18] International Bank for Reconstruction and Development, *The Economic Development of Venezuela* (Baltimore: Johns Hopkins Press, 1961), pp. 204–5.

As a rule, tariff rates are not fixed by congress and embodied in legislative enactment; rather, they are determined by the executive, who has broad authority to raise or lower them by executive decree. Consequently, rates are changed more frequently than in countries where tariff making is primarily a legislative function, with certain discretion delegated to the president.

The duties levied were high enough to protect the sprouting home industries until 1930, when the depression seemingly forced all nations to adopt many new restrictionist trade measures to keep afloat at the expense of their neighbors. The nations of Latin America fell into line. Brazil, for example, required all importers of wheat and wheat flour to mix with their products a certain proportion of native mandioca flour.

The nations during this time also adopted many positive measures to promote economic development. They made loans at a low rate of interest, gave guarantees of a minimum rate of return, and granted subsidies without any obligation of repayment.

Another inducement often successful was special tax treatment given to an industry. In Brazil, a decree of 1932 granting a 10-year exemption from import duties on machinery required in the construction and expansion of plants was designed to promote the development of the cement industry. The tax concession accomplished its purpose, resulting in the establishment of some of the nation's largest cement plants. Tax concessions are still effective inducements for encouraging industry. In 1963, Costa Rica, to encourage light industry, enacted a Protection of Industries Law that offers virtually a 10-year tax holiday to manufacturers of products not previously produced there. The law produced a spate of widely diversified small enterprises, which produced such products as fiber glass, toothpaste, shoe polish, detergents, corrugated roofing, collapsible plastics, wrapping paper, and hairpins.

OBSTACLES TO INDUSTRIAL DEVELOPMENT

There are many obstacles to industrial development in Latin America. The main ones we will consider are: lack of capital, shortage of engineers and skilled labor, high cost of production, political instability and governmental bureaucracy, and antipathetic mores and cultural values.

Lack of capital that industrialists or would-be industrialists need in order to establish, expand, or modernize an enterprise is unquestionably one of the main hindrances to industrialization. This shortage, which is felt by governments and individuals alike, is apparent in many ways. Hardly a week passes that one of the nations—maybe several of them— does not apply to the World Bank or some other international agency to borrow money needed for its economy. As one travels through Latin

America, he sees many tangible evidences of the great need for capital. In city after city, even in the capitals of Bogotá, La Paz, and Buenos Aires, showplaces for the nation and the world, he is impressed by the skeletons of tall buildings whose construction began years ago but could not be completed because of lack of funds.

The scarcity of capital available to the entrepreneur[19] is the result of many significant factors. The disadvantageous terms of trade whereby the region sells its agricultural and other exports at a cheap price but pays dearly for the manufactured products it imports have severely limited its financial resources.

Equally as serious has been the flight of capital from the region. The fantastic wealth that dictators—occasionally constitutional presidents—manage to smuggle out of the nations and deposit to their personal accounts in Swiss, American, or other foreign banks and enterprises is well publicized by the press. Indeed, when a dictator and his entourage are forced into exile after a successful revolution, it is rather assumed that the suitcases, trunks, and other luggage loaded onto departing planes contain the receipts of the national treasury. But even more serious from the standpoint of a nation's economic development is the quiet, little publicized, insidious flight of capital from where it was produced and is greatly needed to areas that have money to spare. In short, many of Latin America's wealthiest citizens have so little confidence in their nations that while they do not mind bleeding them for all they can get, they surreptitiously take their profits elsewhere for investment and safekeeping.

The very threat of the flight of capital is so serious that it can hamstring a government, preventing it from making much-needed reforms—in taxation for instance. Raymond Vernon, referring to Mexico, concludes:

The capacity and willingness to tax are limited by many circumstances, by a long tradition of tax evasion and corruption, by technical limitations in the tax-collecting apparatus, and by a justifiable fear that high taxes will either induce capital flight or generate widespread public unrest, depending on their form. As a result . . . the government seems incapable for the present of collecting more than 10 to 20 per cent of its gross national product in the form of tax revenues.[20]

Capital tiptoes out of the countries so stealthily that even the approximate amount kept in foreign banks or invested in foreign enterprises is unknown. It may be from $5 billion to $20 billion—as much as the United

---

[19] For a breakdown by countries of the sources of savings for gross capital formation, with the relative importance of each source, see William I. Abraham, "Saving Patterns in Latin America," *Economic Development and Cultural Change*, Vol. 12, No. 4 (July, 1964), pp. 380–81.

[20] Raymond Vernon, *The Dilemma of Mexico's Development: The Roles of the Private and Public Sectors* (Cambridge, Mass.: Harvard University Press, 1963), p. 185.

States plans to invest in Latin America during the 10-year program of the Alliance for Progress. "This is money that could be used to build roads, finance land reforms, and perhaps even to hold back a violent social revolution," deplores Tad Szulc. "But the vicious circle of greed still holds Latin America in its grip."[21]

A prominent Latin American is equally as frank in contemplating the problem. "Native capital flees from Latin America," writes Germán Arciniegas. "Only in Montevideo and Mexico City have large fortunes found refuge. *If the amount of Latin American funds on deposit today in the banks of New York and Switzerland were accurately known one would conclude that Latin America possesses all the capital it needs.*"[22]

The shortage of domestic capital available for the entrepreneur is further complicated in many of the countries by the unfavorable climate for foreign investment. Nationalization of foreign properties and disregard of contracts with foreign companies have scared away investment funds from abroad, which Latin America greatly needs. Investors, already leery of Argentina because of its political and economic instability, shied away even further after President Illía, carrying out a campaign pledge in November, 1963, canceled the contracts under which foreign companies had been producing oil or drilling wells in Argentina for the State Petroleum Authority, investing more than $250 million in the operations. Repudiation of the contracts signed with the former Frondizi regime, together with the nationalization of foreign properties in many of the countries, has deprived the nations of much private capital they might otherwise have had.

Lack of capital in the nations is also due to the traditional neglect of agriculture and the resulting inability of this important segment to play its role in materially aiding the economy.[23] The concentration of landownership in relatively few hands, failure to use modern methods or machinery, letting large acreages lie idle, and concentrating on money crops have prevented agriculture from properly feeding the populace or making the contribution it might to the formation of capital.

The priority Mexico has given to land reform should be heeded by the other nations of Latin America. For about 20 years after the civil strife

---

[21] Tad Szulc, *The Winds of Revolution: Latin America Today—And Tomorrow* (New York: Frederick A. Praeger, Inc., 1964), p. 70.

[22] Germán Arciniegas, *The State of Latin America*, trans. Harriet de Onís (New York: Alfred A. Knopf, Inc., 1952), p. 391. Italics in the cited material have been supplied by this author.

[23] Romulo A. Ferrero, "Economic Development of Peru," *Economic Development Issues: Latin America* (Committee for Economic Development, Supplementary Paper No. 21, 1967), pp. 248–49.

"Latin America . . . has begun its industrial revolution without having undergone an agrarian revolution." Jacques Chonchol, "Land Tenure and Development in Latin America," *Obstacles to Change in Latin America*, ed. Claudio Veliz (New York: Oxford University Press, 1965), p. 81.

ended, agrarian reform and agrarian policy were the main interests of the Mexican government. Getting land into the hands of the peasants and carrying out the agrarian revolution were the priority tasks to which the government devoted itself. It was not until after 1940 that its attention shifted sharply from agriculture to industry and the nation began to make great headway in establishing a base for full-scale industrial development.[24]

Genuine land reform is a *sine qua non* of sound economic development and should be given top priority in every state where it is needed. "The future of Brazil," says T. Lynn Smith, "is dependent on the land system it adopts or fails to adopt more than upon any other factor."[25]

Another obstacle industrialists in Latin America often encounter is the shortage of engineers and skilled labor. Since engineering is not regarded as one of the professions of high status, college students have passed it by in preference for law, medicine, or other fields that have a higher status. Consequently, the region is very short of capable, trained engineering talent. The dilemma of Brazil is common to many other nations in the region. Although Brazil is staking its future very largely on its ability to industrialize rapidly, it needs many more engineers to accomplish this. One year, a single factory in São Paulo proposed to hire the entire graduating class of the Polytechnic School, which supplied a large proportion of the nation's engineering graduates.[26]

Eschewing dirty hands or manual labor, even those students who study engineering get a better theoretical than practical education. They balk at putting on coveralls, getting down to earth with machinery, and applying the principles and knowledge they have learned. As a result of this attitude and the emphasis on theoretical rather than practical training, the factories are often far from models of progressive industrial enterprises. In Brazil, a study by the United Nations pointed out many weaknesses in the important textile industry. Overage machines were one problem, but more important were the inadequately specialized techniques of production and improper conditions of manufacture, such as uncleanliness, careless maintenance of machines, and lack of other sound engineering practices.[27]

The shortage of engineers in the region has been greatly aggravated by their desire to emigrate to other nations, particularly the United States, where engineering is not only a very respected profession but also one

---

[24] Mosk, *op. cit.*, p. vii.

[25] T. Lynn Smith, *Brazil: People and Institutions* (rev. ed.; Baton Rouge: Louisiana State University Press, 1963), p. 621.

[26] Richard M. Morse, *From Community to Metropolis: A Biography of São Paulo, Brazil* (Gainesville: University of Florida Press, 1958), p. 231.

[27] *Ibid.*

that pays relatively well. During the period 1951–61, some 3,284 Argentine technicians emigrated to the United States.[28]

An inadequate supply of skilled labor has also been a problem for industrialists. Uneducated and unfamiliar with machinery of any sort as most workers are, training them for the many skilled operations of modern production has been a burden on industry. But illiteracy and the lack of experience have not prevented the natives from becoming skilled productive workers in a short time when they were interested. Indeed, Indians fresh from the *communidades* in the hinterlands and with no training at all for skilled industrial jobs rapidly become proficient in operating machines or performing manual operations that require fast handwork and good coordination. "Moreover, they are artistic perfectionists," a textile engineer explained to the author, "and create beautiful, creative designs when they have the opportunity."

The high costs of production and distribution in Latin America are facts of life that must be reckoned with. An important factor in the high cost of production is the high rate of interest entrepreneurs must pay for establishing or expanding their enterprises. While laws usually specify the maximum rate of interest that can legally be charged, there are many devious ways of getting around them. Consequently, the entrepreneur usually must pay a much higher rate in order to get the capital he needs for his enterprise.

The very limited markets in the region virtually preclude the possibility of mass production, which by its volume would reduce the cost of each unit; the very prevalence of a product in the society would stimulate greater consumer demand for it.[29] The limited market is the result of the interplay of many social and economic conditions. The income of a large part of the population is low, ranging from less than $100 a year in several of the countries to $600 or so in the most advanced ones. The difficulty of even subsisting on the low incomes has been greatly aggravated by inflation, rampant in some of the nations, which works a severe hardship on many members of society because the cost of living almost invariably offsets the increase in wages.

Another cause of the limited market is the high cost of distributing almost any products that are made. The cost of shipping is usually so high that relatively inefficient plants preempt the local markets, since goods manufactured at lower costs elsewhere simply cannot compete. The difficulties in transportation are among the most adverse factors in hinder-

---

[28] *Hispanic American Report*, Vol. XVI, No. 8 (October, 1963), p. 810.

[29] "Latin America's closed industrial system has generated a vicious circle," says Peter Nehemkis. "The coddling effects of protection eliminated the incentive to reduce the high costs. A closed market perpetuated built-in inefficiencies of production, handling of materials, and utilization of manpower." Peter Nehemkis, *Latin America: Myth and Reality* (New York: Alfred A. Knopf, Inc., 1964), p. 200.

ing the development of a national market. As a result of t
the manufacturers of most products gear their production t
market—1 or 2 percent of the populace, maybe as high as 5
Progress is being made toward mass production for a natio
it is slow.

✗ Certain aspects of government have also served to hinc
of industrialization. The well-known governmental instability of nations
in the Caribbean and Central America has discouraged foreign investors.
The instability of Argentina, Brazil, and other nations has also made
foreign investors leery. Moreover, the many dictatorial military regimes
have prevented the development of a healthy, competitive economic
order, and dissipated much of the nations' limited income on large military establishments.[30]

✗ Moreover, with governments assuming a larger role in promoting
economic development, an increasingly large number of trained, efficient
administrators and specialists is needed. Such personnel, however, are in
as short supply as engineers.

The very top-heaviness of government is a great burden on economic
and social development. In Uruguay, padded personnel rolls are a serious
financial drain on the nation. Twenty percent or more of the total
population depend for their livelihood on wages, salaries, and other income from the government, and three fourths or more of the budget is
normally allocated for the payment of personnel.[31] Argentina has a similar problem: according to President Arturo Frondizi, 7 million inhabitants (more than one third of the total population) are dependent on
employment by the national, provincial, or municipal government. "More
than 30 percent of the state's income is spent on wages," said Frondizi,
"and this explains why there is no money to build houses, roads, schools,
or even to repair pavements or give more light to our dark streets."[32]

The cultural values and the mores of Latin America have also served in
many ways to obstruct the progress of industrialization. The upper class,
which might logically be expected to provide entrepreneurial talent, for
the most part disdains such mundane economic pursuits. Even when a
member of this class does enter private business—as president of the
company or chairman of its board of directors—his cultural background
is a hindrance rather than a help. Accustomed to giving orders to peons

---

[30] One of the main reasons for Mexico's rapid, sustained growth is "the existence
and expectation of public order and wide public consensus." Robert J. Shafer, *Mexico: Mutual Adjustment Planning* (Syracuse, N.Y.: Syracuse University Press, 1966),
p. 29.

[31] Russell H. Fitzgibbon, "Uruguay: A Model for Freedom and Reform in Latin
America," *Freedom and Reform in Latin America*, ed. Fredrick B. Pike (Notre
Dame, Ind.: University of Notre Dame Press, 1959), pp. 249–50.

[32] In Lewis Hanke, *South America* (New York: D. Van Nostrand Co., Inc.,
1959), p. 163.

id others who are inferior to him, he cannot help but be authoritarian in his conduct of a modern business enterprise. He may agree with the principle of delegating duties, but the very idea of delegating to inferiors the authority necessary to operate effectively is culturally repugnant to him. Even more repugnant is sitting in a staff meeting and listening to the opinions and recommendations of subordinates.

Also obstructing industrialization are the deeply ingrained investment habits antithetical to the widespread mobilization of large capital on which modern industry depends. Most persons with money to invest prefer to put it into farms, office buildings, or apartment buildings, all of which are socially respectable as well as tangible types of property. They are loath to use their money to buy stocks and bonds or any other "mere pieces of paper." In fact, unless they personally know the individuals or group they are dealing with, they have little confidence in them. As a result of this suspicious attitude, it is most difficult for corporations to float large issues of stocks and bonds, or for banks and insurance companies to develop. Many family businesses have been converted into corporations for tax advantages and other purposes, but their stocks are tightly held by members of the family and are not open to the public.[33]

Certain other cultural habits are in contradiction to the regimentation found necessary by modern industry, such as getting to work on time and leaving on time, and putting in eight hours of work a day for five days a week, with reasonable time off for lunch. In siestaland, it is the almost universal custom to take a two- or three-hour break in the middle of the day. Neither the pressure of business nor noisy, crawly traffic jams have been able to change this hallowed custom, desecrated only by the American Embassy and AID staffs and American companies whose personnel bring their lunches with them or eat in the company cafeteria.

Even more frustrating to the production schedules of modern industry are the many days taken off for *fiestas*, celebrations of religious or national holidays or of births, weddings, and burials. The celebrations are marked by "untiring dancing and drinking. . . . The expense . . . (when combined with the purchase of coca leaves) tends to absorb available surplus income and also to reduce working time and labor efficiency. As long as this primitive pattern of habits prevails, it is almost impossible to achieve improvements in standards of living."[34] The Bolivian pueblo of Mairana in the province of Florida had a total of 107 days off from work in 1960 for such *fiestas*.[35]

---

[33] The effects of personalism and family ties on industrial development are discussed by John P. Gillin in "Some Signposts for Policy," *Social Change in Latin America Today* (Council on Foreign Relations) (New York: Harper & Bros., 1960), pp. 29–40.

[34] John Lindberg, "Bolivia: Mines Without Industry," *Current History*, Vol. 22 (March, 1952), pp. 145–46.

[35] Alfredo Chavarria Frias, "Estudio Socio-Económica de la Provincia Florida Realisado por la Agencia de a Extensión," (unpublished report, Santa Cruz, Bolivia, 1961).

INTERVENTION OF GOVERNMENT IN ECONOMIC DEVELOPMENT

In every one of the Latin American nations, the government plays a very active role in promoting economic development. It performs or directly controls many services that in capitalistic nations are customarily regarded as being within the province of individual entrepreneurs. Even as early as the 1920's, several of the governments, particularly those of Uruguay and Chile, adopted programs of social welfare that were quite advanced for the time.

In Chile, the greatly expanded activity of government in promoting economic development and utilizing tax funds and public credit was the result of an accident of history—some would say a dispensation of divine providence. The awesome earthquake of January 24, 1939, which killed more than 30,000 people, injured 50,000 others, and destroyed most of the large cities of Concepción and Chillán, as well as many smaller towns and villages, was one of the most destructive in history. However, it provided the needed stimulus for a program of action that greatly benefited the nation and the other countries of Latin America too. A temporary emergency program of reconstruction was adopted to provide all aid possible to the stricken areas. Of greater social significance, however, was the companion governmental program for promoting long-range economic development in the whole nation—a program not only ambitiously wide in scope but also so challenging as to bring out the latent possibilities of every segment of the economy.

The resulting Chilean Fomento, or Development Corporation, unique in the annals of Latin America, was the prototype of other similar government authorities which have greatly influenced public policy and the course of economic development throughout the region.

Chile's Fomento, designed both to rehabilitate the earthquake-stricken regions and to promote economic progress in general, was endowed with wide authority and charged with weighty responsibilities. These included: drawing up a comprehensive plan for stimulating production so as to raise the standard of living; making studies to discover the most effective means of increasing production; conducting experiments in producing and selling goods; and aiding domestic producers to gain a larger share in the nation's industrial and commercial activities.

The Fomento, regarded by some as the epitome of governmental interference in the economic realm, had as a primary aim stimulating production by assisting private efforts. It invested its funds in carefully selected enterprises that needed help, often running the risk of a loss, and later pulled out, turning the operations over to private ownership when they became going concerns.

The funds the Fomento needed for its activities were derived from certain allocated taxes, mainly a special tax on copper; loans from the Export-Import Bank of the United States; and revenues derived from government enterprises. To protect the interests of the public when tax moneys were invested either in mixed public-private or completely private undertakings, the government usually had several representatives on the board of directors but did not presume to dictate policy. Rather, in the contractual agreements with the enterprises, it established the terms and conditions deemed to be in the public interest and had inspectors for checking to see that the agreements were observed.

In promoting economic development, the Fomento gave needed assistance to just about every phase of the economy: sources of energy and fuel, such as hydroelectric projects, coal mines, or oil wells; industries of every sort, including metallurgical, chemical, textile, cement, and timber and forestry; mines producing a wide variety of minerals, including manganese, cobalt, zinc, lead, tungsten, gold, talc, kaolin, graphite, and aluminum sulphate; land, sea, and air transportation; and agriculture and ranching.

In short, to promote Chile's economic development the Fomento could undertake any project from constructing a modern steel mill or building a huge hydroelectric dam to erecting a silo for a rancher and aiding him to get started in producing purebred cattle.

Exercising a wide authority, Chile's Fomento has played a most important role in the economic development of the nation. Herman Finer wrote:

The initiative, the forethought, the spirit of going out after business and the ability to do so successfully, are evident from first-hand observation of the Corporation's methods and personnel, and show clearly that there is a large fund of ability and public spirit at work. The feeling that Chile is being rebuilt or built for the first time causes a remarkable release of devotion and thinking. Capable young men are being interested and introduced into economic administration at a stage which is both creative and adventurous. This is a most important factor for the future of Chilean development.[36]

Following Chile's lead, the other nations have adopted development corporations of one sort or another, and their governments have been taking a very active part in promoting and participating in economic development. As evidence of this, public investment constitutes a relatively large proportion of the total investment. In Latin America, new public investment during the period 1950–56 averaged approximately 25 percent of the total amount.

---

[36] Herman Finer, "The Chilean Development Corporation: A Study in National Planning to Raise Living Standards," *International Labour Office, Studies and Reports* (New Series No. 5) (Montreal, 1947), p. 80. A more recent, brief account of Fomento's activities may be found in Alvin Cohen, *Economic Change in Chile, 1929–1959* (Latin American Monograph Series) (Gainesville: University of Florida Press, 1960), pp. 31–36.

The extensive intervention of government in Latin Am̄ mote economic development is due to many deeply rooted (is in short supply, and domestic capital, which should carry load, often is not interested in investing in local enterprise noted. Hoping to change this attitude, the International Bai times recommended that a nation establish a *fomento*, whose main purpose would be to encourage individuals to invest their capital in productive domestic undertakings.[37]

Government intervention is also largely the result of a frequently expressed prejudice against reliance on foreign capital as a possible alternative for financing economic development. The region has long been dependent on outside capital for underwriting its economic growth. Objections to foreign capital have come from many sources. Military leaders, motivated by considerations of national security, are opposed to foreign control of such sensitive operations as communications systems, which explains why most Latin American governments own the telephone companies.[38]

Besides military leaders, many others are opposed to the entry and influence of foreign capital if it can possibly be avoided. Rising local entrepreneurs are convinced that it puts them at a distinct competitive disadvantage, even when their competitors are large native operators financed by foreign capital.[39] Ardent nationalists also have often been resentful at what they regard as the intrusion of foreign capital. Some have drawn the line at foreign exploitation of petroleum. To maintain the national *dignidad* and derive what they regard as full advantage from the resource, they prefer to let it lie underground where it has been for a million years or so and can remain for awhile longer until they are in a position to exploit it.

Other ardent nationalists have been opposed to foreign investment in general. In Uruguay, the government's extensive participation in the economic realm began with the vigorous nationalistic doctrine that José Batlle y Ordóñez directed against the foreign businessman.

This antiforeignism combined with the conviction that domestic private enterprise lacked the capacity to replace foreign capital led to State intervention in the economy. Subsequently the preference for State enterprises has stemmed more from the failure of private initiative to make the expected contribution

---

[37] In Nicaragua, the International Bank figured that if the upper 1 percent of the income recipients invested just 10 percent of their incomes in such enterprises, the existing current rate of investment would increase by 50 percent. International Bank for Reconstruction and Development, *The Economic Development of Nicaragua*, 1953, p. 12.

[38] If many of these companies operated as the one in Managua, the capital of Nicaragua, control of the system even by the enemy would only serve to confuse and frustrate him. For it often takes so long to make a telephone call there that the caller gives up in disgust and sends a telegram or a message by a runner. (*Ibid.*, p. 250.)

[39] Mosk, *op. cit.*, p. 26.

to output and services and less from any strong belief in fundamental social theories.[40]

In intervening to promote economic development, governments have been motivated by still other considerations. Besides finding useful the revenues produced by publicly owned projects, they can speed up the tempo of economic development by vigorous, intelligent intervention. Moreover, they can promote balanced and diversified development which private initiative is not concerned about. In Venezuela, foreign and domestic private capital has been lopsidedly concentrated in one area alone—the exploitation of oil. Consequently, governmental activity has been necessary to take care of the many neglected aspects of the economy.

THE PROMISE OF INDUSTRIALIZATION FOR SOCIAL PROGRESS

In the developing nations of Latin America, as in similar nations elsewhere, there has been considerable difference of opinion as to whether the governments with their limited resources should emphasize rather immediate social goals or more long-range economic ones. James W. Wilkie's study of the Mexican Revolution, pragmatically measuring the accomplishments of its three main ideological periods, reaches an interesting conclusion regarding the fundamental issue.

The ideology of the first period, extending until 1934, was political; that of the second period, 1934–40, social; and that of the third period, 1940–58, economic.

The Social Revolution instigated by President Cárdenas aimed to bring immediate direct benefits to the masses in the form of land for the landless, education for the illiterate, and many other benefits. Cárdenas' social programs were financed by an unusually large percentage of the total national expenditures: a ratio of 2 to 1 vis-à-vis economic development. During the period 1940–58, the emphasis was decidedly on industrialization and economic infrastructure; the government's expenditures for economic development as compared with those for social betterment were at a ratio about 4 to 1, sometimes 5 to 1.

To objectively assess the accomplishments of each period, Wilkie established a Poverty Index for the nation, statistically based on census figures showing those who: (1) are illiterate, (2) speak only an Indian language, (3) live in a community of less than 2,500 persons, (4) go barefoot, (5) wear sandals, (6) regularly eat tortillas instead of wheat bread, and (7) are without sewage disposal.

---

[40] John J. Johnson, *Political Change in Latin America: The Emergence of the Middle Sectors* (Stanford, Calif.: Stanford University Press, 1958), p. 56.

As Table 8–5 shows, Wilkie found that the poverty index decreased at a more rapid rate during the period when emphasis was on economic development than during the period when it was on direct social benefits.

TABLE 8–5

DECREASE IN THE POVERTY INDEX DURING ERAS OF
POI ʼICAL, SOCIAL, AND ECONOMIC REVOLUTION

	Political		*Social*		*Economic*	
	1910	*1921*	*1930*	*1940*	*1950*	*1960*
Index (1940 = 100) ..	123.7	115.4	108.7	100.0	85.7	72.0
Percent Change		−6.7	−5.8	−8.0	−14.3	−16.0

SOURCE: James Wallace Wilkie, *The Mexican Revolution: Federal Expenditure and Social Changes Since 1910* (Berkeley: University of California Press, 1967), p. 258.

Only since 1940 has social change for the masses become relatively rapid, Wilkie concludes, and even then it may be debated whether or not a rate of 14 to 16 percent can be considered revolutionary. Yet, considering the nature and extent of the poverty that existed in Mexico for centuries, the decrease in the poverty index since 1940 is very impressive.[41]

The experience of Cuba under the Castro regime affords another lesson: rapid industrialization can be misguided and unsound. After Castro took over, his government was obsessed with the objective of industrializing rapidly. Cuba would no longer be content to rank number five among the industrially advanced nations of the region, but was to soon become number one, setting the pace for all the other nations. In the judgment of Theodore Draper, the program adopted for accelerated industrialization was almost childishly simple. Dozens of factories would be physically transported in a hurry over thousands of miles and transplanted in Cuba, either on the basis of long-term credits from the Communist nations or outright gifts from them. But the government had given no thought whatever to the cost of the raw materials that would be needed for the new factories. Indeed, it was shocked to find, as in the case of two factories brought over from Czechoslovakia to make picks and shovels, that the raw materials cost almost as much as the imported finished articles. The nation would obviously be much better off if it imported the finished products from Eastern Europe instead of investing

---

[41] For this information regarding the Mexican Revolution, see James W. Wilkie, *The Mexican Revolution: Federal Expenditure and Social Change Since 1910* (Berkeley: University of California Press, 1967), pp. 127–55, 204–43, and 259–69.

A provocative analysis of the post-World War II development achievements of 10 nations as measured by various indexes, such as capital formation, changes in tax structure, agrarian reform, social services, and others, is given by Charles W. Anderson, *Politics and Economic Change in Latin America: The Governing of Restless Nations* (Princeton, N.J.: D. Van Nostrand Co., Inc., 1967), chap. 11.

in costly factories and having to import raw materials whose cost would be a heavy drain on the nation's limited foreign exchange.

As Che Guevarra admitted, the revolution made two fundamental errors: the "declaration of war on sugarcane," and "the decision to have factories without thinking of the raw materials for them."[42]

SUGGESTED READINGS

Alexander, Robert J. *The Bolivian National Revolution,* chaps. 6, 9, 11. New Brunswick, N.J.: Rutgers University Press, 1958.

Anderson, Charles W. *Politics and Economic Change in Latin America: The Governing of Restless Nations,* Part II. Princeton, N.J.: D. Van Nostrand Co., Inc., 1967.

Benham, F., and Holley, H. A. *A Short Introduction to the Economy of Latin America.* Royal Institute of International Affairs. New York: Oxford University Press, 1960.

Burgess, Eugene W., and Harbison, Frederick H. *Casa Grace in Peru.* Second Case Study, United States Business Performance Abroad. National Planning Association, 1954.

Cline, Howard F. *Mexico: Revolution to Evolution: 1940–1960,* chaps. xxix and xxx. Royal Institute of International Affairs. New York: Oxford University Press, 1962.

————. *The United States and Mexico,* chaps. 16 and 17. Rev. ed. Cambridge, Mass.: Harvard University Press, 1963.

Cohen, Alvin. *Economic Change in Chile, 1929–1959.* Latin American Monograph Series. Gainesville: University of Florida Press, 1960.

Committee for Economic Development. *Economic Development Issues, Latin America.* Supplementary Paper No. 21, August, 1967.

Finer, Herman. *The Chilean Development Corporation.* Montreal: International Labour Office, 1947.

Fitzgibbon, Russell H. *Uruguay: Portrait of a Democracy,* chap. vii. New Brunswick, N.J.: Rutgers University Press, 1954.

Furtado, Celso. *The Economic Growth of Brazil: A Survey from Colonial to Modern Times.* Trans. Ricardo W. de Aguiar and Eric Charles Drysdale. Berkeley: University of California Press, 1963.

Gordon, Wendell C. "Freedom and Reform in Urban and Industrializing Latin America," *Freedom and Reform in Latin America* (ed. Fredrick B. Pike), pp. 177–202. Notre Dame, Ind.: Notre Dame Press, 1959.

————. *The Political Economy of Latin America.* New York: Columbia University Press, 1965.

Hughlett, Lloyd (ed.). *Industrialization of Latin America.* New York: Mc-Graw-Hill Book Co., Inc., 1946.

---

[42] Theodore Draper, *Castroism: Theory and Practice* (New York: Frederick A. Praeger, Inc., 1965), pp. 145, 147, 153, and 157.

International Bank for Reconstruction and Development. *The Economic Development of Venezuela,* chaps. 2, 4, 7, 10, and Annex I. Baltimore: Johns Hopkins Press, 1961.

Lauterbach, Albert. *Enterprise in Latin America: Business Attitudes in a Developing Economy.* Ithaca, N.Y.: Cornell University Press, 1966.

Lieuwen, Edwin. *Venezuela,* chap. iv. Royal Institute of International Affairs. New York: Oxford University Press, 1961.

MacGaffey, Wyatt, and Barnett, Clifford R. *Cuba.* Survey of World Cultures, chaps. 3 and 16. New Haven, Conn.: HRAF Press, 1962.

May, Stacy (dir.), *et al. Costa Rica: A Study in Economic Development,* chaps. 2, 6, 9 and 10. New York: Twentieth Century Fund, 1952.

May, Stacy, and Plaza, Galo. *The United Fruit Company in Latin America.* Seventh Case Study, United States Business Performance Abroad. National Planning Association, 1958.

Morse, Richard M. *From Community to Metropolis: A Biography of São Paulo, Brazil,* chaps. 14–18. Gainesville: University of Florida Press, 1958.

Mosk, Sanford A. *Industrial Revolution in Mexico.* Berkeley: University of California Press, 1954.

Nehemkis, Peter. *Latin America: Myth and Reality,* chaps. 6, 10, 12, and 13. New York: Alfred A. Knopf, Inc., 1964.

Osborne, Harold. *Bolivia: A Land Divided,* pp. 106–34. Royal Institute of International Affairs. London: Oxford University Press, 1954.

Pierson, William W., and Gil, Federico G. *Governments of Latin America,* chap. 15. New York: McGraw-Hill Book Co., Inc., 1957.

Stark, Harry. *Social and Economic Frontiers in Latin America,* chaps. 1, 4, 9, 12–14, 18–28. 2d ed. Dubuque, Ia.: W. C. Brown Co., 1963.

Tannenbaum, Frank. *Mexico: The Struggle for Peace and Bread,* chaps. 11–13. New York: Alfred A. Knopf, Inc., 1954.

Taylor, Wayne C., and Lindeman, John, with the collaboration of Victor López R. *The Creole Petroleum Corporation in Venezuela.* Fourth Case Study, United States Business Performance Abroad. National Planning Association, 1955.

Urquidi, Marjory (trans.). *Mexico's Recent Economic Growth.* Essays. Austin: University of Texas Press, 1967.

Veliz, Claudio (ed.). *Obstacles to Change in Latin America,* pp. 9–46, 145–61, 206–29. New York: Oxford University Press, 1965.

Vernon, Raymond. *The Dilemma of Mexico's Development: The Role of the Private and Public Sectors.* Cambridge, Mass.: Harvard University Press, 1963.

———. (ed.). *Public Policy and Private Enterprise in Mexico.* Cambridge: Harvard University Press, 1964.

Weyl, Nathaniel, and Weyl, Sylvia. *The Reconquest of Mexico: The Years of Lázaro Cárdenas,* chap. x. New York: Oxford University Press, 1939.

Wilkie, James W. *The Mexican Revolution: Federal Expenditure and Social Changes Since 1910* (Berkeley: University of California Press, 1967).

Withers, William. *The Economic Crisis in Latin America.* New York: Free Press of Glencoe, 1964.

Wood, Richardson, and Keyser, Virginia. *Sears, Roebuck de Mexico, S.A.* First Case Study, United States Business Performance Abroad. National Planning Association, 1953.

Wythe, George. *Industry in Latin America.* 2d ed. New York: Columbia University Press, 1949.

9

FOREIGN AID, ECONOMIC PLANNING, AND ECONOMIC INTEGRATION

FOREIGN AID

As is well known, the per capita income and standard of living in many of the Latin American nations are quite low. In fact, the purchasing power of a large part of the mass is so low that this group is, in effect, really not part of the market economy.

Although certain physical circumstances, such as geographical barriers, are partly responsible for the region's underdevelopment, the primary factor is that the several fundamental revolutions that swept over the nations of the Western world, transforming their societies, have not so far been experienced by most of Latin America. These transforming movements were: the intellectual revolution, based on concepts of progress and the possibility of material change leading to a better world; the political revolution, with its stress on equality and opportunity for all; and the scientific and technological revolution, involving the application of savings and of sciences to most aspects of life.[1] Yet failing to benefit from these three revolutions, the region has begun to suffer from the fourth, or biological, revolution—the population explosion, which is creating momentous new problems.

Because of the skyrocketing increase in population, the gap between the Latin American nations and the more affluent nations in per capita income and standard of living, already quite wide, is rapidly becoming

---

[1] For these revolutions in underdeveloped nations generally, see Barbara Ward, *The Rich Nations and the Poor Nations* (New York: W. W. Norton Co., Inc., 1962), pp. 13–61.

wider. The outpouring of babies threatens to depress even further the low standard of living in most of the region.[2]

As Table 9–1 shows, the percent average annual increase of per capita GNP—already low—is steadily declining. Brazil with approximately a

TABLE 9–1

GROWTH OF GNP IN LATIN AMERICA

(percent annual average increase)

	Total GNP				Per Capita GNP			
	1950–55	1955–60	1960–65	1950–65	1950–55	1955–60	1960–65	1950–65
Total Latin America (17 Republics) ...	5.1	4.8	4.4	4.8	2.3	2.0	1.5	1.8
Argentina	3.1	2.6	3.0	2.9	1.4	0.9	1.3	1.1
Brazil	5.7	5.8	3.3	4.9	2.6	2.7	0.2	1.8
Chile	3.0	4.2	3.9	3.7	0.7	1.9	1.6	1.3
Colombia	5.5	4.0	4.4	4.6	2.6	1.1	1.5	1.7
Mexico	6.2	6.1	5.9	6.0	3.1	3.0	2.8	2.9
Peru	6.0	4.3	6.6	5.6	3.7	2.0	3.7	3.1
Venezuela	9.0	7.1	5.2	7.1	5.1	3.2	1.6	3.1

SOURCE: Agency for International Development, in Committee for Economic Development, Supplementary Paper No. 21, August, 1967, p. 223.

third of the region's population had a mere 0.2 percent increase—virtually none at all—for the period 1960–65. For the region as a whole, the increase was only 1.5 percent. At this rate, it will take approximately 50 years to double the annual income—50 years to raise the $100 income in some nations to $200.

In short, production is barely keeping ahead of the burgeoning population. And it certainly will not provide the plethora of washing machines, television sets, automobiles, and other evidences of a high standard of living that Latin Americans yearn for in their revolution of rising expectations. But in view of the boom in population, predicted to reach 600 million by the year 2000, many in society had better be thinking in terms of scrubboards, radios, and roller skates.

The continuingly widening economic gap between Latin America and the affluent nations, may be attributed to three main conditions. (1) Economic development tends to lag behind demographic expansion, causing the specter evoked by Malthus to rise again; (2) the prices of primary

[2] This threat is overlooked by some, as Remo di Natale who contends that Latin America is really underpopulated, can support and needs a much larger population. Remo di Natale, *America Latina Hoy: Esquemos Populares Democrata Cristianos* (La Paz, 1964), pp. 23–24.

products tend to steadily decline, while the prices of manufactured goods generally tend to increase; (3) economic development is not taking place at the necessary rate because of the lack of adequate capital.[3]

The peculiar motivating force behind the region's industrial development also has adversely affected its economic growth. This development was not motivated by either of the two stimuli responsible for industrialization in most states—a strong social class, advocating changes and pressuring the government to accept them; or the government itself, as in the case of the Soviet Union and Japan, deciding on changes and effectuating them. Rather, the Latin-American industrialization was brought on by the Depression and World War II, which forced the region to fend for itself, lacking the experience necessary to establish a rational, national policy to guide the process.[4]

Among the unfortunate consequences was failure to provide the social infrastructure needed to transform an economy based on the export of raw materials to one based on industrial production. Another was the concentration of investment in industries that produce luxury goods and yield a high rate of return rather than in capital goods industries, whose development was thereby delayed for a long time. Still others were overcapitalization stimulated by generous government subsidies, and overmechanization with expensive, labor-saving machinery designed for the labor-scarce economies of advanced nations rather than for Latin America where labor is cheap, abundant, and should be utilized if possible.[5]

As a result of the tendency of Brazil's industries to overmechanize with labor-saving machinery, the number of industrial workers rose only 2.8

---

[3] For a penetrating analysis of the impact of these conditions, see David Horowitz, "Narrowing the Gap Through International Aid," *Fiscal and Monetary Problems in Developing States,* ed. David Krivine (New York: Frederick A. Praeger, Inc., 1967), pp. 46–47.

According to Andre Gunder Frank, it is capitalism itself, with its internal contradictions, and not the semifeudal structure of society that has "generated the underdevelopment of Chile and determined its forms." Andre Gunder Frank, *Capitalism and Underdevelopment in Latin America: Historical Studies of Chile and Brazil* (New York: Monthly Review Press, 1967), p. 115.

[4] Anibal Pinto, "Political Aspects of Economic Development in Latin America," *Obstacles to Change in Latin America,* ed. Claudio Veliz (New York: Oxford University Press, 1965, pp. 9–13.

[5] Celso Furtado, "Political Obstacles to Economic Growth in Brazil," *Obstacles to Change in Latin America, op. cit.,* pp. 149.

The matter of industry's capacity and responsibility to absorb surplus manpower is a controversial issue, it should be noted. Some argue that development is best promoted by utilizing the most advanced techniques in order to realize the maximum output per worker, even though this means employing as few as possible. Others argue that industry has an obligation to employ as many workers as is economically feasible, thereby providing jobs for the many who need them. Economic Commission for Latin America, *The Process of Industrial Development in Latin America* (New York: United Nations, 1966), p. 35.

percent a year—a rate less than that of the population as a whole, and less than half that of the urban population growth. Thus, the existing widespread unemployment of labor became even more acute during a decade of rapidly expanding industrialization.[6]

In striving to speed up industrialization, the nations have encountered many obstacles, including the shortage of managerial and technical skills and of entrepreneurial initiative. By far the greatest obstacle has been the shortage of capital needed to establish new industries or expand existing ones.

The formation of investment capital is far more difficult today than during the Industrial Revolution in Western Europe. Then, the entrepreneurs managed to accumulate the capital needed by squeezing out every possible ounce of energy, effort, and production from the workers, as *David Copperfield* and other works by Charles Dickens graphically portray. More recently, Soviet Russia managed to accomplish the great industrial leap forward by repressive measures to accumulate capital at the expense of the living standards of the masses. In Latin America today, the mass with its low income would hardly acquiesce in deprivation to form capital, unless it was imposed by a completely dictatorial regime, as that of Castro in Cuba.

In financing Latin America's industrial development, the main sources of domestic capital are profits that may be reinvested and loans that may be obtained from the banks. Although profits reinvested are a major stimulus to industrial expansion in more advanced states, they are so relatively small compared with the total amount of profits in Latin America that they have far less effect on expansion.[7] For Latin American businessmen have a well-known penchant for stashing away their profits in the banks of Switzerland and other foreign nations rather than plowing them back into much needed internal development.[8] In particular, reinvestment has not taken place in the nations with great inflationary pressures; rather, the companies have relied on domestic credit or foreign financing, thus increasing inflationary pressures.[9] But while Latin American businessmen are allergic to keeping their own profits at home and reinvesting them, they feel strongly that foreign-owned firms should

---

6 Furtado, *op. cit.*, p. 150.

7 Economic Commission for Latin America, *The Process of Industrial Development in Latin America, op. cit.*, p. 199.

8 For the extent and impact of the flight of capital, see pp. 249–50 of this book.

9 Organization of American States, *Final Report of the Fourth Annual Meeting of the Inter-American Economic and Social Council* (Washington, D.C.: Pan American Union, 1966), p. 105.

Since three of the most industrially advanced nations are in this category—Argentina, Brazil, and Chile—the major part of the region's industrialization effort is adversely affected. For the heights of inflation that have engulfed these three nations, see Economic Commission for Latin America, *Statistical Bulletin for Latin America: Vol. III, No. 1* (New York: United Nations, 1966), p. 18.

not be allowed to send much of their profits back home, but should be required to reinvest them and to integrate their new investments into the national development program.[10]

Another source of domestic capital consists of loans from the banks. The widespread shortage of credit is reflected in its high costs—costs that, as mentioned earlier, further contribute to the spiral of inflation in those nations where it is rampant. The rate of interest charged may be as much as 15 percent, possibly much higher. For where the commercial banks are not authorized to grant medium- and long-term loans, they usually operate through subsidiary financing enterprises that are not subject to the banking laws and so can charge a much higher rate of interest.[11]

What might be expected to be an important domestic source of capital —the stock market—has hardly materialized in Latin America. There are stock markets after a fashion in only a half-dozen or so of the nations; in many of them, such a trading exchange has not yet been established. As an example of the activity on one of the main exchanges of the region, in Lima in 1963 only 20 industrial enterprises were registered on the exchange, the shares of only 7 were traded that year, and of the total transactions, 93 percent were in the shares of only 4 enterprises. Almost this identical pattern exists in the other exchanges.[12]

Familiar with the tremendous activity of the New York and American Stock Exchanges, one may wonder what accounts for the situation in Latin America. The answer is simple—the importance of the family and the tight control it has over finance. Most enterprises are so largely family owned that there is little reason for selling stock on the market, except possibly an amount so small that the family's control is not affected. Because of the tight control, profits are not distributed as dividends but as emoluments to the directors and the management. The result, of course, is that shares of stock are hardly regarded as negotiable, but rather as a mere reflection of the ownership of the enterprise.[13]

Also available for financing industrial enterprises are two main foreign sources of capital—loans from international and foreign national credit institutions, and direct private investment. The principal exterior lending agencies that assist in the region's industrial development are the United States Export-Import Bank (Eximbank), the International Bank for Re-

---

[10] Albert Lauterbach, *Enterprise in Latin America: Business Attitudes in a Developing Economy* (Ithaca, N.Y.: Cornell University Press, 1966), p. 121.

[11] Economic Commission for Latin America, *The Process of Industrial Development in Latin America, op. cit.*, p. 203.

[12] *Ibid.*, p. 200.

[13] *Ibid.*, p. 212. For detailed information about the organization and operation of the several stock markets, see *ibid.*, pp. 205–16.

construction and Development (IBRD), and the Inter-American Development Bank (IADB). During the period 1940–63, the total amount of external loans for financing industrial activities in Latin America was approximately $1.3 billion, of which Eximbank made 71.5 percent, IADB, 11.9 percent; IBRD and its subsidiaries, 9.8 percent; and the Mutual Security Program and other agencies, the balance.[14]

Two of these agencies are rather regarded in Latin America as Shylock himself. Eximbank, established in 1934 as a Depression measure to stimulate American foreign trade, makes loans at 4 percent or so, and requires that purchases for which the loan is granted be made in the United States, even though prices are often higher there than elsewhere. Eximbank has also been criticized for extending most of its loans to only several nations, and to only several industries there. The IBRD is regarded with almost as much disfavor, since its policy is to charge the going rate of interest and to avoid granting loans that might compete with private capital from other countries. Only the IADB is popular in Latin America because of its policy of soft loans, which bear a low rate of interest, extend for a long period, and may be granted even for nonamortizable projects.[15]

The other principal external source of funds for the region's industrialization is direct capital investment, meaning in most cases a foreign company's establishing a subsidiary there. But while Latin Americans strongly prefer the mixed, domestic-foreign type of enterprise in which they can buy stock and share in the benefits,[16] most United States companies that operate in South America prefer to own most or all the stock themselves. In fact, 85 percent of the capital of these companies is invested in enterprises in which the parent company owns 95 percent or more of the business; 12 percent, in which it owns 50 to 95 percent; and only 3 percent in which it owns less than a 50 percent interest.[17]

Some American companies welcome local participation in the ownership of the enterprises. Among these is Sears, Roebuck and Company, which has stores in Brazil, Colombia, Mexico, Peru, and Venezuela. (Its first store, opened in Havana, Cuba, in 1942, was a casualty of Castro.) Two of the stores in 1962 had profit sharing funds; the other stores planned to establish them shortly. Employee members of the funds contribute 5 percent of their salaries up to a maximum amount; the company contributes to the funds 5 percent of its net profits before federal income taxes. The major portion of each fund is used to purchase stock in the local company. As of 1962, the Mexican employees owned 20 percent of

14 *Ibid.*, p. 217.
15 *Ibid.*, pp. 216–18.
16 Lauterbach, *op. cit.*, p. 122.
17 U.S. Department of Commerce, *U.S. Business Investments in Foreign Countries* (Washington, D.C., 1960), p. 101.

Sears de Mexico, and the Venezuelan employees owned 13 percent of Sears de Venezuela.[18]

During the past four decades, the estimated rate of return on United States direct investments in Latin America has risen sharply. In 1929, the return was about 6 percent of book value, a figure that rose to 11.2 percent in 1945, and 20.5 in 1951. The highest yields were those earned in the petroleum industry—about 31.1 percent—and in distribution—about 28.1 percent.[19]

Yet, despite this sharp increase in the rate of return, the relative importance of United States investments in Latin America is far less in recent years than formerly. These investments, which in 1929 represented almost half of United States foreign investment throughout the world, steadily dwindled to 40 percent in 1950, to 34 percent in 1955, and to less than 23 percent in 1962.[20]

Although Latin Americans often lament the intrusion of foreign capital, especially American, they lament far more when such capital passes them by, more interested in other areas of investment. Patterns of the flow of capital, concludes the Corporation for Economic and Industrial Research, show that non-U.S. foreign private investment, like foreign governmental loans and grants, tends to concentrate in areas of political influence, as the Commonwealth or French community—a tendency that will undoubtedly become more pronounced. Most U.S. private foreign investment goes to developed countries, and the balance selectively to a few rapidly developing countries, mainly in Latin America, and to the oil and mineral rich regions—a trend which can be expected to continue.[21]

In their frustration, Latin Americans sometimes openly express their disillusionment at American investors going elsewhere when they are supposedly obligated to Latin America. But are they really so obligated? The Corporation for Economic and Industrial Research succinctly summarizes the issue. "The private patterns of investment are understandable; important as their efforts are, private investors are not in the business of economic development per se. Development is a by-product. If private

---

[18] John F. Gallagher, "The Sears, Roebuck & Company Venture in Latin America," *Foreign Investment in Latin America* (New York: United Nations, 1959), p. 162.

For a more detailed account of Sears' operation in Mexico, see Richardson Wood and Virginia Keyser, *United States Business Performance Abroad: The Case Study of Sears, Roebuck de México, S.A.* (National Planning Association, 1953).

[19] United Nations, Department of Economic and Social Affairs, *Foreign Capital in Latin America, op. cit.*, pp. 3–15.

[20] Economic Commission for Latin America, *The Process of Industrial Development in Latin America, op. cit.*, p. 220.

[21] Corporation for Economic and Industrial Research, Inc., "Private Investment and United States Foreign Policy," *Foreign Investment in Latin America, op. cit.*, pp. 232–33.

investment is to go to areas and for purposes important to U.S. foreign policy, specific incentives will need to be devised for specific purposes."[22]

Beset by the urgency of economic development, the Latin American nations are obviously in a dilemma. Domestic sources of capital have for one reason or another been far from adequate. And foreign sources have failed to provide the assistance needed, while at the same time for a number of reasons have been resented by the society.

The resentment in Mexico is summed up by Gustavo Romero Kolbech.

External funds were available but costly. . . . the government was able to obtain only small loans that were generally subject to relatively stiff conditions (tied, short-term loans at a high rate of interest) . . . direct investment in one way or another was excessively oriented to the needs of the country of origin and did not necessarily accommodate itself to urgent development needs. What is more, the servicing of this class of investment in the forms of dividends, royalties, and other items was more costly to Mexico than the servicing of loans, especially of long-term loans.[23]

Getting back to Latin America's urgent need of rapid economic development in the face of many obstacles, what is the solution to the region's problem? Many have hoped to provide the answer.

Among these is Raúl Prebisch, well-known economist of Argentina. The so-called Prebisch theory for the most part recapitulates the sentiments and convictions of Latin Americans for many decades past. Latin America's traditional peripheral position has been producing raw materials and food for the centers that produced manufactured goods. The prices of primary products have tended to decline but those of manufactured goods to increase. The failure of manufactured goods prices to become cheaper relative to those of primary goods is due to the high wages and prices monopolistically established in the centers, especially in the United States. The answer to Latin America's dilemma, Prebisch contends, is in obtaining more foreign loans and aid, not in inducing more domestic capital accumulation or increasing the volume of exports.[24]

Another proposal for providing the assistance needed by Latin

---

[22] *Ibid.*, p. 233.

[23] Kolbech, *op. cit.*, pp. 187–88.
Mexico today has such an excellent credit rating and record of stability that it is able to obtain credit on much better terms than apparently any other country in Latin America. Foreign suppliers bidding on equipment to be purchased by Mexico have offered up to 14 years credit on the total cost.
Mexico gained access to an invaluable source of credit when it was able to sell its government bonds in international markets under conditions similar to those enjoyed by bonds of wide acceptance. *Ibid.*, p. 188.

[24] For a summary and interpretation of Prebisch's views, see William Withers, *The Economic Crisis in Latin America* (New York: The Free Press of Glencoe, 1964), pp. 73–77.

America and other underdeveloped regions is that advanced by David Horowitz, governor of the Bank of Israel. Far more aid should be provided and on more generous terms, he contends. However, in most of the donor countries public opinion and congressional sentiment have become opposed to this course. The way out of the dilemma is for governments of the developed countries to raise in their own financial markets the necessary amount of aid capital by guaranteeing repayment of the amounts raised and by subsidizing interest payments to cover the difference between the market rates of interest and the soft terms on which the money will be made available to developing countries.[25]

Another proposal for the rapid economic development of the region has quite a different emphasis from the others. Instead of concentrating on increasing capital investment, Lauchlin Currie advocates placing initial emphasis on the social and economic infrastructure of the society. Currie would create a comprehensive program for the provision of urban housing, public services, and wage goods. Such a program would have many benefits: it would furnish the employment and, of course, income that a large part of the mass critically needs; at the same time it would provide the social and economic facilities that constitute a sound infrastructure for economic development.[26] Currie reasons that jobs providing an income and basic facilities for fulfilling educational and other needs would break the vicious cycle of poverty, illiteracy, and hopelessness generating more poverty, illiteracy, and hopelessness. He terms his approach "the breakthrough plan."[27]

The Alliance for Progress

The most comprehensive and ambitious program for speeding up the economic and social development of Latin America is, of course, the Alliance for Progress. President John F. Kennedy on March 13, 1961, ad-

---

[25] Horowitz, *op. cit.*, p. 51.

[26] "The achievement of the country's (Colombia's) growth goals requires considerable public investments to provide economic infrastructure facilities and social services, as well as foreign exchange for the importation of capital equipment," concludes Wolfgang G. Friedmann and others in *International Financial Aid* (New York: Columbia University Press, 1966), p. 154.

The creation of an infrastructure by means of a sustained program of public works was an important factor in Mexico's great progress. "These public works permitted the gradual realization of the aspirations of important groups and facilitated geographic and social mobility introduced by the Revolution." Gustavo Romero Kolbech, "Economic Development of Mexico: Financing the Infrastructure," *Economic Development Issues, Latin America* (Supplementary Paper No. 21) (Committee for Economic Development, August, 1967), p. 180.

[27] Lauchlin Currie, *Accelerating Development: The Necessity and the Means* (New York: McGraw-Hill Book Co., Inc., 1966), pp. 86–94. For the application of Currie's breakthrough plan to Colombia, see chap. 14.

dressing the assembled representatives of the Latin American republics and members of the United States Congress, proposed that the American republics work together in the Alliance, "to satisfy the basic needs of the American people for homes, work and land, health and schools." The following August, at Punte del Este, Uruguay, concrete plans for carrying out the Alliance were drafted at a special meeting of the Inter-American Economic and Social Council at the ministerial level.[28]

The Alliance, recognizing that the total inflow of external financing into the Latin American countries from all sources was only about $1 billion a year or less, aimed to at least double this amount to the minimum of $20 billion over a decade. About half of the total would come from various U.S. official programs, including development loans of up to 50 years and "at very low or zero rates of interest." The other $10 billion would come from 3 separate groups, each contributing an estimated $3 billion or more: U.S. private investors; international agencies, such as the International Bank for Reconstruction and Development and the Inter-American Development Bank; and European and Japanese public and private sources.

In return for this financial assistance, the Latin Americans agreed to strive for a number of goals: institute agrarian, tax, and monetary reforms; eliminate illiteracy; provide better housing, health, and sanitation; assure fair wages and satisfactory working conditions for all workers; improve and strengthen democratic institutions; accelerate economic and social development; and promote the economic integration of Latin America.

After almost a decade of operation, the Alliance has achieved a measure of success, a measure that falls far short of the expectations of most persons. On the plus side, tax receipts increased 26 percent between 1960 and 1964. Moreover, the necessary national and international institutions have been established, including the Inter-American Committee for the Alliance for Progress, national planning agencies, development banks, agrarian institutes, and loan associations. Also, comprehensive programs of economic and social reform have been formulated in most of the nations, and attempts have been made to translate the ambitious plans into law. The very goals of the Alliance have alerted many leaders to the necessity for and inevitability of reform.

On the negative side, while planning agencies have been active in formulating reform after reform, relatively few of these reforms have been adopted to date. Especially ominous are certain statistics that indicate that the Alliance is failing in several of its most important goals. Instead of a per capita increase in the Gross National Product of at least

---

[28] The Charter of Punte del Este is given in John C. Dreier (ed.), *The Alliance for Progress: Problems and Perspectives* (Baltimore: Johns Hopkins Press, 1962), pp. 118–41.

2.5 percent annually, as was envisaged, the increase has sagged to a much lower level. And instead of the much more abundant food supply needed for the expanding population, the per capita food production has actually declined. In other realms, too, such as housing, public health facilities, and potable water, the progress made to date is considerably short of what was intended.[29]

Regarding the Alliance's progress, there is no end to reasons, excuses, or blame for why it has not accomplished more. From the beginning, it was probably oversold; many a Latin American, reading the bold figure of $20 billion without bothering to follow the fine print, assumed it was a Marshall Plan for Latin America—a massive program of aid which he felt the region was entitled to. He did not realize until later that the program was essentially an underwriting one, seeking to guarantee a minimum flow of external aid, much of which was already being provided and in the very same forms.[30]

The very countdown of the program's takeoff was delayed in many countries by the required formulation of a comprehensive national plan of development. In most of the nations, planning was not a bad word, as in the United States when the Tennessee Valley Authority's bold program was launched in 1933; with their easy-going way of life, they simply had not felt the need for it. Uruguay's comprehensive plan[31] was not completed until 1965, and for good reason: the nation hardly knew what was going on inside, for it had not bothered to take a census since 1908.[32]

Other more formidable obstacles to the success of the Alliance have been the consuming inflation in Argentina, Brazil, and Chile, which makes planning virtually impossible and keeps the society in a turmoil; the flight

---

[29] These accomplishments and shortcomings are given in Robert N. Burr, *Our Troubled Hemisphere: Perspectives on United States–Latin American Relations* (Washington, D.C.: Brookings Institution, 1967), pp. 223–24.

For a brief summary of the activities and accomplishments of the Alliance in each of the states, see J. Warren Nystrom and Nathan A. Haverstock, *The Alliance for Progress: Key to Latin America's Development* (Princeton, N.J.: D. Van Nostrand Co., Inc., 1966), pp. 88–112.

[30] This reaction is understandable. But what is surprising to an American researcher is the widespread lack of interest among Latin American entrepreneurs and businessmen in the Alliance, as well as ignorance of what it actually is. As Albert Lauterbach found, a sizable number of those replying to the question, "What is the Alliance?" admittedly had not kept up with it and knew little about it. Even many who thought they were well informed about it showed only a hazy understanding of it. Lauterbach, *op. cit.*, pp. 127–28.

[31] Centro de Estudiantes de Ciencias Económicas y de Administración (CECEA), *Plan Nacional de Desarrollo Económico y Social, 1965–1974* (Montevideo, 1966), Tomo I y Tomo II.

[32] Uruguayans may be absentminded for a half-century or so about a census, but when they take one, they plan for it with a vengeance. When the census was taken on October 16, 1963, the carefully selected date was chosen because a 50-year study of rainfall showed that it should be a fair day for the undertaking.

of capital, especially from these same nations, as industrialists and businessmen daily invest their pesos and cruzeiros abroad, well knowing that their inflationary policies will make them worth even less at home tomorrow; and the lack of courage on the part of most Latin American leaders to wholeheartedly support the Alliance. The Alliance has been the butt of much criticism. Its structure and procedures are so bureaucratic that they delay rather than expedite plans for economic development, some critics charge. Its assistance, intended mainly to benefit the masses, seldom gets down to them, others are convinced.[33]

Undoubtedly one of the most vehement critics of the Alliance for Progress is Victor Alba. But unlike most Latin Americans, he does not blame the United States; instead, he aims his broadsides directly at Latin America itself. There, the calls for liberty, representative democracy, progress, and racial equality are myths and myths only, he bitterly concludes. And while the society professes to want progress, the ruling upper and middle classes strongly oppose it. The only way whereby the Alliance can achieve its basic goal of transforming Latin America's semi-feudal society into a modern, democratic one is to circumvent the ruling classes and make a new Alliance directly with the huge mass who yearn for its benefits.[34]

ECONOMIC PLANNING

For the past several decades some of the nations of Latin America have utilized economic planning to establish national goals and work toward their realization. In recent years, planning has been greatly stimulated by the Alliance for Progress' requirement that a nation have an acceptable plan of development in order to be eligible for assistance. Consequently, every one of the nations today has one or several such plans.

In the past, the nations have experimented with various types of planning organizations. In Mexico, the 19 or so planning bodies to date have had full-time or part-time staffs, headed by a single director or a board, and "almost every permutation of organizational characteristics."[35] To-

---

[33] Such a critic with figures to back up his charge is Josué de Castro. The entire Brazilian Northeast with its 25 million impoverished inhabitants received only half as much aid from the Alliance as did the relatively prosperous state of Guanabara with only 4 million people. Josué de Castro, *Death in the Northeast* (New York: Random House, Inc., 1966).

[34] Victor Alba, *Alliance Without Allies: The Mythology of Progress in Latin America* (New York: Frederick A. Praeger, Inc., 1965).

[35] Bertram M. Gross, "The Dynamics of Competitive Planning: A Prefatory Comment," in Robert J. Shafer, *Mexico: Mutual Adjustment Planning* (Syracuse, N.Y.: Syracuse University Press, 1966), p. xii.

For a brief account of the planning organization and activities in each nation, see Economic Commission for Latin America, *Economic Survey of Latin America* (New York: United Nations, 1966), pp. 334–45.

day, however, the national planning bodies follow a rather uniform pattern. Usually, there is a council consisting of ministers and other high-level officials responsible for economic and social affairs. The presiding officer is often the president of the republic; in Venezuela, CORDIPLAN, the national authority, is even housed in Miraflores, the presidential palace in Caracas, and benefits by its prestigious propinquity to the president himself.[36] If the president of the republic does not head the council, the minister of economic affairs discharges this duty. The main functions of the council are to establish the basic policies and guidelines for a national plan, and to approve the plan when completed. The body that actually formulates the plan, translating the broad goals into specific objectives with the means of obtaining them, is in some cases the secretariat of the council; in others, it is an independent, specialized agency.

The plans formulated and adopted fall into several main categories. The overall plans deal with the development problems and goals of the nation as a whole, linking the welfare of the main segments in society with the pace of national development. The public investment plans establish the priorities for governmental assistance and the domestic or external means of financing. The sectoral plans relate to specific areas of the economy that need attention, such as public power, transportation, public health, or education.[37]

Planning at the lower levels of government receives less attention but is nevertheless quite important. Sharing the spotlight at these levels are the regional, state, and municipal plans. Among the regional plans, several are especially well known. Mexico's Papaloapan Project for developing agriculture in one of the nation's tropical areas is a "Mexican TVA"—an ambitious, multipurpose project for flood control, irrigation, generation of power, transportation, and the integral economic and social development of the region.[38] Brazil's Superintendency for Development of the Northeast (usually referred to as SUDENE) has accomplished much by regionwide planning "to create an economy resistant to the drought, and to restructure the agrarian economy and intensify industrial investments."[39] Venezuela's regional development program undertaken by the Guayana Corporation represents a massive effort to transform part of the country into a major center of heavy industry, with its hydroelectric

---

[36] John Friedmann, *Venezuela: From Doctrine to Dialogue* (Syracuse, N.Y.: Syracuse University Press, 1965), p. 34.

[37] For the content and scope of educational planning and the remodeling of the school system to prepare the mass for the region's anticipated economic development, see Economic Commission for Latin America, *Economic Bulletin for Latin America*, Vol. XI, No. 2 (New York: United Nations, 1967), pp. 1–57.

[38] Thomas T. Poleman, *The Papaloapan Project: Agricultural Development in the Mexican Tropics* (Stanford, Calif.: Stanford University Press, 1964), pp. 94–95.

[39] Stefan H. Robock, *Brazil's Developing Northeast: A Study of Regional Planning and Foreign Aid* (Washington, D.C.: Brookings Institution, 1963), p. 107.

installation, a steel plant using local iron ores, and a new city built around a core of new basic industries.[40]

Regarding planning at the level of the states and municipalities, Brazil has made noteworthy progress with its many agencies and projects.[41]

Whatever the level of a planning agency—national, regional, state, or municipal—there are several requisites for the effective discharge of its responsibilities. Not only a nation's public administration but also its entire governmental machinery must so function as to enable planning decisions to be carried out. When this is not the case, as Kilty concludes about Peru, any program of planning will be stifled by the instability of ministerial leadership, bureaucratic inertia, and the relative autonomy of the independent public sector.[42] Another requisite relates to the composition of the planning bodies: all the major sectors and groups concerned with development should be brought into the planning process, as they have much to contribute and will be affected by decisions that are made. In Peru, failure of the National Planning Institute to include the private sector in the planning process has been a notable weakness in the whole procedure.[43] Other requisites are that the planners establish targets that are realistic and can possibly be attained; also, that when they adopt a plan, they supervise its execution to assure that it is carried out as intended, periodically revising a medium- or long-range plan if it seems necessary.

Planning is crucial to the development of Latin America, asserts William Withers, even though it may be regarded by some as dangerous "Prebischism." In fact, the Latin American nations should go one step beyond the two promising young common markets—that is, set up a comprehensive plan for all Latin America, including its economic relations with the United States.[44]

Brazil—an Unstable Nation with Haphazard Planning[45]

Brazil is indeed exasperating to anyone who is convinced of the need and efficacy of planning. For in Brazil there is little or no correlation between planning activity and economic development. From all the

---

[40] John Friedmann, *op. cit.*, pp. 59–60.

[41] For the types and responsibilities of Brazil's state planning organizations, their dates of founding, and state in which located, see Economic Commission for Latin America, *Economic Bulletin for Latin America, op. cit.*, p. 71.

[42] Daniel R. Kilty, *Planning for Development in Peru* (New York: Frederick A. Praeger, Inc., 1967), pp. 158–59.

[43] *Ibid.*, pp. 90–91 and 159.
This exclusion, whatever the reason for it, is unfortunate. For the private sector has a dynamism that has achieved spectacular results, sometimes without any sort of governmental support. Rómulo A. Ferrero, "Economic Development of Peru," *Economic Development Issues, Latin America, op. cit.*, p. 229.

[44] Withers, *op. cit.*, pp. 84 and 125.

[45] The information in this section comes from Robert T. Daland, *Brazilian Planning: Development Politics and Administration* (Chapel Hill: University of North Carolina Press, 1967).

evidence, Brazil appears to have made its progress without relying on planning.

The nation's first significant experience with planning began in 1942, with a joint Brazilian–United States survey of the nation as a pilot area for testing modern methods of industrial development. The plan produced was to cover a 10-year period and cost $4 billion. It was kept secret for many years and, with the end of the war and Vargas thrown out of office, was quietly dropped.

Since that initial effort in 1942, there have been five main plans or agencies, each supposedly intending to remedy whatever was wrong with the nation: the Salte Plan of 1949–53, to coordinate existing plans; the National Development Bank, created in 1952 to obtain funds from international as well as domestic sources; the Program of Goals of 1956–60, the first plan with specific goals for every major segment in the economy; the *Plano Trienal* of 1963–65 to coordinate the plans and activities of the regional agencies as well as foreign aid to Brazil; and the Program of Action of 1964–66, which Castelo Branco hoped would institute effective planning and control over the economy.[46]

As these plans show, planning in Brazil has been haphazard and hit-or-miss. The chief executives and other politicians have either not really understood the benefits that might accrue to the nation from planning or have understood only too well how it could be used as a political gimmick that had popular appeal. As a result, the nation has not had even the first effective national planning institution. Whatever planning has been done at this level has been mainly *projectismo*. Plans are formulated, even when there is no government agency for carrying them out.

Mexico—a Stable Nation with "Incomplete Formal Planning"[47]

In 1933, Mexico adopted its first Six-Year Plan of Economic Development, and in 1939 its second Six-Year Plan. Both were expressed in general, often ambiguous, terms more reflective of political oratory than of definite goals and specific data one expects to find in a plan. Consequently, both have been branded as mere scraps of paper or pious exhortations.

Apparently, Mexico was ever ready to give at least lip service to central planning. For over the past four decades (including the 12 years covered by the first and second six-year plans), the nation has had approximately a score of agencies designated by the government as central planning bodies. They invariably encountered fierce opposition from competing governmental agencies and usually died in infancy.

---

[46] These plans, analyzed and compared in much detail, comprise most of Daland's study.

[47] The information in this section is from Shafer, and Preface by Gross, *op. cit.*

After the demise of the second Six-Year Plan in 1945, the nation showed no further interest in a formal, comprehensive plan until 1962. Then, a frightening slowdown in economic development plus the Alliance for Progress requirement of a plan in order to receive assistance impressed on the government the need for a comprehensive plan of development.

The result was the Plan of Immediate Action for 1962–1964. As plans go, this one was unique in many respects. Its provisions? They have never been made public—are as closely guarded a secret as the production costs of General Motors or Ford Motor Company. (The text of the plan was not even available for Robert Shafer's study of planning in the nation.) Who drew up the plan? Not even that is known except "that it was done by a small group of men, and that Victor Urquidi of the Bank of Mexico was prominent among them." The procedures followed in drafting the plan? This, too, was apparently closely guarded, top-secret information.

Despite Mexico's many years of interest in planning, it has never had a single, central agency, like CORDIPLAN in Venezuela, empowered to establish goals of development and to supervise the execution of its plans. It is no wonder, then, that some scholars, such as Sanford Mosk and Howard F. Cline, have concluded that Mexico's development has been "planless"; and that another scholar, Miguel S. Wionczek, has stated that it has been the result of "incomplete formal planning."

Although Mexico has not practiced conventional planning, Robert J. Shafer concludes that the nation, in effect, has practiced its own peculiar form of planning—a form that has been quite beneficial as shown by the remarkable economic and social progress of the last several decades. This progress was mainly the result of the planning, not of a single overall agency, but rather of the nation's homegrown system, as indigenous as its own social revolution. In brief, this system consists of four powerful institutions: the Presidency, the Ministry of Finance, the Bank of Mexico, and Nacional Financiera.[48] These four institutions, far more powerful than their counterparts in other countries, constitute a "central guidance cluster" that, working closely together, has planned the nation's course of economic and social development. The cluster, together with hundreds of organs of government and enterprises in which the government participates in one fashion or another, constitutes "a web of institutions and policies and devices," all engaged in planning and promoting development. Under the system, planning is quite decentralized and is so largely the result of competition among the many groups that it is often referred to as "competitive" or "mutual adjustment planning."

---

[48] Nacional Financiera's main responsibility is to finance industrial development by all means possible—making loans, buying securities, and guaranteeing foreign and domestic bank credit and investment.

In addition to the formulation of overall programs, there has been much planning for the main sectors of the nation, especially agriculture and irrigation, manufacturing, transportation, electric power, and petroleum. There has also been effective planning at the regional level, as shown by the Papaloapan and similar projects, also by the attention given to state and municipal problems.

Venezuela—a Relatively Stable Nation with Comprehensive Formal Planning[49]

Following the overthrow of Pérez Jiménez in January, 1958, the new democratic regime set as one of its top priorities the formulation of a comprehensive plan of economic and social development. When the commission was appointed to draft the proposal for a national system of planning, all major political parties in the nation were represented. For the planning to be done would be in the interest of the whole nation, transcending the interest of any one party.[50] The commission's labors bore fruit when, on the following December 30, the Congress established the Central Office of Coordination and Planning, usually referred to as CORDIPLAN.

No haphazard offspring but the brainchild of planned parenthood, CORDIPLAN from the very beginning was accorded a high status and deference. Housed in Miraflores, the presidential palace, the agency enjoyed the unique distinction of being the only one within constant earshot of the president. This favored position at the very apex of the national power pyramid virtually implied that the director of national planning would be a man who had great personal prestige and enjoyed the close confidence of the president.

Also contributing to CORDIPLAN's apparently successful operation was the appointment of a permanent consultative commission composed of representatives from government, business, labor, and the Association of Economics to give advice on questions of national planning. Consequently, planning has become almost universally accepted by the more articulate sectors of public opinion as a means to promote national development. Even the essentially skeptical, if not downright hostile, business community has been won over to the idea of national planning.

The legislation establishing planning applied to all officials at all levels of government who were responsible for preparing programs of work and carrying them out. Comformably to this guideline, CORDI-

---

[49] The information in this section unless otherwise indicated is from John Friedmann, with preface by Gross, *op. cit.*

[50] The broadly representative composition of the commission was similar to that of another commission hammering out one of the new regime's main objectives—a complete program of agrarian reform.

PLAN has striven to make planning and coordination important govern-mentwide functions. It also encourages establishing new planning units and strengthening existing ones in the various ministries and other public agencies.

Seeking the support of all segments of society, as of communists and priests to build a schoolhouse, CORDIPLAN has operated on the assumption that to get its work done only minimal public consensus is required. It has also operated on the assumption that it may be necessary to yield a little, maybe a lot, to get a plan adopted or carried out.

Besides promoting economic development, national planning in the nation has also had five latent but important functions: (1) strengthening the president, who can rely on CORDIPLAN for confidential, trust-worthy, and expert advice on economic questions; (2) improving the political process by introducing technical data and reasoning when appropriate; (3) creating a development society by setting up national goals as powerful symbols of progress, also creating a new mentality for achieving them; (4) reducing social conflict by preventing a polarization of social forces into ideologically extreme positions, and reconciling competing interests into what appears to be the national interest; (5) taking advantage of the assistance provided by the Alliance for Progress.

The first three Venezuelan plans were: Plan de la Nación, 1960–64; Plan de Desarrollo Económico y Social Para 1962, which replaced the first plan; and Plan de la Nación, 1963–66. In evaluating the effectiveness of these plans on the basis of goals achieved, Fred D. Levy, Jr. concludes that the first plan was a marked failure, that the second was not appreciably better, but that the third was somewhat more successful, mainly during the first half of the plan. "If the plans were, indeed, a meaningful expression of public policy," Levy states, "their poor record, with regard to target fulfillment, would seem to indicate flaws in the plans themselves, or a pronounced weakness of public policy in influencing the national economy."[51]

Cuba—a Revolutionary Nation with Experimental Planning[52]

During the first two years or so after Castro took over, the methods of work and administration that prevailed throughout the government were known by the Cubans as *Por la Libre*, "freely, without restraints," with everyone on his own, freewheeling, so to speak. Whether organizations were cooperatives, people's stores, factories, or other agencies, they

---

[51] Fred D. Levy, Jr., *Economic Planning in Venezuela* (New York: Frederick A. Praeger, Inc., 1968), pp. 104, 107, 111, and 116. Levy gives a detailed statistical evaluation of these plans in chap. 4.

[52] The information in this section is from Edward Boorstein, *The Economic Transformation of Cuba* (New York: Monthly Review Press, 1968), chap. 5.

wheeled freely with little outside guidance or control. The ministries resembled independent fiefs, each concentrating almost exclusively on its own responsibilities.

By mid–1960, with the strategic parts of the economy nationalized, it was obvious that *Por la Libre* would have to go and some system of national planning instituted in its place. However, the Czech Economic Delegation that arrived toward the end of 1960 to provide technical assistance in planning apparently contributed as many problems as answers. For in the Czech plan, everything was done by the book, meaning, of course, Czechoslovakia's book, which had but little bearing on Cuba's specific problems. In planning sessions, Czech answers given to Cuban questions were sometimes ludicrous. When an economist from the Cuban Ministry of Foreign Commerce posed the question of whether his government should operate a system of warehouses at the ports, the Czech advisers regarded the question as irrelevant. Czechoslovakia, they explained, does not have any warehouses at ports.

On February 13, 1961, the government announced that 1962 would be the Year of Planning, when the economy would for the first time be directed under a single, comprehensive economic plan. Drafting the plan presented many more problems than had been anticipated. Organization-wise, the chart might call for 20 people with training and experience in the analysis of pricing and commodity markets; but if the director had only 2 persons qualified for the responsibility and preferred to operate temporarily with them, he was told he had to have 18 more live bodies to comply with planning directives. Another frustration—the forms for planning, appropriate for Czechoslovakia rather than for Cuba, often asked for accounting information from economic units in which accounting systems had not yet been installed. Perhaps most exasperating of all were the innumerable reports that had to be made—reports whose statistics were gauged more by their quantity than by their accuracy.

As finally formulated in spite of obstacles, the 1962 plan established many key goals for the nation: the number of houses, schools, hospitals, roads, and factories to be constructed; the quantity of sugar, tobacco, coffee, textiles, and other commodities to be produced; and the amount of goods available for export to obtain needed foreign exchange.

Despite all the feverish planning, when the 1962 plan was put into effect certain defects in the system became immediately apparent. The style of work became bureaucratic, with emphasis on rules of procedure instead of on getting a job done. Every office was flooded with papers and spent most of its time battling red tape. Staff meetings were almost endless, developing a momentum of their own. The top-heavy bureaucracy was such a serious problem that the leaders of the Revolution were troubled about it. Castro even gave a long speech, castigating bureaucracy at the National Bank.

Other defects of the plan were obvious in time. Most goals were fixed at impossibly high levels, reflecting revolutionary exuberance or possibly deliberate intent to stimulate the workers to work harder. Compounding the problem of overhigh goals was the failure to set up adequate reserves or to establish margins for error and unforeseeable contingencies.

As a participant in making and carrying out Cuba's plan for 1962, Edward Boorstein concludes that it failed mainly because the planners developed an ivory tower of their own, became oblivious of the real needs of their fellow citizens and the nation. In their ivory tower, the planners made a fetish of planning, which they believed would automatically solve the problems and run the economy.

Despite the plan's many shortcomings and apparent lack of success, it should not be regarded as entirely a failure, Boorstein contends. For it was an excellent exercise in planning; when the plans did not work out as intended, the planners reevaluated their procedures and goals, reassessing them in terms of individual and national aspirations rather than merely statistics in an agency report.

The nation's plan for 1963 was completed on time. Although it, too, suffered from countless flaws—none comparable to those of the year before—the plan was workable. In 1963 the Cuban economy for the first time operated in accordance with an overall economic plan.

ECONOMIC INTEGRATION[53]

The fragmentation of Latin America into 20 sovereign nations after independence was for many years a challenge to political dreamers, who could envisage the many relatively weak states as a strong United States of Latin America. In recent years, the fragmentation of Latin America into 20 economies competing with one another to sell their primary products cheaply for the expensive wares of industrially advanced nations has been a challenge to economic planners, who can envisage the many relatively weak national markets as a strong regional common market that will greatly stimulate economic development.

In Latin America, as in other underdeveloped areas, the national markets are too restricted to provide an adequate volume of demand for mass production industries. In any one country, productivity is lower because of the larger number of different industrial products it attempts to manufacture and because its industries are limited to producing for the home market only. The resulting low productivity and high costs

---

[53] The official documents relative to the establishment of the Central American Common Market and the Latin American Free Trade Association are contained in Inter-American Institute of International Legal Studies, *Instruments Relating to the Economic Integration of Latin America* (Dobbs Ferry, N.Y.: Oceana Publications, Inc., 1968).

invariably lead to high protective tariffs. But there is a way out of this nationalistic, protectionist dilemma, as the Latin American and other underdeveloped nations have discovered. That way out is a regional common market that enables them to trade freely with one another, unhindered by tariffs but at the same time protected by a common tariff barrier against advanced outside competition.[54] The exhaustive study that the Economic Commission for Latin America made regarding the possible benefits from a common market for the region[55] was largely responsible for the two concrete steps toward economic integration taken the next year.

In February, 1960, a treaty signed in Montevideo established the Latin American Free Trade Area, usually referred to as LAFTA. Under the agreement, the member nations pledged themselves to progressively remove over a 12-year period the customs duties and other restrictions that hinder intraregional trade. They would lower tariffs on all goods at an average minimum rate of 8 percent a year; by the end of 12 years, all products traded among them would be completely duty-free. All the nations of South America (with the exception of Bolivia) and Mexico belong to LAFTA.

Another treaty, signed in Managua in December, 1960, established the Central American Common Market, usually referred to as CACM. According to the provisions of the treaty, all tariffs levied on goods traded among the member nations would be progressively reduced each year until they were completely eliminated by 1966. All the nations of Central America are members of the regional common market, with the exception of Panama, which is seriously considering joining.

Of the two integrated trade areas, the Central American Common Market has made far greater progress in achieving its goals. In fact, tariffs have been removed from more than 95 percent of all the items traded, though some important products, such as coffee, cotton, and sugar, which represent 20 percent of the group's total trade, have not yet been classified duty-free. As a result of the removal of tariff barriers, trade between the member nations has greatly increased; in 1965 it was 19 percent of their total exports, having quadrupled in value (from $32.7 to $136 million) since the regional trade agreement went into effect. The most spectacular achievement of CACM has been the expansion of trade in industrial goods, which rose by 532 percent during this period.[56]

---

[54] For an extensive treatment of the need for economic integration, see Sidney Dell, *A Latin American Common Market?* (New York: Oxford University Press, 1966), chap. 2.

[55] Economic Commission for Latin America, *The Latin American Common Market* (New York: United Nations, 1959).

[56] Joseph S. Nye, Jr., "Central American Regional Integration," *International Conciliation,* No. 562 (March, 1967), pp. 13 and 38.

For additional information on this increase in trade, see Dell, *op. cit.,* pp. 58–59.

Particularly encouraging is the fact that that trade is not mainly an exchange of foodstuffs and raw materials as with LAFTA; rather, in 1965 it consisted of: manufactures, 40 percent; chemicals and raw materials, 21; machinery and vehicles, 3; fuels and lubricants, 5; and food and beverages, 31.[57] No wonder that with the stagnation of the Arab Common Market, decline of the East African Common Market, and bogging down of LAFTA, CACM is easily the most successful of the several integrated trade groups today.[58]

In attaining its large measure of success, CACM enjoyed several distinct advantages. Ever since the member states were united in the Federal Republic of Central America, which lasted from 1824 to 1838, the ideal of political union has persisted[59] and has made economic integration much easier than it would otherwise have been. Too, certain peculiarities of the region's political culture played a role. Heads of state, even such dictatorial rulers as General Anastasio Somoza, indulgently allowed the technicrats—new members of the elite with economic and technical training—to putter with integration, little expecting it to materialize. Also a helpful assist—at least the early stages of CACM have not been really costly to the governments. Although they derive from a third to almost half of their revenues from import duties, the loss from tariffs eliminated on intramarket trade has been compensated by duties on increased imports from outside CACM, as well as by consumption taxes.[60]

Despite CACM's signal success to date, it does face some serious problems. As Table 9–2 shows, Honduras and Nicaragua have derived less

TABLE 9–2

Distribution of Regional Trade

(percent share of sales and [percent of purchases])

	1960	1963	1965
Guatemala	22.2 (23.2)	28.8 (27.3)	28.6 (23.2)
El Salvador	38.7 (41.3)	39.8 (38.7)	33.9 (31.2)
Honduras	22.7 (16.2)	19.4 (18.4)	16.3 (19.4)
Nicaragua	10.5 (8.5)	5.8 (10.2)	7.4 (15.5)
Costa Rica	5.7 (10.8)	6.2 (5.3)	13.8 (10.8)

Source: Andrew B. Wardlaw, "The Operation of the Central American Common Market," mimeographed (Guatemala: ROCAP, 1966), p. 31, in Joseph S. Nye, Jr., "Central American Regional Integration," *International Conciliation*, No. 562 (March, 1967), p. 41.

[57] Rómulo A. Ferrero, "The International Trade of Latin America" (translation of a study by the Inter-American Council for Commerce and Production) in *Regional Integration and The Trade of Latin America* (Supplementary Paper No. 22) (New York: Committee for Economic Development, 1968), p. 97.

[58] Nye, *op. cit.*, p. 9.

[59] For the region's experiment with federal union and the many proposals that have been made even until recently to reconstitute the union, see Thomas L. Karnes, *The Failure of Union: Central America, 1824–1960* (Chapel Hill: University of North Carolina Press, 1961).

[60] Nye, *op. cit.*, pp. 14–49.

benefit from the common market than have the other three members. As a result, their demand for compensatory benefits became such a hot issue that the committees of the common market were unable to meet for almost five months prior to September, 1966, when a compromise was finally reached, giving Honduras the right to allow a 20 percent greater exemption on import duties for 5 years in order to attract industry. Nicaragua's demands for special treatment were turned over to the Economic Commission for Latin America for study.[61]

A far more complex problem arises from the wide variations in the levels of industrial development of the member nations. While they recognize that large-scale industries that take advantage of the total market must be established and encouraged within the region, a bitter dispute has arisen as to where these industries, given marketwide preference, will be located. One camp, basing its reasoning on accepted principles of economics, would locate new industries in the areas most favorable for them—areas with the best combination of transport and power facilities, trained labor, and ample raw materials. The other camp, following what is known as the "integration industries" principle, would disregard the accepted criteria of economics and locate industries so as to promote "balanced development," which among the less developed members simply means "balanced *industrial* development." So far, contentions of the second camp have prevailed. But if Honduras continues to lag in its rate of industrial growth because of its poor infrastructure, bitter division of opinion regarding balanced industrial development may well wreck the regional market.[62]

As compared with progress of the CACM, LAFTA has managed to make only modest gains, if that much. Between 1961 and 1966 there were six rounds of negotiations to lower tariffs, and concessions were granted on about 9,800 items traded intraregionally. About 80 percent of these concessions were granted during the first several years of LAFTA. But far more important than the total number of concessions granted are the many critical products that continue to remain on the tariff schedules. Indeed, very few concessions have been made on manufactured goods, whose free flow within the integrated area is absolutely essential for industrial development; concessions made to date have been limited to simply the raw or semiprocessed materials that have long comprised the bulk of Latin America's intraregional trade. Also, if a nation proposes a reduction in tariffs on a significant product, this invariably indicates that it intends to benefit shortly by exporting this item. If, on the other hand, a nation strenuously opposes reduction of the tariff on a significant

---

[61] *Ibid.*, p. 40.
[62] Dell, *op. cit.*, pp. 64–69; and Nye, *op. cit.*, pp. 38 and 58.

product, it shows that the nation regards it as important to its national economy.[63]

LAFTA's failure to achieve even a moderate measure of success as gauged by its goals can be attributed to many factors, no one of which has been determining, but which acting together threaten to virtually stymie future progress.

The economic level of development of any member, whether low or high, has been a potential economic damper on areawide agreement; the nations bogged down in agriculture fight for the best terms to achieve industrial development; and the nations that have managed to achieve a partial degree of industrialization scrap among themselves, determined to hold and expand any industrial beachhead they have taken. The answer to such infighting may be complementarity agreements, such as the one made between Brazil and Chile regarding the production of automobiles and trucks. Since 60 or so Latin American corporations are engaged in such production, and the regional market could be supplied more efficiently by a half-dozen or less companies, Brazil and Chile have agreed to produce only several specified makes of the vehicles. Furthermore, each nation will produce only certain specified parts of these vehicles and trade them with the other nation—each of them enjoying a sort of parity in producing automobiles and trucks for the limited regional market.[64]

While such complementarity agreements will no doubt be helpful in preventing ruinous competition, thereby enabling infant industries to become well established, they are by no means the answer to the long-term requirements for industrial developments. As the Latin American Iron and Steel Institute advocates, the infant iron and steel industries of the region should be protected from competition with industrially developed nations, and should be allowed, with other similar industries, to compete for the regional market.[65] But supplying a regional market, limited as it is, will not be sufficient in time to justify an industry's existence. It must be able to export and compete with other producers on the international market.

The difficulties of transportation and communication have been other handicaps to LAFTA's attempts to achieve its goals. Most of the trade between members of the common market is by boat, but service is poor and rates are high. It is ironic that the cost of shipping goods from Buenos

---

[63] Roy Blough and Jack N. Behrman, "Problems of Regional Integration in Latin America," *Regional Integration and The Trade of Latin America, op. cit.,* pp. 26–27; and Rómulo A. Ferrero, "The International Trade of Latin America," *op. cit.,* pp. 83–84.

[64] For details on this and other complementarity agreements, see Dell, *op. cit.,* p. 144; and Placido Garcia Reynoso, "Problems of Regional Industrialization," *Latin American Economic Integration: Experiences and Prospects,* ed. Miguel S. Wionczek (New York: Frederick A. Praeger, Inc., 1965), pp. 165–66.

[65] William E. Cole, *Steel and Economic Growth in Mexico* (Institute of Latin American Studies) (Austin: University of Texas Press, 1967), pp. 143–44.

Aires to Vera Cruz on the Gulf of Mexico is 25 percent less when the goods are routed through Southampton rather than shipped directly. When and if needed changes are made, emphasis should be placed on improving maritime service, especially at the ports, rather than on protecting LAFTA ships. As Robert T. Brown concludes, "Inefficient ports and undisciplined port workers represent, at present, the single most important obstacle in this transport sector to economic integration in South America."[66] The development of highways within a nation and from one nation to another is also a potent force for promoting national and regional integration.[67]

Other obstructions in the path of LAFTA are the steep inflation and monetary instability in three of its key members—Argentina, Brazil, and Chile. Regardless of their effects within a nation, whether favorable or otherwise, their effects within the regional trading group are undoubtedly quite adverse. The instability of the exchange rate with its rapid fluctuation, invariably upward, is discouraging to international trade, and even more so, to investment made in one of the other nations.

Still another hindrance to LAFTA's progress is the tradition-bound thinking of Latin American entrepreneurs. Despite the challenging, unlimited opportunities that the pioneering free-trade area offers entrepreneurs throughout the region, from all indications these opportunities have had little impact on entrepreneurial thinking. Unlike managerial reactions in Guatemala and El Salvador, where businessmen were genuinely excited about the possibilities of the Central American Common Market, the reactions in South America have been for the most part either indifference or negativism. Entrepreneurs have given little thought to expanding their operations to member nations, much less to making investments there.[68] Rómulo A. Ferrero states the problem rather bluntly: "Psychological attitudes include the timidity of entrepreneurs in venturing from their home markets; the unawareness of expansion possibilities in the region; and, notably, the deep-rooted protectionist attitude, which has shaped the development of sheltered industries that now fear competition even from within the region."[69]

Yet another obstruction confronting LAFTA is nationalism, whose

---

[66] Robert T. Brown, *Transport and the Economic Integration of South America* (Washington, D.C.: Brookings Institution, 1966), p. 218.

For shorter studies on the region's maritime and river transport, see Dell, *op. cit.,* chap. vi; and Enrique H. Angulo, in Wionczek, *op. cit.,* chap. xi.

[67] For studies that show the impact that construction of highways has had on economic development, see George W. Wilson, Barbara R. Bergmann, Leon V. Hirsch, Martin S. Klein, *The Impact of Highway Investment on Development* (Washington, D.C.: Brookings Institution, 1966).

Wilson's conclusions regarding a transport policy—embracing ocean, river, and land—which must be adopted if the intraregional trading program is to succeed, is given in chap. ix.

[68] Lauterbach, *op. cit.,* pp. 124–25 and 138–42.

[69] Ferrero, *op. cit.,* p. 87.

precise relationship to economic integration has led to differing conclusions. LAFTA "is not a negation of the trend toward nationalism," Gerhard Masur maintains, "but rather its fulfillment . . . based on . . . continental nationalism . . . and will integrate the individual republics as nations."[70] Possibly, for that is what LAFTA may have to do if it is to succeed. LAFTA is only one of the several "side-effects of continental nationalism," Arthur P. Whitaker and David C. Jordan conclude.[71]

In the opinion of other scholars, nationalism continues to be a potent force operating against economic integration. ". . . the process of forming free trade areas has probably served as much to heighten sensitivities to national interests as it has served to diminish nationalistic sentiments," Charles W. Anderson observes.[72] Among the many barriers to LAFTA's goals "is the strident nationalism characteristic of contemporary Latin America that manifests itself both in reluctance to cooperate with traditional rivals and in the desire of each nation to possess all the trappings and symbols of modernization," Robert N. Burr states.[73]

While there are still other obstacles, there are also forces operating in favor of the trade areas. Notable among these is the strong stand taken by the sixth Latin American Congress of Christian Democracy in its 1964 meeting in Caracas. The Congress not only strongly backed economic integration but also went much further. It proposed that steps be taken toward political union by estabishing two supranational councils—one in the field of education and the other in economics—and a parliament representing the legislative bodies of all the nations of the regions.[74]

From recent developments, the respective merits and possible attainments of CACM and LAFTA may forever be speculative. For in 1965, in response to a suggestion from President Eduardo Frei of Chile, four of the most respected leaders in Latin American development—Raúl Prebisch, Carlos Sanz, Felipe Herrera, and José Antonio Mayobre—issued a statement of policy stressing the need for acceleration of economic integration and for a single common market as opposed to two regional associations. In 1965, a meeting of the Latin American foreign ministers also gave strong support to the new integration movement.[75]

The movement for change was successful when at Punta del Este the heads of state of the United States and the Latin American nations (only

---

[70] Gerhard Masur, *Nationalism in Latin America: Diversity and Unity* (New York: Macmillan Co., 1966), p. 249.

[71] Arthur P. Whitaker and David C. Jordan, *Nationalism in Contemporary Latin America* (New York: The Free Press, 1966), p. 172.

[72] Charles W. Anderson, *Politics and Economic Change in Latin America: The Governing of Restless Nations* (Princeton, N.J.: D. Van Nostrand Co., Inc., 1967), p. 61.

[73] Burr, *op. cit.*, p. 220.

[74] *Ibid.*, pp. 86–87.

[75] *Ibid.*, pp. 222–23.

Cuba excepted) adopted, on April 14, 1967, an "Action Program" for economic integration and development. According to the program, steps that LAFTA and CACM would take progressively for cooperation and close ties, beginning in 1970, would by the end of 15 years combine them into a single Latin American Common Market.[76] Whether combining a going CACM with a lagging LAFTA into a single common market within a period of only 15 years is merely *projectismo* or genuine planning, the 15 years beginning in 1970 will tell the story.[77]

SUGGESTED READINGS

Alba, Victor. *Alliance Without Allies: The Mythology of Progress in Latin America*. New York: Frederick A. Praeger, 1965.

Anderson, Charles W. *Politics and Economic Change in Latin America: The Governing of Restless Nations*, Part II. Princeton, N.J.: D. Van Nostrand Co., Inc., 1967.

Bernstein, Marvin D. (ed.). *Foreign Investment in Latin America: Cases and Attitudes*. New York: Alfred A. Knopf, Inc., 1966.

Brown, Robert T. *Transport and the Economic Integration of South America*. Washington, D.C.: Brookings Institution, 1966.

Burr, Robert N. *Our Troubled Hemisphere: Perspectives on United States–Latin American Relations*, chap. viii. Washington, D.C.: Brookings Institution, 1967.

Committee for Economic Development. *Economic Development Issues, Latin America*. Supplementary Paper No. 21. New York, 1967.

———. *Regional Integration and The Trade of Latin America*. Supplementary Paper No. 22. New York, 1966.

Currie, Lauchlin. *Accelerating Development: The Necessity and the Means*. New York: McGraw-Hill Book Co., Inc., 1966.

Dell, Sidney. *A Latin American Common Market?* New York: Oxford University Press, 1966.

Daland, Robert T. *Brazilian Planning: Development Politics and Administration*. Chapel Hill: University of North Carolina Press, 1967.

Dreier, John C. (ed.). *The Alliance for Progress: Problems and Perspectives*. Baltimore: Johns Hopkins Press, 1962.

Economic Commmission for Latin America. *The Process of Industrial Development in Latin America*. New York: United Nations, 1966.

Friedmann, John. *Venezuela: From Doctrine to Dialogue*. Syracuse, N.Y.: Syracuse University Press, 1965.

---

[76] The Declaration and Action Program of the American Chiefs of State, adopted at Punta del Este on April 14, 1967, are given as an Appendix to *Regional Integration and The Trade of Latin America, op. cit.*

[77] According to Roy Blough and Jack N. Behrman, a period of only 15 years is very unrealistic, based on the experience of the European Common Market. Blough and Behrman, *op. cit.,* p. 50.

Friedmann, Wolfgang G. *et al. International Financial Aid*, pp. 152–72. New York: Columbia University Press, 1966.

Inter-American Institute of International Legal Studies. *Instruments Relating to the Economic Integration of Latin America*. Dobbs Ferry, N.Y.: Oceana Publications, Inc., 1968.

Kilty, Daniel R. *Planning for Development in Peru*. New York: Frederick A. Praeger, Inc., 1967.

Lauterbach, Albert. *Enterprise in Latin America: Business Attitudes in a Developing Economy*. Ithaca, N.Y.: Cornell University Press, 1966.

Levy, Fred D., Jr. *Economic Planning in Venezuela*. New York: Frederick A. Praeger, Inc., 1968.

Nye, Joseph S., Jr. "Central American Regional Integration," *International Conciliation*, No. 562 (March, 1967).

Nystrom, J. Warren, and Haverstock, Nathan A. *The Alliance for Progress: Key to Latin America's Development*. Princeton, N.J.: D. Van Nostrand Co., Inc., 1966.

Raynolds, David R. *Rapid Development in Small Economies: The Example of El Salvador*. New York: Frederick A. Praeger, Inc., 1967.

Robock, Stefan H. *Brazil's Developing Northeast: A Study of Regional Planning and Foreign Aid*. Washington, D.C.: Brookings Institution, 1963.

Shafer, Robert J. *Mexico: Mutual Adjustment Planning*. Syracuse, N.Y.: Syracuse University Press, 1966.

Veliz, Claudio (ed.). *Obstacles to Change in Latin America*, pp. 9–46, 91–115, and 145–61. New York: Oxford University Press, 1965.

Violich, Francis, and Astica, Juan B. *Community Development and the Urban Planning Process in Latin America*. Los Angeles: University of California Press, 1967.

Wilson, George W. *et al. The Impact of Highway Investment on Development*. Washington, D.C.: Brookings Institution, 1966.

Wionczek, Miguel S. (ed.). *Latin American Economic Integration: Experiences and Prospects*. New York: Frederick A. Praeger, Inc., 1965.

10

LABOR:
A Fair Share or Else

Labor is a third member of the economic triumvirate, along with agriculture and industry. It was late to organize and exert the weight of its collective influence in Latin America. However, it plays a strong role in the political dynamics of the region today and is a force to be increasingly reckoned with. Large landowners, military leaders, and high officials of the Church—traditional representatives of established power and influence—all recognize and respect the power of this new revolutionary force that has an important role in shaping the region's development.

ORIGIN AND DEVELOPMENT OF TRADE UNIONISM[1]

Trade unionism was relatively late in coming to Latin America. In some countries, the stirrings of the labor movement can be traced as far back as the 1860's and 1870's to the workers in the cotton gins and cottonseed oil mills, flour mills and grain elevators, sugar mills and refineries, and many other local enterprises, including the hat and shoe factories of the Pittsburgh of South America. Up until World War I,

---

[1] Much of this background is from Moises Poblete-Troncoso and Ben G. Burnett, *The Rise of the Latin American Labor Movement* (New Haven, Conn.: College and University Press, 1960), pp. 13–19.

For the development of the labor movement in the individual countries of Latin America, see Victor Alba, *Historia del movimiento obrero en América Latina* (Mexico, D.F.: Libreros Mexicanos Unidos, 1964), chaps. ix–xvii; *Politics and the Labor Movement in Latin America* (Stanford, Calif.: Stanford University Press, 1968), Part III; and Robert J. Alexander, *Organized Labor in Latin America* (New York: The Free Press, 1965), chaps. iv–xvii.

organized labor, like its counterpart, industry, was struggling to establish itself and make its influence felt in the society.

Just as World War I gave industrial development a potent shot in the arm, it gave a strong stimulus to the organization of labor. As new industries were established and expanded during and after the war, often enabling their owners to reap great fortunes, they also redounded to the good fortune of the workers, who made higher wages and joined labor unions in increasing numbers.

Later, during the 1930's and 1940's, just as industry developed during the depression and particularly during and after World War II, so did the labor movement expand and increase in stature. The total number of organized workers increased enormously. In many of the countries, especially Argentina and Mexico, practically all the presently organizable workers belong to a union.

In their evolution, labor unions have passed through three stages of development. In the early days of the movement, they were mutual benefit societies, which in return for small contributions from members provided them with night schools and libraries to enable them to get ahead and also paid for their medical treatment, drugs, and funeral expenses.

In the second stage, labor groups became societies of resistance. No longer content with being merely mutualist associations whose main purpose was to pass the hat around for the mutual protection of one another, they now felt ready to stand up to employers and assert what they believed their rights should be as partners in the enterprises. This new posture of labor resulted in long and bitter conflict with capital—a strike against a mine, a factory, or a workshop, or sometimes against an entire industry. Almost every gain labor made, however small, was accomplished at the price of violence, bloodshed, and often loss of life.

Finally, organized labor graduated into its third and current stage of development, when as a modern, strong trade union movement it has become recognized as one of the powerful pressure groups in society, representing the interests of a large part of the citizenry.

In achieving their present status, the unions have had to surmount or circumvent many a formidable obstacle. Employers were very hostile to the growing power of their laborers and did their best to stifle it by means of lockouts, blacklists, and various other methods of coercion. The government was an even more formidable adversary. Representing the interests of the large landowners and other wealthy members of society, it usually did not hesitate to put labor in its place, which normally meant beating it to its knees. Since it controlled the armed might of the civilian police and the army, the government was virtually in a position to break a strike at will by summarily putting recalcitrant workers into uniform and shipping them to distant parts of the country for months and even years, and by dealing even more summarily with labor agitators, simply shooting them on the spot or putting them before a firing squad.

Other obstacles have stood in the way of labor's determined efforts to organize and achieve recognition. Ideological differences of anarchosyndicalism, socialism, and communism have often divided workers into hostile factions that fought one another even more bitterly than they fought any outside adversary.[2] Moreover, the lack of able, honest leadership was a great disadvantage in dealing with competent, sophisticated employers, who often resolved a labor dispute by the simple expedient of buying off the labor representatives. The illiteracy of workers, together with their lack of information and experience, also impeded the growth of trade unionism; workers with such handicaps could hardly comprehend the goals they were collectively striving for, much less the responsibilities they as members of the union should assume.

DISTINCTIVE FEATURES OF THE LABOR FORCE

There are several distinctive features of the labor force in Latin America. Much of it is either underemployed or unemployed—a condition that reduces the region's productivity and constitutes quite a problem for anyone in need of a job. A large proportion of the women are employed, mainly in the lower and middle classes; and many legal safeguards have been adopted for their protection. Child labor, too, is common throughout the region; laws adopted in behalf of minors seek to minimize the dangers to them and also to assure that work will not interfere with their education.[3]

Underemployment, characteristic of the economies of underdeveloped nations, may be either visible or invisible. Visibly, workers are employed only part time or less than normal periods of work, although they could work full time and prefer to do so. Invisibly, productivity or earnings are abnormally low, and jobs do not permit workers to fully use their capacities or skills.[4]

In Latin America, underemployment exists at practically all levels in

---

[2] Syndicalism, although similar in some respects to *corporatismo* (trade unionism), democratic socialism, anarchism, and Marxism, is essentially different from them. Hubert Lagardelle, "Características del Sindicalismo," *Teoría y Práctica del Sindicalismo*, ed. Guillermo Davalos (Buenos Aires, 1958), pp. 67–89.

[3] Still another distinctive feature, forced labor, was discussed in Chapter 2. Peonage in the form of *concertaje, yanaconazco, shirongaje, acasillaje,* and *mita* has long been a problem in Latin America, despite the many legal measures the nations have adopted aimed at abolishing it. Miguel Mejía Fernández, *El Problema del Trabajo Forzado en América Latina* (Mexico, D.F.: Instituto de Investigaciones Sociales, Universidad Nacional, n.d.), pp. 7–30.

[4] International Labour Office, *Employment and Economic Growth* (Studies and Reports, New Series, No. 67) (Geneva, Switz.: 1964), p. 25.

the society. The shortage of well-paying positions in the private sector forces many young men and women with college educations to seek employment in government. The fact of too little work to go around mainly accounts for the top-heavy government bureaucracies, especially those in Argentina and Uruguay, noted earlier. The clamor to squeeze into the bureaucracy, already overcrowded, reminds one who has visited Latin America of the determination of many to ride an overcrowded streetcar, even if it means hanging outside on the rear bumper, holding on for dear life as the motorman guns his vehicle.

Another evidence of underemployment among urban workers is the relatively large percentage of them engaged in services of various kinds, as compared with the other major areas of work. The proportion of persons so employed is increasing, too. In 1948, 54 percent of the total labor force was engaged in agriculture; by 1955, however, only 50 percent were so employed. During the same period a constant 18 percent were engaged in manufacturing and construction. But during this time those engaged in the many service occupations increased from 25 to 30 percent. The increase in the number of service and white-collar employees, who are paid lower than average wages, reflects the fact that the population of working age is increasing more rapidly than are job opportunities in industries producing physical goods.[5]

Underemployment is especially prevalent in agriculture, where for many reasons, such as poor farming practices, failure to use machinery, or concentration on one or two crops, the ability and potential productivity of the farm laborer is barely tapped. Probably the most serious aspect of underemployment in agriculture is the farm laborer's being employed only part time. A rural worker works an average of 218 days a year in Argentina, 210 in Chile, about 200 in Colombia, and barely 180 in El Salvador. In areas where a single main crop is grown for export—usually coffee, sugar cane, and cotton—the situation is far worse than any national average can portray. In such areas, the rural worker actually works only from 80 to 100 days a year and often has to travel a long way to obtain employment.[6]

One of the proudest achievements of the Castro regime in Cuba is providing of full-time jobs for all members of the labor force, using them

---

[5] A. J. Jaffe, *People, Jobs, and Economic Development* (A Case History of Puerto Rico, Supplemented by Recent Mexican Experiences) (Glencoe, Ill.: Bureau of Applied Social Research of Columbia University, 1959), pp. 264–65.

[6] United Nations Economic Commission for Latin America, "An Agricultural Policy to Expedite the Economic Development of Latin America," *Economic Bulletin for Latin America*, Vol. VI, No. 2 (October, 1961), p. 4.

In Cuba during the *zafra* (the cane harvest), there has been such a great demand for labor that workers have been imported from Jamaica and Haiti to help harvest the crop. Yet, during the 7 months of the dead season between harvests, about 20 percent of the farm labor was unemployed. Wyatt MacGaffey and Clifford R. Barnett, *Cuba* (Survey of World Cultures) (New Haven, Conn.: HRAF Press, 1962), pp. 139–40.

in a wide variety of developmental projects. Of those formerly unemployed for most of the year, a much higher percentage is favorable to the Castro regime than of those who had employment for 10 months a year or more: 86 percent of the formerly unemployed as compared with 62 percent of the employed. Significantly, too, only 5 percent of the unemployed were hostile to the regime and 9 percent undecided; the respective percentages for the employed were 25 and 13.[7] Consistent with the ideology of a Marxist-Socialist regime, payment on a piecework basis was rejected, and a system of voluntary labor was adopted. However, each class of work is assigned a minimum production goal within a given unit of time; if a worker produces more than the minimum, he is paid a bonus; if he produces less, his wage is cut proportionately.[8] Apparently, compulsory military service has been resorted to as a form of cheap labor; new recruits spend three or four months a year cutting sugarcane or picking coffee beans.[9]

With Latin America's rapid increase in population, there will be 38 million additional persons in the work force by 1975. However, if the present rate of employment does not improve, only 5 million new jobs will have been created by then. The introduction of modern technical methods in industry, mining, and farming will make the situation worse, since it will reduce employment instead of creating additional jobs.[10]

Although the progress of industrialization in underdeveloped non-Western nations has been hindered by a high rate of turnover of labor, this apparently has not been so in Latin America, and certainly not in Peru. There, according to a recent study made in the textile industry, the turnover in the labor force is at a low level. Moreover, managerial policy in firing or laying off workers is responsible for more separations than is the voluntary leaving of workers. Peruvian managers are frequently anxious to get rid of older workers before normal retirement in order to avoid having to pay them a pension. As a result, those who are discharged are usually the older workers with more seniority.[11]

---

[7] Maurice Zeitlin, *Revolutionary Politics and the Cuban Working Class* (Princeton, N.J.: Princeton University Press, 1967), pp. 49, 51, 55, 64–65.

[8] Andrés Suárez, *Cuba: Castroism and Communism, 1959–1966* (Cambridge: Massachusetts Institute of Technology Press, 1967), pp. 199–200.

[9] Boris Goldenberg, *The Cuban Revolution and Latin America* (New York: Frederick A. Praeger, Inc., 1965), pp. 287–88.

[10] Eduardo Frei Montalva, "Paternalism, Pluralism, and Christian Democratic Reform Movements in Latin America," *Religion, Revolution, and Reform: New Forces for Change in Latin America*, eds. William V. D'Antonio and Fredrick B. Pike (New York: Frederick A. Praeger, Inc., 1964), p. 27.

[11] David Chaplin, *The Peruvian Industrial Labor Force* (Princeton, N.J.: Princeton University Press, 1967), chap. 6.

Victor Alba, it should be noted, is very critical of urban workers generally. Most of them are from the country and cannot be depended on, he says. In many instances when they are needed most, they leave their jobs at the factory to go back home and spend many days enjoying a fiesta or helping with the harvests. Alba, *op. cit.*, pp. 322–23.

Since a large proportion of the women, mainly in the lower class but also in the middle, are gainfully employed, governments have found it advisable to adopt many laws designed to protect them. According to most constitutions and labor codes, women are not allowed to do unhealthy or dangerous work, sometimes spelled out as working in quarries or underground in mines. Nor may they be employed to do very strenuous tasks, such as lifting weights above a specified amount. With the exception of certain occupations, such as those of nurses, telephone operators, and entertainers, they are not allowed to work during the night hours.

Pregnancy and maternity are given special consideration. An expectant mother is given a prescribed time off both before and after the birth of her child, with pay and without any prejudice to her job. During the period of lactation, she is given time off in both the morning and afternoon for nursing the baby.

Brazil affords what is perhaps the most chivalrous protection of all; it exempts women from military service, letting them perform such duties as the law may establish.[12]

In the more advanced nations, which have a higher standard of living, child labor has been almost eliminated. In Canada the percentage of minors under age 15 and gainfully employed is 0.4 boys and 0.3 girls; in Switzerland the figure is even lower—0.1 percent. However, in Latin America, where a large proportion of the children are under age 15, many in this age group are gainfully employed. Percentages range from a low in Chile of 1.6 for boys and 2.0 for girls to 11.4 for both sexes in Honduras. The percentage in certain other countries is: Colombia, 3.8 and 5.8 for boys and girls, respectively, excluding the indigenous population; Peru, 5.6 and 9.1; and Brazil, 6.7 and 10.8.[13]

Most of the young workers are found in agriculture, where it is customary for children of the many peon or sharecropper families to help with such farming operations as planting, cultivating, and harvesting the crops. In Brazil, according to the 1950 census, 20.1 percent of the children between ages 10 and 14 were employed in agriculture. Many young workers are found in the cities, too. The percentage of those who work is known to be high; no reliable figures are available, however, because a large number are secretly employed in many small workshops or independently carry on minor street trades.

As in the case of women, the law tries to protect the minor worker in many ways, such as prohibiting his being employed at night or doing certain heavy or dangerous work, and requiring that he be given a

---

[12] Constitution of 1946, Article 181, Section 1.

[13] This information is mainly from "Youth and Work in Latin America," *International Labour Review*, Vol. XC, No. 1 (July, 1964), pp. 1–23.

minimum number of hours rest. Moreover, he cannot be employed unless permission is given by official authorities. To obtain this permission, certain documents must be submitted, such as the father's or guardian's consent, proof of age, state of health, and amount of schooling. If the authorities are satisfied, permission to work is given in the form of a card or employment book specifying the conditions of employment. Such permission is not necessary, however, for employment in agriculture and domestic service, two sectors that employ a large percentage of children.

The many laws adopted for the benefit of minors have no doubt afforded a measure of protection they would not otherwise have enjoyed. However, the basic problem of eliminating child labor cannot be resolved until two fundamental conditions are met—an income high enough for adult workers to take care of all young members of the family and a school system that can provide an education for all pupils.

GOALS AND GAINS

In every one of the republics, labor is recognized in the constitution, labor code, or both, as having the right to organize and strike.

This right, accepted as matter of fact today, represents for the working man a revolutionary gain that has been achieved only within the last several decades. In Mexico the Penal Code of 1872 prevented any effective attempts on the part of workers to improve their conditions, punishing by arrest and fine "those who make a tumult or riot, or employ any other method of physical or moral violence for the purpose of raising or lowering the wages of the workers, or who impede the free exercise of industry and labor." In 1907, when textile workers who toiled for 13 hours a day in damp, hot, lint-filled rooms humbly petitioned for better conditions, they were locked out, to be starved into submission. When another group, maddened by hunger, raided the company store, troops massacred 200 men, women, and children, and sent others to the dungeons of San Juan de Ulloa.[14]

Such atrocities, commonplace in most of the countries until only a few decades ago, are hardly conceivable today, thanks to the recognition and status organized labor now enjoys.

The large mass of labor laws and codes that confer many rights on labor also impose certain restrictions. Most of the countries specify that the objectives of the union must be economic and social, not political. Moreover, no one can be coerced into joining the union against his will. Furthermore, certain groups are specifically forbidden to organize. In Brazil there are four categories of such workers: domestic help, farm

---

[14] Ernest Gruening, *Mexico and Its Heritage* (New York: D. Appleton-Century Co., Inc., 1934), p. 335.

laborers, government employees at all levels, and employees of semistate autonomous bodies.[15]

One of the main objectives of organized labor has been to obtain higher wages for its members. Consequently, as a result either of bargaining with employers or of direct governmental action, members of the unions frequently obtain increases in wages. Indeed, from the tenor of press accounts from these nations, one may understandably conclude that extravagant wage demands have been mainly responsible for the soaring inflation in many of them.

Unquestionably, wage increases have often proved to be illusory gains in terms of real income—the amount of bread or potatoes or medicine that it would purchase. For often when granting a wage increase with its right hand, government was taking action with its left which completely nullified the supposed gain. Thus, when Chile in 1937 adopted a minimum wage law tied to the cost of living index, the intent of the law and any possible advantage to be derived from it by the intended recipients was nullified by the printing presses flooding the country with new bills.

Another tactic that frequently nullifies any possible gain to be derived from a wage increase is the delay of the government, intentional or otherwise, in taking action to put it into effect. In Brazil several months pass from the time a minimum wage board is named until new wage levels are decreed; during this time the businessmen boost prices even more than the normal increase. As a result, the anticipatory price rise has already more than offset the increase in wages when the increase finally goes into effect.[16]

Though some may benefit from inflation—or at least learn to live comfortably with it—this is not true of the great majority of workers. In fact, they suffer severely from inflation. Wage increases cannot and do not keep up with the inflationary price spiral that benefits some others in the society. In both Brazil and Chile, the industrial worker apparently had a lower real income in 1956 than in 1940.[17] This is apparently true in 1968, too.

In wondering what is going on, the worker might feel better—or perhaps worse—if he could read and understand some of the economic explanations for his problems. For one thing, his developing society is basically different from the earlier ones in that there are many more goods and services for which he can beneficially spend his income today than there were a century or so ago. The conveniences and necessities he knows about and aspires to possess are far more numerous than they were

---

[15] Robert J. Alexander, *Labor Relations in Argentina, Brazil, and Chile* (New York: McGraw-Hill Book Co., Inc., 1962), p. 86.

[16] *Ibid.*, p. 125.

[17] Alexander, *op. cit.*, p. 6.

in the wealthy nations when these had the income levels now common to Latin America.[18]

Another thing that might make the worker unhappy, even antisocial, is to realize that by virtue of his low real wages in a time of rising prosperity he is being called on to pay for the cost of industrialization. He is doing just this in Brazil, where his "real wages are kept down to provide the large profits characteristic of the Brazilian economy, most of which are to a large degree ploughed back into its further development."[19] He is doing the same thing in Mexico, too, where it may "correctly be said that the true hero of the Mexican investment boom is the ordinary Mexican worker, whose acceptance of a declining real income has in effect 'subsidized' much of the nation's building."[20]

The plight of the mass of workers whose wages are low while much of the rest of society enjoys affluence is at least widely recognized, although little has been done about it to date. In Argentina President Illia in his inaugural address of October, 1963, stressed the hardships of the workers and promised that a major goal of his administration would be to see that they got "just wages with real purchasing power."[21]

Although labor's voice was hardly heard despite its lagging remuneration, noted W. Brand, ". . . it might be mainly the increased power of wage earners that will lead, even in the undeveloped countries, to resistance against inflation as a means of capital formation, and to the insistence that increased investment shall lead to increased consumption for the masses with only a modest lag."[22]

Another primary objective of organized labor has been to reduce the hours of labor and establish a workday and workweek of reasonable length. Before labor became organized, there were no effective ground rules whatever for governing the length of time laborers were required to be on the job. In Mexico's textile plants, the workers were required to put in 13 hours a day. In the bakeries, they were not even allowed to leave the shop except to hear mass on feast days, and then always accompanied by an overseer who never let them out of sight.[23]

Within recent decades and due mainly to the power of organized labor, the hours of work have been reduced to humane and reasonable limits. Today the eight-hour day and five-and-a-half- or six-day week

---

[18] Wilbert E. Moore and Arnold S. Feldman, *Labor Commitment and Social Change in Developing Areas* (New York: Social Science Research Council, 1960), p. 214.

[19] Alexander, *op. cit.*, p. 134.

[20] Oscar Lewis, "Mexico Since Cárdenas," *Social Change in Latin America Today* (Council on Foreign Relations) (New York: Harper & Bros., 1960), p. 326.

[21] *Hispanic American Report*, Vol. XVII, No. 5 (July, 1964), p. 447.

[22] Brand, *op. cit.*, p. 245.

[23] Gruening, *op. cit.*, p. 335.

exist throughout the region. About the only ones now who do not enjoy this privilege are the groups, mainly domestic help and farm laborers, that are forbidden by law to organize or belong to labor unions. As recently as 1962, Nicaragua adopted certain "labor reforms" applying to domestic servants. One of the main reforms was limiting their working day to 14 hours!

One of the high-priority goals from the first days of organized labor was to obtain better working conditions for the laborer. Until labor became organized and had a voice that was at least respectfully listened to, the worker performed his tasks in unhealthy, even dangerous surroundings. Ill-lighted, poorly ventilated, and with no regard for safety, the factories and workshops, quarries and mines debilitated and slaughtered workers who were, in effect, just so many expendables. The advent of unions with their demands for better working conditions did not bring about the millennium but did serve to ameliorate some of the harsher conditions.

The efforts of the unions, as well as other influences, have made employers more conscious of their responsibilities. But a great deal still remains to be done to afford workers the healthy and safe conditions of employment they should have. There are still many dangerous hazards in their working environments that need to be and can be corrected. Accidents occur at least six times as frequently in the mines and industries in Latin American nations as in the older industrialized countries. Moreover, occupational diseases are still very prevalent in Latin America, although in other countries many of them have practically disappeared. Silicosis remains a serious problem; another is poisoning from toxic metals, gases, vapors, or smoke. "The application of preventive measures to control occupational accidents and diseases is practically unknown in some countries and is only in its beginning stages in others. Social legislation has placed greater emphasis on compensation than on prevention."[24]

Lack of regard for the safety of workers, besides causing untold misery and suffering, imposes a huge economic burden on the whole society. Economic losses caused by the high rate of worker disability amount to approximately 15 percent of the total national income, and equal from 50 to 100 percent of the countries' national budgets.[25]

Workers in Latin America, like those elsewhere, enjoy eating regularly and have a dread of losing their jobs. Responsive to the unions' influence and concern, the labor laws contain many provisions designed to afford the worker security of tenure and to protect him from being fired summarily. Sometimes the safeguards have been carried so far as to make it virtually impossible for an employer to fire a worker, however much he

---

[24] "Report from the Outposts," *Américas,* Vol. 14, No. 7 (July, 1962), p. 35.
[25] *Ibid.*

deserves to be dismissed. In Cuba the laws were so rigid that the inability to fire workers was known as *inamoviladad* (immobility). Even though workers had stolen from the company, beaten up other employees, sexually molested female workers, committed acts of sabotage, or refused to perform the duties they were assigned, they still could not be fired.[26]

"The inability to fire workers, even for cause, was perhaps the most acute problem faced by employers," say Wyatt MacGaffey and Clifford R. Barnett. "It was commonly said that it was more difficult to fire a worker than to divorce a wife (although it was often easier to find a new wife than a new job)."[27]

The overconcern for job security and the excessive safeguards for providing it have sometimes provoked backlashes that largely defeated the purpose of the measures. In Brazil, although the labor law was intended to give workers greater stability of employment and to protect their jobs, in many instances it has had exactly the opposite effect. An employer who wants to dismiss a worker who has *estabilidade* (tenure) finds that it is very difficult to get the necessary permission from the labor court; the only way he can get rid of him is to buy him off at a high price. As a result, many employers refuse to allow their workers to acquire 10 years' tenure, which gives them such a claim to their jobs that they cannot be dismissed except for grave misbehavior or *force majeure*, adequately proved. Determined to maintain a free hand over employees, employers have dismissed their workers after nine years so as not to be bound by the law. However, labor courts, noting this practice, held that it amounted to an attempt to circumvent the laws; accordingly, they ruled that workers with nine years' standing were regarded as having tenure. But employers are by no means ready to give up on the issue; to keep from being bound by the law, they often fire employees after seven and a half or eight years, regardless of ability.[28]

Organized labor has had many other goals, too, including profit sharing. Foreign enterprises, domestic ones also, have often boasted of making large profits—50 percent a year, sometimes 75, 100, or more. To workers hardly paid enough to keep body and soul together, a larger share of the take has seemed quite a legitimate goal. Getting this incorporated into the labor laws was a relatively easy matter, for the Latin American will pass a law on anything as the easy way out, just so long as he does not have to enforce it. But like many another law, one requiring profit sharing has been easier to enact than to enforce. For the governments in time proceeded to tax away a large part of the profits of foreign enterprises; much of the governments' revenues come from this source. Moreover, com-

[26] International Bank for Reconstruction and Development, *Report on Cuba* (Baltimore: Johns Hopkins University Press, 1951).

[27] MacGaffey and Barnett, *op. cit.*, p. 148.

[28] Alexander, *op. cit.*, p. 121–22.

panies often had bad years when there were no profits to tax, much less to share. Yet, wedded to the concept of profit sharing, organized labor clings to it as a possible means of raising the income of its members. To date, the legal requirements on industry to share profits with labor have been just so much verbiage; yet, nations continue to adopt such social measures.

One of the most recent to adopt profit sharing is Mexico. An amendment added to its constitution on November 20, 1962, gives the government power to force both Mexican and foreign concerns to share their profits with workers. A special committee representing government, management, and labor are to rule on how much of a company's profits shall go to the stockholders and how much to the workers.[29]

Having some say-so in policy is another goal unions aspire to. In most of the countries, however, they have not had much success. Even in Argentina, Brazil, and Chile, which have some of the most progressive labor policies, employers are still very jealous of the "prerogatives of management" and are loath to share these with either the unions or the government. They are determined as far as possible to keep under their control the important powers of making rules and enforcing them.[30]

In Mexico, however, the unions have become so strong and so favored by government that they have a voice in rulemaking and enforcement.

The power of the *sindicatos* has so increased that in addition to having established the common closed-shop and seniority principles, the labor organization in some instances has taken over many functions of management and even of the community. . . . The *sindicato* not only determines most policies at levels below that of the general manager (representing the owner), with whom the labor organization works in friendly cooperation, but acts also as the disciplinary agent in the factory and in the town.[31]

A comprehensive program of social security is still another goal of the unions. Mainly as a result of labor's prodding, all the nations have adopted such programs. Usually they consist only of health insurance, occasionally including pensions for the aged, and only rarely unemployment benefits. In most of the countries, however, these programs exist more on paper than in reality. Even in the several nations where they are most effective, some persons are convinced that their impact on society is more harmful than beneficial. Argentina, Brazil, and Chile all have systems of social security that afford extensive protection for the ill, the aged, and the disabled. They were passed, according to Robert J. Alexander, to gain

---

[29] *Hispanic American Report*, Vol. XVI, No. 11 (January, 1963), p. 994.
[30] Alexander, *op. cit.*, p. 19.
[31] Wilbert E. Moore, *Industrialization and Labor: Social Aspects of Economic Development* (Institute of World Affairs) (Ithaca, N.Y.: Cornell University Press, 1951), pp. 283–84.

political support from the workers, with little or no consideration of their heavy costs and the ability of the nations to sustain such programs, however desirable.[32]

Other scholars, too, are very critical of the programs.

. . . Latin American policy makers [would] do well to re-examine social security and labor legislation passed during the past two decades. They have attempted to impose upon their economies some of the most extreme social security programs seen in the world and, by doing so, have injured the class they intended to benefit, have hampered their own programs of internal economic development, and have made more difficult a profitable participation in international economic relationships.[33]

Organized labor has also been hurt by many unscrupulous leaders who did not hesitate to betray the trust and interests of their followers for their own personal advantage. Sometimes they played one union against another in order to increase their personal power; sometimes they used collective bargaining to enrich themselves instead of to promote the welfare of the workers. Just such a reprehensible character was Luis N. Morones, head of the Mexican labor movement during the 1920's and 1930's. Unscrupulously profiting from his position, he amassed a large fortune and lived lavishly, sporting at least a half-dozen automobiles, a swank retreat for entertaining guests, and diamonds that were the talk of the nation.[34]

On the plus side, the very formation of a union and the transaction of its business are novel and educational experiences for most of the membership. The adoption of a constitution and bylaws, the parliamentary conduct of a meeting, the debate as to whether or not to strike, and the election of officers and selection of delegates to regional and national conclaves are all exercises in democratic responsible citizenship, albeit elementary, even though control is often exercised by an inner clique or boss.

In addition to affording training in citizenship, the labor union, like the army, is an important avenue of social mobility, providing an outlet for leadership and an opportunity for advancement to persons who would otherwise be barred by their social status from exercising political and economic influence. In Cuba Negroes were active in both agricultural and industrial unions. Lázaro Peña, powerful leader of the national labor

---

[32] Alexander, *op. cit.,* p. 17.

[33] Harry Stark, *Social and Economic Frontiers in Latin America* (2d ed.; Dubuque, Ia.: Wm. C. Brown Co., 1963), p. 398.

Wilbert Moore terms Latin America's program as "overly advanced labor legislation" and concludes: "It is doubtful if all existing legislative standards in . . . Latin America could be immediately enforced without a greater economic disruption than the good accomplished for the workers." Moore, *op. cit.,* p. 144.

[34] Gruening, *op. cit.,* p. 390.

confederation, is a Negro, and until 1960 most labor federations had special committees to deal with the problems of Negro members.[35]

LABOR–MANAGEMENT RELATIONS AND COLLECTIVE BARGAINING

In the realm of labor–management relations, employers have had certain advantages, which they exploited in dealing with labor. The industrialists, for example, were a closely knit group who had long had their local and national associations of manufacturers. The Sociedad de Fomento of Chile was organized in 1883, the Unión Industrial Argentina in 1887, and the Sociedad National de Industrias of Peru in 1896. Well established, tightly organized, and having a close community of interests, the industrialists were in a good position to influence government by presenting their point of view.[36]

Moreover, with their large financial resources the corporations do not hesitate to vie with the unions for the allegiance of their employees. In Chile, many employers have formed company unions subject to the influence or control of the employers. These unions are especially numerous in the textile industry. In Brazil, some employers provide extensive fringe benefits for their employees. The Varig Aviation Company, through a related foundation, gives the following benefits to its personnel: a loan fund from which employees can borrow money interest-free to build homes; big, low-priced stores located in the airports of Porto Alegre, Sáo Paulo, and Rio where employees only can trade; vacation spots belonging to the company, with transportation provided gratis for employees and their families; and pensions to superannuated personnel.[37]

While individual companies may have their own benefits, Brazilian employers as a group have a unique program for wooing their employees and winning their allegiance. Many paternalistic services are provided for them by SESI (Serviçio Social de Industria) and SESCI (Serviçio Social de Commercio), nationwide institutions that perform a wide variety of social services for employees on behalf of employers. Financed by compulsory contributions from all employers on the basis of 2 percent of their payrolls, SESI and SESCI render about every social service a union could hope to provide—and more. Commissaries with a wide variety of

---

[35] MacGaffey and Barnett, *op. cit.*, p. 151.

[36] George Wythe, *Industry in Latin America* (2d ed.; New York: Columbia University Press, 1949), p. 74.

In some of the presently developing nations, a labor movement may become a political force before the native capitalists do, reversing the historical experience of the West, including Latin America. John H. Kautsky (ed.), *Political Change in Underdeveloped Countries: Nationalism and Communism* (New York: John Wiley & Sons, Inc., 1962), p. 23.

[37] Alexander, *op. cit.*, pp. 18 and 105–6.

low-priced goods, company dining rooms with cheap meals, and medical and dental service at çost are all soothing to the employee pocketbook. In addition, some 1,800 schools provided by SESI have afforded an education for many thousands of students, and have taught many adult illiterates how to read and write. A corps of lawyers is available to handle family legal problems and to give advice to workers on employment problems— advice that is probably not antagonistic to the interests of employers. In São Paulo, SESI is even engaged in a social orientation program designed to develop future union leaders. The purpose is not to develop leaders who will be subservient to the wishes of employers, SESI asserts—surely tongue in cheek—but to develop leaders who will counteract the union activities of the Communist Party.[38]

But when it comes to sitting down at the bargaining table and dealing directly with employees, most employers find it a very trying task. In Mexico, the older industrialists were decidedly hostile to the unions, regarding themselves as the victims of laws that tipped the scales in favor of labor leaders in the settlement of industrial disputes. However, the new small manufacturers, sometimes referred to as the New Group, were more favorably inclined to the unions; often having risen recently from the ranks of labor to ownership of their small businesses, they welcomed negotiations with the unions.[39]

The process of collective bargaining in Latin America is very different from the process in most industrially advanced nations. It is neither free nor collective nor really bargaining.[40] Special labor courts often hear the disputes and decide them. In actuality, government usually has the whip hand and exercises it to bring about an agreement. The process, as meticulously prescribed in the labor codes, is usually quite different from what actually takes place to resolve a dispute, as is shown in the case of Mexico.

According to Mexico's Federal Labor Law of 1931, if the employer and the union are not able to reach an agreement, the union may call a strike after complying with certain conditions. It must give the employer written notice of the proposed strike at least 6 days before it is to take place, or 10 days for public services such as transportation, communications, light, gas, water, and hospitals. It also notifies a board of conciliation and arbitration, which, in turn, notifies the employer, giving him 48 hours to reply to the union's statement. At the end of this time, the board

---

[38] *Ibid.,* pp. 106–9.

[39] Sanford A. Mosk, *Industrial Revolution in Mexico* (Berkeley: University of California Press, 1954), pp. 27–31.

[40] Analyzing the process in Chile, one scholar concludes: "Generally speaking, there is little direct bargaining between the parties, and, technically, very few collective agreements are ever signed." James O. Morris, *Elites, Intellectuals, and Consensus: A Study of the Social Question and the Industrial Relations System in Chile* (New York State School of Industrial and Labor Relations) (Ithaca, N.Y.: Cornell University, 1966), p. 20.

tries to get the parties to reach an agreement. If this fails, it then declares the strike to be legal, and the walkout takes place. The strike is ended in time by an agreement reached between the employer and the union, by a decision of an arbitral body chosen by the parties, or by a decision of the board of conciliation and arbitration.[41]

In practice, however, labor disputes in Mexico are settled quite differently from the procedure described in the labor law. While they are almost always settled by arbitration or conciliation—more frequently by conciliation—the minister of labor plays a key role in bringing about a settlement.

He:

. . . opens and shuts the valves of labour militancy. He largely determines whether the publicly demanded changes will be made in wages or conditions. The wage policy he imposes must be accepted by labour: any changes must come through peaceful means. . . . When strikes persist beyond acceptable limits [he] can and will invoke all necessary party and government apparatus to bring the situation back into line.[42]

However desirable real collective bargaining might be, it has not been practicable in Latin America, for the process has almost invariably lacked three essential conditions: accurate information about wages, earnings, and other relevant factors; mutual confidence and good will; and genuine freedom of the parties to reach an agreement between themselves.

Regarding information needed, since unions cannot afford to employ economists, statisticians, engineers, and lawyers, they really have no expert opinion on which to base their wage demands; consequently the raise they seek is determined arbitrarily and may be 25 percent, 50 percent, or 200 percent.

Moreover, with class lines drawn as rigidly as they are and with the authoritarian attitudes of those who wield power, it is not surprising that a patrician industrialist and a plebeian union leader can hardly sit down together at the same bargaining table. In fact, employers have often refused to deal with unions at all except through their lawyers, and labor leaders have frequently viewed the differences between them as a class struggle. Even attempts to negotiate a working arrangement directly with management are often viewed with disdain by union members, as though such attempts were collaboration with an enemy.[43]

Finally, the large role played by government in determining the labor contract is fatal to genuine bargaining. In Cuba:

---

[41] William P. Tucker, *The Mexican Government Today* (Minneapolis: University of Minnesota Press, 1957), pp. 316–28.

[42] Howard F. Cline, *Mexico: Revolution to Evolution: 1940–1960* (Royal Institute of International Affairs) (New York: Oxford University Press, 1962), p. 226.

[43] MacGaffey and Barnett, *op. cit.,* p. 153; and Poblete and Burnett, *op. cit.,* p. 149.

. . . the machinery provided by law for the settlement of disputes often failed to function. There was no effective civil service system to promote the development of a body of trained conciliators in the Ministry of Labor, and since most officials were political appointees, both labor leaders and employers distrusted their impartiality. During the 1940s the strongest unions were able to pack the Ministry of Labor with friendly officials.[44]

The labor unions in Peru have their own distinctive methods of trying to achieve their demands. Since labor is so abundant that any striking worker could easily be replaced, most strikes against management would almost inevitably fail. Consequently, if a union has not been able to achieve a satisfactory settlement of its demand after following the prescribed legal procedure, it often resorts to political bargaining—a strike directed not against management but against the president of the nation. When deemed necessary, the union resorts to acts of mass violence, including demonstrations, parades, hunger strikes, sit-down strikes, general strikes, and even assaults on public officials or on government buildings. The objective is to bring tremendous pressure on the president to intervene in behalf of labor.[45]

The government's nationalization of many enterprises and the establishment of many government-owned and controlled enterprises whose workers are employees of the state poses a sensitive question: what right, if any, do the workers have to strike? In most nations, the laws specifically prohibit strikes against the government; however, since government enterprises are so prevalent, especially in some nations, such as Uruguay, the prohibition has not been strictly enforced. The government does have a potent weapon if it is strong enough and minded to use it. After the railroad workers of Argentina staged a series of strikes in late 1950 and early 1951, despite governmental restrictions on the right to strike, Perón acted decisively by drafting the railroad workers for national service—a drastic measure which broke the strike.[46]

LABOR ELITE

With labor's becoming increasingly important as an economic, social, and political force, the backgrounds, orientations, and goals of the labor leaders become increasingly important. Their social profiles can perhaps best be portrayed in terms of educational level, political role and goals, ethical practices, and recent professionalization.

---

[44] MacGaffey and Barnett, *op. cit.*, p. 154.

[45] James L. Payne, *Labor and Politics in Peru: The System of Political Bargaining* (New Haven, Conn.: Yale University Press, 1965), chaps. 1, 3, and 4.

[46] Perón's relations with the railroad unions are given in Samuel L. Baily, *Labor, Nationalism, and Politics in Argentina* (New Brunswick, N.J.: Rutgers University Press, 1967), pp. 102–3, 115, 130, and 133.

Although their formal education may be limited because they did not have the opportunity of acquiring a university education, they are fairly well informed, especially on current social problems. And although usually lacking a university degree, they have acquired considerable sophistication from their wide travels in other Latin American countries, the United States, and Western Europe, and perhaps the countries behind the Iron and Bamboo curtains.[47]

Besides being the head of a union, a labor leader is usually also a politician; his election to head of the union often occurs because he belongs to or has the support of a particular political party. Indeed, he is prone to regard his office in the union as mainly a step to a political career. Because of this close relationship between the union and politics, many of the labor leaders not only are party officials but also hold elective political office.[48]

Their political and economic goals are usually moderate, designed to provide limited benefits for labor but not to overturn and reconstruct society. In the competition for positions of leadership, the moderate progressives usually win over the extremists.[49] The majority of labor leaders in Venezuela are not alienated from the existing society, and are not advocates of immediate revolutionary change.[50] In Peru, a large majority of the strikes called have only limited economic aims and no implication whatever of political designs.[51]

Honest and conscientious, most of the labor leaders are loyal to the interests of their unions. However, their code of ethical behavior varies from nation to nation, reflecting the prevailing standards of ethics and public morality in each. Several decades ago, some of the leaders in Brazil and Mexico were guilty of such widespread corruption as to blacken the

---

[47] Robert J. Alexander, "The Latin American Labor Leader," *Industrial Relations and Social Change in Latin America*, eds. William H. Form and Albert A. Blum (Gainesville: University of Florida Press, 1965), pp. 76–78.

Some labor leaders have been very well educated. Vicente Lombardo Toledano, who organized the Confederación General de Obreros y Campesinos de México and who has long been an influential figure in Mexico, is a former university professor, specializing in labor law, and later governor, congressman, and senator. For Lombardo's many contributions as labor leader and statesman, see Robert Paul Millon, *American Marxist: Vicente Lombardo Toledano* (Chapel Hill: University of North Carolina Press, 1966).

[48] Alexander, in *Industrial Relations and Social Change . . . op. cit.*, pp. 78–79.

[49] Henry A. Landsberger, "The Labor Elite: Is It Revolutionary?" *Elites in Latin America*, eds. Seymour Martin Lipset and Aldo Solari (New York: Oxford University Press, 1967), pp. 264, 269, and 271.

[50] *Estudio de conflictos y concenso, serie de resultados parciales I: muestra de líderes sindicales* (Caracas: CENDES, Universidad Central de Venezuela, 1965), p. 107.

[51] James L. Payne, *Labor and Politics in Peru: The System of Political Bargaining* (New Haven, Conn.: Yale University Press, 1965), pp. 264–65.

image of the labor movement—make it almost synonymous with corruption.[52]

Today, the labor leaders are increasingly becoming well-trained professionals. Many of them have attended leadership training schools in Mexico and Venezuela, where they study not only labor–management relations but also the broader economic problems confronting the unions. In many of the countries, including Argentina, Brazil, Mexico, and Venezuela, the unions have some type of checkoff that affords sufficient funds to pay an administrative staff to look after union interests. Many of these staff members work full time for their organizations, and often enjoy long tenure in their positions. The professionalization of leaders will greatly strengthen the union movement and give it a stronger voice in national affairs.[53]

INVOLVEMENT IN POLITICS

Before World War I, many of the trade unions inserted in their bylaws provisions that they would remain aloof from politics and that none of their leaders could hold public office. Nevertheless, some of the leaders took an active part in politics to promote the interest of the union, or sometimes, as did Luis Morones of Mexico, to promote the cause of labor and also the cause of Morones.

Abstaining from active participation in politics or from pledging themselves to support a certain party or faction was good strategy; labor could thereby play off one group against another and give its support to the one that best served its interests.

Abstention from participation in politics, however, proved to be better in theory than in practice. In Mexico, for example, the small but influential labor movement in 1928 made a well-nigh fatal decision. It decided not to support either Calles or Obregón, believing that it should be an independent labor movement and was strong enough to go it alone. On its own however, it almost disintegrated. "It has not made that error again, nor is it likely to."[54]

As the trade union in Mexico and the other nations well realizes, it is dependent on government in many ways. In order even to exist and carry on its many activities, it must first be recognized by government as a

---

[52] For the unsavory, corrupt practices that set back the labor movement in Mexico, see Marjorie Ruth Clark, *Organized Labor in Mexico* (Chapel Hill: University of North Carolina Press, 1934), pp. 106 ff.

For the widespread corruption of Brazilian union officials, contemptuously called *pelegos,* who administered the union tax and labor welfare funds to their advantage, see Alexander, *Labor Relations in Argentina, Brazil, and Chile, op. cit.,* pp. 65 and 75.

[53] Alexander, in *Industrial Relations and Social Change, op. cit.,* pp. 77 and 82–83.

[54] Cline, *op. cit.,* p. 223.

legitimate legal entity—failure of government to grant a birth certificate has snuffed out the life of many a would-be young union. Even if it is recognized and becomes a dynamic, going concern, government can still destroy it by the mere stroke of a pen. In Chile, when unions conducted strikes against the railroads and mining operations in 1936, President Arturo Alessandri resolved the dispute by the most direct executive action—a presidential decree that forthwith dissolved the unions.

Unions are also very dependent on government and politicians for funds they need in order to operate. The dues of members are small as one would expect from their low incomes. But unions need money for many purposes, from paying the expenses of the organization to rendering various services to members. In Latin America, unions operate on a shoestring—a short one at that.

Brazil has solved the problem of the need for union funds by a very simple expedient. The *imposto sindical*, or trade union tax, is levied on all workers who belong to unions and is collected by the government. Of the tax collected, 60 percent goes back to the individual unions; 15 percent is paid to the federation to which the union belongs; and 5 percent goes to the confederation to which the federation belongs. The remainder, as well as any other funds not used by the unions, federation, or confederation, goes into the Fundo Social Sindical, which provides theater and other recreational facilities, educational activities, and special social services, all of which benefit the workers in an area, regardless of whether they belong to a union.[55]

Moreover, however independent labor might like to be, it is also very dependent on government for aid in collective bargaining. The worker who leaves his job to join in a strike is taking a great risk. He probably has enough beans and bread at the house to last the family for a day or two, maybe several pesos too. But the very idea of being able to hold out for 60 days, 90 days, 120 days, or sometimes much longer, as unions in other nations sometimes do, is inconceivable.[56] With the far greater resources management in Latin America has—some of it a part of his own wages helping to finance industrialization—the worker on strike is in no position to hold out for more than a few days. It is thus critical that a decision to resolve the dispute be made promptly, whether in his favor or against him. Obviously the only one in a position to require this is government.

The benefits obtained from reliance on government have a price tag, of course. In return for its help to labor, government exacts the price of submission to governmental control in certain key areas—mainly in supervision of union funds, general control over union elections, and

---

[55] Alexander, *op. cit.*, pp. 85–86.
[56] In Peru, 46 percent of the strikes last only from 1 hour to 1 day; and 89 percent no longer than 10 days. Payne, *op. cit.*, p. 266.

having the final word in the legality of the strike and the nature of the settlement.

Regarding supervision of funds, unions in Mexico can acquire only those assets absolutely necessary to carry out their legitimate objectives. They cannot engage in any kinds of commercial activities with the view of making a profit. Moreover, union leaders must render a semiannual accounting for all revenues. In Chile, union funds do not belong to the workers but to the organization. They must be deposited in an account in the National Savings Bank in the name of the union, and the manager of the bank and the government inspector will determine how they are to be invested. In Brazil, every union is required to submit its next year's budget for the approval of the Ministry of Labor, Industry, and Commerce. The regional labor delegate representing the government also checks the union's books when they are submitted.[57]

In return for supporting labor, government also insists upon the power to supervise union elections and important union decisions. Thus, when leaders are to be elected or a strike is to be voted on, an inspector from the department of labor is apt to be on hand, in accordance with the labor law in the nation. This law also prescribes the conditions for voting. A secret ballot is usually required. In Brazil, members who have belonged to the union for more than 6 months may vote, provided they are at least 18 years of age. In Chile, anyone who has belonged to the union more than three years has the right to cast two ballots.[58]

Government also insists on having the final word on any agreement reached. Unions come to expect this as the *quid pro quo*.

In return for recognition—a place at the council tables of party and Government [in Mexico], labour has tacitly accepted certain limitations, as full co-partners in the Revolution. It cannot engage in all-out warfare against industry, nor exert full economic pressure against the Government to obtain more desirable wages and conditions. In the total system, the claims of labour for more wages, for example, must be weighed by the Government against such national considerations as trade balances, export prices, the level of domestic prices, the preservation of an attractive climate for domestic and foreign investment, and other elements producing general economic development, now a major goal of the Revolution.[59]

In most of the nations, governmental supervision is extensive in normal times; it is far more so during dictatorships, even those that profess to be labor governments. During the Vargas regime in Brazil, labor as a group had no political rights. Strikes and lockouts were forbidden as "antisocial, harmful to labor and capital, and incompatible with the supreme interests of national production." Only those unions that were thoroughly under

---

57 Poblete and Burnett, *op. cit.*, p. 30; Alexander, *op. cit.*, p. 84.
58 Poblete and Burnett, *op. cit.*, p. 30.
59 Cline, *op. cit.*, pp. 225–26.

government's thumb were allowed to continue in existence.[60] In Argentina, Perón's 10 years or so of *justicialismo* provided many benefits for the urban workers but also exacted strict subservience to the state.[61]

Deeply involved as labor is in politics, whether it would prefer it that way or not, it has a varied arsenal of weapons for slugging it out if necessary to survive or further its goals. The ballot, the general strike, and even armed might are potent weapons, which even labor's most powerful adversaries have learned to respect.

Where workers are allowed under law to vote freely and are not barred by literacy requirements, the ballot is an effective means of their expressing approval or disapproval of an administration. When it is one that has won their approval and support, it is almost sure to receive a strong vote of confidence from the labor sector. In Bolivia, only 126,125 persons voted in the 1951 presidential election. But following the 1952 revolution, which practically remade the society and established universal suffrage without literacy requirements, the workers gave their massive, unqualified support to the new regime. Of the 955,412 votes cast, the MNR, the party responsible for the revolution and the workers' improved status, received 786,792.[62]

Knowing which side its bread is buttered on—one does not have to be able to read and write to know this—organized labor has thrown the weight of its support solidly behind the party regarded as most favorably disposed toward its interests.

The socialist parties of the several nations, which have championed the cause of the workers, have traditionally received labor's support. However, the communist parties in recent decades have managed to chisel in, directing their appeal mainly to the workers, especially members of the urban working class. The Aprista parties have also drawn much labor support, although they are not avowedly labor parties. Other parties, too, such as the Christian Democrats, Liberals, and Argentine Radicals, have appealed to and received much support from labor.

While the ballot is the usual means whereby labor expresses its preference for an administration, the general strike is much more formidable. Its use—or even threatened use—represents, in effect, throwing down the gauntlet and squaring off for a bitter struggle if necessary. The strike is, of course, more effective in the more highly industrialized nations, a large proportion of whose citizens are dependent on a regular supply of needed goods and services for their comfort and even daily existence. It is apt to fail when the government is determined to have a showdown and is willing to risk heavy loss of life to maintain its point of view. But it often

---

[60] Lowenstein, *op. cit.*, p. 342.

[61] George I. Blanksten, *Perón's Argentina* (Chicago: University of Chicago Press, 1953), pp. 257–75.

[62] *Political Handbook of the World, 1957*, p. 14.

succeeds in toppling or helping to topple a regime, or in putting one in power.

In Argentina, labor stepped into the picture at a critical moment to throw its support behind Juan Perón. The idol and boss of the trade union movement, he appeared to be washed out when he was shunted aside by a faction of the army opposed to his personal ambitions and was sent to the prison island of Martín García. But the myriad of workers loyal to him staged a virtually spontaneous general strike throughout the country. In Buenos Aires and the suburbs, the packinghouse workers from nearby La Plata and Avellaneda filled the streets, taking over the city. Bowing to the will of this unprecedented display of popular support, the army permitted Perón to return from Martín García. From October 17, 1945, when he returned to power, until June 16, 1955, Perón exercised strong control with the support of organized labor and the armed forces.

Besides customarily using the ballot and occasionally the general strike for putting its program over, labor has sometimes even supplied armed might to support a regime that has been favorable to its interests. In Mexico, Venustiano Carranza, engaged in a civil war with the forces of Pancho Villa and Emiliano Zapata in 1915, made a deal with the weak Mexican labor movement in return for its support of Carranza's bid for power. The unions were promised the support of his government in unionization and in trade disputes in return for six red battalions of workers who enlisted in Carranza's army.[63]

Years later, President Lázaro Cárdenas, 1934–40, was determined to complete his program of land reform and nationalization of certain industries, especially oil. Doubting the political dependability of the army, he fell back on the organized unions and provided arms to his labor supporters, who organized a labor militia. In return for this support, they received many benefits, among which were wage increases and better working conditions.

Labor also took up its cudgels to support the new revolutionary movement in Bolivia in April, 1952. When the national police who led the revolt appeared to be beaten after two days of fighting, the tide was turned by the determined support of the organized workers of La Paz and the tin mines. According to popular accounts, the organized Indian women who had their established places for selling in the marketplace did their bit, too, in turning the tide of battle. Many a woman offered herself to one of the raw army recruits fighting for the government, then disarmed him and turned him over to the rebel forces.[64]

---

[63] Henry Bamford Parkes, *A History of Mexico* (3d ed. rev.; Boston: Houghton Mifflin Co., 1960), p. 352.

[64] Labor's support is given in detail by Robert J. Alexander, "Organized Labor's Role in the National Revolution," *Bolivian National Revolution* (New Brunswick, N.J.: Rutgers University Press, 1958), chap. 7.

Any participation in politics, especially such all-out support, is risky business. When labor hitches its star to the wrong party or cause, the consequences can be disastrous. But when the gamble is successful, it pays off handsomely, as Mexico's labor movement can attest. Howard F. Cline observed:

As a favourite child of the Revolution, Mexican labour has had a somewhat unique experience. It has never faced some of the other issues that inevitably trouble organized labour seeking to establish a partnership in an economy: survival and permanence, ideology, appropriate structure, discipline, and programmes. These are all provided by the Revolution.[65]

Regarding its future, organized labor in Latin America should feel optimistic. It has won for its members many benefits that they would never otherwise have had; union members realize this and strongly support their organization. Moreover, organized labor represents the largest single bloc of voters in many of the nations; their weight in elections is bound to increase as industrialization advances and more workers become organized, or as the less progressive nations relax their voting requirements to permit illiterates to vote. Furthermore, the labor unions constitute the only organized group in the society strong enough to counterbalance or possibly curb the long entrenched power of the armed forces.

As organized labor becomes stronger, as it almost surely will, it can be expected to participate less directly in politics and devote more of its efforts to the economic objectives for which unions were founded. But the battle is a long way from being won. No one realizes this better than the maid in Nicaragua who still has to work 14 hours a day!

SUGGESTED READINGS

Alba, Victor. *Politics and the Labor Movement in Latin America.* Stanford, Calif.: Stanford University Press, 1968.

Alexander, Robert J. *The Bolivian National Revolution,* chap. 7. New Brunswick, N.J.: Rutgers University Press, 1958.

———. *Labor Relations in Argentina, Brazil, and Chile.* New York: McGraw-Hill Book Co., Inc., 1962.

———. *Organized Labor In Latin America.* New York: The Free Press, 1965.

Baily, Samuel L. *Labor, Nationalism, and Politics in Argentina.* New Brunswick, N.J.: Rutgers University Press, 1967.

Chaplin, David. *The Peruvian Industrial Labor Force.* Princeton, N.J.: Princeton University Press, 1967.

---

[65] Cline, *op. cit.,* p. 222.

Cline, Howard F. *Mexico: Revolution to Evolution: 1940–1960*, chap. xxiii. Royal Institute of International Affairs. New York: Oxford University Press, 1962.

Furtado, Celso. *The Economic Growth of Brazil: A Survey from Colonial to Modern Times*, pp. 127–54. Trans. Ricardo W. de Aguiar and Eric Charles Drysdale. Berkeley: University of California Press, 1963.

Gruening, Ernest. *Mexico and Its Heritage*, pp. 335–90. New York: D. Appleton-Century Co., Inc., 1934.

International Labour Office. *Indigenous Peoples: Living and Working Conditions of Aboriginal Populations in Independent Countries*, Studies and Reports, New Series, No. 35, pp. 199–264. Geneva, Switz., 1953.

———. "Youth and Work in Latin America," *International Labour Review*, Vol. XC, No. 1 (July, 1964), pp. 1–23.

Landsberger, Henry A. "The Labor Elite: Is It Revolutionary?" *Elites in Latin America* (eds. Seymour Martin Lipset and Aldo Solari, chap. 8. New York: Oxford University Press, 1966.

MacGaffey, Wyatt, and Barnett, Clifford R. *Cuba*, chap. 7. Survey of World Cultures. New Haven, Conn.: HRAF Press, 1962.

Millon, Robert Paul. *Mexican Marxist—Vicente Lombardo Toledano*. Chapel Hill: University of Northa Carolina Press, 1966.

Moore, Wilbert. *Industrialization and Labor: Social Aspects of Economic Development*, Part II, chaps. ix–xii. Institute of World Affairs. Ithaca, N.Y.: Cornell University Press, 1951.

Morris, James O. *Elites, Intellectuals, and Consensus*. New York State School of Industrial and Labor Relations. Ithaca, N.Y.: Cornell University, 1966.

Payne, James L. *Labor and Politics in Peru: The System of Political Bargaining*. New Haven, Conn.: Yale University Press, 1965.

Pierson, William W., and Gil, Federico G. *Governments of Latin America*, chap. 14. New York: McGraw-Hill Book Co., Inc., 1957.

Poblete-Troncoso, Moises, and Burnett, Ben G. *The Rise of the Latin American Labor Movement*. New Haven, Conn.: College and University Press, 1960.

Stark, Harry. *Social and Economic Frontiers in Latin America*, chap. 11. Dubuque, Ia.: Wm. C. Brown Co., 1963.

Tannenbaum, Frank. *Mexico: The Struggle for Peace and Bread*, chap. 7. New York: Alfred A. Knopf, Inc., 1954.

———. *Peace by Revolution: An Interpretation of Mexico*, chaps. 19–23. New York: Columbia University Press, 1933.

Zeitlin, Maurice. *Revolutionary Politics and the Cuban Working Class*. Princeton, N.J.: Princeton University Press, 1967.

PART IV

Dynamics of Political Change:
Bullets or Ballots

CAUDILLOS AND REVOLUTIONS:
Bullets, if Necessary

Latin America is often referred to as one of the largest areas in the world embracing democratic government. In reality, however, only a few of the nations have developed genuinely democratic governments. Most of them have been plagued by dictatorships during much of their history. "They have been so numerous," concludes J. Fred Rippy, "their sway has been so constant, that the national history of most of the countries of the area is to a large extent the biography of these imperious personalities."[1]

CAUDILLOS

Origin and Duration

The *caudillos*, Latin America's indigenous variety of dictators, first rose to power during the wars of independence as leaders of the armies that fought the Spanish forces. Commanding what was often a fanatical devotion from their personal armies, these men on horseback were not only to throw off the Spanish yoke but also to be the future rulers of their countries. So strong was their influence that the early decades of independence are often referred to as the era of the *caudillos*.

It is easy to ascertain when the dictators first appeared on the national scene, with their heroic exploits in battle and later strong-man rule of

---

[1] J. Fred Rippy, "Dictatorships in Spanish America," in Guy Stanton Ford (ed.), *Dictatorship in the Modern World* (Minneapolis: University of Minnesota Press, 1935), p. 51.

their countries. But it is more difficult to be sure how long *caudillismo* or dictatorship has continued in the various countries. Several of them managed to escape fairly early from its grip; by the middle of the 19th century, four of them were able to rid themselves of at least its more violent aspects. Chile, which shook off *caudillismo* about 1830, was followed later by Uruguay, Brazil, and Argentina. In succeeding decades, other nations have been largely able to throw off the yoke of these dictatorial rulers.

But, unfortunately, *caudillismo* is far from dead in Latin America; quite to the contrary, it shows a surprising vitality. Indeed, several of the nations, including the Dominican Republic, Haiti, Nicaragua, and Paraguay, have made little, if any, progress in freeing themselves from its clutches. Their strong-man rulers, although they have more *savoir faire* and probably a crease in their pants, are every bit as much *caudillos* as their predecessors of a century and a half ago.

In addition to these four states, many others—a majority of the total number—vacillate between absolutism and constitutionalism, bogging down much of the time in absolutism. Indeed, the recent history of even some of the more democratic states, such as Argentina and Brazil, shows that there is always the danger of slipping back into its insidious grip.

In fact, judged by the record of the last several decades apparently only four states—Chile, Costa Rica, Uruguay, and Mexico—are not in danger of a serious relapse. These states have developed "the capacity to make the transition from one administration to another of opposing political views without resort to arms," which is the test for determining whether a nation has emerged from *caudillismo*.[2] One of the four states, Mexico, is governed by a single political party, Partido Revolucionario Institucional, known as PRI, which easily wins every election and is hardly representative of the best democratic practice.

The deep discontent of the masses whose aspirations Getulio Vargas supported during his 15-year rule, 1930–1945, is almost as acute today as it was then. The same is true of the masses in Argentina whose aspirations Perón supported during his decade in office. The military regimes in each country may be able to thwart for the time being the deep yearnings of the popular classes, but *caudillos* in years to come may champion them again.

Fidel Castro has given the institution of *caudillismo* such a vitality and significance that it merits serious study. A decade ago, Americans would hardly have dreamed that a *caudillo* would dare establish a socialist regime in a nearby nation, form an alliance with the Communist East,

---

[2] J. Fred Rippy, *Historical Evolution of Hispanic America* (3d ed.; New York: Appleton-Century-Crofts, Inc., 1945), p. 166.

defy the might of the United States, and even instigate guerrilla uprisings in other nations.

Background and Characteristics

Most of the dictators have been military leaders who became political bosses and absolute rulers in their countries, as Getulio Vargas, Anastasio Somoza, Fulgencia Batista, Leonidas Trujillo, and Juan Perón. On the other hand, some were civilians, as François Duvalier and Fidel Castro. But whether a military man or a civilian, it was absolutely necessary for the dictator to have control of the armed forces and to be able to count on their loyalty and support.[3] Because of the dependence on the military, *caudillismo* has a symbiotic relationship to militarism, since the armed forces are the most important single power group in most of the nations.

Although many of the *caudillos* governed an entire nation, most of them controlled only a region or perhaps an isolated district in their country. One of the most powerful and colorful of the many regional bosses was Pancho Villa of Mexico, who led a private army of 40,000 and controlled a large part of northern Mexico. In the various nations, these regional and local *caudillos* spent much of their time and energy fighting one another to achieve hegemony. Usually, one of them managed to emerge supreme, and the nation then had a dictator as its chief of state. Some of the dictators, as Leonidas Trujillo, came from a humble background. Trujillo's father was a small trader and had difficulty eking out a living.[4] Others however, such as Fidel Castro, came from families of comfortable circumstances.[5]

Some were unrecognized *naturales* who resented the stigma attached to bastardy and were themselves resented by the society they controlled.[6]

The racial backgrounds of the *caudillos* were as varied as their family origins and environments. Some of them were whites; a few were Negroes or mulattoes; but the large majority were mestizos. But whether

---

[3] To this end, Castro instituted the politicization of the armed forces. See pp. 178–79.

[4] For Trujillo's background, see Robert D. Crassweller, *Trujillo: The Life and Times of a Caribbean Dictator* (New York: Macmillan Co., 1966).

[5] For Castro's background, see Jules Dubois, *Fidel Castro: Rebel–Liberator or Dictator?* (New York: Bobbs-Merrill Co., Inc., 1959).

[6] Bernardo O'Higgins was the illegitimate son of a Creole mother and the Irish Ambrosio O'Higgins who served as governor of Chile and later as viceroy of Peru. Bernardo, sometimes called the George Washington of Chile, was dictator from 1818 to 1823 and instituted a number of reforms that gave the young nation a good start toward democracy. But the blue bloods of Santiago opposed his reforms and finally managed to throw him out; they "could not stomach a bastard son of an Irishman as the standard-bearer for their new nation." Hubert Herring, *A History of Latin America from the Beginnings to the Present* (2d ed. rev.; New York: Alfred A. Knopf, Inc., 1961), p. 576.

Negro or mulatto, Indian or mestizo, "no sooner did these men reach power," says Tad Szulc, "than they made themselves the hubs of hero elites, even if it was in the crudest sense of the word, and provided a monotonous repetition of the old story of how power corrupts."[7]

Their educational backgrounds also differed widely. Some of the *caudillos*, as Juan Vicente Gómez of Venezuela, had only the rudiments of an education. Gómez' "mother taught him his numbers, and a neighbor's daughter, expounding the alphabet to the children of the neighborhood, taught him reading and writing."[8] But other dictators had excellent educations. François Duvalier is a Doctor of Medicine, having obtained his degree from Tulane University. Fidel Castro received the degree of Doctor of Laws from the University of Havana.

While some of the *caudillos* were upright, moral individuals, others were gamblers, drunkards, gluttons, and unrestrained libertines. Some had their own peculiar brand of morality. Gómez never smoked, drank, or got married. But he had a roving eye for feminine pulchritude and apparently aspired quite literally to be the father of his country. He managed to possess almost any lady in the nation whom he desired, and is said to have sired 200 or so illegitimate children in these unions.[9]

A few of the *caudillos* have been outright crackpots. Maximiliano Hernández Martínez, president of El Salvador from 1930 to 1944, was regarded by many of his fellow countrymen as a madman who attempted to bewitch the peons by prescribing magic drinks for curing their illnesses and for increasing their harvests. A theosophist, he is remembered for saying: "It is a greater crime to kill an ant than a man, because when a man dies, he is reincarnated, but the ant dies forever." Martínez never killed an ant, but in 1932 alone he killed more than 20,000 peasants who had rebelled because of hunger.[10]

By almost any criteria the *caudillos* have been a very heterogeneous lot. But however much they may differ in other respects, they have several basic characteristics in common.

They are inordinately ambitious, with little or no sense of their personal limitations and with complete self-confidence in their ability to rule the nation. The erstwhile dictator of the Dominican Republic from 1930 to 1961, Generalissimo Rafael Leonidas Trujillo Molina, was not one to hide his candle under a bushel. According to Abelardo R. Nanita, he rose to the top because of his physical stamina, mental acumen, dy-

---

[7] Tad Szulc, *Twilight of the Tyrants* (New York: Henry Holt & Co., 1959), p. 16.

[8] John Lavin, *A Halo for Gómez* (New York: Pageant Press, 1954), p. 10.

[9] The amorous interests of Gómez are given in Thomas Rourke, *Gómez: Tyrant of the Andes* (New York: William Morrow & Co., 1936), pp. 140–46; and in Lavin, *op. cit.*, pp. 157–66.

[10] Alfredo Pareja Diezcanseco, "Thinkers of the Americas: Alberto Masferrer," *Américas*, Vol. 14, No. 4 (April, 1962), p. 10.

namism, discipline, persevering effort, and unswerving pursuit of a goal. "Trujillo is a man who never loses sight of his main objective," effuses Nanita. "He knows what he wants and how to obtain it. He leaves nothing to chance and all his plans include alternate courses to meet any contingencies that may arise. It is difficult to catch him unaware . . ."[11]

Another characteristic common to the *caudillos* is their unusual ability. Regardless of family background, race, or education, in the fiercely competitive milieu of Latin American politics they had to be very able individuals in order to rise to the top and to rule their countries, with the many pressing problems they presented.

Still another characteristic common to the *caudillos* is their extreme vanity. Their self-appreciation is boundless and is well reflected by the honors they so generously bestow on themselves. Among the many titles they have freely assumed are: Benefactor of the Fatherland, Liberator, Restorer of Liberty, The Only Man Capable of Saving the Country, National Regenerator, Illustrious American, Deliverer of the People from Chains, Voice of the People, and Restorer of Financial Independence.

Nothing pleases the dictator more than the ubiquitous signs of his benign being. In this respect, Rafael Leonidas Trujillo of the Dominican Republic was one of the vainest of the lot. The name of the national capital was changed from Santo Domingo to Ciudad Trujillo, or Trujillo City, and along its main street were huge neon signs reading, "Trujillo Forever" and "God and Trujillo." Every automobile license plate in the nation shouted, "Viva Trujillo," and every school and other public building proclaimed in bold bronze letters, "Era of Trujillo." On all four walls of every government office were photographs of the nation's ruler. The drinking fountains along the highway long carried the inscription, "God and Trujillo supply you with water." But Trujillo, like other dictators, disliked sharing the credit with anyone; in time the inscription was changed to read, "Trujillo is the only one who gives you water."

Rise to Power and Exercise of Authority

The *caudillo* may obtain supreme power in the nation by one of several means. The one most frequently used is revolution against the established government, with the *caudillo* taking over the presidential office if the revolution is successful. The first revolution may not succeed. But if an ambitious would-be leader is able, persistent, and determined, he has a good chance of eventually toppling the government. Several dictators, however, became heads of nations with popular approval and in con-

---

11 Abelardo R. Nanita, *Trujillo* (5th ed. rev.; Ciudad Trujillo, D.R.: Editora del Caribe, C. por A., 1954), pp. 100 and 114–15.

formity with constitutional and legal requirements. Juan Perón was elected president in 1946 and reelected in 1951.[12]

Sometimes the election whereby a dictator attains the presidency is a mere sham, with only the barest semblance of legality. When President Horacio Vásquez of the Dominican Republic was overthrown by a revolution in 1930, Leonidas Trujillo, head of the well-equipped, American-trained constabulary, managed to win presidential office through the façade of legal election, after his henchmen had beaten, terrorized, and killed many of his opponents. With the opposition so mauled that it finally withdrew from the campaign, Trujillo's election was proclaimed to be "virtually unanimous."[13]

In exercising power once he gets it, the *caudillo*, although unquestionably the most powerful man in the nation, may prefer not to become president at all but, rather, to remain behind the scenes where he can exercise control through his puppet president. Thus, Fulgencio Batista, who became Cuba's strong man in August, 1933, after throwing out Gerardo Machado, did not assume the presidency in his own name until 1940. In the intervening seven years, he ruled through puppets—seven in seven years. But such indirect exercise of power is unusual; ordinarily, a dictator prefers to govern in his own name.

However the dictator chooses to exercise power, whether through puppets or by becoming president himself, one thing is certain: there is no doubt whatever in the nation as to where plenary power really lies. The *caudillo* is a "monarch in republican dress," and an absolute monarch at that. In effect, he is the constitution, the government, and the law. Whatever he says goes; regardless of the nation's forms and trappings of democracy, he rules the country with as wide a latitude as he chooses.

Almost no ruler in Latin America likes to be regarded by his fellow countrymen or the rest of the world as an interloper. Accordingly, he makes every effort to give his regime the appearance of legitimacy and constitutionality. To this end, one of the first things he does after becoming head of the nation is to promulgate a new constitution, tailored to legitimize his accession to power and his exercise of governmental authority.

Sometimes the *caudillo*'s determination to have his regime legitimized by a constitution and to present a democratic front to the world tends to run riot. During the 27 years in which Vicente Gómez exercised dictatorial control over Venezuela, he promulgated a total of six constitutions.

---

[12] For an excellent account of both elections, see George I. Blanksten's *Perón's Argentina* (Chicago: University of Chicago Press, 1953), pp. 63–86.

[13] For a very different account, portraying Trujillo as fairly and democratically elected, see a typical sycophant's version—Lawrence de Besault, "Rise to the Presidency," *President Trujillo: His Work and the Dominican Republic* (2d ed.; Washington Publishing Co., 1936), chap. iii.

Each succeeding constitution professed to establish democracy more firmly in the nation and to guarantee the basic liberties of citizens, while at the same time concentrating more and more absolute power in Gómez' hands.

Besides showing respect for a constitution, however much it has been perverted to serve his own ends, the *caudillo* also prefers to govern through the regular, constitutionally established organs of government, since they give his regime the appearance of democracy. But the legislative and judicial branches had better resign themselves to being merely subservient rubber stamps, ready, willing, even eager to carry out his wishes. In Peronist Argentina, after the Supreme Court of Justice presumed to exercise its independent authority and to declare unconstitutional a number of executive decrees, Perón instigated a purge of the entire court—a purge that extended throughout the nation's judicial system.[14]

The Argentine Congress was likewise reduced to a bootlicking body, with little semblance of any independent exercise of authority. The 1948 session mirrored the complete control that Perón exercised over the body. The members of the Chamber of Deputies, consisting mainly of Peronistas, adopted an 8.6 billion peso ($1.8 billion) budget, hardly bothering to look at the mimeographed budget report on their desks. And in just four hours they passed a total of 28 bills, including one that gave Perón dictatorial powers by authorizing him to mobilize men and resources by decree whenever he thought the nation's welfare demanded it.

In maintaining dictatorial control over the nation, the *caudillo* shows consummate skill. He must satisfy his henchmen and supporters, especially the members of the armed forces whose unswerving allegiance is essential to his continuance in office. To assure the support of them all and to keep them happy, he gladly shares with them the spoils of office, tapping every possible source of wealth. Funds in the public treasury, customs duties and taxes, land comprising the national domain, and the confiscated property of his opponents are all utilized to keep his following in line. The military are usually given additional benefits.

Also critically important to the dictator is control of the opposition. The policies and techniques for accomplishing this vary widely. Sometimes a *caudillo* is very indulgent with members of the opposition, permitting them to exercise their constitutional rights, possibly to criticize him publicly or to campaign against him politically. And sometimes even when he catches them red-handedly conspiring to overthrow his regime, he metes out only mild punishment, such as sending them into exile. But this kind of treatment of adversaries is not subscribed to by most dictators, and for good reason. Many a conspirator released to go

---

[14] Blanksten, *op. cit.*, pp. 122–32.

into exile has later returned to institute a successful revolution against the regime in power—possibly, too, to execute the deposed head of state whose brand of *realpolitik* did not work.

More often, the *caudillo* instinctively realizes that any opposition is a challenge to his power and may eventually undermine him. With this in mind, he is apt to be ruthless in ferreting out opposition and brutal in suppressing it. The most sadistic tortures are often inflicted on the regime's opponents. In Cuba the security police of Batista did not hesitate to extract information by any means they chose, whether by yanking out fingernails with pliers, or carbonizing hands and feet in red hot vises. Castrating males was another technique often employed.

Dealing with known members of the opposition is a primary concern of the *caudillo;* keeping the mass of people in line is another. An effective means he uses for this purpose, in addition to rumors of torture that spread among the people, is fear—a paralyzing fear of what will happen to them if they dare to oppose him. To impress this on them, as well as to seek out any incipient opposition, he usually has an elaborate system of espionage, as did Gómez in Venezuela. Relying heavily on his secret police, Gómez is said to have spent two and a half times more for this suppressive force than for public education![15]

Maintaining his power by violence and terror, the *caudillo* is himself infected with the very fear he disseminates among the populace. Feared by his subjects and bitterly hated by his enemies, he knows that he can trust no one. Lurking in any shadow or mixed in any group may be a victim or a relative determined to inflict revenge. Many a fellow country-man would gladly give his life for the privilege of assassinating him. Not even the closest associate can be completely trusted, for he may be jealous of the chief's authority and have ambitions of his own. Since the *caudillo* owes his success to violence, he well realizes that he will probably meet his end by violence too.[16]

The *caudillo*, realizing that his regime will probably fall by the sword, just as it was established by the sword, usually makes elaborate prepara-tions for a hurried departure from the nation should a turn of fortune

---

[15] For the many cruel means of torturous punishment used, see Lavin, *op. cit.*, pp. 208–20, and Rourke, *op. cit.*, pp. 147–54 and 231–37. For Gómez' all-seeing, all-hearing, and omnipresent spy system, see Lavin, *op. cit.*, pp. 313–21.

[16] Francia of Paraguay, president from 1811 to 1840, was so obsessed with his safety that he had all the trees cut down around the presidential mansion, removing vantage points where an assassin might lurk. Hoping to thwart a potential assassin, Francia slept in a different room in the presidential mansion every night, and even personally doled out the cartridges to the supervisors of prisons and powder maga-zines to ensure as far as possible that the bullets would be used against his enemies and not against him. Rengger and Longchamps, *The Reign of Doctor Joseph Gaspard Roderick de Francia, In Paraguay: An Account of a Six Years' Residence in that Republic, from July, 1819 to May, 1825,* trans. J. R. Rengger (London: Thomas Hurst, Edward Chance & Co., 1827), p. 44.

make this necessary. Anticipating this possibility, he smuggles his vast loot out of the country and stores it safely in banks in the United States, Switzerland, and elsewhere. In times of unusual tension, his suitcase is packed and a plane is warming up at the airport to whisk him away on short notice.

But however great are the risks inherent in exercising dictatorial power, the *caudillo* is quite willing to gamble with his safety and even with his life. For "in his own view, the *caudillo* is an indispensable man," says George I. Blanksten, ". . . the only figure on the national scene who can 'save the country.' He . . . bears a striking resemblance to Max Weber's 'charismatic' leader, who feels an 'inner call.' "[17] When Doctor François Duvalier of Haiti—"Papa Doc," his admiring followers call him—had himself installed as president for life in April, 1964, he told his crowd of well-wishers that he considered himself an exceptional man— the kind of man that Haiti can produce only once every 50 or 75 years.[18]

Effects of Dictatorship[19]

Throughout the century and a half of *caudillismo*, although representing the antithesis of democratic government the *caudillos* have nevertheless helped their nations in many important ways. Seeking to improve communication and transportation, if only to strengthen and consolidate their power, they built telegraph lines and roads that tied the various sections of the nations together. And usually concerned with economic development, if only to increase their personal revenues, they stimulated agriculture and industry, developed local resources, and increased foreign trade. Sometimes, they supported public education, building schools and public libraries, thereby adding to their long list of titles that of Patron of Arts and Learning. But education of the mass was a recognized hazard, so concern for public education was apt to be mere talk; a citizenry that was educated might catch on to their machinations and turn the rascals out.

Another contribution of the *caudillos* has been the intense nationalism they have fostered. During the critical early years of independence, when the young nations were threatened with fragmentation by internal anarchy or dismemberment by foreign invasion, a strong national leader and his stress on patriotism was sometimes the only force that held the nation together. Thus, Argentina owes its very existence as a nation today largely to Juan Manuel de Rosas, whose 23 years of dictatorial rule kept the nation together during the turbulent early period when it was

---

[17] George I. Blanksten, *Ecuador: Constitutions and Caudillos* (Berkeley: University of California Press, 1951), p. 35.

[18] *New York Times*, April 2, 1964, p. 1, col. 6.

[19] For a detailed appraisal of the balance sheet of the Vargas regime in Brazil, see Karl Lowenstein, *Brazil Under Vargas* (New York: Macmillan Co., 1942), pp. 316–62.

threatened with dissolution. Nationalism has also been a dynamic force in the social revolutions of more recent years that have transformed Mexico, Bolivia, and Cuba.[20]

Still another noteworthy contribution of the dictators has been the order and stability they were able to maintain. Although their methods were ruthless and violent, they nevertheless managed to curb the turbulence and anarchy that all but swamped the young nations. In the Buenos Aires area alone, there were 12 revolutions in a single year (1820), and other parts of Latin America were almost as chaotic. The rule of the *caudillos* might be strong, even tyrannical, but it afforded the young republics still struggling to maintain themselves a measure of law and order they sorely needed.

However much a dictator might be disliked or even hated because of his strong rule while in power, he was often sorely missed the moment he was overthrown. Thus, when Bernardo O'Higgins of Chile was forced out in 1823 after five years of firm but enlightened rule, there followed seven years of ruinous disorder. During this period, there were at least 10 governments and 3 different constitutions. Presidents came and went so fast it was almost impossible to keep track of them. "National life reached a very bad state," says J. Fred Rippy, with "'vandalism in the country, commerce paralyzed, industry at a standstill, finance in disorder, credit vanished, and politics revolutionary.' The Chilean people passed 'from liberty to license, and from license to barbarism.'"[21]

Yet another contribution made by many of the *caudillos* was their emphasis on efficiency in government. Often, they reorganized the governmental structure to make the operating agencies more effective and streamlined their procedures to enable them to operate more expeditiously. The dictator sometimes even demanded scrupulous honesty on the part of his officials and personnel—a yardstick he seldom applied to himself or to his cronies.

But whatever the *caudillos* contributed to the welfare of their nations, these contributions were usually very dearly paid for, as the debit side of the ledger clearly shows. Some of the dictators, such as Rosas of Argentina, were quite honest. A wealthy man when he came to power, Rosas carried almost nothing away with him when he went into exile and died virtually a pauper in England in 1877.

But such honesty was quite the exception. Usually, at the same time the *caudillo* was demanding scrupulous honesty on the part of his officials, he had his hand deep in the national till, taking everything he wanted,

---

[20] Arthur P. Whitaker and David C. Jordan, *Nationalism in Contemporary Latin America* (New York: The Free Press, 1966), chaps. iii and viii; and Gerhard Masur, *Nationalism in Latin America: Diversity and Unity* (New York: Macmillan Co., 1966), chaps. v, vii, and xi.

[21] Rippy, *Historical Evolution of Hispanic America, op. cit.*, p. 197.

including land, money, and lucrative concessions. Although not many *caudillos* were large landowners before they came into power, they were usually among the largest *hacendados* in the nation afterward.

They enjoy accumulating money as well as land, and have stolen public funds in fantastic amounts. Dictators who have been overthrown within the last decade have set quite a record for peculation. Juan Perón is believed to have left Argentina after his overthrow in 1955 with an estimated $700 million, enough to enable him to live comfortably in his old age. Pérez Jiménez of Venezuela and Fulgencio Batista of Cuba, both of whom were overthrown in 1958, were bush leaguers by comparison, but each is supposed to have taken more than $250 million with him to ease the pangs of exile.

Besides helping himself to all funds in the national treasury, the *caudillo* often regards the nation as his private preserve and bleeds it as much as he can. In the Dominican Republic, Rafael Trujillo and members of his family had a monopoly on practically every commodity the people needed—meat, milk, rice, coffee, vegetable oils, cacao, tobacco, and salt— as well as on lumber and furniture. But the Trujillos were not satisfied with just the profit from commodities, which amounted to millions of dollars a year thanks to high fixed prices that were charged. They also set up for themselves monopolies on such profitable services as sea and land transportation; the sale of accident insurance; iron and steel used by the government for construction purposes; and even the laundry concession for all the nation. No source of easy money was overlooked. One of the brothers even had a monopoly on houses of prostitution![22]

Sometimes, even more harmful to a nation than the graft and corruption of a *caudillo* and his gang are his economic policies. Those of Rojas Pinilla, who guided Colombia's destiny with a firm hand from 1953 to 1957, provided needed benefits for the mass but were very expensive to the nation.[23] Perón's economic program left Argentina with a legacy of internal stagnation and in virtual economic collapse. Indeed, the nation's instability, which has continued since his overthrow in 1955, is largely due to his economic policies; he left virtually bankrupt a country that had enjoyed prosperity until he came into power.[24] The eminent Argentine economist, Raúl Prebisch, has estimated that Perón's rule cost the nation more than $3 billion—a tremendous sum for the country—which spelled the difference between enjoying economic stability and prosperity or

---

[22] Albert C. Hicks, *Blood in the Streets: The Life and Rule of Trujillo* (New York: Creative Age Press, Inc., 1946), pp. 65–74.

[23] Vernon Lee Fluharty, *Dance of the Millions: Military Rule and the Social Revolution in Colombia, 1930–1956* (Pittsburgh, Pa.: University of Pittsburgh Press, 1957), pp. 237–58.

[24] For Argentina's disastrous economic situation in 1955, see Arthur P. Whitaker, *Argentine Upheaval: Perón's Fall and the New Regime* (New York: Frederick A. Praeger, Inc., 1956), pp. 37–38 and 161–64.

teetering on the brink of economic chaos. But while Argentines sweat it out today at home, Perón manages to live comfortably on the $700 million or so he took with him into exile.

Why *Caudillismo* Continues to Flourish

The persistence and frequency of dictatorships have provoked much soul-searching on the part of Latin Americans and analytical thought on the part of others. The explanations that have been offered are many and varied.[25]

Geography has had a very important effect. Much of the area is covered by lofty mountains or tropical jungles, tremendous obstacles to easy intercourse between the different regions of a nation. There are few roads—usually poor ones—for reaching regions isolated from the seat of government. As a result, there is a strong feeling of regional loyalty, which makes it easy for a local *caudillo* to rise to power and difficult for the central government to suppress an insurrection once it has begun. Pancho Villa, notorious regional *caudillo* in Mexico, managed to avoid capture by the Mexican government and even by the United States Army under General Pershing, sent across the border to apprehend him.[26]

Also a factor that has made for *caudillismo* is the tradition of strong-man rule in the history of the several races of Latin America; this is true of the Spanish and Portuguese as well as of the Indian and Negro. Each of these races has long been accustomed to the dictatorial rule of a monarch or cacique. The Inca, for example, was one of the most absolute rulers to be found anywhere. He was the supreme chief of the nation, the leader of the army, the high priest of the religion, and the supreme law giver. Owing him blind obedience, the mass of Indians were accustomed to forced labor without pay and were not even permitted to choose their occupations. In fact, every aspect of their life conditioned them to absolute rule.

The heterogeneous racial composition of the region has also been a very influential factor. In most of the nations, a large part of the population is Indian or mestizo, with culture, mores, and interests quite different

---

[25] For some provocative explanations, see W. W. Pierson (ed.), "Pathology of Democracy in Latin America: A Symposium" (Arthur P. Whitaker, "A Historian's Point of View"; Russell Fitzgibbon, "A Political Scientist's Point of View"; Sanford A. Mosk, "An Economist's Point of View"; and W. Rex Crawford, "Discussion: A Sociologist's Point of View"), *American Political Science Review*, Vol. 44, No. 1 (March, 1950), pp. 100–49; also Rippy, "Dictatorships in Latin America" (2d ed.), *op. cit.*, pp. 179–85; and Charles Edward Chapman, *Republican Hispanic America: A History* (New York: Macmillan Co., 1937), chap. vii.

[26] For a graphic account of Villa's relations with the United States, see Clarence C. Clendenen, *The United States and Pancho Villa: A Study in Unconventional Diplomacy* (Ithaca, N.Y.: Cornell University Press, 1961).

from those of the whites and Negroes. Strong animosities are generated by these differences, and the resulting tensions in society are tempting targets for demagogues, who often rise to power by playing off one racial group against another.

"Our political backwardness," wrote Lucas Awarragaray about anarchy and *caudillismo* in Argentina, "is and always has been simply a phenomenon of the psychology of race; a hybrid mind has been the source of Creole, that is, hybrid anarchy. The mestizo element has been the cause of the most fundamental defects in our character."[27]

Another influence often regarded in Latin America as encouraging to dictatorship is the Spanish temperament, certain aspects of which are conducive to violence and strong rule. Among the traits regarded as typically Spanish are arrogance, conceit, selfishness, impulsiveness, verbosity, an exaggerated sense of dignity, and a theatrical sense of the heroic. "To die for a principle, how glorious!" thinks the Latin American, a born revolutionary. "But to live for a principle, how dull." Moreover, the Spaniards who came to the New World were intensely individualistic, impatient with authority, and unwilling to regard themselves as subject to law. With few restraining influences on them in the new society, their tendencies toward aggrandizement and turbulence were given free rein. Strong government was necessary to hold them in check.

The high rate of illiteracy prevailing in Latin America has also been a factor conducive to dictatorship. Man's political history has shown that where a large part of the citizenry is illiterate this uneducated group cannot adequately assume its responsibilities in a democracy. Latin America has proved no exception to the rule. There, the ignorant masses have often been the easy prey of demagogues who prated about the rights of man, harangued them into an emotional frenzy, and enlisted their enthusiastic support for a revolution. But the demagogues promptly forgot about the rights of man after they managed to get control of the government, and set up just another dictatorship in the long, monotonous pattern of the region.

Still another factor conducive to dictatorships was the lack of apprenticeship in self-government during the more than 300 years of colonial status.[28] The only self-government enjoyed then was participation in the *cabildos* or town councils. Consequently, the citizens of the new independent nations, denied wider political experience, lacked the habits of independent judgment, self-direction, and self-restraint that citizens of a truly democratic nation must have.

---

[27] In Pierson, *op. cit.*, p. 106.

[28] The *caudillo* is "the receiver of the bankrupt colonial regime of Latin America. In a few of these countries his function has already been fulfilled." George S. Wise, *Caudillo: A Portrait of Antonio Guzmán Blanco* (New York: Columbia University Press, 1951), p. x.

In short, the people really were not ready for self-government. Simón Bolívar was fully convinced of this and was very pessimistic about Latin America's future. "For centuries we were political ciphers [under Spanish rule]," he declared in his famous Jamaica letter of 1815. "That is why it is so hard for us to rise to the enjoyment of freedom. . . . Events have already shown that completely representative institutions are not suited to our present character, habits, and educational background."

The economic conditions and problems of the region have also done much to further dictatorship. The extremes of great wealth for the few and blighting poverty for the mass are mainly responsible for the sharp cleavage between social classes and the bitter social conflicts that often result. Members of the mass, who eke out a bare subsistence and live in miserable squalor, are receptive to almost any appeal that promises somehow to improve their condition.

An additional factor that has played a part in the continuance of *caudillismo* is the role of foreign capital in the society. Lacking the means to develop their own economic resources, the countries have had to rely heavily on the investments of foreign companies, particularly those of the United States, Britain, Germany, and Japan. Foreign capital has been invested in a variety of enterprises, including mines and petroleum, railroads and rapid transit companies, and banks and public utilities. Although capital from abroad was badly needed and usually eagerly welcomed, its presence was often a disturbing influence that could easily be exploited for political purposes. Ofttimes, the foreign companies were bitterly criticized and charged with making excessive profits, wasting irreplaceable natural resources, exploiting native labor, paying inadequate taxes to the government, enjoying undeserved privileges through concessions, favors, and exemptions, and intervening in local politics to protect their privileges and interests. Aroused by these criticisms, public opinion in Latin America has been decidedly antiforeign and strongly nationalistic. Charges of economic imperialism, whether solidly or superficially supported, have often proved to be an effective technique that enabled an ambitious demagogue and incipient *caudillo* to rise to power.

A last influence that has figured prominently in the persistence of dictatorships is personalism—the tendency of citizens to support or oppose a leader for such purely personal reasons as his personal appeal or family background, rather than for the program he espouses or party he represents. Taking advantage of this tendency, the *caudillos* with their dynamic personalities and flair for the dramatic are easily able to capture the attention and support of a following by their personal magnetism.[29]

---

[29] Sometimes a *caudillo* resorts to personalism as his sole claim to leadership. ". . . Guzmán Blanco has no background to relieve his sheer insistence on his personal glory. There is no assurance behind his claims. He must assert his lone self because he has nothing else to assert." (*Ibid.*, p. 172.)

But Latin America pays a high price for personalism, because it results in the rule of men, often capricious, arbitrary, and absolute, rather than in the rule of law, uniform, impartial, and fair.

REVOLUTIONS AND VIOLENCE

One of the most characteristic features of the political process in Latin America is the resort to revolution to bring about changes in political power. So frequently has violence been used for this purpose in the past that change of administration by revolution is regarded as the normal pattern in many of the countries. While such revolutions were more frequent during the 19th century, they have continued to thwart the orderly, constitutional processes of government and constitute an accepted means of transfer of political power from one administration to another.

The term "revolution" is used quite loosely in referring to changes in political power brought about by violence. In fact, the term has come to connote three very different political phenomena: (1) the wars for independence during the first quarter of the 19th century; (2) struggles for political power involving the use of force; and (3) fundamental change in the political structure accompanied by basic changes in social institutions.[30]

The Wars of Independence

Regarding the wars for independence in the various nations, the successful struggles for freedom resulting in transfer of sovereignty from the mother country to the colonies are usually referred to as revolutions, in the same sense that we refer to the revolution of the 13 original colonies as the American Revolution. And just as the American Revolution did relatively little at the time to basically change the new nation's political and social structure, the Latin American revolutions made few, if any, basic changes.

The wars for independence, as in the case of the American Revolution, were led for the most part by conservatives who were determined to maintain their vested interests in the new nations. They had no intention whatever of overturning the existing political, economic, and social structure

---

[30] Categorizing the purposes of violence in Latin America's experience, Martin Needler classifies them as: anomic violence, which does not consciously aim to affect the political system; representational violence, whereby grievances and demands are brought directly to the attention of the president, buttressed by a direct or veiled threat to be effective; and revolutionary violence, which aims to change personnel only, or policy, or the political system itself. Martin Needler, *Political Development in Latin America: Instability, Violence, and Evolutionary Change* (New York: Random House, Inc., 1968), pp. 46–54.

Esquire, *January, 1961, p. 69. Reproduced by permission.*

"Congratulations! We've changed our minds—you're the new President!"

and remolding it into a true democracy. Consequently, although the masses had contributed mightily to the success of the national revolts, supplying most of the soldiers that eventually humbled the military might of Spain, they were to benefit but little from the newly won independence. "The heroic struggle for Bolivian independence did nothing to relieve the Indian of his miserable state," concludes Eduardo Palomo, "although . . . the majority of those who fought and died for independence were Indians. . . . As far as the Indian was concerned, one feudal master had been substituted for another."[31]

---

[31] Eduardo Palomo, "Agrarian Reform," (in collaboration with Eugene C. Reichard and Clifford Belcher) (La Paz, Bolivia: Servicio Agrícola Interamericano, January 20, 1961), p. 1.

In the political realm, the Creole elite, who were now in the saddle after displacing their envied superiors, the *peninsulares,* preempted all political offices and political rights for themselves. In the social realm, they continued the rigid class system that had existed from the early days of the colonial era. In the economic realm, too, they condoned and accepted the great extremes of wealth that had so long burdened the society. These basic disparities—political, social, and economic—were to be veritable millstones around the necks of the struggling young nations —millstones that still threaten to submerge them almost a century and a half after independence.

Thus, the wars for independence, which made no basic changes in the semifeudal society, can hardly be said to have been revolutions in the true sense of the term. Indeed, the very fact that such changes were not made earlier and have not been made even to date is the main reason for the unrest and instability that prevails throughout most of the region. In fact, many who are very interested in Latin America are quite convinced that the nations will still have to undergo a true revolution in order to achieve the democratic society they profess to aspire to. The liberal leaders of Latin America "know that their own countries must go through a social as well as a political reorganization . . . ," says A. A. Berle, Jr. "The outstanding necessity is to put an end to the division between age-old oligarchic, irresponsible power cliques and a proletariat living out its life in hunger and disease, without hope of improvement."[32]

Struggles for Political Power Involving the Use of Force

Besides designating the wars for independence, the term "revolution" is used to denote the many struggles for political power involving the use of force. In such cases, only the presidency, cabinet positions, and other high executive offices are usually affected. The courts may continue to function as before, along with the congress and the administrative machinery of government. These typically Latin American revolutions are of two kinds: the *golpe de estado,* or *coup d'état,* and the *cuartelazo,* or barracks revolt.

According to William S. Stokes, "the *golpe de estado* . . . is the fastest and potentially the most dangerous of the forceful methods of establishing and changing governments in Latin America. The *golpe* is a direct assault on power, which means the immobilization of the president either through assassination, detention, or exile."[33]

---

[32] A. A. Berle, Jr., "Latin America: The Hidden Revolution," *The Reporter,* Vol. 20, No. 10 (May 28, 1959), p. 20.

[33] William S. Stokes, *Latin American Politics* (New York: Thomas Y. Crowell Co., 1959), p. 319.

Speedy and effective, this supraconstitutional means of seizing political power by force is frequently used in Latin America. Sometimes it is quite dramatic. In August, 1947, José María Velasco Ibarra, president of Ecuador since June, 1944, was forced to relinquish his presidential office and depart in haste when Colonel Carlos Mancheno, minister of defense, managed to get into the presidential mansion and compel him at gunpoint to resign in his favor. Mancheno tried to justify his seizure of the presidential office on the ground that "the members of the Armed Forces see ourselves in the necessity of taking over the government temporarily."

Another novel application of the *golpe* was staged in Paraguay in February, 1949, when President Raimundo Rolón and most members of his government were invited to dinner by Felipe Molas López. The host, who had surrounded his home with his own henchmen, summarily announced to the group, "Gentlemen, the jig is up." It was, and López thereupon became president of Paraguay.

The *golpe* as a political instrument has several distinct advantages over other violent methods used in taking over the presidential office. For one thing, it is relatively easy to organize. Only a small number—a single individual, in fact—may be able to successfully accomplish the seizure. And while a ranking military figure would probably have a better chance of succeeding, even a civilian leader with sufficient daring and finesse might be able to finagle his way into the presidential mansion and successfully accomplish his mission.

The *golpe* also has the advantage of obtaining a prompt, often immediate, decision. No widespread seizure of critical installations, no assault in force on the presidential palace or fighting in the streets by military and police, is necessary. If the *golpe* is adroitly planned and executed, the decision is apt to be speedy and irrevocable. A president can say uncle and disappear fast when he sees the menacing barrel of a loaded 38 or 44.

Another effective means of bringing about a change in government at the top by violence is the *cuartelazo*, or barracks revolt, which has its origin in the *cuartel* or barracks. The most extensive and careful planning is necessary for its success—planning that is as painstaking as the architect's for constructing a building sturdy enough to withstand the earthquakes that beset the Andean region. Many critical questions must be answered, and answered correctly. What leaders can be counted on to sympathize with the revolt, throw in their forces to make it successful, and be willing to risk their careers, and perhaps lives, on its outcome? What specific program should be adopted that will appeal to the people and justify the new regime's revolting and taking over? How much force will be necessary to achieve control, and just when, where, and how will it be exercised? In short, a successful *cuartelazo* requires consummate strategy, for in essence it is a form of military statesmanship.

The timing of the revolt is of the utmost importance. It is usually set for a Sunday or a holiday, when the president is apt to be alone or lightly guarded, the security forces relaxed, the government offices closed, and the various facilities for communication either closed or on a standby basis. Moreover, the populace will be at the soccer games or at the races, more concerned at the moment with the fate of a five peso bet than with the safety of governmental authority.

If everything goes as planned, the *cuartelazo* is executed quickly and precisely. All key military and governmental centers, including armories and supply depots, TV and radio stations, governmental buildings and banks, are speedily seized. Using the seized media of communication, the leader of the *cuartelazo* announces to the people that a revolt has taken place and that his group has taken over governmental authority. The rascals of the overthrown regime will be properly dealt with, and all of their abuses, which are many, will be corrected in short order. The people are assured that the nation is now in good hands, and their co-operation is requested in restoring and maintaining order.

There have been many such *cuartelazos* in Latin America, some of them brilliantly planned and executed. In fact, whichever side one is on, he cannot help but admire the skill and finesse responsible for their success.

One of the most brilliant *cuartelazos* of all time was that executed by Fulgencio Batista of Cuba on March 10, 1952, which put him back in power. During the preceding two decades, he had been a leader to be reckoned with in Cuban politics. A chief figure in the revolt that forced President Machado to resign in 1933, he had dominated the government from then until 1940, and was president from 1940 to 1944. By 1952, after eight years of democratic government, the nation was thoroughly disillusioned by the widespread corruption and abuse of authority. Sensing that it was time for a change. Batista organized a *cuartelazo* that will long rank as a classic in Latin America's revolutionary history.

Precisely at 2:43 A.M. on March 10, 1952, while the nation was asleep, Batista's forces acted with split-second timing, seizing air force, naval, supply, and other critical installations. The skillfully synchronized and coordinated maneuver was so adroitly planned and executed that by 4:00 A.M.—just 1 hour and 17 minutes later—every important military installation was in control of the insurgents. And by 8:30 A.M., President Carlos Prio and members of his cabinet had thrown in the sponge and taken refuge in the Mexican Embassy. In a region that rather prides itself on the skill of its revolts, this was indeed one to remember.

Most *cuartelazos*, however, are not so well planned and executed. Indeed, the slightest slipup can mean the difference between success and failure. A couple of such flukes in execution doomed to failure a revolt attempted in Colombia in May, 1958. Diehard military men who were determined to keep Alberto Lleras Camargo from being selected as bipartisan president of the nation concocted a brazen plot to kidnap him

A. B. C. IN LATIN AMERICA

THIS IS A SYNTHESIS OF MILITARY POLITICS IN LATIN AMERICA.

1 IN COUNTRY "A" GENERALÍSIMO "B" RULES.—HE IS A DICTATOR.

2 COLONEL "C" REBELS.— THE PEOPLE BACK HIM.

3 THE REVOLUTION SUCCEEDS.

4 THE DICTATOR "B" FLEES WITH ALL THE MONEY.

5 THE COUNTRY IS BROKE.— THEY MUST START ALL OVER.

6 COLONEL "C" PROMISES ELECTIONS AND REFORMS...

7 THE U.S.A. RECOGNIZES HIM.

SOURCE: Abel Quezada, *The Best of Impossible Worlds* (Englewood Cliffs, N.J.: Prentice-Hall, Inc.). Reproduced by permission.

and also the five members of the military junta who were temporarily ruling the nation.

But the best-laid schemes of generals, as of mice and men, "gang aft a-gley." The conspirators managed to seize Lleras and were carrying him to the military barracks in a panel truck when they committed the tactical error of driving too fast past the presidential palace. It was a careless mistake. Palace guards stopped the truck for speeding, recognized with astonishment the prisoner in the back, and with rifles leveled at the kidnappers escorted Lleras Camargo to safety. Meanwhile the *cuartelazo* was further bungled by failure to capture a fifth member of the military junta, Vice-Admiral Ruben Piedrahita. Temporarily in charge of the government, he ordered all loyal armed forces to aid in suppressing the insurrection, which they did, thus ending the fiasco.

A frequent cause of bungling a *cuartelazo* is failure to secure the cooperation of all branches of the armed forces, as was shown by the unsuccessful revolt in Ecuador in November, 1961. When José María Velasco Ibarra resigned as president of the crisis-ridden nation, Carlos Julio Arosemena, the vice president, prepared to take over. Because of his leftist leanings, however, the army refused to recognize him as president, and backed Camilo Gallegos Toledo, chief justice of the Supreme Court and a political moderate. But the air force refused to acquiesce in this decision, and backed up its conviction with force. Three jet planes firing rockets and machine guns swooped low over the legislative palace, where army men were holding Arosemena virtually prisoner, and within minutes the radio stations announced that army-backed Gallegos Toledo had dropped his claim to the presidency. Apparently, the air force was more astute politically than militarily. Its political sights were better than its bombsights, for despite its low-level attack, dead on target, there was not a single hit.

With many such revolts taking place, whether *golpes* or *cuartelazos*, one may wonder why they have not accomplished the reforms so badly needed in the political, social, and economic structure of the society. The answer is simple. In the 19th century and well into the 20th, the many *golpes* and *cuartelazos*, popularly known as "revolutions," were hardly more than palace revolts—a sort of in-fighting among members of the ruling class who had a virtual monopoly on the domain of politics. Since they all had about the same vested interests to protect, they could hardly be expected to advocate basic changes in society that would adversely affect these interests—possibly seriously jeopardize them.

Although they usually agreed on fundamental issues, members of the upper class were apt to disagree on several main points.[34] Foremost was *personalismo*, or attraction to a leader because of his personal or family appeal. So widespread has been *personalismo* that it inspired the political axiom, "in Latin America, almost every 'ism' is a 'somebodyism.'" Juan Perón of Argentina gave rise to *peronismo*, and José Batlle y Ordoñez of Uruguay to *batllismo*. If President Richard Nixon were head of a Latin American state instead of the United States, his program and doctrines

---

[34] George I. Blanksten, "Revolutions," in Harold Eugene Davis (ed.), *Government and Politics in Latin America* (New York: The Ronald Press Co., 1958), p. 144.

would be known as *nixonismo*. But whatever the ism or ismo, it is not nearly as important as the dynamic, colorful leader who espouses it.

Another main cause of division within the ruling class was regionalism, which is largely the result of the area's topography. Loyalties to different regions often conflict, causing serious tension within the nation. In Ecuador, a competitive and unhealthy rivalry has long existed between Guayaquil, the liberal coastal metropolis, and Quito, the conservative capital located in the sierra.

Still another cause of disagreement among members of the upper class was the conflict in opinion and conviction on social issues that confronted the nations. A very controversial one was the status of the Roman Catholic Church and the rights, privileges, and immunities it should be allowed to enjoy.

The many revolutions occurring in Latin America have not resulted in fundamental change in most of the nations. But the very persistence of revolt as an institution indicates that it does have some utilitarian value. ". . . revolution is . . . a cure for governmental longevity and self-perpetuation," concludes Harris Gaylord Warren, "since it is an axiom in Latin American politics that the government does not lose an election."[35] Revolt and the resort to violence are often the only possible means of expressing dissent and protest. For an election may be so rigged that it is a farce, and opposition groups may boycott the polls in disgust, hoping thereby to register their disapproval. This is usually a rather futile gesture, however, for the *caudillo* cites the vote in his favor to show his nation and the world that there is little opposition to his regime. And in a statistically minded world, the election returns are what count most.

The courts of the nation may be frail reeds for members of the opposition to rely upon to protect their constitutional rights. For the courts of Latin America, as elsewhere, tend to follow the election returns.

But instituting a revolution is one means of protesting that is bound to be heard and recognized for what it is. The state of siege decreed by the president in effect proclaims to his nation that there is serious opposition within the country. And press dispatches in Washington, London, and Moscow carry the news, which is adverse publicity for the government.

Thus, any revolt in Latin America is a significant one, whatever its locale, objectives, or backing. Even one that is unsuccessful, whether crushed by overwhelming force or fizzling out, may accomplish the purpose for which it was intended. For the president ponders the open challenge to his power, dramatically presented for public consideration. And however strongly he is ensconced in power, if he is wise he will consider the demands of the opposition and make some concession toward satisfying them.

---

[35] Harris Gaylord Warren, *Paraguay: An Informal History* (Norman: University of Oklahoma Press, 1949), p. 266.

In the 20th century, most of the revolutions that have taken place have involved, not mainly the interests of the upper class, as earlier, but those of the middle class. During the early decades of the century, the rising middle class demanded a stronger voice in politics and greater opportunity in economic life—demands that won acceptance mainly because of the support of the military in Uruguay,[36] Chile,[37] Brazil,[38] and other nations.

In achieving its demands, the rising new class did not constitute any real threat to the existing order. For it did not challenge the validity of the economic system or threaten to change it fundamentally; its aspirations were limited to freer participation in the economic life of the nation and enjoyment of equality of opportunity.

But the entry of the urban proletariat into the political arena—sometimes supported by the heads of state such as Vargas in Brazil and Perón in Argentina—posed a serious threat to the whole existing basic structure. The large popular class demanded fundamental reforms which would virtually remake the society. The reforms, if made, would be mainly at the expense of the middle class—politically, economically, and socially.

With its hard-won gains thus threatened, the middle class has not hesitated to put its interests above its principles. And when necessary to safeguard its interests, it has not hesitated to call on the armed forces, most of whose leadership is middle class in origin and sympathy.

Analyzing the relationship between the interests of the middle class and military coups, José Nun concludes,

. . . it is the Armed Forces which assume the responsibility of protecting the middle class. It was with their support that the middle class achieved, at the beginning of the century, political recognition from the oligarchy; it was with their protection that it later consolidated itself in power; and now it is with their intervention that it seeks to ward off the threat posed by the popular sectors that it is incapable of leading.[39]

Social Revolutions

The third type of violent revolt against established authority in Latin America is the social revolution. It is quite unlike the *golpe* or *cuartelazo*, whose objective is to capture control of the government primarily for the privilege of filling government offices, exercising governmental authority,

---

[36] Milton I. Vanger, *José Batlle y Ordóñez of Uruguay: The Creator of His Times, 1902–1907* (Cambridge, Mass.: Harvard University Press, 1963), p. 167.

[37] Federico G. Gil, *The Political System of Chile* (Boston: Houghton Mifflin Co., 1966), p. 58.

[38] Thomas E. Skidmore, *Politics in Brazil, 1930–1964: An Experiment in Democracy* (New York: Oxford University Press, 1967), pp. 58–59.

[39] José Nun, "The Middle-Class Military Coup," *The Politics of Conformity in Latin America*, ed. Claudio Veliz (New York: Oxford University Press, 1967), p. 103.

and looting the national treasury as well as the rest of the nation. While the social revolution, too, seeks to get control of the government, this is only a means to an end—a means of accomplishing a fundamental reorganization of the whole society.

With such a fundamental objective, the social revolution is the only one of the several types of revolts by violence that really deserves to be called a revolution. To date, only three nations in Latin America—Mexico, Bolivia, and Cuba—have undergone the arduous but fruitful ordeal of remaking their society: ". . . shatter it to bits—and then remold it nearer to the heart's desire." While only these three so far have dared to attempt a social revolution, many of the other nations, burdened with their semifeudal social structure, power cliques, and elite values, teeter on the brink of chaos, either too timid to undergo the needed social surgery or preferring to risk all rather than make fundamental changes in their society.

While the social revolutions of Mexico beginning in 1910 and Bolivia in 1952 have resulted in many mistakes and have found the going exceedingly rough at times, the radical programs undertaken by both nations have accomplished impressive results. Neither nation has achieved all that its visionary idealists hoped to, but the retooling and restyling have obviously taken hold. And although neither nation has accelerated to a 1969 tempo, each is far ahead of the burro pace that still characterizes much of Latin America.

Regarding their ideologies, Mexico and Bolivia have accepted as national values the democratic idealism the United States and most nations of the Western world have long embraced. More specifically, both nations are striving to apply to their new societies the democratic principles professed since the first day of independence. Every individual, regardless of his race, class, educational attainment, or economic worth is recognized to be a full member of society, entitled to all its rights and privileges.

The application of these democratic, egalitarian principles has been a severe blow to the deeply entrenched groups that long enjoyed a privileged status in these nations. Thus, in Mexico the Roman Catholic Church was stripped of most of its vast wealth and severely limited in its activities. (In Bolivia, the Catholic Church was not nearly so strong, and hence has not been a major concern of the revolutionary regime.) The armed forces, too, have felt the mighty impact of the social reform: in Mexico, their power has been greatly curbed, as was described in Chapter 6; in Bolivia, the old army, which tried to suppress the revolution, was disbanded and a new one established, much smaller in size and believed to be loyal to the regime. In both countries, the small, aristocratic, and wealthy elite has also been adversely affected, losing its privileged status as well as much of its wealth.

Although these formerly privileged groups have suffered, the mass of citizens of both Mexico and Bolivia have greatly benefited by the many changes instituted in their behalf. In the political realm, the suffrage requirements have been so broadened as to enable almost every adult to vote in elections and thereby express his opinion of how he should be governed. The extension of the suffrage has greatly increased the size of the electorate. In Bolivia's 1951 presidential election, held the year before the revolution, only 126,125 persons voted out of a population of approximately 3 million. However, in the 1956 election, the first one held under the new revolutionary government, a total of 955,412 ballots were cast in electing the president and members of Congress. (These elections are treated in more detail in the next chapter.)

In the economic realm, the social revolutions of Mexico and Bolivia have resulted in many changes designed to give the former underdogs a chance. In both nations, an extensive program of land reform has been undertaken—a program basically designed to break up the large landed estates whose land was unused or underutilized and to give at least a few acres to the rural farm worker who lives on the land, makes his living from it, and craves a few acres of his own. The extensive programs of land redistribution have made both Mexico and Bolivia primarily societies of many small farmers who work their own private acreages.

The social revolution in Cuba has been different in many respects from those in Mexico and Bolivia. Castro's decision to transform the nation into a socialist society has given it many distinctive characteristics.

Socially, there have been many changes that should make for a more democratic society. The government has conducted an intensive campaign to promote education. In 30 months it opened more classrooms than preceding governments had opened in 30 years; in December, 1961 the government proudly proclaimed that Cuba was the first Latin American country without illiterates.[40] Intensive efforts have been made to achieve a classless society—efforts that included permitting or forcing to leave their homeland most members of the middle class unsympathetic to the Revolution. Castro's opening up the formerly swank hotels, beaches, and resorts to the mass of citizens, black and white alike, has deeply impressed them.[41]

Politically, although Castro promised many times that his government would hold elections "and if the people do not want us because they are tired of us or because we are failing, then we shall go . . .", soon after

---

[40] Boris Goldenberg, *The Cuban Revolution and Latin America* (New York: Frederick A. Praeger, Inc., 1965), pp. 215 and 217.

[41] Maurice Zeitlin and Robert Scheer, *Cuba: Tragedy in Our Hemisphere* (New York: Grove Press, Inc., 1962), pp. 74–78.

assuming power he changed his mind and openly expressed his aversion to elections.[42] But apparently this has not bothered most citizens; in answer to questions regarding elections and influence, they overwhelmingly expressed the opinion that the country should not have elections "soon," and that workers had more influence on government then than before the Revolution.[43]

Economically, the adoption of socialism and its application throughout the economy have maximized public ownership and correspondingly minimized private ownership. Most industries and businesses, large or small, are now owned and operated by the state. Land reform has been very different from what was promised by the guerrilla chieftain in the Sierra Maestra Mountains. Instead of tracts individually owned by many small farmers, lands expropriated from large and small landowners alike have been converted into *granjas del pueblo*—state farms where those who work the soil are, in effect, wage laborers.[44]

Insurgency, Counterinsurgency, and Civic Action

When on January 1, 1959, Fidel Castro overthrew Fulgencia Batista, whose regime seemed to be invincible, it was apparent that a new technique for revolution had succeeded in Latin America. By such a technique, determined civilian insurgents, inspired by a messianic leader, had managed to invade their homeland, establish themselves in a rugged, mountainous region, and conduct guerrilla warfare, until finally they swooped down on the capital and destroyed the remnants of a disintegrating army.[45]

Castro's eventual triumph after two years of guerrilla fighting in the Sierra Maestra Mountains was hardly due to support from the local peasants, few of whom joined his band (estimates of the total strength of Castro's forces range from only several hundred to 2,000 or so), or to support from the cities, either, as shown by the complete failure of the general strike called by Castro from the mountains in April, 1958. But the shift in tactics from occasional skirmishes in the mountains to widespread sabotage in the populous areas proved to be the turning point

---

[42] Andres Suárez, *Cuba: Castroism and Communism, 1959-1966*, trans. Joel Carmichael and Ernst Halperin (Cambridge: Massachusetts Institute of Technology Press, 1967), p. 47.

[43] Zeitlin and Scheer, *op. cit.*, p. 38.

[44] Edward Boorstein, *The Economic Transformation of Cuba* (New York: Monthly Review Press, 1968), pp. 44–45; and Goldenberg, *op. cit.*, pp. 221-35.

[45] For a graphic account of the guerrillas' hardships, such as surviving on broiled snake, edible cactus, and prickly pears, see Robert Taber, *M-26: Biography of a Revolution* (New York: Lyle Stuart, 1961), p. 66.

in the struggle. Batista countered the sabotage with such vengeful cruelty as to completely alienate the populace.[46]

Castro's overthrow of the established government was heady wine for the Cuban revolutionaries. Che Guevara, a member of the brain trust, even formulated a basic set of principles that supposedly governed the organization of the guerrilla movement, the fighting force itself, and the tactics of warfare.[47]

Since Castro's victory in 1959, guerrilla insurgency has been a serious threat to the governments of many of the Latin American nations, especially those of Bolivia, Guatemala, Peru, and Venezuela. Much if not most of the insurrectionary activity has been instigated and supported by Castro, who hoped by this means to export his "new order" to other nations in the hemisphere deemed ripe for social revolution. Many Latin Americans agreed with this appraisal. "The Cuban revolution is a national revolution," says Senator Salvador Allende of Chile, "but it is also a revolution of the whole of Latin America. It has shown the way for the liberation of all our peoples."[48]

Aware of Castro's designs and of the serious threat they posed, the United States in cooperation with its southern neighbors took vigorous measures to counter possible insurgency. Rigorous programs of training in guerrilla warfare were instituted at several selected military installations in the United States and Panama, and members of the Latin American military were invited to participate.[49]

The training in counterinsurgency paid off handsomely when in early October, 1967, the prized Cuban revolutionary, Che Guevara himself, was finally cornered in the rugged mountainous vastness of Bolivia's Santa Cruz Province. Among the detachments of the Bolivian Army engaged in the successful operation was the Second Ranger Battalion, which had completed four months of rugged training in jungle fighting. These were apparently the troops Guevara was referring to when he wrote in his diary: "They are good fighters. How they have pursued us. They do not fear death, their chiefs coolly command. I never thought the Bolivian army was so stubborn."[50]

---

[46] For a brief summary of Castro's problems and tactics, see Theodore Draper, *Castro's Revolution: Myths and Realities* (New York: Frederick A. Praeger, Inc., 1962), pp. 11–15.

[47] *Che Guevara on Guerrilla Warfare*, trans., with an introduction by Major Harries-Clichy Peterson, USMCR (New York: Frederick A. Praeger, Inc., 1961).

[48] Boris Goldenberg, *op. cit.*, p. 311.

[49] Jay Mallin, " 'Che' Guevara: Some Documentary Puzzles," *Journal of Inter-American Studies*, Vol. X, No. 1 (January, 1968), pp. 81–82.

These training programs are given by Willard F. Barber and C. Neale Ronning, *Internal Security and Military Power: Counterinsurgency and Civic Action in Latin America* (Columbus: Ohio State University Press, 1966), chap. 5.

[50] Mallin, *op. cit.*, pp. 81–82.

Che's choice of Bolivia as a base for his revolutionary activities was apparently based on conditions that must have seemed ideal to him—the vast jungle area . . . a Bolivian Army supposedly inept and poorly trained . . . chronic internal turmoil . . . the nation's location in the heartland of South America from which a guerrilla movement could be extended into Argentina, Brazil, Chile, Paraguay, and Peru. But what Guevara over-looked were certain forces working inexorably against him—the suspicion of him as a foreigner, the little support given him by the peasants who now owned their own land after the agrarian revolution ("What could Che offer them?" a high Bolivian official commented, "Cabinet posts?") . . . and an army trained in the specialized techniques of counter-insurgency.[51]

Guevara's masterminded guerrilla movement, which ignominiously ended in his capture and execution, and in the earlier arrest (April 20, 1967) of Régis Debray, young French philosopher and radical writer, hardly did credit to the two revolutionaries' basic premises. Guevara's rules for guerrilla warfare, successful in Cuba, were as alien to Bolivia as was the thinking of the Czech planning mission to Cuba, which dismissed the problem of government warehouses at ports simply because Czechoslovakia had no ports. But the outcome in Bolivia certainly verified Debray's conclusion that of the three stages guerrilla warfare seems to pass through—establishment, development, and offensive—by far the most difficult is the first stage.[52] For the movement in Bolivia did not survive even that one.

Another strategy that has proved quite effective in countering insurgency is a program of civic action. Under such a program, the armed forces are used for many developmental projects that will benefit the people,[53] especially those in rural areas, and also make them less susceptible to the appeals of insurgents who promise reform in order to win support to overthrow the government. The projects of civic action, designed to improve the nation's social and economic infrastructure, may be either small and with immediate impact, such as a potable water system, or more long range, such as a power dam or all-weather road to market. While the projects are no substitute for basic social and economic reforms that need to be undertaken, and may even be perverted to strengthen an existing military regime, they have nevertheless served to

---

[51] *Ibid.*, pp. 79–81.

[52] Régis Debray, *Revolution in the Revolution? Armed Struggle and Political Struggle in Latin America*, trans. Bobbye Ortiz (New York: Grove Press, Inc., 1967), p. 32.

[53] "Civic action programs of the Armed Forces are playing an important role in bringing progress to Peru," says President Fernando Belaúnde Terry. Fernando Belaúnde-Terry, *Peru's Own Conquest* (Lima, Peru: American Studies Press S.S., 1965), p. 203.

improve the lot of the rural people and keep them loyal to the government.[54]

SUGGESTED READINGS

Barber, Willard F., and Ronning, C. Neale. *Internal Security and Military Power*. Columbus: Ohio State University Press, 1966.

Blanksten, George I. *Ecuador: Constitutions and Caudillos*, chaps. iii and ix. Berkeley: University of California Press, 1951.

———. *Perón's Argentina*. Chicago: University of Chicago Press, 1953.

Che Guevara. *Guerrilla Warfare*. Introduction by Major Harries-Clichy Peterson. New York: Frederick A. Praeger, Inc., 1961.

Crassweller, Robert D. *Trujillo: The Life and Times of a Caribbean Dictator*. New York: Macmillan Co., 1966.

Crist, Raymond E. "Geography and Caudillismo: A Case Study," *Dictatorship in Spanish America* (ed. Hugh M. Hamill, Jr.). New York: Alfred A. Knopf, Inc., 1965.

Debray, Régis. *Revolution in the Revolution? Armed Struggle and Political Struggle in Latin America*. Trans. Bobbye Ortiz. New York: Grove Press, Inc., 1967.

Dubois, Jules. *Fidel Castro: Rebel—Liberator or Dictator?* Indianapolis, Inc.: Bobbs-Merrill Co., Inc., 1959.

Dulles, John W. F. *Vargas of Brazil: A Political Biography*. Austin: University of Texas Press, 1967.

Fluharty, Vernon Lee. *Dance of the Millions: Military Rule and the Social Revolution in Colombia, 1930–1956*. Pittsburgh, Pa.: University of Pittsburgh Press, 1957.

Gilmore, Robert L. *Caudillism and Militarism in Venezuela, 1810–1910*. Athens: Ohio University Press, 1964.

Goldenberg, Boris. *The Cuban Revolution and Latin America*. New York: Frederick A. Praeger, Inc., 1965.

Gruening, Ernest. *Mexico and Its Heritage*, pp. 91–108. New York: D. Appleton-Century Co., Inc., 1934.

Hicks, Albert C. *Blood in the Streets: The Life and Rule of Trujillo*. New York: Creative Age Press, Inc., 1946.

Horowitz, Irving Louis, de Castro, Josué, and Gerassi, John (eds.). *Latin American Radicalism: A Documentary Report on Left and Nationalist Movements*, Part III. New York: Random House, Inc., 1969.

Lavin, John. *A Halo for Gómez*. New York: Pageant Press, 1954.

Lieuwen, Edwin. *Venezuela*, chaps. 2 and 3. Royal Institute of International Affairs. New York: Oxford University Press, 1961.

Lowenstein, Karl. *Brazil Under Vargas*. New York: Macmillan Co., 1942.

---

[54] For an extensive treatment of civic action, see Barber and Ronning, *op. cit.*, chaps. 6 and 7.

MacGaffey, Wyatt, and Barnett, Clifford R. *Cuba*, chap. 13. Survey of World Cultures. New Haven, Conn.: HRAF Press, 1962.

Needler, Martin C. *Anatomy of a Coup d'Etat: Ecuador 1963*. Washington, D.C.: Institute for the Comparative Study of Political Systems, 1964.

————. *Political Development in Latin America: Instability, Violence, and Evolutionary Change*. New York: Random House, Inc., 1968.

Nun, José. "The Middle-Class Military Coup," *The Politics of Conformity in Latin America* (ed. Claudio Veliz), pp. 66–119. New York: Oxford University Press, 1967.

Pierson, William W., and Gil, Federico G. "Dictators and Revolutions," *Governments of Latin America*, chap. 6. New York: McGraw-Hill Book Co., Inc., 1957.

Pierson, W. W. (ed.). "Pathology of Democracy in Latin America: A Symposium," (Arthur P. Whitaker, "A Historian's Point of View"; Russell Fitzgibbon, "A Political Scientist's Point of View"; Sanford A. Mosk, "An Economist's Point of View"; and W. Rex Crawford, "Discussion: A Sociologist's Point of View"), *American Political Science Review*, Vol. 44, No. 1 (March, 1950), pp. 100–49.

Rengger and Longchamps. *The Reign of Doctor Joseph Roderick de Francia, in Paraguay; An Account of a Six Years' Residence in that Republic, from July, 1819 to May, 1825*. Trans. J. R. Rengger. London: Thomas Hurst, Edward Chance & Co., 1827.

Rourke, Thomas (pseud.), Clinton, Daniel Joseph. *Gómez: Tyrant of the Andes*. New York: William Morrow & Co., 1936.

Stokes, William S. "Violence," *Latin American Politics*, chap. 13. New York: Thomas Y. Crowell Co., 1959.

Street, John. *Artigas and the Emancipation of Uruguay*. London: Cambridge University Press, 1959.

Suárez, Andrés. *Cuba: Castroism and Communism, 1959–1966*. Trans. Joel Carmichael and Ernst Halperin. Cambridge: Massachusetts Institute of Technology Press, 1967.

Szulc, Tad. *Twilight of the Tyrants*. New York: Henry Holt & Co., 1959.

————. *The Winds of Revolution: Latin America Today and Tomorrow*. New York: Frederick A. Praeger, Inc., 1963.

Tannenbaum, Frank. *Mexico: The Struggle for Peace and Bread*, chap. 4. New York: Alfred A. Knopf, Inc., 1954.

Vandercook, John Womack. *Black Majesty: The Life of Christophe: King of Haiti*. New York: Harper & Bros., 1928.

Warren, Harris Gaylord. *Paraguay: An Informal History*, chaps. xi, xii, xiii. Norman: University of Oklahoma Press, 1949.

Whitaker, Arthur P. *Argentine Upheaval: Perón's Fall and the New Regime*, pp. 1–54. New York: Frederick A. Praeger, Inc., 1956.

Wilgus, A. Curtis (ed.). *South American Dictators During the First Century of Independence*. Washington, D.C.: George Washington University Press, 1937.

Wise, George S. *Caudillo: A Portrait of Antonio Guzmán Blanco.* New York: Columbia University Press, 1951.

Wolf, Eric R. and Hansen, Edward C. "Caudillo Politics: A Structural Analysis," *Comparative Studies in Society and History,* Vol. 9, No. 2 (January, 1967), pp. 168–179.

12

POLITICAL PARTIES AND ELECTIONS:
Ballots, Preferably Honest

In nations that have achieved political democracy, political parties play an important role in the formulation and expression of public opinion and in the election of candidates to public office. Parties play such an important role, in fact, that the vitality of democracy may be gauged by the freedom and effectiveness of party activities.

In the 20 republics of Latin America, where there is a great variation in per capita income and national wealth, literacy, and degree of political sophistication and stability, the operation of political parties has been uneven—successful in some of the nations but ineffectual in others.

GENERAL ATTRIBUTES OF PARTIES

There are several general attributes of political parties in Latin America. These include, especially: personalism, party and membership instability, identification of government with a political party, and intolerance of the opposition.

The primary basis for most political parties in the nations has been personalism—the intense, unswerving allegiance to a dynamic leader. So strong has been the influence of leaders that most parties are identified by their names rather than by the official names of the parties. In Mexico, although the Institutional Revolutionary Party has long been dominant, even factions within it take their names from certain of the leaders. The *alemanistas* were followers of former President Miguel Alemán; the *callistas, cardenistas,* and *ruizcortinistas* are the names of other factions that supported particular presidents. In Uruguay, the two major parties,

350

or at least leading wings of them, have been known as *batllistas* and *herreristas* as commonly as by the official names, Colorados and Blancos.

Whether known by its leader's name or not, a party often exists for one reason alone—to promote his political career. In Venezuela, one of the minor parties in the 1950's was *Movimiento Electoral Nacional Independiente*, known as MENI. This small party of apparently only about 15,000 members was the personal vehicle of Vice-Admiral Wolfgang Larrazabal to support his candidacy for the presidency. Soon after he was defeated in the 1958 election, the "party" disbanded.

Although long a main influence on political parties, personalism is on the wane. "A reasonable hypothesis," K. H. Silvert says, "is that the more national a country the less personalistic will be the parties, the more they will adjust conflicting interests within their own mechanisms, the greater will be their concern for institutional self-preservation and the winning of elections as a good in itself."[1]

The political parties are also characterized by a transient, precarious existence and high rate of mortality, sometimes with reincarnation under a slightly different format or name. The main exception to this instability has been the Communist Party, whether operating under its own name or under some other label and whether in the open or underground. Following an ideological line, this party offers a program from which it rarely deviates in principle.

The Christian Democratic Parties have also developed an ideology, most of whose principles are accepted by every party. But a national party apparently has considerable leeway in interpreting and applying these principles in its own nation. In Chile, the party has proposed many reforms of particular interest to political scientists, such as: giving more power to the executive, permitting him to submit to a national referendum bills he proposed but Congress refused to pass; simplifying congressional procedures to make the congress more effective and responsible; limiting campaign expenditures to curb the influence of large economic interests; and lowering the age required for voting.[2]

Democratic Action in Venezuela also has its distinctive ideology: the party's program and doctrine are based mainly on the programmatic statement adopted in 1958, envisaging basic reforms in many broad areas.[3]

---

[1] K. H. Silvert, "Political Change in Latin America," *The United States and Latin America*, ed. Herbert L. Matthews (American Assembly) (2d ed.; New York: Columbia University Press, 1963), p. 78.

[2] Ernst Halperin, *Nationalism and Communism in Chile* (Cambridge: Massachusetts Institute of Technology Press, 1965), pp. 196–203; Federico G. Gil and Charles J. Parrish, *The Chilean Presidential Election of September 4, 1964: Part I: An Analysis* (Washington, D.C.: Institute for the Comparative Study of Political Systems, 1965), pp. 28–30; and Edward J. Williams, *Latin American Christian Democratic Parties* (Knoxville: University of Tennessee Press, 1967), pp. 96–97.

[3] John D. Martz, *Acción Democrática: Evolution of a Modern Political Party in Venezuela* (Princeton, N.J.: Princeton University Press, 1966), pp. 228–34.

There are many reasons for the instability of political parties. However capable and respected leaders they may develop, the socio-economic structure of most of the nations is so lacking in integration, cohesion, and maturity that the parties find it almost impossible to enforce effective internal discipline, as even the communist parties have shown by their many schisms and dissensions.[4]

Another reason for instability in many of the nations is the relative ease with which a new political party may be formed and obtain legal recognition. In Uruguay, a legal minimum of only 50 citizens is all that is necessary in order to register a group as a certified political party.

Apparently, it has been even easier to form political parties in Bolivia, Ecuador, and Peru. According to Luis Terán Gómez:

In these times, nothing is simpler than to found a political party. To form a political party, only three people and one object are necessary: a president, a vice-president, a secretary, and a rubber stamp. The party can get along even without the vice-president and the secretary. . . . There have been cases in which the existence of only the rubber stamp has been sufficient.[5]

In Mexico, however, the situation is quite different; the requirements for obtaining recognition as a national party are stringent. To qualify as a national party, a political group must have at least 75,000 qualified voters; of these, a minimum of 2,500 must reside in each of two thirds of the nation's 29 states, 2 territories, and the Federal District. The group is also required to present a comprehensive party program for the solution of national problems.

The membership of parties, like the bodies themselves, is quite unstable. Even in Chile, one of the most politically sophisticated nations in the region, the vast majority of the electorate does not belong to any particular political party or profess loyalty to any party. A public opinion poll conducted by Eduardo Hamuy, Director of the Center of Socio-Economic Studies of the University of Chile, showed that in 1964 more than 90 percent of the Chileans did not belong to any political party. But when pressed to select the party that represented ideas nearest to their own, 40.1 percent named the Christian Democrats, and the next highest percentage, 12.6, chose the Socialist Party. Approximately half of the respondents either had no preference as to parties or were completely indifferent to all the major parties.[6]

In Latin America, a newly elected regime has no qualms about showing undisguised favoritism to the party responsible for its victory. It appoints

---

[4] Russell H. Fitzgibbon, "The Party Potpourri in Latin America," *Western Political Quarterly*, Vol. X, No. 1 (March, 1957), p. 13.

[5] In George I. Blanksten, "The Politics of Latin America," *The Politics of the Developing Areas*, eds. Gabriel A. Almond and James S. Coleman (Princeton, N.J.: Princeton University Press, 1960), p. 483.

[6] Gil and Parrish, *op. cit.*, pp. 14–17.

to high office or favors with lush government contracts only party stalwarts. Favoritism is also shown in the lower echelons of government. While most governments permit their civil servants to affiliate with political organizations, it is understood that this permission applies only to joining a political group that supports the administration. Joining any other group is practically asking for dismissal. In fact, government employees are expected to be not only public servants but also party faithfuls who can always be depended on to promote the interests of the party along with carrying out whatever governmental duties they have.

Staffing the government with political supporters who change with each new administration has been a great deterrent to the development of a qualified, professional, nonpartisan civil service.

Victorious parties have usually shown a strong intolerance of their political opponents. Sometimes, mere allegiance to the regime is not enough; it must be publicly displayed for all others to see. In Colombia after the outbreak of civil war in 1948, coloration was not so much to decorate as to indicate the wearer's political allegiance. Red was the distinctive color of the liberal party, and blue of the conservative. In the conservative communities, the women wore blue skirts; in the liberal, they wore red. Even the containers for beer were red or blue, depending on the community. Wearing the wrong color was interpreted as an insult to the rest of the community; its wearer was very apt to be vilified and beaten up.[7]

THE TRADITIONAL PARTIES

From the time of independence, there were traditionally two main political parties, the conservatives and the liberals. The conservatives, having something to conserve, championed the vested interests of the landowners and the Church. The liberals, representing mainly the new professional, business, and commercial groups, were professedly interested in liberating the society from its semifeudal stodginess by providing free secular schools, broadening the suffrage, and encouraging foreign trade and immigration. However, these differences were often more theoretical than real.

As a rule, during the 19th century both the liberals and conservatives belonged to the upper class, which had a virtual monopoly on government office and political influence. Ordinarily, the scrapping between the two parties did not involve the whole community and reflected only superficial differences between them. However, they differed sharply on

---

[7] Orlando Fals-Borda, *Peasant Society in the Colombian Andes: A Sociological Study of Saucío* (Gainesville: University of Florida Press, 1962), p. 210.

two highly controversial issues: the role the Catholic Church should be allowed in the new nations, and centralized versus decentralized exercise of governmental authority.

The role of the Church was an explosive issue which split many a nation into two warring camps. In the United Provinces of Central America, when the liberals under the leadership of Francisco Morazán were victorious in 1829 and occupied Guatemala City, they celebrated their triumph by a plethora of anticlerical laws that outlawed the religious orders and ended state support of the Church. But when the conservatives regained control of the government in 1838, led by the illiterate fanatic, Rafael Carrera, it was with the vengeful battle cry and program of "Long Live Religion and Death to the Foreigners."[8] Morazán's forces were destroyed and their leader exiled. Elsewhere, too, virulence and violence invariably marked the contests to determine the status and role of the Church.

Another bitter issue between the liberals and conservatives was whether the nation should adopt political centralism or federalism. The centralists, advocating a tightly knit unitary government, wanted all power to be vested in the national government; the federalists, on the other hand, insisted on a large measure of autonomy for the states, provinces, departments, or other component political units. The centralist-federalist debate resulted in many bloody struggles, especially in Argentina, Brazil, Colombia, Mexico, and Venezuela.

Local autonomy was often championed so strongly that it was almost impossible to govern the nation as a whole. This played into the hands of local *caudillos,* who had to be either suppressed or paid off again and again. The doctrine of states' rights in Latin America was a fetish that greatly impeded the political and economic development of the region.[9]

For the most part, the conservative–liberal division resulted in a gross oversimplification of issues. As René León Echaíz of Chile perceptively observed, there were "two parties which contested for political supremacy during the early years of Latin America's independence. The banner of one party carried a slogan, 'Liberty Even If It Results in Anarchy'; the banner of the other read, 'Order Even If It Means Depotism.' In the case of both groups, the slogans were sometimes inscribed in bloody letters."[10]

Even today, nations sometimes show the lingering effects of the earlier liberal–conservative controversy. The bitter divisiveness in Colombia re-

---

[8] Hubert Herring, *A History of Latin America from the Beginnings to the Present* (2d ed. rev.; New York: Alfred A. Knopf, Inc., 1961), pp. 450–51.

[9] J. Fred Rippy, *Latin America: A Modern History* (Ann Arbor: University of Michigan Press, 1958), pp. 180–82.

[10] René León Echaíz, *Evolución histórica de los partidos políticos chilenos* (Santiago, Chile, 1939), pp. 26–27.

sulted in a costly, fratricidal civil war that began in 1948; the nation has not yet fully recovered from it.[11]

THE ONE, TWO, AND MULTIPARTY SYSTEMS

One-Party Systems

Regarding their political parties, the nations of Latin America may be classified on the basis of having a one-party, two-party, or multiparty system.[12]

As a rule, the effective existence of only one political party has been almost prima facie evidence that the government is dictatorial and has suppressed all opposition, probably by ruthless means. For many a dictator in the past has asserted his unquestioned control over the nation by allowing only one party, the official one, to exist.

The Dominican Republic during the long tyrannical rule of Rafael Leonidas Trujillo exemplifies one type of one-party government at its worst. With an amazing display of *caudillo* temerity, Trujillo aspired to erase any effective opposition to his regime not only at home but also in the United States, its main ally. The drugging and kidnapping of Dr. Jesús Galíndez, a member of the staff of Columbia University and an unsparing critic of Trujillo, was a presumptuous extension of dictatorial one-party rule. Trujillo stretched his tyrannical power even further by disposing of the incriminating evidence—Gerald Murphy, the American pilot who apparently flew the private plane containing drugged Galíndez to the Dominican Republic.[13]

Recalling the brutally oppressive nature of Trujillo's regime—there have been others like it, too—one may jump to the conclusion that the one-party system per se connotes dictatorial rule. This is not true, however, as the experience of Mexico well shows. In the new revolutionary

---

[11] The background and effects of the civil war are given by Robert H. Dix, *Colombia: The Political Dimensions of Change* (New Haven, Conn.: Yale University Press, 1967), chaps. 4 and 5.

[12] In the opinion of some scholars this categorization is too general and does not provide an adequate basis for classifying political parties. J. Austin Ranney and Willmore Kendall, "The American Party Systems," *American Political Science Review*, Vol. XLVIII (1954), pp. 480-81. However, if the basic differences within a category are properly noted, this classification can afford a realistic and manageable consideration of parties.

[13] For an account of the drugging and abduction of Dr. Galíndez, and the role that Murphy unwittingly played in it, see *Life*, February 25, 1957, pp. 24-30; Robert D. Crassweller, *Trujillo: The Life and Times of a Caribbean Dictator* (New York: Macmillan Co., 1966), chap. 21.

For later revealing his role, Murphy, knowing too much, was apparently thrown over the cliff to the sharks.

society, the new order has been so popular that one party has all but cornered popular support.

In Mexico, the Partido Revolucionario Institucional, freely translated as the "Party of Revolutionary Institutions" and better known as PRI, is unquestionably the dominant party in the nation. Its revolutionary program, which virtually remade the formerly semifeudal nation, was designed to better the condition of the great mass of citizens, especially by land reform and benefits to the urban workers. As a result, on election day the citizens turn out en masse to give their support to the party that has helped them.[14]

Being able to count on this widespread popular appeal and determined to carry out the revolutionary goals, PRI's governmental practices often reflect its assured position. The new president has usually been selected months, maybe years, before by the incumbent president and given a position of such responsibility as to indicate clearly that he will inherit the mantle.[15] Mexican practice appears to be at first glance *imposición*, or an arbitrary determining of the presidential successor. But Mexico has no vice president who would be the logical successor, receiving the outgoing president's support. Mexico apparently has not suffered from not having a vice presidency—an office that in most of the Latin American nations has not furthered constitutionalism but has complicated it by jealousy and intrigue.

Long recognized as the groomed successor, the designee matter-of-factly accepts the nomination in a national convention and is selected by acclamation.

Although PRI operates with the confidence of a champion (as when the Mexican Tourist Bureau gave the *New York Herald Tribune* a photograph of Díaz Ordaz captioned "Mexico's president-elect" a week before the election), it is by no means the only political party in the nation. In 1963, there were four other registered parties: Partido Acción Nacional (PAN); Partido Popular Socialista (PPS); Partido Nacionalista

---

[14] For an organizational breakdown of the party into its labor, agrarian, and popular sectors, see Frank R. Brandenburg, "Political Parties and Elections," *Government and Politics in Latin America*, ed. Harold E. Davis (New York: The Ronald Press Co., 1958), pp. 208–9.

In the 1964 presidential election, PRI received 89 percent of the total votes cast. There were many reasons for this overwhelming endorsement, including: the saturation campaign of propaganda conducted by the party for a full year before an election, the identification of the party on the part of many voters with the revolution of 1910 and the social goals it established, the great patronage of the administration, and the party's policies, which are skillfully designed to appeal to an extremely wide range of voters, from conservative businessmen to urban workers and landless peasants. Martin C. Needler, "Changing the Guard in Mexico," *Current History*, Vol. 48, No. 281 (January, 1965), p. 27.

[15] A detailed account of the procedure of selecting a president is given by Frank Brandenburg, *The Making of Modern Mexico* (Englewood Cliffs, N.J.: Prentice-Hall, Inc., 1964), chap. 4.

de México (PNM); and Partido Auténtico de la Revolución Mexicana (PARM).

Although the minor parties have won very few of the local, state, or national elections they have competed in, they have played an important role as political gadflies by alerting the electorate to alternatives other than those presented by the government, as well as by pricking the public conscience.[16] These parties that operate freely have paradoxically not been the main threat to PRI in presidential elections. Rather, the main opposition in the past has been an *ad hoc* party headed by a prominent member of the regime who was disappointed at not receiving the nomination.[17]

PRI's choice for president, selected six months or so before the scheduled date of the election, is as sure of winning as is the Democratic gubernatorial candidate in Mississippi. Nevertheless he conducts a vigorous campaign in all parts of the nation. To PRI's presidential designate, campaigning as he does provides an opportunity to visit all parts of the nation and learn firsthand the grass-roots sentiments and gripes. Visiting these areas serves another purpose, too. Many an obscure citizen who has probably never even heard of the candidate before thereby has the opportunity of seeing or meeting the new *jefe*.

After his inauguration, the president must cater to the power groups within PRI and also to the major interests of the country, which are organized into large and influential pressure groups. To keep them loyal to the official party, he must be responsive to their demands.[18]

Another well-known one-party system was that of Bolivia from 1952 to 1964. The Movimiento Nacional Revolucionario, the Nationalist Revolutionary Movement usually known as the MNR, led the sweeping social

---

[16] L. Vincent Padgett, *The Mexican Political System* (Boston: Houghton Mifflin Co., 1966), pp. 66–67.

[17] The *realpolitik* of conflicting political philosophies is confined to PRI itself, where left, middle, and right battle it out for supremacy. Recent years have seen the rise of the right, according to David L. Graham. "The real struggle between the right and the left in the nation goes on silently but firmly inside PRI, not at the polls." David L. Graham, "The Rise of the Mexican Right," *Yale Review*, Vol. LII, No. 1 (Autumn, 1962), pp. 104 and 110.

[18] Karl M. Schmitt and David D. Burks, *Evolution or Chaos: Dynamics of Latin American Government and Politics* (New York: Frederick A. Praeger, Inc., 1963), p. 221. One of the most interesting of these pressure groups is the Instituto de Investigaciones Sociales y Económicas (Institute of Social and Economic Research), a nonprofit organization that aims at the long-range molding of public opinion rather than at influencing the passage or defeat of any particular governmental measure. (Merle Kling, *A Mexican Interest Group in Action* (Englewood Cliffs, N.J.: Prentice-Hall, Inc., 1961), pp. 1 and 4.

In seeking to please all his constituents, the president may thereby have relinquished much or even most of his presidential authority, Raymond Vernon concludes. Raymond Vernon, *The Dilemma of Mexico's Development: The Role of the Private and Public Sectors* (Cambridge, Mass.: Harvard University Press, 1963), pp. 188–89.

revolution that began in April, 1952. Like PRI, the MNR was a heterogeneous political conglomeration; there was deep division of opinion on
each of the many reforms that was adopted. The bitter issue of party
leadership and presidential succession proved to be the party's undoing
when Paz Estenssoro decided in 1964 to change the constitution in order
to succeed himself, thus provoking a military take-over.

Although the military accepted most of the MNR's reforms, they
were very critical of the party's corruption; its harsh methods of political
control, especially of surveillance, arrest, interrogation, and incarceration;[19] and its decision to arm the militia and the police to counterbalance
the power of the army.

Two-Party Systems

Several nations today have a two-party system. Uruguay has traditionally had only two main parties, the Colorados and Blancos. They
were not very evenly matched, however. Up to 1958 the Colorados, or
liberals, had governed the country for the preceding 90 years, although
the Blancos, or conservatives, representing mainly the large landholders,
strongly contested every election. In view of this very one-sided score,
most thoughtful observers hardly considered Uruguay as possessing a
two-party system. However, in the elections of both 1958 and 1962, the
Blancos were victorious, mainly because of the nation's deepening economic crisis and the Colorados' neglect of rural development. In view of
the Blancos' two successive victories, "Uruguay has laid to rest any
doubts about her two-party system."[20] However, the Colorados returned
to power in the November, 1966, election when both the Blancos and the
plural executive were ditched.

Colombia adopted a unique two-party system in 1957 to restore
orderly, constitutional government after nine years of internecine civil
war and dictatorship. Under the bipartisan agreement reached between
the conservatives and the liberals, a National Front government would be
established to last until 1974. The presidency would alternate between the
two parties, offices at all levels and branches would be equally divided
between them, and certain types of legislation would require a two thirds
majority vote for approval. But while the two parties would jointly

---

19 After the demise of the Paz regime and the 12-year rule of the MNR, there
was a rash of books recounting alleged brutalities and atrocities of the regime. Among
these are Hernán Barriga Antelo, *Laureles de un Tirano* (La Paz, Bolivia), 1965;
Loauza Beltrán, *Campos de Concentración en Bolivia* (La Paz, Bolivia), 1966; Hernán
Landívar Flores, *Infierno en Bolivia* (La Paz, Bolivia), 1965; René López Murillo,
Bolivia Cementerio de la Libertad (La Paz, Bolivia), 1966; and Mario Peñaranda
Rivera, *Entre Los Hombres Lobos de Bolivia* (La Paz, Bolivia: Instituto de Ediciones
Americanas), 1965.

20 Schmitt and Burks, *op. cit.*, p. 207.

participate in governing the nation, each would still be free to criticize and oppose the administration. The unusual pact has worked out well in some ways but has fallen short in others.[21]

Brazil is the most recent nation to adopt a semblance of the two-party system. Institutional Act No. 2, issued by Dictator-President Castelo Branco on October 27, 1965, dissolved all the existing political parties. In their place, an official government party, the National Renovation Alliance, was created, as well as an official opposition party, the Brazilian Democratic Movement.[22]

Multiparty Systems

Most of the nations have a multiplicity of parties. Chile is the only nation where the parties fall into a left-center-right framework, resembling the traditional pattern of multiparty systems. The political spectrum from left to right consists of: four leftist parties—Communist, Socialist, National Democratic, and National Vanguard of the People; two of the center—the Christian Democratic and Radical; and three of the right—Liberal, United Conservative, and Democratic Front. In addition, there are a number of minor parties.[23]

Chile's multiparty system has existed for the past 100 years, and the number of parties has varied greatly from time to time. It reached a maximum in 1953 when 24 new parties, in addition to the 12 already represented in Congress, registered to run candidates in the municipal and congressional elections. Since then, the number of parties has decreased considerably. Only 11 parties sponsored candidates for national office in 1961, of which only 8 managed to win representation.[24]

There are several explanations for Chile's complex system of political parties. Foremost is the nation's unfortunate experience from 1891 to 1925 with parliamentary government.

. . . if the liberal democratic party [which instituted it] had deliberately set about the work of undermining the credit and authority of parliament it could not have succeeded better than it actually has, through forcing upon the

---

[21] The vicissitudes and accomplishments of the National Front are treated at length in Dix, *op. cit.*, chaps. 7 and 13.

[22] Jordan M. Young, *The Brazilian Revolution of 1930 and the Aftermath* (New Brunswick, N.J.: Rutgers University Press, 1967), p. 116.

The sudden abolition of political parties after two decades of existence did not cause the slightest commotion among the public, disillusioned by the many shortcomings of the party system. Vladimir Reisky de Dubnic, *Political Trends in Brazil* (Washington, D.C.: Public Affairs Press, 1968), pp. 95–101.

[23] For a brief history of each of these parties, together with its strength as shown in elections of the past two decades, see *Chile: Election Factbook*, September 4, 1964 (Institute for the Comparative Study of Political Systems) (Washington, D.C.: Operations and Policy Research, Inc., 1963), pp. 22–29 and 32–41.

[24] *Ibid.*, pp. 13, 21, and 13.

various groups and parties of parliament the necessity of making shifting and temporary alliances and coalitions. . . . It has gained this success not by consistently following any definite policy of government, but rather by making opportune arrangements with this or that party or faction.[25]

The d'Hondt system of proportional representation in Chile has also tended to encourage the formation of many minor political groups. Moreover, the ease of registering as a political party, by presenting its statutes, the composition of its executive committee, and the signatures of 10,000 registered voters, is also greatly responsible for the large number of parties.[26]

As a result of the nation's multiparty system, no single party received more than one fourth of the total popular vote cast in a national election during the 20 years preceding 1964. Moreover, since no candidate received an absolute majority of the total votes, as required by Article 64 of the constitution, it became the responsibility of congress to select the president in the elections of 1946, 1952, and 1958. The constitution merely specifies that the choice must be between the two high candidates. In every case, however, the congress has overwhelmingly endorsed the voters' first choice.

In the crucial September, 1964, election, however, the Christian Democrats supporting the moderate leftist Eduardo Frei scored a smashing victory over the Socialist-Communist combination supporting the far leftist, Salvador Allende, leader of the Socialist-Communist Coalition. The Christian Democrats won 56 percent of the total vote, proving that even in the multiparty system a presidential candidate may receive an absolute majority of the votes.

THE NATIVE LIBERAL PARTIES

In many of the nations, native liberal parties have arisen within the last several decades to challenge the old order and strenuously advocate a wide range of social reforms. Some of these parties no longer exist but have nevertheless left their indelible imprint on the nation. The Peronista Party, which espoused a broad program of social reform during Perón's decade in office, has not been allowed to operate as a political party—a very controversial issue before the military took over in 1966. The MNR in Bolivia, during its 12 years in power put through a broad program of

---

[25] Paul S. Reinsch, "Parliamentary Government in Chile," *American Political Science Review*, Vol. III (1909), p. 521.

[26] For the operation of proportional representation and registration of political parties and candidates in Chile, see Federico G. Gil, *The Political System of Chile* (Boston: Houghton Mifflin Co., 1966), pp. 215–20; and *Chile: Election Factbook, op. cit.*, pp. 30–31 and 42–43.

basic social reforms that completely transformed the nation—reforms that the present administration is supporting.

Several of the native liberal parties are in power now. The National Liberation Party of Costa Rica, founded in 1949 by José Figueres, the liberal leader of the 1948 revolution and later president of the nation, has been the dominant party during the past two decades and can claim credit for much of the nation's social progress. The Democratic Action Party of Venezuela, founded in 1936, in control of the government by revolution and election from 1945 to 1948 and legally in power since 1958, has accomplished a broad program of social reform that has made Venezuela one of the most dynamic nations in the whole region.

Paradoxically, the one native party that has exercised by far the most widespread influence over all of Latin America is a party that has never been in control of the government, even though it is still very much alive. This is the Aprista, or People's Party, of Peru. Founded by Victor Haya de la Torre while a student at San Marcos University in Lima, the party has agitated for a comprehensive, idealistic program of reform. The maximum program, intended to benefit all the nations of Latin America, had five main objectives: stemming imperialistic penetration of the region, unifying Latin America, nationalizing land and industry, placing the Panama Canal under the joint ownership and control of all the nations of America, and promoting solidarity with the rest of the world.

The party's minimum program, intended for Peru alone, advocated a wide range of reforms that would benefit the nation. Assistance to agriculture, development of the economy generally, help to urban workers, improvement of public administration, reform of the judicial system, control of the armed forces, and separation of church and state are objectives the party has long striven for.

Because of a long-standing feud with the army, the party has been outlawed much of the time, and Victor Haya de la Torre has been forced to spend much of his life in hiding in his native land, in exile abroad, or in the Colombian Embassy in Lima, where he spent more than five years—from 1949 to 1954.

Whether in power or in ominous opposition, the native liberal parties are a dynamic force in Latin America today.

THE TRADITIONAL COMMUNIST PARTIES

Every one of the nations has a communist party operating either openly when legal or clandestinely when outlawed. When the party is forced to go underground, as frequently happens, it sometimes continues to function under another name. In Guatemala when the party was declared illegal, it ceased to exist officially but operated under the name Partido Guatemalteco del Trabajo, or Guatemalan Labor Party. Sometimes, to play it safe, the party follows a policy of dual Communism; one branch of the party operates openly and the other underground.[27]

Since the actual number of party members is top-secret information, with many of them functioning underground, the strength of a party in a nation can only be estimated. In Table 12–1 Rollie Poppino gives an

TABLE 12–1

ESTIMATED MEMBERSHIP OF LATIN AMERICAN
COMMUNIST PARTIES IN SELECTED
POSTWAR YEARS

Country	1947	1952	1957	1963
Argentina	30,000	30,000	90,000	50,000
Bolivia	negligible	2,000	5,000	4,000
Brazil	150,000	60,000	50,000	35,000
Chile	50,000	35,000	25,000	30,000
Colombia	5,000	3,000	5,000	8,000
Costa Rica	3,000	2,000	300	300
Cuba	50,000	25,000	12,000	80,000
Dominican Republic	500	negligible	negligible	negligible
Ecuador	2,500	2,000	1,000	3,000
El Salvador	negligible	500	500	500
Guatemala	negligible	1,000	1,000	1,000
Haiti	500	negligible	negligible	negligible
Honduras	negligible	negligible	500	2,000
Mexico	10,000	5,000	5,000	5,000
Nicaragua	500	500	200	300
Panama	500	500	negligible	150
Paraguay	8,000	1,000	500	500
Peru	30,000	10,000	6,000	7,000
Uruguay	15,000	10,000	3,000	4,000
Venezuela	20,000	10,000	9,000	30,000
	375,500	197,500	214,000	260,750

SOURCE: Rollie Poppino, *International Communism in Latin America: A History of the Movement, 1917–1963* (New York: The Free Press, 1964), p. 231.

estimated number of party members in the nations in selected postwar years.

As Table 12–1 shows, communism was relatively strong in 1947; Russia had been a valiant ally in World War II, and its strength and progress were much admired. But when the cold war began and most of the nations aligned with the United States, the number of members declined sharply. The notable increase by 1963 reflects the impact Castro and the Cuban Revolution had on the nations. As the table also shows, the esti-

[27] Robert J. Alexander, *Communism in Latin America* (New Brunswick, N.J.: Rutgers University Press, 1957), p. 293.

mated membership is very small in many of the countries, but rather large in others, especially Cuba, Argentina, Brazil, Chile, and Venezuela.

The almost incredible triumph of communism in Cuba, only 90 miles from the United States, has been a heartening shot in the arm to communists throughout Latin America. In many nations, they are displaying a growing confidence in the inevitable victory of their cause, and are showing an increasing willingness to call openly for revolution, even risk a show of force.[28] For they are convinced that conditions in the region make it ripe for a communist social revolution: the poverty, illiteracy, and feeling of futility of the masses; the rigid social structure; dominance of the military to maintain the status quo; and the increasing fervor of nationalism.[29]

While the communists are piddling in number, constituting only about 1 percent of the total population, they nevertheless count on drawing support from certain important segments of the population.[30] As could be expected, urban wage earners constitute most of the rank-and-file members of the parties. In the countries where labor is well organized, communists have often managed to worm their way into key positions where they can exert considerable influence—possibly determine the policies of the unions.[31] In Guatemala, control of labor was the key to the success of the communist take-over of the nation. "Organized labor played a crucial role . . ." concludes Ronald M. Schneider. "Without control of the labor movement, the communists could hardly have become a major political force; with it they automatically were."[32] But the communists have learned that they cannot always count on the support of labor. In Chile's 1963 election, strategists for the Popular Action Front, of which the Communist Party was a member, assumed that the working-class vote was safe for its candidate, Salvador Allende—an assumption that was disproved by the election results.[33]

---

[28] Rollie E. Poppino, *International Communism in Latin America: A History of the Movement, 1917–1963* (New York: The Free Press, 1964), pp. 3–4.

[29] Alexander, *op. cit.*, chap. 1, and *ibid.*, pp. 18–21.

[30] These are discussed by Poppino, *op. cit.*, in chap. 5, "Who are the Communists?"

[31] For a survey of communist activities in the labor movement, see Alexander, *op. cit.*, chap. iv; and Víctor Alba, *Politics and the Labor Movement in Latin America* (Stanford, Calif.: Stanford University Press, 1968), chap. 6.

[32] Ronald M. Schneider, *Communism in Guatemala: 1944–1954* (New York: Frederick A. Praeger, Inc., 1958), p. 123. During the days of Chile's Popular Front, communist tactics were not to impose their own leaders but to attract those already selected by the unions, then to corrupt them and make them subservient to communist dictation. (Eudocio Ravines, *The Yenan Way* [New York: Charles Scribner's Sons, 1951], pp. 175–76.)

For the devious course the Communist Party in Argentina has pursued, utilizing labor and other support, see Jorge Abelardo Ramos, *El Partido Communista en la Politica Argentina: Su Historia y Su Crítica* (Buenos Aires, 1962).

[33] Halperin, *op. cit.*, pp. 237–38.

The rural farm areas have been for the most part barren ground for communist ideological tillage. Party leaders, usually urban in background and outlook, have found it difficult to contact the farm workers, scattered as they are throughout the countryside, and even more difficult to win the confidence of the illiterate, apathetic, suspicious workers—much less arouse their enthusiasm. Probably the greatest communist success in rural areas has been in drought-stricken, poverty-stricken northeastern Brazil, where peasant leagues flourished during the first half of the 1960's. But rural unions sponsored by the Catholic Church and organized by priests have won over many of the workers there.

Still another large segment of society to which the communists appeal and in which they find much support is the *petit bourgeoisie*, the lower middle class. For its white-collar members with their modest salaries suffer from the same economic pressures that oppress the many members of the mass.

Another group—one especially susceptible to the appeal of communism—are the students. Even though most of them come from upper and middle class families, their political attitudes and actions are determined by their sensitivity to social and economic injustice and by fervent nationalism rather than by their financial and class interests. In fact, during the fling of their student years and following the long tradition of student participation in politics, they are ardent opponents of the status quo and of the classes they come from.

One group the communists have had very little success in winning over, despite intensive wooing, is the women, with their naturally conservative outlook and devotion to the Catholic Church. Even in Argentina, Brazil, Chile, and Uruguay, where the party has made its greatest pitch to win their support, they constitute no more than 10 to 15 percent of the party membership. In the Chilean election of 1964, most significant because it appeared that the Communist Party supported by leftist allies might for the first time legally win control of a government in a popular election, it was the women voters who determined the outcome of the election and put Christian Democrat Eduardo Frei in office. The female vote was approximately two to one in favor of Frei over Allende; however, the male vote was almost evenly divided.[34] And even in Cuba where Castro's regime has championed the rights of women, aiming to give them equality in the society, women have nevertheless been notably less enthusiastic than men in supporting the regime. A study of attitudes toward the revolution by sex showed that among the men 83 percent were favorable, 10 indecisive, and 16 hostile. Among the women, 62 percent were favorable, 12 indecisive, and 25 hostile.[35]

---

[34] Institute for the Comparative Study of Political Systems, *The Chilean Presidential Election of September 4, 1965, Part II* (Washington, D.C., 1965), pp. 10 and 11.

[35] Maurice Zeitlin, *Revolutionary Politics and the Cuban Working Class* (Princeton, N.J.: Princeton University Press, 1967), pp. 126–27.

Although the communists have several sources of strong or potentially strong support, have what in most cases is a tight, effective party organization that is freewheeling in propagandizing, and are not tainted by the accusation of imperialistic exploitation, they nevertheless have certain weaknesses that explain why they have made no more progress than they have in Latin America. Their internationalism and close ties with the Soviet Union, shown in toeing the party line, run counter to the ardent nationalism of Latin America—a nationalism that demands independence from all foreign powers. Also, communists are guided by a rationalistic philosophy and by opportunistic considerations, while young Latin American intellectuals highly prize voluntarism and an uncompromising radicalism. Too, the communists are accustomed to an impersonal discipline, which they have tried to impose on Latin Americans who are individualists and personalists.[36]

With these and other weaknesses, including bitter factionalism and schisms, the parties have had to forego the usual communist revolutionary goals and settle for far more limited ones, such as winning friendship for Russia and provoking hostility toward the United States.

In Mexico, the communist movement has split into three political parties and appears to be actually declining, despite five decades of activity there. There are many reasons for this decline. Their propaganda has often been so blatant and inconsistent as to defeat its purpose. But the main reason for communism's lack of success is simply that Mexico had already experienced its social, economic, and political revolution—a homegrown variety—some years before the Russian Revolution took place. Proud of its new society, the Mexican Government has long followed the policy of trying to promote the welfare of all groups and of remedying as far as possible any discontent before it assumes serious proportions.[37] Yet, despite communism's weakness in playing the role of political gadfly, it has helped to educate the public by stressing alternatives other than those offered by the government. It has also served to prick the public's conscience and thereby encourage the airing of some policy questions.[38]

The Communist Party of Chile, although of small size and limited popular following, is probably the most politically effective communist party in Latin America. Its disproportionately large influence is due to its discipline and its faculty for exploiting popular issues.[39] Moreover, by

---

[36] Boris Goldenberg, *The Cuban Revolution and Latin America* (New York: Frederick A. Praeger, Inc., 1965), p. 308.

[37] Karl M. Schmitt, *Communism in Mexico: A Study in Political Frustration* (Austin: University of Texas Press, 1965), pp. 220–22 and 227–29; and Howard F. Cline, *Mexico: Revolution to Evolution: 1940–1960* (New York: Oxford University Press, 1963), p. 178.

[38] Padgett, *op. cit.*, pp. 66–67.

[39] Federico G. Gil, *The Political System of Chile* (Boston: Houghton Mifflin Co., 1966), pp. 277–78. For the Party's reaction to momentous events on the international

collaborating with Socialists and bourgeois groups and by professing a policy of legitimacy and respect for elections as the means of attaining political power, the party has won much support at the polls. Its tactic of professing a gradualist, peaceful road to power, together with its strong appeal in labor and intellectual circles and its stance as being just a political party, have helped to extend its national influence.[40]

In Colombia, although the long-range goal of the Communist Party is the revolutionary reconstruction of the society, the Party throughout most of its existence has favored the peaceful road to power. It supported the positive aspects of the 1957 plebiscite and the election of Lleras Camargo in 1958, regarded as steps toward the restoration of constitutional order. Nevertheless, the Party has been highly critical of what it regards as the negative features of the National Front—its oligarchic nature, alternation, the allowance of only two political parties, and the dependence of Colombia on the imperialist United States.[41]

Since Castro took over in 1959, the communists in most of the nations have been considerably more active than before.[42] For they have felt confident that his success in gaining power and instituting a new social order could be emulated in the other nations of Latin America. The fires of their hopes have been vigorously fanned by Castro, who has resorted to propaganda, subversion, and even direct attack in attempting to export his revolution to the other nations.[43]

THE COMMUNIST PARTY IN CUBA

The Communist Party in Cuba has long been one of the most important and powerful of all the Latin American communist parties. It was the first such party to place one of its members in the national cabinet; it also graphically proved that by cooperating with a dictator communists could achieve power in the labor movement and in politics.[44] In the years since Castro embraced Marxism-Leninism and aligned himself with Russia, the Party's star has risen to its zenith.

During the two years of Castro's guerrilla struggle to overthrow the

---

scene, such as Castro's take-over in Cuba, the Bay of Pigs invasion, and the Cuban missile crisis, see Halperin, *op. cit.*, chap. 7.

[40] Gil, *The Political System of Chile, op. cit.*, p. 278.

[41] Dix, *op. cit.*, pp. 273 and 278.

[42] A helpful but biased account of their activities is given by Jules Dubois, *Operation America: The Communist Conspiracy in Latin America* (New York: Walker & Co., 1963); and *Danger Over Panama* (New York: Bobbs-Merrill Co., Inc., 1964).

[43] Goldenberg, *op. cit.*, pp. 305–22; and Nicolás Rivero, *Castro's Cuba: An American Dilemma* (Washington, D.C.: Luce, 1962), pp. 110–42.

[44] Alexander, *op. cit.*, p. 270. In chap. xiii, Alexander traces the development of the party in the nation.

Batista regime, the Communist Party played a negligible role. Of all the groups actively opposing Batista, they did the least fighting and suffered the smallest losses. They did organize several small guerrilla bands during autumn, 1958, while at the same time infiltrating those led by Castro. An officer of the revolutionary army succinctly described the Party's minuscule role. "In all the countryside you won't find any Communists," he said. "They're all in Havana. No one of them was with us in the mountains. They joined us at the last minute."[45]

There were several reasons for the Communist Party's uncooperative, even hostile attitude toward Castro's campaign. First, they had fared relatively well under Batista, who had welcomed their support (thinly disguised under another party name); five of their senior leaders had joined the Batista Party, providing the dictator with the popular support that he needed.[46] Second, Castro's leader-instigated guerrilla revolution was abhorrent to the Communist Party's Marxist theology of revolutions; according to the book, revolutions were supposed to be instigated by the proletariat and led by its vanguard, the Communist Party.[47] No wonder the party regarded Castro with his ragtag guerrilla force as a "bourgeois romantic putschist."[48] Finally, the party just plumb misfigured. As Che Guevara frankly stated on August 24, 1963, "the Communist Party did not see clearly; it did not properly understand the method of struggle; it erred in its estimation of the movement's chances of success."[49]

But once Castro was in power, the Communist Party with its flexibility and adaptability managed to climb on the bandwagon—to become, in time, the sole and governing party under Castro's leadership. The transition of the Party from disfavor to power is interesting to follow. For the first year or so after the revolution succeeded, Castro frequently denounced communism, and even termed the communists as counterrevolutionaries because of their agitation for higher wages.[50] And outwardly, the Party appeared to be lukewarm to the new regime, as shown at their 1960 convention.

But by 1961 the picture was changing radically. Edwin Tetlow writes, "I confirmed to my own satisfaction that Cuba had been delivered to Communism when I went to Havana in January, 1961, to see just what had happened after the final diplomatic break with the United States.

---

[45] Goldenberg, *op. cit.*, p. 146.

[46] Alexander, *op. cit.*, pp. 292–94; and Goldenberg, *op. cit.*, p. 165.

[47] Andrés Suárez, *Cuba: Castroism and Communism, 1959–1966*, trans. Joel Carmichael and Ernst Halperin (Cambridge: Massachusetts Institute of Technology Press, 1967), pp. 26–29 and 124–27.

[48] Maurice Zeitlin and Robert Scheer, *Cuba: Tragedy in Our Hemisphere* (New York: Grove Press, Inc., 1963), p. 117.

[49] Goldenberg, *op. cit.*, p. 166.

[50] Zeitlin and Scheer, *op. cit.*, pp. 107–11.

There were telltale signs of the conversion." Among these telltale signs were the economy's change from free private enterprise to state control, Communists in charge of all the big unions, a growing furtive surveillance by military and political agents, and the existence of only one radio network and one television channel.[51]

During late 1961—scholars still have not been able to pinpoint the exact date—the Communist Party made its first great leap forward when Castro decided to merge the three main political groups in the nation into a single political party to be known as the Integrated Revolutionary Organization, or ORI as it is popularly called. The amalgamation of the 26th of July Movement, the student Directorio Revolucionario, and the Communist Party was, in reality, a farce. For the 26th of July Movement had long been gutted, and the Directorio suffered an even more shadowy existence. They were no match for the Communist Party.[52]

The growing role of the communists was due to the radicalization of the revolution, and to the fact that they alone had a program, collective discipline, and real organization, with trained cadres supported by thousands of members. As Boris Goldenberg concludes, "No wonder that the old communists tended to become the head and the backbone of the revolution."[53] When ORI in 1963 became the United Party of the Socialist Revolution (known as PURS), the change was primarily to weed out some of the older communists and turn over the reins to younger, more dynamic members of the party.

The communists' star reached its zenith in 1965 when the party replaced PURS, an event publicized extensively. It signified that the political system of a communist nation was for the first time being actually established in Cuba.[54]

The Communist Party that governs Cuba today is structured conformably to the model of a governing communist political organization. There is a Central Committee composed of 100 members, 69 percent of whom belong to the military; and capping the political hierarchy is the Secretariat of 6 members, 5 of whom belong to the military. The secretary-general and head of the party is, of course, Fidel Castro, who exercises power in the dual capacity of premier of the government and head of the party. Adoption of the new system was designed to strengthen the

---

[51] Edwin Tetlow, *Eye on Cuba* (New York: Harcourt, Brace & World, Inc., 1965), p. 116.

[52] Theodore Draper, *Castro's Revolution: Myths and Realities* (New York: Frederick A. Praeger, Inc., 1962), p. 120. Draper concludes that "Fidel could not simply join the PSP (Communist Party) without losing face." *Ibid.*, p. 122. In Draper's *Castroism: Theory and Practice* (New York: Frederick A. Praeger, Inc., 1965), pp. 34–36, he interprets the formation of ORI as a transition from Castro–Communist alliance to Castro–Communist fusion.

[53] Goldenberg, *op. cit.*, pp. 245 and 298.

[54] Suárez, *op. cit.*, p. 227.

Party's grip over the nation and to concentrate power into the hands of the premier, who controls the nation's armed forces.[55]

THE CHRISTIAN DEMOCRATIC PARTIES

Auguring well for the future of Latin America is the meteoric rise to prominence of the Christian Democratic parties. Their rise has been so fast that it has largely escaped the notice of observers of the Latin American scene. But in only a few years the parties have won wide acceptance —have had a great effect on the politics and aspirations of the region.

The Christian Democratic Party of Chile has the distinction of being the first such party to win control of the government, as it did in the hotly contested presidential election of 1964 and the congressional elections of the next year. The Christian Democratic Party of Venezuela, long known as COPEI (the Committee for Independent Political Electoral Organization), won the presidency with its candidate, Rafael Caldera, in the December, 1968, election but did not get control of the congress. In other countries too, the mostly fledgling parties have fared well. The party in El Salvador gained second place in the 1963 congressional elections; and in the Dominican Republic it came in third. In the same year, the party in Peru formed a coalition with Popular Action to elect to the presidency Belaúnde Terry, candidate of the Popular Action Party. In several other countries, particularly Argentina, Guatemala, and Uruguay, the parties have become an important political force. The parties exist in the other nations, too, with the exception of Brazil (where only two parties, the Official Party and the official opposition party, are allowed), Haiti, Honduras, and, of course, Cuba. Attempts made to form a party in Cuba in 1960 were unsuccessful when the leaders were either threatened with violence or were exiled.[56]

These parties have been successful largely because they offer a meaningful alternative to the widespread threat of communism. Rafael Caldera, for many years head of COPEI in Venezuela, has characterized Christian Democracy as ". . . the only growing democratic political force in Latin America today . . . the best, and perhaps the only hope of Latin America."[57]

Christian Democracy is not a movement composed of Catholics only and designed for Catholics only. As Eduardo Frei emphasizes—and many

---

[55] *Ibid.*, pp. 227–29.

[56] Goldenberg, *op. cit.*, p. 202.

[57] Rafael Caldera, "Christian Democracy and Social Reality," *Social Revolution in the New Latin America: A Catholic Appraisal*, ed. John J. Considine (Notre Dame, Ind.: Fides, Inc., 1965), pp. 65 and 74.

According to Vladimir Reisky de Dubnic, in Brazil "Christian Democracy is the only force which is at least ideologically prepared to supply democratic guidance in case of a basic social and economic structural change." de Dubnic, *op. cit.*, p. 74.

others do, too—its call goes out to all citizens, including Catholics, those of other faiths, and those with no faith at all. In Chile, many Protestants, Jews, and agnostics have joined the party, which is glad to have them as members.[58]

The widespread acceptance the parties have won in only a short time is attributable to several factors, especially their effective organization, broad basis of support, and appealing revolutionary ideology.

The parties have a complex internal structure that is federal, sometimes confederal. In its comprehensiveness and effectiveness, it is second only to that of the communist and some socialist parties. The party organization reaches all levels, from the neighborhoods where local groups carry on the grass-roots activities, up to the state or provincial conventions and committees, and culminating in the national convention, whose annual or biennial session determines policy, and the national committee, which, in effect, runs the party. Membership requirements generally include a minimum age, usually 18, and acceptance of the party's principles and program, also obligations that may range from not criticizing the party before a stranger to contributing to it a certain percentage of one's income. Membership cards are issued to dramatize the ties that bind a member to the party.[59]

With their goals of far-reaching reform, the parties enjoy a broad base of popular support. Liberals are attracted by the comprehensive ideology, which challenges both the intellect and the conscience. Young people are among the most ardent supporters, accepting Christian Democracy as a sort of secular faith whose tenets will lead the way to a new, reformed social order. Women, too, have given the movement their fervent support because reforms it envisages have Christian rather than communist methods and goals.[60] And workers, both urban and rural, have been drawn to the party by its promises of a better life for the many members of the large, underprivileged mass.

Easily the main reason for the movement's success is its idealistic ideology and program. These stress that man is a being of spirit and matter, and is by nature social as well as spiritual. Whatever his status, he should be encouraged to participate actively in the society; involvement gives him a stake in it and makes for a genuine social stability. Liberty and justice in society would be achieved by means of pluralism, mani-

---

[58] Eduardo Frei Montalva, "Paternalism, Pluralism, and Christian Democratic Reform Movements in Latin America," *Religion, Revolution, and Reform: New Forces for Change in Latin America*, eds. William V. D'Antonio and Fredrick B. Pike (New York: Frederick A. Praeger, Inc., 1964), pp. 37–38.

[59] Williams, *op. cit.*, pp. 81–88. For the structure and organization of the party in Chile, see Gil, *op. cit.*, pp. 274–76.

[60] For the decisive role women have played in recent elections in Chile, especially the crucial one of 1964, see Gil, *op. cit.*, pp. 212–15.

fested in the existence of numerous intermediate societies within the body politic.[61]

The program of reform that the Christian Democrats advocate is basic and comprehensive. In the social realm, the parties aim to rapidly improve and extend education as well as to strengthen the family, which, rather than the individual, is regarded as the basic social unit. Society should provide every family with an allowance that is adequate for its support. The rights of women should be recognized in both public and family life; for example, they should be allowed to own and inherit property. While the issue of divorce is controversial throughout the continent, there is almost united opposition (Chile being an exception) to birth control. The rationale is not that of traditional Catholic theology but, rather, that Latin America is underpopulated and needs many more persons to fully exploit the continent's resources. Overpopulation is a remote threat, they assert. In fact, the region is underpopulated and needs a boom in population, not a curtailment![62]

In the economic realm the parties likewise advocate many reforms. They would strengthen the labor movement, especially by guaranteeing the right to strike and by the depoliticalizing trade unionism, making it independent of the government and any political party—presumably of the Catholic Church, too. They also stress the necessity of a genuine agrarian reform, and have introduced many specific proposals intended to accomplish this, including the program of land reform adopted in Chile in July, 1967.

But the parties go far beyond merely proposing specific changes. A basic credo of faith is economic humanism that will supply the material necessities to all persons at the expense of the wealthy few in society. This economic humanism is based on five main principles: "The precedence of moral over material gain, the precedence of consumption over production, the precedence of labor over capital, replacement of patronage by coownership, and the replacement of salary by profit-sharing."[63]

As a short-range goal, they foresee the establishment of a mixed economy, where private initiative and state intervention work jointly together. Some large-scale undertakings will be jointly owned by private concerns and the state. Although private ownership is the key ingredient of economic development, the right of private property is not absolute but is limited by considerations of the common good. Moreover, the present relationship between labor and management must be restructured, and the present economic system must be reformed to provide for labor's

---

[61] Miguel H. Benjamin, *Democracia Cristiana* (La Paz, 1966), pp. 78–84; and Williams, *op. cit.*, pp. 51–60.

[62] Williams, *op. cit.*, pp. 94–96; and Remo Di Natale, *América Latina Hoy: Esquemas Populares Democrata Cristianos* (La Paz, 1964), pp. 23–24.

[63] Williams, *op. cit.*, p. 112.

coparticipation, codetermination, and co-ownership. The ultimate goal is communitarian property, whereby wages and salaries and profit sharing are eliminated, the means of production are owned by the workers, and the society is transformed into a complete system of cooperatives. Achievement of this idealistic goal would eliminate the age-old division of men into the haves and the have-nots.[64]

In the political realm, the parties advocate many badly needed reforms, such as strengthening the legislative and judicial branches of government, instituting a civil service for the selection of governmental employees, and adopting universal suffrage by the abolition of literacy as a requirement for voting. A more radical reform they espouse is the adoption of functional representation in the national congress, whereby occupational groups may be able to influence public policy directly instead of through the intermediary of geographically elected representatives.

These proposed reforms are obviously revolutionary; if and when achieved, they would completely remake society. That is the goal of the Christian Democrats, who frankly and boldly proclaim that they are revolutionaries and will use revolutionary measures to attain revolutionary goals. To attain them, a revolution is not only necessary but inevitable. Yet, violence is not necessary; legal methods can and must be used in the revolution, which is to be Christian in principle, leadership, and ultimate goal.[65]

Perhaps the really unique feature of the movement is its political stance. The parties, finding themselves in a polarized world and forced to choose between what they regard as two extremes—capitalism and communism—reject them both and take a third position, selecting the best from each system. Although liberal capitalism stands accused of causing the proletarianization of the masses and of alienating man from his work, his community, and even his own soul, it has made great technological progress yielding material benefits, and has stressed human liberty. And although communism is atheistic and materialistic, it has recognized and mitigated the struggle between the classes and has stressed justice. The synthesis the parties strive for would reconcile liberty as exemplified by liberal capitalism, with justice as exemplified by disciplined communism. The synthesis would stress the dignity of the individual and integrate him fully into a humanistic society.[66]

In the various countries, the programs of the Christian Democratic parties are rather tailored to the existing situation. In Chile, the party advocates giving more power to the Executive, permitting him to submit to a national referendum the bills he has proposed but Congress has re-

---

[64] Miguel, *op. cit.*, pp. 73–78 and 224–26; Williams, *op. cit.*, pp. 113–18; and Halperin, *op. cit.*, pp. 196–98.

[65] Williams, *op. cit.*, pp. 36–41.

[66] Miguel, *op. cit.*, pp. 88–105.

fused to pass; simplifying congressional procedure so as to make Congress more effective and responsible; and limiting campaign expenditures to curb the influence of powerful economic interests. In Colombia, where the party is barred from elective office until 1974, its leaders—reformers rather than revolutionaries—express hope that the system can be revised before then by a popular plebiscite.[67]

In striving to achieve its visionary, messianic goals, Christian Democracy may have an advantage in the long run. But a pressing question is: What can be accomplished today or perhaps tomorrow? For the fervor of the movement has attracted militants who are "hell-bent for reform." It has aroused the hopes of many, too, that the millennium can be attained now or sooner.[68] Indeed, the enunciation of lofty principles may win an election, as the party found in Chile in 1964. But almost immediately, practical problems arise over how to effectuate them. President Frei critically needs the support of the private sector; without it, he will be forced to adopt a type of socialism he neither advocates nor desires. However, winning the support of the private sector in the short run while aiming to take over the sector as a long-range goal is no easy task, as Frei is finding out.[69]

Nevertheless, Christian Democracy is confident that it is the wave of the future—the alternative the region will choose instead of communism. As Rafael Caldera well expresses it:

Communism is one of these coherent systems, seeking to interpret all the phenomena of the cosmos, from the origin of matter to the final destiny of man; Christian Democracy is the only other system that is able to offer a similar cohesion, with the advantage that it nurtures in the spirit of youth, its faith in absolute values, and makes you feel that not everything ends with death or has its only expression in material terms."[70]

CAMPAIGNS AND ELECTIONS

Consistent with democratic practice, universal suffrage is increasingly becoming the rule in Latin America. Indeed, many of the nations have not only gone about as far as they can to extend the suffrage but have also made it obligatory.

There are three main requirements today which determine whether or not one is eligible to vote: age, literacy, and citizenship. In a majority of the nations, the minimum age for voting is 21; and with the exception of Cuba, which has set a minimum of age 20, the others permit 18-year-olds

---

[67] Dix, *op. cit.*, p. 288.

[68] Williams, *op. cit.*, pp. 230–32.

[69] Leonard Gross, *The Last, Best Hope: Eduardo Frei & Chilean Democracy* (New York: Random House, Inc., 1967), pp. 139–47.

[70] Rafael Caldera, *op. cit.*, pp. 69–70.

to vote. In several of the countries, the voting age for married persons is lowered to 18, or no minimum age is required.

Literacy continues to be a requirement in five of the nations; four of these—Chile, Colombia, Ecuador, and Peru—are located in the Andean region and have a large number of illiterate Indians. In the fifth, Brazil, the literacy requirement is aimed at disqualifying the large number of illiterate Negroes. In the nations where illiteracy is high but illiterates are allowed to vote, rapport is established by the simple expedient of printing the ballots—election posters, too—of candidates in different colors. *VOTO ROJO!* some posters shriek in living color, urging the voters to "Vote Red!" while others urge them to vote *negro, blanco, amarillo,* or whatever is the distinctive color of their party and candidates.

Citizenship is ordinarily a qualification, too. Several of the nations, however, permit foreigners to vote in municipal elections after a certain minimum period of residence, usually five years. Sometimes a *caudillo,* anxious to prove that his regime is really democratic and to roll up a larger majority in his favor, relaxes the requirements. In Venezuela's 1958 election when dictator Pérez Jiménez was the only candidate on the ballot, he gave all foreigners the right to vote and urged them to cast a ballot. Americans, who constituted the largest number of foreigners, were warned by the State Department that they ran the risk of losing their American citizenship if they voted in the election.

Women, now allowed to vote in every one of the nations, have raised some peculiar problems with regard to the suffrage. A main reason they were for so long denied the privilege of voting was the fear that their votes might be influenced by the clergy; it is the women in the family who attend church more regularly and are more heedful of the admonitions of the priests. Another male fear has been that, if allowed to vote, the women might vote as a bloc, take over, and possibly institute such absurd reforms. Obviously reflecting masculine misgivings, in giving women the right to vote the Panamanian constitution seeks to avoid open conflict between the sexes by specifying that no political party shall be based on sex alone. Women's suffrage, supposedly based upon the premise of equality, is nevertheless slightly tipped in favor of femininity. Since women are so averse to revealing their age, many of the election laws in deference to such top secrecy chivalrously exempt them from the requirement of giving their exact age when registering to vote or when voting; they are allowed to state merely that they are over 21.

Masculine fears that feminine voters may possibly decide the outcome of elections have a fairly substantial basis, as the crucial September, 1964, election in Chile clearly showed. It was the women who elected Eduardo Frei president, giving him his large majority. Since Chilean women use separate ballot boxes, their preference could easily be ascertained. While the masculine vote was split about evenly between Allende and Frei, the women gave Frei almost 63 percent of their vote, enough to assure his election.[71]

To enable all to vote who are qualified, yet eliminate the possibility of election frauds, all the nations require registration as a prerequisite for voting. In Venezuela, to make it easier for voters to register, municipal electoral boards are open all working days from 6 to 9 P.M.; in rural areas, they are also open on Sundays and holidays from 7 A.M. to 1 P.M. Citizens are registered in the order in which they appear.[72] In Chile, registration is compulsory for everyone who is eligible to vote. Any eligible voter who fails to register is subject to a prison term of up to 60 days, commutable to one-half an escudo a day.[73] But the requirement of a birth certificate for registration in Peru and several of the other nations prevents many *naturales* and Indians from voting.

In the political campaign, just about anything goes. With the hope of getting elected, the candidates promise anything and everything to the voters. In Uruguay's 1946 presidential campaign, Domingo Tortorelli, a prosperous produce dealer and candidate, set a fast pace for the other aspirants. He promised that if he were elected, there would be two fountains on every Montevideo street corner, one with milk for the children, the other with wine for adults. The capital would have a roof built over it to protect its residents in inclement weather. And since gasoline was in very short supply at the time, a superhighway from Montevideo to Colonia would be built to run downhill both ways in order to save gas! Tortorelli's nightly speeches sometimes drew crowds estimated as high as 150,000. They often pelted him with vegetables, which, of course, helped his business. In fact, they gave him more vegetables than votes; despite all his promises, he ended up another also-ran.[74]

According to the constitutions and laws, the political opposition has the rights of freedom of speech, press, and assembly. In those nations where constitutional government is more firmly established, the opposition can wage a vigorous and highly critical campaign. In the nations less accustomed to democratic procedures, however, the rub comes when in a heated campaign the opposition takes these rights seriously and criticizes the government. Sensitive of his *dignidad,* many a president effectively copes with a bothersome opponent by the simple expedient of declaring him a traitor to the homeland and giving him a choice of exile or jail. When President Ydígoras of Guatemala was advised of ex-president Aré-

---

[71] Women have come to play an almost decisive role in Chilean elections, says Federico Gil; consequently, the political parties assiduously court this segment of the electorate. Gil, *op. cit.*, p. 214.

[72] *Venezuela: Election Factbook, op. cit.*, p. 31.

[73] *Chile: Election Factbook, op. cit.*, p. 14.

[74] Russell H. Fitzgibbon, *Uruguay: Portrait of a Democracy* (New Brunswick, N.J.: Rutgers University Press, 1954), p. 152.

valo's contemplated return to Guatemala, he laid down the law that his political opponent would not be allowed to return under any circumstances. "There would be only two doors open for him—one at the border and another at the penitentiary."[75]

Another means of effectively disposing of political opposition is to brand it as communistic. Guatemala's 1956 constitution in Article 62 specifies that any individual or joint communist action may be punished. But since no definition is given of what constitutes communist activity, the executive is free to formulate his own definition; it often means more liberal tendencies than he deems expedient.[76]

Still another means of throttling the opposition is to proclaim a state of siege. The proclamation, whether justified or not, keeps the opposition within close bounds as effectively as a yoke placed around the neck of a fence-jumping maverick. For during a state of siege the opposition cannot campaign freely in the countryside because travel is restricted; it cannot even get its message across via TV, radio, or the press because all news is censored—in the national interest, of course.

Yet in most elections the opposition does have the opportunity, after a fashion, to present its case to the electorate. But the ins who are determined to remain in, and the outs who want in are very wary of one another. Indeed, any election is apt to be a no-holds-barred contest, where chicanery may well determine the outcome. One of the various chicane practices is stealing the ballots of the opposition party. In many of the nations there is no official ballot, but each party is allowed by law to print and distribute its own ballots. If for any reason these are not available, its partisans are, of course, deprived of their vote. Thus, stealing ballots before elections has become a widespread practice in some of the nations.

In Bolivia, on the eve of the 1960 presidential election, Guevara Arze charged that more than 200,000 ballots that were to have been used by his supporters had been seized by an armed militia. The seizures, he alleged, could cost him the election. In the hotly contested campaign, it was apparently open season for swiping the ballots of political opponents. Paz Estenssoro's ballots had allegedly been stolen by Guevara supporters in Oruro, Bolivia's third largest city, and Paz' henchmen apparently were retaliating in similar fashion.

When election day comes, members of the armed forces are on duty at all polling places. Their very presence supposedly symbolizes law and order; moreover, by being on hand, they can cope with any disorders that take place and can make sure that the loser acquiesces in the results. But sometimes the opposition is as distrustful of the military supervision

---

[75] *New York Times*, October 24, 1959, p. 7, col. 3.

[76] Nathan L. Whetten, *Guatemala: The Land and the People* (Caribbean Series, 4) New Haven, Conn.: Yale University Press, 1961), p. 399.

as it is of the political regime it is fighting. In 1961, opposition leaders in Nicaragua urged the OAS to supervise the election, alleging that if the national guard under Chief of Staff Anastasio Somoza was in charge, fraud and terrorism would prevail. In 1962, United States and Mexican journalists toured El Salvador at the invitation of the ruling junta so they could see for themselves that the armed forces were not used to influence the outcome of the presidential election. In 1966, representatives of the Organization of American States observed the July, 1966, election in Bolivia at the invitation of the interim military regime.

In the nations that have universal suffrage, the voter turnout is usually heavy. To the millions of underprivileged but enfranchised citizens, the opportunity of casting a ballot for electing the president, members of congress, or even local officials is substantial proof that they are full citizens of the republic. The laws that make voting compulsory are also largely responsible for the heavy turnout. In Chile, failure of an eligible voter to vote makes him subject to a prison term of up to 60 days, commutable to one half escudo a day, and the loss of his citizenship for a period up to 10 times as long as the prison term.

When the voters are strongly moved to register their disapproval or protest, they resort to one of several means for venting their feelings. Sometimes they stage a mass boycott of the election, a form of political passive resistance intended to discredit the election in the eyes of the country and the rest of the world. Sometimes they cast blank ballots to express disapproval of the alternatives open to them. In Argentina, where the Peronista Party or candidates have been outlawed for most of the past decade, millions of Peronistas have taken the trouble to go to the polls and cast blank ballots. In some nations, instead of turning in their ballots, voters sometimes turn in only the envelopes, filled with black beans, as a protest against the high cost of living and the shortages of such staples as beans and meat.

In Brazil, dissidents have their own unique way of registering their disapproval. In São Paulo's 1959 municipal election, there was a popular revolt against politics and politicians. The largest number of votes for city councilman, easily leading all other candidates, was received by Cacareco, who was not even a registered candidate. In fact, Cacareco was a 2,400 pound rhinoceros, the third to be born in captivity and the first to be elected city councilman in São Paulo. Cacareco was never sworn into office, however; she was disqualified on the technicality of having her legal residence in Rio, from whose zoo she was temporarily on loan to São Paulo.[77]

---

[77] *New York Times*, October 8, 1959, p. 1, col. 8; and October 9, 1959, p. 2, col. 2. Cacareco, it should be noted, is not the first animal to win an election in Brazil. In 1954, a goat named Smelly was chosen city councilman in Jaboatão, Pernambuco.

Irregularities in voting or tabulating the ballots often vitiate the whole electoral process. Indeed, more elections have been won or lost there than in all the hustings of Latin America. A common tale in El Salvador is the boast of a United States citizen about the efficiency of his voting machines. "Our polls close at 6 P.M.," he brags, "and by 10 we know who is going to be our next President." "So what?" replies the Salvadorean, "We know that three months in advance."

There are many techniques for stealing elections. Stuffing the ballot box is naturally a favorite method. It is sometimes so blatant that it backfires. The heated 1958 contest in the Iguala district of Guerrero, Mexico, was just such an occasion. Profesora María López Díaz, running as a candidate for PRI, received 54,852 votes as opposed to only 2,542 for her opponent, a feminine labor leader, Macrina Rabadán. The plurality was most impressive—so impressive, in fact, that it completely discredited itself. For according to official records there were only 42,000 registered voters in the district. Although Macrina received only 2,542 votes out of a possible 42,000, she was declared the winner in the contested election.[78]

Another election obviously won by falsification of returns was the Venezuelan election of 1952. The military junta, having earlier declared Democratic Action, the largest party, to be illegal and ineligible to run, was so confident the junta's candidates could win in a fair election that it permitted Democratic Action and other parties to enter candidates. However, when the early returns indicated that the junta was about to suffer a resounding defeat, it declared a state of siege and gave out no further news about the election until the official announcement two days later that the government's candidates had won.

To guarantee the fairness of elections, 13 of the nations have established electoral courts, either by constitutional provision or by statute. One of the most effective of these is the *Corte Electoral* of Uruguay, established in January, 1924, and composed of four members elected by the national assembly as partisan representatives and five members who are elected as "guarantors of impartiality."[79] The effectiveness of the court, which has gone far toward assuring the fairness of elections, is largely responsible for the reputation Uruguay enjoys as one of the most democratic nations in the world.

---

[78] Ward M. Morton, *Woman Suffrage in Mexico* (Gainesville: University of Florida Press, 1962), pp. 119–21.

Justice has not always triumphed, however. During the wasteful, profligate dictatorship of Antonio Guzmán Blanco, 1870–88, the results of one election were: Blanco, 239,691; General Pulido, 9; General Colina, 6; and 1 each for 3 other candidates. (George S. Wise, *Caudillo: A Portrait of Antonio Guzmán Blanco* [New York: Columbia University Press, 1951], p. 91.)

[79] For the operation of the electoral court in Uruguay, see Phillip B. Taylor, "The Electoral System in Uruguay," *Journal of Politics,* Vol. 17, No. 1 (February, 1955), pp. 19–42.

Electoral reform is badly needed in many of the nations. In Argentina, the famous Sáenz Peña election law of 1912 provided for universal and compulsory male suffrage, the secret ballot, and a strict system of registration of voters. Designed to put an end to electoral fraud, the law enabled the Argentine people to freely elect a president for the first time in 1916. Thanks to President Sáenz Peña who sponsored the law, Argentine elections, when held, have been among the fairest in Latin America.

SUGGESTED READINGS

Alba, Víctor. *Politics and the Labor Movement in Latin America,* chap. 6. Stanford, Calif.: Stanford University Press, 1968.

Alexander, Robert J. *The Bolivian National Revolution,* chaps. 3 and 12. New Brunswick, N.J.: Rutgers University Press, 1958.

———. *Communism in Latin America.* New Brunswick, N.J.: Rutgers University Press, 1957.

Arévalo, Juan José. *Anti-Kommunism in Latin America.* Trans. Carleton Beals. New York: Lyle Stuart, Inc., 1963.

Blanksten, George I. *Ecuador: Constitutions and Caudillos,* chaps. iii and iv. Berkeley: University of California Press, 1951.

———. *Perón's Argentina,* chaps. 14–16. Chicago: University of Chicago Press, 1953.

Cline, Howard F. *Mexico: Revolution to Evolution: 1940–1960,* chaps. xv and xvii. Royal Institute of International Affairs. New York: Oxford University Press, 1962.

Considine, John J. (ed.). *Social Revolution in the New Latin America: A Catholic Appraisal,* chaps. 4–6. Notre Dame, Ind.: Fides, Inc., 1965.

De Dubnic, Vladimir R. *Political Trends in Brazil,* chaps. iii and iv. Washington, D.C.: Public Affairs Press, 1968.

Dix, Robert H. *Colombia: The Political Dimensions of Change,* chaps. 6, 8, 9, and 10. New Haven, Conn.: Yale University Press, 1967.

Dubois, Jules. *Danger Over Panama.* New York: Bobbs-Merrill Co., Inc., 1964.

———. *Operation America: The Communist Conspiracy in Latin America.* New York: Walker and Co., 1963.

Fitzgibbon, Russell H. "The Party Potpourri in Latin America," *Western Political Quarterly,* Vol. X, No. 1 (March, 1957), pp. 3–22.

———. *Uruguay: Portrait of a Democracy,* chap. x. New Brunswick, N.J.: Rutgers University Press, 1954.

Gil, Federico G. *Genesis and Modernization of Political Parties in Chile.* Gainesville: University of Florida Press, 1962.

———. *The Political System of Chile,* chaps. 5 and 6. Boston: Houghton Mifflin Co., 1966.

———. "Central American Political Parties: A Functional Approach," *Western Political Quarterly,* Vol. 15, No. 1 (March, 1962), pp. 125–39.

Goldenberg, Boris. *The Cuban Revolution and Latin America.* New York: Frederick A. Praeger, Inc., 1965.

Gómez, R. A. *Government and Politics in Latin America,* chap. 3. Rev. ed. New York: Random House, Inc., 1964.

Gross, Leonard. *The Last, Best Hope: Eduardo Frei & Chilean Democracy.* New York: Random House, Inc., 1967.

Halperin, Ernst. *Nationalism and Communism in Chile.* Cambridge: Massachusetts Institute of Technology Press, 1965.

Kantor, Harry. *The Ideology and Program of the Peruvian Aprista Movement.* Berkeley: University of California Press, 1953.

Kling, Merle, *A Mexican Interest Group in Action.* Englewood Cliffs, N.J.: Prentice-Hall, Inc., 1961.

Martz, John D. *Acción Democrática: Evolution of a Modern Political Party in Venezuela.* Princeton, N.J.: Princeton University Press, 1966.

Morton, Ward M. *Woman Suffrage in Mexico.* Gainesville: University of Florida Press, 1962.

Padgett, L. Vincent. *The Mexican Political System,* chap. 2. Boston: Houghton Mifflin Co., 1966.

Pierson, William W., and Gil, Federico G. *Governments of Latin America,* chap. 13. New York: McGraw-Hill Book Co., Inc., 1957.

Pike, Fredrick B. "The Old and the New APRA in Peru," *Inter-American Economic Affairs,* Vol. 18, No. 2 (Autumn, 1964), pp. 3–45.

Poppino, Rollie E. *International Communism in Latin America: A History of the Movement, 1917–1963.* New York: The Free Press, 1964.

Ravines, Eudocio. *The Yenan Way.* New York: Charles Scribner's Sons, 1951.

Schmitt, Karl M. *Communism in Mexico: A Study in Political Frustration.* Austin: University of Texas Press, 1965.

Schneider, Ronald M. *Communism in Guatemala: 1944–1954,* chaps. 4, 5, and 9. New York: Frederick A. Praeger, Inc., 1959.

Scott, Robert E. *Mexican Government in Transition,* chaps. 5–7. Rev. ed. Urbana: University of Illinois Press, 1964.

Stevenson, John Reese. *The Chilean Popular Front.* Philadelphia: University of Pennsylvania Press, 1942.

Stokes, William S. *Honduras: An Area Study in Government,* pp. 206–64. Madison: University of Wisconsin Press, 1950.

Suárez, Andrés. *Cuba: Castroism and Communism, 1959–1966.* Trans. Joel Carmichael and Ernst Halperin. Cambridge: Massachusetts Institute of Technology Press, 1967.

Taylor, Phillip B. "The Electoral System in Uruguay," *Journal of Politics,* Vol. 17, No. 1 (February, 1955), pp. 19–42.

Williams, Edward J. *Latin American Christian Democratic Parties.* Knoxville: University of Tennessee Press, 1967.

Ydígoras Fuentes, Miguel (with Mario Rosenthal). *My War with Communism.* Englewood Cliffs, N.J.: Prentice-Hall, Inc., 1963.

PART V

Structure and Operation
of Government in a
Developing Society

13

CONSTITUTIONS, FEDERALISM, AND PRIVATE RIGHTS:
In Theory and in Practice

CONSTITUTIONS

General Characteristics

Many of the constitutions are quite youthful as constitutions go. In fact, seven of them, one third of the total number, were adopted during the years 1960–69 and are still wet behind the ears. These most recent ones are Bolivia's and Venezuela's, 1961; El Salvador's, 1962; the Dominican Republic's, 1963; Haiti's, 1964, and Brazil's, Ecuador's, and Guatemala's in 1967.

A few of the constitutions are notable for their longevity, especially the following: Mexico, 1857–1917, or 60 years; Costa Rica, 1871–1940, 69 years; Colombia, 1886 to the date of writing, 83 years; Uruguay, 1830–1919, 89 years; and Chile, 1833–1925, 92 years. The top honor for longevity goes to Argentina's 1853 constitution, which was 96 years old when it was abrogated by Perón in 1949 (it was reinstated in 1957).

The life expectancy of a constitution is very short in Latin America. The mortality rate is high during constitutional infancy, and even higher during adolescence. Only a small percentage of them live to a ripe old age. Among the many cases of short-lived constitutions are the two that Colombia had in a single year, 1811, and the two that Bolivia had in 1839. The Dominican Republic set a record for the region that will probably stand for quite a while. In the eight-year period 1874–81, the nation had seven new constitutions—one for each year of the period except 1876.

Not a single one of the 20 republics has the constitution that was originally adopted after independence was won.

Compared with the Constitution of the United States, which fills nine pages or so plus another half-dozen pages of amendments, the constitutions of Latin America are quite lengthy. There are several reasons for this. Sometimes, they go into excessive detail to spell out minutely the functions of government, the organization of governmental departments, and the powers the several branches of government will exercise. Thus, in the Mexican constitution, adopted in 1917 and about 60 pages long, the Congress is authorized to levy taxes on, among other things, matches and *aguamiel,* the unfermented juice of the maguey plant—which ferments quickly in the warm climate.

Another reason for the length of the constitutions is the inclusion of many provisions that are strictly temporary. Sometimes, a new constitution will specify by name who the new president is to be and the conditions under which he will hold office. The constitution of Colombia in particular has many such transitory provisions, all hopefully designed to promote respect for constitutional government and end civil strife.

Still another reason for the length of Latin American constitutions is their inclusion of many new functions and responsibilities vested in the government. Mexico's 1917 constitution, embodying the concepts and goals of its social revolution, set a pattern for many later constitutions in Latin America. Thereafter, the organic laws were to contain articles and even whole chapters that embodied a new philosophy of government and new governmental responsibilities. Under these new constitutions, the government was to concern itself with such matters as ownership of lands and waters within the national boundaries and the government's right to expropriate them, the permissible role and activities of religious institutions, distribution of land to the landless, education and culture, labor and social security, and public health and social assistance.

Also among the distinctive characteristics of Latin American constitutions are the many discrepancies between how government is described in the constitution and how it actually functions. Some such inconsistencies exist in every nation, but in Latin American nations they are quite pronounced. There, constitutions all declare that the people are sovereign, but dictators exercise control much of the time. Constitutions lay down the principle of separation of powers and checks and balances, but in most nations the executive dominates the government. They enumerate private rights in great detail, but genuine civil liberty is the exception.

Since the written constitutions are so different from the actual operation of government, one may well wonder why the nations bother to have a constitution. For one thing, in the more advanced nations the constitutions do prescribe the organization, structure, and powers of government and pretty well chart the course that it will follow. And in the nations generally, constitutions usually contain the programs government will follow and the goals it will strive for. Thus, Brasilia, Brazil's brave new capital imaginatively located well inward so as to develop the large interior, was more than a campaign slogan or promise of President Juscelino Kubitschek. The visionary goal of moving the capital inward— as radical a step as moving the American capital from Washington to Chicago—was written indelibly into the constitution of 1946, which largely accounted for the realization of Kubitschek's dream.

Even in those countries often dominated by dictators, constitutions have a purpose. They serve to legitimize the existing regime and to give it at least a façade of respectability in the eyes of the populace.

Lastly, constitutions express the ideals the society—at least certain influential articulate members of it—aspires to.[1] The aspirations, however, have often led nowhere. "In brief hours of ecstasy," wrote J. Fred Rippy, referring to the earlier days of the republics, "fledgling political philosophers had written into virgin constitutions all the idealism of their time, but it was as if they had attached wings to lead. The constitutions served as a mighty stimulus to individualism, but they were without power to impose restraints."[2]

Formulation and Adoption

In formulating and adopting their constitutions, the Latin American republics have utilized three main instrumentalities: the constitutional convention, whose members were elected specifically to draft new constitutions; the congress, either reconvening in extraordinary session or with its members elected after the president announced the purpose of drafting a new organic law; and the president, acting solely on his own responsibility.

Constitutional conventions can claim the credit for having drawn up many of the present constitutions. The 1917 constitution of Mexico, under which the nation is governed today, was drawn up by a constituent convention, which met in Querétaro in December, 1916, and completed its gigantic task in two months. Brazil's constitution of 1946, the most

---

[1] ". . . although the spirit of the written constitutions may be violated, the very fact that it is preserved in a written document is indeed a 'homage paid by vice to virtue,' proof of the vitality of the ideals of the people." Vincente Herrero, *La organización constitucional de Iberoamérica* (México, 1944), p. 15.

However, unless the discrepancy between the real and paper constitutions is adjusted in realistic fashion, unrest and even active resistance will result in reform or abolition of the constitution. Aurelio García, *Ciencia del estado* (Quito, Ecuador: Imprenta de la Universidad Central, 1947), pp. 259–60.

[2] J. Fred Rippy, "Dictatorships in Spanish America," *Dictatorship in the Modern World*, ed. Guy Stanton Ford (Minneapolis: University of Minnesota Press, 1935), pp. 55–56.

democratic in the nation's history, was also drawn up by a popularly elected constitutional convention. Such a specially elected body also drew up El Salvador's constitution of 1962 and the Dominican Republic's constitution of 1963. The Dominican Republic, for some years in the doghouse after three decades of tyrannical government under *caudillo* Rafael Leonidas Trujillo, made a special bid to adopt a constitution recognized as legal and aboveboard. Justice William O. Douglas of the United States Supreme Court, long a friend of President Bosch, was invited to advise the constituent assembly, which he did.

While the constitutional convention is generally considered to be the most democratic means of formulating and adopting a new constitution, it is by no means immune to political shenanigans. The selection of delegates to Mexico's constituent convention of 1916 was tainted by fraud; only constitutionalists (those who followed President Carranza) were eligible to be elected, which automatically excluded representatives of many opposition groups.[3] The constituent convention of El Salvador, which drew up its 1962 constitution, is vulnerable for the same reason. Politically, it was a monolithic body, since all of its 54 delegates were members of the Party of National Conciliation—the party backed by the civil-military directorate.

But however desirable it may be to observe legality and fair play in the selection and functioning of the constituent assembly, they afford no assurance of success. Indeed, they may completely stymie the convention and prove to be its undoing. Thus in Argentina Provisional President Aramburu, who headed the caretaker government that liquidated the Perón regime, was so anxious to enforce fair play in the 1957 Constituent Assembly that its efforts came to naught. In the elections of members, held on July 28, 1957, which Aramburu decreed should be held under proportional representation, no less than 16 parties were represented in the assembly of 205 members. Although a majority of the members favored reforming the 1949 Peronista constitution, they could not agree on the exact reforms to be made, split as they were into 16 parties. Such a hopeless deadlock immediately developed that shortly after the convention met, President Aramburu remarked that the nation was in a state of "paralysis."[4]

New constitutions are sometimes drafted by the congress, which ordinarily meets for the purpose in special session. Sometimes, to enable congressional membership to more closely reflect public opinion on the proposed new fundamental law, a new election will be held. Bolivia's 1961 constitution was formulated by a special session of congress, with the

---

[3] For the problems and work of the body see Ward M. Morton, "The Mexican Constitutional Congress of 1916-1917," *Southwestern Social Science Quarterly*, Vol. 33, No. 1 (June, 1952), pp. 7–27.

[4] *New York Times*, July 31, 1957, p. 9, col. 1, and September 1, 1957, p. 4, col. 5.

vice president presiding. The extraordinary session accomplished its mission, although under considerable difficulties. There was no quorum on the opening day; many senators and deputies were loath to attend because a state of siege was still in force. Members of the leading opposition parties either boycotted the special session or walked out in protest when they could not be heard. Despite these complications, a new constitution was drawn up, adopted, and printed not only in Spanish but also in three Indian languages—Quechua, Aymara, and Guaraní.[5]

Brazil's new controversial constitution was approved by the congress 25 minutes after midnight in the early morning of January 22, 1967. President Humberto Castelo Branco was given power under the original bill to promulgate both the constitution and an equally controversial new press law if they were not passed by midnight. In order to technically beat the deadline, President of the Congress Senator Auro Mozra Andrade stopped all the clocks in the chamber at 10 minutes to midnight.[6]

A third means of drawing up and promulgating new constitutions is by executive action alone. This method was frequently used during the first century of independence but is seldom used today. Smacking of dictatorship and absolutism, this direct method is offensive to the democratically inclined nations in Latin America, as elsewhere. A president may wield a big stick, getting almost exactly the sort of document he wants from a subservient congress or constituent assembly, but at least he is careful to observe the prescribed formalities. One of the few instances in recent times of a constitution drafted and put into effect solely by executive action without even a pretense of congressional or constituent assembly participation was the Brazilian constitution of 1937, promulgated by a decree of dictator-president Getulio Vargas.[7]

The Many Constitutions Most Nations Have Had

Latin Americans are undoubtedly the most experienced constitution makers in the world. For a century and a half, they have had a field day in discarding old constitutions and writing new ones. All together, the 20 republics have adopted a total of approximately 200 constitutions, an average of 10 apiece, as Table 13–1 shows. Panama with three and Cuba, Paraguay, and Uruguay with four have the best record for writing an organic law and being willing to live with it, for richer or for poorer, in

---

[5] *Hispanic American Report*, Vol. XIV, No. 7 (September, 1961), pp. 633–34.
[6] *New York Times*, January 22, 1967, p. 20, cols. 3–4.
[7] In a nationwide broadcast, Vargas explained to the nation that he, with the backing of the armed forces, was putting the constitution into effect as an emergency measure to bring an end to disorder and grave threats to the nation's very existence. John W. F. Dulles, *Vargas of Brazil: A Political Biography* (Austin: University of Texas Press, 1967), pp. 171–77.

TABLE 13-1

LATIN AMERICAN CONSTITUTIONS

Country	Number	Dates of Constitutions
Argentina	5	1811, 1819, 1826, 1853, 1949 (1957, back to 1853)
Bolivia	17	1825, 1831, 1834, 1839 (two), 1843, 1851, 1861, 1868, 1871, 1878, 1880, 1931, 1938, 1945, 1947, 1961
Brazil	5	1824, 1891, 1934, 1937, 1946, 1967
Chile	9	1811, 1812, 1814, 1818, 1822, 1823, 1826, 1833, 1925
Colombia	6	1821, 1843, 1853, 1858, 1863, 1886
Costa Rica	7	1825, 1844, 1847, 1859, 1869, 1871, 1917, 1949
Cuba	4	1901, 1934, 1935, 1940
Dominican Republic	21	1844, 1854, 1865, 1868, 1872, 1874, 1875, 1877, 1878, 1879, 1880, 1881, 1887, 1896, 1908, 1924, 1927, 1934, 1942, 1947, 1963
Ecuador	16	1820, 1825, 1843, 1845, 1851, 1852, 1861, 1869, 1878, 1884, 1897, 1906, 1929, 1938, 1945, 1946, 1967
El Salvador	12	1824, 1841, 1864, 1871, 1872, 1880, 1883, 1886, 1939, 1945 (back to the 1886, 1950, 1962)
Guatemala	6	1839, 1851, 1879, 1945, 1954, 1956, 1967
Haiti	13	1801, 1805, 1806, 1843, 1849, 1867, 1879, 1889, 1918, 1935, 1946, 1957, 1964
Honduras	11	1825, 1839, 1848, 1865, 1873, 1880, 1894, 1904 (restored 1894), 1924, 1936, 1957
Mexico	6	1824, 1835, 1837, 1843, 1857, 1917
Nicaragua	7	1826, 1838, 1858, 1893, 1905, 1911, 1939, 1950
Panama	3	1904, 1941, 1946
Paraguay	4	1813, 1844, 1870, 1940
Peru	17	1823, 1826, 1827, 1828, 1834, 1836 (two), 1839, 1855, 1856, 1860, 1867, 1868, 1879, 1880, 1920, 1933
Uruguay	4	1830, 1918, 1934, 1951
Venezuela	22	1830, 1857, 1858, 1864, 1874, 1881, 1891, 1893, 1901, 1904, 1909, 1914 (two), 1922, 1925, 1928, 1929, 1931, 1936, 1947, 1953, 1961

SOURCE: Russell H. Fitzgibbon (ed.), *The Constitutions of the Americas* (Chicago: University of Chicago Press, 1948); and *Statesman's Yearbook: Statistical and Historical Annual of the States of the World* (ed. S. H. Steinberg) (New York: Macmillan Co.).

sickness or in health. But most other nations have taken their constitutional vows more lightly. Nine of them have had from five to ten constitutions. Seven of them have had eleven or more. These include: Honduras with 11 constitutions; El Salvador, 12; Bolivia, Ecuador, and Peru, 17; and the Dominican Republic, 21. The brass ring goes to Venezuela, which heads the list with 22 constitutions; the nation has changed constitutions almost as frequently as it has changed presidents.

Constitutions have sometimes been changed so frequently and in such circumstances that there is a difference of opinion as to just how many constitutions a nation has actually had. For puzzling questions arise that cannot be categorically answered. Was a "new" constitution really a new one or merely the old one altered by a few amendments? Most new constitutions contain relatively little that is really new. Thus, El Salvador's constitution promulgated in January, 1962, represented a bare minimum of retouching, such as shortening the president's term from six years to five and moving the date of his inauguration from September 15 to July 1.

And what about a constitution drawn up and promulgated but never actually put into effect? Honduras has had three such documents—those of 1831, 1898, and 1921. Should they be counted as constitutions too?

Brazil had more than its share of constitutional confusion during the 15-year regime of Getulio Vargas. The constitution of 1937, which he formulated on his own responsibility and promulgated by executive decree, was despite its visionary goals and lofty phraseology a "ghost constitution . . . devoid of living reality." It never really went into effect. Indeed, the nation was never quite sure whether it was living under the 1937 Constitution or the 1934 Constitution, or whether it was experiencing the phenomenon of being governed simultaneously by two constitutions.[8]

The large number of organic laws that most of the republics have had can be attributed to several causes. In the politically unstable society where revolution before breakfast is almost as popular as bullfighting, a new constitution serves to legitimize the political *naturale* and to emphasize to the nation and the rest of the world that the republic is under new management. Moreover, the foreign practices and institutions so lavishly borrowed by the constitution makers were political quicksand on which to build sound constitutional structures; often unworkable, they have been a ready justification for scrapping old constitutions and writing new ones. The idealistic Latin American constitution makers would have done well to follow the advice of Juan Bautista Alberdi, father of the Argentina Constitution of 1853. A nation's constitution, he strongly believed, should be based on and reflect its history, its customs and habits, and its ideas and values.

Foreign Influences[9]

One of the main sources that the independent young Spanish republics relied upon in formulating their earlier constitutions was the Spanish constitution of 1812. Formulated by idealists who were intoxicated by French republicanism, the document was quite radical for its time. Under its

---

[8] Karl Lowenstein, *Brazil Under Vargas* (New York: Macmillan Co., 1942), pp. 46–49.

[9] In Colombia, these influences had the harmful effect of interrupting historical continuity. Luis Carlos Sáchica, *Constitucionalismo Colombiano: Historia, Teoría y Realidad del Sistema* (Bogotá, Colombia: Universidad de la Gran Colombia, 1962), pp. 23–25.

provisions, the king was to be a mere figurehead, subordinate to the congress; many class privileges were to be abolished; and many private rights were to be guaranteed to citizens. The document with its various radical provisions had a considerable impact on the early constitutions of Latin America.

France was another country from which Latin American constitutionalism borrowed heavily. "The finely developed logic of early French constitutions and the artistic symmetry of their political institutions," says Russell Fitzgibbon, "had a strong effect as the Latin Americans essayed their first steps in these directions."[10] Thus the new Latin American constitutions reflected not only the egalitarian and republican idealism of France but also many of its governmental institutions and practices. These include: the council of state; the system of ministries, especially the ministry of *gobernación;* the requirement of ministerial signatures for authenticating acts of presidents; parliamentary interpellation; decree legislation; separate courts of administrative litigation; municipal administration; police organization; proportional representation; and structure of codes of law.

The political experience of the United States was also another source that the constitution makers of Latin America found quite helpful, particularly in the early days of independence. It was natural that the young nations would look to their northern neighbor for help and guidance. For it, too, had had a long colonial history, and the successful operation of its government during the preceding four decades of independence had given it considerable prestige. Among the Latin American constitutions most influenced by the political experience of the United States were Venezuela's constitution of 1811, Mexico's of 1824, Argentina's of 1853, and Brazil's of 1891.

The influence exerted by the United States has been most profound in Argentina, Brazil, Mexico, and Venezuela, all of whom adopted a federal system of government patterned largely after that of the United States.[11]

---

[10] Russell H. Fitzgibbon (ed.), *The Constitutions of the Americas* (Chicago: University of Chicago Press, 1948), p. 6.

[11] There is considerable difference of opinion, however, about how much influence was actually exerted. At one extreme, Nicolás A. Calvo held that the Argentine constitution was copied from the United States Constitution; its only defects were in those respects in which it was different. Nicolás A. Calvo, *John Story, Comentario sobre la Constitución Federal de los Estados Unidos* (1888).

At the other extreme, Alberdi maintained that despite superficial similarities, the two documents were entirely different; even to compare them was to "misrepresent and bastardize" the Argentine constitution. Juan Bautista Alberdi, *Bases y Comentarios a la Constitución Argentina* (Buenos Aires, 1929), pp. 335 and 346.

Yet, a comparison of the two documents shows that 44 sections are practically identical, 22 similar, and 41 different, with 60 sections of the Argentine constitution not found in the American. Segundo V. Linares Quintana, "Comparison of the Constitutional Bases of the United States and Argentine Political Systems," *University of Pennsylvania Law Review,* Vol. 97, No. 5 (April, 1949).

A detailed comparison of the two documents is given in Viamonte, *Manual de Derecho Constitucional* (1944), pp. 355–80.

Thus, the principles of tripartite division of government, separation of powers, and checks and balances were woven into the constitutional fabric of these federal republics. The influence of the United States is further shown in the organization of the congress, the extensive list of private rights, and provisions for the admission of new states.

For the last five decades, Mexico has had the most influence on new constitutions adopted in the other Latin American republics. Its landmark constitution of 1917 embodied the new goals and values of a revolutionary society. Article 27 advanced a new concept of private property; it is regarded by the society as having a social function, and rights of private ownership are subordinate to social welfare. Article 123 of the constitution was likewise quite radical. Often referred to as Latin American labor's Magna Charta, its constitutional guarantees afforded Mexican labor a degree of protection and multiplicity of benefits that were far in advance of similar provisions in most other countries, including the United States. Of much significance, too, the 1917 constitution was thoroughly Mexican, expressing the strong nationalism and aspiration welling up within the republic. Influenced by Mexico's bold step, other Latin American nations adopting new constitutions have included in them the new concepts of human rights and their precedence over property rights. Adapting these concepts to their own situations, the nations are at last following Alberdi's advice by having their constitutions more nearly reflect their own history and practices, customs and habits, and ideas and values.

Amendment

Three usual methods for amending are prescribed in the constitutions. The one most often specified is by action of the congress alone, with certain variations from the usual requirements for enacting a law. Bolivia, which is one of the nations that follows this method of amendment, requires a two-thirds vote of all members of congress who are present. Ecuador specifies that the change must be approved by an absolute majority of the total membership.

A second method of amendment involves proposal by the congress, usually with a two-thirds vote, and ratification by a constitutional convention held later. This is the method of amendment followed by Argentina.

In a third method, used in Mexico and Venezuela, the states, too, play a role in the amending process—a distinctive feature of their federal form of government. In Mexico, a proposed amendment must be approved first by the congress, specifically two thirds of the members present, then subsequently approved by a majority of the legislatures of the states. In Venezuela, an amendment can be proposed by the legislatures of two thirds of the states, then adopted by the congress.

The frequency of amendment varies widely among the 20 nations. Mexico has adopted well over 100 amendments, many of which were found necessary to modify or repeal details included in the organic law. Quite different from Mexico's experience, Argentina's 1853 constitution was amended only twice in the whole 96 years of its existence prior to 1949, even though the process of amendment was easier than in the United States. Austin F. Macdonald concludes:

This difference may be due in part to the fact that Argentine constitutional provisions have always been regarded as somewhat elastic. The president acts in accordance with his own interpretation of the fundamental law, or even in more or less defiance of it. Members of congress and publicists deplore this deviation from the constitutional ideal, but virtually nothing is done to correct the situation.[12]

In frequency of amendment to constitutions, Honduras enjoys a unique distinction. The nation to date has had 11 constitutions, including the one of 1957 now in effect. Although each of these documents included a method of amending, not a single amendment has ever been adopted.

FEDERALISM

Background

A very controversial issue that has often convulsed the nations of Latin America is whether or not to adopt a federal form of government. The unitary type of governmental organization was quite familiar to them; they had lived under it for more than three centuries of colonial rule. Under this form of government, the central authority located in the national capital exercises full and complete power over the whole nation. There is no such thing as state or provincial and local autonomy—states' rights as we would think of it. From its vantage point in the capital city, the central government completely dominates the country, making all the laws, local as well as national, and directly or indirectly appointing all officials.

After independence, there was strong sentiment in most of the new nations to discard the old system of highly centralized supervision and control. In its place, a federal system of government would be adopted under which states or provinces would exercise a wide measure of self-government, with their powers and functions guaranteed by the constitution itself.

---

[12] Austin F. Macdonald, *Government of the Argentine Republic* (New York: Thomas Y. Crowell Co., 1942), p. 144.

Federalism and decentralization of governmental authority had a tremendous appeal in the young republics. It apparently was working very successfully in the United States, which only several decades before had thrown off colonial rule. Impressed as they were by this experience, many Latin Americans were convinced that federalism was a political shortcut that could advance their nations by one simple step from medieval to modern government.

Arguments For and Against

For most of the first century of independence, the issue of whether to adopt federalism or retain a unitary form of government was a lively one. Whenever federalists and *unitarios* got together, whether in a constitutional convention, session of congress, or bull session, the issue of federalism sooner or later was bound to come up—usually sooner. When it did, the fur would fly; rational discussion would shortly give way to invective and often end in physical violence.

Very cogent arguments were advanced by proponents of each of the two systems of government. In Ecuador, for example, authorities on the internal organization of their republic offer five main reasons why the unitary system is better suited to the nation's needs. This system, they claim, ensures administrative uniformity throughout the country, strengthens the national government in combating regionalism, makes for a more efficient administration, ensures the administration of laws with greater equality and justice, and facilitates the maintenance of order throughout the country.[13]

The partisans of decentralized control were just as convinced that federalism was the political prescription for democratic, efficient government. According to them, it stimulates grass-roots initiative, makes local and provincial government viable and meaningful, recognizes local differences and their contribution to the nation, and encourages a society of free men rather than of robots controlled from the capital.

Convulsed by the acrimonious controversy over federalism, the largest republics tried one system and then the other, depending on which faction was in control of the government. Chile briefly adopted federalism in its constitution of 1826, dividing the nation into eight provinces and assigning to each a large measure of autonomy. But after just two years' trial, this incursion into federalism was quickly dropped. Colombia

---

[13] George I. Blanksten, *Ecuador: Constitutions and Caudillos* (Berkeley: University of California Press, 1951), pp. 144–46.

In Peru, the reality of geography in the opinion of some made unitary government a necessity. "Without a centralized system of government," says José Pareja Paz-Soldan, "Perú would not be Perú." *Derecho Constitucional Peruano* (tercera edición; Lima, Perú: Ediciones del Sol, 1963), pp. 381–82.

was another of the larger nations that unsuccessfully experimented with federalism. After a federal plan of government was inaugurated under its constitution of 1853, Colombia became less a nation and more a federation of semi-independent states, beset by numerous bloody uprisings and several years of full-scale civil war. The principle of federalism was discarded in the 1886 constitution, and Colombia once more became a unitary nation with a strong central government.

Federalism has sometimes been a bitter issue in the smaller states, too. In Honduras, a battle to the death took place between federalists and *unitarios;* the federalists finally won out. Accordingly, the constitution of 1824 provided for a federal system. After a few years of trial, however, the nation reverted to the unitary system in its constitution of 1831. William Stokes says:

A federal union modeled on the American principle of delegated or enumerated powers for the federal government and reserved or inherent powers for the states was unrealistic. Actually, the new states had never enjoyed any inherent powers. As colonies they were part of a unitary system of government in which their functions were outlined and controlled by the central government. They were therefore not prepared by their experience to make this kind of federalism work.[14]

Federalism in Operation

In the states that have the federal system of government today, the principles governing the distribution of power are far from uniform. Argentina follows the same principle as the United States; the national government possesses only those powers delegated to it expressly or by implication, and all other powers are reserved to the provinces. The reservation, at least in theory, of large residual powers to the provinces was the logical result of their having been independent entities before the formation of the federal government, just as were the colonies in the United States.

Brazil follows a similar principle of distribution of power, though stated negatively. According to Article 18 of the 1967 constitution, "All powers which, implicitly or explicitly, are not forbidden to them by this Constitution are reserved to the States."

But regardless of the principle of distribution followed, the power of the national government has usually far overshadowed that of the states or provinces. In Brazil, the national government possesses not only those powers that ours does but also many more. For example, it is authorized to legislate in such broad fields as production and consumption, which, in effect, makes federal regulation apply to almost all economic activities.

---

[14] William S. Stokes, *Honduras: An Area Study in Government* (Madison: University of Wisconsin Press, 1950), p. 66.

Moreover, the congress under its constitutional power has enacted codes of criminal, civil, and commercial law. As a result of this sweeping legislative power, almost every criminal act in the nation is a federal offense, and every dispute arising from the terms of a contract or will is covered by some federal statute.

With the national government exercising such far-reaching powers, federalism as it operates in the four nations is generally regarded as a sham. Speaking of Mexico's federalism, Emilio Portes Gil, former president of the nation, has bluntly called it "a great lie."[15]

A major reason for the federal system's functioning so ineffectually is the preeminent taxing power enjoyed by the national government. In raising revenue, it utilizes customs duties, taxes on incomes, production and consumption, business transactions, and documents. While it is required by the constitution to share a part of these revenues with the states, apportioning the money on the basis of population, area, and other factors, it nevertheless spends most of the money; as a result, the state and local governments are greatly handicapped by not having sufficient revenue for their needs.

In Mexico, as Table 13–2 shows, the federal government spends about 71 percent of the public revenue collected, the state governments 26 percent, and the local 2 to 3 percent.[16]

TABLE 13–2

INCOME IN MEXICO: FEDERAL, STATE, AND LOCAL SHARES
IN SELECTED YEARS, 1900–1960

Year	Total*	Percent	Federal	State	Local
1900	63	100.0	63.0	24.1	12.9
1923	84	100.0	72.6	14.5	12.9
1929	101	100.0	71.1	21.2	7.7
1932	86	100.0	64.0	27.1	8.9
1940	122	100.0	71.4	23.3	5.3
1950	180	100.0	78.3	18.4	3.3
1960	369	100.0	71.1	26.3	2.6

° In pesos per capita of 1950.
SOURCE: México, Dirección General de Estadística, *Anuario Estadístico* (cited as *Anuario Estadístico*) *1906,* 222–24; *1923–1924,* II, 285; *1926,* 285; *1940,* 741, 745, 747–48; *1942,* 1245; *1954,* 695, 697–98; *1960–61,* 585, 587, 592.
In James W. Wilkie, *The Mexican Revolution: Federal Expenditure and Social Changes Since 1910* (Berkeley: University of California Press, 1967), p. 147.

---

[15] August O. Spain, on the other hand, strongly challenges this point of view. Citing many instances of assertion of state power, state nullification of national authority, and successful state resistance to intervention, he maintains that federalism in Mexico, far from being a myth or sham, may well be the nation's peculiar brand of federalism, stemming from its peculiar background. August O. Spain, "Mexican Federalism Revisited," *Western Political Quarterly,* Vol. 9, No. 3 (September, 1956), pp. 620–32.

[16] Some *municipios* may have to run on a budget as low as $40 a year, says L. Vincent Padgett; as a result, municipal services suffer. L. Vincent Padgett, *The Mexican Political System* (Boston: Houghton Mifflin Co., 1966), p. 151.

Still another reason for the federal systems' not functioning effectively in Latin America is intervention in the states or provinces by the national government. In each of the four federal republics, the president has frequently intervened, with or without congressional approval, to displace state or provincial authorities and take over their powers.[17] Sometimes, he is requested to intervene by the state or province, usually when the governor and the legislature are feuding with each other, or when the election for governor is contested by one or several candidates.

In Mexico, the question of the legality of a state government frequently comes before the federal government because two and sometimes three governors, each with his own legislature, claim to have been elected by a huge majority. The several competing groups establish themselves as near the state capitol as possible, organize a government, and bombard the president, secretary of the interior, and senate with telegrams, each seeking to be recognized as the legal government of the state. The Permanent Committee of the Senate, probably strongly influenced by the president, makes the decision as to which governor and legislature were elected. If the national government did not resolve the issue, there would be civil war in the state.[18]

Of the four republics that have a federal system, only in Brazil have the regional units been able to take courses of action independently of the national government.[19] Indeed, prior to 1930, the states enjoyed most of the privileges of self-government, even raising part of their revenues from levies on interstate commerce. The wealthy, progressive, industrialized state of São Paulo twice during the present century revolted against the central government, protesting that it bore a disproportionate share of the nation's expenses and would be better off as an independent nation. São Paulo had a large and well-equipped army that was much more than a mere militia. Moreover, the state maintained quasi-diplomatic relations with foreign countries, sending its agents abroad to negotiate with foreign governments on questions pertaining to immigration and the all-important coffee trade. When the state flag was displayed in the public schools, it was often above the emblem of the nation.[20]

---

[17] See Chapter 14.

[18] Tannenbaum, *op. cit.,* p. 87.

[19] This is not true in time of dictatorship, of course. "What has become of the United States of Brazil?" asked Karl Lowenstein, referring to the Vargas administration. "The state's rights have become completely obliterated by the steamroller of the centralizing dictatorship," he concluded. "Practically no field of legislative action is left in which the state can act without approval of the president of the republic." Lowenstein, *op. cit.,* p. 70.

This is not true, either, of the *municipios,* the primary unit of local government, according to L. Donald Carr, who concludes that local self-government in Brazil has not really developed to any appreciable degree. (Donald L. Carr, "Brazilian Local Self-Government: Myth or Reality?" *Western Political Quarterly*, Vol. 13, No. 4 (December, 1960), pp. 1043–55.

[20] William Lytle Schurz, *Latin America* (rev. ed.; New York: E. P. Dutton & Co., Inc., 1949), p. 110.

Until the military take-over in 1964, the Brazilian states sometimes followed such an independent course of action as to seriously embarrass the national government. Just such an action was the expropriation of the United States–owned telephone system by Governor Leonel Brizola, head of the state of Rio Grande do Sul. The expropriation was very disconcerting to the national government—the United States government, too, since the Congress was in the process of passing the foreign aid bill, a perennial bone of contention, and Brazil was the principal Latin American beneficiary. Governor Brizola's action was as embarrassing to the Brazilian government as was the 1906 rule of the San Francisco school board to our own national government. That measure segregated all Japanese, Chinese, and Korean children into a separate oriental school and created such an international furor that President Theodore Roosevelt himself stepped in and got the board to rescind its action.

In the Brazilian action, the constitution of Rio Grande do Sul permits expropriation "in the public interest," with "prior and adequate compensation in money," and without the approval of the national government. Indeed, the foreign office promptly advised Washington that the expropriation was not carried out with the approval of the national government and did not reflect its policy toward foreign investments in the nation. Moreover, the government would use its good offices to obtain fair payment for the American property that had been taken over.

The Brazilian press praised the reaction of President Kennedy, who forthrightly served notice to Congress that nothing could be more unwise than congressional action to halt aid to Brazil because of the expropriation. Said *O Jornal*, one of the leading newspapers of the nation: "The imposing of a sanction on the Brazilian people for what Governor Brizola did would be the same thing as condemning all the American nation as racist because of Governor Faubus."[21]

PRIVATE RIGHTS

Respect for Rights Generally

In every one of the 20 republics, the constitution contains an imposing list of private rights—usually a half-dozen or more pages of them. When read, they sound as appealing as the nations' travel ads and literature, shrewdly designed to lure tourists with their dollars, pounds, or other currency. The rights set forth in the constitutions are genuinely respected in some of the countries, as much so as in Britain or the United States. But in some of the others that have never really known democ-

---

[21] *New York Times*, February 18, 1962, p. 1, col. 4, and March 10, 1962, p. 8, col. 3.

racy, the rights are more shadow than substance—paper rights in a paper constitution.

The enjoyment of private rights as set forth in the constitutions may be vitiated in a number of ways. The 1946 constitution of Ecuador contains an impressive list of rights, almost as long, in fact, as the whole Constitution of the United States. But the many guarantees are hedged with numerous qualifications and restrictions, the most common of which is the phrase, "with such exceptions as the law may indicate."

Besides such constitutional loopholes, private rights are often severely limited by the imposition of a state of siege, which all Latin American nations are quite familiar with—both the more democratic ones sometimes imposed as emergency measures, and the many others that are practically a way of life. Wherever imposed, the state of siege very adversely affects the enjoyment of private rights. Sometimes, the emergency as proclaimed is of a limited nature, and only a few of the citizens' rights will be affected, such as the right to move freely around the country or to join in any large assembly, whether to participate in a political rally or see the matador jab the bull. The Latin American Marquis of Queensbury rules may even be politely enforced. These rules specify, among other things, that political opponents arrested during the emergency may not be transferred from one part of the country to the other—for instance, from the coast to the sierra or vice versa—and that a political opponent if arrested cannot be thrown into an ordinary prison but must be detained under house surveillance or allowed to go into exile.

But more often, a state of siege ignores such gentlemanly amenities and plays havoc with a bill of rights, suspending virtually all its long list of meticulously drafted guarantees. Citizens are arrested by the secret police in the dead of the night and thrown into prison to languish for weeks, months, maybe even years, in flagrant disregard of constitutional provisions relating to rights of persons accused of crimes.

Among the main private rights usually spelled out in much detail in the constitutions are the following: freedom of speech and the press; freedom of religion; rights of persons accused of a crime; social and economic guarantees; and political asylum.

Freedom of Speech and the Press

Freedom of speech and the press exists in all the nations, at least according to their constitutions. In some of the nations, this freedom is quite genuine and is comparable to that of the Western democracies. "The communication of thought by word, written privately, or published in the press, or by any other method, without necessity of previous censorship, is entirely free," states Article 28 of the constitution of

Uruguay; "authors and, as the case may be, printers or distributors, remain liable, according to law, for abuses that may be committed." Under Uruguay's living constitution, freedom of speech exists as much in reality as on paper.

In most of the nations, however, various restrictions are imposed on the press, many common to other nations but some peculiar to Latin America. For instance, there has been a strong effort to free the national press from undue outside influence, thereby better enabling it to reflect national values and aspirations and to be responsible only to the nation. Thus, according to Article 42 of Colombia's constitution, no newspaper can receive a grant from a foreign government or corporation except with the permission of the Colombian government.

Chile also has acted to make its press independent of direct foreign influence. Under the Press Control Law, passed in January, 1964, the owners of all newspapers, magazines, and periodicals, as well as the concessionaires of all radio and TV stations, are required to be citizens of Chile. The managers of such operations must also be Chileans, and Chilean capital must constitute 85 percent or more of the economic backing.[22] Restrictions on freedom of the press are usually imposed either by presidential decree or legislative enactment, supposedly under authority of the constitution.

The main threat to the press stems from the president himself. When it comes to taking criticism, he is notably thin-skinned. He can dish it out vehemently and profusely to his political opponents and others, but he does not stand up very well under public scrutiny, especially the critical scrutiny of a free press. As former President Truman would aptly put it, he cannot stand the heat in the kitchen. R. A. Gómez says:

> In keeping with the cultural emphasis on personal dignity and pride, Latin American presidents are ordinarily exceedingly sensitive to personal affronts that would be considered "part of the game" elsewhere. And, in many cases, the personal affront may be nothing more than just opposition. Thus, there is likely to be legislation to protect the president from "disrespect" (*desacato*). . . . A hard-hitting article in a newspaper or magazine, a speech delivered during a political rally, even actors providing entertainment can sometimes be punished for offending the dignity of the president. Opposition leaders may be jailed for alleged "disrespect" and find themselves still incarcerated at election time.[23]

With *desacato* interpreted so broadly, it is not smart to blame the president directly for anything but to aim all complaints at his subordinates, pointing out that they failed to advise him properly. For the president has many potent weapons with which he can beat the press to its

---

[22] *Hispanic American Report*, Vol. XVII, No. 1 (March, 1964), pp. 69–70.

[23] R. A. Gómez, *Government and Politics in Latin America* (rev. ed.; New York: Random House, Inc., 1964), pp. 79–80.

knees if he so desires. Newspapers that oppose him too strongly may suddenly find themselves beset by labor problems—government-inspired, of course—or suddenly short on newsprint which is allocated by the government. Sometimes, the president does not deign to use these indirect methods; preferring to flaunt his authority and teach the press a lesson, he has the editor thrown into jail and the newspaper padlocked.

Journalists, whose stock in trade is freedom of speech and expression, have many causes for complaint, more in some nations than in others. Two of the worst recent abuses did not occur in the insular republics or those of Central America in the warm climate with its low human boiling point. Quite to the contrary, the much criticized restrictions on the press were those imposed by two of the most progressive nations of the region, Chile and Mexico.

Chile's very controversial Press Control Law of 1964, passed with strong government backing, was designed to correct, according to the administration, "abuses of publicity." Significantly though, all the nation's major press associations and schools of journalism strenuously opposed the law, alleging among other things that it was merely an attempted cover-up of the scandals of the Alessandri regime. Opposition parties termed the law the *"Ley Mordaza"* (muzzle law). The very first infraction of the law that the Ministry of the Interior seized on to prosecute went far toward proving the contention of its opponents. The ministry seized a world encyclopedia published in Buenos Aires because the part of Antarctica claimed by Chile appeared as Argentine territory.[24]

But the impact of Chile's Press Control Law was mild compared with that of Mexico's far more controversial Law of Social Dissolution. The Mexican law applies to those persons who obstruct "the path of the legitimate aims of the government." The definitions of crimes under the law are vague and ambiguous; anyone accused of them is virtually at the mercy of the prosecution. Cracking down under the law, the government arrested a world-renowned Marxist artist, David Alfaro Siqueiros, and a newspaperman, Filomeno Mata, allegedly for conspiring against the government. Apparently, the real reason for their arrest was their engaging in a demonstration supported by the Teachers Organization in behalf of political prisoners.

After spending a year and a half in prison, the two men had their first public hearing. Siqueiros, who was 65 years old, and Mata, even older, both had to remain standing during the 11½-hour ordeal in a small, dismal courtroom. The spirit and even express provisions of the constitution were flagrantly violated; no specific charges had been filed against the two defendants, nor had any supporting affidavits been furnished, as are

---

[24] *Hispanic American Report*, Vol. XVII, No. 1 (March, 1964), p. 69; and No. 2 (April, 1964), p. 101.

required under Article 16 of the constitution. The lengthy imprisonment of Siqueiros and Mata, without even the pretense of observing constitutional and legal requirements, has been quite a *cause célèbre* in Mexico, showing how frail a reed freedom of speech and the press really is in the nation.[25]

On July 13, 1964, Siqueiros was given a pardon by President López Mateos, after serving almost four years of an eight-year sentence. According to the president, the pardon was granted so that the famous artist could complete his murals, a task regarded as very much in the national interest. In the opinion of some observers, however, the pardon was a gesture to former President Lázaro Cárdenas and other leftists for their support of Díaz Ordaz, or perhaps a gesture by the government to win the support of leftists within PRI.[26]

Under Brazil's sweeping press law, the government has virtual control over all news media in the nation. According to its provisions, the president will be immune from criticism; even proving the truth of allegations will not protect the writer, editor, or publisher, or all three of them, from possible jail terms. The measure also contains many restrictions on what can be published, and provides fines and imprisonment for journalists who in the government's view break the law.[27]

Freedom of Religion

Compared with the daily and highly combustible issue of freedom of speech and the press, freedom of religion, which all the nations profess, has been in recent years a relatively mild issue that seldom makes the headlines. The right of the individual to worship as he pleases is guaranteed in every one of the constitutions.

In times past, the role of the Catholic Church in national life and the measure of freedom worshipers of other faiths could enjoy were issues so controversial as to divide many a nation into two hostile, vituperative camps. One political regime, such as that of García Moreno of Ecuador, might try to establish a theocratic Roman Catholic state and dedicate the whole nation to the sacred heart of Jesus. But the next regime that came into power would reject the measures of the religious zealots and would divest the Church of its gains under the theocratic administration, as well as much of what it had had before.

During the 19th century, religious freedom to most Latin Americans meant freedom within the teachings and precepts of the Catholic Church. The decision of many of the faithful to disregard Church teachings and

---

[25] *Ibid.*, Vol. XV, No. 2 (April, 1962), p. 111; and No. 12 (February, 1963), p. 1086.
[26] *Ibid.*, Vol. XVII, No. 7 (September, 1964), p. 592.
[27] *The New York Times*, January 22, 1967, p. 20, cols. 3–4.

decide problems on their own was primarily a family affair, with Catholic liberals challenging a Catholic hierarchy.

In the past several decades, however, religious liberty has taken on a wholly new dimension. Many of the Protestant faiths, viewing Latin America as a fertile field for evangelization, have devoted much of their financial and ministerial resources to carrying Protestantism to the region, as was shown in Chapter 4. As a result, the question of freedom of religion in Latin America today refers not so much to the traditional battle of the faithful against Lucifer as to one Christian faith in competition with another. In one nation, the competition was so acrimonious as to amount to a direct confrontation. Protestantism versus Catholicism was one of the fiery issues in the no-holds-barred, internecine civil war that wracked Colombia for more than a decade. Since then, both Catholic and Protestant faiths have arrived at a sort of informal concordat, which recognizes that freedom of religion, regardless of its outcome, will be tolerated in the nation.

Physical Liberty

There are many constitutional provisions and laws aimed to guarantee the physical liberty of the inhabitants. Thus, it is specifically stated in the constitutions that slavery is forbidden. Moreover, one cannot be imprisoned because of indebtedness or required to give his personal labor without his free consent and just compensation.

Besides these general provisions, there are many specific ones to guarantee certain rights to anyone accused of having committed a crime. He cannot be tried and convicted under a law that applies retroactively unless it is in his favor. If he is a civilian, he cannot be tried and convicted by military court or board. Moreover, he cannot be arrested and imprisoned except for offenses specified by law and under a procedure established by law. If imprisoned, he must be advised in writing of the reasons for his detention, and must within 48 hours be brought before a judge qualified to pass on the legality of his arrest and detention. He is not to be subjected to psychological pressure or physical brutality, especially during the interrogation.

But these and many other rights which sound so impressive on paper are frequently violated with impunity, even in those nations that have a respect for due process of law. In Argentina, as in all the other republics, habeas corpus has long been recognized as a constitutional right, sometimes under the name of *amparo*, a similar judicial weapon. But in Argentina, habeas corpus is regarded as a "legalized farce" because of the excessive delays that destroy its practical value. An application for the writ may not be considered for days or even weeks, despite the explicit wording of the law requiring prompt action. Since no way has been found to compel speedier consideration, most citizens who are imprisoned make no effort whatever to exercise their right to obtain a writ for a prompt hearing.[28]

Political Asylum

The right of political asylum, whereby political offenders may obtain refuge in the embassy of a foreign country, is recognized by every one of the nations. Because of the prevalent political instability and the usual practice of regarding political opponents as enemies of the regime in power, the right of asylum is frequently exercised. Indeed, hardly a month passes when political offenders in one country or another do not flee for their lives to the safety of a foreign embassy, often with the police or military in hot pursuit, firing at them as they frantically clamber over embassy walls or bang in desperation on embassy doors, pleading for admittance.

According to the ground rules of asylum, the seeker is to be given not only refuge but also safe-conduct out of the country. But on rare occasions, a nation will obstinately refuse to grant a guarantee of safe-conduct, and a political refugee will be forced to reside for years as a guest of a foreign embassy. In 1948, the previously mentioned leader of the Aprista Party in Peru, Victor Haya de la Torre, sought refuge in the Colombian Embassy in Lima. However, the Peruvian government, insisting that he was not a political refugee but a common criminal, refused to guarantee him safe-conduct out of the nation. The refusal was the subject of bitter and prolonged dispute until 1954, when Peru finally agreed to give Haya de la Torre the customary guarantee of safe-conduct.

The record for the longest time spent as a political refugee in a foreign embassy is held by two Argentines, Carlos and Luis Amadeo Cardoza, brothers and former Peronista secret police terrorists who fled to the Paraguayan Embassy in Buenos Aires in September, 1955, after Perón was overthrown. For years, Argentina adamantly refused to grant safe-conduct. However, it finally yielded in December, 1963, reportedly only on condition that extradition proceedings to return them to Argentina would be begun as soon as they reached Paraguay.[29]

On even rarer occasions, nations have flagrantly disregarded the universally recognized immunity to local jurisdiction enjoyed by foreign embassies. In 1915, an irate mob in Haiti's capital, Port-au-Prince, invaded

---

[28] Macdonald, *op. cit.*, pp. 137–38.
[29] *Hispanic American Report*, Vol. XVI, No. 11 (January, 1964), p. 1100; and No. 12 (February, 1964), p. 1194.

the French legation to drag out and lynch President Guillaume Sam, who had fled there for refuge. In April, 1963, Haiti again disregarded international law when authorities entered the chancellery of the Dominican Republic, searching for political refugees being sheltered there. The violation so incensed the Dominican Republic that it deployed its armed forces so as to be ready to strike. The two nations were perilously close to war when President Duvalier of Haiti withdrew the guard from the Dominican embassy grounds and gave guarantees of safe-conduct for the 24 refugees and 3 Dominican diplomats there.[30]

The practice of asylum sometimes has its lighter moments too. One ambassador, roused by shouts from his garden, looked out and saw his butcher clutching two babies and trying to raise his arms over his head in response to the orders of two armed militiamen. When the ambassador opened the door, the butcher appealed frantically for asylum. Why? the diplomat wanted to know.

"It's my wife," the butcher explained. "We've had a terrible fight and I've decided that I must take asylum with my children." The ambassador admitted him, let him sleep it off, and persuaded him the next morning to go home.[31]

SUGGESTED READINGS

Blanksten, George I. "Constitutions and the Structure of Power," *Government and Politics in Latin America* (ed. Harold E. Davis), chap. 9. New York: Ronald Press Co., 1958.

———. *Perón's Argentina*, pp. 161–85. Chicago: University of Chicago Press, 1953.

———. *Ecuador: Constitutions and Caudillos*, pp. 38–42 and 51–54. Berkeley: University of California Press, 1951.

Busey, James L. *Latin America: Political Institutions and Processes*, pp. 16–21, 57–60, 100–105, 132–38, New York: Random House, Inc., 1964.

Carr, L. Donald. "Brazilian Local Self-Government: Myth or Reality?" *Western Political Quarterly*, Vol. 13, No. 4 (December, 1960), pp. 1043–55.

Christensen, Asher N. (ed.). *The Evolution of Latin American Government: A Book of Readings.* New York: Henry Holt & Co., 1951. Readings 2, 15, and 23–26.

Cline, Howard F. *Mexico: Revolution to Evolution: 1940–1960*, chaps. xiii and xix. Royal Institute of International Affairs. New York: Oxford University Press, 1962.

Fitzgerald, Gerald E. (ed.). *The Constitutions of Latin America.* Chicago: Henry Regnery Co., 1968.

---

[30] *Ibid.*, Vol. XVI, No. 4 (June, 1963), pp. 354–55.
[31] *New York Times* (May 23, 1963), p. 24, col. 1.

Fitzgibbon, Russell H. (ed.). *The Constitutions of the Americas.* Chicago: University of Chicago Press, 1948.

———. "Constitutional Development in Latin America: A Synthesis," *The American Political Science Review,* Vol. XXXIX, No. 3 (June, 1945), pp. 511–22.

Gómez, R. A. *Government and Politics in Latin America,* chap. 2. Rev. ed. New York: Random House, Inc., 1964.

Lowenstein, Karl. *Brazil Under Vargas,* pp. 3–105: 237–84. New York: Macmillan Co., 1942.

Macdonald, Austin F. *Government of the Argentine Republic,* chaps. 7 and 9. New York: Thomas Y. Crowell Co., 1942.

Mecham, J. Lloyd. "Mexican Federalism—Fact or Fiction?" *Annals of the American Academy of Political and Social Science,* Vol. 208 (March, 1940), pp. 23–38.

Morton, Ward M. "The Mexican Constitutional Congress of 1916–1917," *Southwestern Social Science Quarterly,* Vol. 33, No. 1 (June, 1952), pp. 7–27.

Needler, Martin C. *Latin American Politics in Perspective,* pp. 123–27; 155–59. Princeton, N.J.: D. Van Nostrand Co., Inc., 1963.

Pan American Union. Constitutions of Individual Republics in Latin America. Washington, D.C.

Pierson, William W., and Gil, Federico G. *Governments of Latin America,* chaps. 5 and 7, and pp. 192–95. New York: McGraw-Hill Book Co., Inc., 1957.

Spain, August O. "Mexican Federalism Revisited," *Western Political Quarterly,* Vol. 9, No. 3 (September, 1956), pp. 620–32.

Stokes, William S. *Honduras: An Area Study in Government,* chaps. iii and iv. Madison: University of Wisconsin Press, 1950.

———. *Latin American Politics,* pp. 457–64. New York: Thomas Y. Crowell Co., 1959.

Tucker, William P. *The Mexican Government Today,* chap. 5. Minneapolis: University of Minnesota Press, 1957.

14

EXECUTIVES:

Democratic Caesars and Democrats

TYPES OF EXECUTIVES SINCE INDEPENDENCE

During the 170-odd years of its existence, the United States has had only the presidential form of executive. Quite in contrast, however, during Latin America's approximately century and a half of independence the republics have experimented with several very different types of executives. The main ones have been: monarch and emperor, both constitutional and absolute; life president and life consul; parliamentary government; and committee or council.

After becoming independent, Haiti was ruled by an emperor from 1804 to 1806 and from 1847 to 1859, and the northern part of the country was ruled by a monarch from 1806 to 1820. Under both emperor and king (as well as under most of its presidents), the government was oppressive and tyrannical. Its violence and brutality were relieved only by some of its comic opera aspects, as those surrounding the nobility created by Henri Christophe, King Henri I, a nobility that included the "Duke of Marmalade" and the "Count of Lemonade."

Contrasting sharply with Haiti's experience was Brazil's Empire, which lasted from October 12, 1822, when Pedro I was proclaimed constitutional emperor until November 16, 1889, when his son, Pedro II, was deposed by the army and ordered to leave the country. Under the liberal constitution of 1824, which remained in effect until the establishment of the republic in 1889, the emperor had a "moderative power" that gave him an active and significant role within the framework of effective representative government. In reality, if not in form, Brazil under the reign of its two able emperors, especially the second, was a republic—a democracy with a permanent president. When President Rojas Paul of Venezuela heard the news of the empire's collapse in 1889, he declared: "The only republic which existed in America has come to an end: the Empire of Brazil."

Brazil even today is deeply indebted to the Empire, particularly to the enlightened rule of Pedro II. It gave the young nation a long period of political stability and saved it from dangerous contention over the form of government to be adopted or who should exercise authority. Moreover, it enabled the country to maintain its territorial integrity and to enjoy a long era of freedom from serious internal strife. In brief, the Empire greatly aided the nation's development.

Uneasy lies the head that wears a crown, especially in Latin America. For emperors and kings alike usually met a tragic fate. Jacques I, emperor of Haiti, 1804–6; Augustín I (Iturbide), emperor of Mexico, 1822–23; and Maximilian, emperor of Mexico, 1864–67, were all assassinated or executed. And King Henri I of Haiti managed to avoid death at the hands of his enemies by killing himself.

Haiti's life president, Jean Pierre Boyer, who governed the southern part of the country from 1818 to 1820 and the whole country until he was overthrown by revolution in 1843, was one of the best rulers the nation has had. Perhaps his greatest achievement was maintaining the young nation's independence and preventing its reabsorption by France, who still had designs on her former colony. More recently, Haiti acquired another self-styled life president when François Duvalier graciously bestowed that title on himself on April 1, 1964—apparently not as an April fool joke.

Paraguay's life consul was José Gaspar Rodríguez Francia. One of the country's two consuls from 1813 to 1814, he was named sole ruler in 1814 on a temporary basis and consul for life in 1816; his tenure lasted until 1840. During his long dictatorial reign, he instituted various measures for improving the lot of the Indians and mestizos. However, he greatly retarded Paraguay's development generally by completely sealing it off from all contact with the outside world, even refusing to have diplomatic relations with other nations.

Several nations in Latin America have experimented with the parliamentary system; Chile and Brazil are interesting examples. In Chile, the bases for cabinet government were established by the constitution of 1833, which provided among other things that members of the cabinet could be chosen from the senate or chamber of deputies, and that ministers might attend sessions of congress and debate but not vote. By 1891, the practice was firmly established that the president would select the members of his cabinet from among the majority party in congress and that he should not govern without the support of a majority in congress. The parliamentary system, which lasted from 1891 to 1925, was marred by ministerial instability and frequent cabinet changes.

Brazil instituted cabinet government as an emergency measure in September, 1961, in an effort to avert civil war. When President Jânio Quadros unexpectedly resigned on August 25, 1961, after only seven months in office, a military uprising threatened to prevent the vice president, João Goulart, head of the Brazilian Labor Party and a confirmed leftist, from becoming president. Civil war was averted only by a compromise that permitted Goulart to be inaugurated on condition that his legal power would be sharply curtailed by a constitutional amendment changing the government from a presidential to a parliamentary system.

During the 16 months of parliamentary government—from September, 1961, to January, 1963—three men served as prime minister. Instead of exercising executive authority, each became simply a servant of the president; the lines of authority were so confused that the nation had no national administration. As the situation became more chaotic, the citizens in a plebiscite in January, 1963, expressed a preference for the presidential system, which was restored soon afterward.[1]

Still another type of executive has been tried in Latin America—the committee or council. The first Venezuelan republic had a committee for its executive; the weakness and indecision of the committee when strong direction was critically needed were largely responsible for the failure of the first republic.

Another form of plural executive, the *colegiado* of Uruguay, was without doubt the most provocative experiment with executive organization and power undertaken in Latin America. The *colegiado* was the brainchild of José Batlle y Ordóñez, president from 1903 to 1907 and from 1911 to 1915, and one of the great Latin American statesmen of all time. Very much concerned about the threat of dictator-presidents to democratic government and individual liberty, Batlle while on an extended tour of Europe studied the Swiss Council of seven members, which deeply impressed him. This was the answer to dictatorship, he was convinced; and on his return to Uruguay, he proposed that the nation adopt the *colegiado* or plural executive. His proposal was adopted and was in effect from 1917 until 1933, when President Gabriel Terra discarded the system after a successful *golpe de estado*. Adopted a second time in 1951, the *colegiado* was Uruguay's executive authority until discarded by the electorate in November, 1966.

The *colegiado*, or National Council, was composed of nine members who constitute the executive branch. The nine councilors were elected directly by the people of the entire nation, which constituted a single

---

[1] Jordan M. Young, *The Brazilian Revolution of 1930 and the Aftermath* (New Brunswick, N.J.: Rutgers University Press, 1967), pp. 111–13.

electoral district, from lists of candidates submitted by the political parties and their factions for the electorate's consideration. The party or coalition that received the largest number of votes was allotted six seats on the National Council, and the party or coalition with the next largest number of votes was given three seats. The National Council appointed nine ministers who served as heads of the administrative departments. These ministers were responsible to the council and also to the congress; they had to resign if the congress in a joint session voted to censure them.

Uruguay's weak plural executive, regarded by its supporters as the cornerstone of the nation's democracy, proved to be very inept in coping with the nation's domestic and foreign problems. When it was discarded by an overwhelming popular vote in 1966, a presidential form of government with greatly increased powers for the executive was adopted.[2]

THE PRESIDENT TODAY[3]

The constitutions of Latin America, borrowing heavily from the political experience of the United States, established a tripartite division of government, consisting of the executive, legislative, and judicial branches, all equal and coordinate.[4] And under the correlative principle

---

[2] For a survey of the *Colegiado's* 14-year existence and evaluation of its performance, see Alexander T. Edelmann, "The Rise and Demise of Uruguay's Second Plural Executive," *Journal of Politics*, February, 1969.

For an objective treatment of the adoption of the *colegiado* and the likelihood of its success, see Russell H. Fitzgibbon, "Adoption of a Collegiate Executive in Uruguay," *Journal of Politics*, Vol. 14, No. 4 (November, 1952), pp. 616–42; and Milton I. Vanger, "Uruguay Introduces Government by Committee," *American Political Science Review*, Vol. 48, No. 2 (June, 1954), p. 500.

[3] For an earlier, but still valid, summary of the presidency in each of the republics, see Miguel Jorrín, *Governments of Latin America* (New York: D. Van Nostrand Co., Inc., 1953), pp. 92–96.

For a provocative analysis of the major types of Latin American executives, classified according to constitutional presidents, demagogic *caudillos*, military guardians, or paternalistic *caudillos*, see R. A. Gómez, "Latin American Executives: Essence and Variations," *Journal of Inter-American Studies*, Vol. 3, No. 1 (January, 1961), pp. 81–95.

For a penetrating study of the executive in Venezuela, see Leo B. Lott, "Executive Power in Venezuela," *American Political Science Review*, Vol. L, No. 2 (June, 1956), pp. 422–41.

[4] In Ecuador, however, the traditional doctrine of separation of powers and equality of the three branches of government has been discarded, in theory at least. While the nation's first 13 constitutions referred to the executive, the congress, and the judiciary as "powers," the constitutions adopted in 1945 and 1946 refer to these organs as "functions." The emphasis of the earlier constitutions was on separation of "powers"; the emphasis today is on coordination of "functions." Furthermore, while the earlier constitutions stressed that the three branches of government were equal, the 1946 constitution, in effect in 1964, specifies that the executive and the judicial functions are subordinate to the legislative. George I. Blanksten, *Ecuador: Constitutions and Caudillos* (Berkeley: University of California Press, 1951), p. 85.

of separation of powers, each branch of government was to exercise the powers it was given under the constitution, but no more.

But constitution making is one thing, and the practice of government is sometimes quite another. In most of the republics, instead of being equal and coordinate, the executive so far overshadows the other two branches of government that for all practical purposes the president *is* the government. "L'état c'est moi," boasted Louis XIV of France; in many of the Latin American nations, the president comes close to being a 20th-century version of the French monarch. Mexico is ordinarily regarded as one of the more politically advanced nations in Latin America; yet, "the feudalistic traditions of Mexico, like those of most of Latin America, make *el presidente* the political *patrón* for the entire republic," says James L. Busey. "In a political sense, Mexico is his *hacienda*. He is father-image and boss-image for all the people of the country."[5]

But not all the presidents in Latin America possess and exercise such wide power as is commonly assumed. Quite to the contrary, in those nations where democracy is more firmly established, the president is expected to perform the functions and exercise the powers vested in him by the constitution—these and only these. Nations that hold their president to such accountability include Chile, Costa Rica, and Uruguay.

In his annual state of the nation address on May 21, 1962, Chile's President Jorge Alessandri Rodríguez sharply criticized the congress with which he had many bitter disagreements. The nation's economic health was good, he contended, but continued progress was contingent on reform of the 1925 constitution.[6] On September 18, 1963, he addressed the nation about the need for a drastic revision of the constitution. Deeply concerned with pressing economic problems and with the often uncooperative attitude of congress, he urged that the constitution be changed to provide for a stronger executive. Moreover, whenever disputes occurred between the president and congress, they should be resolved by submitting the issues to a plebiscite or by dissolving the congress and holding another election to enable public opinion to express itself. Furthermore, congress should be prohibited from initiating legislation in the fields of taxes and public investment.[7]

In Costa Rica, too, the president often feels a sense of diminished

---

[5] James L. Busey, *Latin America: Political Institutions and Processes* (New York: Random House, Inc., 1964), p. 29.

[6] *Hispanic American Report,* Vol. XV, No. 5 (July, 1962), pp. 447–48.

[7] *New York Times,* September 19, 1963, p. 12, col. 5.

Budgetary anarchy in the nation has resulted from frequent congressional delay in approving the budget, a tactic employed by parliamentary cliques against the executive. However, at present, if the budget presented by the president is not approved by the congress by the end of four months it automatically becomes effective. Federico G. Gil, *The Political System of Chile* (Boston: Houghton Mifflin Co., 1966), p. 96.

TABLE 14-1

EXECUTIVES—JANUARY, 1969

Country	Incumbent	Date Taking Office	Const. Length of Term	Political Party of Incumbent
Argentina	Juan Carlos Onganía	6-66	—	Seized power by military coup, 6-28-66, indefinite term
Bolivia	René Barrientos Ortuño	8-66	4	Frente de la Revolución Boliviana (FRB)
Brazil	Artur da Costa e Silva	3-67	4	Partido de Reforma Democrática (PAREDE)
Chile	Eduardo Frei Montalva	11-64	6	Partido Democrática Cristiano (PDC)
Colombia	Carlos Lleras Restrepo	8-66	4	Frente Nacional (a coalition party since 1957 pact)
Costa Rica	José Joaquín Trejos Fernandez	5-66	4	Partido de Unificación Nacional (PUN)
Cuba	Fidel Castro Ruz (Prime Min., dictator)	7-59	—	Partido Communista Cubano (PCC), only legal party
				Pres. Osvaldo Dorticos Torrado
Dominican Republic	Joaquín Balaguer	7-66	4	Partido Reformista Dominicano
Ecuador	José María Velasco Ibarra	11-68	4	Conservador
El Salvador	Fidel Sánchez Hernández	7-67	5	Partido de Conciliación Nacional (PCN)
Guatemala	Julio César Méndez Montenegro	7-66	6	Partido Revolucionario (PR)
Haiti	François Duvalier	6-64	—	Elected for life; no political parties exist
Honduras	Osvaldo López Arellano	6-65	6	Partido Nacional (military coup 10-63; elected president, 6-65)
Mexico	Gustavo Díaz Ordaz	12-64	6	Partido Revolucionario Institucional (PRI)
Nicaragua	Anastasio Somoza Debayle	5-67	5	Partido Liberal Nacionalista (PLN)
Panama	Colonel José M. Pinilla	10-68	—	Seized power by military coup, 10-11-68, indefinite term
Paraguay	Alfredo Stroessner	8-68	5	Partido Colorado (official party for Stroessner's dictatorship)
Peru	General Juan Velasco Alvarado	10-68	—	Seized power by military coup, 10-3-68, indefinite term
Uruguay	Jorge Pacheco Areco	12-67	4	Assumed office after death of Gestido, who took office 3-37, Partido Colorado
Venezuela	Raúl Leoni	3-64	5	Partido Acción Democrática (AD)

SOURCE: James L. Busey, *Latin American Political Guide* (El Paso: Texas Western Press, 1967).

importance, since his powers and status have been purposely deemphasized. He has no assurance whatever that his program will be approved by the congress unless his party constitutes a majority of the membership; even then, some members of his party may balk and fail to give him the support he needs.

Congress regards the president as just another citizen; the rest of the nation does too. James L. Busey says:

[He] is likely to drive his own car, pick up friends whom he sees on the streets, and fill his time with interviews with callers who come to praise, or condemn. Though the President is kept busy with the pleas of friends and enemies, he shares none of the *patrón*-like features that are common to many other countries of Latin America. Everyone feels free to criticize the President, and unless his party enjoys a large and unshakable majority in the Legislative Assembly, no one expects much from him.[8]

QUALIFICATIONS FOR THE PRESIDENT

As elsewhere, the constitutions in Latin America have established various qualifications for persons elected president. Three qualifications in particular are found in all the nations. First is citizenship. The president must be a native-born citizen, born in the national territory and subject to its jurisdiction, or, if born abroad, a child of native-born citizens. However, Nicaragua goes one step further and requires that the president must not only be the offspring of Nicaraguan parents but also born within the homeland. A second requirement common to all the countries is a minimum age. The minumum age is 30 in 7 of the nations; 35 in 9 nations; and 40 in 2. A third requirement found in all the constitutions is a minimum period of residence there; this varies all the way from 1 year in Mexico to 10 years in Peru.

Various other qualifications are specified in the several constitutions. In Colombia, to qualify for president one must have held one of the other high offices of the nation, such as member of the cabinet, ambassador or minister, head of a department, or judge of one of the higher courts. He might also qualify by having been a university professor for at least five years or having practiced a "liberal profession with a university degree." Costa Rica requires that the president must own property worth at least 500 *colones* or have an annual income of at least 200 *colones*. Costa Rica also adds a modest requirement that the president should "be able to read and write." The Paraguayan constitution specifies that the president must "meet the moral and intellectual requirements qualifying him to exercise the office," and El Salvador's stipulates that he must be "of known honesty and learning." Several of the states require that he be a Roman

---

[8] Busey, *op. cit.*, p. 75.

Catholic (apparently, not necessarily a practicing one), while others require that he be a member of the laity.

Besides these formal qualifications specifically stated in the constitutions, some of the nations have informal, unwritten qualifications that go a long way toward determining one's chances for the presidency. In Argentina, if one aspires to be president, it helps to be a resident of Buenos Aires; since 1860, only two Argentines who did not live there have been elevated to the presidency. Or if one lives in Brazil, the chance of becoming president is far better if one lives in either Minas Gerais or São Paulo. It has long been the custom in the nation to choose presidents alternately between these two dominant states; only occasionally is a candidate selected from Rio Grande do Sul or one of the northern states of the nation. And in Mexico, besides measuring up to all of the qualifications specified in the constitution, one ought to be the protegé of the incumbent president, who virtually designates his successor.

To discharge all his responsibilities and accomplish all that is expected of him, the president should have the superhuman qualities of Superman himself. As Lleras Camargo, president of Colombia from 1958 to 1962 and one of the great statesmen of Latin America, aptly expressed it, a president of Colombia must be "a magician, prophet, redeemer, savior, and pacifier who can transform a ruined republic into a prosperous one, can make the prices of the things we export rise and the value of the things we consume drop."[9]

In addition to the various qualifications established for the presidency, the constitutions contain a number of disqualifications which automatically rule out persons in certain categories. Those usually disqualified include: a close relative of either the president or vice president; one who has actively served in the armed forces of the nation during the previous six months, year, or other specified time before taking office; the leader of a *golpe de estado* or one of his relatives; and a member of the priesthood. Mexico also disqualifies anyone who has ever served as president, in whatever capacity and for whatever period of time.

The caliber of those who have filled the presidential office has varied considerably. Some of the presidents have been persons of quite modest endowment and background. Enrique Peñaranda, who was pushed into the presidency of Bolivia by conservative army elements, was a *cholo* of little education. When the news of his election reached his mother, the old woman supposedly said: "Why, if I had known Enrique would be president, I would have sent him to school."[10]

---

[9] *Time*, May 5, 1958, p. 33.

[10] Hubert Herring, *A History of Latin America from the Beginnings to the Present* (2d ed. rev.; New York: Alfred A. Knopf, Inc., 1961), p. 559. But perhaps, as Herring adds, any lack of earlier book learning was offset in 1943 when, visiting the United States, Peñaranda was awarded an honorary doctorate of laws by Columbia University.

But Peñaranda by no means typifies the Latin American presidents. Usually, they are well educated, having prepared for one of the professions. Many of them have been lawyers, since law is regarded as a natural steppingstone to politics. Some of them, such as Lleras Camargo or Café Filho of Brazil, were journalists and reached the presidency after a stormy career of advocating reform. Others, among whom were José María Guido of Argentina and François Duvalier of Haiti, were doctors of medicine; and still others, as Arturo Frondizi of Argentina, were professors at the university. In this respect, Latin America is more broad minded than the United States; there, the egghead is regarded as presidential timber.

Many of the presidents have been relatively young men; they may have climbed fast via the armed forces or have received recognition for their intellectual competence. Among those who were under 40 when they took the oath of office are Arbenz Guzmán of Guatemala, Fulgencio Batista of Cuba, and Pérez Jiménez of Venezuela.

The presidents as a group are rather widely traveled, too, sometimes by their own choice, as visitors or students, but more often as political exiles at the choice of a successful new revolutionary regime. The period of residence specified in the constitution to qualify one for the presidency is aimed largely at these exiles. The length of the period required is quite significant. The rule of thumb is that the shorter the residence requirement, the more democratic a nation is apt to be, and, conversely, that the longer the requirement, the less democratic a nation is likely to be.

TERM OF OFFICE AND ELIGIBILITY FOR REELECTION

Generally, the presidential term of office ranges from four to six years. With dictators, Cuba and Argentina have indefinite terms at the present time. The four-year term is found in eight countries: Bolivia, Brazil, Colombia, Costa Rica, Dominican Republic, Ecuador, Panama, and Uruguay. The five-year term exists in four countries: El Salvador, Nicaragua, Paraguay, and Venezuela. The six-year term is found in five countries: Chile, Guatemala, Honduras, Mexico, and Peru. One nation, Haiti, is in a class by itself; the constitution adopted on June 14, 1964, provided that the president's term would be for life, paving the way for the national assembly's action a week later which declared François "Papa Doc" Duvalier permanent president of the country.

The average of the terms established in the constitutions, excluding Haiti's, is approximately five years, which is sometimes said to be approximately the same as the average term of presidents in the United States. But this statistical computation can be misleading. The American presidents have actually served an average term of about five years; in Latin America, however, the actual term is far less than this. For example, although the president's term of office in Ecuador has traditionally been four years, only 23 percent of the presidents have been able to serve out the full term for which they were elected. As a result, presidents actually remain in office an average of only 2.47 years.[11] In Honduras, too, the actual term of office has been much shorter than the constitutional term. Throughout the nation's history, the presidency has seldom changed hands peacefully; changes in regime, usually the result of revolution, have been swift and frequent. In fact, from 1824 to 1950, a period of 126 years, the presidency changed hands 116 times![12]

Eligibility for reelection has been one of the most sensitive problems confronting constitution makers in Latin America. The republics have had so many dictators who served their term of office and then had themselves reelected many times that the history of some of the countries has seemed to consist largely of the interminable rules of several long-lived presidents. With this bitter experience in mind, most of the nations have set up strong constitutional safeguards to try to prevent a president from perpetuating himself in office.[13]

Courtesy of Ross Lewis and the Milwaukee Journal

. . . and there's where El Presidente lives when we have one!

---

[11] Blanksten, *op. cit.*, p. 88.

[12] William S. Stokes, *Honduras: An Area Study in Government* (Madison: University of Wisconsin Press, 1950), p. 181. For the list of presidents who held office from 1824 to 1949 and the dates they assumed office, see pp. 329–31.

[13] These safeguards and the countries embracing them are given in José Miranda, *Reformas y Tendencias Constitucionales Recientes de la América Latina (1945–1956)* (Instituto de Derecho Comparado) (México D.F.: Universidad Nacional Autónoma de México, 1957), pp. 278–83.

The main safeguard is the provision regarding eligibility for reelection. Only three of the republics permit a president to seek reelection and continue in office for another term or more. Paraguay permits a president to be reelected, but only for one additional term. Brazil and the Dominican Republic have no express prohibitions against immediate reelection; presumably a president in either of these two countries could be reelected any number of times. In Brazil, however, a sort of tradition against immediate reelection has been established. Prior to the regime of Getulio Vargas, no president had served more than one term except Francisco de Paula Rodríques Alves, who was president from 1902 to 1906 and from 1918 until his death less than a year later. In Argentina, the Peronista constitution adopted in 1949 permitted the president to be reelected—a practice that had been forbidden for nearly a century. But in 1957, the 1853 constitution was readopted, and a president is prohibited from succeeding himself in office.

In the other republics, provisions written into the constitutions are unequivocal in forbidding a president to succeed himself in office. Guatemala's constitution of 1945 was one of the many that contained such a provision—and a unique penalty for violating it.

According to Articles 132 and 133:

The presidential term is six years and cannot be prolonged, and one who has exercised the presidency may not be reelected except after twelve years from having ceased in the exercise of it. The author or authors of a proposal that tends in any form to vitiate the principle of alternability in the presidency of the Republic, and any person, official, or employee who co-operates, directly or indirectly, for such a purpose, whatever may be the motives that are invoked and the means that are employed, commit the crime of treason to the Fatherland, cease in the discharge of their respective offices, and, as the case may be, remain permanently disqualified for the exercise of any public function and automatically lose, furthermore, all their ranks. Responsibility for acts that violate or restrict or tend to violate or restrict the principle of alternability in the office of President of the Republic is imprescriptible.

Most of the constitutions do not intend to bench a president permanently after he finishes his term of office, but are determined that he shall sit on the sidelines for a term or two. Ten of the nations require the lapse of at least one term before he can be reelected, and five require two terms or more.

The prohibition in most of the constitutions against immediate reelection has by no means terminated the careers of former presidents. Indeed, it is quite common for them to make a comeback and be elected again to the high office. Among the ex-presidents within the last decade who have been elected after skipping a term are Rómulo Betancourt of Venezuela, Ibáñez del Campo of Chile, Getulio Vargas of Brazil, and Velasco Ibarra of Ecuador. Ibarra has become almost a perennial candidate in Ecuador, having been elected to the presidency five times, but each time he was overthrown before he could complete his term. "Ecuador is a very difficult country to govern," he has said.

Unfortunately, the many constitutional prohibitions against immediate reelection are not self-enforcing. Politically immature as most of the nations are, their governments represent the rule of men rather than of law. Once he is in office, the enjoyment of power is heady wine to many a president. Basking in the adulation and plaudits of his fellow countrymen, toward the end of his term he conveniently forgets the constitutional restrictions against reelection, as well as the cogent reasons behind them. Or if he remembers them, he is sure his case is different from that of other presidents. The program he had hoped to complete during his term is only partly finished, and he is the only one who can be sure of seeing it through. Moreover, the nation is facing many critical problems, as everyone realizes. Thanks to his experience in the presidency, he and he alone understands them and has the answers for their solution.

Determined that his invaluable experience and insight shall not be lost, he decides that by one means or another he must be reelected—for the good of the country, to be sure. His reelection and that of many other like-minded presidents are flagrantly contrary both to the intent and expressed provisions of the constitution, and are usually accomplished by the adoption of an amendment permitting the incumbent to succeed himself. This practice of reelection, which is widespread throughout Latin America, is known as *continuismo,* which connotes continuance in office beyond the legal term by the use of peaceful constitutional methods. *Continuismo* has been practiced mainly by the republics of Central America and the Caribbean.[14]

In attempts to forestall *continuismo,* the republics have set up many kinds of constitutional roadblocks. Guatemala's 1945 constitution even legalized rebellion as a means of blocking continuation in office after the presidential term of six years had expired. "The principle of alternate succession in the exercise of the office of President of the Republic is imperative for the national political system," asserted Article 2 of the constitution, "and the people may have recourse to rebellion should anyone venture to violate this principle."[15]

---

[14] For the reasons why it has been so successful in these nations, see Russell H. Fitzgibbon, "Continuismo in Central America and the Caribbean," *Inter-American Quarterly* (July, 1940), pp. 442–44.

[15] This provision is not in the 1956 constitution. The drafters of that document were much more circumspect. The sanction of rebellion was dropped and a proper, innocuous provision adopted that could hardly ruffle any feathers. It reads: "Reelection or any other means used to prolong the term of office of a President is punishable in accordance with the law, and the mandate which a person so doing claims to exercise shall be void ipso jure."

The right of rebellion has often been asserted in other Latin American nations besides Guatemala. Regarding the feasibility and possibility of establishing this principle in constitutional form, see Ricardo Gallardo, *Estudios de Derecho Constitucional Americano Comparado* (Madrid: Ediciones Cultura Hispanica, 1961), pp. 118–42.

But despite legalizing rebellion or other drastic tactics that have been resorted to, *continuismo* continues to be a threat in most of the republics. There are many devious means whereby a shrewd president can circumvent the constitutional prohibition against immediate reelection and still stay in the good grace of his people. Getulio Vargas of Brazil utilized a tried and true method; after serving as "provisional president" from 1930 to 1934, he convoked a constitutional convention that rewrote the nation's fundamental law and obligingly elected him as the first "constitutional president" to serve under its provisions.

In El Salvador, Maximiliano Hernández Martínez executed this effective maneuver twice, convoking constituent assemblies that elected him to a new term in 1939 and again in 1944. Bolivia's constitution of 1961, adopted by the congress, repealed the earlier provision forbidding a president to succeed himself, thereby permitting President Paz Estenssoro to be reelected in 1964.

A novel means of finagling to continue in office was contrived in 1961 by President François Duvalier of Haiti. In the election for members of congress which occurred midway during the presidential term, Duvalier had his name printed at the top of the ballot that gave the names of the candidates, then announced after the election that he had been reelected president for a new term without opposition.

MEANS OF SELECTION AND TRANSFER OF THE OFFICE

During the 19th century, the presidents of most of the republics were chosen by one of several means of indirect election—namely, by national congresses, by electoral congresses, or by state or provincial assemblies. Indirect election by these means continued in some nations until several decades ago. Among the last to provide for direct popular election were Chile, Cuba, and Peru, which discarded their old method of electoral colleges, and Haiti, which changed from election by the national congress.

Prior to the military take-over of Argentina by Lieutenant General Juan Carlos Onganía in June, 1966, suspending all vestiges of constitutional authority, Argentina was the only one of the nations whose president was indirectly elected. According to the 1853 constitution, citizens do not cast their votes directly for the president but for presidential electors who cast the deciding votes. Each of the 16 provinces is entitled to twice as many electors as the total number of its representatives in both houses of congress. The federal capital is also represented on the same basis. After their election, the electors meet at a specified time in their respective provincial capitals and in Buenos Aires and cast their ballots for the president—a system of indirect election that closely resembles the election of the President in the United States.

Under Brazil's new constitution, adopted in January 1967, the president is elected indirectly by an electoral college composed of members of the congress and others who are elected by the state legislatures.

After a presidential election has been held, the national congress, in accordance with most of the constitutions, examines the results and declares elected the candidate who has received the specified majority. Some of the more recent constitutions assign this function to special electoral courts, which are regarded as less susceptible to political pressures.

In the event that no candidate receives a legal majority of the votes cast, the usual procedure is for the congress to choose between the several highest candidates. Sometimes, the full congress is designated by the constitution to make this choice; sometimes, it is the lower house alone, as in the United States. The vote cast by the congress or by the chamber of deputies sometimes results in a tie; then, there are some unique methods for resolving it. In Costa Rica, the older candidate is declared to be the winner; in Ecuador, the choice is made by lot.

Having been declared by the congress or the special electoral court to be duly elected, the winning candidate takes his oath of office, swearing to uphold the constitution and to discharge faithfully his duties as president. In most of the countries, the oath of office is usually taken before the full congress. Some nations specify, however, that it shall be taken before the supreme court, the council of state, or the chamber of deputies. Having taken the oath before one of these bodies, the president is now vested with the great powers of his office.

POWERS OF THE PRESIDENT

The powers the president should have are as controversial today as they were a century or so ago. In Argentina, Alberdi at that time urged the constitutional convention to endow the executive with very great power. Within recent decades, however, a fellow Argentine, González Calderón, is convinced that such a concentration of power is "anachronistic and antirepublican," contrary to the development of a democratic nation.[16] The threat of "democratic caesarism" has prompted Peru to adopt a semiparliamentary system of government,[17] and other nations to try

---

[16] J. A. González Calderón, *Derecho constitucional* (1931), p. 286.

[17] "The mistake that the partisans of 'democratic caesarism' make is to seek to perpetuate what has been only a historical accident. Our Latin American nations by tradition, environment, and circumstances require a president who is strong and resolute. But this primacy and effectiveness of presidential authority should not degenerate into tyranny, dictatorship, and personalist *caudillismo* or in the absorption

other restrictive measures. But regardless of the system or the measures, the power of the executive in most of the nations is great—far greater than in most democratic nations, as the following analysis of his specific powers will show.

Armed Forces

The constitutions vest in the president quite extensive military powers. In every one of the republics he is specifically designated as commander in chief of the armed forces, in which capacity he is charged with the responsibility for preserving internal order and defending the nation against external aggression. To these ends, he may decree partial or total mobilization to cope with a serious internal or external threat. As a rule, he may declare war only after having been authorized to do so by congress, but if aggression from the outside occurs and congress is not in session, he can declare war on his own authority. In the normal exercise of his military powers he appoints the officers of the armed forces. Legislative approval is ordinarily necessary for the highest officers, except for appointment on the field of battle. The president may also be authorized to determine the size of the armed forces, as in Venezuela, as well as their organization and distribution to cope with a particular situation.

The president is usually authorized to take personal command of troops if he believes it advisable. However, he has seldom done so, even if formerly an officer, because of the pressure of other responsibilities and duties. In Peru, he is specifically forbidden to take personal command without the permission of congress; and if he does assume command he has only the powers of a commander in chief, subject to the military and other laws of the republic. In Chile, if the president decides to don a uniform the appropriate minister in the legal order of succession substitutes for him with his regular duties under the title of vice president.

On several occasions, presidents have found it advisable to exercise their constitutional power of taking personal command of the armed forces. Presidents Mitre and Sarmiento of Argentina both did this in the 19th century. And more recently, in the turmoil following the Mexican revolution the presidents of Mexico have several times assumed their constitutional prerogative of exercising direct command, the last time in the spring of 1938, when President Lázaro Cârdenas took to the field to crush an uprising led by General Cedillo.

The extent to which provisions in the constitutions actually determine

by the executive of the other powers of state." José Pareja Paz-Soldan, *Derecho Constitucional Peruano* (Tercera Edición; Lima, Perú: Ediciones del Sol, 1963), p. 192.

a president's power over the armed forces varies greatly among the 20 republics. In those nations that are more advanced politically and where the armed forces are nonpolitical, the president exercises his constitutional prerogatives, and the armed forces are subject to civilian control.[18] But in less advanced countries where the armed forces dominate politics, the president is often the mere tool of the military powers that be.

Sometimes the rivalry between the civilian president and the military strong man in the nation is undisguised. In Nicaragua, President Luis Somoza apparently wanted to comply with at least the form of democratic procedure by arranging for the election of an "independent" who could be depended on not to endanger the vast Somoza fortune; however, his brother Anastasio, who commanded the National Guard, felt strongly that this course would be disastrous and that the strong-man tradition should be continued to protect the family's interests. President Luis won out; on May 2, 1963, René Schick was sworn in as president for a four-year term, and on his death on August 3, 1966, Lorenzo Guerrero Gutiérrez took office for the unexpired term.

In Honduras, the rivalry between civilian and military authorities has been especially bitter as a result of Article 318 of the nation's 1957 constitution. It states: "The Armed Forces shall be under the direct command of the Chief of the Armed Forces; through him the President of the Republic will exercise his constitutional function respecting this institution. Merely administrative functions shall be entrusted to the Secretary of State for Defense." The effect of this provision has been to create a duality of authority making the armed forces autonomous and their chief virtually independent of the president, who controls the Civil Guard. As a result, the president and the chief of the armed forces vie with each other for supremacy, and the jealous rivalry between the armed forces and the Civil Guard has resulted in several fatal clashes.[19]

Administration

In each of the republics, the president is also responsible for seeing that the laws are faithfully executed and that the multifarious functions of government, such as delivering the mail or educating the youth, are properly carried out. In discharging this responsibility, the president is the apex and final authority of the national administative machinery that, day in and day out, conducts a great variety of activities and performs countless services for the citizenry.

As head of the national administrative setup, the president usually has a wide measure of authority that would indeed be the envy of the president

---

[18] See Chapter 6.
[19] *Hispanic American Report*, Vol. XIV, No. 2 (April, 1961), p. 103; and Vol. XVI, No. 9 (November, 1963), p. 856.

of the United States. In Mexico, for example, the president has a much wider leeway. Although executive departments are created by law, their number and organization are purposefully left quite elastic to suit the desires of each president. But as in the United States, the coordination and supervision of the many independent and semi-independent agencies has been a frustrating problem.[20]

In Venezuela, the president is given even greater leeway than in Mexico. When a serious emergency arises and congress is not in session, he can create new public services or modify, even abolish, those already in existence, with the authorization of the permanent committee of congress known as the "Delegated Committee."[21]

Appointment and Removal

In exercising wide control over the many government departments and agencies, the president has virtually unlimited power to appoint administrative officials and the large number of government employees. As the constitutions neatly express it, the president has the power to appoint "freely." With only lip service paid to civil service, the president and his trusted lieutenants also have almost complete control over the tenure of government employees as well as over their salaries, promotions, pensions, leaves of absence, and retirement.

In the appointment of high officials, such as ambassadors and ministers, judges of the higher courts, and ranking officers of the armed services, constitutions usually require that the president's choice must be approved by the senate, the council of ministers, or some other body. This approval, however, is more theoretical than real, as Mexico's Senate was to find out when it took its power of approval seriously.

Soon after President Ávila Camacho was inaugurated, he submitted a number of nominees for the Supreme Court of Justice to the senate for approval. To the great surprise of the capital, apparently of the president too, the senate, meeting in closed session, turned down three of the president's choices, terming them "reactionaries." (Although politically naïve, the senate was on sound constitutional ground, for Article 89, section 18 of the constitution specifically gives it the authority to pass on the president's appointments to the Supreme Court of Justice.) When the president was informed by a committee of senators of the body's action, he apparently blew a gasket, for the members of the committee hurried back to the chamber to set things right. The next day the senate backtracked and capitulated, ratifying the entire list. Explained the president

---

[20] Robert E. Scott, *Mexican Government in Transition* (rev. ed.; Urbana: University of Illinois Press, 1964), pp. 281–83.

[21] Venezuela's 1961 constitution, Article 190, Section 11. For the composition and functions of the Delegated Committee, see Article 178.

of the senate, earlier press reports on the secret session were erroneous; the senate had never refused to approve the nominees. It had merely delayed taking action until more information about them could be gathered.[22]

Legislative

Another very important power of the president relates to his participation in the legislative process. One of his many duties in this realm is to preside at the opening of each annual session, when he gives a state of the nation address and advises congress—the nation, too, indirectly—of significant national conditions and problems and, especially, his recommendations for dealing with them.

The president also has considerable control over the sessions of congress. Since the constitutions usually specify that he must be present at the opening session, his absence on occasion has delayed congress from officially convening and beginning its legislative duties. This has caused some speculation about whether by boycotting a session entirely, a president might thereby prevent congress from meeting at all during its constitutionally authorized session. Whether this is so or not, the president unquestionably has other controls over sessions of the legislative body. He is authorized in most of the nations to prorogue the regular session and also to call congress back into extraordinary session if he deems that a matter of great importance requires it.

Besides exercising these powers, the executive has a very imposing role in lawmaking. He is authorized by the constitution to present bills to the congress, and most of the laws enacted are measures he has proposed. In Honduras, during the period from 1896 to 1941, 93 percent of the bills drafted by the executive branch were approved by congress. In 12 different years, the body approved without change every bill submitted by the executive branch. "Certainly during the greater part of the history of Honduras," concludes William S. Stokes, "the Congress has acted as a rubber stamp for the legislative proposals of the executive."[23]

Mexico is another of the many nations in Latin America where the president dominates. There, as in Honduras, he enjoys almost absolute control over the congress. Since his party is the only one represented in the senate and overwhelmingly controls the chamber of deputies, his measures presented to the congress have a monopoly on the green light. Bills initiated by individuals are virtually unknown. Thus, in the 3-year term of the 41st Congress, some 138 bills were passed by both houses and enacted into law. Of these, only seven were initiated by the congress

---

[22] For this episode, see Scott, *op. cit.,* pp. 264–65.
[23] Stokes, *op. cit.,* p. 287.

itself, mainly from the Chamber of Deputies' Comisión de Estudios Legis-lativos.[24]

Controlling the congress as completely as he does, the president of most countries finds that his power of the veto is a superfluous weapon. Why should he want to veto a bill that was written in the first place by one of his own ministers and passed without the slightest alteration by congress? Enjoying a legislative field day as he does, it is no wonder that since the Revolution, presidents of Mexico have cast only two vetoes and both of these on minor technical questions.[25]

But in a few of the nations that are proud of a long tradition of democratic government, the president does not enjoy such easy sailing. There, limited to exercising only the powers he is granted by the constitution and having to deal with a congress that is also zealous in discharging its responsibilities, the president sometimes finds that the veto is a very useful weapon. Thus, in Chile President Alessandri, in his basic disagreements with congress over social security for urban workers and other measures he regarded as inflationary, cast veto after veto to prevent these measures from becoming law—at least 17 vetoes in the period of a few weeks.[26]

As a rule, however, vetoes by the president are rare in Latin America, and still rarer is the item veto. The constitution of Argentina does not even refer to the power to veto items in a bill, so presumably the president does not possess it. However, several presidents have vetoed certain items in budget bills, then put the remainder into effect. The item veto was exercised by Irigoyen in 1918, by Justo in 1932, and by Ortiz in 1939. Irogoyen even went so far as to strike out objectionable clauses from laws and imposing taxes and regulating the exportation of sugar, then promulgated the laws in this partially vetoed form. Strong protests were made in the public press and also in congress, but the legislation stood as promulgated.[27]

Decree

Another very important power of the president is his authority to issue decrees. In democratic states today, it is accepted practice for laws to be formulated in rather general terms, leaving to the executive considerable discretion for implementing them by administrative regulations. In this way laws can be interpreted and applied to all kinds of situations and

---

[24] Scott, *op. cit.*, pp. 263–64.

[25] *Ibid.*, p. 263.

[26] *Hispanic American Report*, Vol. XVI, No. 10 (December, 1963), p. 1000.

[27] Austin F. Macdonald, *Government of the Argentine Republic* (New York: Thomas Y. Crowell Co., 1942), p. 202.

problems, thereby carrying out their basic intent. But in Latin America, this universally exercised practice of filling in the details of legislation to make it applicable to the innumerable problems of everyday living has been so grossly perverted as to translate it into a usurpation of the powers belonging to congress. Exercising this unbridled, limitless power, the presidents in most of the nations have acted as a supraconstitutional legislative authority, whose far-reaching decrees were as authoritative as those that in earlier times came from Mount Olympus.[28]

While recognizing that the president and the executive branch of government must have the power to issue supplementary regulations, the constitution makers have done their best to direct the purposes and intended boundaries of decrees. The Argentine constitution, after giving the president the power to issue decrees, states that he should be "careful not to modify their spirit with exceptions in the regulations." The Nicaraguan constitution vests in the executive the power to issue regulations to implement the laws, but "without transgressing or emasculating them."

But these and many other constitutional restrictions intended to limit the decree power of the executive have been of little or no avail. Mexico's experience after 1917 shows how far the power of the president can be exercised to supplant the constitutional authority of the congress. Acting under the authority of Article 29 of the constitution of 1917 which provides for the suspension of constitutional guarantees "in case of invasion, of serious disturbance of the public peace, or any other emergency that may place the people in great danger or conflict," the president has stretched the power of issuing decrees to cover any matter of legislation that he has chosen, regardless of how basic and comprehensive it was. Thus, from 1920 to 1938 most of the important legislation was in the form of decrees issued by the president under the justification of a supposed state of grave emergency when, in fact, there was no emergency at all. But when the president requested that congress delegate to him the power to issue decrees, it willingly did so. Among the many fundamental and far-reaching laws enacted during this period solely on the authority of the president were the following: regulations governing the Church, the Commercial Code, Federal Penal Code and Code of Penal Procedure, Agrarian Code, Law of the Nationalization of Property, General Insurance Law, and General Law on Cooperative Societies.

This unwarranted exercise by the president of powers granted to congress by the constitution lasted until 1938, when a constitutional amend-

---

[28] In Chile, there are two types of presidential decrees: *decretos-leyes* (decree laws) and *decretos con fuerza de ley* (decrees having the force of law). The first, enacted without authorization by delegation of power by the congress, is regarded as a clear usurpation of the powers of the congress. The second are issued under the authorization of such a delegation. Gil, *op. cit.*, p. 100.

ment was adopted to end such blanket decrees unless a grave national emergency existed.[29]

Honduras, like Mexico, has felt the full impact of the president's authority to issue decrees. There, too, the president's control over congress was so strong and the body was so subservient that it virtually surrendered its prerogative of lawmaking to the executive. In 1880 and 1889, the congress gave the president carte blanche to enact legislation in the important fields of war and police activities, finance, public instruction, court organization, and *fomento*. And in 1899, having again conferred blanket legislative powers on the president, the congress approved without discussion the penal, mining, and commercial codes he had formulated and submitted for formal adoption.[30]

Finance

The president also has very broad powers over the nation's finance and economy. Under the constitution, he is required to propose to the congress a budget for each fiscal year, giving an estimate of the revenues to be received and the expenditures to be made. He is also required to collect the public revenue he spends through his ministers who head the various departments. In a brave attempt to give the congress some control over the president's tremendous financial power, the constitution usually specifies that he must render an annual accounting of the receipts and expenditures for the preceding year. But this requirement is virtually meaningless, because neither the congress nor any other public body makes an independent audit of public receipts and expenditures, and what information the president supplies can hardly be relied on.

Even in some of the most democratic countries of Latin America, the congress sometimes delegates to the president an extremely wide measure of discretion and authority in public finance and related fields. In 1959, the congress of Chile gave its able, industrialist president, Jorge Alessandri, virtually absolute control over the nation's economy for one year. Under this unusual grant of power, he was authorized to establish a new monetary system, reorganize the tax structure, and modify the nation's system of banking. He was also empowered to reorganize public utilities, consolidate government or semigovernment agencies, control monopolies and practices that restrict free trade, and fire civil servants. These drastic powers, most unusual for one of the democratic nations of Latin Amer-

---

[29] For the evolution and exercise of extraordinary decree powers in Mexico, see Stephen S. Goodspeed, "The Development and Use of *Facultades Extraordinarias in México*," *Southwestern Social Science Quarterly*, Vol. 34, No. 3 (December, 1953), pp. 17–33.

[30] Stokes, *op. cit.*, p. 286.

ica, were granted because of the nation's acute economic problems, particularly the severe budgetary deficit it incurred in 1959.[31]

Foreign Relations

Still another area in which the president has broad and significant powers is foreign relations. His is the primary responsibility for determining the nation's politics toward other nations, as well as for setting the prevailing tone of friendliness and cooperation or possibly bellicosity and antagonism. A president who is amicably inclined and interested in the peaceable development of his country may contribute greatly to its progress. Just such a president was Pedo II of Brazil. With its huge territory, Brazil—the colossus of the south it is sometimes called—has common borders with all but two of the nations of South America. This propinquity has involved the nation in many boundary and other disputes with its neighbors. But Pedro I and II, as well as the presidents since Brazil became a republic, followed the course of settling these disputes peacefully by arbitration or friendly negotiation. This wise course is largely responsible for the fact that only six major wars have occurred in Latin America; Brazil participated in only three of them.

A president of a very different stripe was Francisco Solano López of Paraguay, who recklessly plunged his nation into a five-year war with Argentina, Brazil, and Uruguay, the most savage and sanguinary war in the whole history of Latin America. The internecine struggle that Paraguay lost was disastrous for the nation. Its economy was wrecked; its population was reduced from an estimated 525,000 in 1865 to 221,079 in 1871, of whom only 28,746 were men.[32]

In recent years, a matter of particular concern to the United States has been the attitudes and policies of Latin American presidents in the cold war. Some of the presidents, such as José Figueres of Costa Rica and Rómulo Betancourt of Venezuela, have been staunch friends and supporters of the free world ideals and programs. However, some of the other presidents, such as João Goulart of Brazil, have shown such leftist leanings as to greatly disturb the United States, their own nations, and their immediate neighbors as well. Of course, the greatest disturbing leftist influence in the hemisphere has been the bearded prime minister who has openly converted his island nation into a communist state.

Besides being the final voice in determining foreign policy and in directing foreign relations, the president has other related responsibilities. Among these, he concludes and signs treaties of peace, alliance, mutual

---

[31] *New York Times*, March 23, 1959, p. 10, col. 2.

[32] Harris Gaylord Warren, *Paraguay: An Informal History* (Norman: University of Oklahoma Press, 1949), p. 243.

assistance, neutrality, trade and navigation, and boundaries. In addition, he appoints ambassadors and ministers who represent his country in other nations and receives the envoys these nations send to him.

Judicial

In the judicial realm, too, the president has extensive authority. In accordance with the constitution, he is required to oversee the general administration of justice in the nation to make sure that it is impartial and fair to all citizens. As the chief executive charged with enforcing the law, he is also required to see that judicial decisions are enforced. He checks, too, on the operation of the courts to make sure that the official conduct of judges comports with the national dignity and with their official responsibilities.

Among his important judicial powers, the president may also grant pardons, either full or conditional, as well as commute sentences. Often, on a national holiday or just before going out of office he grants pardons freely to friends and political followers. In an effort to prevent abuse of the pardon power, constitutions often limit it in various ways, such as by making persons convicted of electoral frauds or crimes ineligible for pardon until they have served at least a third of their sentence.

A presidential judicial power one occasionally reads about in the newspapers is amnesty—a blanket pardon extended to large groups, usually political offenders. With its frequent exercise, the amnesty is as thoroughly Latin American as *machismo, chicha,* or the siesta. For in most of the nations, the regime in power has incarcerated a large number of political prisoners who may have been in jail for years, whether from having committed such a serious offense as overtly trying to overthrow the government or such a trivial one as speaking disparagingly of the president. Every so often the president proclaims an amnesty for certain or all political offenders, possibly motivated by the goodness of his heart or, more than likely, by the assurance of his established power or by a desire to favorably impress foreign opinion.

Intervention

Another power the president exercises in those states that have a federal form of government is intervention in the states or provinces. As envisaged by constitution makers, intervention is a drastic exercise of federal authority, to be used only for the most cogent reasons and in conformity with the requirements laid down in the constitutions. In Argentina, the national government may intervene in a province in order to repel a foreign invasion, guarantee a republican form of government, support provincial authorities if they request federal assistance, or re-establish them if they have been overthrown. In Brazil, besides these justifications, the federal government may also intervene to assure the execution of a judicial order or decision, reorganize the finances of a state under certain conditions, prohibit the immediate reelection of governors and prefects, and assure the autonomy of municipalities.

Practice among the several federal republics varies somewhat as to who makes the decision about intervention. In Brazil, the president can inter-vene on his own discretion or, in certain circumstances, with the concur-rence of the federal supreme court. In Argentina, however, it is a moot constitutional question which branch of government has the authority to make the decision. On many occasions the congress has assumed this responsibility when it was a powerful force in the affairs of the republic, but the president has made the decision much more often. Of the 129 interventions that occurred between 1860 and 1942, 83 were made by presidential decree, the other 46 by law.[33]

Intervention by the national government in the states and provinces has been intended by constitution framers as a strong weapon to be used discreetly and sparingly; it was designed to preserve the authority and dignity of the national government and the autonomy of the states or provinces. But in practice it has deviated far from its intended purpose; it has degenerated into a political bludgeon which the president uses at will to keep the states or provinces politically in line. It is not, wrote Austin F. Macdonald,

an occasional practice—a last resort used only for the purpose of averting anarchy. Far from it. In the Argentine constitutional system it has long been accepted as part of the established routine. Sometimes it is justified by extreme circumstances; more commonly it arises from trifles that can scarcely be considered matters of federal concern. But always the result is the same: the federal government assumes control of provincial affairs.[34]

The practice of frequent and widespread intervention in Argentina began with the administration of Hipólito Irigoyen, the leader of the Radical Party who became president in 1916. Thanks to the Sáenz Peña electoral law of 1912, which in effect gave the nation truly universal suffrage, Irigoyen was the first freely elected president in the history of the nation. After taking over the presidential office, Irigoyen began a

---

[33] Macdonald, *op. cit.*, p. 180.

For an analysis of interventions 1860–1930 by administrations, provinces, and duration, see Rosendo A. Gómez, "Intervention in Argentina, 1860–1930," *Inter-American Economic Affairs*, Vol. 1, No. 3 (December, 1947), pp. 55–73.

[34] *Ibid.*, p. 170. Many Argentines have felt strongly that interventions were undermining the federal system. Estrada, however, defended them as a legitimate use of power to maintain order in a society in a state of turbulence. José M. Estrada, *Curso de derecho constitucional* (2d ed.; Buenos Aires, 1927), Vol. III, pp. 152–53.

systematic campaign of interfering in the affairs of the provinces, replacing the conservative governors, legislators, and other officials with federal officials who could be trusted to enforce the liberal policies of his regime. During his term of office, the president intervened 20 times in the provinces. While intervention had been used in previous administrations for political ends, it had never been used on such an extensive scale.

Irigoyen's political opponents showed that they could play the same political game. Back in office in 1930 under José Uriburu, one of the first things they did was to intervene in 12 of the 14 provinces and "toss the rascals out." The two provinces spared were already controlled by the conservatives.[35]

In Brazil, too, the power of the central government to intervene in the states has been very much twisted from its original constitutional intent. After Getulio Vargas seized control in 1930, he dismissed all governors of the states except Benedeto de Valladares, governor of Minas Gerais, an able and respected administrator who was regarded as loyal. Just as Irigoyen had done in Argentina, Vargas was to set the pattern in Brazil for wholesale intervention in the states for purely political purposes. "The right of intervention, though defined concretely in line with eventual state deficiencies and failures, is so wide as to place the states fully at the mercy of the federal government, that is, of the president . . .", concludes Karl Lowenstein. "As a matter of fact, although the appearances are carefully preserved, the states are reduced to the status of territorial subdivisions under full central control."[36]

In Mexico, the national government has frequently exercised its power of intervention in the states. The Senate declares that the constitutional powers of a state have "disappeared," warranting the appointment of a provisional governor. Senatorial declarations of disappearance of state powers under Article 76 of the constitution were numerous in the chaos of the early years of the revolution but have been infrequent in recent years.[37] When resorted to, however, intervention has been abusively used for political purposes, some observers are strongly convinced.[38]

State of Siege

Easily one of the most important powers of the president is his authority to proclaim an *estado de sitio,* or state of siege, also known as the suspension of constitutional guarantees. This emergency power is

---

[35] Macdonald, *op. cit.,* pp. 170–71.

[36] Karl Lowenstein, *Brazil Under Vargas* (New York: Macmillan Co., 1942), p. 51.

[37] Felipe Tena Ramírez, *Derecho constitucional mexicano* (2d ed.; México, 1949), pp. 126–27.

[38] Scott, *op. cit.,* pp. 273–75.

authorized by the constitutions to be used if the nation is threatened by foreign invasion or serious internal disturbances. The state of siege is somewhat similar to martial law in the United States, the main difference being that under the state of siege the civilian police and regular organs of government continue to function, while under martial law civilian control is superseded by military.[39]

The constitutions of the republics invariably provide that the state of siege may be authorized only by the Congress—a bold bid for control of this important emergency power. In practice, however, the president usually asks the congress for authority to exercise the power. If the body is not in session, he is empowered to take action on his own authority or possibly with the concurrence of members of a permanent legislative commission—a sort of congressional watchdog that functions between sessions of congress. In either event, the president is required to call a special session of congress within a specified period of time, ranging from 2 to 60 days.

The emergency recognized by the state of siege vests extraordinary powers in the president and authorizes him to take drastic steps that affect most aspects of national life. He may, for example, increase the size of the standing army or call up additional reserves that may be needed. The president may also divert national taxes and income to military purposes and even make forced loans if the government critically needs the money. Another measure that affects all citizens is the suspension of certain private rights guaranteed by the constitution, especially those of freedom of speech and the press, peaceable assembly, privacy of one's home and correspondence, and freedom to move about in the country. In some nations, such as the Dominican Republic, virtually all constitutional guarantees are suspended for the duration of the emergency.

The presidents of some nations resort to the state of siege on the least provocation, as when, for instance, there is a possibility of political opponents' winning in a forthcoming election; other nations, however, use the emergency power quite sparingly. In the nations that are especially politically unstable or that have long been accustomed to the rule of dictators, a state of siege is practically the normal way of life. In Haiti and the Dominican Republic, the nations of Central America, and Paraguay, the citizens have long been inured to the president's cracking the whip through the medium of the *estado de sitio.*

Even in some of the more democratic and stable nations, the state of siege may have a long duration. Argentina lived under four and a half years of emergency rule prior to Perón's election on February 24, 1946, when the state of siege was lifted for 48 hours to permit the holding of

---

[39] While Argentina, like the other nations, does not recognize martial law, it does recognize a state of prevention and alarm, as well as a state of siege. Pablo A. Ramella, *Derecho Constitucional* (Buenos Aires, 1960), pp. 417–20.

the election. With this brief respite over, Argentina was to endure emergency rule during much of Perón's long dictatorship. Likewise, when Colombia was beset by civil war that took a toll of 200,000 lives during the 10 years 1948–58, the nation was under a state of siege most of the time.

Sometimes, one of the most politically stable nations resorts to this emergency power for dealing with what is commonly regarded as a routine problem of local authorities in maintaining law and order. Taking advantage of the emergency power, Chile declared a state of siege in 1946 to cope with a strike in the nitrate mines, and again in 1947 when a general strike occurred in the coal mines. In addition to being used on other occasions to deal with violence in labor disputes, the state of siege was also used in 1948 to break up a strike led by university students who were protesting increases in bus fares.

Fully cognizant of possible abuse in the suspension of constitutional guarantees, the constitutions and laws have tried to hold it within bounds by many restrictions. As the Bolivian constitution tersely states in Article 38, the authorization of emergency powers for the president is not intended to "grant the Executive extraordinary powers, the total of the public power, or accord him supremacy by which the life, honor, and property of Bolivians are placed at the mercy of the government or of any person." Other constitutions and national laws likewise aim to restrict the president's use of emergency powers. Thus, he is usually limited in the time he may maintain a state of siege, and in order to extend it he is required to obtain the approval of congress. Moreover, he is usually required to make a detailed report to the congress, explaining specifically what dangers justified the emergency measures and describing the steps taken by the administration for coping with the emergency. If congress is not satisfied with the president's explanation, it can call him to account for abusing his authority.

Costa Rica has done a particularly effective job in guarding against possible abuses of the state of siege. The constitution makes it clear that the suspension is a legislative act and can occur only with the approval of two thirds of the legislative assembly. Moreover, the suspension is definitely limited in scope and can affect only certain specified provisions of the constitution. And the suspension can continue for only 30 days, thus precluding its dragging on for months or even years, as is often the case in other nations. Finally, if the assembly is not in session when the emergency arises, the president may order the suspension of constitutional guarantees, but his act serves automatically to convene the assembly within 48 hours to approve or disapprove of his action.[40]

---

[40] Constitution of 1871 (in effect in 1969 and the second oldest in Latin America), Article 82, Clause 7, and Article 109, Clause 3.

THE CABINET

Next in importance to the president in the national administration are his ministers, who act as his chief advisers, and head and supervise the various administrative departments of the government. Collectively, they constitute the cabinet, although the constitutions of Latin America, as in the United States, do not recognize its existence.

The number of ministers varies considerably among the 20 republics, ranging from 8 or 9 in the smallest countries to 25 or so in the largest. Certain ministries are regarded as a must in every one of the countries— those of war or defense, *gobernación* ("government" or interior), *hacienda* (treasury), agriculture or economy, education, public health and social welfare, labor and social security, and foreign affairs.

In selecting his ministers, the president takes into account many weighty considerations,[41] for the dependability and competence of his ministers may well determine the success of his administration. The main criterion he applies is trustworthiness. His ministers will be his trusted confidants and advisers; his programs, his accomplishments, even possibly his very life, will depend on their loyalty and faithful performance of duty.

A second important consideration in the selection of a cabinet member is his political affiliation and participation in the party rough-and-tumble in the nation. As a rule, the president selects as ministers only members of his own political party, especially when it represents a large majority of voters and elects heavy majorities in the congress. Thus, in Mexico where the *Partido Revolucionario Institucional*, popularly known as PRI, represents the overwhelming majority of voters, any president would be regarded as loco if he included in his cabinet a member of one of the small opposition parties. But in other nations, such as Chile or Peru, where the president may have to look to his allies or even to the opposition for the additional support he needs, it is common for his cabinet to include members of these parties.

Certain ministerial posts are regarded as political; they are plums given to the most trusted, most influential, and most likely to be tapped by the president to succeed himself. Such a political post is that of secretary of *gobernación*, who is often second only to the president in power and influence. As the number two man in government, he exercises the sensi-

---

[41] These considerations are given in Blanksten, *op. cit.*, pp. 98–99; and Martin Needler, *Latin American Politics in Perspective* (Princeton, N.J.: D. Van Nostrand Co., Inc., 1963), pp. 147–49.

The qualifications of cabinet members and the role of the cabinet in the decision-making process is treated by Gil, *op. cit.*, pp. 104–6; and L. Vincent Padgett, *The Mexican Political System* (Boston: Houghton Mifflin Co., 1966), pp. 157–60.

tive functions of administration of elections, supervision of provincial and local government, and especially control of the national police. The minister of war or defense is also regarded as a political member. Frequently, he is a ranking officer in the armed forces who has doffed his uniform but not his rank, perquisites, affiliations, and loyalty. Often, he is simply a militarist in civilian garb. When he controls the loyalty of the armed forces and manifests political aspirations, the president had better treat him gingerly, for he is a power to be reckoned with.

A third criterion the president follows in sizing up a prospective minister is his qualification for handling the post. Some of the ministries require a highly professional or technical background and experience to qualify the individual for effectively discharging his duties. Such ministries are those of agriculture, mining, education, justice, and foreign affairs. The minister of foreign affairs is seldom a practicing politician and is not selected for the high post on the basis of party considerations. Rather, he is selected because he is a distinguished figure in his country— a respected jurist, scholar, or man of letters. Recognition abroad of his scholarly achievement is quite an asset too. However, he is seldom regarded as presidential timber. Indeed, the very fact of his having lived abroad and acquired cosmopolitan tastes and thinking is apt to make him suspect by many of his fellow countrymen.

Sometimes, in selecting a cabinet a president tosses political considerations to the winds and chooses the men who in his honest opinion are most qualified for the important responsibilities. President Jorge Alessandri of Chile was one who chose his cabinet on the basis of ability rather than political considerations. It was a blue-ribbon cabinet, and even Alessandri's strongest critics admitted that it was the most able and the most honest that Chile had ever had.

The president frequently makes changes in his cabinet; he can remove any minister at will, and often does. Sometimes, he relieves a single minister of his duties, usually without the courteous amenities that the President of the United States observes in easing out a member of his administration. Indeed, the president in Latin America does not hesitate to throw out his whole cabinet unceremoniously, without apology or compunction. On April 22, 1957, President Carlos Ibáñez of Chile asked his whole cabinet to resign because in his absence from the capital the minister of interior had caused four lawyers representing *Horizonte*, a communist newspaper, to be arrested and exiled to distant provinces.

Why are there so many changes in the cabinet, one may wonder, in view of the president's being so careful in selecting his trusted lieutenants? For one thing, he regards them as expendable. When some political fiasco or snafu occurs, which often he himself is directly responsible for, he must do something to satisfy his political opponents' cry for blood. To shunt any blame from himself and to preserve his *dignidad* unsullied before the nation, he is quite willing to regard his ministers as the scapegoats of the matter and throw them to the wolves.

There is another explanation for the frequent changes in the cabinet, whether individual or collective. They have a definite psychological impact on the citizenry, showing them who is unquestionably the boss, thus reinforcing and maintaining the strong centralized power of the executive.

According to most of the constitutions of Latin American republics, the president cannot take any official action whatever without the approval and signature of the appropriate minister. However, this requirement of ministerial responsibility is entirely theoretical and of no practical significance. For the strong president who dominates the government in most of the nations does not need the approval of any subordinate before exercising any of his executive powers. He alone makes the decision on a policy to be adopted or course of action to be followed. Cabinet members are expected to give their opinions, even possibly to dissuade him if they believe he is making a mistake, but their disagreement with him cannot force him to change his mind. He knows that he is the only one whom the nation holds responsible for discharging the important duties of his office. With this in mind, the president does not take very seriously the constitutional requirement that his ministers must approve and countersign every one of his official acts, especially since he alone selects his ministers and can dismiss them any time he chooses. If conceivably a minister refused to sign one of his official documents, he would be relieved of his duties pronto, and another minister who would sign would be appointed.

The constitutional requirement of ministerial responsibility is "either a dead letter or a redundancy," wrote Austin F. Macdonald, "a dead letter, if it means that the ministers are responsible to Congress or the people, for they are not; or a redundancy, if it indicates that they are responsible to the president, for such a responsibility is already assured through the chief executive's absolute power of appointment and removal."[42]

METHODS OF EXERCISING PRESIDENTIAL CONTROL[43]

In running the government and putting his program into effect, the president resorts to a varied assortment of weapons and methods.

His power over patronage at all governmental levels is extensive. For he has the final word, directly or indirectly, in the selection of the vast number of government officials and employees, ranging from the minister

---

[42] Macdonald, *op. cit.*, p. 196.

[43] For a provocative treatment of this subject, see William W. Pierson and Federico G. Gil, *Governments of Latin America* (New York: McGraw-Hill Book Co., Inc., 1957), pp. 227–31.

of *gobernación* to dogcatcher and garbage collector. In those countries that have unitary systems of government, this is no constitutional problem, since the president by constitutional authorization controls the entire machinery of government even in the most remote localities of the nation. In those countries that have a federal form of government, his power of appointment is potent, too, for the provincial or state governors are either his trusted friends or they are removed forthwith. Consequently, his influence in appointments is felt by public employees all down the line, even to the outer edges of government.

A judicious exercise of the principle of checks and balances is another technique presidents apply instinctively. They may not understand all its theoretical nuances, but they thoroughly appreciate its practical application. Thus, when the army has proved to be a serious threat, the president has sometimes counterbalanced or neutralized its power by strengthening the capability of the national police. And when this does not suffice, the president may even organize and arm a peasant and worker militia that his government can rely on.

Influencing and controlling the news as much as he can is another method every president utilizes. The odds are heavily in his favor. Almost every government has its own official newspaper or papers, which serve as the official mouthpiece and enjoy the advantage of a hot line directly to the presidential office. Any other newspaper that is cooperative and follows the government line is also given favored treatment. Papers or radio stations that oppose him, however, get an official cold shoulder or worse.

The president asserts control over the government and the nation by many other means, such as designating the members of a constituent assembly to draw up a new constitution, influencing the selection of members of congress, creating an official political party, and controlling the dreaded secret police. On occasion, the president has found that the most effective method of dealing with congress is the straightforward, direct approach. In Argentina in 1908, after President Figueroa Alcorta had had many strong disagreements with congress, he finally ordered its members to adjourn and go home. When they balked, he used federal troops to enforce his order.

PRESIDENTIAL RESPONSIBILITY

According to the constitutions, the president is responsible to the congress for any of his acts of omission or commission that violate either the constitution or the laws. These acts comprise a wide range of offenses. In Brazil, they include any "attempt" against: the federal constitution and, in particular, the existence of the Union; the free exercise of the legislative power, judicial power, and constitutional powers of the states; the exercise of social and political rights; the internal security of the country; probity in the administration; the safekeeping and legal use of public funds; and the enforcement of judicial decisions.

If the president is alleged to have violated the constitution or laws of his country, he may be impeached and tried by the congress to determine his innocence or guilt. According to the usual procedure, action against him is instigated in the lower house, which appoints a committee to investigate the charges; after the committee makes its report, the house debates on whether or not the charges are sufficiently substantial to warrant putting the president on trial. To recommend this, a two thirds vote is necessary. If the impeachment charges are adopted, the upper house has no choice but to proceed with the trial, converting itself into a court presided over by the chief justice of the supreme court.

In those republics that have a unicameral congress, this body acts just as the lower house of a bicameral congress, and the president is then tried before the supreme court. In Panama, however, the one-house national assembly not only prefers charges against the president but also conducts the trial.

Whichever procedure is followed for the trial, a two thirds vote is necessary to convict the president of the charges. If convicted, he is removed from office as well as disqualified from holding public office indefinitely or for a specified period. If he has also committed an indictable offense, after being removed from office he may be brought before the ordinary courts and tried as any other citizen of the republic.

Since the president dominates the congress in most of the countries, his impeachment and conviction by that body have been very rare occurrences. In Cuba, President Miguel Mariano Gómez was impeached and removed from office in 1936 when Batista, controlling the government from behind the scenes, brought pressure to bear on the Congress. More recently, the acting president of Panama, José Ramón Guizado, who held office after the assassination on January 2, 1955, of President José Antonio Remón, was tried and convicted of complicity in the assassination of his predecessor. Guizado was removed from office by the national assembly and sentenced to six years' imprisonment.[44]

In March, 1968, the Panamanian Congress voted to impeach and remove President Marco A. Robles for attempting to designate his successor in the election scheduled for two months later. However, Robles defied the congress, charging that its action was unconstitutional; he was successful when the army gave him military support, and the Supreme Court the blessing of legality.

---

[44] A detailed account of the drama of Guizado's impeachment and trial is given in John D. Martz, *Central America: The Crisis and the Challenge* (Chapel Hill: University of North Carolina Press, 1959), pp. 293–304.

In some nations, the president is held accountable on charges of crimes against the state only during his term of office. In other nations, however, this accountability lasts for 6, maybe 12, months after he leaves office. Whatever period is specified, the president is required to remain within the country during this time.

A celebrated case in which a former president was tried for having committed offenses against the state during his term of office was that involving Rojas Pinilla, dictator-president of Colombia from 1953 until his overthrow in 1957. Following his overthrow, the government appointed a bipartisan national commission to investigate allegations of corruption and illegal acts on the part of Rojas and his officials. Acting on the findings of the commission, the chamber of deputies voted 107 to 7 in favor of filing criminal charges. As a result, Rojas was tried by the Senate and found guilty of having acted "in violation of the national constitution" and of "abuse of power by improper conduct in the exercise of the office of president." Specifically, he was found guilty of ordering customs officials to admit duty-free the purebred cattle imported by a friend, and of forcing banks to lend $7 million to friends, relatives, and himself without collateral. The Senate vote for conviction was overwhelming—62 to 4 on the first charge and 65 to 1 on the second, with several senators abstaining. Following conviction, the senate deprived Rojas of his political rights, thereby barring him from voting, holding political office, or serving further in the army. He was also deprived of his honors and titles, as well as of his $3,000 a month pension which the nation gives to ex-presidents.

The charges against Rojas were then supposed to go automatically to the Supreme Court, which would try him for "common crimes." But after Rojas had been detained under house arrest for nearly two years without any action being taken by the court, he was finally released on the payment of 5,000 pesos (about $750) bond, apparently closing the case.[45]

EXPOSURE TO THE PUBLIC—A RISK OF THE GAME

In Latin America, unless the president is a dictator it is customary for him to appear freely in public without a bodyguard or other armed protection. He strolls down the boulevard, mingles with the people, and enjoys himself as any other citizen without any special precautions for his safety—a practice quite different from that in the United States.

Sometimes the risk to his personal safety is especially great, as when a president on occasion has defied danger to perform a dramatic act of

---

[45] The information about Rojas is from the *New York Times*, May, 1957–October, 1960.

heroism. In Chile, when a group of *Nacistas*–Chilean Nazis–opened fire on the presidential palace for the purpose of storming it, mortally wounding a policeman on duty nearby, President Alessandri rushed out to aid the dying man, dragging him to shelter while bullets whizzed around him.[46] And in Bolivia, when an infuriated mob took out its wrath against *Time* magazine by storming the American Embassy and sacking the U.S. Information Office, President Hernán Siles took to the streets in an attempt to calm the mob, even crossing the heavy police lines that guarded the embassy, and addressing the throng from the nearby headquarters of the MNR, urging it to obey the law and maintain order.[47]

Running as many risks as they do, it is inevitable that some of the presidents meet with violence. Several have been assassinated. In Mexico, during the turbulent early years of the revolution two of the presidents were assassinated–Madero in 1913 and Carranza in 1920–as was president-elect Álvaro Obregón in 1928. In Ecuador, two of the presidents were assassinated–Gabriel García Moreno in 1875 and Eloy Alfaro in 1911. Among other presidents who suffered a similar fate were: José Balta in 1872 and Luis Sánchez Cerro in 1933, both of Peru; Anastasio Somoza of Nicaragua and Carlos Castillo Armas of Guatemala, both in 1957; and most recently, Rafael Leonidas Trujillo of the Dominican Republic in 1961. A president of Panama, José Remón, was murdered in 1955. The number of presidents who have met violent ends would be much larger if many a beleaguered president had not fled to a foreign embassy and been saved by the grant of political asylum.

But sometimes a president is not so fortunate when a bloodthirsty mob overturns his government. When this happened to President Gualberto Villarroel of Bolivia in 1946, the vengeful mob dragged him out of an upstairs closet in the presidential palace where he was hiding, beat him up, shot him, then threw him out of the window where those on the street below lynched him, stringing him up to a lamp post that stands in front of the building. President Vilbrun Guillaume Sam of Haiti was another president whose career was ended by violence with a vengeance when in 1915 a mob even entered the French legation to seize their quarry.

Breaking into the legation, they cornered the President in the bathroom where he had taken refuge, pulled him out, dragged him down the steps into the courtyard, and pulled him along the path leading to the locked gate. Throwing Sam's body over the gate, where it became impaled on the iron spikes, the mob dragged it to the ground and poured shot after shot into it.

Even this did not satisfy the passions of the mob. Machetes appeared out of nowhere and Sam's arms, legs, and head were hacked off, impaled on spikes

---

[46] Austin F. Macdonald, *Latin American Politics and Government* (New York: Thomas Y. Crowell Co., 1949), pp. 297–98.

[47] For a vivid account of the mob violence and Siles's role, see *New York Times,* March 3, 1959, p. 8, col. 3.

and paraded through the streets, followed by his bloody torso dragged at the end of a rope. . . .[48]

SUCCESSION TO THE PRESIDENTIAL OFFICE WHEN VACANT

We in the United States attach much importance to the office of vice president. As the number two man in government, who has twice within the last two decades stepped into the breach to take over for a president who had fallen, he represents a shared political experience, continuity of policy, and orderly succession to the high office in time of national crisis.

In Latin America, too, the vice president performs some useful functions. He helps to balance the ticket, as important in Latin America as in the United States, thereby contributing to party and national unity. Thus, in Bolivia during the presidency of Victor Paz Estenssoro from 1952–56 and 1960–64, the vice president for much of this time was Juan Lechín. President Paz was a middle-of-the-roader whose policies and methods decidedly moderated the social revolution Bolivia has been undergoing since 1952. But Lechín was a far leftist, an admitted communist who would have used far more drastic methods and policies to push the nation's social revolution more rapidly ahead. His selection as vice president was to recognize the influential left-wing miners and other labor groups, and to get their needed cooperation and support.

In Ecuador, the vice president has helped to balance the ticket by giving recognition to one of the two sensitive regions in the nation. Political parties have found it wise and expedient to have both the coast and the sierra represented in an administration; accordingly, the president customarily represents one of these regions and the vice president the other.

Another important function of the vice president is to preside impartially over the upper house, casting his vote on any issue when it is necessary to break a tie. His most important function, of course, is to take over the presidential office if for any reason the president is unable or unwilling to discharge his duties.

But in Latin America, the office of vice president—a transplant from the United States—has never really taken root and flourished. In fact, only half of the 20 republics have a vice president. These are: Argentina, Bolivia, Brazil, Chile, Costa Rica, Cuba, Ecuador, Honduras, El Salvador, and Panama. Two of these nations, Costa Rica and Panama, have two vice presidents.

The general tendency of the other 10 nations that have no vice president—even, sometimes, of those who do—is to be very leery of the office.

---

[48] James H. McCrocklin, *Garde D'Haiti, 1915–1934* (Annapolis, Md.: United States Naval Institute, 1956), pp. 15–16.

It has never acquired much stature in the region. The vice president, usually representing a different faction or even party, and frequently ambitious and chafing at being relegated to second place, has often forgotten his oath of office and sparked a revolt that managed to throw out the president.

Wary of such possible machinations by the vice president, 10 of the nations have made other arrangements for succession to the presidential office in case it is vacant. In Colombia and Nicaragua, a *designado* appointed by the congress and having the same qualifications required of a presidential candidate would take over the office in an interim capacity. In Mexico, a provisional president would be selected by the Congress. In other nations, the president of the supreme court, the president of the chamber of deputies, or a minister would temporarily take over the presidential duties.

EX-PRESIDENTS

Latin America has been notably imaginative in utilizing the interests, talents, and experience of its ex-presidents. In a number of the republics, including Nicaragua and Venezuela, the constitutions provide that a former president is to be honored by being made a member of the Senate for life. In Mexico, President Adolfo López Mateos did some thinking up about the nation's seven living ex-presidents; he offered every one of them a very responsible position in the government as project director or adviser to himself. Every one of the former presidents accepted the offer, including several who had previously been expending their energies in opposing the government.[49] President López' course was a wise one for many reasons. It solved a long-standing problem of how to recognize the honor and prestige of former presidents, and it also brought back into the government invaluable experience and expertise.

Perhaps most important of all, López' recognition enabled restless ex-presidential political volcanoes to expend their energies usefully instead of possibly spewing political volcanic ashes of unrest, conspiracy, and revolution that would endanger the government.

SUGGESTED READINGS

Blanksten, George I. *Ecuador: Constitutions and Caudillos*, chap. v. Berkeley: University of California Press, 1951.

Busey, James L. *Latin America: Political Institutions and Processes*, pp. 28–33; 57–60; 72–75; 110–12; 159–61. New York: Random House, Inc., 1964.

---

[49] *New York Times*, March 18, 1962, p. 40, col. 1.

Davis, Harold Eugene. *Government and Politics in Latin America,* chap. 10. New York: Ronald Press Co., 1958.

Edelmann, Alexander T. "The Rise and Demise of Uruguay's Second Plural Executive," *Journal of Politics,* Vol. 31, No. 1 (February, 1969).

Fitzgibbon, Russell H. "'Continuismo' in Central America and the Caribbean," *The Inter-American Quarterly,* Vol. 2, No. 3 (July, 1940), pp. 56–74.

———. "Executive Power in Central America," *Journal of Politics,* Vol. 3, No. 3 (August, 1941), pp. 297–307.

———. "Adoption of a Collegiate Executive in Uruguay," *Journal of Politics,* Vol. 14, No. 4 (November, 1952), pp. 616–42.

Gil, Federico G. *The Political System of Chile,* pp. 92–106. Boston: Houghton Mifflin Co., 1966.

Gómez, R. A. *Government and Politics in Latin America,* chap. 5 and pp. 27–28. Rev. ed.; New York: Random House, Inc., 1964.

———. "Latin American Executives: Essence and Variations," *Journal of Inter-American Studies,* Vol. 3, No. 1 (January, 1961), pp. 81–95.

———. "Intervention in Argentina, 1860–1930," *Inter-American Economic Affairs,* Vol. 1, No. 3 (December, 1947), pp. 55–73.

Goodspeed, Stephen S. "The Development and Use of *Facultades Extraordinarias* in Mexico," *Southwestern Social Science Quarterly,* Vol. 34, No. 3 (December, 1953), pp. 17–33.

Jorrín, Miguel. *Governments of Latin America,* chap. 4. New York: D. Van Nostrand Co., Inc., 1953.

Lott, Leo B. "Executive Power in Venezuela," *American Political Science Review,* Vol. L, No. 2 (June, 1956), pp. 422–41.

Macdonald, Austin F. *Government of the Argentine Republic,* chaps. 8 and 10. New York: Thomas Y. Crowell Co., 1942.

Needler, Martin. *Latin American Politics in Perspective,* pp. 135–52. Princeton, N.J.: D. Van Nostrand Co., Inc., 1963.

Padgett, L. Vincent. *The Mexican Political System,* chap. 6. Boston: Houghton Mifflin Co., 1966.

Pierson, William W., and Gil, Federico G. *Governments of Latin America,* chap. 8. New York: McGraw-Hill Book Co., Inc., 1957.

Scott, Robert E. *Mexican Government in Transition,* chap. 8. Rev. ed. Urbana: University of Illinois Press, 1964.

Stokes, William S. *Honduras: An Area Study in Government,* chap. 7 and pp. 285–88. Madison: University of Wisconsin Press, 1950.

———. *Latin American Politics,* chap. 16. New York: Thomas Y. Crowell Co., 1959.

Tucker, William P. *The Mexican Government Today,* chap. 7 and pp. 81–82. Minneapolis: University of Minnesota Press, 1957.

Vanger, Milton I. "Uruguay Introduces Government by Committee," *American Political Science Review,* Vol. 48, No. 2 (June, 1954), pp. 500–518.

15

LEGISLATURES:
Echoes and Voices

LEGISLATIVE–EXECUTIVE RELATIONS

The legislature or congress in Latin America is theoretically an equal partner with the other two branches of government, the executive and the judiciary. However, this equality is usually more fiction than fact. In most of the nations, the legislative body is greatly overshadowed by the president and does not even enjoy as much independence or influence as the judiciary.

"The unicameral legislature is almost always a rubber stamp of the president's wishes," write John and Mavis Biesanz, referring to Panama; "most of its members being concerned chiefly with seeing that they get their share of the government pork barrel."[1] This description of the legislature in Panama accurately characterizes the role of the body in most of the other nations too. The legislatures ordinarily kowtow to the president, cater to his slightest whims, and enjoy no more independence or popular respect than political sycophants could expect to.

There are many reasons for the predominance of the president and the minor supporting role played by most legislatures. In many of the nations, the legislature is a hand-picked body, with the long, influential hand of the president doing the picking. Often it is impossible to be elected without his personal approval.[2] Even when the president does not per-

---

[1] John and Mavis Biesanz, *The People of Panama* (New York: Columbia University Press, 1955), p. 141.

[2] For the influence the president has exercised in Mexico, see Frank Tannenbaum, *Mexico: The Struggle for Peace and Bread* (New York: Alfred A. Knopf, Inc., 1954), pp. 89–90 and 96; L. Vincent Padgett, *The Mexican Political System* (Boston:

sonally pass on his party's candidates for the legislature, they may owe their election entirely to riding into office on his coattails and therefore be beholden to him.

Besides owing their election to the president, the legislators in most of the nations are well aware that in a power struggle he holds most of the trumps, especially the high ones such as the support of the armed forces and the national police. In a showdown of strength, he does not hesitate to play them, either. In Haiti, dictator Duvalier had no compunction about ousting six members of the senate on the trumped-up charge that they were betraying their national trust.[3] In Venezuela, President Betancourt, one of the most consistent liberals and supporters of constitutional government, reluctantly but forcefully "threw the book" at communist members of the congress who in his judgment were masterminding the sabotage and terrorism designed to paralyze the nation and prevent it from holding the elections scheduled for December, 1963. Despite their congressional immunities, President Betancourt had them put under house arrest and later put into prison.[4]

Many other factors help to explain the inconsequential role of the legislature in many of the nations. The prevailing illiteracy, poverty, and lack of political experience have had much to do with it. Denied the privilege of voting because of illiteracy, and hardly knowing what was going on even when given the suffrage, the great majority of citizens have never been really interested in the legislature's work, problems, or degree of independence. Conversely, the tradition of the strong leader who can capture the imagination of the mass has also served to relegate the repesentative body to a position of minor importance.

In most of the nations, as is illustrated in the case of Panama, the legislatures are merely rubber stamps. But this is certainly not true of some of the most important countries of the region, both large and small.

In Brazil, the congress has been far from being a lackey. "Despite the Brazilian habit of strong presidential leadership," says James L. Busey, "the Congress is no pliant tool in the hands of the executive. . . . Though the President is strong, he cannot be sure that all his legislation will be approved, and provisions on the veto and means whereby it may be overridden, as well as on the various legislative powers of the Congress, are more than mere empty gestures to the forms of democratic government."[5] But since the military take-over in 1964, Brazil's Congress is merely an echo of the military.

Houghton Mifflin Co., 1966), pp. 147–48; and Robert E. Scott, *Mexican Government in Transition* (Urbana: University of Illinois Press, 1964), pp. 262–63.

For presidential influence in Argentina, see Austin F. Macdonald, *Government of the Argentine Republic* (New York: Thomas Y. Crowell Co., 1942), p. 205.

[3] *New York Times,* October 11, 1959.

[4] *Hispanic American Report,* Vol. XVI, No. 10 (December, 1963), pp. 978–79.

[5] James L. Busey, *Latin America: Political Institutions and Processes* (New York: Random House, Inc., 1964), p. 113.

The congress is even less a pliant tool in some of the other nations. In Chile at the opening session of May, 1961, members of the opposition rudely showed their lack of respect for the president by staging a slow march across the speaker's platform, interrupting the president's State of the Union Address.[6] While disagreement is usually not so crudely expressed, Chilean legislators are traditionally quite independent in expressing their opinions, in supporting or opposing presidential programs, and most important of all, in casting their votes. This legislative independence is largely the result of the country's multiparty system.

In Costa Rica also, members of the legislature are not the least bit awed by the president. Only when his party has a large majority can he be assured that his program will be approved, and even then some members of his party may defect and oppose it. He cannot even be sure of the respectful attention of legislators during the reading of his annual message, which in most of the nations is a very ceremonious, pompous, and solemn event. His remarks may be greeted with derisive laughter, boos, hisses, and catcalls.[7]

In Uruguay, too, the congress insists on exercising the power and influence granted to it by the constitution. Although there, as in other nations, the role of the executive tends to be increasingly prominent,[8] the legislative branch has anomalously become more important too. "Its job is legislation, policy making if you will," writes Russell Fitzgibbon, "but more basically and more subtly it has the correspondingly greater responsibility of retaining fundamental control over the executive and the administrative machine. Uruguay's parliament well realizes and exercises that responsibility."[9]

Peru is another nation where the legislature has been anything but a sycophant, lackey, or pliant presidential tool. In fact, it was very obstructive to the program of President Belaúnde. Although he easily won in the June, 1963, election, receiving almost 100,000 more votes than his closest challenger, the perennial APRA candidate Victor Haya de la Torre, nevertheless his party and coalition supporters were able to elect only 20 of the 45 members of the senate, and only 52 of the 140 members in the chamber of deputies.

When Belaúnde tried to bargain with the opposition, offering several ministerial posts in exchange for a commitment to pass a specified minimum of his planned legislation and to give his party members several of the official positions in the senate and chamber of deputies, APRA and UNO spurned the proposal. Instead of cooperating with Belaúnde, they

---

[6] *Hispanic American Report,* Vol. XIV, No. 4 (July, 1961), p. 439.

[7] Busey, *op. cit.,* p. 74.

[8] This is, of course, a well-nigh universal trend. For a provocative discussion, "The Decline of Legislatures?" see K. C. Wheare, *Legislatures* (New York: Oxford University Press, 1963), chap. 9.

[9] Russell H. Fitzgibbon, *Uruguay: Portrait of a Democracy* (New Brunswick, N.J.: Rutgers University Press, 1954), pp. 155 and 161.

signed a pact giving their members all important posts in both houses of
the legislature, including committee chairmanships. The alliance between
the supposedly liberal APRA and the ultraconservative UNO consisting of supporters of Manuel A. Odria, dictator of the nation from
1948 to 1956, was one of the oddest coalitions in Peruvian legislative
history. Earlier bitter enemies and not even on speaking terms, they were
now kissing kin. Because of their control of the legislature, President
Belaúnde's program has been almost hamstrung.[10]

LEGISLATIVE EXPERIMENTATION

Whatever their legislative shortcomings, the nations have certainly
shown a willingness to experiment with various forms and practices.

Seven of the countries—Costa Rica, El Salvador, Guatemala, Haiti,
Honduras, Panama, and Paraguay—have unicameral legislatures. The
decision to have only one house was usually made for cogent objective
reasons. The nations are small and relatively homogeneous, have a unitary
system of government, and prefer to economize by supporting just one
house.[11]

However, the decision to adopt the unicameral system has not always
been made on such an objective basis. In the spring of 1961, dictator-
president Duvalier of Haiti in *caudillo* fashion arbitrarily reduced the
bicameral legislature to a single-house body in preparation for the April
30 election. A single list of 58 candidates, all of them his personal supporters, was sponsored by the government and elected. By making the
change, Duvalier eliminated the handful of followers of his opponent in
exile, Louis Dejoie, who had held seats in the previous legislature.[12]

Another innovation, at least in the western hemisphere, is Ecuador's
trial of functional representation since 1929. There are four national
functional senators, representing public education, private education,
journalism and the scientific and literary societies, and the armed forces.
In addition, there are eight regional functional senators apportioned
equally between the sierra and the coast, representing for each region
agriculture, commerce, industry, and labor. The 12 national and regional

---

[10] *Hispanic American Report,* Vol. XVI, No. 6(August, 1963), pp. 597–98; and
Vol. XVI, No. 7 (September, 1963), pp. 705–6.

[11] For a concise analysis of the bicameral system in federal and nonfederal states
and the unicameral system in nonfederal states, see Inter-Parliamentary Union,
*Parliaments: A Comparative Study on the Structure and Functioning of Representa-
tive Institutions in Forty-One Countries* (New York: Frederick A. Praeger, Inc.,
1961), pp. 4–13.

[12] Karl M. Schmitt and David D. Burks, *Evolution or Chaos: Dynamics of Latin
American Government and Politics* (New York: Frederick A. Praeger, Inc., 1963),
pp. 179–80.

senators are elected every four years by electoral colleges so organized as to best reflect the interests of the particular group involved.[13]

Functional representation in the Ecuadorian Senate accomplishes two main purposes. It enables certain groups that are basic in the power structure to better protect their interests. It also tends to prevent any catastrophic disruption of the delicate balance of power between the sierra and the coast.[14]

Another bit of creative thinking on the legislative front led to the selection of *suplentes*, or alternate members, who take office if a regular member for any reason cannot perform his duties. The practice has many points in its favor. During a session, members often drop out for illness or other reasons. If this occurs, the *suplente* steps in to perform the duties. Elected in the same manner and required to have the qualifications of a member of the legislature, he is logically the best suited for taking over.[15]

Also an interesting device is the Permanent Committee which is composed of members of both houses and functions between sessions of the legislature. Acting as a sort of watchdog, it keeps a close eye on the activities of the president and executive departments, passes on the president's request for a state of siege, and calls the legislature back into session if the circumstances warrant.[16]

Still another experiment tried in some of the nations has been that of parliamentary or semiparliamentary government. Where this system has been practiced, members of the cabinet may attend sessions of the legislature and participate in debate but may not cast a vote. They may even be required to attend sessions and be subjected to grueling questioning. In Peru and Uruguay, if the legislature approves a motion of censure the minister or ministers involved are removed.[17]

---

[13] For the composition of each of the electoral colleges, see *Special Memorandum No. 21: Methods of Electing National Executives and National Legislatures in Latin American Countries* (Washington, D.C.: Institute for the Comparative Study of Political Systems, n.d.), pp. 16–17.

[14] George I. Blanksten, *Ecuador: Constitutions and Caudillos* (Berkeley: University of California Press, 1951), pp. 106–7.

[15] This system is superior in many respects to that in the United States. If for any reason a congressional seat becomes vacant, the district is often without representation until the next election. If a senatorial seat is involved, the governor may arrange to appoint anyone he pleases, including himself, even though the appointee may belong to a political party different from that of the former holder, and for this or some other reason would hardly have been chosen by the electorate.

[16] In Mexico where the Permanent Committee has a considerable number of duties, constitutional authorities criticize it on the grounds that it has no fixed rules or minority members, and might possibly become dominant over the congress. However, there is apparently no strong move to abolish the committee. William P. Tucker, *The Mexican Government Today* (Minneapolis: University of Minnesota Press, 1957), pp. 98–99.

[17] For an extended discussion of this subject, see William S. Stokes, "Parliamentary Government in Latin America," *American Political Science Review*, June, 1945, pp. 522–36.

Many of the nations have also experimented with unusual means for the introduction of laws. State legislatures in Mexico are empowered by the constitution to propose laws to congress. The Cuban people under the nation's 1940 constitution could initiate a law by having 10,000 voters sign a petition. Members of the judiciary and judicial officers in some of the nations prepare bills or assist in their preparation. In Honduras, any bill that amends or repeals code law either must originate in the supreme court or its opinion must be heard by congress before the bill is enacted into law.

The legislative commission established in Ecuador in 1944 represents one of the most novel experiments in the introduction of legislation. The commission, designed to prepare bills of major importance, is a very select, broadly representative body. The five-member group is composed of one senator, one deputy, one representative of the president, one representative of the judiciary, and the dean of the faculty of juris-prudence at the Central University at Quito. Bills formulated by the commission are presented directly to a joint session of congress and are not considered by a standing committee of either chamber. A measure once passed by a two thirds vote of the joint session is sent to the president for his signature and promulgation, with no choice of veto on his part.[18]

SELECTION OF MEMBERS

Qualifications

Citizenship is a requisite for legislators in every one of the nations. A majority of the countries, in fact, specify that legislators must be natural-born citizens. In others, however, persons are eligible who have been citizens for a specified number of years or, in a few countries, from the moment they become citizens.

With regard to age, in countries that have the bicameral system, a member of the upper house in 6 of the nations must be at least 30 years old, in 4 at least 35, and in 1 at least 40. The Dominican Republic specifies 25, and Brazil 21. One is eligible for the lower house at age 25 in 8 nations, age 30 in 1, and age 35 in 1. Brazil and Venezuela specify 21; and Chile, only that one be eligible to vote. In the 7 unicameral nations, 21 is the minimum age in 2, 25 in 4, and 30 in 1, Haiti.

Residence within the nation for a minimum period preceding the election is sometimes required. In the Dominican Republic, if one is a naturalized citizen, two years' continuous residence immediately preceding

---

[18] Blanksten, *op. cit.*, pp. 115–16.

the election is required. Some nations also specify that members must reside in the state, province, department, district, or other unit from which they are elected. Uruguay does not have a residence requirement, however; consequently, congressmen are often elected from departments other than the ones in which they reside.

Three of the nations have noteworthy additional requirements for members of the upper house. Argentina requires an annual income of 2,000 pesos, and Costa Rica an income of 200 colones or property valued at 500 colones. Colombia emphasizes experience, specifying that besides fulfilling the other requirements a candidate for the senate must have served as president of the republic, minister in the cabinet, chief of a diplomatic mission, governor of a department, or magistrate of a court, or have been a university professor for at least five years, or be a lawyer, doctor, or other professional person and have a university degree.

Besides establishing certain qualifications, the constitutions and laws also set up various disqualifications which can automatically bar election to the legislature. Those most usually disqualified are specified government officials, clergymen, members of the armed forces, persons who have contracts with the government or are in debt to the treasury, and close relatives of the president, vice president, and cabinet members.

Apportionment

Members of the upper house are usually apportioned equally among certain specified electoral areas. This is true in both federal and unitary states. In Argentina, two senators are allotted to each province and the federal capital, and in Bolivia two to each department. Colombia follows a different principle, however. It apportions seats on the basis of population, one for every 190,000 inhabitants; each department has a minimum of three senators. In Peru, too, senators are apportioned on the basis of population.

Brazil's 1946 constitution had the unusual feature of permitting one to be a candidate for the senate from several of the states simultaneously, and at the same time run for the lower house from several districts too. After Getulio Vargas was deposed by the military in October, 1945, he ran for election to both houses of the congress in the election of December, 1945. His popularity among the workers was so great that he was elected Senator from São Paulo and from Rio Grande, also Congressman from six states in the central district.[19]

Members of the lower house are usually chosen from the same electoral areas as senators, but on the basis of population. Paraguay with its

---

[19] John W. F. Dulles, *Vargas of Brazil: A Political Biography* (Austin: University of Texas Press, 1967), p. 281.

TABLE 15-1

Bicameral Legislatures
(senate)

Country	No. of Members	Term— Years	Qualifications	Basis of Apportionment	Special Features
Argentina	46	9; ⅓ every 3 years	Age 30, citizen for 6 yrs., annual income of 2,000 pesos, 2 yrs. residence in province or born there	2 to each province and the federal capital	Indirect election: in provinces, by plurality vote of provincial legislatures; in federal capital, by electoral college
Bolivia	27	6; ⅓ every 2 years	Age 35; others as for deputies	3 to each department	⅓ or ⅔ of members elected every 4 years, respectively
Brazil	66	8	Age 21; citizen by birth	3 to each state and the federal district	20 or 25 elected every 4 years, respectively
Chile	45	8	Age 35; citizen, eligible to vote	5 to each provincial senatorial grouping or district	Membership equally divided under parity formula
Colombia	98	4	Age 30, citizen by birth, have held high political, administrative, diplomatic, or judicial office or been professor or practiced profession, with degree	At least 3 to every department, 1 : 190,000	
Cuba	—	—	—	—	Last elections, Nov. 3, '58, annulled by revolutionary gov't in '59. None held since.

Country			Qualifications	Apportionment	Election system
Dominican Republic	74	2	Age 30, citizen 8 years, 2 years continuous residence preceding election	To provinces and the national district, 1 : 50,000	A plurality when only 1 is elected, otherwise by PR
Ecuador	73	2	Age 25, citizen by birth enjoying rights of citizen	At least 2 to a province, 1 : 50,000	In all pluripersonal elections, a closed list, PR
Mexico	178	3	Age 25, citizen by birth, possessed of his rights, a native or resident of state for 6 months preceding election	At least 2 to a state, 1 : 200,000; 1 to a territory with less than 200,000	Renewed in entirety
Nicaragua	42	4	Age 25, citizen in the exercise of his rights, secular status	To departments, 1 : 30,000	Election according to PR
Peru	182	6	Age 25, citizen by birth, eligible to vote, a native of the dept. or 3 years continuous residence	2 to a department with population up to 100,000, to a maximum of 24 for departments over 2,000,000	Renewed in entirety
Uruguay	99	4	Age 25, citizen for 5 years in exercise of his rights	At least 2 to a department, figured on a quotient of representation	—
Venezuela	50	6	Age 21, citizen by birth	At least 2 to a state and 1 to the Federal Territory, 1 : 50,000	Closed list, PR

TABLE 15-2

Bicameral Legislatures
(chamber of deputies)

Country	No. of Members	Term—Years	Qualifications	Basis of Apportionment	Special Features
Argentina	192	4: ½ every 2 years	Age 25, citizen 4 years, 2 years residence or born in province	At least 2 to a province and the federal capital, 1 : 85,000	Closed list, PR
Bolivia	72	4: ½ every 2 years	Age 25, citizen by birth, completion of military duties, inscription in the civic register	At least 4 to a department, 1 : 100,000	Open list, PR
Brazil	409	4	Age 21, citizen by birth	7 to 20 to a state, 1 : 150,000. Above 20, 1 : 250,000. Every territory a minimum of 1	Renewed in entirety, open list, PR
Chile	147	4	Citizen, eligible to vote	1 : 30,000	Renewed in entirety, open list, PR
Colombia	181	2	Age 25, citizen with full rights	At least 3 to a department, 1 : 90,000	Membership equally divided under parity formula, closed list, PR
Dominican Republic	27	4	Age 30, citizen for 10 years with 2 years continuous residence preceding election	1 to each province and the national district	

Country	Number	Qualifications	Apportionment	Remarks
Ecuador	51	4	Age 25, citizen by birth	2 to each province and 1 to Archipelago of Colon, directly; also 12 functional senators chosen by electoral colleges	Renewed in entirety
Mexico	60	6	Age 35, others as for deputies	2 to each state and the federal district	Presidential runner-up and popularly elected ex-presidents are members
Nicaragua	19	4	Age 40, citizen, secular status	1 to every department	Renewed in entirety. Closed lists, PR
Peru	53	6	Age 35, citizen by birth, eligible to vote	At least 1 to a department; for those over 400,000, up to a maximum of 9 for departments over 2,000,000	
Uruguay	31	4	Age 30, citizen 7 years	All members elected from the whole republic regarded as a single electoral district	Closed lists, PR
Venezuela	50	6	Age 30, citizen by birth	2 to each state and the federal district; also a number awarded by a national quotient	Past presidents also members

TABLE 15-3

UNICAMERAL LEGISLATURES

Country	No. of Members	Term— Years	Qualifications	Basis of Apportionment	Special Features
Costa Rica	57	4	Age 21, literate, property valued at 500 colones or annual income of 200 colones, citizen, resident for 4 years after naturalization	To provinces, 1 : 30,000	No immediate reelection. PR
El Salvador	54	2	Age 25, citizen by birth, of known integrity and education, a native or resident of the district	To departments, 1 : 50,000	Renewed in entirety. Party with highest vote in department gets all the seats
Guatemala	66	4: ½ every 2 years	Age 21, citizen by birth, in the exercise of rights, secular status	At least 2 to an electoral district. In districts over 100,000, 1 additional for each 50,000	If three or more positions, a closed list, PR
Haiti	58	6	Age 30, citizen by birth, in enjoyment of civil and political rights, resident of department 2 years	1 to a district	
Honduras	58	6	Age 25, citizen by birth, in exercise of rights, native or resident of department	At least 1 to a department, 1 : 30,000	No immediate reelection
Panama	53	4	Age 25 and a citizen	At least 1 to a province, 1 : 25,000	
Paraguay	60	5	Age 25 and a citizen by birth	All members elected from the whole republic regarded as single electoral district, 1 : 25,000	Renewed in entirety. Open list, PR

SOURCES, Tables 15–1, 15–2, 15–3: *Methods of Electing National Executive and National Legislatures in Latin American Countries*, Special Memorandum No. 21. Institute for the Comparative Study of Political Systems; and *Political Handbook and Atlas of the World*. Used by permission. Also constitutions of the several countries.

unicameral legislature is an exception. The whole nation constitutes a single electoral district, and every member represents the nation as a whole.

The great increase in population has been accompanied by a corresponding increase in the size of the legislature. In Honduras, many observers have been of the opinion that the population boom would soon result in a body of unwieldy proportions.[20] In Brazil, the chamber of deputies is apparently already approaching the limit of manageable size. Although the population of the country is little more than a third that of the United States, the size of its lower house, 409 members, is almost as large as the United States House of Representatives.

The massive trek to the city, especially to the national capital, is creating both a population and electoral imbalance. In Argentina, the federal capital and province of Buenos Aires are allotted 85 out of the 192 deputies in the lower house—almost half of the total number. In Uruguay, Montevideo and adjacent Canelones department together have more than half—51 out of the 99 representatives in the lower house. As the migration to the city continues unabated, the lower house threatens to become in time in some nations mainly a national city council.

Method of Election

Members of the lower house are without exception elected by direct popular vote. In the upper house, members with two exceptions are elected in similar fashion. In Argentina, the two senators from each province are chosen by the provincial legislature and the two from the federal capital by an electoral college. In Ecuador, the 12 functional senators are also selected by electoral colleges.

ORGANIZATION OF THE LEGISLATURE

To discharge its functions effectively and expeditiously, the legislature as a first order of business proceeds to organize itself into a deliberative body. Most constitutions provide in detail for the internal organization which is adopted.

In a bicameral system, the vice president—if there is one—is the presiding officer over the upper house. The lower house, in contrast, selects all its officers, including the president and one or more vice presidents and secretaries. Ordinarily, they are chosen to serve for the entire session. In Mexico, however, they are elected for only a month at a time, which obviously lessens their influence over the body. As a rule the president of

---

[20] William S. Stokes, *Honduras: An Area Study in Government* (Madison: University of Wisconsin Press, 1950), p. 269.

the nation has considerable influence as to who will be selected as presiding officers in those nations where he dominates the legislature, he practically dictates his choice.

As its presiding officer, the president of the body is in many countries virtually in a position to control its deliberations and to determine what measures will be enacted into law. His power to recognize speakers on the floor is important; if he chooses, he may recognize only loyal party supporters, thereby denying the opposition an opportunity to be heard. Sitting in the prestigious speaker's chair, he also has the power to restrict debates, maintain order, and decide points of law. In addition, he designates those who will serve on standing committees.

The selection, work, and importance of committees are quite different among the countries. In those where the president calls the tune, hardly challenged, the committees are puny; they seldom hold public hearings on proposed measures or permit witnesses from outside the executive branch to be heard. As a result, most committee work is very superficial and does not constitute a serious review of the proposals submitted for examination. However, this is certainly not so in those nations where the legislature really has powers and responsibilities. Especially in Chile, Costa Rica, and Uruguay, the committees are an important part of the legislative machinery and have a considerable influence on the outcome of legislation.[21]

THE LEGISLATIVE PROCESS

Most of the important bills considered by the legislature are formulated and presented by the executive. He alone is responsible to the whole nation for getting needed laws passed. Ordinarily, he alone has the assistance of experts in drafting legislative proposals. Moreover, he is in a better position to be informed about the need for new legislation and what laws should be passed to cope with national problems. Accordingly, most constitutions recognize that the president has an important role in the legislative process. He is given exclusive authority to prepare and submit the national budget. Often, the legislature is even specifically prohibited from increasing proposed expenditures unless it provides additional revenues to make up for the difference. In other fields, too, the president sometimes has the exclusive right of initiating legislation. In Paraguay, for example, only the executive council may initiate proposals regarding the public debt or increases in government personnel, salaries, retirement benefits, and pensions.

---

[21] In Chile, although committee members are nominated by the presiding officer in each house, they are, in reality, selected by the party caucus. The bulk of legislation originates, not with the president as in most of the Latin American nations, but with the 13 committees in the chamber of deputies and 14 in the senate. Federico G. Gil, *The Political System of Chile* (Boston: Houghton Mifflin Co., 1966), p. 111.

Private members are, of course, allowed to introduce bills, but they usually receive casual, if any, consideration. Consequently, to save face and preserve his *dignidad,* a member customarily does not propose a specific bill but instead merely presents his idea to the body. If it is favorably received, he may then embody it in a bill he introduces.[22] In contrast, bills that originate with the executive enjoy favorable treatment throughout the legislative process. Given preferential treatment, they are seldom subjected to close scrutiny either by the legislature as a whole or by a committee.

Normal procedure for the passage of a bill conforms to the general practice of democratic legislatures. A bill presented either by the executive branch or by a member of congress is assigned to a certain committee, which may consider the measure in private, hold a public hearing on it, or not consider it at all. Whichever course the committee follows, it must report a bill; it is not allowed, as in the United States, to pigeonhole a measure. In accordance with customary procedure, the measure is given three readings and usually is debated only on the second and third. In the 13 nations that have a bicameral system, the approval of both houses is necessary before a measure is submitted to the president for his signature and promulgation.

Sometimes, the two houses disagree in a bitter battle between themselves. A bill introduced into the Argentine Congress in 1958 to give private universities the right to award degrees and professional titles, thus ending the traditional system of state education at the university level, provoked just such a controversy. The senate favored and approved the bill, but the chamber of deputies vigorously opposed it. The bill passed when the chamber in a tumultuous night session failed to get the two thirds majority necessary to override the senate's approval.[23]

Such disagreement is quite the exception, however. Ordinarily, the order of business, who will do what, and even the outcome of the proceedings, is a foregone conclusion. In fact, open debate in the legislature is mainly window dressing for the nation. Thus, in Ecuador, any one in the know could reliably predict in advance such important matters as who would make what motions, who would speak against them, how long the floor debate on a given issue would last, what aspects of the issue could not be debated because they were delicate or inconvenient, and what the final vote on the issue would likely be.[24]

In discharging its constitutional duties as an independent policymaking

---

[22] In Chile, however, any member of either house of the congress may introduce a bill. The motion introducing it should not be signed by more than 10 deputies or 5 senators, but in practice most bills are signed by more than this number of sponsors. *Ibid.,* p. 115.

[23] *New York Times,* September 21, 1958, p. 33, col. 4; September 25, 1958, p. 18, col. 6; and October 2, 1958, p. 10, col. 3.

[24] Blanksten, *op. cit.,* p. 117.

body, the legislature usually has many strikes against it. The selfish, narrow interests of its members often completely preclude their visualizing national interests and needs. Moreover, the president's enjoyment of the national spotlight enables him to readily mobilize public opinion on his side if he needs to. Easily one of the legislature's greatest drawbacks is a self-imposed one—the intransigent unwillingness of the dominant party in some of the nations to accord any rights or even respect to members of the opposition. Often they are given no recognition whatever—not recognized by the speaker and given the privilege of participating in debates on the floor or assigned to committees where they might express their dissenting convictions. The opposition in such circumstances has no status and is allowed to make no contribution whatever. As a result, all it can do is resort to obstructionist tactics, such as boycotting sessions, hoping thereby to prevent the legislature from having the quorum needed to transact business. In Honduras, one frustrated member of the opposition resorted to the ultimate in obstructionist tactics when he set fire to the legislative palace with the intention of destroying it.

In view of the lack of respect, even vengefulness, shown members of the opposition, it is no wonder that members often challenge one another to duels and that violence sometimes occurs within the legislative chamber itself. On September 8, 1949, a dramatic and tragic gun battle erupted in the Colombian Congress, a microcosm of the nationwide interparty bitterness. Conservative members of the house opened fire on the liberals with pistols, killing the member who held the floor and mortally wounding another. In all, more than 100 shots were fired.[25]

In October, 1961, the Ecuadorian Congress was also a scene of wild disorder. It apparently began when rocks and bottles were thrown from the gallery at antigovernment congressmen. The uproar ended in gunfire with the congressmen taking cover under their desks. In the ensuing volley, Vice-President Carlos Arosemena, who was presiding over the session, grabbed his chair as a shield, fired his revolver wildly at the ceiling, and fled.[26]

SESSIONS

The length of sessions ranges from two months or so in Costa Rica, the Dominican Republic, and Ecuador to five months in Argentina, eight in Brazil, and nine in Uruguay. Often, a certain period will be specified by the constitution, with the proviso that the legislature may extend its sessions for another 30 days if the pressure of business warrants.

---

[25] Vernon Lee Fluharty, *Dance of the Millions: Military Rule and the Social Revolution in Colombia, 1930–1956* (Pittsburgh, Pa.: University of Pittsburgh Press, 1957), pp. 112–13.

[26] *Hispanic American Report*, Vol. XIV, No. 10 (December, 1961), p. 917.

Members are usually paid on a per diem basis, which apparently has often tempted them to prolong sessions. Indeed, one of the most common criticisms of the legislature is that it stays in session unnecessarily long[27] —a sort of legislative boondoggle. The stretch-out is well shown by the Mexican legislature, which in accordance with the constitution meets for up to four months a year. During most of that time, however, the body convenes for business only two or three days a week and for no more than an hour or two a day.

Attendance at meetings is notoriously poor. The constitutions have long taken cognizance of this and embody many provisions intended to remedy the situation, such as an absentee's losing his per diem or, after so many absences, being replaced by the *suplente*. The written penalties are almost never enforced, however, so legislatures are sometimes obviously handicapped. In Colombia, sessions of the lower house often had to be adjourned during October, 1963 for lack of a quorum. The body's idleness, lack of responsibility, and apparent unconcern with the nation's serious problems were sharply criticized throughout the nation. To lessen absenteeism, the president of the house initiated a system of paying representatives' salaries on the basis of their attendance at the session.[28]

Although Brasília is a daring experiment in national planning, it has been a problem in efficient operation of the congress. Most congressmen still insist on living in Rio de Janeiro, with its glamorous metropolitan life, and commuting back and forth, usually only for several days during the middle of the week. Most sessions are so poorly attended that it is often very difficult to obtain the quorums necessary for transacting business.[29]

The duration of sessions when unnecessarily prolonged, the skimpy hours of business, and poor attendance all attest to the relative insignificance of the legislature and the predominance of the executive.

POWERS AND FUNCTIONS

The constitutions endow the legislatures with an impressive number of powers and functions, which cover the gamut of those usually given to policymaking bodies. Whether they exist only on paper or are actually exercised, they may be broadly classified into four main groups: legislative, constitutive, electoral, and judicial.

---

[27] Blanksten, *op. cit.*, p. 104–5; Stokes, *op. cit.*, p. 271; and Fitzgibbon, *op. cit.*, p. 171.

[28] *Hispanic American Report*, Vol. XVI, No. 10 (December, 1963), p. 895.

[29] Jordan M. Young, *The Brazilian Revolution of 1930 and the Aftermath* (New Brunswick, N.J.: Rutgers University Press, 1967), p. 112.

Legislative Powers

The legislative power basically comprises the formulation of public policy and the passage of laws for carrying it out. In the realm of finance, the legislature levies the taxes necessary to support the government and carry out its many activities. The legislature also approves loans obtained on the credit of the nation as well as the terms of their repayment. It provides, too, for the issuance or coinage of money and, theoretically at least, regulates its value.

The legislature's war powers, too, are quite significant. They involve determining the size of the armed forces in time of peace and appropriations for their support, authorizing the president to declare a state of war, and approving the use of national troops anywhere outside the republic.

The regulatory power extends to many aspects of national life. The legislature has control over the free navigation of interior rivers, also over land and maritime trade with foreign nations or between states or provinces. It creates or abolishes governmental departments and bureaus, and authorizes increases in governmental personnel, salary, or other benefits. It may even have to approve the president's leaving the country for a goodwill tour abroad or a visit to a foreign capital to promote the interests of the nation.

The legislature also functions as a sort of custodian of the national territory, probably largely a holdover from earlier days when such *caudillos* as Melgarejo of Bolivia gave away huge chunks of the national domain. Legislative authorization is necessary for the entry of foreign troops into the country and determines the length of their stay. The legislature must also act to create new provinces or departments, determine their boundaries, and keep the principal ports in good condition. Argentina's borders for most of the past century have been quite secure; but the constitution authorizes the congress "to provide for the security of the frontiers, to maintain peaceful relations with the Indians, and promote their conversion to Catholicism."[30]

The legislative power, however, may be exercised negatively as well as positively; the policymaking body sometimes asserts its constitutional prerogatives by refusing to pass legislation the president urgently requests. The Chilean Congress in 1952 turned thumbs down on President Carlos Ibáñez' request for dictatorial powers to deal with a nationwide strike but did give him special powers to combat inflation. The Ecuadorian Congress caused a national crisis by concluding its 1962 session on November 7 of that year without taking action on the president's request for the promotion of 24 high ranking officers of the army, navy, and air force. The officers affected all turned in their resignations and requested

---

[30] *Argentine Constitution* of 1853, Article 67, Paragraph 15.

to be retired, a move calculated to put pressure on the government. When the president's proposal to call a special session was vigorously opposed by the two largest labor unions, the disaffected members of the military backed down, stating that they would accept any decision taken by the congress and would respect the constitution.[31]

In exercising its legislative powers, a determined congress sometimes even overrides a presidential veto. In 1962, the Colombian Congress passed a bill, to be effective in 1964, that would increase the salaries of the president, members of the cabinet, and congressmen. When President Valencia vetoed the measure, citing "the very difficult fiscal circumstances which the nation confronts," the congress overrode his veto and enacted the measure into law.[32]

Constitutive Powers

The legislature also plays a very significant role in the adoption of new constitutions or the amendment of existing ones. Since constitutions in some countries are changed so frequently and in others are amended so often, the power of congress to participate in the process is of no little importance.

If a new constitution is to be adopted, congress' role may be limited to calling a special constituent convention to formulate a new organic law. Six of the countries specify that this will be the procedure when a general revision is to be made.[33] In other nations, however, a new constitution may be formulated by congress itself, usually convened in special session, and also ratified by the congress, normally after a new election of members in order to give the electorate an opportunity to indicate its opinion. The 1961 constitution of Bolivia and 1964 constitution of Haiti are among those adopted under this procedure. Besides formulating and adopting new constitutions, the congress is frequently empowered by the constitution to propose and adopt amendments.

Another indication of the close tie between the legislative and the constitutive power is the frequency with which a constitutive convention, after having formulated a new constitution, becomes the nation's legislative body until new elections are held. In El Salvador, a constituent assembly, convoked by the civil-military directorate, formulated and adopted a new constitution, which went into effect on January 25, 1962. Thereafter, the constituent assembly became the legislative assembly; its term ended May 31, 1964.

---

[31] *Hispanic American Report,* Vol. XV, No. 11 (January, 1963), p. 1035.
[32] *Ibid.,* Vol. XVI, No. 10 (December, 1963), p. 934.
[33] Argentina, Costa Rica, Cuba, El Salvador, Honduras, and Uruguay.

Electoral Powers

The legislature has a number of important responsibilities pertaining to elections. Among these, it passes laws that govern the conduct of elections, and may determine whether their procedure will be genuinely democratic or merely farcical.

In the election of the president especially, the legislature plays an important role. It canvasses the returns and officially proclaims who is the winner. Where elections are close and candidates contest or refuse to recognize the results, the duty is a delicate, unenviable one. In the multiparty nations, the legislature must sometimes even choose the president of the republic. In fact, the multiparty system tends to put the selection in the lap of the legislature. Peru and Venezuela, which have the plurality rule, accept the results of the polls as final, even though it often means having presidents who received a decided minority of the total vote. Chile, on the other hand, requires that the winning candidate must receive a majority of the total votes cast. Since no candidate received such a majority in elections from 1942 to 1964, responsibility for making the choice fell to the lot of congress, which in every case respected as much as possible the wishes of the electorate by selecting the candidate with the largest number of votes.

Judicial Powers

As a check on the other two branches of government, the legislature may impeach and try the president, vice president, officials in the executive departments, and judges. The lower house is charged with the duty of investigating the allegations made against them and drawing up a formal indictment if the evidence seems to warrant. The upper house then conducts a formal trial of the accused. In several of the nations that have unicameral legislatures, the trial is conducted by the supreme court. Although impeachment has often been threatened, only rarely have presidents been put on trial and removed from office. President Balmaceda of Chile was removed in 1891, Eloy Alfaro of Ecuador in 1933, and José Ramón Guizado of Panama in 1955.

An unusual power of the congress is that of approving a request from the president for permission to leave the country. Arnulfo Arias, elected president of Panama in the May, 1968, election, was removed from the presidential office he held in 1941 after he had flown to Havana to visit his oculist without receiving legal permission. His cabinet then declared the office vacant and named a successor.[34]

---

[34] Hubert Herring, *A History of Latin America from the Beginnings to the Present* (New York: Alfred A. Knopf, Inc., 1963), p. 475.

When President Eduardo Frei of Chile routinely requested permission in January, 1967 to be allowed to leave the country for a trip to the United States to discuss important matters of policy, the senate, controlled by the opposition, refused by a vote of 23 to 15 to grant the permission. The action not only provoked much embarrassment but also impeded the president in his important constitutional responsibility of conducting foreign relations.[35]

LEGISLATIVE PRIVILEGES AND IMMUNITIES

In politically democratic nations, members of the legislature enjoy certain unusual privileges and immunities. The free and untrammeled expression of their different points of view, though sometimes offensive, is absolutely necessary. In recognition of this, constitutions in Latin America accord to legislators a freedom of expression and action that ordinary citizens do not enjoy. They cannot be held responsible for statements made or acts committed in pursuance of their legislative duties. Thus, remarks made during the course of debate, however derogatory and vitriolic, are privileged and not subject to the laws of defamation or slander. In addition, legislators may not be arrested for ordinary offenses or subject to civil suit.

Some nations, such as Argentina, recognize immunity as extending over the legislator's entire term of office and protecting him against all but the most serious crimes. "No Senator or Deputy may be arrested," states Article 61 of Argentina's 1853 constitution, "from the day of his election until he ceases in office, except in case of being surprised *in flagrante delicto,* in the commission of a crime that deserves the penalty of death, or an infamous or other distressing one." In the Dominican Republic, on the other hand, immunity according to Article 28 of the constitution extends only to the duration of the legislative session. In practice, the constitutionally provided immunity is sometimes flagrantly violated, but it is usually respected and affords legislators the scope of freedom needed for performing their duties.

In retrospect, one may safely say that the legislature has not lived up to what has been expected of it and what it might have accomplished.

In short, as it now operates [in Mexico] the legislative branch of the national government is not really fulfilling its constitutional duties. . . . On the whole, it serves as little more than a convenient training ground for ambitious young politicians who wish to spend a few years in the national capital, as a kind of convenient patronage for certain political and functional interest association leaders, or as a quiet tapering-off appointment for older politicians who no

---

[35] *New York Times,* January 29, 1967, p. 4, cols. 3–6.

longer are as efficient as they once were but are not quite ready to retire, or perhaps more nearly correctly, to remove their names from the public payroll.[36]

Yet, despite the legislature's imperfections it is a main wheel in the governmental machinery. Its measure of effectiveness is probably the best single index of the true level of democracy.

SUGGESTED READINGS

Blanksten, George I. *Ecuador: Constitutions and Caudillos,* chap. vi. Berkeley: University of California Press, 1951.

Christensen, Asher N. *The Evolution of Latin American Government: A Book of Readings,* No. 30. New York: Henry Holt & Co., 1951.

Cox, Isaac Joslin. "Chile: The Pseudo-Parliamentary Regime, 1891–1914," *Argentina, Brazil, and Chile Since Independence* (ed. A. Curtis Wilgus), chap. 30. Washington, D.C.: George Washington University Press, 1935. Reissued in 1963 by Russell and Russell, New York.

Gil, Federico G. *The Political System of Chile,* pp. 106–22. Boston: Houghton Mifflin Co., 1966.

James, Herman G. *The Constitutional System of Brazil,* chap. iii. Washington, D.C.: Carnegie Institution of Washington, 1923.

Jorrín, Miguel. *Governments of Latin America,* chap. 5. New York: D. Van Nostrand Co., Inc., 1953.

Macdonald, Austin F. *Government of the Argentine Republic,* chaps. 12 and 13. New York: Thomas Y. Crowell Co., 1942.

Scott, Robert E. "Legislatures," *Government and Politics in Latin America* (ed. Harold Eugene Davis), chap. 11. New York: The Ronald Press Co., 1958.

Pierson, William W., and Gil, Federico G. *Governments of Latin America,* chap. 10. New York: McGraw-Hill Book Co., Inc., 1957.

Stokes, William S. *Honduras: An Area Study in Government,* pp. 268–93. Madison: University of Wisconsin Press, 1950.

———. *Latin American Politics,* chap. 17. New York: Thomas Y. Crowell Co., 1959.

———. "Parliamentary Government in Latin America," *American Political Science Review,* Vol. XXXIX, No. 3 (June, 1945), pp. 522–36.

———. "The Cuban Parliamentary System in Action, 1940–1947," *Journal of Politics,* Vol. 11, No. 2 (May, 1949), pp. 335–64.

Tucker, William P. *The Mexican Government Today,* chap. 6. Minneapolis: University of Minnesota Press, 1957.

---

[36] Scott, *op. cit.,* p. 265.

16

COURTS AND LAW:
The Last Word, Fact or Fiction

The administration of justice is one of the most important functions of government. The legal and equitable decision of controversies that arise from conflicting rights of citizens or of citizens and the state is the weighty responsibility of the courts. The administration of justice in Latin America, as elsewhere, has never been easy. The Aztecs, who did not develop a systematic script to form an alphabet or syllabary, represented the purport of their laws and kept judicial records by means of painted pictures. The Incas devised a more ingenious system. The courts of justice kept records of their sentences by means of knots made on cords of various colors, the color signifying the kind of offense that had been punished. Small threads, also of various colors, attached to the cords indicated the punishment meted out.[1]

The courts today do not have to draw pictures to portray concepts of justice or knot variegated cords to record judicial decisions, but the administration of justice is still a difficult as well as important responsibility.

PECULIAR ATTRIBUTES OF LATIN AMERICAN LAW

A Blend of Legal Systems

By far the major influence on the legal systems of the Latin American nations has been the Roman law, their common cultural heritage. The Roman or civil law had for many centuries provided the basis and much

---
[1] John H. Wigmore, *A Kaleidoscope of Justice* (Washington, D.C.: Washington Law Book Co., 1941), pp. 567 and 587–90.

of the content of the law in both Spain and Portugal. "Remaining long under Roman dominion," writes John Thomas Vance, "Spain's inhabitants became thoroughly Romanized. . . . Roman dominion introduced Roman law into Spain on the basis of cultural influence."[2]

The civil law as recognized in Spain and Portugal was transplanted to the New World by the conquistadors and settlers. It was as much a part of the Iberian culture in the New World as was the use of the Spanish and Portuguese languages. During the three centuries or more of colonial rule, the colonies all had the legal systems in effect in the mother countries. The civil law was as firmly rooted there by the time of independence as was the English common law in the 13 colonies that formed the United States.

Since independence, civil law transplanted from continental Europe has continued to have a strong influence on the legal systems of Latin America. A code of commerce promulgated in 1829 by Spain had a great effect on the region's mercantile law, as did the renowned Code Napoleon and 1864 civil code of Italy on its civil and criminal law.

While the civil law has undoubtedly been the major influence, the legal systems also strongly reflect the impact of the English common law. Moreover, among the American influences the doctrine of judicial supremacy has been gradually adopted—sometimes with interesting modifications, as in Colombia and Panama, with their *acción popular,* to provide an immediate test of the constitutionality of statutes and executive acts. Advisory opinions, following the practice of a few American state courts, have also been occasionally provided for. The writ of habeas corpus has also been adopted in most of the countries, under that name in Cuba and some others. In Brazil, it is known as *mandado de seguranca,* and in Mexico and Central America, as the more comprehensive *amparo.* The homestead law, common-law marriage, and legal grounds for divorce are found, too, in the legislation of many of the countries.[3]

The constitutional law and practice of the United States have also had a considerable influence in Latin America, especially in the federal republic of Argentina and to a lesser extent in the federal republics of Brazil, Mexico, and Venezuela. In Argentina, court decisions, lawyers' briefs, and writings of commentators frequently contain citations of decisions rendered or works written in the United States.[4] However, in Colombia, whose practice is much more typical of Latin America, judges and scholars have not been interested in the judicial precedents of the

---

[2] John Thomas Vance, *The Background of Hispanic-American Law* (New York: Central Book Co., 1943), pp. 30–32.

[3] Phanor James Eder, "The Impact of the Common Law on Latin America," *Miami Law Quarterly,* Vol. IV, No. 4 (June, 1950), pp. 436–38.

[4] Segundo V. Linares Quintana, "Comparison of the Constitutional Bases of the United States and Argentine Political Systems," *University of Pennsylvania Law Review,* Vol. 97, No. 5 (April, 1949), pp. 641–64.

United States. If a judge or scholar wants to study precedents elsewhere, he turns to French or other continental sources.[5]

Extensive Borrowings

Another characteristic of Latin American legal systems is their propensity for borrowing or adopting from European nations, the United States, or one another. Bolivia in 1830 adopted verbatim the French civil code. Ecuador and Colombia, as well as several of the Central American republics, copied Chile's civil code of 1855. Paraguay in 1886 adopted the Argentine civil code of 1869. Our Uniform Negotiable Instruments Law was adopted practically word for word by Colombia and in slightly revised form by Chile.

But Latin America has by no means relied solely on Europe or the United States in fashioning its legal systems. In fact, those laws which have been the most effective are the ones that were forged on the anvil of native experience and were adapted to the conditions and requirements of the region. Just such laws were the mining legislation of Peru and Mexico, which were formulated to meet local needs and which form the basis of the mining codes of the nations today. These codes have also greatly influenced mining law in the United States and in many other nations throughout the world. Mexico's unique agrarian reform laws have also won international attention and have been adopted in at least a modified form by several nations.

Embodiment of the Law in Codes

Another basic characteristic of Latin American law is its embodiment in codes that are compact, precise, and systematic formulations of the law. Practically ignoring judicial precedent, as well as custom and usage, the codes adopted by the congress are a concise statement of the law of the land. And as the Latin American realizes, there are certainly some advantages in code law. Its very brevity is intriguing. The whole Codigo Civil, or Civil Code, of Venezuela, for example, can be printed in a 485-page, pocket-size edition, weighing about 10 to 12 ounces. In this code, as well as in the many others in Latin America, the law is succinctly laid down in unequivocal terms, which anyone can read for himself. Moreover, "there is logic, composition, and symmetry which is impressive," concludes William S. Stokes. "The writing is usually lucid. The intent is to achieve certainty in the law. Everything is defined in detail. Standards are exact. Procedure is specific and definite."[6]

---

[5] J. A. C. Grant, " 'Contract Clause' Litigation in Colombia: A Comparative Study in Judicial Review," *American Political Science Review*, Vol. XLII, No. 6 (December, 1948), p. 1126.

[6] William S. Stokes, *Latin American Politics* (New York: Thomas Y. Crowell Co., 1959), p. 468. Another scholar, Phanor J. Eder, has expressed great respect for Latin

These codes of Latin America are indeed a contrast to law as we know it in the United States. Based largely on the English common law, our jurisprudence leans heavily on the doctrine of *stare decisis* and judicial precedent, and recognizes custom and usage as important sources of law. Thus, law in the United States consists not only of statutes passed by Congress and state legislatures but also of many judicial decisions, national and state, which interpret the law and refine its meaning. Consequently, while the federal government—and every one of the states, too—has its own code of laws, these are bulky, detailed affairs that fill many large volumes and are replete with judicial decisions as well as laws enacted by the legislative bodies.

The common law, bulky though it is, has certain distinct advantages over the civil law. In applying common law, a judge has more discretion in interpreting the law in its application to many diverse circumstances. The common law has thus tended to be a dynamic, living body of law reflecting social customs and experience. In this respect, it is decidedly superior to code law, whose rigid provisions as applied by judges who exercise little discretion are sometimes ill-adapted to the peculiar circumstances of the case before the court.

In one respect, however, common and constitutional law operate under a decided disadvantage. Since they both consist largely of case law and judicial precedent, the study and practice of law become progressively unwieldy as a body of precedent grows. "Case law is gold in the mine—a few grains of precious metal to a ton of useless matter—while statute law is coin of the realm, ready for immediate use." In 1947, the student of common law faced the formidable problem of having to consider "325,000 pages of United States statute law and a yearly production of 500 volumes of court decisions."[7]

ORGANIZATION AND OPERATION OF THE COURTS

In most of the republics, the constitutions give much less attention to the courts than to the executive and legislative branches of government. In fact, these two are usually authorized by the organic law to fill in the many necessary details concerning judicial structure, jurisdiction, and pro-

American jurisprudence. "North Americans could learn much from Latin American legislation. We need more scientific method of our law. We need to rid ourselves of our fear of the philosophy of law and of abstract reasoning. . . . As regards form, we could well imitate the clarity and simplicity of the Codes and learn to avoid the excessive verbosity and prolixity of many Anglo-American statutes. Every legislator ought to study the Code Napoleon." Phanor James Eder, *Anglo-American and Latin-American Law* (New York: New York University Press, 1950), p. 142.

[7] In Helen L. Clagett, "Law and Court Systems," *Government and Politics in Latin America*, ed. Harold Eugene Davis (New York: The Ronald Press Co., 1958), p. 334.

cedure. However, unlike the other nations, Mexico and Uruguay have in their constitutions lengthy articles that provide in detail for the organization and operation of the courts.

The Supreme Court

The judicial system in each of the republics is headed by a supreme court, known by such various names as supreme court of justice, supreme tribunal, high federal court, or supreme federal tribunal.

The number of justices who compose the court varies sharply among the nations. Paraguay is very parsimonious; its court has only three members. Despite its small size, Cuba is quite lavish by comparison; its supreme tribunal of justice according to the 1940 constitution has 31 members, and is the largest of the bodies. In between these extremes, such courts in half of the nations number 10 members or less; the others have more than 10. According to the Constitution of Brazil, the composition of its federal supreme tribunal is notably flexible. It must have a minimum of 11 members, the constitution specifies, but the number can be increased on the recommendation of the body itself.

The constitutions and laws establish specific and exacting qualifications for membership on the supreme court. Invariably, candidates must be native-born citizens, fully able to exercise a citizen's political and civil rights. To pin this down more specifically, Mexico adds a residence requirement, specifying that a prospective member of its supreme court of justice must have resided in the country during the preceding five years, except in case of absence in the service of the republic for a period of more than six months.

Age is another qualification. Many of the nations establish both a minimum age for appointment as well as a maximum age. To be eligible for the supreme court, one must be at least 30 years old in Argentina, the Dominican Republic, El Salvador, Haiti, Honduras, and Venezuela; and at least 40 in Cuba, Ecuador, Nicaragua, Peru, and Uruguay. The maximum age is 65 in Mexico, 70 in El Salvador, and 75 in Peru. Besides establishing maximum ages for appointment, some of the nations also specify that retirement is compulsory at a certain age; in Brazil, Mexico, and Uruguay it is age 70.

Exacting professional qualifications are also established for members of the high court. In a number of the nations, they must be qualified members of the bar and have practiced law for a minimum number of years. Colombia requires a minimum of 4 years legal practice; Mexico 5; Haiti 7, Chile, Ecuador, and Panama 15; and Peru 20. Other nations also require that members of the court must have had judicial experience as judges in the lower courts—thus coming up from the ranks. Several require competitive examinations.

Good conduct and reputation are still other qualifications established for members. Brazil's constitution requires that candidates must be of "spotless reputation"; Nicaragua sets its sights high, too, by requiring "irreproachable conduct and good reputation." By comparison, Mexico is quite charitable and more willing to overlook human frailties. Its constitution states that candidates for the supreme court of justice must enjoy a good reputation and not have been convicted of any crime punishable by imprisonment for more than one year in the penitentiary.

Still another requirement usually specified by law or the constitution is that a candidate possess good eyesight and hearing.

Sometimes, extraconstitutional requirements figure largely in the acceptability of a prospective member of the high court. In Ecuador, for example, the geographical division of the nation and prevailing political pattern practically requires that a careful balance be maintained in allocating the 15 judgeships between the jealous and highly competitive coast and sierra.[8]

There are also disqualifications that bar persons from being appointed to the court. Being a member of the priesthood automatically disqualifies an individual in most of the nations. Being related to either the president, who would normally make the nomination, or to a member of congress, who would confirm it, is another disqualification.

Once he becomes a member of the bench, there are many restrictions on a justice's activities. He cannot engage in the private practice of law, hold any other elective or appointive office, or participate in any sort of partisan political activity. In Ecuador, he is not even permitted to vote. Peru, however, gives members of its supreme court of justice considerably more leeway than they are allowed in most other nations. According to Article 226 of the constitution, they may have a diplomatic assignment, teach at the university, aid codifying or amending commissions for the laws, represent the nation in international or scientific congresses and conferences, and act as arbiter or attorney in tribunals of international arbitration in which any Peruvian right may be disputed.

Although there are various differences in detail and refinements in practice, there are three main methods for selecting members of the supreme court.

The president may be empowered by the constitution to make the appointment. In Haiti, he appoints solely on his own responsibility the judges of all judicial tribunals from the top to the bottom. In Chile, the president appoints a member to the high court from a list of five indi-

---

[8] George I. Blanksten, *Ecuador: Constitutions and Caudillos* (Berkeley: University of California Press, 1951), p. 121.

viduals proposed by the court itself. The two ranking members in point of seniority on the court of appeals must be included in the list.

The president nominates members for the high court, with or without the advice or approval of some body as the council of state, and both houses of congress—maybe only one of them—confirm the appointment. In some instances, the president does not recommend a specific individual but submits a list from which the congress may choose. This plan in its general outline is the one followed by Argentina, Mexico, Panama, Paraguay, and Peru. In Brazil, the federal supreme tribunal itself has a strong voice in the selection of its members; when a vacancy exists, the tribunal may nominate an individual, who is usually chosen by the joint action of the president and the senate. In Cuba, nominations for the supreme tribunal of justice under the 1940 constitution were made by a nine-member electoral college, of whom four were proposed by the tribunal itself, three were designated by the president, and two were members of the faculty of law at the University of Havana.

The members of the court may be chosen by the congress—a procedure followed in Bolivia, Colombia, Guatemala, Honduras, Nicaragua, El Salvador, Uruguay, and Venezuela. Congressional action has many variations. In Bolivia, the senate approves a list of nominees for the high office, and the chamber of deputies makes the final selection. In Colombia, the two houses of congress have a strictly equal voice in approving the membership of the court. Six members of the body are named by the senate, and six by the chamber of deputies.

The nations have experimented with many methods for appointing members to the supreme court and obviously have reached no conclusion as to which method is best. Concludes Helen L. Clagett:

If a generalization may be ventured, it is that the participation of both executive and legislative branches in judicial appointments has been found the most satisfactory method. The use of competitive examinations, the practice of appointing career judges, and the use of slates or panels prepared by other agencies, even by the judicial branch itself, have in some countries contributed to reducing political pressure in appointments.[9]

Permanence of tenure, subject only to the requirements of good behavior and proper discharge of duty, is essential for the independence of the courts. However, it has made slow progress in Latin America. Only six of the nations—Argentina, Brazil, Chile, Cuba, Mexico, and Peru—provide that the judges of the supreme court will hold office during "good behavior," the legal term for permanent tenure.[10] Most of

---

[9] Clagett, *op. cit.*, p. 357.

[10] In Argentina, a judge can be removed only for failure to perform his duty, immoral conduct, or commission of a crime. Pablo A. Ramella, *Derecho Constitucional* (Buenos Aires, 1960), p. 643.

the republics prefer to establish specific terms of office. Four of the nations have relatively long terms; 10 years in Bolivia, Haiti, and Uruguay; and 18 years in Panama.

The other 10 nations, however, keep a much closer checkrein on their justices. Costa Rica has a term of eight years; Ecuador, Honduras, and Nicaragua six; and Colombia, the Dominican Republic, Paraguay, and Venezuela five. In Guatemala, the term of a justice is even less than that of the president, four years as against six. And El Salvador has the shortest term of all, three years. A member of the Salvadorean high court has hardly taken the oath of office, gotten his bench warm, and acquired a judicial mien before he must run for reelection.

The provisions for reelection also vary widely among the nations. Colombia permits a justice to be reelected indefinitely, but Uruguay stipulates that he cannot be reelected except after a lapse of five years. El Salvador and Guatemala, with their short terms of three and four years, respectively, have added their own distinctive touches to permanence of tenure. If a member of the supreme court in El Salvador serves three consecutive elective terms of three years each, or in Guatemala two such terms of four years each, he is regarded as having tenure for life until the compulsory retirement age.

The supreme court is presided over by a *presidente* or chief justice. In some nations, he is directly appointed to this position, as in the United States; usually, however, he is selected by his colleagues. The basis of choice may be seniority, rotation in office, or vote of the members. The term a member serves as chief justice may be one year, a number of years, or the entire duration of his service.[11]

In performing their judicial duties, the supreme courts of nine nations —Argentina, Brazil, the Dominican Republic, Haiti, Honduras, Nicaragua, Panama, Paraguay, and Uruguay—always function as a unit; members of the court sit in on all cases and have a voice in deciding them. In the other nations, however, instead of sitting as a single body the court divides its members into what are known as *salas* or *cámaras*. Each *sala* specializes in a certain type of judicial controversy. In Colombia, for example, the court is divided into four such groups to correspond to: cases under original jurisdiction, civil law appeals, criminal law appeals, and miscellaneous business.

The division into *salas* has its advantages; it enables members of the court to specialize in certain fields of law and consequently to weigh more expertly the many complex issues that come before them. Moreover, the division of labor helps to expedite the rendition of justice.

---

[11] There are many variations in ground rules. In Peru, where the president of the supreme court is elected for a term of one year, the custom has been to reelect a president who is approaching retirement. José Pareja Paz-Soldan, *Derecho Constitucional Peruano* (Tercera edición; Lima, Perú: Ediciones de Sol, 1963), p. 306.

In Ecuador, as in the majority of the nations, the supreme court of 15 justices is divided into *salas,* three chambers of five judges each. But the rationale underlying the division is quite different from that of the other courts in Latin America. Each of the chambers handles all types of cases. The only principle in distribution of cases is that of chance, and this has been stressed in Ecuadorian law as an element of justice. Distribution on this basis has another advantage. Under this system, no one of the chambers is overburdened with cases while the other two have relatively light dockets.[12]

The selection of *suplentes* and *fiscales* have also served to ease the burden of the courts. The *suplentes* are alternate or substitute judges who may be called on to serve whenever a regular member of the body is unable to. In some nations, a *suplente* is elected for each incumbent justice; in others, a panel of substitutes is named from which one is selected in the event of the death, serious illness, or resignation of a justice. The substitute justices, incidentally, must have the same qualifications as those established for regular members of the court.

The *fiscales,* or technical advisers, are also of great assistance to the court in the discharge of its responsibilities. They often make investigations for the justices, and their findings and recommendations become part of the official record of the case.

The supreme court, as its name implies, is the judicial body of last resort for the nation. To assure the uniform and equitable administration of justice, it is given a wide appellate jurisdiction over constitutional and legal questions.

The court also enjoys original jurisdiction over certain classes of cases that are of special importance to the nation or have international implications. Original jurisdiction usually extends to all cases involving: proceedings against the president, members of the cabinet, national judges, diplomats, and other officials representing the central government; disputes between foreign countries and the nation; issues involving international law; and, in the case of federal states, conflicts between the union and the states or between states.

To effectively discharge its responsibilities, the court must have its own independent power to enforce respect for its operations. In Colombia, for example, contempt of court is a serious offense. The justices may order arrest, limited to six days, or impose fines of from 5 to 50 pesos to compel parties to comply with court orders duly issued. In Panama, too, justices can impose heavy penalties for contempt of court.[13]

The supreme court in the several nations has a number of special duties that are quite important. In Ecuador, the president of the body attends

---

[12] Blanksten, *op. cit.,* pp. 121–22.
[13] Eder, *Anglo-American and Latin-American Law, op. cit.,* p. 154.

the first meeting of the congress and personally reads his message regarding the administration of justice in the whole nation. On the basis of his information, observations, and recommendations, the congress will later pass legislation relating to the administration of justice.

In all the nations, the supreme court has extensive control over the lower courts in the land. It appoints or recommends for appointment the judges of these courts and closely supervises their work. Members of the high court are required by the constitutions or laws to visit the lower courts personally and observe at firsthand how they are conducted. These visits are not announced in advance. Another aspect of the high court's supervisory control is its broad power to discipline judges of the lower courts and to correct any malfeasance or misfeasance in the exercise of judicial duty. In Honduras, the supreme court has the right to summarily impose a fine as large as 30 *lempiras* on a member of the lower judiciary. In extreme cases where a judge's bad conduct is clearly proved after a hearing, the court may order his removal from office. But it can reward as well as penalize; it can recognize good service by granting vacations with or without pay and by recommending promotions.[14]

In addition to supervising the lower courts and being responsible for its own employees, budgetary needs, and other housekeeping duties, the court determines the caliber of lawyers who practice before it. Their preparation, ability, and performance have a direct influence on the effectiveness of the court and the quality of justice it dispenses. Recognizing this, the court under legal or constitutional authorization establishes standards and qualifications that lawyers who practice before it must meet, and disqualifies from appearing before it any attorneys who fail to meet these requirements.

Easily one of the more unusual extraneous duties of a supreme court is that imposed in Mexico by Article 97, of the 1917 constitution. Under this article, the court is "to investigate . . . any act or acts constituting a violation of any individual guarantee or abuse of the public vote, or any other offense punishable by the federal law." Under this sweeping grant of investigatory power, the court must conduct an investigation if one of the constitutional officers or agencies requests it, but it can use its own discretion about whether or not to act if a nongovernmental or private group makes the request.

In practice the High Court never has attempted spontaneously to investigate a political dispute resulting from an election, and its record of acting on request points up clearly that political factors influence its decisions. A review of the cases in which the court did act demonstrates that requests from a national authority, and especially the executive, are likely to produce an investigation

---

[14] William S. Stokes, *Honduras: An Area Study in Government* (Madison: University of Wisconsin Press, 1950), p. 137.

but that almost from the first years of the present constitutional era, starting in 1917, the court has preferred not to accede to petitions from state officials to review elections at that or the municipal level, on the grounds that such action would invade state sovereignty. This despite the clear mandate to do so in the constitution. Petitions from opposition political parties, which seem to come as a matter of course after every election now that the revolutionary party has become all-powerful, are even more apt to receive short shrift.[15]

The Lower Courts

The supreme court, whose organization and operation we have discussed at length, is, of course, only the superstructure of the judicial system. By far the greater part of the judicial load in every nation is carried by the many lower courts, which are on the front line so to speak, grappling with judicial controversies in the villages, towns, and cities.

In the unitary nations, which have a single hierarchy of courts, the understructure of the judicial system is very simple. At the bottom is the justice of the peace or a similar official who can try persons accused of less serious criminal offenses and can adjudicate the less important run-of-the-mine civil controversies that arise between citizens. The quality of justice rendered by these judges varies considerably between the nations. In Uruguay, for example, to be eligible for appointment as a justice of the peace one must have a law degree, which attests to his legal qualifications and assures a professional disposition of cases that come before the court.

In Honduras, however, where illiteracy is high, the J.P. courts have never been very satisfactory, mainly because of the difficulty of securing competent personnel. The quality of the justices who obtained office by popular election was so low that selection by appointment was adopted in 1924. The change, however, has not greatly improved the quality of justices of the peace. Moreover, raising the requirements for the position is hardly likely to provide the needed qualified justices. "It is not logical to criticize the low educational and professional requirements demanded for qualification for the office," says William S. Stokes, "because, if they were raised it is doubtful that all the positions could be filled."[16]

The district courts located in the larger towns have both original and appellate jurisdiction. Besides reviewing appeals from decisions of justices of the peace, they also try civil and criminal cases. Above the district courts in the judicial pyramid is the departmental court, located in the capital of the department and ranking next to the supreme court of the nation. Like the district court, it also has original and appellate jurisdiction. In several of the nations, there is also a court of appeals with appel-

---

[15] Robert E. Scott, *Mexican Government in Transition* (Rev. ed.; Urbana: University of Illinois Press 1964), pp. 270–71.

[16] Stokes, *Honduras, op. cit.,* p. 128.

late jurisdiction only and ranking between the departmental and supreme courts.[17]

In the federal states, the administration of justice is more complicated. A dual system of courts, both federal and state or provincial, is charged with the responsibility of administering justice. The federal courts, established to maintain the supremacy of the union and to pass on national questions, have the lion's share of the jurisdiction, commensurate with the activities and power of the national government. The state or provincial courts have a far more restricted jurisdiction; they often twiddle their thumbs for lack of judicial business while the federal courts are overburdened with work.

The dual system of courts in the federal nations has not proved to be very successful. Venezuela experimented with both the unitary and federal judicial systems until 1945, when it merged the two sets of courts into one national system. Brazil has long had misgivings about the wisdom of a dual system. In 1937, it acted to centralize the judicial power and eliminate duplication by merging federal and state courts at the intermediate levels, with the exception of a single federal court of appeals. In Mexico, the dual system still exists; the national and state governments both have their own courts.

Special Courts

There are many special courts and jurisdictions in Latin America today. They are by no means new to the region. During colonial days, special tribunals existed for such narrow ranges of offenses as cockfighting, crimes committed in uninhabited places, and crimes committed by doctors, pharmacists, or barbers.[18]

Special courts have long handled a wide range of specialized cases. Military courts, for example, have long functioned to try members of the armed forces who commit offenses against military law, maybe even against national law. Special courts exist, too, for juveniles and to handle disputes over taxes, accounts, and elections.

As the role of government has greatly expanded in recent decades, the number of special courts has greatly increased. They deal with a wide range of modern social problems. The labor courts, for example, which are found in most of the nations, were established because the regular courts lacked the specialized knowledge and trained personnel for coping with complex labor–management problems. Moreover, such cases should have special consideration because of the need for a speedy solu-

---

[17] In Honduras, an appraisal of the intermediate courts shows that they have discharged their responsibilities quite competently. *Ibid.*, pp. 130–35.

[18] Helen L. Clagett, *Administration of Justice in Latin America* (New York: Oceana Publications, Inc., 1952), p. 55.

tion of conflicts that might drag on interminably if processed through the regular courts of law, with great detriment to the employer, the employee, and the nation.

Although the special courts have many strong points in their favor, there are strong arguments against them too. "The principal objection [against them] . . .," says Helen L. Clagett, "is not so much that they are alien to the Judicial Power, but rather that they are exempt from its control. Another objection is that where executive and judicial functions are combined, the judge and one of the parties to the controversy became merged in a single person, which element fosters the danger of despotism."[19]

INDEPENDENCE OF THE JUDICIARY

As one of the three coequal branches of government, the judiciary according to law and theory should enjoy an independence of authority and function within its constitutionally allotted sphere of operation. To bolster or further this independence, various measures have been adopted in the several republics.

Selection on the basis of professional qualifications rather than political partisanship is becoming increasingly accepted in the region. The voice the supreme court often has in the selection of its own members and judges of the lower courts, also the requirement of competitive examinations in some nations, are commendable steps in the right direction. They aim to make judicial service a professional career rather than the bailiwick of political favorites or hacks.

Permanence of tenure is likewise of great importance to the independence of the judiciary. Although only six of the nations provide for it at present, several others, as we noted earlier, grant it to justices who have been reelected successively.

In some of the nations, the courts have been able to achieve or approximate the independence of function the constitution envisaged. In Brazil, they have attained a "respected and generally independent position in the constellation of Brazilian governmental organs," according to James L. Busey. The respect that very strong presidents, including Vargas, have accorded them is unusual in the quasidictatorial republics of Latin America.[20]

---

19 *Ibid.*, p. 57. In pp. 59–115, the author discusses at length the different kinds of special courts in Latin America and gives a country-by-country description of the courts found in each one.

20 James L. Busey, *Latin America: Political Institutions and Processes* (New York: Random House, Inc., 1964), p. 114. In the opinion of Martin Needler, however, the fact that milder dictators, such as Vargas, permit the courts to continue to function as usual should not be regarded as an evidence of their strength but rather as an indication of their ultimate political weakness. Martin C. Needler, *Latin American Politics in Perspective* (Princeton, N.J.: D. Van Nostrand Co., Inc., 1963), p. 155.

In Costa Rica the judiciary enjoys a degree of independence and respect seldom found in Latin America. "The Costa Rican Constitution uses all the ingenuity of human invention to guarantee the autonomy of the seventeen-member Supreme Court," says Busey. "There is no doubt that the Costa Rican judiciary is free of presidential control. . . . In Costa Rica, the judiciary functions as an independent branch, and can and does issue judgments which are contrary to presidential policy or design."[21]

But in most of the other nations, the judiciary is not nearly so fortunate. There, independence is a high-sounding phrase in the paper constitution and bears little resemblance to reality.

As a part of the tripartite division of government, the courts have many highly significant relations with the other two branches of government. These relations afford the executive and the congress many opportunities to undermine the independence of the judiciary if they want to.

In performing his constitutional duties, the president exercises many powers that have a direct and vital bearing on the independence and integrity of the courts. As we have seen, he appoints or nominates members of the supreme court, often judges of the lower courts as well, thus deciding or having a strong voice in who will sit on the bench. He also initiates legislation relating to the courts. His proposals may greatly help both the institutional and personal interests of the judges; they may also very adversely affect them. The executive also grants pardons and reprieves. He can exercise this power with restraint, as the constitution no doubt intends, or he can use it vindictively, to free convicted offenders wholesale and to undermine the prestige and very *raison d'être* of the courts. The president has still another whip hand over the courts. Responsible for executing the laws of the nation and commanding its various enforcement agencies, he may respect the rulings of the courts and assiduously enforce them, or he may show his disdain by making no effort to carry them out.

With these strong controls over the courts, the president usually has decidedly the upper hand in his relations with the judiciary. In most of the nations, he can easily dominate the judicial branch if he so desires. He often does, too.

The complaints against undue presidential influence or even dictation are legion. In Peru, criticism of the executive has been restrained and pitched to a relatively low key. To remedy his undue influence, a new law has been formulated.[22]

In most of the other nations, however, the president is often accused not just of influencing the courts but of actually controlling them.

---

[21] Busey, *op. cit.*, pp. 78–79.

[22] R. J. Owens, *Peru* (Royal Institute of International Affairs) (New York: Oxford University Press, 1963), p. 69.

Panama well typifies the situation in these nations. Say John and Mavis Biesanz:

Even the Supreme Court appears to be putty in the president's hands. Although the five justices are appointed for ten-year terms, they rarely express a majority opinion contrary to that of the current president, for dissenters can be retired with pay. Only when he flagrantly violates the rules of the political game or arouses public opinion against him do the . . . justices venture to oppose him.[23]

The congress has a number of controls over the judiciary. Sometimes, these are exercised in subservience to the president; sometimes, they represent quite independent expressions of congressional design. The congress may approve nominations for the court made by the president or may itself appoint the members. It also has the power to pass legislation regarding the organization and jurisdiction of the courts, thus being able to determine their structure, size, authorized agenda, and many other matters of fundamental importance. Control of the purse strings is also significant.

Congress' power of removal is in some nations a bludgeon for intimidating the judiciary. In Mexico, although the justices supposedly enjoy permanence of tenure, this is a blatant farce. For in accordance with Article 111 of the 1917 constitution, they may be removed at the drop of a hat—a presidential hat, of course—and approval by an absolute majority of a rubber-stamp congress.

Congress' power to amend the constitution, whether exercised independently or under presidential pressure, also has a critical bearing on the role and authority of the courts, as the experience of Guatemala shows. Nathan L. Whetten writes:

The process of change is so simple in fact that a president in power who has complete control over his political party may change the Constitution almost at will. The role of the Supreme Court as interpreter of the Constitution has therefore been relatively unimportant. It may declare laws unconstitutional but in the past this has had little significance because any powers desired by the government could easily be obtained through amendment of the law.[24]

In most countries, the judiciary even in normal times find it an uphill battle to maintain its supposed independence. In times of repressive dictatorship, its chances of independence are far less. Sooner or later it is almost certain to get the dictatorial axe, wielded either as a naked display of power or in compliance with at least the formalities of constitutionality. In Argentina, Lonardi's provisional government reconstituted the

---

[23] John and Mavis Biesanz, *The People of Panama* (New York: Columbia University Press, 1955), p. 141.

[24] Nathan L. Whetten, *Guatemala: The Land and the People* (Caribbean Series, 4) (New Haven, Conn.: Yale University Press, 1961), p. 326.

supreme court by executive fiat, dismissing four of the five Peronista judges and filling their places with his own appointees. He used the direct approach because he had no congress to assist him or to approve his actions against the justices. By contrast, when Perón purged the Supreme Court in 1946 to make way for his appointees, he used the slower process of impeachment as provided by the constitution, having congress firmly under his control.

Dictatorship almost invariably plays havoc with judicial independence. Yet, while many a Latin American matter-of-factly accepts its aberrations, he shrinks with dread from the very idea of social revolution which he realizes will completely overturn the government as well as the rest of society. Paradoxically, the courts of Mexico and Bolivia have enjoyed more independence of action during the course of the social revolutions than many courts do under many a normal dictatorship in Latin America. In Mexico, even during the most hectic days of the revolutionary government's attempts to put into effect its land reform program by expropriating properties in accordance with law, the courts not only were very much in business but for several years even greatly obstructed the government's program of reform.[25]

In Bolivia, too, the new revolutionary regime that came into power in 1952, bent on accomplishing a full-scale social revolution, respected the independence of the judiciary. The nation's crash program of land reform was, like Mexico's, greatly impeded by the revolutionary regime's respect for due process of law.

"One of the principal causes for the slowness of the execution of the agrarian reform decree," says Robert J. Alexander "was the fact that there were four stages at which the landowner could appeal the decision to expropriate his holding. . . . Most landholders took full advantage of this right to appeal. The result has been that many cases have lingered on for years."[26]

CIVIL AND CRIMINAL PROCEDURE

Judicial procedure in Latin America is very different from that of Britain or the United States. Since the procedure of Argentina in civil and criminal cases is similar to that of the other nations, it warrants close study.

---

[25] James G. Maddox, "Mexican Agrarian Reform," *American Universities Field Staff Reports Service* (Mexico, D.F., July 3, 1957), p. 22. Eyler Simpson terms the government's efforts to expropriate land "the battle of injunctions." Eyler N. Simpson, *The Ejido: Mexico's Way Out* (Chapel Hill: University of North Carolina Press, 1937), pp. 113–15.

[26] Robert J. Alexander, *The Bolivian National Revolution* (New Brunswick, N.J.: Rutgers University Press, 1958), p. 69.

In accordance with Argentine practice,[27] the suitor in civil actions must rely almost entirely on written forms for presenting his case. After his attorney prepares the complaint and the necessary affidavits and presents them to the court, the trial in time takes place. It is usually a private hearing, closed to the public. A secretary presides over the proceedings and attempts to record verbatim everything that is said—sometimes in longhand, incidentally. Witnesses appear both for and against the suitor. Lawyers for both sides ask them as many questions as they want and prepare rebuttals for each other's arguments. The lawyers' questions, rebuttals, and summaries often run to great length. The whole proceeding, or more exactly, as much as can be faithfully recorded in longhand, is transcribed on stamped paper.

The judge seldom bothers to put in an appearance; usually, he does not come face to face with the participants in a case unless they happen to be friends or acquaintances. His august judicial judgment is based solely on the book of evidence—the voluminous notes the secretary has taken from the testimony of witnesses, and the arguments, rebuttals, and summaries of opposing attorneys.

Justice rendered under such a procedure is perforce under a handicap. "If the secretary takes notes in longhand—which some of them do, and if in addition the handwriting is almost indecipherable—which sometimes it is, then the judge may be forced to guess the exact meaning of many sentences or paragraphs. There is no assurance, moreover, that the secretary's notes are accurate. Yet the judge has no other guide."[28]

In criminal cases, too, the procedure is very different from that of Great Britain or the United States. Anyone arrested and charged with a penal offense is taken before an instruction judge (*juez de instrucción*) who functions as a combination committing magistrate and grand jury. In a preliminary hearing, he decides whether or not the accused will be held for trial and, if so, whether he will be required to wait in jail until the trial begins or released on bail, personal recognizance, or the assurance of a responsible person that he will appear for trial. Meanwhile, the accused may be held incommunicado for days while the police attempt to obtain incriminating evidence, apparently sometimes by what are commonly regarded as third-degree methods.

Eventually, the trial takes place. As in the case of civil suits, it is usually conducted behind closed doors. Sometimes the trial judge may preside over a part of the proceedings, but he seldom presides over the entire trial. As in a civil action, he bases his judgment almost entirely on the book of evidence a secretary has prepared for him.

---

[27] This account is from Austin F. Macdonald, *Government of the Argentine Republic* (New York: Thomas Y. Crowell Co., 1942), pp. 270–73.

[28] *Ibid.*, p. 272.

There are other notable variations from Anglo-American criminal procedure. If convicted, the accused may appeal from the court's decision, but the public prosecutor may appeal the verdict, too. Consequently, a person found innocent in the lower court may be adjudged guilty in the court of appeals or may have his penalty increased.

Another significant variation is the lack of a jury for deciding on the innocence or guilt of the accused. Juries are not used, although the constitution of 1853, in Article 24 and in Article 67, clause 11, clearly authorized the congress to adopt the jury system.[29]

JUDICIAL REVIEW

Probably the single greatest influence that Anglo-American law has had on Latin American law is judicial review. The practice, borrowed from the United States where it appeared to work so well, is used in some form by the courts in every one of the nations today.

In Brazil, the constitution in Article 101 provides for court review of the acts of the other branches of government. In Argentina, judicial review is the result of decisions made by the court itself. Just as the Supreme Court of the United States in the landmark case of *Marbury* v. *Madison* successfully staked out its claim for authority to review and invalidate government actions in violation of the Constitution, the Supreme Court of Argentina in two cases of 1875 and 1884 successfully asserted its own right of review—one considerably more limited than that of courts in the United States.[30]

Borrowing the doctrine of judicial review from the United States was a simple matter. All constitution makers had to do was add a relevant section, a paragraph, or even a sentence. But making it really effective has been quite a problem. Several basic questions have arisen.

Who should have the authority to review laws or acts of government officers when their constitutionality is challenged? About three fourths of the nations confer a limited power of review on the courts. The others, however, have decided that the function should be shared jointly by congress and the courts, or should be exclusively a responsibility of congress. Popularly elected, congress in the opinion of many best represents the national will; any law it passes should therefore be nullified only by another act of congress itself.

---

[29] In compliance with the constitutional provision, the Argentine senate did pass a measure providing for the jury system, but the chamber of deputies sidetracked the measure by proposing that the president appoint a commission to study the question and make a report. The commission was appointed and the report made to congress in 1874. However, no further action was taken on the matter. (*Ibid.*, p. 273.)

[30] *Fallos de la Corte Suprema de Justica Nacional*, Series II, Vol. 13 (1875), p. 458; and Series II, Vol. 3 (1884), p. 197.

If the courts are to exercise the power of review, what should be the scope of this review? In Argentina, whose constitutional experience most nearly parallels that of the United States, judicial review has been interpreted to mean that the federal courts may declare unconstitutional an executive, legislative, or judicial act in violation of the constitution. Yet, in practice the court does not challenge the executive on any important issue or declare unconstitutional a major law enacted by the congress.

In the other nations, judicial review is limited only to a decision of the particular case before the court. The body has no authority whatever to declare that an act of either the president or the congress is unconstitutional.

A unique form of judicial review is Mexico's writ of *amparo*, provided by Article 103 of the 1917 constitution and expanded by the Law of *Amparo*, enacted in 1936. Under this law, any citizen may apply to one of the federal courts for redress if a law or act of a government official or judge impairs any rights guaranteed to the citizen by the first 29 articles of the constitution.[31] A decision made by the court applies only to a specific case and does not presume to declare unconstitutional, or even to question the constitutionality of, an act of congress or of the president.

"It is clear," concludes Busey, referring to court decisions involving *amparo*, "that the courts never take a position contrary to that of executive policy. No writs of *amparo* are issued against actions by the President, by members of his official family, by leading members of the PRI, or against federal legislation which has been passed by the congress."[32]

The writ of *amparo* is a home-grown institution, as native to the region as maize. For almost three decades, it has been Mexico's prized contribution to the protection of private rights.

"The practice of the amparo," justifiably boasts Felipe Tena Ramírez, associate justice of the Federal Supreme Court of Mexico, "has made that institution, not a defense of the paramount law, but a means of protecting the individual rights recognized by the Constitution; the comparative lack of effectiveness of the *amparo* as a direct and authentic defense of constitutionality has been compensated for by its extraordinary effectiveness as a safeguard of human rights."[33]

The writ of *amparo* has made quite an impression on other nations too. The Universal Declaration of Human Rights, proclaimed by the United Nations General Assembly on December 10, 1948, contained a modified version of *amparo* in Article 8. Moreover, both Costa Rica and Nicaragua

---

[31] A detailed statement of these rights is given in Ignacio Burgoa, *Las Garantias Individuales* (México: Ediciones Botas, 1944).

[32] Busey, *op. cit.*, p. 39.

[33] Felipe Tena Ramírez, "The International Expansion of the Mexican Amparo," *Inter-American Law Review*, Vol. I, No. 1 (January–June, 1959), p. 163.

in their constitutions of 1950 adopted *amparo* as a protection for the rights of citizens.

Yet, while protecting the citizen in individual cases, *amparo* falls far short of being real judicial review. Hundreds, even thousands, of *amparo* cases may be the result of a single act of congress, which, in the opinion of the justices, infringes on private rights and should be amended or repealed. But all the justices can do is to give relief to each suppliant and hope that the president or congress will take cognizance of their findings and change the law.[34]

However, while the court is wishfully hoping for a change in the law it is deluged with a flood of appeals for redress. By 1950, it was falling so far behind with its work that, although it handled 33,957 matters of judicial business, it still had a backlog of 27,026 cases, almost all concerning writs of *amparo*. To ease the court's critical situation, an amendment in 1951 to the Organic Law of the Judicial Branch temporarily added a fifth *sala* to assist in cleaning up the backlog of cases. Even with this extra help, the number of *amparo* cases continued to increase so fast that in 1955 the supreme court found it necessary to establish stricter rules for obtaining the writ.[35] The provision in the Law of *Amparo* whereby five uniform supreme court decisions create *jurisprudencia* or precedent has apparently been of limited aid to the court.

In most of the other nations, judicial review does not afford, as in Mexico, an effective protection to private rights, and extends only to administration of the law, not to the law itself. In Ecuador, two types of unconstitutionality are recognized—procedural and substantive. The supreme court has the power to declare an action procedurally unconstitutional but does not have the authority to find a measure substantively unconstitutional.[36]

Restricting the courts to deciding specific cases and denying them the authority to rule on questions of law have largely been responsible for the slight attention given to precedent. Although supreme court cases are reported in every one of the nations, they are published in volume form in only a few of them—in Argentina, Brazil, Costa Rica, Uruguay, and Venezuela. Not a single nation has a complete record of decisions of its supreme court since independence. Decisions of lower courts are seldom reported. Even in Argentina, whose judicial records are probably the most complete of all the nations, court opinions until 1903 were so brief and sketchily written that it was almost impossible to tell how the judges arrived at their decisions. In that year, however, Antonio Bermejo, a distinguished jurist, became a member of the court and served for 25

[34] Scott, *op. cit.*, p. 267.
[35] *Ibid.*, pp. 268–69.
[36] Blanksten, *op. cit.*, pp. 137–38.

years. Under his influence, supreme court decisions became more complete and more lucid.[37]

The minor role that precedent plays in the decision of cases also explains why law students spend most of their time in studying legal theory and philosophy. For a case, however interesting it may seem at the moment, is soon judicially forgotten. But as the student knows, a thorough knowledge of the codes and skillful application of logic are always helpful in a case before the bench.

CRITICISMS OF THE COURTS

Various scholarly appraisals made of the courts of specific nations have in general been complimentary. In Honduras, the caliber of justices of the supreme court has been high; consequently, they have been honored and respected. The major weakness of the court has been its hesitancy to assert its leadership and supervise the administration of justice, a hesitancy that is being gradually overcome.[38] In Uruguay, the courts are "a good complement to her congress and to her executive branch."[39] In Ecuador, "of the three national functions, the judiciary has operated most effectively."[40]

However, in many countries there have been notable criticisms of judicial procedure and the administration of justice. The recording of legal testimony on stamped paper is quite expensive, greatly adding to the cost of a lawsuit. Lawyers with their volubility further aggravate the problem of court costs, since their fees are based on the volume of testimony recorded on the expensive legal paper.

Another criticism often made of the courts refers to the cumbersome, antiquated judicial procedure. The judges' reliance on the book of evidence, prepared by a secretary and often giving only longhand bits of the testimony, is contrary to more advanced concepts of justice. Certainly, few judges would care to have their fate determined by the same consideration they directly give to cases they decide.

Probably the most trenchant criticism of all is the long delay in the rendition of justice, a situation that from reliable indications seems true in every one of the republics. In Colombia, the courts have a tremendous backlog of cases waiting to be tried, estimated unofficially to be 150,000. Some of these have been on the docket for as long as 22 years; as a result, there is little incentive for instituting legal actions today.[41]

---

[37] Macdonald, *op. cit.*, p. 279.

[38] Stokes, *Honduras, op. cit.*, p. 138–39.

[39] Russell H. Fitzgibbon, *Uruguay: Portrait of a Democracy* (New Brunswick, N.J.: Rutgers University Press, 1954), p. 164.

[40] Blanksten, *op. cit.*, p. 172.

[41] *Hispanic American Report*, Vol. XVI, No. 9 (November, 1963), pp. 887–88.

In Peru, also, the wheels of justice grind slowly in spite of the large number of practicing lawyers. In December, 1956, 9,558 prisoners were in Peruvian jails; 7,395 (77.5percent) were still awaiting trial. The time spent in jail just waiting to be tried is sometimes even longer than the sentence subsequently meted out. To make matters worse, "prison conditions are poor," says R. J. Owens. "As many as twelve men may now occupy one small room, sleeping on the floor, before even having their depositions before a judge."[42]

The Goddess of Justice is usually portrayed as blindfolded, supposedly symbolizing impartiality and fairness. One sometimes wonders, however, if the blindfold may not be intended to spare the Goddess the anguish of seeing the travesties committed in the name of justice.

SUGGESTED READINGS

Blanksten, George I. *Ecuador: Constitutions and Caudillos*, chap. vii. Berkeley: University of California Press, 1951.

———. *Perón's Argentina*, pp. 122–32. Chicago: University of Chicago Press, 1953.

Cabrera, Lucio A. "History of the Mexican Judiciary," *Mexico: A Symposium on Law and Government*, pp. 23–31. University of Miami School of Law; Inter-American Legal Studies, No. 3. Coral Gables, Fla.: University of Miami Press, October, 1958.

Clagett, Helen L. *Administration of Justice in Latin America*. New York: Oceana Publications, Inc., 1952.

———. "Law and Court Systems," *Government and Politics in Latin America* (ed. Harold E. Davis), chap. 12. New York: The Ronald Press Co., 1958.

Eder, Phanor J. *Anglo-American and Latin-American Law: A Comparative Study*. New York: New York University Press, 1950.

———. "The Impact of the Common Law on Latin America," *Miami Law Quarterly*, Vol. IV, No. 4 (June, 1950), pp. 435–40.

Grant, J. A. C. " 'Contract Clause' Litigation in Colombia: A Comparative Study in Judicial Review," *American Political Science Review*, Vol. XLII, No. 6 (December, 1948), pp. 1103–26.

———. "Judicial Control of Legislation: A Comparative Study," *The American Journal of Comparative Law*, Vol. III (1954), pp. 186–98.

———. "Judicial Review by Executive Reference Prior to Promulgation: the Colombian Experience," *Southern California Law Review*, Vol. XXXI, No. 2 (February, 1948), pp. 154–71.

Gruening, Ernest. *Mexico and Its Heritage*, pp. 497–514. New York: D. Appleton-Century Co., Inc., 1934.

---

[42] Owens, *op. cit.*, p. 69.

Inter-American Legal Studies. *Mexico: A Symposium on Law and Government.* No. 3. Coral Gables, Fla.: University of Miami Press, 1958.

James, Herman G. *The Constitutional System of Brazil,* chap. v. Washington, D.C.: Carnegie Institution of Washington, 1923.

Jorrín, Miguel. *Governments of Latin America,* chap. 6. New York: D. Van Nostrand Co., Inc., 1953.

Linares Quintana, Segunda V. "Comparison of the Constitutional Bases of the United States and Argentine Political Systems," *University of Pennsylvania Law Review,* Vol. 97, No. 5 (April, 1949), pp. 641–64.

Macdonald, Austin F. *Government of the Argentine Republic,* chap. 14. New York: Thomas Y. Crowell Co., 1942.

Pierson, William W., and Gil, Federico G. *Governments of Latin America,* chap. 11. New York: McGraw-Hill Book Co., Inc., 1957.

Stokes, William S. *Honduras: An Area Study in Government,* pp. 106–50. Madison: University of Wisconsin Press, 1950.

———. *Latin American Politics,* pp. 465–83. New York: Thomas Y. Crowell Co., 1959.

Tena Ramírez, Felipe. "The International Expansion of the Mexican Amparo," *Inter-American Law Review,* Vol. 1, No. 1 (January–June, 1959), pp. 163–66.

Tucker, William P. *The Mexican Government Today,* chap. 8. Minneapolis: University of Minnesota Press, 1957.

Vance, John Thomas. *The Background of Hispanic-American Law.* New York: Central Book Co., 1943.

Washington Foreign Law Society. *A Symposium on the Law of Latin America.* Washington, D.C.: George Washington University Law School, 1959.

INDEXES

INDEX OF AUTHORS

INDEX OF SUBJECTS